AMERICANS
OF
ROYAL DESCENT.

COLLECTION OF GENEALOGIES SHOWING THE
LINEAL DESCENT FROM KINGS OF SOME
AMERICAN FAMILIES.

REPRODUCED FROM RECOGNIZED AUTHORATIVE GENEALOGICAL WORKS, FROM PRINTED
FAMILY HISTORIES, AND VERIFIED INFORMATION SUPPLIED IN MANUSCRIPT PEDIGREES.

CHARLES H. BROWNING,

MEMBER OF THE AMERICAN HISTORICAL ASSOCIATION; THE HISTORICAL
SOCIETY OF PENNSYLVANIA, ETC.

SEVENTH EDITION.

Southern Historical Press, Inc.
Greenville, South Carolina

This volume was reproduced
from a personal copy located in
the Publishers private library

All rights reserved. No part of this publication may be reproduced,
stored in a retrieval system, transmitted in any form, posted
on the web in any form or by any means without the
prior written permission of the publisher.

Please direct all correspondence and book orders to:
SOUTHERN HISTORICAL PRESS, Inc.
1071 Park West Blvd.
Greenville, SC   29611

Seventh Edition Printed 1911
ISBN #978-1-63914-625-3
Printed in the United States of America

THE PEDIGREE OF ORVILLE D. BALDWIN

	ROGER BIGOD			
HENRY DE BOHUN	HUGH BIGOD			
Margery de Newburg.	Ralph Bigod.			
Alice de Mauduit.	Isabel Fitzpiers.	GEOFFREY DE SAY	ROBERT FITZWALTER	
Isabel de Beauchamp.	John Fitzjohn.	William de Say.	Walter Fitzrobert.	
William de Beauchamp, m.	Maud Fitzjohn.	William de Say.	Ela Odingsells.	
	Guy de Beauchamp.	Geoffrey de Say.	Ida de Clinton.	
	Maud de Beauchamp, m.	Geoffrey de Say.	John de Clinton.	

Idonae de Say, m John de Clinton.

Sir Baldwin de Montfort=Lady Margaret de Clinton
Sir William de Montfort, Knt.=Margaret de Peche.
Sir Baldwin de Montfort, Knt.=Joanna de Vernon.
Robert Montfort, of Bescote, Staff.=(Name unknown.)
Katharine Montfort, heiress=Sir George Booth, of Dunham-Massie.
Sir William Booth, of Dunham-Massie.=Ellen Montgomery, of Thornley.
Jane Booth (widow)=Sir Thomas Holford, of Holford, Cheshire.
Dorothy Holford (2d wife)=John Bruen, of Bruen-Stapleford, Cheshire.
John Bruen, of Bruen-Stapleford=Margaret . . . . . . (3d wife).
Marie Bruen (See pages 316-319)=John Baldwin, d. 1681, at Milford, Conn.
Abigail Baldwin b. 1658=Samuel Baldwin, of Fairfield, Ct., 1665-1696.
Nathaniel Baldwin, of Guilford, Conn., 1693-1760=Elizabeth Parmalee, of Guilford, 1690-1786.
Samuel Baldwin, of Guilford, Conn., 1725-1804=Mercy Stanley, m. 26 Nov. 1744, d. 1768.
Samuel Baldwin, of Goshen, N. Y., 1755-1838=Lucina Hill, of Goshen.
Harvey Baldwin, of Lexington, N. Y., 1784-1852=Nellie Calkins (1st wife).
Orin Calkins Baldwin, of Rensselaerville, N. Y.=Jane Wightman Luce, b. Middleburg, N. Y.
Orville Dwight Baldwin, of San Francisco, Member of the Order of Runnemede.=Millie Eva, daughter of Charles and Catharine (Rohé) Wehn, of Philadelphia, Pa.

Blanche Evelyn, of the Society of Colonial Dames.=John McGaw, of Brentford, England.		Orville Raymond Baldwin=Anna, dau. Eugene Deuprey. of Lake Co., Cal.		
Baldwin.	Evelyn Victoria.	Doris.	Orville Dwight.	Drusilla. Dalthea.

AMERICANS OF ROYAL DESCENT

PEDIGREE I.

HENRY III., King of England, *m.* Eleanor, daughter of Raymond, Count of Provence, a grandson of Alphonso, King of Aragon, and had:

EDMUND, Earl of Leicester, etc., lord high steward of England, who *m.* Blanche, widow of Henry, King of Navarre, and daughter of Robert Count of Artois, (by his wife, Matilda, daughter of Henry, Duke of Brabant), son of LOUIS VIII., King of France, and had:

HENRY, Earl of Leicester, etc., who *m.* Lady Maud, daughter of Sir Patrick, Lord Chatworth, by his wife, Lady Isabel de Beauchamp, also of Royal Descent, and had:

LADY ELEANOR PLANTAGENET, widow of John, Lord Beaumont, who *m.* Sir Richard Fitzalan, K. G., Earl of Arundel and Surrey, and had:

JOHN FITZALAN, Lord Maltravers, second son, *d.* 15 December, 1379. His and his wife's wills, given in Nicolas's "Testamenta Vetusta." He *m.* Lady Eleanor, *d.* 10 January, 1405, daughter of John, Lord Maltravers, and had:

JOHN, Lord Fitzalan de Arundel, eldest son, *d. v. p.*, who had:

SIR THOMAS FITZALAN, younger son. His will given in "Testamenta Vetusta." He *m.* Lady Katherine, daughter of Sir John Dynham, and sister to Sir John, Lord Dynham, K. G., and had:

LADY ELEANOR FITZALAN, who *m.* Sir Thomas Browne, treasurer of the household to King Henry VI., and had:

SIR ANTHONY BROWNE, standard bearer to Henry VII., who had:

LADY ELIZABETH BROWNE, who *m.* Henry, second Earl of Worcester, *d.* 1549, also of Royal Descent, (see Ped. LXXXIX.), and had:

SIR WILLIAM, Earl of Worcester, K. G., *d.* 1589, who *m.* Lady Christian, daughter of Edward, Lord North, and had:

SIR EDWARD, Earl of Worcester, K. G., *d.* 1628, who *m.* Lady Elizabeth, daughter of Francis Herbert, Earl of Huntingdon, and had:

LADY CATHERINE SOMERSET, *d.* 31 October, 1624, (see Dugdale's "Baronage," and Foster's "Royal Descents," p. 86), who *m.* 8 November,

1596, William, second Lord Petre, of Writtle, *b.* 24 June, 1575, *d.* 5 May, 1627, (see Morant's "Essex," and Bridge's "Topographer," April, 1789, p. 13), and had:

THOMAS PETRE, (brother to Robert, third Lord Petre, *d.* 1638), who *m.* Ursula, daughter of Richard (or Walter) Brooke, of Lapsley Hall, Suffolk, and had:

WINIFRED PETRE, *d.* 1771, who *m.* George Atwood, of Beverlyin, *d.* 1794, and had:

GEORGE ATWOOD, who *d.* at Warburton manor, Maryland, 1744. He *m.* Anne Petre, and had:

ANNE ATWOOD, who *m.* 3 June, 1739, William Digges, of Warburton manor, Md., also of Royal Descent, (Pedigree XVII.), and had:

GEORGE DIGGES, of Warburton manor, Prince George County, Md., which was patented 20 October, 1641. He *m.* Catherine, daughter of Robert Brent, by his wife, Anne, daughter of Daniel Carroll, of Upper Marlboro, Md., by his wife, Eleanor, daughter of Col. Henry Darnall, by his wife, Anne, daughter of Col. William Digges, Dep. Gov. of Md. (p. 76), (and sister to Charles, father of William, *m.* Anne Atwood), and had:

WILLIAM DUDLEY DIGGES, of "Green Hill," Prince George County, who *m.* Eleanor, daughter of Daniel Carroll, of "Duddington," by his wife, Anne, daughter of William Brent, of "Richlands," Stafford County, Va., by his wife, Eleanor, sister to John, Archbishop of Baltimore, and daughter of Daniel Carroll, of Upper Marlboro, aforesaid, and had:

NORA DIGGES, (a grand-daughter, on her mother's side, of Daniel Carroll, of "Duddington," D. C., see p. 304), who *m.* in 1854, James Ethelbert Morgan, M. D., of Washington, D. C., and had seven children, (see Corrigenda, B), of whom:

ADA MORGAN, youngest daughter, a member of the Maryland Society of the Colonial Dames of America, (see pp. 76, 304), who *m.* in 1869, Richard Smith Hill, Jr., of Prince George Co., Md., and had *Nora Digges* and *Elizabeth Snowden*, twins, *Ada Morgan, Eleanor Carroll*, and *Anna Brent Mosher*.

PEDIGREE II.

CHARLEMAGNE, Emperor of the West, King of the Franks, had by his third wife, Lady Hildegarde, *d.* 783, daughter of Childebrand, Duke of Suabia:

PEPIN, KING OF LOMBARDY and Italy, who *m.* Lady Bertha, daughter of William, Count of Thoulouse, and had:

BERNARD, KING OF LOMBARDY, who had by his wife, Lady Cunegonde:

PEPIN, COUNT OF VERMANDOIS and Peronne, 840, who had:

HERBERT I., COUNT DE VERMANDOIS, *d.* 902, who had:

HERBERT II., COUNT DE VERMANDOIS, *d.* 943, who had:

ALBERT I., THE PIOUS, COUNT DE VERMANDOIS, *d.* 987, who *m.* Princess Gerberga, daughter of Louis IV., King of France, and had:

HERBERT III., COUNT DE VERMANDOIS, who had:

OTHO, COUNT DE VERMANDOIS, 1021–1045, who had:

HERBERT IV., COUNT DE VERMANDOIS, 1045–1080, who *m.* Lady Hildebrante, Countess of Valois and Amiens, heiress, and daughter of Raoul III., Count de Valois, and had one child:

ADELHEID, COUNTESS OF VERMANDOIS, 1080–1117, who *m.* (his third wife) Hugh Magnus, Duke of France and Burgundy, Marquis of Orleans, Count of Paris, Valois and Vermandois, son of Henry I., King of France, grandson of Hugh Capet, King of France, and had:

LADY ISABEL DE VERMANDOIS (also called Elizabeth), *d.* 1131 (widow of Robert de Beaumont, Earl of Mellent and Leicester, *d.* 1118), who *m.*, secondly, William de Warren, second Earl of Surrey, *d.* 113–, also of Royal Descent, and had:

WILLIAM DE WARREN, third Earl of Surrey, *d. s. p. m.* in 1148. He *m.* Lady Adela, *d.* 1174, daughter of William de Talvas III., Count of Alencon and Ponthieu, also of Royal Descent, and had:

LADY ISABELLA DE WARREN, Countess of Surrey, *d.* 1199 (widow of William de Blois, *d.* 1160), who *m.*, secondly, 1163, Hameline Plantagenet, fifth Earl of Warren and Surrey, *d.* 1202, and had:

LADY ISABELLA PLANTAGENET DE WARREN, who *m.* (his first wife) Roger Bigod, created Earl of Norfolk in 1189, steward of England, a surety for the Magna Charta, also of Royal Descent, *d.* 1220, and had:

HUGH BIGOD, second Earl of Norfolk, one of the sureties for the Magna

Charta, d. 1225; m. Lady Maud Marshall, daughter of William, Earl of Pembroke, protector of England during the nonage of Henry III. and his wife Lady Isabel de Clare, also of Royal Descent, and had:

SIR RALPH BIGOD, KNT., third son, who m. Lady Berta de Furnival, and had:

LADY ISABEL BIGOD (widow of Gilbert de Lacie, Lord of Meath, d. 1241), who m., secondly, John Fitzgeoffrey, of Barkhampstead and Kirtling, sheriff of Yorkshire, 1234, justiciary of Ireland in 1246, son of Geoffrey Fitz Piers, Earl of Essex, justiciary of England, and had:

JOHN FITZJOHN, chief justice of Ireland, 1258, father of:

MAUD FITZJOHN (widow of Gerard de Furnival, of Sheffield, d. 1280), who m., secondly, William de Beauchamp, of Elmley, created Earl of Warwick, d. 1298, also of Royal Descent, and had:

LADY SARAH DE BEAUCHAMP, who m. Richard, sixth Baron de Talbot, of Goodrich, d. 1306, also of Royal Descent, and had:

LADY GWENTHELLEAN DE TALBOT, who m. Sir Payne de Turberville, custos of Glamorganshire, 134–, and had:

SARAH DE TURBERVILLE, who m. William de Gamage, sheriff of Gloucestershire in 1325, and had:

GILBERT DE GAMAGE, of Rogiad, who m. Lettice, daughter of Sir William Seymour, of Penhow, and had:

SIR WILLIAM GAMAGE, of Rogiad and Coyty, who m. Mary, daughter of Sir Thomas de Rodburg, and had:

SIR THOMAS GAMAGE, of Rogiad and Coyty, who m. Matilla, daughter of Sir John Dennis, and had:

JANE GAMAGE, who m. Roger ap Arnold ap Arnholt-Vychan, of Llanthony Manor, in Monmouthshire, also of Royal Descent, and had:

THOMAS ARNOLD, eldest son, succeeded to Llanthony Manor. He m. Agnes, daughter of Sir Richard Wairnstead (or Warnstead), and had: JOHN, eldest son and heir, who owned Hingham Manor, Churcham parish, Gloucestershire; d. 15 September, 1545, and

RICHARD ARNOLD, second son, who resided in Street parish, Somersetshire. He m. Emmote, daughter of Pearce Young, of Damerham, Wiltshire, and had:

RICHARD ARNOLD, eldest son, who resided on Bagbere Manor, in Middleton parish, Dorsetshire, before 1549. His will, dated 15 May, 1593, was proved 9 July, 1595. He owned, besides Bagbere—the old Bagbere Manor house was demolished in 1870—the manors of Alton Pancras, Buckland Newton, Cheselbourne and Melcombe Horsey, all in Dorsetshire. He was buried in July, 1595, in the Milton Church. He was twice married, and of his children by his first wife, whose name has not been preserved, JOHN, eldest son and heir, and

THOMAS ARNOLD,* named in his father's will. He resided on Melcombe Horsey Manor, in Dorsetshire (Subsidy Rolls, 1598), and removed to Cheselbourne Manor, in this county. He *m.*, first, Alice, *b.* 29 September, 1553, daughter of John Gully, of Northover Manor, in Tolpuddle parish, Dorset; the name of his second wife has not been preserved (*See* H. Q. Somerby's Arnold pedigree, "compiled in 1870 from the Herald's Visitations, Inqui. P. M., Subsidy Rolls, parish registers," *etc.* N. E. His. Geneal. Register, October, 1879, and the Family Records kept by the immigrant William Arnold and his son, N. E. His. Gen. Reg., vol. 33, p. 427). By his first wife he had:

WILLIAM ARNOLD, *b.* 24 June, 1587. He was appointed 23 November, 1616, guardian of the children of his brother John, of Cheselbourn, 1585–1616. He sailed from Dartmouth with his wife and four children Friday, 1 May, 1635, and arrived in New England 24 June, 1635; came to Providence, Rhode Island, 20 April, 1636, and to Newport 19 November, 1651. He had many grants of land and filled important offices of trust in the Colony of Rhode Island. He was one of the thirteen original proprietors of the Province Plantations; was a signer of the agreement for a form of government in the colony in 1640, and was commissioner for Providence to the Court of Commissioners in 1661 (see Austin's "Genealogical Dictionary of Rhode Island"). He *d.* about 1676, having issue by his wife, Christian, *bapt.* 15 February, 1583, daughter of Thomas Peake, of Muchelney, Somersetshire, of whom:

1.—ELIZABETH ARNOLD, *b.* 23 November, 1611, *d.* in 1683; *m.* William Carpenter, of Providence, *d.* 7 September, 1685, and had:

    I.—BENJAMIN CARPENTER, of Providence, *m.* Mary, daughter of Pardon and ——— (Butterworth) Tillinghast. She was *b.* October, 1661, and *d.* 1711 (about). Their son:

        BENJAMIN CARPENTER, *b.* 1673, *d.* 16 December, 1766; *m.* Prudence, daughter of Nathaniel and Christian (Cole) Kingsley. She was *b.* 23 August, 1714, and *d.* 29 July, 1801. Their son:

        OLIVER CARPENTER, *b.* 1 September, 1739, *m.* Susanna, daughter

---

* The following ladies, members of the National Society of the Colonial Dames of America, are also of Royal Descent through Thomas Arnold:

MRS. LEWIS T. HOYT, New York State Society.

MRS. CHARLES S. SARGEANT, Massachusetts State Society.

MRS. S. VAN R. THAYER, Massachusetts State Society.

MRS. GEORGE V. CRESSON, Pennsylvania State Society.

MRS. B. JONES TAYLOR, Maryland State Society.

MRS. D. GIRARD WRIGHT, Maryland State Society.

MRS. A. L. DANIELSON, Rhode Island State Society.

MRS. LEWIS BUCKNER, Kentucky State Society.

of Benjamin and Jemima (Williams) Potter. She was *b.* 3 July, 1755. Their daughter:

CHARLOTTE CARPENTER, *m.* Allen Gladding, son of Jonathan and Susanna (Cary) Gladding, of Bristol, Rhode Island. He was *b.* 14 November, 1764, and *d.* 22 May, 1837. Their daughter:

SUSAN CARY GLADDING, *m.* John Holden Ormsbee, son of John and Barbara (Holden) Ormsbee. He was *b.* 1780 and *d.* 5 September, 1860. Their daughter:

CHARLOTTE BARBARA ORMSBEE, *m.* Alexander Farnum, and had:

MARGARET BARBARA FARNUM, a member of the Rhode Island Society of the Colonial Dames of America, who *m.* Charles Warren Lippitt, of Providence, former Governor of Rhode Island, and had: *Charles Warren* (deceased); *Alexander Farnum* (deceased); *Jeanie Barbara* (deceased); *Charles Warren, Jr., Alexander Farnum*, and *Gorton Thayer*.

II.—TIMOTHY CARPENTER, of Providence, *d.* 19 August, 1726, who *m.* Hannah, daughter of William and Hannah (Wickes) Burton, and had:

ELIZABETH CARPENTER, who *m.* Peleg Williams, *d.* 1766, and had:

FREELOVE WILLIAMS, 1713–1791, who *m.*, 1732, Daniel Fiske, 1710–1804, also of Royal Descent, and had:

DANIEL FISKE, 1753–1810, who *m.*, 1785, Freelove Knight, and had:

CELIA FISKE, 1787–1859; *m.*, 1815, Stephen Burlingame, *d.* 1837, and had:

COLONEL STEPHEN BURLINGAME, 1819–1890; *m.*, 1841, Elsie Maria Tillinghast, 1820–1884, and had:

SARAH MARIA BURLINGAME, a member of the New Hampshire Society of the Colonial Dames of America, who *m.*, 12 December, 1877, Prentiss Webster, of Lowell, Mass., 1851–1898, and had: *Susan H., Adeline B., Prentiss B., Helen B.*, and *Dorothy P.*

2.—BENEDICT ARNOLD, of Providence, *b.* 21 December, 1615. Governor of the Rhode Island Colony, 1663–1678; *d.* 19 June, 1678; *m.*, 17 December, 1640, Damaris Westcott, of Stukeley, and had:

CAPTAIN JOSIAH ARNOLD, of Jamestown, Rhode Island, *b.* 22 December, 1646, *d.* 26 December, 1724–1725; *m.*, first, 14 September, 1683, Sarah Mills, 1665–1704, and had by her:

ABAGAIL ARNOLD, *b.* 14 December, 1685, *d.* 14 December, 1705–1706; *m.*, 14 February, 1704–1705, Governor Jonathan Law, *b.* Milford, Connecticut, 6 August, 1674; chief justice of Connecticut 1725–

1741, governor of the Connecticut Colony, 1741–1750, d. 6 November, 1750, and had:

JONATHAN LAW, JR., b. Milford, 5 December, 1705–1706, d. 24 September, 1790; m., 11 January, 1737, Eunice Andrew, b. 16 August, 1720, d. 2 March, 1762, a descendant of the Rev. John Eliot, the celebrated apostle to the Indians; of Governor William Brenton, of Rhode Island; of Rev. Samuel Andrew, of Milford, Connecticut, a founder and second president of Yale College; of Governor Robert Treat, of Connecticut, etc., and had:

BENEDICT ARNOLD LAW, b. Milford, 20 December, 1740, d. at North Milford, 19 November, 1819; m., 4 January, 1770, Sarah, b. 24 April, 1749, d. 26 November, 1785, daughter of Captain Richard Bryan, of Milford, and had:

SARAH BRYAN LAW, b. North Milford, 9 November, 1785, d. at Philadelphia, Pennsylvania, 19 February, 1854; m., 14 January, 1808, Ebenezer Johnson, Jr., b. 30 April, 1774, d. 8 July, 1863, and had:

CHARLOTTE AUGUSTA JOHNSON, b. New Haven, Connecticut, 5 July, 1823, who m., 27 August, 1846, Dewitt Clinton Morris, of Philadelphia, Pennsylvania, b. 1821, d. 28 July, 1868, a descendant of Lewis Morris, chief justice of New York; governor of New Jersey, and had:

CHARLOTTE JOHNSON MORRIS, of Brunswick, Maine, a member of the New York and Maine Societies of the Colonial Dames of America, who m., at New Haven, Connecticut, 11 July, 1876, Professor William Addison Houghton, of Bowdoin College, and had: *William Morris, Charles Andrew Johnson,* and *Harriet Cecil.*

3.—JOANNA ARNOLD, b. 27 February, 1617, d. 1692; m., first, 1646, Zachariah Rhodes, of Providence, 1603–1665, a signer of the Compact of 3 July, 1644; was constable 1660, deputy 1664, town treasurer 1665, a town councilman 1665, etc.; will proved 29 May, 1666, and had: *Mary,* (see below) and

I.—REBECCA RHODES, d. 1727 (widow of Nicholas Power), who m., secondly, 2 December, 1676, Daniel Williams, of Providence, b. February, 1642, d. 14 May, 1712, and had:

MARY WILLIAMS, d. after 1740, who m. Epenetus Olney, of Providence, b. 18 January, 1675, d. 18 September, 1740, and had:

JAMES OLNEY, of North Providence, d. 10 February, 1770; m., 1 March, 1733, Hannah Winsor, of Providence, b. 26 August, 1711, d. 27 December, 1777, and had:

EMOR OLNEY, of Johnston, Rhode Island, b. 28 November, 1741, d. 29 March, 1830; m., 1760, Amy Hopkins, 1742–1782, and had:

PARIS OLNEY, b. 18 October, 1770, d. 1850; m. Mercy Winsor, b. 31 August, 1769, and had:

MARY ANN OLNEY, b. 21 June, 1803, d. 11 September, 1878; m., 25 December, 1822, Clark Sayles, of Pawtucket, b. 18 May, 1797, d. 8 February, 1885, and had:

WILLIAM FRANCIS SAYLES, of Pawtucket, b. 20 September, 1824, d. 7 May, 1894; m., 30 October, 1849, Mary Wilkinson Fessenden, also of Royal Descent, and had:

MARY FESSENDEN SAYLES, a member of the Rhode Island Society of the Colonial Dames of America, who m., 21 May, 1872, Roscoe Stetson Washburn, of Providence, and had: *Maurice King, Roscoe Clifton, William F. S.* (deceased), and *John Fessenden* (deceased).

II.—JOHN RHODES, of Warwick, Rhode Island, b. 1658, d. August, 1716; m., first, 12 February, 1685, Waite, 1668–1711, daughter of Resolved Waterman, 1638–1670, and his wife Mercy, 1640–1705, daughter of Roger Williams, 1599–1683, the founder of the Rhode Island and Providence Plantations, and had:

PHEBE RHODES, b. 30 November, 1698, d. 1761, who m., first, Anthony Holden, d. 13 May, 1720, and had:

CATHARINE HOLDEN, only child, b. 13 October, 1717, d. 4 May, 1807; m., 2 January, 1736, Christopher Lippitt, b. 29 November, 1712, d. 7 December, 1764, and had:

I.—CHARLES LIPPITT, b. 2 March, 1754, d. 17 August, 1845; m., 12 January, 1783, Penelope, b. 5 February, 1758, d. 27 August, 1889, daughter of John Low, and had:

   1.—JULIA LIPPITT, b. 29 January, 1784, d. 22 March, 1867; m., 9 September, 1814, Joseph Sweet, b. 5 December, 1782, d. 9 January, 1878, and had:

      I.—JULIA SWEET, a member of the Rhode Island Society of the Colonial Dames of America, who m., 7 June, 1849, John Henry Weir, of Providence, Rhode Island, b. 27 August, 1819, d. 12 September, 1858.

      II.—CATHARINE SWEET, a member of the Rhode Island Society of the Colonial Dames of America.

   2.—WARREN LIPPITT, b. 25 September, 1786, d. 22 January, 1850, who m., 7 July, 1811, Eliza Seamans, b. 20 February, 1792, d. 7 April, 1881, and had:

      HENRY LIPPITT, b. 9 October, 1818, d. 5 June, 1891, who m., 16 December, 1845, Mary Ann Balch, b. 7 October, 1823, d. 31 August, 1889, and had:

I.—JEANIE LIPPITT, *b.* 6 January, 1852, a member of the Rhode Island Society of the Colonial Dames of America, who *m.*, 18 April, 1893, William Babcock Weeden, of Providence, Rhode Island. *No issue.*

II.—MARY BALCH LIPPITT, *b.* 14 July, 1858, a member of the Rhode Island Society of the Colonial Dames of America, who *m.*, 7 January, 1892, Charles John Steedman, of Philadelphia. Issue: *Charles Richard, b.* 31 July, 1897.

III.—ABBY FRANCES LIPPITT, *b.* 31 October, 1861, a member of the Rhode Island Society of the Colonial Dames of America, who *m.*, 24 January, 1893, Duncan Hunter. Issue: *Mary L., Frances G.,* and *Janet Malise.*

II.—COLONEL CHRISTOPHER LIPPITT, *b.* 28 October, 1744, *d.* 17 June, 1824; *m.*, 23 March, 1777, Waite Harris, *b.* 1775, *d.* 8 September, 1836, and had:

WILLIAM LIPPITT, *b.* 21 November, 1786, *d.* 8 October, 1872; *m.*, 1 January, 1809, Rhobey Sheldon, *b.* 19 October, 1790, *d.* 3 January, 1865, and had:

SARAH WILLIAMS LIPPITT, *b.* 7 February, 1832, who *m.*, 15 June, 1859, John Tyler Mauran, *b.* 20 November, 1826, *d.* 23 December, 1882, and had:

JULIA LIPPITT MAURAN, of Providence, Rhode Island, *b.* 25 June 1860, a member of the Rhode Island Society of the Colonial Dames of America.

4.—STEPHEN ARNOLD, of Pawtuxet, *b.* 22 December, 1622, *d.* 15 November, 1699. He was a deputy to the general court for thirteen years, and governor's assistant nine years. He *m.*, 24 November, 1646, Sarah, 1629–1713, daughter of Edward Smith, of Newport, *d.* 1675, governor's assistant six years, commissioner to the court of commissioners two years and deputy to the general court seven years, and had:

I.—PHŒBE ARNOLD, 1670–173—, who *m.*, 25 December, 1691, Benjamin Smith, Jr., of Warwick, Rhode Island, son of Benjamin Smith, 1631–1713, governor's assistant nineteen years, deputy to the general court eight years, and his wife Lydia, also of Royal Descent, daughter of William Carpenter, *d.* Providence, 1685 (and his wife Elizabeth, a daughter of the aforesaid William Arnold, 1587–1676), one of the thirteen original proprietors of the Providence Plantations, commissioner, deputy, assistant, *etc.*, and had:

PHŒBE SMITH, *b.* 5 December, 1699, who *m.* James Cargill, Jr., of North Kingston, Rhode Island, and had:

LUCY CARGILL, who *m.* Nathan Arnold, of Cumberland, Rhode Island, a descendant of Thomas Arnold, *d.* 1674, and had:

PEDIGREE II.—Continued.

CAPTAIN NATHAN ARNOLD, of Cumberland, who *d.* from wound received in battle 29 August, 1778; *m.* Esther Slack Darling, also of Royal Descent, and had:

SETH ARNOLD, of Smithfield, Rhode Island, who *m.* Mrs. Belinda (Mason) Streeter, a descendant of Captain Roger Williams, the founder of Rhode Island and the Providence Plantations, and president of the Colony, and had:

FRANCES ARNOLD, who *m.* William Henry Hathaway, of Dighton, Massachusetts, also of Royal Descent, and had:

BELINDA OLNEY HATHAWAY, a member of the Rhode Island Society of the Colonial Dames of America, Society Daughters of the American Revolution, Order of the Crown, *etc.*, who *m.* Joshua Wilbour, of Bristol, Rhode Island.

II.—ESTHER ARNOLD, *b.* 22 September, 1647, *d.* 1688. She *m.*, first, 1671, James Dexter, *d.* 1676, and *m.*, second, 30 October, 1680, William Andrews, by whom she had an only child:

MARY ANDREWS, who *m.* Simon Smith, son of Benjamin Smith, 1631–1713, and his wife, Elizabeth (Lydia), *d.* 1 October, 1711, daughter of William Carpenter, of Providence, Rhode Island, *d.* 7 September, 1685, and his wife, Elizabeth, 1611–1683, a daughter of the aforesaid William Arnold, and had:

SIMON SMITH, who *m.*, 23 March, 1766, Freelove, *b.* 13 July, 1743, daughter of Arthur Fenner, 1699–1788, and had:

SIMON SMITH, 1710–1753, who *m.* Elizabeth Turpin, and had:

SARAH SMITH, *b.* 28 May, 1780, who *m.*, 25 June, 1803, John Carpenter Bucklin, *d.* 1842, and had:

JEANNETTE BUCKLIN, *b.* 1814, *d.* 25 June, 1854, who *m.*, February, 1849, George Davis, *b.* 5 April, 1811, *d.* 14 October, 1895, and had:

MARY DAVIS, *b.* 9 June, 1851, a member of the Rhode Island Society of the Colonial Dames of America, who *m.*, 23 January, 1873, George Corlis Nightingale, of Providence, Rhode Island, and had: *Jeannette Davis, Mary Greene, George Corlis,* and *Alice Bucklin.*

III.—ISRAEL ARNOLD, *b.* 30 October, 1649, *d.* 15 September, 1716, who *m.*, 16 April, 1677, Mary (widow of Elisha Smith), *d.* 19 September, 1723, daughter of James Barker, of Newport, 1623–1702, one of those named in the Royal Charter, 1663; was ensign, 1648; commissioner for three years, assistant for nine years, deputy for twelve years and deputy governor, 1678–1679, and had:

SARAH ARNOLD, *d.* Warwick, Rhode Island, 26 November, 1727, who *m.*, 21 December, 1708, Silas Carpenter, Jr., of Providence, Rhode Island, *b.* 27 July, 1709, *d.* 13 June, 1751, also a descendant of the aforesaid William Arnold, and had:

MARY CARPENTER, b. 14 February, 1714, who m., 29 April, 1733, Benjamin Westcott, 3d, of Providence, b. 1716, and had:

JAMES WESTCOTT, of Providence, b. 25 March, 1740, d. 17 March, 1814; m., 1767, Martha, b. 9 September, 1747, d. 18 August, 1790, daughter of William and Lydia (Harris) Tillinghast, of Providence, and had:

JAMES WESTCOTT, JR., of Providence, b. 28 June, 1773, d. 2 June, 1853; m., 23 August, 1795, Mary Dewer, b. Providence, 1776, d. 2 June, 1853, and had:

STEPHEN T. WESTCOTT, b. 22 November, 1799, d. West Roxbury, Massachusetts, 13 June, 1874; m., 22 June, 1826, Mary Smith Barker, b. Salem, Massachusetts, 23 December, 1800, d. West Roxbury, 29 September, 1860, and had:

EMMA WESTCOTT, a member of the Rhode Island Society of the Colonial Dames of America and the Order of the Crown, who m., 23 December, 1868, Jonathan Russell Bullock, of Bristol, Rhode Island, and had:

EMMA RUSSELL BULLOCK, only child, who m., 6 May, 1897, Albert Stanton Cheseborough, of Bristol, Rhode Island.

IV.—ELIZABETH ARNOLD, b. 2 November, 1659, d. 5 June, 1728; m., 16 December, 1680, Peter Greene, of Warwick, Rhode Island, b. 7 February, 1654–5, d. 12 August, 1723, and had:

WILLIAM GREENE, b. 29 July, 1690, d. 17 March, 1766; m., 14 February, 1712–13, Sarah Medbury, of Rehoboth, Massachusetts, b. 27 April, 1689, d. 6 April, 1763, and had:

JAMES GREENE, b. 1713, d. 30 May, 1792; m., 15 June, 1738, Desire Slocum, of Warwick, b. 14 January, 1720, d. 22 November, 1794, and had:

JAMES GREENE, b. 26 October, 1754, d. 14 October, 1825; m., 17 November, 1782, Rebecca Pitman, b. 11 March, 1763, d. 7 July, 1806, and had:

ELIZA GREENE, b. 1 August, 1791, d. 23 March, 1820; m., 3 December, 1809, Stephen Harris, of Warwick, b. 29 October, 1786, d. 10 October, 1858, and had:

CYRUS HARRIS, b. 16 October, 1812, d. 23 June, 1887; m., 26 August, 1836, Abby Spalding, of Centreville, Rhode Island, b. 12 November, 1816, d. 21 November, 1888, and had:

ABBY GREENE HARRIS, b. 31 December, 1851, a member of the Rhode Island Society of the Colonial Dames of America, who m., 28 February, 1876, Samuel Ames, of Providence, Rhode Island, b. 10 April, 1849. *No issue.*

THE ROYAL DESCENT
OF
MRS. JONATHAN R. BULLOCK,
OF BRISTOL, R. I.

HUGH CAPET, King of France=Lady Adela of Aquitaine.
Princess Hedewige=Ranigerus V., Count of Hainault.
Lady Beatrix d'Hainault=Eblo I., Count de Reimes de Rouci.
Adela, Countess de Rouci=Hildwin, Count de Montdider de Rouci.
Lady Margaret de Rouci=Hugh, Count de Clermont.
Lady Adeliza de Clermont=Gilbert, 2d Earl of Clare.
Lady Adeliza de Clare=Alberic de Vere.
Lady Juliana de Vere=Hugh Bigod, Earl of Norfolk.
Roger Bigod, Earl of Norfolk=Lady Isabella de Warren.
Hugh Bigod, Earl of Norfolk=Lady Maud Marshall.
Sir Ralph Bigod, Knt.=Lady Berta de Furnival.
Lady Isabel Bigod=John Fitz-Piers Fitz-Geoffrey.
John Fitz-John=(Name unknown).
Lady Maud Fitz-John=William, Earl of Warwick.
Lady Sarah de Beauchamp=Richard de Talbot, of Lintone.
Lady Gwenthellean de Talbot=Sir Payne de Turberville, of Glamorganshire.
Lady Sarah de Turberville=William de Gamage, of Gloucestershire.
Gilbert de Gamage=Lady Lettice Seymour.
Sir William Gamage=Mary de Redburg.
Sir Thomas Gamage=(Name unknown).
Lady Jane Gamage=Roger ap Arnholt, of Llanthony.
Thomas Arnold, of Llanthony=Agnes Wairnstead.
Richard Arnold, of Somersetshire=Emmote Young, of Wiltshire.
Richard Arnold, of Dorsetshire=(First wife, name unknown).
Thomas Arnold, of Dorsetshire=Alice Gully, of Dorsetshire.
William Arnold, of Providence, R. I.=Christian Peake.
Stephen Arnold, of Pawtuxet, R. I.=Sarah Smith.
Israel Arnold=Mary Barker.
Sarah Arnold=Silas Carpenter, of Providence.
Mary Carpenter=Benjamin Westcott, 3d, of Providence.
James Westcott, of Providence=Martha Tillinghast, of Providence.
James Westcott, of Providence=Mary Dewer.
Stephen T. Westcott, West Roxbury, Mass.=Mary Smith Barker.
Emma Westcott, member of the National Society of the Colonial Dames of America=Jonathan Russell Bullock, of Bristol, Rhode Island.
Emma Russell Bullock=Albert S. Cheseborough, of Bristol, Rhode Island.

PEDIGREE III.

ROBERT BRUCE, King of Scotland, had by his first wife, Lady Isabel, daughter of Donald, Earl of Marr:

PRINCESS MARGERY BRUCE, *d.* 1315-16, who *m.*, 1315 (his second wife), Walter, lord high steward of Scotland, 1293-1326, and had, only child:

ROBERT II., King of Scotland, *b.* 2 March, 1315-16, who had by his first wife, Lady Elizabeth, daughter of Sir Adam Mure, of Rowallan:

PRINCESS CATHERINE STUART, who *m.* Sir David Lindsay, of Glenesk, created, in 1389, Earl of Crawford, *d.* before 1412, and had:

LADY MARJORY LINDSAY, sister of Alexander, second Earl of Crawford, who *m.* Sir William Douglas, of Lochlevan and Lugton, and had:

SIR HENRY DOUGLAS, of Lochlevan and Lugton, who *m.* Lady Elizabeth, daughter of Sir Robert Erskine, of that Ilk, *d.* 1453, and had:

ROBERT DOUGLAS, of Lochlevan and Kincross, *k.* at Flodden, who had by his first wife, Elizabeth, daughter of David Boswell, of Balmuto:

SIR ROBERT DOUGLAS, Knt., of Lochlevan, only son, who *m.* Margaret, daughter of David Balfour, of Burleigh, and had:

THOMAS DOUGLAS, of Lochlevan, only son, *d. v. p.*, who *m.* Elizabeth, daughter of Archibald Boyd, son of Sir Robert, first Lord Boyd, of Kilmarnock, regent of Scotland 1466, justiciary and lord high chamberlain, and had:

ELIZABETH DOUGLAS, third daughter (sister of Sir Robert Douglas, of Lochlevan, *k.* at Pinkie, 1547, father of Sir William Douglas, seventh Earl of Morton, and Robert Douglas, Earl of Buchan), who *m.*, before 26 August, 1529, Alexander Alsynder (or Alexander), of Menstrie, *d.* 1545 (see Wood's "Douglas Peerage of Scotland," ii., 536-39; Brown's "Genesis of the United States," p. 813; Roger's "House of Alexander," *American Heraldic Journal*, iv., p. 59; Hewlett's "Scotch Dignities," p. 160), and had:

ANDREW ALEXANDER, of Menstrie, eldest son, *d.* before 26 August, 1529, father of:

JOHN ALEXANDER, of Gogar, 1541, second son (only uncle of William Alexander, created Earl of Stirling, who had descendants), father of:

PEDIGREE III.—Continued.

ALEXANDER ALEXANDER, of Millnab, only son, father of:

DAVID ALEXANDER, of Muthill, second son, father of:

JAMES ALEXANDER,* b. 1691, second son, who came to America in 1716, and became surveyor-general of New Jersey in 1714. He was for many years a member of the King's council and attorney-general, and auditor-general of New Jersey and New York, d. in 1756, and had by his wife, Mary, d. 1760, daughter of John Sprott, of Wigton, in Scotland, and widow of Samuel Prevost or Provost:

1.—MARY ALEXANDER, b. 16 October, 1721, d. 24 April, 1767, who m., 1739, Peter Van Brugh Livingston, of New York, a son of Philip Livingston, second lord of Livingston Manor, New York, and had:

I.—CATHERINE LIVINGSTON, 1743–1798, who m., 20 April, 1762, Nicholas Bayard, of New York, and had:

1.—KATHERINE ANNE BAYARD, who m. Robert Charles Johnson, of New York, and had:

KATHERINE ANNE JOHNSON, who m. Thomas Pollock Devereux, and had:

JOHN DEVEREUX, who m. Margaret Mordecai, and had:

ELLEN DEVEREUX, a member of the North Carolina Society of the Colonial Dames of America, the Order of the Crown, *etc.*, who m. John Wetmore Hinsdale, of Raleigh, North Carolina, and had: *Margaret*, wife of John Cotton Engelhard; *Samuel Johnson, Elizabeth Christophers, John Wetmore, Ellen Devereux*, and *Annie Devereux.*

2.—ELIZA BAYARD, d. 1846, who m., 30 April, 1791, John Houston McIntosh, of Darien, Georgia, also of Royal Descent, and had:

I.—JOHN HOUSTON MCINTOSH, b. Cumberland Island, Georgia, 7 June, 1802, d. 4 May, 1852; m., 13 September, 1832, Mary Randolph, daughter of Joseph and Elizabeth Higbee, of Trenton, New Jersey, and had:

MARY RANDOLPH MCINTOSH, a member of the Ohio Society of the Colonial Dames of America, who m., 12 March, 1861, John Kilgour, of "The Pines," Mt. Lookout, Cincinnati, Ohio, and had: *Charles, Bayard Livingston, Elizabeth, Louise*, and

I.—MARY KILGOUR, a member of the New York Society of the Colonial Dames of America, who m., 16 April, 1890,

---

* MRS. WALTER KENNEDY, a member of the Tennessee State Society of the National Society of the Colonial Dames of America is also of Royal Descent, through James Alexander.

Edmund E. Miller, of Cincinnati and New York, and had: *Mary Kilgour*, b. Cincinnati, 4 April, 1891.

II.—CHARLOTTE KILGOUR, a member of the New York Society of the Colonial Dames of America, who m., 21 April, 1896, Captain Ashton B. Heyl, M.D., United States Army, and had: *John Kilgour*, b. 2 March, 1897, at Fort Riley, Kansas.

II.—ELIZA BAYARD MCINTOSH, who m. Duncan L. Clinch, United States Army, and had:

ELIZA BAYARD CLINCH, who m. General Robert Anderson, United States Army, and had:

ELIZA MCINTOSH CLINCH ANDERSON, a member of the New York Society of the Colonial Dames of America, who m. James M. Lawton, of New York City.

II.—SARAH LIVINGSTON, who m. Major John Ricketts, of Jamaica, and had:

MARIA ELIZA RICKETTS, m. William Palmer, of Suffolk, and had:

SARAH JULIA PALMER, m. William Fisher, of Philadelphia, and had:

ELIZABETH FISHER, a member of the Society of the Colonial Dames of America, who m. Edward King, of New York City. *Issue.*

2.—ELIZABETH ALEXANDER, who m. John Stevens, of Perth Amboy, New Jersey, and had:

JOHN STEVENS, of Hoboken, New Jersey, who m. Rachel Cox, and had:

EDWIN AUGUSTUS STEVENS, who m., secondly, Martha Bayard Dod, and had by her:

CAROLINE BAYARD STEVENS, a member of the Society of the Colonial Dames of America, who m. Archibald Alexander, of New York City. *Issue.*

3.—CATHERINE ALEXANDER, who m. (his first wife) Major Walter Rutherfurd, of the British Army, and had:

JOHN RUTHERFURD, of Edgarstown, New Jersey, b. 1760, d. 23 February, 1840, United States Senator from New Jersey, 1791–1798, who m., 1781, Magdalene, daughter of General Lewis Morris, chief justice and governor of New Jersey, a member of the Continental Congress and a signer of the Declaration of Independence, and had:

ROBERT WALTER RUTHERFURD, of New York, 1778–1851, who m. his cousin, Sabina E., daughter of Colonel Lewis Morris, Jr., and had:

JOHN RUTHERFURD, of New York, d. 1871, who m. Charlotte, daughter of James Kane Livingston, of New York, and had:

HELENA RUTHERFURD, a member of the New York Society of the Colonial Dames of America, who m. Alfred Ely, of Newton, Massachusetts.

4.—WILLIAM ALEXANDER, b. 1726, major-general in the American Army; surveyor-general of New Jersey; he assumed the title "Earl of Stirling," as under Scottish law and custom he inherited it, according to a decision of the Chancery Court of Scotland in 1759, which declared him the nearest heir-male to the last Earl of Stirling (see sketch of General Alexander, by his grandson, Judge Duer, in "Proceedings of the New Jersey Historical Society," 1847), but was denied the right to it, and forbidden by the English House of Lords to use it. Before his case was argued, 10 March, 1762, "Lord Stirling" d. in Albany, New York, 15 January, 1783, leaving issue by his wife Sarah, daughter of Philip Livingston, second lord of the Manor of Livingston, New York:

CATHERINE ALEXANDER, 1755-1826, who m., first, 27 July, 1779, at "Basking Ridge," New Jersey, Colonel William Duer, of the New York Line, Continental Army, and had:

I.—JUDGE WILLIAM ALEXANDER DUER, of New York, 1780-1858, president of Columbia College, 1829-1842, who m., 1806, Marie, daughter of William Denning, of New York, and had:

ELIZABETH DENNING DUER, b. 1821, a member of the Society of the Colonial Dames of America, who m., 1845, Archibald Gracie King, of New York, and had:

MARIA DUNNING KING, a member of the Society of the Colonial Dames of America, who m., 4 October, 1871, John King Van Rensselaer, of New York. *Issue.*

2.—SARA GRACIE KING, a member of the Society of the Colonial Dames of America, who m., 1 December, 1875, Frederic Bronson, of New York City. *Issue.*

II.—MARIE THEODORA DUER, 1789-1837, who m., 1816, Beverly Chew, of New Orleans, Louisiana, and had:

ALEXANDER LAFAYETTE CHEW, of Geneva, New York, who m. Sarah Augusta Prouty, also of Royal Descent, and had:

KATHERINE ADELAIDE CHEW, a member of the New Jersey Society of the Colonial Dames of America, who m. Samuel Winship, of Morristown, New Jersey. Issue: *Theodora Augusta.*

PEDIGREE IV.

CHARLEMAGNE, King of France and Emperor of the West,
d. 814, had by his third wife, Hildegarde, *d.* 783, daughter of Childebrand, Duke of Suabia:

PEPIN, KING OF LOMBARDY and Italy, second son, who *m.* Lady Bertha, daughter of William, Count of Thoulouse, and had:

BERNARD, KING OF LOMBARDY, who had by his wife, Cunegonde:

PEPIN, Count of Vermandois and Peronne, a lay abbot, 840, father of:

PEPIN DE SENLIS DE VALOIS, Count Berengarius, of Bretagne, father of:

LADY POPPA DE VALOIS, who *m.* (his first wife) Rollo the Dane, founder of the royal House of Normandy and England, first Duke of Normandy, 912, *d.* 932, also of Royal Descent (see Anderson's "Royal Genealogies"), and had:

WILLIAM THE LONGSWORD, second Duke of Normandy, father of:

RICHARD I., third Duke of Normandy, father of:

GODFREY, Count of Eu and Brion, in Normandy, father of:

GISLEBERT-CRISPIN, Count of Eu and Brion, father of:

BALDWIN DE BRION, who accompanied his relative, William of Normandy, to England, and became high sheriff of Devonshire. He *m.* Lady Albreda, daughter of Richard-goz d'Abrancis, Viscount d'Auveranchez (who accompanied the Conqueror and was granted the Earldom of Chester, in 1086), and his wife, Lady Emme, half-sister of King William the Conqueror, and had:

RICHARD D'AUVERANCHE de Redvers, Baron of Oakhampton, created Earl of Devon, *d.* 1137; *m.* Lady Adeliza, daughter of William Fitz-Osborne, Count of Bretoille, lieutenant and steward in Normandy, created Earl of Hereford, and had:

BALDWIN DE REDVERS, second Earl of Devon, *d.* 1155; *m.* Lady Lucia, daughter of Dru de Balm, and had:

WILLIAM DE REDVERS de Vernon, who succeeded as sixth Earl of Devon, *d.* 1216. He had by his wife, Lady Mabel de Bellomont, also of Royal Descent, daughter of Robert the Consul, Earl of Mellent and first Earl of Gloucester, *d.* 1147:

LADY MARY DE REDVERS (widow of Robert de Courtenay, of Oakhampton, *d.* 1242), who *m.*, secondly, Peter Prouz, of Eastervale, Devonshire (see Vivian's "Devonshire Visitations"), and had:

WILLIAM PROUZ, father of:

WALTER PROUZ, who had by his wife, a daughter of Baron Dinham:

WILLIAM PROUZ, who had by his wife, daughter and heiress of Giles de Gidley, in Devonshire:

SIR WILLIAM PROUZ, Knt., Lord of Gidley, m. Alice, daughter and heiress of Sir Fulke Ferners, of Throwleigh, and had:

WILLIAM PROUZ, of Orton, Devonshire, m. Alice, daughter of Sir Hugh de Widworthy, and had (see Vivian's "Devonshire Visitations"):

LADY ALICE PROUZ, who m. Sir Roger Moels, Knt., and had:

LADY JOAN MOELS, who m. John Wotton, of Widworthy, in Devonshire, and had:

JOHN WOTTON, of Widworthy (see Westcote's "Devonshire Pedigrees"), who m. Engaret, daughter of Walter Dymoke, and had:

ALICE WOTTON, who m. Sir John Chichester, Knt., b. 1385, who was in the retinue of Le Sieur de Harrington at Agincourt, son of Sir John Chichester, of Treverbin, Cornwall, and had:

RICHARD CHICHESTER, b. 1424, sheriff of Devonshire, 1469, 1475, d. 25 December, 1496; m. Margaret, daughter of Sir Nicholas Keynes, of Winkleigh, and had:

NICHOLAS CHICHESTER, b. 1447, who m. Christian, daughter of Sir William (or Nicholas) Pawlet, and had:

JOHN CHICHESTER, of Rawleigh, Devon, b. 1472, d. 22 February, 1537-8; m., secondly, Joan, daughter of Robert Bright, or Brett, and had:

AMIAS CHICHESTER, of Arlington, Devon, b. 1527, d. 4 July, 1577; m. Jane Giffard, will proved 16 April, 1596; daughter of Sir Roger Giffard, of Brightley, d. 1 May, 1547, and had:

FRANCES CHICHESTER (see N. E. His. Gen. Reg., April, 1897), who m. John Wyatt, bapt. Braunton, Devon, 27 November, 1558; admitted to the Inner Temple in 1576, son of Philip Wyatt, steward and town clerk of Barnstaple, Devon, 1562-3, d. 1592, and had:

MARGARET WYATT, who m. at Braunton, 2 February, 1626, Matthew Allyn,* bapt. Braunton, 17 April, 1605; came to New England, resided at Cambridge, 1632; at Hartford, 1637; at Windsor, 1648. He was a representative to the general court of Massachusetts, 1636; was excommunicated at Hartford; was deputy and assistant in the Connecticut

---

* MRS. HENRY GILBERT HART, a member of the New York State Society of the National Society of the Colonial Dames of America, is also of Royal Descent, through Matthew Allyn and Margaret Wyatt.

Colony, 1648–67; a commissioner to the United Colonies, 1660, 1664; d. 1 February, 1670–71, and had:

LIEUTENANT-COLONEL JOHN ALLYN, *bapt.* Braunton, 24 February, 1630; came to New England with his father; was cornet of troop, 1657–58; town clerk of Hartford, 1659–96; deputy, 1661; magistrate, 1662; secretary of Connecticut, 1663–65, 1667–95; d. 16 November, 1696. (See the pedigree chart of his ancestry, compiled by Messrs. Waters, F. Olcott Allen, Jeremiah Allyn, and Bolton, 1898.) He *m.*, 19 November, 1651, first, Ann, daughter of Henry Smith, and granddaughter of Colonel William Pynchon, treasurer of the Massachusetts Colony, *etc.*, and had:

MARY ALLYN, 1657–1724; *m.*, 6 October, 1686, William Whiting, *b.* 1659, and had:

CHARLES WHITING, 1692–1738; *m.*, 10 January, 1716–1717, Elizabeth Bradford, 1696–1777, and had:

WILLIAM BRADFORD WHITING, 1731–1796; *m.*, 24 July, 1757, Amy Lathrop, 1735–1815, and had:

DANIEL WHITING, 1768–1855; *m.*, 19 January, 1804, Elizabeth Gilbert Powers, 1782–1859, and had:

HENRY LAURENS WHITING, 1821–1897; *m.*, 3 November, 1851, Anna Frances Johnson, *b.* 1830, and had:

VIRGINIA WHITING, *b.* Philadelphia, Pennsylvania, 20 March, 1857, a member of the California Society of the Colonial Dames of America, who *m.* (his second wife), 20 July, 1882, Edwin White Newhall, of San Francisco, California, and had: *Edwin White, b.* 21 April, 1883; *Virginia Whiting, b.* 20 March, 1889, and *Frances Henrielle, b.* 2 October, 1890.

PEDIGREE V.

HENRY I., King of France, had, by his third wife, Anne of Russia:

HUGH-MAGNUS, Duke of France and Burgundy, Marquis of Orleans, Count of Paris, Valois and Vermandois, who had, by his third wife, m., 938, Adelheid (or Hadwid), daughter of Herbert IV., Count of Vermandois:

LADY ISABEL DE VERMANDOIS, third daughter (called also Elizabeth), d. 1131. She m., first, 1096, Robert de Beaumont, Earl of Mellent and first Earl of Leicester, d. 1118, and m., secondly, William de Warren, second Earl of Surrey, d. between 1131 and 1138, and had:

LADY GUNDREDA DE WARREN, who m., first, Roger de Bellomont de Newburgh, second Earl of Warwick, d. 1153, and had:

WALERAN DE NEWBURGH, fourth Earl of Warwick, d. 1205, who had, by his second wife, Alice, daughter of John de Harcourt and widow of John de Limesi:

LADY ALICE DE NEWBURGH, who m. William, Baron Mauduit, of Hanslape, heritable chamberlain of the exchequer, d. 1256, and had:

LADY ISABEL DE MAUDUIT, d. before 1268 (sister of William Mauduit, seventh Earl of Warwick, d. s. p. 1268), who m. William, fifth Baron Beauchamp, of Elmley Castle, will 7 January, 1268, and had:

WILLIAM DE BEAUCHAMP, Baron Beauchamp, created Earl of Warwick, d. 1298, who m. Maud, daughter of John Fitz-John, chief justice of Ireland, in 1258, and widow of Gerard de Furnival, and had:

GUY DE BEAUCHAMP, second Earl of Warwick, 1275–1315, who m. Lady Alice, daughter of Ralph de Toni, and widow of Thomas de Leyburne, and had:

LADY MATILDA DE BEAUCHAMP, who m. Geoffrey, second Baron de Say, admiral of the King's Fleet, d. 1359, and had:

LADY IDONES DE SAY, who m. Sir John Clinton, of Mantoch, third Baron Clinton, 1326–1397, and had:

LADY MARGARET CLINTON, who m. Sir Baldwin de Montfort, and had:

SIR WILLIAM DE MONTFORT, d. 1453, who m. Margaret Peche, and had:

SIR BALDWIN DE MONTFORT, b. 1445, d. 1475, who m. Joanna Vernon, and had:

ROBERT MONTFORT, of Bescote, Staffordshire, who had:

KATHERINE MONTFORT, who m. Sir George Booth, d. 1483, son of Sir William Booth, sheriff of Chester, and had:

SIR WILLIAM BOOTH, d. 1519, who m. Ellen, daughter of Sir John Montgomery, and had:

JANE BOOTH, who m., secondly, Sir Thomas Holford, of Chester, and had:

DOROTHY HOLFORD, who m. (his second wife) John Bruen, of Bruen-Stapleford, Cheshire, b. 1510, d. 14 May, 1580 (see Ormerod's "History of Cheshire," ii., 322), and had:

JOHN BRUEN, of Stapleford, b. 1560, d. 18 January, 1625, buried at Tarvin, who had, by his third wife, Margaret:

MARY BRUEN, bapt. 14 June, 1622, came to New England with her half-brother, Obadiah Bruen, who m., 1653 (his second wife), John Baldwin, Sr., one of the founders of Milford, Connecticut, d. 1681 (see "The Baldwin Family History," Pond's "Old Milford Tombstones," Caulkin's "History of New London"), and had:

HANNAH BALDWIN, b. 20 November, 1664, who m., 17 January, 1682, Dr. John Fiske, of Milford, Connecticut, b. 12 December, 1654, d. 1715, and had:

BENJAMIN FISKE, b. 1683, d. 14 February, 1765; m., 24 July, 1701, Abigail Bowen, and had:

DANIEL FISKE, b. 16 December, 1710, d. 27 June, 1804; m., 24 December, 1732, Freelove Williams, b. 13 November, 1713, d. 20 April, 1791, also of Royal Descent, and had:

DANIEL FISKE, b. 28 April, 1753, d. 5 May, 1810; m., 13 April, 1785, Freelove Knight, b. 21 January, 1766, d. 20 May, 1819, and had:

CELIA FISKE, b. 17 February, 1787, d. 7 May, 1859; m., 16 November, 1815, Stephen Burlingame, b. 2 October, 1789, d. 20 August, 1837, and had:

COLONEL STEPHEN BURLINGAME, b. 3 December, 1819, d. 15 November, 1890; m., 30 October, 1841, Elsie Maria Tillinghast, b. 3 January, 1820, d. 20 May, 1884, and had:

SARAH MARIA BURLINGAME, b. 10 February, 1855, a member of the New Hampshire Society of the Colonial Dames of America, and of the Massachusetts Society of the Descendants of Colonial Governors, who m., 12 December, 1877, Prentiss Webster, of Lowell, Massachusetts, b. 24 May, 1851, d. 26 October, 1898, and had: *Susan Hildreth, Adeline Burlingame, Prentiss Burlingame, Helen Burlingame,* and *Dorothy Prentiss.*

PEDIGREE VI.

CHARLEMAGNE, Emperor of the West, King of the Franks, had by his third wife, Lady Hildegarde, daughter of Childebrand, Duke of Suabia:

PEPIN, KING OF LOMBARDY, who m. Lady Bertha, daughter of William, Count of Thoulouse, and had:

BERNARD, KING OF LOMBARDY, who had by his wife, Lady Cunegonde:

PEPIN, Count of Peronne and Vermandois, father of:

PEPIN DE SENLIS, Count Berengarius, of Bayeux and Valois, father of:

LADY POPPA, who m. (his first wife) Rollo the Dane, first Duke of Normandy, d. 932, son of Rognvald the Mighty, Jarl of Möre, in Upland, Norway, and of the Isles of Orkney and Shetland Isles (see "Royal House of Sweden," in Anderson's "Royal Genealogies"), and had:

WILLIAM (LONGUE-EPEE), second Duke of Normandy, who had:

RICHARD I. (Sanspeur), third Duke of Normandy, who had:

RICHARD II. (le Bon), fourth Duke of Normandy, who had:

RICHARD III., fifth Duke of Normandy, who had by Lady Adela, daughter of Robert the Pious, King of France:

LADY ALICE (half-sister of Queen Maud of England), who m. Radulfe, Viscount of Bayeux, and had:

RANULF DE BRISQUESART, de Meschines, b. ante 1066, Viscount of Bayeux, created, 1119, Earl Palatine, of Chester, d. 1128; m. Lady Maud (or Margaretta), sister of Hugh (lupus), Earl of Chester, and daughter of Rubard, Viscount de Auveranches, created, 1086, Earl of Chester, and his wife, Lady Margaret (Emme), a half-sister of King William the Conqueror (see Banks's "Extinct Peerages" and Doyle's "Official Baronage"), and had:

RANULF DE MESCHINES DE GERNON, b. ante 1109, fifth Earl Palatine, of Chester, d. 1153; m. Lady Maud, daughter of Robert the Consul, Earl of Gloucester and Mellent (see Planche's "The Conqueror and His Companions"), and had:

HUGH DE KYVELIOC, Earl Palatine of Chester, d. 1181, who had by his wife, Lady Bartred, daughter of Simon, Earl of Evereux, in Normandy:

LADY DE MESCHINES, sister of Ranulph, Earl of Chester and Lincoln, who m. (see Banks's "Baronage" and "Stemmata Anglicana," and Edmondson's "Baronagium Genealogicum) Reginald Bacun, son of Robert, son of Roger, son of George de Bacunsthorp, in Norfolk (see Kimber's "Baronetage," 1771; *Notes and Queries*, First Series, and Blomefield's "Norfolk"), and had:

RICHARD BACUN, benefactor of Bury Abbey and founder of the Priory of Roucester, Staffordshire, who m. Alice de Multon, and had:

SIR ROBERT BACON, of Bacunsthorp, who m. daughter of Sir Richard d'Ingham, and had:

SIR THOMAS BACON, who m. Elizabeth ——, living 1249, and had:

SIR HENRY BACON, 1270 (brother to Sir Bartholomew Bacon, a justice itinerant, Sir Stephen Bacon, and "Friar Bacon"), who had:

SIR HENRY BACON (brother to John Bacon, chamberlain to the Exchequer and secretary to the King; master of the Rolls, etc.), who m. Margaret Ludham, and had:

SIR ROGER BACON (brother to Sir John Bacon, justice itinerant), a celebrated commander in the wars of Edward II. and III., who m. Felicia Kirton, and had:

BEATRICE BACON, heiress, who m. Sir William Thorpe (see "New England His. and Geneal. Register," April, 1883), and had:

WILLIAM THORPE, who m. (see Playfair's "British Family Antiquity") Margery, daughter of John Quadladde (or Quadlop), and had:

JOHN THORPE, whose daughter and heiress:

MARGERY THORPE, m. (according to Playfair) John Bacon, of Drinkstone, son of John, son of John Bacon, of Hessett and Bradfield, Suffolk, and had:

EDMUND BACON, of Drinkstone, who m. Elizabeth Crofts, and had:

JOHN BACON, of Drinkstone, d. 1500, who m. Agnes, daughter of Thomas Cockfield (or Cokefield), and had:

ROBERT BACON, of Drinkstone (*bur.* at Hessett, with his wife), who m. Isabel, daughter of John Cage, of Pakenham, Suffolk, and had:

JAMES BACON, alderman of London, d. 15 June, 1573, *bur.* St. Dunstan's, East London (a brother of Sir Nicholas Bacon, Lord Keeper of the Great Seal, 1509–1579, whose son was the celebrated Sir Francis, Lord Bacon), who m., secondly, Margaret, daughter of William Rawlings, of London, and widow of Richard Gouldston, and had by her:

SIR JAMES BACON, Knt., of Friston Hall, Suffolk, d. London, 17 January, 1618; m. Elizabeth, daughter and heiress of Francis and Anne (Drury) Bacon, of Hessett (see Cullome's "History of Hawstead") and had:

PEDIGREE VI.—Continued.

REV. JAMES BACON, rector of Burgatt, Suffolk, d. 9 November, 1649, will probated 23 January, 1649-1650, who m. Martha Honeywood, d. 25 August, 1670, and had:

MARTHA BACON (sister of Colonel Nathaniel Bacon, b. 1620, member of the Virginia Council for forty years, d. in York county, Virginia, 1692—see his will in New England His. Geneal. Reg., vol. xxxvii., p. 194), who m., ante 1652, Anthony Smith, of Colchester, Virginia, d. 1667, and had:

ABIGAIL SMITH, b. 11 March, 1656, d. 12 November, 1692, who m. (his first wife) Major Lewis Burwell, of White Marsh, Gloucester county, Virginia, and had:

1.—JOANNA BURWELL, 1674-1727; m., 1693, Colonel William Bassett, Jr., of "Eltham," New Kent county, Virginia, 1670-1723, a member of the Virginia Council, son of Captain William Bassett (see Henning's "Virginia Statutes," ii., 220, and Keith's "Ancestry of Benjamin Harrison") and his wife, Bridget, daughter of Miles Cary, of Virginia, and had:

COLONEL WILLIAM BASSETT, of "Eltham," b. 8 July, 1709, d. 174–, burgess in 1743, who m., 1729, Elizabeth, daughter of William Churchill, of "Barkby Park," Middlesex county, Virginia, a member of the Virginia Council, 1705, and had:

HON. BURWELL BASSETT, of "Eltham," b. 1734, member of the house of burgesses, of the Virginia convention of 1788, etc., d. 4 January, 1793; m., secondly, 7 May, 1757, Anna Maria Dandridge, b. 30 March, 1739, d. 17 December, 1777, sister of Mrs. George Washington, and daughter of John Dandridge, of New Kent county, Virginia, and had:

JOHN BASSETT, JR., of "Eltham" and "Farmington," Hanover county, Virginia, b. 30 August, 1765 (second son, and heir to his elder brother, Burwell), d. 1826; m., 12 September, 1786, Betty Carter, daughter of William Burnet Browne, of "Elsing Green," King William county, Virginia, also of Royal Descent, and had:

GEORGE WASHINGTON BASSETT, of "Eltham," b. 23 August, 1800, d. 28 August, 1878 (he was a grandnephew of Mrs. George Washington, who was his godmother), who m. his cousin, Betty Burnet, daughter of Robert Lewis (a nephew and private secretary of General Washington), also of Royal Descent, and his wife, Judith Walker Browne, also of Royal Descent, and had:

I.—ANNA VIRGINIA BASSETT, who m. Major John Hayes Claiborne, of Richmond, Virginia, also of Royal Descent, and had:

DELIA CLAIBORNE, a member of the Virginia Society of the Colonial Dames of America, who m., 10 June, 1885, General

PEDIGREE VI.—Continued.

Simon B. Buckner, of "Glen Lily," Hart county, Kentucky, former Governor of Kentucky, and had:

SIMON BOLIVAR BUCKNER, b. 18 July, 1886.

II.—ELLA BASSETT, a member of the Virginia Society of the Colonial Dames of America, d. 1898, who m. Lewis William Washington. *Issue.*

2.—NATHANIEL BURWELL, who m. Elizabeth Carter, also of Royal Descent, and had:

I.—LEWIS BURWELL, of "White Marsh," who m. Mary Willis, and had:

REBECCA BURWELL, who m. Jacqueline Ambler, and had:

ANNE AMBLER, who m. George Fisher, and had:

ELIZA JACQUELINE AMBLER, who m. Thomas Marshall Colston, and had:

RALEIGH COLSTON, who m. Gertrude Powell, and had:

JANE COLSTON, a member of the Virginia Society of the Colonial Dames of America, who m., 12 September, 1871, Conway Robinson Howard, of Richmond, Virginia, and had: *Mary Eloise*, m. Francis Elliott Sharp; *Gertrude, Jeanie C.*, and *Conway R.*

II.—ELIZABETH BURWELL, who m. William Nelson, of Yorktown, president of the Virginia Colony, and had:

ROBERT NELSON, who m., secondly, Susan Robinson, and had:

PEYTON RANDOLPH NELSON, who m. Sallie Berkeley Nicolson, also of Royal Descent, and had:

WILLIAM WILMER NELSON, who m. Sally Browne Catlett, and had:

SALLY BERKELEY NELSON, of Richmond, Virginia, a member of the Virginia Society of the Colonial Dames of America, who m. William Todd Robins, Colonel Confederate States Army. Issue: *Ruth Nelson, Elizabeth Todd, Augustine Warner, Wilmer Nelson*, and *Sally Berkeley Nicolson*.

III.—CARTER BURWELL, who m. Lucy Grymes, and had:

NATHANIEL BURWELL, who m. Lucy (Page) Baylor, also a descendant of Robert Carter, 1663–1732, and had:

GEORGE H. BURWELL, who m. Agnes Atkinson, and had:

ISABELLA DIXON BURWELL, who m. Peter H. Mayo, and had:

AGNES ATKINSON MAYO, a member of the Virginia Society of the Colonial Dames of America, who m. Thomas Nelson Carter, of Richmond, Virginia, also a descendant of Robert Carter, 1663–1732, and had: *Isabelle Burwell.*

IV.—COLONEL ROBERT CARTER BURWELL, of Isle of Wight county, Virginia, m. Sarah Nelson, and had:

FRANCES BURWELL, who m. Governor John Page, of "Rosewell," also of Royal Descent, and had:

FRANCES PAGE, who m., secondly, Dr. Carter Berkeley, of "Edgewood," and had:

CATHERINE FANNY BERKELEY, who m. Lucius Horatio Minor, of "Edgewood," also of Royal Descent, and had:

MARY WILLIS MINOR, of Baltimore, a member of the Maryland Society of the Colonial Dames of America.

3.—MARTHA BURWELL, seventh child, b. November, 1685, who m. Colonel Henry Armistead, of Gloucester county (son of John Armistead, a Virginia councillor—see *William and Mary Quarterly*, July, 1898, p. 445; Keith's "Harrison Pedigree," pp. 36–37), and had:

WILLIAM ARMISTEAD, will probated 30 December, 1755, who m., 1739, Mary, daughter of James Bowles, d. 1728, and his wife, Rebecca, daughter of Colonel Thomas Addison, and had:

COLONEL JOHN ARMISTEAD, who m., 1764, Lucy, daughter of Colonel John and Lucy (Walker) Baylor, and had:

GENERAL WALKER KEITH ARMISTEAD, United States Army, who m. Elizabeth, daughter of John and Elizabeth (Wright) Stanly, and had:

CORNELIA ARMISTEAD, who m. Major Washington I. Newton, United States Army (son of Thomas Newton, of Norfolk, Virginia, M. C., 1801–1833), and had:

ELIZABETH STANLY NEWTON, a member of the California Society of the Colonial Dames of America, who m. Pedro Merlin Lusson, of San José, California, and had:

CORNELIA ARMISTEAD NEWTON LUSSON, a member of the Virginia Society of the Colonial Dames of America, who m. George A. Crux, of Portland, Oregon.

4.—ELIZABETH BURWELL, d. 1734, who m. Benjamin Harrison, of "Berkeley," 1673–1710, colonial treasurer and attorney-general of Virginia (see Keith's "Ancestry of Benjamin Harrison"), and had:

BENJAMIN HARRISON, of "Berkeley," high sheriff, burgess, *etc.*, d. 1744, who m., 1722, Anne, daughter of Robert Carter, of "Carotoman," also of Royal Descent, and had:

I.—BENJAMIN HARRISON, of "Berkeley," 1726–1791, member of the Continental Congress, a signer of the Declaration of Independence, governor of Virginia, *etc.*, who m. Elizabeth, b. 1730, daughter of Colonel William Bassett, Jr., of "Eltham," son of Colonel William Bassett, of

PEDIGREE VI.—Continued.

"Eltham," New Kent county, Virginia, member of the Virginia council, and his wife, Joan Burwell, aforesaid.

GENERAL WILLIAM HENRY HARRISON, of Ohio, 1773-1841, President of the United States, who m. Ann Tuthill, daughter of Judge John Cleves Symmes, of Ohio, and had:

1.—JOHN SCOTT HARRISON, of Cleves, Ohio, 1804-1878, m., 1831, ELIZABETH IRWIN, and had:

GENERAL BENJAMIN HARRISON, of Indiana, President of the United States, who m., first, Caroline Scott, and had by her:

MARY SCOTT HARRISON, a member of the Virginia Society of the Colonial Dames of America, who m., 5 November, 1884, James Robert McKee, of Indianapolis, Indiana, and had: *Benjamin Harrison* and *Mary Lodge*.

2.—LUCY SINGLETON HARRISON, 1800-1826, who m. (his first wife) Judge David Kirkpatrick Este, of Cincinnati, also of Royal Descent, and had:

LUCY ANN HARRISON ESTE, who m. Joseph F. Reynolds, of Hagerstown, Maryland, and had:

ANNA HARRISON REYNOLDS, who m. John Law Crawford, and had:

LUCY ESTE CRAWFORD, a member of the Maryland Society of the Colonial Dames of America, who m. George C. Woodruff, of Litchfield, Connecticut. *No issue.*

II.—NATHANIEL HARRISON, a member of the Virginia State Senate, 1780, who m. Mary, daughter of Edmund Ruffin, of Prince George county, Virginia, and had:

EDMUND HARRISON, of Amelia county, Virginia, 1761-1826, who m. Martha Wayles Skipwith, also of Royal Descent, and had:

WILLIAM HENRY HARRISON, of Amelia county, 1812-1884, who m. Lucy A. Powers, and had:

PROF. EDMUND HARRISON, of Louisville, Kentucky, who m. Kate Steger, and had:

1.—LELIA SKIPWITH HARRISON, a member of the Virginia Society of the Colonial Dames of America, who m. Howard D. Hoge, of Richmond.

2.—LULIE HARRISON, a member of the Virginia Society of the Colonial Dames of America, who m. Dana Henry Rucker, of Richmond, Virginia, and had: *Edmund Harrison*, b. 18 February, 1898.

3.—JENNIE HARRISON, a member of the Virginia Society of the Colonial Dames of America, who m. Charles H. Chalkley, of Hopkinsville, Kentucky.

III.—CARTER HENRY HARRISON, of "Clifton," who married Susan, daughter of Isham Randolph, of "Dungeness," and had:

ROBERT CARTER HARRISON, who *m.*, Anne Cabell, and had by her:

MARY HOPKINS HARRISON, who *m.* Samuel Q. Richardson, and had:

ROBERT CARTER RICHARDSON, who *m.* Marie Louise Harris, and had:

MARY CABELL RICHARDSON, of Covington, Kentucky, a member of the Virginia Society of the Colonial Dames of America, founder of the Order of Colonial Governors, etc.

PEDIGREE VII.

EDWARD I., King of England, had by his first wife, *m.* 1254, Princess Eleanor, only child of Ferdinand III., King of Castile and Leon:

PRINCESS JOAN PLANTAGENET D'ACRE, *d.* 1305, who was the second wife of Gilbert, ninth Earl of Clare, seventh Earl of Hertford, and third Earl of Gloucester, *d.* 1295, also of Royal Descent, by whom she had:

LADY MARGARET DE CLARE (widow of Piers de Gravestone, Earl of Cornwall), who *m.*, secondly, Hugh, second Baron d'Audley, created, in 1337, Earl of Gloucester, *d.* 1347-1349, and had:

LADY MARGARET D'AUDLEY, heiress, who *m.* (his first wife) Sir Ralph de Stafford, K.G., second Baron de Stafford, created, in 1351, Earl of Stafford, *d.* 1372, and had:

SIR HUGH DE STAFFORD, K.G., second Earl of Stafford, 1344-1386, who *m.* Lady Phillippa, daughter of Sir Thomas de Beauchamp, K.G., third Earl of Warwick, 1313-1369, also of Royal Descent, and had:

LADY MARGARET DE STAFFORD, *d.* 9 June, 1370, who *m.* (his first wife) Sir Ralph de Neville, K.G., fourth Baron de Neville, of Raby, created, in 1397, Earl of Westmoreland; Earl Marshal of England, *d.* 1425, and had:

LADY MARGARET DE NEVILLE, *d.* 1463, who *m.*, first, Richard, third Baron Scrope, of Bolton, *d.* at Rouen, 29 August, 1420, also of Royal Descent, and had:

SIR HENRY LE SCROPE, fourth Baron Scrope, of Bolton, *d.* 1459, who *m.* Lady Elizabeth, daughter of John, Baron Scrope, of Masham and Upsal, and had:

LADY MARGARET LE SCROPE, who *m.* John Bernard, of Abingdon, Northamptonshire, 1437-1485, and had:

JOHN BERNARD, of Abingdon, 1469-1508; *m.* Margaret, daughter of John Daundelyn, and had:

JOHN BERNARD, of Abingdon, 1491-1549; *m.* Cicely, daughter of John Muscote, of Earls Barton, and had:

FRANCIS BERNARD, of Abingdon, 1530-1609; *m.* Alice, daughter of John Hazlewood, of Maidwell, and had:

FRANCIS BERNARD, of Kingsthorpe, Northamptonshire, *bur.* 21 November, 1630, who *m.* Mary, daughter of Anthony Woodhouse, of Glasswell, and had:

COLONEL WILLIAM BERNARD, of Nansemond County, Virginia, member of the Virginia Council, 1642–1659, *d.* 31 March, 1665, who *m.* Lucy, daughter of Captain Robert Higginson (she *m.*, second, Major Lewis Burwell, and *m.*, third, Colonel Philip Ludwell), and had:

LUCY BERNARD (see *Virginia Mag. of His. and Biog.*, vi., 409), who *m.* Dr. Edmund Gwynne, of Gloucester county, Virginia, will dated 10 March, 1683, and had:

LUCY GWYNNE, who *m.* Thomas Reade, of Gloucester county, Virginia, will 4 January, 1694, also of Royal Descent, and had:

I.—MILDRED READE (see *Virginia Mag. of His. and Biog.*, iv., 204), who *m.* Major Philip Rootes, and had:

ELIZABETH ROOTES, who *m.* (his second wife) Rev. John Thompson, of St. Mark's parish, Culpeper county, Virginia, will proved 16 November, 1772, and had by her:

PHILIP ROOTES THOMPSON, of Culpeper, Virginia, M.C., 1801–1807; *m.*, secondly, Sally, daughter of Robert Slaughter, of "The Grange," Culpeper county, Virginia, and had by her:

JUDGE R. AUGUSTUS THOMPSON, of San Francisco, who had by his first wife:

—— THOMPSON, a member of the Virginia Society of the Colonial Dames of America, who *m.* S. C. Hine, of San Francisco, and had:

SALLIE HELENA HINE, a member of the Virginia Society of the Colonial Dames of America, who *m.* her cousin, William Thompson.

JUDGE R. AUGUSTUS THOMPSON had by his second wife, Elizabeth Jane Early:

1.—RUTH HOUSTON THOMPSON, a member of the Virginia and California Societies of the Colonial Dames of America, who *m.* William Craig, of San Francisco, California.

2.—ROBERTA THOMPSON, of San Francisco, a member of the Virginia and California Societies of the Colonial Dames of America.

II.—MARY READE, who *m.* Captain Mordecai Throckmorton, of Virginia, 1696–1768, also of Royal Descent, and had:

LUCY THROCKMORTON, who *m.*, 16 June, 175–, Robert Throckmorton, J. P., of Culpeper county, Virginia, *b.* 20 November, 1736, son of Major Robert Throckmorton (brother of the aforesaid Captain Mordecai Throckmorton), and his wife, Mary Lewis, also of Royal Descent, and had:

FRANCES THROCKMORTON, *b.* 29 February, 1765, who *m.*, 20 December, 1783, General William Madison, of "Woodbury Forest," Madison county, Virginia (see Hayden's "Virginia Genealogies," p. 257–259), and had:

REBECCA CONWAY MADISON, *b.* at "Montpelier," Orange county, Virginia, 31 March, 1785, *d.* March, 1860, who *m.*, 1803, Reynolds Chapman, *b.* at "Chericoke," King William county, Virginia, 22 July, 1778, *d.* at "Berry Hill," Orange county, Virginia, 184–, and had:

JUDGE JOHN MADISON CHAPMAN, *b.* at "Berry Hill," 1810, *d.* 31 March, 1879; *m.*, 3 August, 1841, Susannah Digges Cole, also of Royal Descent, and had:

1.—SUSIE ASHTON CHAPMAN, *b.* 18 December, 1845, a member of the Tennessee Society of the Colonial Dames of America, the Order of the Crown, *etc.*, who *m.*, 3 October, 1878, Calvin Perkins, of Memphis, Tennessee, and had: *Blakeney, b.* 4 April, 1880; *Belle Moncure, b.* 7 October, 1881; *Ashton Chapman, b.* 27 January, 1883; *Mamie Anderson, b.* 11 April, 1884; *Louis Allen, b.* 10 April, 1885, and *William Alexander, b.* 23 March, 1886.

2.—BELLE CHAPMAN, *b.* November, 1858, a member of the Virginia Society of the Colonial Dames of America, the Order of the Crown, *etc.*, who *m.*, 12 November, 1878, William Moncure, of Richmond, Virginia, and had: *William, b.* Orange County, Virginia, 1 October, 1880; *Belle Perkins, b.* Richmond, Virginia, 17 November, 1882, and *Vivienne Daniel, b.* Franklinton, North Carolina, 17 February, 1885.

3.—ASHTON ALEXANDER CHAPMAN, *b.* Orange county, Virginia, 22 August, 1867; *m.*, 23 January, 1895, Nannie Eaton, daughter of Colonel Roger O. Gregory, of Oxford, North Carolina.

THE ROYAL DESCENT
OF
MISS MARGARET VOWELL SMITH,
OF ALEXANDRIA, VA.

EDWARD I., King of England=Lady Eleanor of Provence.
    Princess Joan Plantagenet=Gilbert de Clare, Earl of Gloucester and Hertford.
        Lady Margaret de Clare=Hugh de Audley, Earl of Gloucester.
            Lady Margaret de Audley=Sir Ralph de Stafford, K. G., Earl of Stafford.
Sir Hugh de Stafford, K. G., Earl of Stafford=Lady Philippa de Beauchamp.
            Lady Margaret de Stafford=Sir Ralph de Neville, K. G., Earl of Westmoreland.
Ralph de Neville, of Oversley, Warwickshire=Lady Mary de Ferrers.
    John de Neville, of Wymersley, Yorkshire=Lady Elizabeth de Newmarch.
            Joan de Neville=Sir William Gascoigne, of Gawthrope, Yorkshire.
Sir William Gascoigne, of Gawthrope, York=Lady Margaret de Percy.
            Lady Elizabeth Gascoigne=Gilbert de Talboys, of Kyme.
      Sir George de Talboys, of Kyme=(Name unknown.)
            Lady Anne de Talboys=Sir Edward Dymoke, of Scrivelsby, Lincolnshire.
            Lady Frances Dymoke=Thomas Windebank, of Haines Hill, Berkshire.
            Lady Mildred Windebank=Robert Reade, Linkenholt Manor, Southampton.
    Col. George Reade, of Gloucester Co., Va.=Elizabeth Martian.
            Mildred Reade=Col. Augustine Warner, Jr., of "Warner's Hall."
      Mary Warner (*m.* 17 February, 1680)=John Smith, of "Purton," Gloucester Co., Va.
    Augustine Smith, of "Purton," 1687–1756=Sarah Carver.
John Smith, of "Shooters' Hill," Va., 1715–1771=Mary Jacqueline.
Augustine Smith, of "Shooters' Hill," 1738–1774=Margaret Boyd.
      Mary Jacqueline Smith, 1773–1846=John Cripps Vowell, of Alexandria, Va.
Sarah Gosnelle Vowell, member of the National=Francis Lee Smith, of Fauquier Co., Va.
Society of the Colonial Dames of America

Margaret Vowell Smith, of Alexandria, Va., member of the National Society of the Colonial Dames of America, the Order of the Crown, etc.

PEDIGREE VIII.

ROBERT BRUCE, King of Scotland, had by his second wife, Lady Elizabeth de Burgh, daughter of Richard, Earl of Ulster:

PRINCESS MARGARET BRUCE, sister of King David II., who *m.*, 1344 (his first wife), William, Earl of Sutherland, *d.* 1370, and had:

JOHN, sixth Earl of Sutherland, only son, *d.* 1389, who *m.* Lady Mabilla Dunbar, daughter of Patrick, tenth Earl of March, and had:

NICHOLAS, eighth Earl of Sutherland, second son, *d.* 1399, who *m.* Elizabeth, daughter of John Macdonald, Lord of the Isles, and had:

ROBERT, ninth Earl of Sutherland, *d.* 1442, who *m.* Lady Mabilla, daughter of John, second Earl of Murray, and had:

ALEXANDER SUTHERLAND, of Dunbeath, third son, who had:

LADY MARGARET SUTHERLAND, *m.* William Sinclair, third Earl of Orkney, and Earl of Caithness, and had:

LADY MARJORY SINCLAIR, who *m.* Andrew, Lord Leslie, who *d. v. p.*, 1502, son of George Leslie, first Earl of Rothes, and had:

WILLIAM LESLIE, third son, third Earl of Rothes, who *m.* Lady Margaret, daughter of Sir Michael Balfour, of Mountquhanie, and had:

GEORGE, fourth Earl of Rothes, *k.* in France, in 1558, who had by his third wife, Margaret Crichton:

LADY HELEN LESLIE, second daughter, widow of Gilbert de Seton the younger, who *m.* Mark Ker, Abbot, or Commendator of Newbottle, 1546, extraordinary lord of session, *d.* 1584, second son of Sir Andrew Ker, of Cessford, and Agnes, daughter of William, Lord Crichton, and had:

MARK KER, eldest son, succeeded his father in office, was made a baron 28 July, 1587, and created, 10 February, 1606, Earl of Lothian, *d.* 8 April, 1609. He *m.* Lady Margaret, daughter of John, fourth Lord Maxwell, and Lord Herries, in right of his wife, Agnes, daughter of William, Lord Herries, and had:

LADY JEAN KER, who *m.*, first, the Hon. Robert Boyd, Master of Boyd, *d. v. p.*, eldest son of Thomas, fifth Lord Boyd, and his wife Margaret, daughter of Sir Matthew Campbell, of Loudon, and had:

JAMES, eighth Lord Boyd, of Kilmarnock, second son, *d.* 1654, who *m.* Catherine, daughter of John Craik, of York City, and had:

PEDIGREE VIII.—Continued.

WILLIAM, ninth Lord Boyd, created Earl of Kilmarnock, 7 August, 1661, d. 1692, who m., 25 April, 1661, Lady Jean Cunningham, daughter of William, ninth Earl of Glencairn, chancellor of Scotland, and had:

ROBERT BOYD, of Kilmarnock, fourth son, b. 6 August, 1689, d. 1761; m. Margaret Thompson, by whom he had:

JAMES BOYD, b. in Kilmarnock, 8 May, 1732, d. 30 September, 1798. In 1756 he came to America with a patent from George II. for sixty thousand acres in New Brunswick. During the Revolution he sided with the Colonies, and thereby forfeited his grant. He m., 11 August, 1757, Susannah, daughter of Colonel Joseph Coffin, of Newburyport, and had:

1.—ROBERT BOYD, b. October, 1758, d. 18 January, 1827; m., 1 November, 1791, Ruth, daughter of David Smith, of Portland, and had:

WILLIAM BOYD, b. 16 December, 1800, graduated at Harvard 1820, d. Portland, Maine, 10 May, 1875. He m., 10 September, 1832, Susan Dayton, daughter of Charles Harrod, of New Orleans, Louisiana, and his wife Hannah Dayton, granddaughter of Major-General Elias Dayton, of Elizabethtown, New Jersey, and had:

MAJOR CHARLES HARROD BOYD, of Portland, Maine, a member of the Military Order of the Loyal Legion, and the societies of the Grand Army of the Republic, Sons of the American Revolution and the Colonial Wars, b. 4 July, 1833, m., 1 September, 1858, Annette Maria, daughter of Colonel Greenlief Dearborn, United States Army, who served in the War of 1812 and in the Florida War, and great-granddaughter of Major-General Henry Dearborn, secretary of war under Jefferson, commander-in-chief of the army under Madison, and minister to Portugal under Monroe, and had:

I.—ANNIE FRANCES HARROD BOYD, a member of the Maine Society of the Colonial Dames of America, the Order of the Crown, etc.

II.—AUGUSTA DEARBORN; III.—JULIA WINGATE; IV.—EMILY DEARBORN.

2.—JOSEPH COFFIN BOYD, of Portland, Maine, b. Newburyport, 23 July, 1760, d. 12 May, 1823; m., 24 January, 1796, Isabella, daughter of Judge Robert Southgate, of Scarboro', Maine, and had:

JUDGE SAMUEL STILLMAN BOYD, of Natchez, Mississippi, b. 27 May, 1807, d. 21 May, 1869; m., 15 November, 1838, Catherine Charlotte Wilkins, of Natchez, and had:

ANNA MARIA WILKINS BOYD, b. 10 March, 1859, a member of the Pennsylvania and Mississippi Societies of the Colonial Dames of America, the Order of the Crown, etc., who m. William Benneville Rhodes, of Natchez, and had: *Catherine Charlotte Boyd*, b. 1890, and *Dorothy Marie*, b. 1894.

PEDIGREE IX.

HUGH CAPET, King of France, 987, had by his wife, Lady Adela, daughter of William, Duke of Aquitaine:

PRINCESS HEDEWIGE, who *m.* Raginerus IV., Count of Hainault, and had:

LADY BEATRIX, who *m.* Eblo I., Count of Rouci and Reimes, and had:

ADELA, Countess de Rouci, who *m.* Hildwin IV., Count de Rouci and Montdider, and had:

LADY MARGARET DE ROUCI, who *m.* Hugh, Count de Clermont and de Beauvais, and had:

LADY ADELIZA DE CLERMONT, who *m.* Gilbert de Tonsburg, in Kent, second Earl of Clare, and had:

LADY ADELIZA DE CLARE, who *m.* Alberic, second Baron de Vere, appointed by Henry I. great high chamberlain of England, and had:

ALBERIC DE VERE, third Baron, created, in 1135, Earl of Oxford and great high chamberlain, *d.* 1194; *m.*, secondly, Lady Lucia, daughter of William, third Baron d'Abrancis, and had by her:

ROBERT DE VERE, third Earl of Oxford; one of the twenty-five Barons selected to enforce the Magna Charta; *m.* Lady Isabel, daughter of Hugh, second Baron de Bolbec, and had:

HUGH DE VERE, fourth Earl of Oxford, great high chamberlain, *d.* 1263; *m.* Lady Hawise, daughter of Saher de Quincey, Earl of Winchester, one of the twenty-five Magna Charta Barons, and had:

ROBERT DE VERE, fifth Earl of Oxford, *d.* 1296; *m.* Lady Alice, daughter of Gilbert, Baron Saundford, chamberlain in fee to Eleanor, Queen of Henry III., and had:

ALPHONSO DE VERE, second son, who *m.* Lady Jane, daughter of Sir Richard Foliot, Knt., and had:

JOHN DE VERE, seventh Earl of Oxford, killed at Rheims, who *m.* Lady Maud, daughter of Bartholomew, first Baron Badlesmere, executed in 1322, and widow of Robert Fitz-Payn, and had:

AUBREY DE VERE, second son (uncle of Robert, ninth Earl of Oxford, and Duke of Dublin, declared a traitor to King Richard, and outlawed and attainted, and *d.* in exile, 1292), who was restored to the honors, titles and estates of Oxford, and was the tenth Earl of Oxford; *m.* Lady Alice, daughter of John, Lord Fitz-Walter, and had:

PEDIGREE IX.—*Continued.*

RICHARD DE VERE, eleventh Earl of Oxford, *d.* 1417; *m.* Lady Alice, daughter of Sir John Sergeaux, Knt., of Cornwall, and had:

ROBERT DE VERE, second son, who *m.* Lady Joan, daughter of Sir Hugh Courtenay, Knt., also of Royal Descent, and had:

JOHN DE VERE, who *m.* Alice, daughter of Walter Kelrington, and had:

SIR JOHN DE VERE, K.G., who succeeded as fifteenth Earl of Oxford; great lord high chamberlain of England, *d.* 1539, who *m.* Elizabeth, daughter of Sir Edward Trussel, of Cublesdon, and had:

LADY ANNE DE VERE, who *m.* Edmund Sheffield, created Lord Sheffield, of Butterwicke, in 1547, killed in battle, 1548–49, and had:

JOHN, second Lord Sheffield, who *m.* (her first husband) Lady Douglas, daughter of William, Lord Howard, of Effingham, and had:

SIR EDMUND SHEFFIELD, K.G., third Lord, a celebrated naval officer, who for the part he took in the defeat of the Armada was made a Knight of the Garter, and Governor of Brill, and in 1626 created Earl of Mulgrave, *d.* 1646, aged 80 years; *m.*, first, Lady Ursula, daughter of Sir Robert Tirwhit, of Ketleby, and had:

LADY FRANCES SHEFFIELD, who *m.* Sir Philip Fairfax, Knt., of Stenton, and had:

SIR WILLIAM FAIRFAX, of Stenton, 1610–1692, who *m.* Frances, daughter of Sir Thomas Chalomer, chamberlain to Prince Henry; *k.* in 1644, at Montgomery Castle, and had:

ISABELLA FAIRFAX, *bapt.* at Stenton, 16 August, 1637; *d.* 25 October, 1691; who *m.* Nathaniel Bladen, of Hemsworth, Yorkshire, councillor, *etc.; bapt.* at Bolton Percy, son of Rev. Dr. Thomas Bladen, dean of Oxford, and had:

WILLIAM BLADEN,* 1670–1718, clerk of the Maryland House of Burgesses 1497, clerk of the Prerogative Office 1699 and commissary-general of Maryland 1714, who had by his first wife, Letitia, daughter of Judge Dudley Loftus, LL.D., deputy judge advocate in Leinster, Ireland, in 1651; a master in chancery, and vicar-general of Ireland till his death in 1695:

ANNE BLADEN, who *m.* Benjamin Tasker, of Annapolis, 1690–1768,

---

* The following ladies, members of the National Society of the Colonial Dames of America, are also of Royal Descent through William Bladen:

MISS LIZINKA C. BROWN (deceased), Maryland State Society.
MRS. EDWARD S. BEALL, Maryland State Society.
MISS LOUISA OGLE BEALL, Maryland State Society.
MRS. CHARLES S. SHAWHAN, Maryland State Society.
MISS MARY WINN, Maryland State Society.

president of the council for thirty-two years, and deputy-governor of the Province of Maryland 1752, commissioner to Pennsylvania 1752, a delegate to the Colonial Congress at Albany, New York, 1754, *etc.*, and had:

1. REBECCA TASKER, who *m.* Daniel Dulany, mayor of Annapolis 1764, member of the council from 1757, and secretary of State of Maryland from 1761, *b.* 1721, *d.* 19 March, 1797, and had:

    COLONEL BENJAMIN TASKER DULANY, of Virginia, who *m.*, 1773, Elizabeth, daughter of Daniel French, of "Clairmont," Fairfax county, Virginia, and had:

    I.—DANIEL FRENCH DULANY, of Virginia, who *m.* Sarah, daughter of Commodore Thomas Tingey, United States Navy, and had:

    MARY DULANY, who *m.* Mottrom Ball, of Virginia, and had:

    REBECCA BALL, a member of the Virginia Society of the Colonial Dames of America, who *m.* John Addison, of Richmond, Virginia.

    II.—BENJAMIN TASKER DULANY, who *m.* Miss Rozier, of "Notley Hall," Prince George county, Maryland, and had:

    MAJOR ROZIER DULANY, United States Army, who *m.* Fannie Carter, of "Sabine Hall," Virginia, also of Royal Descent, and had:

    REBECCA DULANY, who *m.* Colonel Richard H. Dulany, of "Welbourne," Virginia, and had:

    FRANCES ADDISON CARTER DULANY, a member of the Maryland Society of the Colonial Dames of America, who *m.* J. Southgate Lemmon, of Baltimore.

2.—ELIZABETH TASKER, who *m.* Christopher Lowndes, and had:

    CHARLES LOWNDES, 1765–1846, who *m.* Eleanor, *d.* 18 August, 1805, daughter of Edward Lloyd, of "Wye," Governor of Maryland, and had, besides other children: *Lloyd*, and

    RICHARD LOWNDES, 1801–1844, who *m.*, 22 March, 1832, Louisa Black, and had:

    1.—ELOISE LOWNDES, who *m.*, 11 July, 1864, J. Philip Roman, and had:

        I.—ELOISE LOWNDES ROMAN, a member of the Maryland Society of the Colonial Dames of America, who *m.*, 25 September, 1894, Ernest St. George Lough.

        II.—LOUISA LOWNDES ROMAN, a member of the Maryland Society of the Colonial Dames of America, who *m.* at Annapolis, 15 June, 1899, Arthur J. Hepburn, United States Navy.

        III.—J. PHILIP ROMAN, *m.*, 15 November, 1899, Mary Katherine Clark.

2.—ELIZABETH TASKER LOWNDES, a member of the Maryland Society of the Colonial Dames of America, who *m.*, 2 December, 1869, her first cousin, Lloyd Lowndes, Governor of Maryland, son of the aforesaid Lloyd Lowndes, and had: I. *Elizabeth T., d. inf.;* II. *Lloyd, m.,* 23 November, 1899, Mary Campbell Quinn; III. *Richard T., m.,* 22 October, 1896, Mary McDowell, and had: *Richard Tasker;* IV. *Charles Thomas;* V. *William Bladen;* VI. *Upshur, d. inf.;* VII. *Elizabeth;* VIII. *Tasker Gantt.*

3.—ANNE TASKER, who *m.* Samuel Ogle, 1704-1762, thrice Governor of the Province of Maryland, and had:

ANNE OGLE, who *m.* John Tayloe, of "Mt. Airy," King George county, Virginia, and had:

ANNE OGLE TAYLOE, who *m.* Henry Howell Lewis, United States Navy, and had: *Henry Grosvenor, Theodorick Napier, Anne Ogle, d.,* and

VIRGINIA TAYLOE LEWIS, of Baltimore, a member of the Maryland Society of the Colonial Dames of America.

PEDIGREE X.

EDWARD I., King of England, had by his first wife, Princess Eleanor, daughter of Ferdinand III., King of Castile and Leon:

PRINCESS ELEANOR PLANTAGENET, who *m.* Henri, Comte de Barr, and had:

LADY ELEANOR DE BARR, who *m.* Llewelyn ap Owen, and had:

THOMAS AP LLEWELYN, who *m.* Lady Eleanor, daughter of Philip ap Iver ap Cadivor, and had:

ELEANOR V. PHILIP, who *m.* Griffith Vychan (or Vaughn), Lord of Glyndyfrdwy, and had:

LOWRY VAUGHN (sister of Owen Glendower), who *m.* Robert Puleston, of Emral, and had:

JOHN PULESTON, of Emral, who *m.* Angharad, daughter of Griffith de Hanmer, and had:

MARGARET PULESTON (see Dunn's "Visitations of Wales"), who *m.* David ap Ievan ap Einion, constable of Harlech Castle in 1468, and had:

EINION AP DAVID, of Coyniarth, in Edermon, who had:

LLEWELYN AP EINION, who had:

GRIFFITH AP LLEWELYN, who *m.* Mary, daughter of Howell ap Harry, and had:

CATHERINE V. GRIFFITH, who *m.* Edward ap Ievan, of Llanwddyn parish, Monmouthshire, and had:

ELLEN V. EDWARD, who *m.* Lewis ap Griffith, of Yshute, Denbigshire, 1525–1600, and had:

ROBERT AP LEWIS, of Rhiwlas, Merionethshire, 1555–1645, who *m.* Gwyrrll, daughter of Llewelyn ap David, of Llan Rwst, in Denbigshire, and had:

EVAN AP ROBERT AP LEWIS, of Rhiwlas and Vron Gôch, Merionethshire, 1585–1662, who had:

OWEN AP EVAN, of Vron Gôch farm, near Bala, Merionethshire, *d.* 1669, who *m.* Gainor John, *d.* 14 December, 1678, and had:

ELLEN EVANS, who *m.* Cadwalader Thomas ap Hugh, of Kiltalgarth, Llanvawr, Merionethshire, who suffered persecution and imprisonment because he was a Quaker, and had by him, who *d. ante* February, 1682–

PEDIGREE X.—Continued.

1683 (see Glenn's "Merion in the Welsh Tract," and Keith's "Provincial Councillors of Pennsylvania"):

JOHN CADWALADER,* b. 1677–1678, came to Pennsylvania 1697, and was admitted a freeman of Philadelphia, in July, 1705; elected to the Common Council, 1718–1733; member of the Provincial Assembly, 1729–1734; d. 23 July, 1734, intestate. He m. at Friends' Meeting, Merion, Pennsylvania, 29 December, 1699, Martha, d. 16 April, 1747, daughter of Dr. Edward Jones, of Merion, and his wife, Mary, daughter of Dr. Thomas Wynne, of Philadelphia, and had:

1.—THOMAS CADWALADER, M.D., of Philadelphia, a member of the Common Council, 1751–1774; of the Provincial Council, 1755–1776; medical director of the army hospitals, 1776; d. at his country-seat, "Greenwood," Mercer county, New Jersey, 14 November, 1779, aged 72 years. He m., 18 June, 1738, Hannah, d. 1786, aged 74, daughter of Thomas Lambert, of Trenton, New Jersey, and had:

I.—COLONEL LAMBERT CADWALADER, of Philadelphia and Trenton, a member of the constitutional convention; a deputy to the Continental Congress; member of Congress from New Jersey, 1789–1795; d. at "Greenwood," 13 September, 1813, aged 81 years. He m., in 1793, Mary, daughter of Archibald McCall, of Philadelphia, and had:

MAJOR-GENERAL THOMAS CADWALADER, of "Greenwood," b. 11 September, 1795, d. 22 October, 1873. He m., 27 December, 1831, Maria C., daughter of Nicholas Grosverneur, of New York, and had:

MARIA CADWALADER, a member of the Society of the Colonial Dames of America, who m., 29 April, 1880, John Hone, of New York City, and had: *Hester.*

II.—GENERAL JOHN CADWALADER, of Philadelphia, b. January, 1742, d. 10 February, 1786; m., first, Elizabeth, d. 15 February, 1776, daughter of Edward Lloyd, of "Wye House," Talbot county, Maryland, and had:

ELIZABETH MCCALL, b. 1773, d. October, 1824, who m., 1792, Archibald McCall, of Philadelphia, d. 1843 (son of Archibald McCall and his wife, Judith, daughter of Peter Kemble, president of the Provincial Council of New Jersey), and had:

COLONEL GEORGE ARCHIBALD MCCALL, United States Army, of

---

* The following ladies, members of the National Society of the Colonial Dames of America, are also of Royal Descent through John Cadwalader :
MISS MARTHA MORRIS BROWN, Pennsylvania State Society.
MRS. SAMUEL CHEW, Pennsylvania State Society.
MRS. WILLIAM PEARSALL, Pennsylvania State Society.

"Belair," Pennsylvania, *b.* 16 March, 1802, *d.* 26 February, 1868; *m.*, 1853, Elizabeth, daughter of William McMurtrie, and had:

ELIZABETH MCCALL, a member of the Pennsylvania Society of the Colonial Dames of America, who *m.* Edward Fenno Hoffman, of Philadelphia, and had: *Edward F., b.* 27 July, 1888; *John C., b.* 18 Dec., 1889, *d.* 3 March, 1890; and *Phœbe White, b.* 3 Feb., 1894.

2.—HANNAH CADWALADER, *b.* 15 April, 1715, *d.* 15 December, 1787; *m.*, 29 April, 1737, Samuel Morris, of Philadelphia, *b.* 21 November, 1711, *d.* April, 1782. He was commissioned to settle the Braddock expedition accounts, 1756; was a member Common Council of Philadelphia, 1756–1766; vice-president council of safety, and afterwards of the board of war during the Revolution; a founder of the Pennsylvania Hospital, 1752; register of wills, Philadelphia, 1777; a founder of the Philadelphia Library, 1742; justice court of common pleas, 1745, and of the orphans' court, 1747; high sheriff of Philadelphia county, 1752, and had by his wife, Hannah Cadwalader:

ANTHONY CADWALADER MORRIS, of Philadelphia, *d.* 28 September, 1798; *m.*, 12 April, 1770, Mary, daughter of William Jones, and had:

1.—HANNAH MORRIS, *d.* 26 January, 1832, who *m.*, 24 November, 1791, Nathaniel Mitchell, of Laurel, Sussex county, Delaware, *b.* 1753, *d.* 21 February, 1814. He was adjutant of a Delaware battalion under Colonel John Dagworthy, 1775; captain second Delaware battalion, under Colonel Samuel Patterson, 1776–1777; captain in Colonel Grayson's regiment of Virginia line, 1777–1779; major in Colonel Nathaniel Gist's regiment of Virginia and Maryland line, 1779–1781; brigade major and inspector to General Muhlenburg, 1780–1781; prisoner of war on parole, July 18, 1782; member of Delaware Society of the Cincinnati; delegate to first Colonial Congress from Delaware, 1786–1788; Governor of Delaware, 1805–1808, and had by his wife, Hannah Morris:

THEODORE MITCHELL, *b.* 7 January, 1804, *d.* 26 September, 1884; *m.*, 6 June, 1837, Rebecca Ann Earp, *d.* 1 July, 1893, and had:

EMILIE REBECCA MITCHELL, *b.* 22 July, 1850, who *m.*, 7 April, 1869, Robert Edgar Hastings, of Philadelphia, *b.* 12 November, 1843, and had:

I.—FLORENCE HASTINGS, *b.* 11 May, 1870, *d.* 31 July, 1870.

II.—MABEL HASTINGS, *b.* 10 October, 1871, a member of the Pennsylvania Society of the Colonial Dames of America, who *m.*, 2 June, 1898, Henry Burnett Robb, of Philadelphia, and had: *Henry Burnett, b.* 12 February, 1899.

III.—THEODORE MITCHELL HASTINGS, *b.* 16 July, 1876, a member of the Delaware Society of the Cincinnati.

PEDIGREE X.—Continued.

2.—FRANCES MORRIS, 1791–1864; m., 1809, Nathaniel Stout Allison, M.D., 1786–1817, and had:

ELIZABETH ALLISON, 1812–1844; m., 1836, Oliver Spencer Janney, 1810–1861, and had:

FRANCES MORRIS JANNEY, b. 7 December, 1839, a member of the Pennsylvania Society of the Colonial Dames of America, who m., 5 November, 1857, John Steinmetz, of Philadelphia, b. 22 September, 1830, d. 30 July, 1877, and had:

I. OLIVER JANNEY STEINMETZ, b. July 24, 1858, d. August 15, 1858.

II. ELIZABETH MORRIS STEINMETZ, b. May 22, 1859, m. 27 November, 1883, S. Bevan Miller, and had: *Francis Morris*, b. December 4, 1884; *Elise Bevan*, b. December 22, 1886, and *Allison Janney*, b. January 20, 1891.

III. FRANCES ALLISON STEINMETZ, b. October 3, 1860, d. July 17, 1866.

IV. SPENCER JANNEY STEINMETZ, b. July 3, 1863.

V. and VI. JOHN E. W. and DANIEL C., twins, b. 21 August, 1864; d. inf.

VII. MARY ELEANOR STEINMETZ, b. December 7, 1865.

VIII. EDITH ALLISON STEINMETZ, b. July 14, 1867.

IX. JOSEPH ALLISON STEINMETZ, b. March 22, 1870.

X. ANITA MAY, b. May 9, 1874, m., January 27, 1897, Roland L. Taylor, and had: *Anita Marjory*, b. November 26, 1897.

PEDIGREE XI.

EDWARD I., King of England, had by his first wife, Princess Eleanor of Castile:

PRINCESS JOAN D'ACRE, *d.* 1307, who *m.*, first (his second wife), Gilbert de Clare, Earl of Hertford and Gloucester, *d.* 1295, and had:

LADY MARGARET DE CLARE (widow of Piers de Gavestone, Earl of Cornwall), who *m.*, secondly, Hugh d'Audley, Earl of Gloucester, *d.* 1347, and had:

LADY MARGARET D'AUDLEY, who *m.* (his first wife) Sir Ralph de Stafford, K.G., created, in 1351, Earl of Stafford, *d.* 1372, and had:

SIR HUGH DE STAFFORD, K.G., second Earl of Stafford, *d.* 1386, who *m.* Lady Philippa, daughter of Sir Thomas de Beauchamp, K.G., Earl of Warwick, also of Royal Descent, and had:

LADY MARGARET DE STAFFORD, who *m.* (his first wife), Sir Ralph de Neville, K.G., created, in 1399, Earl of Westmoreland, *d.* 1425, and had:

LADY MARGARET DE NEVILLE, who *m.* Richard le Scrope, *d.* 1420, and had:

HENRY LE SCROPE, fourth Baron le Scrope, of Bolton, *d.* 1459, *m.* Lady Elizabeth, daughter of John le Scrope, Lord of Masham and Upsal, and had:

LADY ELIZABETH LE SCROPE, who *m.* Oliver St. John, of Lydiard-Tregoze, Wilts, *d.* 1497, also of Royal Descent, and had:

SIR JOHN ST. JOHN, of Lydiard-Tregoze, only son, knighted by Henry VIII., *d.* at sea, 1512, who *m.* Lady Jane, daughter of Sir John Ewarby, K.B., of Farley, Hants, also of Royal Descent, and had:

JOHN ST. JOHN, of Lydiard-Tregoze, *m.* Lady Margaret, daughter of Sir Richard Carew, of Bedington, Surrey, and had:

NICHOLAS ST. JOHN, of Lydiard-Tregoze, *m.* Lady Elizabeth, daughter of Sir Richard Blount, of Mapledurham, Oxford, and had:

SIR JOHN ST. JOHN, of Lydiard-Tregoze (second son, brother and heir of Oliver, Viscount Grandison), who *m.* Lady Lucy, daughter of Sir Walter Hungerford, of Farley Castle, Wilts, and had:

SIR JOHN ST. JOHN, of Lydiard-Tregoze, knighted in 1608, created a

Baronet in 1611. He *m.*, first, Lady Anne, daughter of Sir Thomas Leighton, of Feckingham, Wilts, also of Royal Descent, and had:

LADY ANNE ST. JOHN, *b.* 5 November, 1614, who *m.*, first, Sir Francis Henry Lee, second Baronet, of Quarendon, *d.* 26 July, 1639, and had:

FRANCIS HENRY LEE, second son (see Foster's "Royal Descents," p. 162), father of:

SIR EDWARD HENRY LEE, of Ditchley, Oxford, third baronet, *d.* 1716, who was elevated to the peerage in 1674, as Baron of Spellesburg, Viscount Quarendon and Earl of Litchfield, which titles became extinct with the death of the fourth Earl, in 1778. He had by his wife, Lady Charlotte Fitz-Roy, a natural daughter of Charles II., King of England, by Lady Barbara Villiers, Duchess of Cleveland:

LADY CHARLOTTE LEE, who *m.*, 2 June, 1698, Benedict Leonard Calvert, fifth Lord Baltimore, of Baltimore, county Longford, Ireland, M.P. for Harwich, who *d.* 16 April, 1715, son of Charles, fourth Lord Baltimore, Governor of the Province of Maryland, 1661 (see Foster's "Yorkshire Pedigrees"), and had:

BENEDICT LEONARD CALVERT, M.P. for Harwich, Governor of the Province of Maryland, *b.* 1700, *d.* 1751-52; *m.*, 20 July, 1730, Lady Mary, daughter of Sir Thomas Jansen, Bart., and had:

ELEANOR CALVERT, *d.* 28 April, 1811, who *m.*, first, 3 February, 1774, John Parke Custis, of "Abingdon" (the stepson of President Washington), *b.* at "The White House," on the Pamunky River, New Kent county, Virginia, 1753, *d.* at "Eltham," 5 November, 1781, son of Daniel Parke Custis (and his wife, Martha Dandridge, who *m.*, secondly, President Washington), and had:

MARTHA PARKE CUSTIS, *b.* at General Washington's "Mt. Vernon," 31 December, 1777, *d.* at "Tudor Place," 13 July, 1854; *m.* at "Hope Park," Fairfax county, Virginia, 6 January, 1795, Thomas Peter, of "Tudor Place," Georgetown, District of Columbia, *b.* 4 January, 1769, at "Peter's Square," Georgetown, *d.* at "Tudor Place," 16 April, 1834, and had:

BRITANNIA WELLINGTON PETER, President of the District of Columbia Society of the Colonial Dames of America, *b.* at "Tudor Place," 28 January, 1815, who *m.*, 8 December, 1842 (his second wife), Commodore Beverley Kennon, United States Navy, also of Royal Descent, accidentally *k.* by the bursting of a gun on the United States Frigate "Princeton," 28 February, 1844, and had:

MARTHA CUSTIS KENNON, *b.* at "Tudor Place," 18 October, 1843, who *m.* at "Tudor Place," 23 April, 1867, Armistead Peter, M.D., of Georgetown, and had: *Armistead.*

PEDIGREE XII.

HUGH CAPET, King of France, had, by his wife Lady Adela, daughter of William, Duke of Aquitaine:

ROBERT THE PIOUS, KING OF FRANCE, who had, by his second wife, Lady Constance, daughter of William, Count of Provence:

PRINCESS ADELA (widow of Richard III., Duke of Normandy), who *m.*, secondly, 1027, Baldwin V., Count of Flanders, *d.* 1067, and had:

BALDWIN VI., COUNT OF FLANDERS and Artois, *m.* Countess Richildis, daughter and heiress of Raginerus V., Count of Hainault, and had:

GILBERT DE GAUNT (nephew of Queen Maud of England), who had:

LADY EMMA, *m.* Alan de Percy, the Great, second Baron Percy, and had:

WILLIAM DE PERCY, third Baron, who *m.* Lady Alice, daughter of Richard Fitz-Gilbert de Tonebridge de Clare, of county Suffolk, created Earl of Clare, justiciary of England, *d.* 1090, and had:

LADY AGNES DE PERCY, who *m.* Josceline de Louvaine, Baron de Percy, son of Godfrey, Duke of Brabrant, Louvain and Lother, d. 1140, also of Royal Descent, and had:

HENRY DE PERCY, eldest son, *d. v. p.*, who *m.* Lady Isabel, daughter of Adam de Brus, and had:

WILLIAM DE PERCY, sixth Baron Percy, *d.* 1245; *m.* Lady Eleanor, daughter of Lord Bardolf, and had:

HENRY DE PERCY, seventh Baron Percy, *d.* 1272; *m.* Lady Margaret de Warren, also of Royal Descent, and had:

HENRY DE PERCY, tenth Baron Percy, *d.* 1315; *m.* Lady Eleanor Fitz-Alan, also of Royal Descent, and had:

HENRY DE PERCY, eleventh Baron Percy, of Alnwick, *d.* 1352; *m.* Lady Imania (or Ida), daughter of Robert, Baron de Clifford, of Appleby, *k.* at Bannockburn, 1313, and his wife, Lady Maud de Clare, both of Royal Descent, and had:

LADY MAUD DE PERCY, who *m.* (his first wife) Sir John de Neville, K.G., third Baron Neville, of Raby, *d.* 17 October, 1389, and had:

SIR RALPH DE NEVILLE, K.G., fourth Baron, created in 1399, Earl of Westmoreland, Earl Marshal of England for life, *d.* 1425, who had, by his second wife, Lady Joane de Beaufort, also of Royal Descent, widow of Sir Robert de Ferrers:

PEDIGREE XII.—Continued.

SIR EDWARD NEVILL, K.G., BARON BERGAVENNY, fourth son, d. 18 October, 1476, who m., first, 1435, Lady Elizabeth Beauchamp, 1415–1447, only child of Richard, first Earl of Worcester, and his wife, Lady Isabel de Despencer, a descendant of King Edward III., and had:

SIR GEORGE NEVILL, Knt., 1440–1492, second Baron Bergavenny, who m., first, Margaret, d. 1485, daughter of Sir Hugh Fenne, sub-treasurer of England, and had:

SIR GEORGE NEVILL, K.B., third Baron Bergavenny, who had, by his third wife, Lady Mary Stafford, daughter of Edward, Duke of Buckingham, who was beheaded on Tower Hill:

LADY URSULA NEVILL, who m. (his first wife) Sir Warham St. Leger, Knt., of Ulcombe, sheriff of Kent, 1560; chief-governor of Munster, 1566; member of the Privy Council, 1585 (see Lodge's " Peerage of Ireland," 1754, vol. iii.). He was a bitter foe of the Irish, and he and Hugh Maguire, Prince of Farmagh, killed each other in a battle while heading their forces, 4 March, 1599. Sir Warham and Lady Ursula had:

SIR ANTHONY ST. LEGER, Knt. (see Berry's " Kent Pedigrees," Foster's " Royal Descents "), of Ulcombe, m. Mary, daughter of Sir Thomas Scott, and had:

SIR WARHAM ST. LEGER, of Ulcombe, d. ante 1632; m. Mary, daughter of Sir Rowland Hayward, lord mayor of London, d. 1593, and had:

URSULA ST. LEGER, 1600–1672, who m. Rev. Daniel Horsmanden, D.D., rector of Ulcombe, Kent, removed by Parliament, 1643, d. 1654, and had:

COLONEL WARHAM HORSMANDEN,* of Purleigh, Essex, came to Virginia in 1649, but returned to England and d. there, who had:

MARIA HORSMANDEN, d. 9 November, 1699, who m. Colonel William Byrd, b. 1652, who came to Virginia in 1674 from London, son of John and Grace (Stegg) Byrd, and d. 1704 (see Munsell's " Byrd MSS.," Dr. Page's " Page Family History," Neill's " Virginia Carolorum," Brown's " Genesis of the United States "), and had:

I.—COLONEL WILLIAM BYRD, 2d, of " Westover," Charles City county, Virginia, 1674–1744, president of H. M. Council in Virginia, etc.; m., first, Lucy, daughter of Colonel Daniel Parke, and had by her:

WILHELMINA BYRD, who m. Thomas Chamberlayne, of New Kent county, Virginia, and had:

EDWARD PYE CHAMBERLAYNE, who had by his second wife, Mary Bickerton Webb:

---

* The following ladies, members of the National Society of the Colonial Dames of America, are also of Royal Descent, through Colonel Horsmanden:

MISS EVELYN B. MCCANDLISH, Maryland State Society.
MRS. ARTHUR E. POULTNEY, Maryland State Society.
MRS. ALEX. B. RANDALL, Maryland State Society.

PEDIGREE XII.—Continued.

LUCY PARKE CHAMBERLAYNE, who m. Robert Carter Williamson, of Brook Hill, Henrico county, Virginia, and had:

MARY AMANDA WILLIAMSON, a member of the Virginia Society of the Colonial Dames of America, who m. John Stewart, of Bute, Scotland, and had:

    1.—MARY AMANDA, d. 1889, wife of Thomas Pinckney. Issue: *Charles Cotesworth.*

    2. ISOBEL LAMONT STEWART, a member of the Virginia Society of the Colonial Dames of America, who m. Joseph Bryan, of Richmond, Virginia, and had: *John Stewart, Robert Coalter, Jonathan Randolph, St. George Tucker,* and *Thomas Pinckney.*

    3. MARION McINTOSH, wife of Rt. Rev. George W. Peterkin, D.D., Bishop of West Virginia. Issue: *Mary Stewart.*

    4. LUCY WILLIAMSON; 5. ANNE CARTER; 6. NORMA; 7. ELIZABETH HOPE.

COLONEL WILLIAM BYRD, 2d, of "Westover"; m., secondly, Maria, daughter of Thomas Taylor, of Kensington, England, and had by her:

I.—MARIA BYRD, who m. (his second wife) Colonel Landon Carter, of "Sabine Hall," Richmond county, Virginia, also of Royal Descent, and had:

    LANDON CARTER, of Pittsylvania county, Virginia; m. Judith Fauntleroy, also of Royal Descent, and had:

    WORMELEY CARTER, m., 1787, Sarah Edwards, and had:

    WORMELEY CARTER, 1792–1821; m., 1815, Lucinda Washington Alexander, and had:

    JUDGE WILLIAM ALEXANDER CARTER, 1818–1881; m., 1848, Mary Eliza Hamilton, and had:

    MARY ADA CARTER, a member of the Pennsylvania Society of the Colonial Dames of America, who m., 1874, Joseph K. Corson, M.D., surgeon United States Army, also of Royal Descent, and had: *Mary Carter,* 1876–1890, and *Edward Foulke, b.* 1883.

II.—ANNE BYRD, who m. Charles Carter, of "Cleve," also of Royal Descent, and had:

    1.—MARIA CARTER, who m. William Armistead, and had:

        ELEANOR BOWLES ARMISTEAD, who m. Judge William McMechen, of Baltimore, Maryland, and had:

        SIDNEY JANE McMECHEN, who m. John Charles Van Wyck, of Baltimore, Maryland, and had:

        SIDNEY McMECHEN VAN WYCK, b. 6 April, 1830, d. at San Francisco, California, 27 April, 1887; m. Nannie Churchill Crittenden, also of Royal Descent, and had:

LAURA SANCHEZ VAN WYCK, of San Francisco, a member of the California Society of the Colonial Dames of America, the Order of the Crown, *etc.*

2.—LANDON CARTER, of "Cleve," *m.* Mildred Willis, also of Royal Descent, and had:

LUCY LANDON CARTER, *m.* General John Minor, of Fredericksburg, Virginia, and had:

LUCIUS HORATIO MINOR, of "Edgewood"; *m.* Catherine Frances Berkeley, also of Royal Descent, and had:

MARY WILLIS MINOR, of Baltimore, a member of the Maryland Society of the Colonial Dames of America.

III.—JANE BYRD, who *m.*, 1746, John Page, of "North End," Matthews county, Virginia (son of Mann Page, of "Rosewell"), a member of the Virginia Council, and had:

1.—JUDITH Page, who *m.*, 1775, Colonel Hugh Nelson, of Yorktown, Virginia (son of William Nelson, president of the Virginia Council), and had:

JANE BYRD NELSON, who *m.*, 1798, Francis Walker, of "Castle Hill," Albemarle county, Virginia, M.C, 1793–1795, and had:

JUDITH PAGE WALKER, 1802–1882; *m.*, 24 March, 1820, William Cabell Rives, of "Castle Hill," Albemarle county, 1793–1868, United States Senator, United States Minister to France, *etc.*, and had:

ALFRED LANDON RIVES, of Mobile, Alabama; *m.*, 1859, Sadie McMurdo, of Richmond, Virginia, and had:

AMÉLIE LOUISE RIVES, a member of the Virginia Society of the Colonial Dames of America, who *m.*, first, John Armstrong Chanler, of New York City, and *m.*, secondly, P. Troubetskoy.

2.—LUCY PAGE, who *m.*, 1792, Francis Nelson, of "Mt. Air," Hanover county, Virginia, son of Governor Thomas Nelson, of Yorktown, Virginia, and had:

JUDITH NELSON, who *m.* (first wife) Mann Page, of Greenland, Virginia, and had:

FRANCIS NELSON PAGE, United States Army, *d.* near Fort Smith, Arkansas, 25 March, 1860; *m.* Susan Duval, and had:

LUCY NELSON PAGE, a member of the Virginia Society of the Colonial Dames of America, who *m.* William A. Hardaway, M.D., of St. Louis, Mo., and had: *Augusta, b.* 29 October, 1877, *d.*

12 December, 1882; *Page, b.* 17 June, 1881, *d.* 8 June, 1890, and *Francis Page, b.* 26 April, 1888.

IV.—COLONEL WILLIAM BYRD, 3d, of "Westover," 1728-1777, who *m.*, first, Elizabeth Hill, daughter of Colonel John Carter, of "Shirley," King's counsel, *etc.*, also of Royal Descent, and his wife Elizabeth, daughter of Edward Hill, King's counsel, and had by her:

THOMAS TAYLOR BYRD, who *m.* Mary Anne, daughter of William Armistead, of "Hesse," Gloucester county, Virginia, and his wife Maria, daughter of Colonel Charles Carter, of "Cleve," also of Royal Descent, and his second wife, Ann, daughter of Colonel William Byrd, Jr., aforesaid, and had:

MARIA CARTER BYRD, who *m.* Judge Philip Narbonne Nicholas, of Richmond, Va., also of Royal Descent, and had:

ELIZABETH BYRD NICHOLAS, of Washington, D. C., a member of the District of Columbia Society of the Colonial Dames of America, and national treasurer of the general society.

COLONEL WILLIAM BYRD, 3d, of "Westover," *m.*, secondly, 29 January, 1761, Mary, 1740-1814, daughter of Charles and Ann (Shippen) Willing, of Philadelphia, Pennsylvania, and had by her:

MARIA HORSMANDEN BYRD, *b.* 26 November, 1761, *m.*, 1784, John Page, of "Broadneck," *b.* 29 June, 1760, *d.* 17 September, 1838, also of Royal Descent, and had:

1.—ABBY BYRD PAGE, *b.* 1798, *d.* April, 1888, who *m.* John Hopkins, of Winchester, Virginia, also of Royal Descent, and had:

WILLIAM EVELYN HOPKINS, Commodore United States Navy, *b.* 10 January, 1821, *d.* 25 October, 1894; *m.*, 8 March, 1852, Louise Kimball, *b.* March, 1832, and had:

MARIA BYRD HOPKINS, a member of the Virginia and California Societies of the Colonial Dames of America, *b.* 2 February, 1853, who *m.*, at Mare Island, California, 30 April, 1873, Colonel Stuart Selden Wright, of Fresno, California, also of Royal Descent, and had:

LOUISE KIMBALL WRIGHT, *b.* 6 December, 1874, a member of the Virginia and California Societies of the Colonial Dames of America, who *m.*, 7 June, 1895, John Mannen McClure, of Oakland, California, and had: *Mannen Wright. b.* 7 April, 1896.

2.—SARAH WALKER PAGE, *m.*, 1815, Major Thomas M. Nelson, United States Army, member of Congress from Virginia, 1816-1819, and presidential elector, 1829 and 1833, and had:

MARIA BYRD NELSON, who *m.* William Gray Woolfolk, of Columbus, Georgia, and had:

ROSA WOOLFOLK, a member of the Maryland Society of the Colonial Dames of America, who m. Robert Ober, of Baltimore, and had: *Gustavus* and *Maria Byrd Nelson*.

II.—ANNE URSULA BYRD, who m. Robert Beverley, of "Beverly Park," Drysdale parish, King and Queen county, Virginia, and had:

COLONEL WILLIAM BEVERLEY, only son, of "Beverley Manor," Essex county, and "Blandfield," Virginia, member of the House of Burgesses, 1748, d. 1756; m. Elizabeth Bland (sister of Colonel Richard Bland, of the Virginia Line), and had:

ROBERT BEVERLEY, only son, of "Wakefield," Culpeper county, Virginia, d. 1800; m. Maria Carter of "Sabine Hall," Virginia, also of Royal Descent, and had:

EVELYN BYRD BEVERLEY, m., first, George Lee, and, secondly, Patrick Hume Douglas, M.D., of Leesburg, Loudoun county, Virginia, d. 1837, and had:

I.—WILLIAM BYRD DOUGLAS, b. at Leesburg, 8 December, 1815, d. Nashville, Tennessee, 13 December, 1882; m., first, Martha Rebecca Bright, and had by her:

MARY MARGARET DOUGLAS, a member of the Virginia Society of the Colonial Dames of America, who m., first, James R. Buckner, of Nashville, and had:

JAMES R. BUCKNER, JR., of Nashville; m. Louise Eve, and had: *Edward Richards*, b. 1 February, 1892, and *Jane Eve*, b. 9 May, 1893.

MARY MARGARET DOUGLAS, m., secondly, Edward D. Richards, of Nashville, and had:

EVELYN BYRD RICHARDS, m. Owen H. Wilson, M.D., of Nashville.

WILLIAM BYRD DOUGLAS, of Nashville, 1815–1882; m., secondly, Mrs. Hannah (Underwood) Cook, and had by her: *Bruce*, m. Ella Kirkman, and had issue, and

ELLEN DOUGLAS, a member of the Virginia Society of the Colonial Dames of America, who m. Dr. G. A. Baxter, of Chattanooga, Tennessee (son of Judge John Baxter, of Knoxville, Tennessee), and had: *Byrd Douglas* and *Bruce Beverley*.

II.—HUGH DOUGLAS, who m. Nancy Hamilton, and had:

EVELYN BEVERLEY DOUGLAS, a member of the Virginia Society of the Colonial Dames of America, who m. John Sergeant Wise, of New York City, and had: *John S.*, d.; *Hugh D.*, *Henry Alexander*, *John S.*, *Hamilton*, d.; *Eva Douglas*, *Jennings C.*, *Margaretta*, and *Byrd Douglas*.

PEDIGREE XIII.

EDWARD I., King of England, had by his first wife, Princess Eleanor, daughter of Ferdinand III., King of Castile:

PRINCESS ELIZABETH PLANTAGENET, widow of John de Vere, who m., secondly, 1306, Humphrey de Bohun, fourth Earl of Hereford and Essex; lord high constable of England, k. 16 March, 1321, and had:

LADY ELEANOR DE BOHUN, who m., 1327, James Butler, lord butler of Ireland and second Earl of Carrick, and Earl of Ormond, and had:

JAMES BUTLER, second Earl of Ormond; lord butler and lord justice of Ireland 1331–1382, who m. Lady Elizabeth, daughter of Sir John d'Arcy, first Baron d'Arcy, of Platten, County Meath; lord justice of Ireland, and had:

LADY ELEANOR BUTLER, d. 1392, who m., 1359, Gerald Fitz-Maurice Fitz-Gerald, fourth Earl of Desmond, lord justice of Ireland, murdered in 1397, and had:

JAMES FITZ-GERALD, seventh Earl of Desmond; Governor of Limerick, Waterford, Cork and Kerry, who m. Lady Mary, daughter of Ulick Burke Mac William-Iachter, a chieftain in Connaught, and had:

LADY HONORA FITZ-GERALD, who m. Thomas Fitz-Maurice, eighth Lord of Kerry, d. 1469 (see Lodge's "Peerage of Ireland," 1754, Vol. I.), and had:

LADY JOAN FITZ-MAURICE, m. (his first wife) Turlogh-donn O'Brien, prince of Limerick and Thomond, d. 1528, a descendant of King Brian Boru, and had:

MURROUGH O'BRIEN, third son, created Earl of Thomond for life, 1 July, 1543, and Baron Inchiquin, d. 1551; m. Eleanor, daughter of Thomas Fitz-Gerald, Knight of the Valley, and had (see Lodge's "Peerage of Ireland," 1754, Vol. IV., page 12, and 1789, Vol. III., page 417, and O'Hart's "Irish Landed Gentry," page 128):

LADY HONORIA O'BRIEN, m. Sir Dermod O'Shaughnassie, Knt., of Gortinshigorie (or Gort), County Galway (see his royal descent in O'Hart's "Irish Pedigrees," 3d edition, pages 393–5, and see Blake-Foster's "The Irish Chieftains," 1872, and Hardiman's "West Connaught"), and had:

LADY MAUD O'SHAUGHNASSIE, who m., about 1560, Edmund Bermingham, fifteenth Baron of Athenry (see Lodge's "Peerage of Ireland," 1754, Vol. IV.), and had:

RICHARD BERMINGHAM, sixteenth Baron of Athenry, 1570–1635; who *m.* "a daughter of the family of Tuite," and had:

EDWARD FITZ-RICHARD BERMINGHAM, seventeenth Baron of Athenry, *d.* 1640; *m.* Mary, daughter of Sir Festus Burke, of Donamon and Glinsk, County Galway, and had:

LADY ANNE BERMINGHAM, who *m.* The O'Connor-Duinn, of Ballintober, Roscommon (see "The O'Connor-Don" family, O'Hart's "Irish Pedigrees"), and had:

CLARE O'CONNOR-DUINN, who *m.* Charles O'Carroll, of Ely, O'Carroll, Kings county, Ireland (see "Stemmata Carrollana," in the Journal of the Royal His. and Arch. Asso. of Ire., Oct. 1883, also O'Ferrell and Betham's O'Clery's "Linea Antiqua," O'Hart's "Irish Land Gentry," *etc.*), and had:

DR. CHARLES CARROLL,* *b.* 1691, who removed to Annapolis, Maryland, about 1737, and was the representative of Annapolis in the Maryland Assembly. He *m.* Dorothy, daughter of Henry Blake and his wife Henrietta Maria, daughter of Philemon Lloyd, speaker of the Lower House of the Assemblies of Maryland in 1681, and granddaughter of Edward Lloyd, a member of the Privy Council and General Assembly of Maryland, and one of the commissioners, under the Lord Protector in 1654, for the governing of the affairs of Maryland, *d.* 29 September, 1755, and had: *Charles*, called the barrister, *b.* 22 March, 1722, *d. s. p.* 28 May, 1783; member of Congress from Maryland, and

MARY CLARE CARROLL, *b.* 13 May, 1727, who *m.*, 21 July, 1747, Nicholas Maccubbin, of Maryland, *d.* 1787, and had: *Mary Clare* and

I.—JAMES MACCUBBIN-CARROLL, who assumed the surname Carroll, under the will of his uncle Charles Carroll, barrister, who *d. s. p.* 28 May, 1783. He *m.* Sophia Dorsey Gough, and had:

    1.—JAMES CARROLL, who *m.* Achsah Ridgely, of Hampton, and had:

        JAMES CARROLL, of Baltimore, Maryland, who *m.* Mary Wethered Ludlow, and had:

        SALLY W. CARROLL, of Baltimore, a member of the Maryland Society of the Colonial Dames of America.

---

* The following ladies, members of the National Society of the Colonial Dames of America, are also of Royal Descent through Dr. Charles Carroll:

MRS. ETHAN ALLEN (deceased), Maryland State Society.
MRS. EDWARD S. BEALL, Maryland State Society.
MISS LOUISE OGLE BEALL, Maryland State Society.
MRS. J. ALEX. PRESTON, Maryland State Society.
MISS MARY WINN, Maryland State Society.
MRS. JOHN O. TURNBULL, Maryland State Society.

PEDIGREE XIII.—Continued.

2.—CHARLES RIDGELEY CARROLL, m. Rebecca Pue, and had:

REBECCA CARROLL, who m. Carroll Spence, son of Commodore Robert Trail Spence, United States Navy, and his wife Mary Clare, sister of the aforesaid James Maccubbin-Carroll, and had:

KATE STYLES SPENCE, a member of the Maryland Society of the Colonial Dames of America, who m, Charles W. Washburn, of Baltimore.

II.—CHARLES MACCUBBIN, of Maryland, b. 1 January, 1757, d. 20 June, 1799; m. 12 May, 1793, Sarah Allen, b. 22 April, 1774, and had:

ELEANOR MACCUBBIN, b. 11 May, 1795, d. 9 December, 1858; m., 27 October, 1812, her cousin, George Mackubin, b. 9 March, 1789, d. 11 January, 1853, treasurer of Maryland, 1826-1843, and had:

1.—CHARLES NICHOLAS MACKUBIN, of Annapolis, Maryland, m. Ellen Fay, of Boston, Massachusetts, and had:

FLORENCE MACKUBIN, of Baltimore, b. at Florence, Italy, a member of the Maryland Society of the Colonial Dames of America.

2.—RICHARD CREAGH MACKUBIN, of "Strawberry Hill," Anne Arundel county, Maryland, b. 8 August, 1815, d. 18 November, 1865; m., 31 October, 1839, Hester Ann Worthington, b. 28 November, 1818, d. 22 February, 1848, and had:

ELEANOR MACKUBIN, a member of the Maryland Society of the Colonial Dames of America, who m., 14 June, 1866, Charles Baltimore Calvert, of "Riversdale" and "Mac Alpine," Prince George county, Maryland, and had:

I.—ELEANOR CALVERT, m., 14 June, 1892, William Gibson Carey, and had: *Charles Baltimore Calvert*, b. Lynn, Massachusetts, 8 November, 1893, and *William G.*, b. Schenectady, New York, 3 July, 1896.

II.—HESTER VIRGINIA CALVERT, m., 20 September, 1899, Henry Walter Lilly, M.D.

III.—CHARLOTTE AUGUSTA; IV. CHARLES BENEDICT (dead); V. RICHARD CREAGH MACKUBIN; VI. GEORGE HENRY; VII. ROSALIE EUGENIA STIER; VIII. CHARLES BALTIMORE; IX. ELIZABETH STEUART.

THE ROYAL DESCENT

OF

MRS. FRANCIS LEE SMITH,

OF ALEXANDRIA, VA.

EDWARD I., King of England=Princess Eleanor of Castile.

Princess Joan Plantagenet=Gilbert de Clare, Earl of Gloucester and Hertford.

Lady Margart de Clare=Hugh de Audley, Earl of Gloucester.

Lady Margaret de Audley=Sir Ralph de Stafford, K. G., Earl of Stafford.

Sir Hugh de Stafford, K. G., Earl of Stafford=Lady Philippa de Beauchamp.

Lady Margaret de Stafford=Sir Ralph de Neville, K. G., Earl of Westmoreland.

Ralph de Neville, of Oversley, Warwickshire=Lady Mary de Ferrers.

John de Neville, of Wymersley, Yorkshire=Lady Elizabeth de Newmarch.

Joan de Neville=Sir William Gascoigne, of Gawthrope, Yorkshire.

Sir William Gascoigne, of Gawthrope, York=Lady Margaret de Percy.

Lady Elizabeth Gascoigne=Gilbert de Talboys, of Kyme.

Sir George de Talboys, of Kyme=(Name unknown.)

Lady Anne de Talboys=Sir Edward Dymoke, of Scrivelsby, Lincolnshire.

Lady Frances Dymoke=Thomas Windebank, of Haines Hill, Berkshire.

Lady Mildred Windebank=Robert Reade, Linkenholt Manor, Southampton.

Col. George Reade, of Gloucester Co., Va.=Elizabeth Martian.

Mildred Reade=Col. Augustine Warner, Jr., of "Warner's Hall."

Mary Warner (*m.* 17 February, 1680)=John Smith, of "Purton," Gloucester Co., Va.

Augustine Smith, of "Purton," 1687–1756=Sarah Carver.

John Smith, of "Shooters' Hill," Va., 1715–1771=Mary Jacqueline.

Augustine Smith, of "Shooters' Hill," 1738–1774=Margaret Boyd.

Mary Jacqueline Smith, 1773–1846=John Cripps Vowell, of Alexandria, Va.

Sarah Gosnelle Vowell, member of the National=Francis Lee Smith, of Fauquier Co., Va.
Society of the Colonial Dames of America. *Issue.*

PEDIGREE XIV.

ETHELRED II., King of England, 978–1016, *m.*, first, Lady Elgiva, or Elgifa, *d.* 1003, daughter of Earl Thorad, and had by her:

PRINCESS ELGIVA (sister of King Edmund Ironsides), who *m.* Uthred, Prince of Northumberland, and had:

LADY ALDIGITHA, who *m.* Maldred (brother of King Duncan I., murdered by his nephew, Macbeath, in 1041), eldest son of Crynan, Lord of the Western Isles and Archthane of Dul Argyle, and his wife Lady Beatrice, daughter of Malcolm II., King of Scots, and had:

COSPATRICK, Earl of Northumberland and Dunbar, who had:

LADY GUNILDA (sister of Cospatrick, first Earl of Dunbar), who *m.* Orme, feudal Baron of Seaton, and had:

COSPATRICK, first feudal Baron of Workington, *d.* 1179, who had:

THOMAS DE WORKINGTON, *d.* 7 December, 1152, who had:

PATRICK DE CURWEN, of Workington, second son, *d.* 1212, who had:

GILBERT DE CURWEN, of Workington, who had:

GILBERT DE CURWEN, of Workington, eldest son, *d.* 1278, who *m.* Edith Harrington, *d.* 1353, and had:

GILBERT DE CURWEN, of Workington, eldest son, *d.* 1370, who had:

GILBERT DE CURWEN, of Workington, *b.* 1403; *m.* Alice Lowther, of Lowther, and had:

WILLIAM DE CURWEN, of Workington, who had by his second wife, Margaret, daughter of Sir John Croft, Knt.:

CHRISTOPHER CURWEN, of Workington (see Cumberland Visitations, 1615), *m.* Elizabeth Hudleston, of Millum, and had:

THOMAS CURWEN, of Workington Hall, Cumberland (see Burke's "Royal Descents," Ped. 37, and Jackson's "Cumberland Pedigrees," p. 288), who *m.* Anne, daughter of Sir Robert Lowther, Knt., and had:

ELIZABETH CURWEN, who *m.* John Cleburne, of Cleburne Hall and Bampton, Westmoreland, *d.* 8 August, 1489 (see O'Hart's "Irish Pedigrees," third series, and O'Hart's "Irish Landed Gentry"), and had:

THOMAS CLEBURNE, of Cleburne Hall, *b.* 1467, who had:

ROBERT CLEBURNE, of Cleburne Hall and Killesby, York, who *m.* Emma, daughter of George Kirkbride, of Kirkbride, Northumberland, and had:

EDMUND CLEBURNE, of Cleburne Hall and Killesby, who *m.* Anne Layton, of Dalemain, Cumberland, and had:

RICHARD CLEBURNE, of Cleburne Hall and Killesby, *d.* 4 January, 1607, who *m.* Eleanor, daughter of Launcelot Lancaster, of Stockbridge and Barton, Westmoreland, and had:

EDMOND CLAIBORNE, of Cleburne Hall, who *m.*, 1 September, 1576, Grace, daughter of Allan Bellingham, of Helsington and Levins, and had:

CAPTAIN WILLIAM CLAIBORNE, of "Romancoke," King William county, Virginia, *b.* 1587. He settled in Virginia in 1621, and was secretary and treasurer of the Virginia Colony, and surveyor-general of the "Old Dominion." Grants of twenty-five thousand acres of land are of record in his name in the Virginia land office. He *m.*, in 1638, in London, Jane Buller, and, dying before 1680, had issue:

I.—LIEUTENANT-COLONEL WILLIAM CLAIBORNE, of "Romancoke," Virginia, who had:

WILLIAM CLAIBORNE, *d.* 1705, who had:

WILLIAM CLAIBORNE, *m.* Elizabeth Whitehead, and had:

PHILIP WHITEHEAD CLAIBORNE, of "Liberty Hall," King William county, Virginia, who *m.* Elizabeth Dandridge, also of Royal Descent, and had:

PHILADELPHIA CLAIBORNE, who *m.* Abner Waugh, and had:

SARAH SPOTSWOOD WAUGH, *m.* James Lyons, and had:

LUCY LYONS, *m.* John Hopkins, and had:

JOHN HOPKINS, *m.* Abby Byrd Page, also of Royal Descent, and had:

WILLIAM EVELYN HOPKINS, *m.* Louise Kimball, and had:

MARIA BYRD HOPKINS, *m.* Stuart Selden Wright, also of Royal Descent, and had:

LOUISE KIMBALL WRIGHT, a member of the Virginia Society of the Colonial Dames of America, who *m.* John M. McClure, of Oakland, California. *Issue.*

II.—LIEUTENANT-COLONEL THOMAS CLAIBORNE, of "Romancoke," *b.* 17 August, 1647, *d.* 7 October, 1683; *bur.* at "Romancoke." He had by his wife, Sarah, whose surname has not been preserved (she *m.*, secondly, Captain Thomas Bray):

CAPTAIN THOMAS CLAIBORNE, of "Sweet Hall," King William county, *b.* 16 December, 1680, *d.* 16 August, 1732, *bur.* at "Sweet Hall." He *m.*, thirdly, Anne, *b.* 20 May, 1684, *d.* 4 May, 1733, daughter of Henry Fox, of King William county, and his wife, Anna West, also of Royal Descent, and had by her:

PEDIGREE XIV.—Continued.

1.—COLONEL NATHANIEL CLAIBORNE, of "Sweet Hall"; m. Jane, daughter of William Cole, of Warwick county, Virginia, and had:

WILLIAM CLAIBORNE, of Manchester, Virginia, d. 29 September, 1809, m. Mary, daughter of Ferdinand Leigh, of King William county, and had:

NATHANIEL HERBERT CLAIBORNE, b. Surrey county, Virginia, 14 November, 1777, d. Franklin county, Virginia, 15 August, 1859. He was for many years a member of both branches of the Virginia Legislature, and a member of the council during the war of 1812; member of Congress, 1825–1837, etc. He m., 1815, Elizabeth Archer Binford, of Goochland county, Virginia, and h .d:

I.—ELIZABETH HERBERT CLAIBORNE, 1829–1855, m., 1851, James Coleman Otey, of Bedford county, Virginia, and had:

LULIE LEIGH OTEY, a member of the Virginia and California Societies of the Colonial Dames of America, who m., 1870, Hervey Darneal, of Alameda, California, and had: *Susan Cole, Herbert Claiborne,* and *Hervey Otey.*

II.—NATHANIEL CHARLES CLAIBORNE, of "Rocky Mount," Franklin county, Virginia, who m. Mildred Kyle Morris, and had:

JENNIE CLAIBORNE, b. 5 September, 1853, at "Rocky Mount," a member of the Missouri Society of the Colonial Dames of America, who m., 21 October, 1874, Robert McCormick Adams, of St. Louis, Missouri, and had: *Hugh Claiborne*, b. 6 September, 1875; *Mildred Kyle*, b. 20 October, 1877, d. 20 October, 1886; *Amanda McCormick*, b. 26 August, 1880; *Nathalie*, b. 19 October, 1882; *Virginia Claiborne*, b. 3 August, 1885; *Robert McCormick* and *Marian Kyle*, twins, b. 17 June, 1890, and *John Alan Bellingham*, b. 7 February, 1896.

2.—SARAH CLAIBORNE, who m. Joseph Thompson, and had:

COLONEL ROGER THOMPSON, who had:

JOSEPH THOMPSON, who m. Elizabeth James, and had:

MARY THOMPSON, who m. Burr Harrison McCown, and had:

ANNIE McCOWN, who m. Alexander Craig, and had:

LOUISE CRAIG, a member of the Virginia and Kentucky Societies of the Colonial Dames of America, who m. Samuel A. Culbertson, of Louisville, and had: *William Stuart*, and *Alex. Craig.*

3.—COLONEL AUGUSTINE CLAIBORNE, of "Windsor," King William county, Virginia, b. 1721, d. 3 May, 1787, an eminent attorney and member of the house of burgesses and State Senate; m., Mary, daughter of Buller Herbert, of "Puddlecock," Dinwiddie county, Virginia, and had:

PEDIGREE XIV.—Continued.

I.—HERBERT CLAIBORNE, of "Chestnut Grove," New Kent county, Virginia, b. 7 August, 1746. He had by his second wife, Mary Burnet Browne, also of Royal Descent:

HERBERT AUGUSTINE CLAIBORNE, of Richmond, Virginia, 1784–1841, m. Delia, daughter of James Hayes, of Richmond, and had:

JOHN HAYES CLAIBORNE, of Richmond, Virginia, Major Confederate States Army, who m. Anna Virginia, daughter of George Washington Bassett, of "Eltham," New Kent county, Virginia, and had:

DELIA CLAIBORNE, a member of the Virginia Society of the Colonial Dames of America, who m., 10 June, 1885, Simon B. Buckner, of "Glen Lily," Hart county, Kentucky, Lieutenant-General Confederate States Army and Governor of Kentucky, and had: *Simon Bolivar*, b. 18 July, 1886.

II.—MARY CLAIBORNE, b. 1744, who m., 1763, General Charles Harrison, of "Berkeley," Virginia, an officer in the Virginia line, Continental Army, d. 1796, and had:

ELIZABETH RANDOLPH HARRISON, who m. General Daniel Claiborne Butts, also of Royal Descent, and had:

DANIEL CLAIBORNE BUTTS, who m. Ariadne Smith, and had:

MARIE ELOISE BUTTS, who m. Robert Dunlop, and had:

1.—AGNES DUNLOP, a member of the Virginia Society of the Colonial Dames of America, who m. William H. Wight, of Cockeysville, Baltimore county, Maryland, and had: *Robert Dunlop*.

2.—MARIE DUNLOP, a member of the Virginia Society of the Colonial Dames of America, who m. Warner Moore, of Richmond, Virginia, and had: *Marie Jean*, and *Warner*.

III.—ANNE CLAIBORNE, b. 1749, who m., 1768, Richard Cocke, and had:

BULLER COCKE, who m. Elizabeth Barron, and had:

ELIZABETH M. COCKE, who m. Louis Trezevant, M.D., and had:

ELIZABETH COCKE TREZEVANT, a member of the Virginia Society of the Colonial Dames of America, who m. George de Benneville Keim, of Philadelphia, and had:

1.—JULIA MAYER KEIM, of Philadelphia, a member of the Pennsylvania Society of the Colonial Dames of America.

2.—SUSAN DOUGLASS KEIM, of Philadelphia.

PEDIGREE XV.

HENRY I., King of France, had by his third wife, Anne of Russia:

HUGH THE GREAT, Duke of France and Burgundy, who had by his third wife, *m.* 938, Lady Adelheid, daughter of Herbert IV., Count of Vermandois:

LADY ISABEL DE VERMANDOIS, *d.* 1131 (widow of Robert, Earl of Mellent, *d.* 1118), who *m.*, secondly, William de Warren, second Earl of Surrey (see Watson's "Ancient Earls of Warren and Surrey"), and had:

WILLIAM DE WARREN, third Earl of Surrey, *d. s. p. m.* 1148. He *m.*, before 1143, Lady Alice de Talvace, also of Royal Descent (or Talvas, see Doyle's "Official Baronage"), *d.* 1174, and had:

LADY ISABELLA DE WARREN, heiress, *d.* 1199 (widow of William de Blois, *d. s. p.* 1160), who *m.*, secondly, 1163, Hameline Plantagenet de Warren, fifth Earl of Surrey, *d.* 1202, and had:

LADY ISABEL DE WARREN, who *m.* Roger, Baron le Bigod, created, 1189, Earl of Norfolk; lord high steward of England, and had:

HUGH, second Earl of Norfolk, *d.* 1225; *m.* Lady Maud Marshall, daughter of William le Marshal, Earl of Pembroke, the celebrated Protector during the nonage of Henry III., and had:

SIR HUGH BIGOD, second son, appointed, 22 June, 1257, chief justice of England, resigned in 1260, *d.* 1266 (see Foss's "Lives of the Chief Justices"), who *m.*, first, Joan, daughter of Robert Burnet, and had:

SIR JOHN BIGOD, Knt., younger brother of Roger, the last Earl of Norfolk, *d. s. p.* 1306, and father of

ROGER BIGOD, Knt., of Settington, youngest son, father of

JOAN BIGOD, who *m.*, 1358, Sir William de Chauncy, Knt., last Baron of Skirpenbeck, Yorkshire, which he sold in 1399, and purchased Stepney in Middlesex, and had:

JOHN CHAUNCY, of Stepney, *d.* 1444–1445, who *m.* Margaret, daughter of William Gifford, of Gedleston, and had:

JOHN CHAUNCY, of Sawbridgeworth, Herts, *d.* 7 May, 1479, who *m.* Anne, daughter of John Leventhorp, of Shingey Hall, and had:

JOHN CHAUNCY, of Sawbridgeworth, *d.* 8 June, 1510, who *m.* daughter of Thomas Boyce, and had:

JOHN CHAUNCY, of Pishobury Manor, *d.* 4 June, 1546, who *m.* Elizabeth Proffit, widow of Richard Mansfield, and had:

HENRY CHAUNCY, of New Place Gifford's, second son and heir, *d.* 14 April, 1587; *m.*, Lucy ——, and had:

GEORGE CHAUNCY, of Yardley-Bury, Hertfordshire, second son, *d.* 1627, who had by his second wife, Anne, daughter of Edward Welsh, of Great Wymondley, and widow of Edward Humberston (see "Chauncy Pedigree," compiled by Stephen Tucker, Somerset Herald in Ordinary; Chauncy pedigree in Sir Henry Chauncy's " History of Hertfordshire," Fowler's " Chauncy Memorials," *etc.*):

REV. CHARLES CHAUNCY, D.D., second President of Harvard College, *b.* 5 November, 1592, *d.* Cambridge, Massachusetts, 19 February, 1671; *m.*, 17 March, 1630, Catherine, *b.* 1601, *bapt.* 2 November, 1604, *d.* 23 June, 1667; daughter of Robert Eyre, of New Sarum and Chilhampton, Wilts, a barrister, *bur.* at St. Thomas's, 8 August, 1638, aged 69, and his first wife, Anne, daughter of Rt. Rev. John Still, D.D., bishop of Bath and Wells in 1592, *d.* 26 February, 1607, and his first wife, Anne, daughter of Thomas Arblaster (or Alabaster), of Hadley, Suffolk (see Somersetshire Visitations, 1623; Wiltshire Visitations, 1623; Bliss's Wood's " Athenæ Oxonienses," ii., 829, and Burke's " Commoners," iv., 538), and had:

1.—REV. ISAAC CHAUNCY, M.D., eldest son, *b.* Ware, Eng., 23 August, 1632, educated at Harvard College, was minister at Woodborough, Wiltshire, and was ejected by the Act of Uniformity, in 1662; *d.* London, 28 February, 1712. He had by his wife, Jane, whose surname has not been preserved:

CHARLES CHAUNCY, of Boston, Massachusetts, *d.* 4 May, 1781; *m.* Sarah, daughter of Judge John Walley, who commanded the land force in the expedition of Sir William Phipps against Canada, and had:

MARY CHAUNCY, 1707–1776; *m.* Jacob Cushing, of Hingham; representative for twelve years to the general court, and had:

CHARLES CUSHING, 1744–1809, a representative and member of the Massachusetts Senate; *m.* Hannah Croade, and had:

PRISCILLA CUSHING, *b.* 1779; *m.* Thomas Stearns, and had:

THOMAS STEARNS, *m.* Charlotte Blood, and had:

CHARLOTTE CHAMPE STEARNS, a member of the Massachusetts Society of the Colonial Dames of America, who *m.* Henry Ware Eliot, of St. Louis, Missouri, and had: *Ada, Margaret Dawes, Charlotte C., Marian Cushing, Henry Ware,* and *Thomas Stearns.*

2.—REV. ISRAEL CHAUNCEY, *b.* 1644, *d.* at Stratford, Connecticut, 1703, had by his first wife, Mary Nichols:

REV. ISAAC CHAUNCEY, *b.* 1670, *d.* at Hadley, Conn., 1745; had by his first wife, Sarah, *d.* 1720, daughter of Richard and Abigail (Hudson) Blackleach:

ABIGAIL CHAUNCEY, *b.* 1701, who *m.* (his second wife) Rev. John Graham, *b.* at Edinburgh, 1694; graduate University of Glasgow; came to New England in 1718; *d.* at Woodbury, 1774, and had:

SARAH GRAHAM, who *m.* Gideon Hurd, and had:

LOVE HURD, who *m.* Phineas Chapin, of Salisbury, and had:

MARY CHAPIN, *b.* 1791, *d.* at Milwaukee, Wisconsin, 1860; *m.*, first, at Chapinville, Connecticut, 25 November, 1810, Ezra Jewell, *b.* 27 January, 1786, *d.* at Lyons, New York, 10 October, 1821, and had:

> HENRY CHAPIN JEWELL, *b.* at Salisbury, Connecticut, 1 December, 1811; *m.*, 1 October, 1833, Mary Anne Elizabeth Russell, *b.* Salisbury, Connecticut, 23 December, 1813, and had:
>
> MARY ELEANOR JEWELL, *b.* Canaan, New York, 3 July, 1842, a member of the Wisconsin Society of the Colonial Dames of America, who *m.*, at Oshkosh, Wisconsin, 18 October, 1864, Edgar Philetus Sawyer, *b.* Crown Point, New York, 4 December, 1842, and had:
>
> 1.—MARIA MELVINA SAYWER, *b.* Fond du Lac, Wisconsin, 18 July, 1865, a member of the Massachusetts Society of the Colonial Dames of America, who *m.*, 2 June, 1886, Charles Curry Chase, of Oshkosh, Wisconsin, and had: *Jewell Sperry, b.* 28 August, 1888; *Mary Henrietta, b.* 2 September, 1892, *d.* 7 September, 1892; *Prescott Sawyer, b.* 20 April, 1899, *d.* 1 Feb. 1900.
>
> 2.—PHILETUS HORACE SAWYER, *b.* 25 October, 1874; *m.*, at Madison, Wisconsin, 12 November, 1896, Caroline, daughter of Governor W. H. Upham, and had: *Kathryn Upham, b.* 3 October, 1899.

MARY CHAPIN (widow of Ezra Jewell) *m.*, secondly, John Ashley Dutcher, of Salisbury, Connecticut, and had:

JOHN ASHLEY DUTCHER, JR., *b.* at Salisbury, *d.* at Milwaukee; *m.* Annette, daughter of Pierpont Edwards, of Kent, Connecticut, and had:

CORNELIA FRANCES DUTCHER, a member of the Massachusetts Society of the Colonial Dames of America, who *m.* Henry Belcher Goodrich, of Milwaukee, Wisconsin, and had: *Cornelia Frances* and *John Dutcher.*

3.—REV. NATHANIEL CHAUNCY, of Hatfield, Massachusetts, *b.* 1639, *d.* 4 November, 1685; *m.*, 12 November, 1673, Abigail, 1645–1704, daughter of John Strong, of Northampton, Massachusetts, and had:

I.—SARAH CHAUNCY, 1683–1767; *m.*, 1712, Rev. Samuel Whittelsey, of Wallingford, 1686–1752, and had:

Rev. Chauncy Whittelsey, of New Haven, 1717–1787; *m.*, 1745, Elizabeth Whiting, 1717–1751, and had:

Chauncey Whittelsey, of Middletown, 1746–1812; *m.*, 1770, Lucy Wetmore, 1748–1826, and had:

Lucy Whittelsey, 1773–1856; *m.*, 1797, Joseph Wright Alsop, of Middletown, 1772–1844, and had:

Charles Richard Alsop, of Middletown, 1802–1865; *m.*, 1833, Margaret Elinor Armstrong, 1814–1897, and had:

Catherine Beatty Alsop, a member of the New York Society of the Colonial Dames of America, who *m.* Rev. Christopher S. Leffingwell, of Bar Harbor, Maine, and had: *Alsop, Mary Mütter, Douglas, Christophea, Aimée G.,* and *Alice G.*

II.—Rev. Nathaniel Chauncy, of Durham, Connecticut, *b.* 21 September, 1681, *d.* 1 February, 1756; he was the first graduate of Yale College; *m.*, 12 October, 1708, Sarah, daughter of Captain James Judson, of Stratford, and had:

1.—Rev. Elnathan Chauncy, of Durham, Connecticut, *b.* 10 September, 1724, *d.* 14 May, 1796; *m.*, 6 February, 1760, Elizabeth, 1733–1793, widow of Colonel Samuel Gale, and daughter of Rev. William and Temperance (Gallup) Worthington, of Saybrooke, and had:

Catherine Chauncy, *b.* 6 August, 1765, *d.* 12 April, 1841; *m.*, 14 March, 1790, Reuben Rose Fowler, of Durham, 1763–1844, and had:

Prof. William Chauncey Fowler, LL.D., of Durham, Connecticut, *b.* 1 September, 1793, *d.* 15 January, 1881; author of "The Memorials of the Chaunceys," etc., who *m.*, 21 July, 1825, Harriet, *d.* 30 March, 1844, widow of Edward Cobb, and daughter of Noah Webster, LL.D., the celebrated lexicographer, and had:

Emily Ellsworth Fowler, *b.* 26 August, 1826, *d.* 23 November, 1893; *m.*, 16 December, 1853, Gordon Lester Ford, and had:

1.—Rosalie Greenleaf Ford, *b.* 28 September, 1858, a member of the New York Society of the Colonial Dames of America, who *m.*, 27 May, 1880, William Rufus Barr, of New York City, and had: *Honor Ellsworth, b.* 7 July, 1881; *Rufus Gordon, b.* 12 November, 1884; *Gillian Webster, b.* 12 August, 1886, and *Lester Stacy, b.* 6 March, 1894, *d.* 29 October, 1895.

2.—Emily Ellsworth Ford, a member of the New York Society of the Colonial Dames of America, who *m.* Roswell Skeel, Jr., of New York City. *No issue.*

2.—Colonel Elihu Chauncy, of Durham, *b.* 24 March, 1710, *d.* 10 April, 1791; commanded a regiment in the French War; chief justice of the County Court, and member of the Connecticut Legislature for thirty-nine years; *m.*, 28 March, 1739, Mary, daughter of Samuel Griswold, of Killingworth, and had:

CATHERINE CHAUNCY, *b.* 11 April, 1741, *d.* 8 April, 1830; *m.*, 1 February, 1759, Rev. Elizur Goodrich, D.D., of Durham, 1734–1797, and had:

I.—JUDGE ELIZUR GOODRICH, LL.D., of New Haven, Connecticut, *b.* 24 March, 1761, *d.* 1 November, 1849. He was member of Congress from Connecticut, 1799; mayor of New Haven, 1803–22; professor at Yale College; collector of the port of New Haven; chief justice of New Haven County Court for thirteen years, judge of the Probate Court for seventeen years, *etc.* He *m.*, 1 September, 1785, Anne Willard, *d.* 1818, daughter of Daniel and Esther (Colton) Allen, of Great Barrington, Massachusetts, and had:

NANCY GOODRICH, *b.* 1 January, 1793, *d.* 15 January, 1847; *m.* Henry L. Ellsworth, of Lafayette, Indiana, 1790–1858, commissioner for Indian affairs under President Jackson; chief of the United States Patent Office, *etc.*, and had:

ANNIE GOODRICH ELLSWORTH, a member of the New York Society of the Colonial Dames of America, who *m.*, 1852, Roswell Smith, of New York City, *b.* 30 March, 1829, *d.* 19 April, 1892, and had: *Julia Goodrich Smith, m.*, 21 April, 1879, George Innis, Jr., of New York, and had: *Elizabeth, Julia,* and *George Ellsworth.*

II.—REV. SAMUEL GOODRICH, of Ridgefield, Connecticut, *b.* 12 January, 1763, *d.* 19 April, 1835; *m.*, 29 July, 1784, Elizabeth, *b.* 22 February, 1764, *d.* aged 72 years, daughter of Colonel John Ely, M.D., and his wife Sarah Worthington, of Pachog, and had:

1.—SARAH WORTHINGTON GOODRICH, *b.* 7 August, 1785, *d.* 14 September, 1842, who *m.*, first, 5 February, 1805, Amos Cook, of Danbury, Connecticut, and had:

ELIZABETH COOK, who *m.*, 31 August, 1824, Richard Wayne Stiles, and had:

ELIZABETH WOLCOTT STILES, who *m.*, 15 September, 1847, Cortlandt Parker, of New Jersey, and had:

MARY FRANCES PARKER, a member of the Massachusetts Society of the Colonial Dames of America, who *m.*, 21 August, 1890, Henry Parkman, of Boston, and had: *Mary Elizabeth, b.* 1891; *Edith Wolcott, b.* 1892; *Henry, b.* 1894; *Penelope, b.* 1896, and *Francis, b.* 1898.

SARAH WORTHINGTON GOODRICH, *m.*, secondly, 21 June, 1815, Frederick Wolcott, of Litchfield, Connecticut, and had:

I.—MARY WOLCOTT, who *m.* Theodore Frothingham, and had:

MARY GOODRICH FROTHINGHAM, a member of the Pennsylvania Society of the Colonial Dames of America, who *m.* Charles A. Brinley, of Philadelphia. *Issue.*

II.—CHARLES MOSELEY WOLCOTT, b. 20 November, 1816, d. 20 November, 1889; m., 26 November, 1849, Katharine A. Rankin, and had:

1.—KATHARINE RANKIN WOLCOTT, b. 29 April, 1855, president of the New York Society of the Colonial Dames of America, who m., 8 April, 1896, Samuel Verplanck, of Fishkill-on-Hudson, New York. *No issue.*

2.—HENRY GOODRICH WOLCOTT, b. 16 July, 1853, m., 22 May, 1879, Julia S. Hutchins, and had: *Oliver*, b. 14 March, 1880, d. 26 December, 1893; *Charles Moseley*, b. 11 August, 1882; *Henry Goodrich*, b. 2 March, 1884, d. 10 August, 1885; *Elizabeth Ellsworth*, b. 8 September, 1886; *Katharine Rankin*, b. 16 August, 1888, d. 7 December, 1893, and *Julia Hutchins*, b. 1 July, 1892.

3.—ANNETTA RANKIN WOLCOTT, b. 29 June, 1857.

2.—CATHARINE GOODRICH, b. 2 December, 1792, d. 15 October, 1873; m., 12 September, 1817, Daniel Dunbar, of Berlin, Connecticut, b. 28 March, 1774, d. 1841, and had:

MARGARET ELIZABETH DUNBAR, b. 28 May, 1828, a member of the New York Society of the Colonial Dames of America, who m., 4 September, 1849, Homer H. Stuart, of New York, b. 1 April, 1810, d. 5 October, 1885, and had:

I.—KATHARINE DUNBAR STUART, a member of the New York Society of the Colonial Dames of America, b. 22 October, 1852, m., 29 September, 1884, John G. Dunscomb, and had: *Margaret Stuart*, b. 1886; *Cecil*, b. 1888; *John C.*, b. 1889, and *Godefroi*, b. 1893.

II.—HOMER HINE STUART, JR., b. 30 January, 1855, m., 3 October, 1888, Margaret Beckwith Kenney, and had: *Homer Howland*, b. 5 July, 1890.

III.—INGLIS STUART, of New York, b. 24 March, 1859.

PEDIGREE XVI.

OWEN GWYNEDD, Prince of North Wales, had:

IEVAN AP OWEN GWYNEDD, whose daughter,

LADY GWENLLIAN, *m.* Hwfa ap Kendrig ap Rhywalon, lord of Christion-ydol-Cynrig and Maelor Cynraig, of the tribe of Tudor Trevor, lord of Hereford, and had:

LADY ANGHARAD, who *m.* Kendrig ap Iorwerth, lord of Brynffenigl and Llansadwrn, a descendant of Brochwel Ysgithrog, Prince of Powys, and had:

EDNYFED VYCHAN ap Kendrig, lord of Brynffenigl and Krigeth, chief chancellor and chief justice to Llewelyn ap Iorwerth, King of North Wales and a commander in the army of Llewelyn in his war with King John, of England. He had by his second wife, Gwenllian, daughter of Rhys ap Griffith, lord of South Wales, and representative of the Sovereign Princess of South Wales (*see* Burke's " Ancestry of the Royal House of Tudor "):

GRIFFITH AP EDNYFED VYCHAN, of Henglawdd, who had by his second wife, Gwenllian, daughter of Howell ap Trehearn, lord of Brecknock:

SIR HOWELL AP GRIFFITH, Knt., who *m.* Tanghost, daughter of David Goch ap Howell, and had:

GRIFFITH AP SIR HOWELL, who had by his second wife:

ROBERT AP GRIFFITH, of Einmal, who had:

RHYS AP ROBERT, from whom derived, sixth in descent (*see* Burke's " Royal Families," vol. ii., p. 39):

MEREDITH AP JOHN, who had:

RT. REV. GEORGE LLOYD, D.D., sixth son, bishop of Sodor and Man, 1600–04, and bishop of Chester, 1604–16, who *m.* Anne, daughter of John Wilkinson, of Norwich, and had:

ANNA LLOYD, who *m.* (his second wife) Theophilus Eaton, first Governor of the New Haven Colony, New England, son of Rev. Richard and Elizabeth Eaton, vicar of Great Polworth, Cheshire, whose will, 11 July, 1616, proved 14 January, 1616–17 (*see* " N. E. His. Gen. Reg." October, 1899), and had:

HANNAH EATON, who *m.*, 4 July, 1659, William Jones, Deputy-Governor of the New Haven Colony, Connecticut, and had:

ELIZABETH JONES, who *m.*, 1689, Captain John Morgan, and had:

PEDIGREE XVI.—*Continued.*

WILLIAM MORGAN, who *m.*, 3 July, 1716, Mary Avery, and had:

WILLIAM MORGAN, JR., who *m.*, 4 July, 1744, Temperance Avery, and had:

CHRISTOPHER MORGAN, who *m.*, 16 February, 1768, Deborah Ledyard, and had:

CHRISTOPHER MORGAN, JR., who *m.*, 15 July, 1805, Nancy Barber, and had:

EDWIN BARBER MORGAN, who *m.*, 23 September, 1829, Charlotte F. Wood, and had:

1.—LOUISE F. MORGAN, a member of the New York Society of the Colonial Dames of America, who *m.*, 28 June, 1865, Nicholas Lansing Zabriskie, of Aurora, New York.

2.—KATHARINE MORGAN, a member of the New York Society of the Colonial Dames of America, who *m.* William Brookfield of New York City.

PEDIGREE XVII.

EDWARD III., King of England, had by his wife, Lady Philippa, daughter of William, Count of Hainault, also of Royal Descent:

SIR EDMUND PLANTAGENET DE LANGLEY, K.G., Duke of York, Earl of Cambridge, *etc.*, fifth son, *d.* 1402, who had by his first wife, Princess Isabel, daughter and heiress of Peter, King of Castile and Leon:

LADY CONSTANCE PLANTAGENET, who *m.* Thomas, Baron le Despencer, created in 1337 Earl of Gloucester, beheaded in 1400, also of Royal Descent, and had:

LADY ISABEL LE DESPENCER, who *m.*, first, Richard de Beauchamp, created in 1421 Earl of Worcester, also of Royal Descent, and had:

LADY ELIZABETH DE BEAUCHAMP, heiress, 1415–1447, who *m.* 1435 (his first wife), Sir Edward de Neville, K.G., Baron Abergavenny, *d.* 1476, also of Royal Descent, and had:

SIR GEORGE DE NEVILLE, second Baron Abergavenny and Lord Latimer, 1440–1492, who *m.*, first, Lady Margaret, *d.* 1485, daughter and heiress of Sir Hugh Fenne, sub-treasurer of England (*see* Foster's "Royal Descents," p. 5), and had:

SIR GEORGE DE NEVILLE, K.B. and K.G., third Baron Abergavenny, *d.* 1535–36; *m.*, thirdly, Lady Mary, daughter of Edward Stafford, Duke of Buckingham, beheaded on Tower Hill, 17 May, 1521, and had by her:

LADY URSULA DE NEVILLE, who *m.* (his first wife) Sir Warham St. Leger, of Ulcombe, Kent, high sheriff, 1560; chief governor of Munster, Ireland, 1566; member of the Privy Council, 1585; *k.* in battle in Ireland 4 March, 1599, (*see* Lodge's "Peerage of Ireland," 1754, iii., and Berry's "Kent Pedigrees"), and had:

LADY ANNE ST. LEGER, *bur.* in St. Mary's, Chilham, 20 January, 1636–37, aged 81. She *m.* Thomas Digges, of Digges Court, in Kent, muster-master general of the English Army in the Low Countries, and had by him, who *d.* 24 August, 1595:

SIR DUDLEY DIGGES, Knt., master of the rolls in 1619, who erected Chilham Castle, in Kent. (*See* Bridge's "Topographer," February, 1791.) He was a member of the London Company for colonizing Virginia, and dying 18 March, was buried in St. Mary's, Chilham, 23 March, 1638. He *m.* Lady Mary, daughter of Sir Thomas Kempe, Knt., of

Olantigh, Kent, and' had by her, who was *bur.* in St. Mary's 5 May, 1631:

EDWARD DIGGES,* third son, *bapt.* 29 March, 1621. He had an interest in the Virginia London Company, and served as Governor of the Virginia Colony, 30 March, 1655, to 13 March, 1658, and was a member of the Governor's Council from 22 November, 1654, till his death, 15 March, 1675. (*See* Brown's "Genesis of the United States," 990). He *m.* Elizabeth Braye (or Page), and had:

1.—COLONEL WILLIAM DIGGES, *b.* at Chilham Castle, came to Maryland in 1679, *m.* Elizabeth Seawell, and had:

CHARLES DIGGES, of Charleston and Warburton Manor, now the site of Fort Washington, who *m.* (Miss Dulany?), and had:

I.—WILLIAM DIGGES, of Warburton Manor, who *m.*, 3 June, 1739, Anne, daughter of George Atwood, Jr., *d.* at Warburton Manor, 1744, also of Royal Descent, and had:

GEORGE DIGGES, of Warburton Manor, who had:

WILLIAM DUDLEY DIGGES, of Warburton Manor and Green Hill, near Washington City, who *m.* Eleanor, daughter of Daniel Carroll, of Duddington Manor, now a part of Washington City, also of Royal Descent, and had:

NORA DIGGES, who *m.*, 1854, James Ethelbert Morgan, M.D., of Washington City, and had:

ADA MORGAN, the youngest of seven children, a member of the Maryland Society of the Colonial Dames of America, who *m.*, 1889, Richard Smith Hill, of Prince George county, Maryland, and had: *Nora Digges* and *Elizabeth Snowden*, twins, and *Ada Morgan*.

II.—ANNE DIGGES, who *m.* Dr. George Steuart, *d.* 1780, commissioner of the Maryland Land Office, 1753–57, mayor of Annapolis, 1759–63, *etc.*, and had:

DR. JAMES STEUART, *m.* Rebecca Sprigg, and had:

---

* The following ladies, members of the National Society of the Colonial Dames of America, are also of Royal Descent, through Edward Digges:

MRS. MARY J. BAUGHMAN, Maryland State Society.
MRS. H. B. DENMAN (deceased), Maryland State Society.
MRS. GEORGE ALONZO JONES, Maryland State Society.
MRS. ALEXANDER B. RANDALL, Maryland State Society.
MRS. EMORY SPEER, Georgia State Society.
MRS. L. McLEAN TIFFANY, Maryland State Society.
MRS. CHARLES P. WILLIAMS, Maryland State Society.

PEDIGREE XVII.—Continued.

GENERAL GEORGE H. STEUART, *m.* Anne Jane Edmondson, and had:

DR. JAMES HENRY STEUART, *m.* Ellen L. Duvall, and had:

1.—MARY ELIZABETH STEUART, of Baltimore, a member of the Maryland Society of the Colonial Dames of America.

2.—HENRIETTA STEUART, of Baltimore, a member of the Maryland Society of the Colonial Dames of America.

2.—DUDLEY DIGGES, of "Bellefield," *b.* about 1663, *d.* 18 January, 1710, councillor and auditor of the Virginia Colony; *m.* Susannah, daughter of Colonel William Cole, of "Denbigh," Warwick, Virginia (and his first wife, Susan Croft), and had by her, who *d.* 9 December, 1708, aged 34 years:

COLONEL COLE DIGGES, of "Bellefield," eldest son, *b.* 1691, *d.* 1744; president of the Virginia Council, *etc.* He *m.* Elizabeth, daughter of Dr. Henry and Mary (Folliott) Power, and had:

1.—DUDLEY DIGGES, of "Bellefield," a member of the Virginia Committee of Correspondence, 1773–74; of the Colonial Convention, 1776, *etc.* He had by his first wife, Martha Armistead:

MARTHA DIGGES, who *m.* Captain Nathaniel Burwell, of the Virginia Line Continental Army, a member of the Virginia Society of the Cincinnati, and had:

THOMAS NELSON BURWELL, who *m.* Elizabeth, daughter of Andrew Nicholson and Judith Wormeley, daughter of Dudley Digges, of "Bellefield," and his second wife, Elizabeth Wormeley, and had:

LUCY CARTER BURWELL, a member of the Virginia Society of the Colonial Dames of America, who *m.* Peterfield Trent, M.D., of Richmond, Virginia, and had: *William Peterfield Trent, M.A., LL.D.,* who *m.* Alice, daughter of Frederick Lyman, of East Orange, New Jersey, and had: *Lucia.*

DUDLEY DIGGES, of "Bellefield," Virginia, member of the Virginia Committee of Correspondence, 1774; of the Convention of the Colonies, 1776, *etc., m.,* secondly, Elizabeth Wormeley, of "Rosegill," and had:

ELIZABETH DIGGES, who *m.* Robert Nicolson, and had:

SALLY BERKELEY NICOLSON, who *m.* Peyton Randolph Nelson, also of Royal Descent, and had:

WILLIAM WILMER NELSON, *m.* Sally Browne Catlett, and had:

SALLY BERKELEY NELSON, of Richmond, Virginia, a member of the Virginia Society of the Colonial Dames of America, who *m.* William Todd Robins, colonel Confederate States Army, and had: *Ruth Nelson, Elizabeth Todd, Augustine Warner, Wilmer Nelson,* and *Sally Berkeley Nelson.*

2.—MARY DIGGES, *d.* 12 November, 1744, aged 27 years, *m.* (his first wife), 23 August, 1739, Nathaniel Harrison, Jr., of "Brandon," Prince George county, Virginia, *d.* 1 October, 1791, aged 78 years, and had:

ELIZABETH HARRISON, *b.* 30 July, 1737, who *m.*, 31 January, 1760, Major John Fitzhugh, and had:

ANNA FITZHUGH, who *m.* George May, and had:

HENRY MAY, M.D., of Petersburg, Virginia, *b.* 30 March, 1804, *d.* 27 December, 1886; *m.* Julia Jones, and had:

SALLY MAY, a member of the Virginia Society of the Colonial Dames of America, the Order of the Crown, *etc.*, who *m.* James H. Dooley, of Richmond, Virginia.

3.—MAJOR WILLIAM DIGGES, of "Denbigh," Warwick county, Virginia, who *m.* Frances, daughter of Major Anthony and Diana (Starkey) Robinson, and had:

SUSANNAH DIGGES, who *m.* William Cole, 3d, of Albemarle county, Virginia, descended from Colonel William Cole, secretary of the Virginia Colony and member of the Council, and his wife Martha, daughter of Colonel John Lear, a member of the Council, and had:

WILLIAM COLE, 4th, of "Swynard," Orange county, Virginia, who *m.* Mary Frances, daughter of Colonel Gerard Alexander, of "Effingham," Prince William county, Virginia, and had:

SUSANNAH DIGGES COLE, *b.* 25 December, 1824, who *m.*, 3 August, 1841, Judge John Madison Chapman, of Orange county, Virginia, 1810–1879, also of Royal Descent, and had:

1.—SUSIE ASHTON CHAPMAN, a member of the Tennessee Society of the Colonial Dames of America, the Order of the Crown, *etc.*, who *m.* Calvin Perkins, of Memphis, Tennessee, *b.* Columbus, Miss. *Issue.*

2.—BELLE CHAPMAN, a member of the Virginia Society of the Colonial Dames of America, the Order of the Crown, *etc.*, who *m.*, 12 December, 1878, William Moncure, of Richmond, Virginia. *Issue.*

3.—ASHTON ALEXANDER CHAPMAN.

PEDIGREE XVIII.

LOUIS VI., King of France, had by his second wife, Lady Adelaide, daughter of Humbert II., Count de Piedmont, *d.* 1103 :

PETER OF FRANCE, Lord of Courtenay, Gastinois, fifth son, who *m.* Lady Alice, daughter of Sir Reginald de Courtenay, first Baron Oakhampton, *d.* 1194, and had :

LADY ALICE DE COURTENAY (sister of Peter, Emperor of Constantinople, 1217), who *m.* Aymer de Taillefer, Count de Angoulême, and had :

LADY ISABEL DE TAILLEFER, *d.* 1246, second wife and widow of John, King of England, *d.* 1216, who *m.*, secondly, Hugh le Brun, Earl of Marche, in Poictou, and had :

LADY ALICE LE BRUN, who *m.* John Plantagenet de Warren, seventh Earl of Surrey, *d.* 1304 (*see* Watson's " Earls of Warren and Surrey "), and had :

WILLIAM DE WARREN, *d. v. p.*, 15 December, 1286, who *m.* Lady Joan de Vere, daughter of Robert, fifth Earl of Oxford, *d.* 1296, and had :

LADY ALICE DE WARREN, who *m.*, 1305, Sir Edmund Fitz-Alan, K.B., eighth Earl of Arundel, beheaded in 1326, and had :

SIR RICHARD FITZ-ALAN, K.G., ninth Earl of Arundel and seventh Earl of Surrey, *d.* 1375, who *m.*, secondly, Lady Eleanor Plantagenet, daughter of Henry, third Earl of Lancaster, also of Royal Descent, and had by her :

LADY ALICE FITZ-ALAN, who *m.* Sir Thomas de Holland, Earl of Kent, *d.* 1397, also of Royal Descent, and had :

LADY MARGARET DE HOLLAND, *d.* 1440, who *m.*, first, John de Beaufort, Earl of Somerset, Marquis of Dorset, Lord High Admiral and Lord Chamberlain, *d.* 1410, also of Royal Descent, and had :

SIR EDMUND DE BEAUFORT, K.G., Duke of Somerset, *etc.*, Regent of France, Lord High Constable of England, *k.* 1455, who *m.* Lady Alianore, widow of Thomas de Roos and daughter of Sir Richard de Beauchamp, K.G., Earl of Warwick and Albemarle, Lord High Steward, guardian of Henry VI., Lieutenant-General of Normandy and France, also of Royal Descent, *d.* 1439, and had :

HENRY DE BEAUFORT, beheaded in 1463, father of :

CHARLES DE SOMERSET, Baron Herbert in right of his wife, created, in

1514, Earl of Worcester, *d.* 1526, who had by his wife, Lady Elizabeth, heiress and daughter of William de Herbert, Earl of Huntingdon :

HENRY DE SOMERSET, second Earl of Worcester, *d.* 26 November, 1549, who *m.* Elizabeth, daughter of Sir Anthony Browne, standard-bearer to Henry VII., also of Royal Descent, and had:

LADY ELEANOR DE SOMERSET, *m.* Sir Roger Vaughan, Knt., of Porthaml, Talgarth, and had:

WATKIN VAUGHAN, of Talgarth, who had by his wife, Joan v. Evan ap Gwilim Ychan, of Peytyn Gwyn:

SIR WILLIAM VAUGHAN, of Porthaml, *d.* 1564, *m.* Catherine v. Jenkin Havard, of Tredomen, and had:

CATHERINE VAUGHAN, who *m.* David ap Evan, of Neath, high sheriff of Glamorganshire, in 1563, and had:

MARY DAVID EVAN, widow of Edward Turberville, of Sutton, who *m.*, secondly, Thomas Basset, of Miscin, and had:

CATHERINE BASSET, who *m.* Richard ab Evan, of Collonna, Glamorganshire, and had :

JANE EVANS, who *m.* Evan ab John, of Treverigg, Llantrisant parish, Glamorganshire, *d.* ante 165—, and had :

JOHN AB EVAN, *alias* " John Bevan, Senior,"* *b.* about 1646. He *m.*, about 1665, Barbara, probably daughter of William Awbrey, of Pencoed, and removed from Treverigg in 1683, with his family, to Pennsylvania, and settled in Merion and became a large landholder (*see* Glenn's "Merion in the Welsh Tract"). He was a member of the Assembly, 1687–1700, a justice in Philadelphia county 1685 and in Chester county 1689, and dying at Treverigg in 1726 (his will proved in Glamorganshire, 21 October, 1726), had by his wife, Barbara, who *d.* 26 January, 1710:

JANE BEVAN, *d.* 12 December, 1703, who *m.*, 1 December, 1687, John Wood, of Darby, Pennsylvania, a member of the Assembly, 1704–1717, son of George Wood, a member of the Assembly, 1682–1683, and had:

ABRAHAM WOOD, of Makefield township, Bucks county, Pennsylvania, *b.* 2 March, 1702, *d.* September, 1733, who *m.* Ursula, 1701–1778, daughter of Philip Taylor, of Oxford, Philadelphia county (*see* Glenn's "Merion in the Welsh Tract"), and had:

ANN WOOD, *b.* 24 January, 1734, *d.* Lancaster, Pennsylvania, 8 March, 1799; *m.*, 1756, William Henry, *b.* Chester county, Pennsylvania, 19

---

* The following ladies, members of the National Society of the Colonial Dames of America, are also of Royal Descent through John Bevan, Sr. :

MRS. DUNCAN L. BUZBY, Pennsylvania State Society.

MRS. THOMAS MCKEAN, Pennsylvania State Society.

May, 1729, d. 15 December, 1786, justice of the peace, 1758, 1770, 1777, associate justice of courts of common pleas and quarter sessions in 1780, and in 1776 elected a member of the Assembly, and in 1777 of the council of safety; treasurer of Lancaster county, Pennsylvania, from 1777 till his death, in 1786 (his wife, Ann, acted as county treasurer for twelve years after his death), and had:

WILLIAM HENRY, b. 12 March, 1757, d. 21 April, 1821; associate justice of the Northampton county courts, 1788–1814; m., 21 November, 1781, Sabina Schropp, and had:

ELIZABETH HENRY, b. 15 October, 1782, d. 15 December, 1844; m., 23 August, 1804, John Jordan, b. 1 September, 1770, Hunterdon county, New Jersey, and had:

ANTOINETTE JORDAN, b. 10 January, 1813, d. 22 December, 1880; m., 18 January, 1849, John Thomas Bell, b. 26 August, 1804, d. 4 March, 1882, and had:

EMILY BELL, of Philadelphia, a member of the Pennsylvania Society of the Colonial Dames of America.

THE ROYAL DESCENT

OF

MISS ALICE HUMPHREYS,

OF SAN FRANCISCO, CAL.

EDWARD I., King of England—Princess Eleanor of Castile.
Princess Elizabeth Plantagenet—Humphrey de Bohun, Earl of Hereford.
William de Bohun, Earl of Northampton—Lady Elizabeth de Badlesmere.
Lady Elizabeth de Bohun—Richard Fitz-Alan, K.G., Earl of Arundel.
Lady Elizabeth Fitz-Alan—Sir Robert Goushill, of Hault Hucknall, Derby.
Lady Joan Goushill—Sir Thomas Stanley, K.G., Lord Stanley.
Lady Margaret Stanley—Sir William Troutbeck, of Prynes Castle, Cheshire.
Lady Jane Troutbeck—Sir William Griffith, of Penrhyn Castle.
Sir William Griffith, of Penrhyn Castle—Jane Puleston of Carnarvon.
Lady Sibill Griffith—Owen ap Hugh, of Bodeon.
Jane Owen—Hugh Gwyn, of Penarth.
Sibill Gwyn—John Powell, of Llanwddyn.
Elizabeth Powell—Humphrey ap Hugh, of Llwyn-du.
Samuel ap Humphrey, of Port Neven—Elizabeth ———.
Daniel Humphreys, of Pennsylvania—Hannah Wynne, of Pennsylvania.
Joshua Humphreys, of Darby, Pennsylvania—Sarah Williams, of Blockley, Pennsylvania.
Joshua Humphreys, of Ponta Reading, Pa.—Mary Davids, of Philadelphia.
Samuel Humphreys, of Georgetown, D. C.—Letitia Atkinson.
William Penn Humphreys, United States Navy—Mary Stencon.
Alice Humphreys, of San Francisco, member of the National Society of the Colonial Dames of America, the Order of the Crown, etc.

PEDIGREE XIX.

HENRY I., King of France, had by his third wife, Anne of Russia:

HUGH THE GREAT, Duke of France and Burgundy, who had by his third wife, m. 938, Lady Adelheid, daughter of Herbert IV., Count of Vermandois:

LADY ISABEL DE VERMANDOIS, d. 1131 (widow of Robert, Earl of Mellent, d. 1118), who m., secondly, William de Warren, second Earl of Surrey (see Watson's "Ancient Earls of Warren and Surrey"), and had:

WILLIAM DE WARREN, third Earl of Surrey, d. s. p. m. 1148. He m., before 1143, Lady Alice de Talvace, also of Royal Descent (or Talvas, see Doyle's "Official Baronage"), d. 1174, and had:

LADY ISABELLA DE WARREN, heiress, d. 1199 (widow of William de Blois, d. s. p. 1160), who m., secondly, 1163, Hameline Plantagenet de Warren, fifth Earl of Surrey, d. 1202, and had:

LADY ISABEL DE WARREN, who m. Roger, Baron le Bigod, created, 1189, Earl of Norfolk; lord high steward of England, and had:

HUGH, second Earl of Norfolk, d. 1225; m. Lady Maud Marshall, daughter of William le Marshal, Earl of Pembroke, the celebrated Protector during the nonage of Henry III., and had:

SIR HUGH BIGOD, second son, appointed, 22 June, 1257, chief justice of England, resigned in 1260, d. 1266 (see Foss's "Lives of the Chief Justices"), who m., first, Joan, daughter of Robert Burnet, and had:

SIR JOHN BIGOD, Knt., younger brother of Roger, the last Earl of Norfolk, d. s. p. 1306, and father of

ROGER BIGOD, Knt., of Settington, youngest son, father of

JOAN BIGOD, who m., 1358, Sir William de Chauncy, Knt., last Baron of Skirpenbeck, Yorkshire, which he sold in 1399, and purchased Stepney in Middlesex, and had:

JOHN CHAUNCY, of Stepney, d. 1444–1445, who m. Margaret, daughter of William Gifford, of Gedleston, and had:

JOHN CHAUNCY, of Sawbridgeworth, Herts, d. 7 May, 1479, who m. Anne, daughter of John Leventhorp, of Shingey Hall, and had:

JOHN CHAUNCY, of Sawbridgeworth, d. 8 June, 1510, who m. daughter of Thomas Boyce, and had:

JOHN CHAUNCY, of Pishobury Manor, d. 4 June, 1546, who m. Elizabeth Proffit, widow of Richard Mansfield, and had:

HENRY CHAUNCY, of New Place Gifford's, second son and heir, *d*. 14 April, 1587; *m*., Lucy ——, and had:

GEORGE CHAUNCY, of Yardley-Bury, Hertfordshire, second son, *d*. 1627, who had by his second wife, Anne, daughter of Edward Welsh, of Great Wymondley, and widow of Edward Humberston (*see* "Chauncy Pedigree," compiled by Stephen Tucker, Somerset Herald in Ordinary; Chauncy pedigree in Sir Henry Chauncy's "History of Hertfordshire," Fowler's "Chauncy Memorials," *etc*.):

REV. CHARLES CHAUNCY, D.D.,* second President of Harvard College, *b*. 5 November, 1592, *d*. Cambridge, Massachusetts, 19 February, 1671; *m*., 17 March, 1630, Catherine, *b*. 1601, *bapt*. 2 November, 1604, *d*. 23 June, 1667; daughter of Robert Eyre, of New Sarum and Chilhampton, Wilts, a barrister, *bur*. at St. Thomas's, 8 August, 1638, aged 69, and his first wife, Anne, daughter of Rt. Rev. John Still, D.D., bishop of Bath and Wells in 1592, *d*. 26 February, 1607, and his first wife, Anne, daughter of Thomas Arblaster (or Alabaster), of Hadley, Suffolk (*see* Somersetshire Visitations, 1623; Wiltshire Visitations, 1623; Bliss's Wood's "Athenæ Oxonienses," ii., 829, and Burke's "Commoners," iv., 538), and had:

SARAH CHAUNCY, *b*. 13 June, 1631, at Ware, England, *d*. 3 June, 1699, Wethersfield, Connecticut; *m*., 26 October, 1659, at Concord, Massachusetts, Rev. Gershom Bulkeley (son of Rev. Peter and Grace Chetwode Bulkeley), *b*. 6 December, 1636, at Concord, *d*. 2 December, 1713, at Glastonbury, a member of the Massachusetts Assembly, 1679, and had:

1.—EDWARD BULKELEY, *b*. 1673, *d*. 27 August, 1748, Wethersfield; *m*., 14 July, 1702, at Wethersfield, Dorothy, *b*. 31 March, 1681, Concord, *d*. 1748, Wethersfield, daughter of Jonathan and Elizabeth (Hoar) Prescott, and had:

I.—CHARLES BULKELEY, *b*. 27 March, 1703, Wethersfield; *m*., 28 May, 1724, Mary, *b*. 9 April, 1699, Middletown, *d*. 24 January, 1771, Wethersfield, daughter of John and Hannah (Starr) Sage, and had:

1.—SARAH BULKELEY, *b*. 20 April, 1733, Wethersfield, *d*. 10 December, 1802, Rutland, Vermont; *m*., 5 August, 1756, at Wethers-

---

* The following ladies, members of the National Society of the Colonial Dames of America, are also of Royal Descent through Charles Chauncy:

MISS ELIZABETH C. WILCOX, Massachusetts State Society.
MRS. JOHN E. THAYER, Massachusetts State Society.
MISS ELLEN R. NYE, New York State Society.
MRS. WILLIAM B. BEEKMAN, New York State Society.
MRS. ETIENNE ST. GEORGE, New York State Society.

field, Cephas Smith, son of Noah and Mary (Johnson) Smith, and had:

CEPHAS SMITH, JR., *b.* 21 October, 1760–1761, Suffield, Connecticut, *d.* 24 January, 1815, Rutland; *m.*, 9 November, 1794, at Preston, Connecticut, Mary, *b.* 25 December, 1775, Preston, *d.* 30 April, 1842, Salem, N. Y., daughter of Nathaniel and Esther (Tyler) Gove, and had:

MARY PAGE SMITH, *b.* 3 June, 1805, Rutland, *d.* 1 April, 1838, Pittsford, Vermont; *m.*, 5 December, 1827, at Rutland, Chester, *b.* 5 July, 1797, Sandisfield, Massachusetts, *d.* 30 January, 1879, Pittsford, son of Simeon and Phœbe (Couch) Granger, and had:

WILLIAM SMITH GRANGER, *b.* 18 September, 1834, Pittsford; *m.*, 12 June, 1871, at Providence, Rhode Island, Caroline, *b.* July 4, 1846, Providence, daughter of John Talbot and Caroline (Richmond) Pitman, and had:

MARY ALICE GRANGER, of Providence, a member of the Rhode Island Society of the Colonial Dames of America.

2.—BRIG.-MAJOR EDWARD BULKELEY, *b.* about 1736, *d.* 30 June, 1787, a member of the Society of the Cincinnati; *m.*, 27 October, 1771, Rachel Lyman Pomeroy, also of Royal Descent, and had:

ROXA LYMAN BULKELEY, *b.* 25 October, 1772, *m.*, 25 February, 1793, Colonel Selah Francis, and had:

ROXA BULKELEY FRANCIS, *b.* 4 July, 1796, *d.* 1868; *m.*, 4 May, 1815, Judge Jesse Booth, who was commissioned Quartermaster in the War of 1812, in the regiment raised by his father-in-law, under Brigadier-General Farrington. He held important offices in State and county, and was a member of the New York Legislature, and also served as judge a number of years, and had:

ELLEN CORDELIA BULKELEY BOOTH, a member of the Connecticut Society of the Colonial Dames of America, who *m.*, 21 November, 1864, Byron Coleman Dick, of Oakland, California. *No issue.*

3.—BENJAMIN BULKELEY, who had:

HANNAH BULKELEY, who *m.* Amos Woodruff, and had:

RUSSELL WOODRUFF, *m.* Maria Smith, and had: *Franklin Amos, Morgan Lewis, Charles Russell, Joseph Bulkeley,* and *H. Estelle*, of New York City.

II.—DOROTHY BULKELEY, *b.* 11 September, 1716, *d.* 7 December,

1801; *m.*, 8 January, 1741, Thomas Curtis, of Wallingford, Connecticut, *b.* 8 October, 1710, *d.* 6 November, 1789, and had:

HEPHZIBAH CURTIS, *b.* 1757, *d.* 4 January, 1807; *m.*, 7 July, 1784, Jason Boardman, of Rocky Hill, Connecticut, *b.* 16 January, 1762, *d.* 10 February, 1844, and had:

RHODA BOARDMAN, *b.* 11 May, 1787, *d.* 10 December, 1852; *m.*, 2 January, 1811, Sabin Colton, of Longmeadow, Massachusetts, *b.* 18 August, 1783, *d.* 10 November, 1857, and had:

SABIN WOOLWORTH COLTON, *b.* 20 February, 1813, at Longmeadow, *d.* 3 May, 1890, in Philadelphia, Pennsylvania; *m.*, 4 August, 1835, Susanna, *b.* 25 December, 1812, daughter of Captain William Beaumont, of Argyleshire, Scotland, and his wife, Euphemia McCall, and had:

JULIA COLTON, *b.* 13 April, 1844, a member of the Pennsylvania Society of the Colonial Dames of America, who *m.*, 29 December, 1869, Harrison Allen, M.D., of Philadelphia, *b.* Philadelphia, 17 April, 1841, *d.* 14 November, 1897, and had: *Harrison*, *b.* 26 February, 1875, *d.* 30 March, 1899, and *Dorothea W.*, *b.* 6 December, 1879.

III.—SARAH BULKELEY, *m.* Joseph Stow, and had:

SARAH STOW, *m.* Josiah Savage, and had:

REBECCA SAVAGE, *m.* Richard Dowd, and had:

REBECCA DOWD, *m.* Enoch Cornwall Roberts, and had:

EBENEZER ROBERTS, *m.* Clarissa Root Bancroft, and had:

FLORENCE ROBERTS, a member of the Connecticut Society of the Colonial Dames of America, who *m.* William Converse Skinner, of "Woodleigh," Hartford, Connecticut, and had: *Marjorie Roberts*, *Roberts Keney*, and *William Converse*.

2.—REV. JOHN BULKLEY, of Colchester, Connecticut, *d.* June, 1731; *m.*, 1701, Patience, daughter of Captain John and Sarah Prentice, of New London, Connecticut, and had:

I.—COLONEL JOHN BULKLEY, of Colchester, *b.* 19 April, 1705, Judge of the Supreme Court of Connecticut, 1745–1753, Commissioner to England, 1745, *d.* 21 July, 1753; *m.*, 29 October, 1738, Mary, widow of John Gardiner, of New London, drowned in 1735, and daughter of Rev. Eliphalet Adams, of New London, and had:

1.—CAPTAIN CHARLES BULKLEY, of Colchester, *b.* 1752, who *m.* Betsy Taintor, and had:

I.—SOLOMON TAINTOR BULKLEY, of Williamstown, Massachusetts, who *m.* Mary Welk, and had:

SARAH TAINTOR BULKLEY, who m. George W. Pleasants, and had:

NANNIE BUELL PLEASANTS, a member of the Virginia Society of the Colonial Dames of America, who m. Samuel Adams Lynde, of Chicago, Illinois.

II.—ESTHER BULKLEY, m. Jesse Sabin, and had:

SARAH ELIZABETH SABIN, m. Robert McClelland, and had:

AUGUSTA MCCLELLAND, b. Monroe, Michigan, 1865, a member of the Massachusetts Society of the Colonial Dames of America, who m. George Nexsen Brady, of Detroit, Michigan, and had:

1.—ROBERT MCCLELLAND BRADY, m. Mary Belle Holland.

2.—MARY AUGUSTA BRADY, a member of the Michigan Society of the Colonial Dames of America, m. Robert Mallory Berry, United States Navy.

2.—COLONEL ELIPHALET BULKELEY, b., Colchester, Connecticut, 8 August, 1746, d. Wilkes-Barre, Pennsylvania, 11 January, 1816; captain Twelfth Regiment, 1773–76, and lieutenant-colonel Twenty-fifth Regiment, Connecticut militia; m., 16 September, 1767, Anna Bulkeley, and had:

JOHN CHARLES BULKELEY, b. Colchester, who m. Sally Taintor, and had:

ELIPHALET ADAMS BULKELEY, b. Colchester, June, 1803, m. Lydia Smith Morgan, and had:

WILLIAM HENRY BULKELEY, b. East Haddam, Connecticut, 2 March, 1840, m., September, 1863, Emma Gweney, of Brooklyn, and had:

SARAH TAINTOR BULKELEY, b. Hartford, Connecticut, 7 November, 1876, a member of the Massachusetts Society of the Colonial Dames of America, who m., 7 November, 1895, Richard Henry Macauley, of Detroit, Michigan, and had: *Richard Bulkeley*, b. 28 August, 1896; *Frances Gweney*, b. 1 February, 1898, and *Sally*, b. 11 January, 1899.

COLONEL ELIPHALET BULKELEY, d. Wilkes-Barre, Pennsylvania, 1816, aforesaid, was the ancestor of

FRANCES BULKELEY, a member of the Pennsylvania Society of the Colonial Dames of America, who m. Asa R. Brundage, of Wilkes-Barre, Pennsylvania, and had:

MARY GILLETTE BRUNDAGE, of Wilkes-Barre, a member of the Pennsylvania Society of the Colonial Dames of America.

PEDIGREE XIX.—Continued.

II.—CAPTAIN GERSHOM BULKELEY, of Colchester, b. 4 February, 1709, m., 28 November, 1733, Abigail Robbins, and had:

SARAH BULKELEY, b. 10 January, 1735, who m., 23 November, 1758, John Taintor, of Colchester, b. 23 February, 1725-26, d. 1798, and had:

JOHN TAINTOR, of Wyndham, Connecticut, b. 23 September, 1760, d. 29 March, 1825, who m., 1786, his cousin, Sarah, b. 12 June, 1770, d. 29 October, 1856, daughter of Enos Hosford (or Horseford), and his wife Abigail, daughter of Ichabod Lord, and his wife Patience Bulkeley, aforesaid, and had:

1.—ABBIE LOUISE TAINTOR, who m. William Gibbons, and had:

SARAH TAINTOR GIBBONS, who m. Ward McAllister, of New York City, and had:

LOUISE WARD McALLISTER, of New York City, a member of the Pennsylvania Society of the Colonial Dames of America.

2.—SARAH TAINTOR, b. 1787, d. 6 June, 1827, who m., 20 February, 1815, Israel Foote, of New York City, b. 19 January, 1783, d. 21 September, 1871, and had:

JOHN TAINTOR FOOTE, of Morristown, New Jersey, b. 27 May, 1819, m. Jordena Cannon, b. 1827, d. 2 November, 1853, daughter of Horatio Turpin Harris, United States Navy, of Newport, Kentucky, 1799-1855, and his wife Keturah L., daughter of General James Taylor, of Newport, Kentucky, and had:

KATHARINE JORDENA FOOTE, a member of the New Jersey Society of the Colonial Dames of America, and Society of the Daughters of the Cincinnati, who m. Philip H. Cooper, captain United States Navy, and had: *Dorothy B.*, b. 9 March, 1889, and *Leslie B.*, b. 24 March, 1894.

PEDIGREE XX.

EDWARD I., King of England, had by his wife, Princess Eleanor, daughter of Ferdinand III., King of Castile and Leon:

PRINCESS ELIZABETH PLANTAGENET, 1289-1316, who *m.*, secondly, 14 November, 1302, Humphrey de Bohun, constable of England, Earl of Hereford and Essex, *k.* in 1321, and had:

LADY MARGARET DE BOHUN, will dated 28 January, 1390-1, who *m.*, 1325, Sir Hugh Courtenay, K. G., second Earl of Devon, *d.* 1377 (*see* notice of Courtenay Royal Descent from Gibbons's " Decline and Fall of the Roman Empire," in Bridge's " Topographer," June, 1789), and had:

LADY MARGARET COURTENAY, who *m.* John, third Baron Cobham, and had:

LADY JOANE COBHAM, who *m.* Sir John de la Pole, Knt., and had:

LADY JOANE DE LA POLE, who *m.* Sir Reginald Braybrooke, and had:

LADY JOANE BRAYBROOKE, who *m.* Sir Thomas Brooke, Lord Cobham, and had:

SIR EDWARD BROOKE, Lord Cobham, *d.* 1464, who *m.* Lady Elizabeth, daughter of James, Lord Audley, and had:

JOHN BROOKE, Lord Cobham, *d.* 1511-12, who *m.*, first, Lady Margaret, daughter of Sir Edward Neville, K.G., Baron Bergavenny, also of Royal Descent, and had by her:

THOMAS BROOKE, Lord Cobham, *d.* 1529, who *m.*, first, Dorothy, daughter of Sir Henry Heydon, Knt., and had by her:

LADY ELIZABETH BROOKE, who *m.*, 1520, Sir Thomas Wyatt, of Allington Castle, Kent, 1503-1544, poet-laureate to Henry VIII., and had:

SIR THOMAS WYATT, of Allington Castle, executed 11 April, 1554, on Tower Hill (*see* Brown's " Genesis of the United States," p. 996), who *m.*, 1536-1537, Lady Jane, daughter of Sir William Hawte, of Bishop Bourne, Kent, and had:

LADY JANE WYATT, who. *m.* Charles Scott, of Egerton, Kent, *d.* 1617, also of Royal Descent, and had:

THOMAS SCOTT, of Egerton, 1567-1635, who *m.*, secondly, 1604, Mary, *d.* 1616, daughter of John Knatchbull, of Mersham Hatch (*see* Berry's " Kent Pedigrees," p. 169), and had by her:

DOROTHEA SCOTT, *bapt.* 22 September, 1611, who came to Oyster Bay,

Long Island, New York, in 1680, with her children by her first husband (*m*. about 1636), Major Daniel Gotherson, of Cromwell's army, who *d*. 1666 (*see* Scull's " Life of Dorothea Scott "); of these:

DOROTHEA GOTHERSON, *m*., 1680, John Davis, of Oyster Bay. They removed to Pilesgrove township, Salem county, New Jersey, in 1705, and had:

JUDGE DAVID DAVIS, of Salem county, New Jersey, *d*. aged 90 years, who *m*. Dorothy Cousins, *d*. 1789, aged 96 years, and had:

1.—AMY DAVIS, who *m*., 1741, John Gill, of Haddonfield, New Jersey, and had:

JOHN GILL, who *m*., first, 17 January, 1788, Anna Lovett Smith, and had:

JOHN GILL, of Camden, New Jersey, 1795–1874; *m*., 6 August, 1817, Sarah Hopkins, and had:

WILLIAM HOPKINS GILL, 1832–1873; *m*., 6 July, 1858, Phœbe Shreve, and had:

MARY R. GILL, a member of the Pennsylvania Society of the Colonial Dames of America, who *m*., 30 December, 1885, Johns Hopkins, of Baltimore, and had: *Johns* and *William Gill*.

2.—HANNAH DAVIS, *b*. 1728, who *m*. Richard Wood, of Salem county, New Jersey, *b*. 18 March, 1727, and had:

RICHARD WOOD, of Haddonfield, New Jersey, *b*. 2 July, 1755, who *m*., secondly, 6 November, 1793, Elizabeth, 1776–1826, daughter of Job Bacon, and had:

1.—RICHARD DAVIS WOOD, of Philadelphia, *b*. 29 March, 1799, *d*. 1 April, 1869; *m*., at the North Meeting, Philadelphia, 16 October, 1832, Julianna Randolph, of Philadelphia, *b*. 21 October, 1810, *d*. 15 March, 1884, and had:

GEORGE WOOD, of Philadelphia, *b*. 31 July, 1842, who *m*., at the Twelfth Street Meeting, Philadelphia, Mary Sharpless Hunn, of Philadelphia, *b*. 23 August, 1844, and had:

LYDIA HUNN WOOD, *b*. 23 March, 1867, a member of the Pennsylvania Society of the Colonial Dames of America, who *m*., at the Haverford Meeting, 23 April, 1892, Charles Winter Bailey, of Philadelphia, *b*. 1 December, 1866, and had: *Mary Hunn Wood*, b. 12 July, 1896.

2.—CHARLES S. WOOD, of Philadelphia, who *m*., 5 June, 1834, Juliana, daughter of George FitzRandolph, and had:

ELIZABETH WOOD, a member of the Pennsylvania Society of the Colonial Dames of America, who *m*., 3 June, 1858, John Hooker Packard, M.D., of Philadelphia, and had, besides other children:

ELIZABETH DWIGHT PACKARD, of Philadelphia, a member of the Pennsylvania Society of the Colonial Dames of America.

PEDIGREE XXI.

EDWARD I., King of England, had by his first wife, m., 1254, Eleanor, d. 1290, daughter of Ferdinand III., King of Castile and Leon:

PRINCESS ELIZABETH PLANTAGENET, 1282–1316, widow of Sir John de Vere, who m., secondly, 14 November, 1302, Humphrey de Bohun, Earl of Hereford and Essex, lord high constable, k. at Boroughbridge in 1321, of Royal Descent, and had:

SIR WILLIAM DE BOHUN, K.G., fifth son, created, 1337, Earl of Northampton, d. 1360; who m. Lady Elizabeth, d. 1356, daughter of Bartholomew, Baron de Badlesmere, executed in 1322, and had:

LADY ELIZABETH DE BOHUN, who m. (his first wife) Sir Richard Fitz-Alan, K.G., tenth Earl of Arundel, beheaded in 1398, also of Royal Descent, and had:

LADY ELIZABETH FITZ-ALAN, d. 8 July, 1425, who m., first, 1378, Sir William Montacute, k. s. p., 6 August, 1383; m., secondly, 1386, his second wife, Thomas, Lord Mowbray, Earl Marshal of England, first Duke of Norfolk and Earl of Nottingham, d. 22 September, 1399; and m., thirdly, Sir Robert Goushill, Knt., lord of Hault Hucknall Manor, county Derby, and had by him, who had been an esquire to the first Duke of Norfolk (she m., fourthly, Gerard de Ufflete, Knt., of Wighill, York, see Glover's "History of Derby," ii., 78):

LADY ELIZABETH GOUSHILL, who m., first, Sir Robert Wingfield, Knt., of Letheringham, Suffolk, d. 1431 (see Lodge's "Peerage of Ireland," 1754, iii., and Camden's "Huntingdonshire Visitations"), and had:

SIR HENRY WINGFIELD, of Orford, Suffolk, younger son, will dated 21 February, 1483. He m., first, Alice ——, and m., secondly, Lady Elizabeth, daughter of Sir Robert Rook, or Rowks, and had:

SIR ROBERT WINGFIELD, of Orford and Upton, Northants, who was present at the memorable interview between Henry VIII. and Francis I. in 1520; m. Margery, daughter of John Quarles, of Ufford, Northants, and had:

ROBERT WINGFIELD, of Upton, M. P., d. 31 March, 1580 (see the "Tinwell Parish Register," Rutland), who m. (her first husband) Elizabeth, daughter of Richard Cecil, of Burleigh, sheriff of Northamptonshire and custodian of Windsor Castle, and sister to the lord high treasurer Cecil, and had:

DOROTHEA WINGFIELD (*see* Lodge's "Peerage of Ireland," iii., 347), *d.* 7 November, 1619 (*see* Marshall's "Genealogist," iii., 327), who *m.*, at St. George's, Stamford, 30 September, 1587 (his first wife), Adam Claypoole, Esq., of Latham, Lincolnshire, and Narborough (*see* "Rutland Visitations," 1618), and had:

SIR JOHN CLAYPOOLE, Knt., of Narborough, Northants, third son, clerk of the Hanaper, knighted by Cromwell (*see* Waylen's "House of Cromwell"), who *m.*, 8 June, 1622, Marie Angell, of London, and had by her, who *d.* 1661:

JAMES CLAYPOOLE, of Philadelphia, *b.* 6 October, 1634, *d.* 1687. He arrived in Pennsylvania in the "Concord," 8 June, 1683, and was a merchant and treasurer of the "Free Society of Traders of Pennsylvania,"—so elected in London, 29 May, 1682 (*see* Graff's "Claypoole Family" and "Pa. Mag.," x.). He *m.*, at Bremen, in Germany, by Conradus Lelius, a Calvin minister, 12 December, 1657, Helen Merces (or Mercer), who *d.* in Philadelphia, in 1688, and had:

JOSEPH CLAYPOOLE, of Philadelphia and Mt. Holly, N. J., *b.* in Scots' Yard, London, 1677, *d.* 1744. He came to Philadelphia with his father, and was high sheriff of Philadelphia county. He *m.*, first, 20 July, 1703, Rebecca Jennings, at Charleston, South Carolina, and *m.*, secondly, 10 April, 1716, Edith Ward, who *d.* 1715.

JOSEPH CLAYPOOLE, had by his first wife:

I.—GEORGE CLAYPOOLE, 1706-1770; *m.*, first, Hannah ——, *d.* 1744, and had by her:

GEORGE CLAYPOOLE, *b.* 1733, who *m.*, 1756, Mary Parkhouse, and had:

WILLIAM CLAYPOLE, M.D., of Wilmington, North Carolina, 1758-1792; *m.*, 1790, Mary Wright (a sister of Judge Joshua Wright, of Cape Fear), and had:

ANNE CLAYPOLE, 1791-1838; *m.*, 1809-10, William Henry Hill, of Wilmington, North Carolina, *d.* 1814, and had:

ELIZA ANN HILL, *b.* 13 May, 1813, *d.* 6 December, 1896; *m.*, 1830, William Augustus Wright, of Wilmington, North Carolina, and had:

1.—ANN CLAYPOLE WRIGHT, *b.* 8 September, 1836, *d.* 27 November, 1887, who *m.* Walker Meares, and had:

I.—WILLIAM AUGUSTUS, *d.* 1858; II. WALKER, *d.* 1862; III. JOSHUA; IV. SUSAN KIDDER; V. GEORGE MORDECAI, *d.* 1876; VI. CLAYPOLE, *d.* 1882.

VII.—ADELAIDE SAVAGE MEARES, of Wilmington, North Carolina, a member of the North Carolina Society of the Colonial Dames of America.

VIII.—ELIZA ANN HILL MEARES, a member of the North Carolina Society of the Colonial Dames of America, who m. William C. Munds, of Wilmington, North Carolina, and had: *Annette Claypole*, and *William Capers*.

IX.—MARGARET ENGELHARD MEARES, a member of the North Carolina Society of the Colonial Dames of America, who m., 1897, William Bennett Thorpe, and had: *William B.*, b. 1898.

2.—WILLIAM AUGUSTUS WRIGHT, m. Louisa Holmes, and had: *Alice, William A.*, and *Sallie*.

3.—FLORENCE WRIGHT, 1849–1884, who m., first, 1869, William Fotterall Potter, and m., secondly, 1881, Colonel John W. Atkinson, and had:

I.—ELIZA POTTER, b. 1871, a member of the North Carolina Society of the Colonial Dames of America, who m., 1897, Thomas Settle, of Greensboro, North Carolina. *No issue.*

II.—SARAH POTTER, b. 1874, a member of the North Carolina Society of the Colonial Dames of America, the Order of the Crown, *etc.*, who m., 1898, Tench C. Coxe, of Asheville, North Carolina, and had: *Franklin*, b. Sept., 1899.

II.—REBECCA CLAYPOOLE, b. 26 November, 1711, d. 1 August, 1762, who m., 1 May, 1729, Henry Pratt, of Philadelphia, b. 30 April, 1708, d. 31 January, 1748, and had:

1.—MATTHEW PRATT, of Philadelphia, an artist, who m. ——, and had:

HENRY PRATT, of "The Hills," Philadelphia county, Pennsylvania, who m. Elizabeth Dundas, also of Royal Descent, and had:

SARAH CLEMENTINA PRATT, 1791–1836; m., 1809, Thomas McKean, Jr., of Philadelphia, 1779–1852, and had:

I.—SARAH ANN MCKEAN, m., 1833, George Trott, and had:

SARAH MCKEAN TROTT, m., 1857, James W. Hazlehurst, and had:

ELIZABETH BORIE HAZLEHURST, a member of the Pennsylvania Society of the Colonial Dames of America, who m., 1887, Daniel Lammot, of Philadelphia, also of Royal Descent.

II.—CLEMENTINA SOPHIA MCKEAN, m., 1843, Charles Louis Borie, and had:

1.—ELIZABETH MCKEAN BORIE, a member of the Pennsylvania Society of the Colonial Dames of America, who m., 1872, John Thompson Lewis, of Philadelphia. *Issue.*

PEDIGREE XXI.—Continued.

2.—EMILY BORIE, a member of the Pennsylvania Society of the Colonial Dames of America, m., 1871, James Mauran-Rhodes, of Philadelphia. *Issue.*

3.—SARAH CLEMENTINA MCKEAN BORIE, a member of the Pennsylvania Society of the Colonial Dames of America, who m., 1886, George C. Mason, of Philadelphia.

2.—HANNAH PRATT, b. 3 April, 1732, who m., 3 May, 1755, her cousin, Enoch Hobart, of Philadelphia, who d. 27 October, 1776, and had:

RT. REV. JOHN HENRY HOBART, D.D., of Auburn, New York, b. 14 September, 1775, d. 12 September, 1830; consecrated P. E. Bishop of New York in 1811; m., 6 May, 1800, Mary Goodin, d. 4 April, 1847, daughter of Rev. Thomas Bradbury and Jane (Emote) Chandler, and had:

ELIZABETH CATHERINE HOBART, b. 27 January, 1810, d. 26 May, 1883; m., 22 June, 1830, Rev. George Emlen Hare, D.D., LL.D., b. 4 September, 1808, d. 15 February, 1892, and had:

CHARLES WILLING HARE, of Philadelphia, b. 31 August, 1835, m. Mary S. Widdifield, and had:

CHRISTINE SINGER HARE, a member of the Pennsylvania Society of the Colonial Dames of America, who m. Newberry Allen Stockton, of Bethayres, Montgomery county, Pennsylvania.

JOSEPH CLAYPOOLE, 1677–1744, had by his second wife:

I.—EDITH CLAYPOOLE, b. 1723, d. 27 February, 1800, who m., first, 1744, David Chambers, of Philadelphia, d. 1759, and had:

REBECCA CHAMBERS, b. 2 September, 1751, d. 1834, who m., 3 March, 1768, Robert Wallace, of Pennsylvania, and had:

REBECCA WALLACE, b. 23 August, 1778, d. 1867, who m., 2 January, 1800, Judge Jacob Burnet, of Cincinnati, a United States senator and son of Dr. William Burnet, a delegate to the Continental Congress from New Jersey, and the first surgeon-general, United States Army, and had:

ELIZABETH BURNET, b. 23 June, 1818, d. 5 April, 1889, who m., 1 November, 1837, Hon. William Slocum Groesbeck, of Cincinnati, b. 24 July, 1815, d. 7 July, 1897, and had:

JULIA GROESBECK, a member of the New York Society of the Colonial Dames of America, who m., 1 June, 1876, Robert Ludlow Fowler, of New York City, and had: *William S. G., Mary Powell, Robert L.,* and *Elizabeth Burnet Groesbeck.*

II.—JAMES CLAYPOOLE, of Philadelphia, b. 22 January, 1720; sheriff of Philadelphia county, Pennsylvania, 1777; m., first, 24 May, 1742,

Rebecca White; *m.*, secondly, Mary, daughter of Dr. David Chambers. By his second wife he had:

CAPTAIN ABRAHAM GEORGE CLAYPOOLE, of Philadelphia and Chillicothe, Ohio, an officer in the Pennsylvania Line, Continental Army, and one of the original members of the Pennsylvania Society of the Cincinnati, *b.* 1756, *d.*, Philadelphia, 10 February, 1827. He *m.*, secondly, in New York, November, 1795, Elizabeth Steele, *d.* 4 November, 1818, and had by her:

1.—JANE BYRNE CLAYPOOLE, *b.* at Trenton, New Jersey, 7 March, 1797, *d.* 2 July, 1864, who *m.*, at Chillicothe, 21 June, 1819 (his second wife), Thomas James, of Chillicothe, *b.*, Maryland, 5 November, 1776, *d.* 13 June, 1856, and had:

WILLIAM JAMES, of St. James, Missouri, *b.* 30 March, 1823, who *m.*, 2 July, 1846, Lucy Ann, *b.* 21 August, 1822, daughter of Robert Dun, of Glasgow, Scotland, and his wife, Lucy Wortham Angus, of Petersburg, Virginia (*see* "Americans of Royal Descent," fourth edition, p. 864), and had:

I.—THOMAS JAMES, of Kansas City, Missouri, *b.* Chillicothe, 21 August, 1847; *m.*, 2 July, 1873, Octavia Ann, *d.* 4 November, 1894, daughter of William Hearst Bowles, M.D., of Maries county, Missouri, and his wife, Augusta Glanville, and had: *Lucy Wortham*, *b.* St. Josephs, Missouri, 13 September, 1880.

II.—LUCY JAMES, *b.* Chillicothe, 29 December, 1848, a member of the Pennsylvania Society of the Colonial Dames of America, a member of the Order of the Crown, *etc.*, who *m.*, first, 15 November, 1871, Colonel William Alexander Rucker, United States Army, *b.* at Grosse Isle, Michigan, 17 March, 1831, *d.* at Chicago, 22 January, 1893, and had: *William James*, only child, *b.* St. James, Missouri, 25 April, 1873, and *m.*, secondly, 31 October, 1899, James Dun.

III.—JANE JAMES, a member of the Maryland Society of the Colonial Dames of America, *b.* Maramec Iron Works, Missouri, 4 October, 1851; *m.*, 31 October, 1881, Captain George Hamilton Cook, United States Army, *d.* 4 October, 1889, and had: *Lucy James*, *b.* 13 December, 1882; *Elizabeth Graham*, *b.* 28 January, 1884; *Jane James*, *b.* 15 July, 1885, and *Frances Swayne*, *b.* 13 December, 1887.

2.—ALICE ANNE CLAYPOOLE, *b.* 7 December, 1798, *d.* 30 September, 1822, who *m.* Major David Gwynne, United States Army, *d.* at "Fair Hope," Jefferson county, Kentucky, 21 August, 1849, and had:

ABRAHAM EVAN GWYNNE, of Cincinnati, Ohio, who *m.* Cettie Moore, daughter of Henry Collins Flagg, mayor of New Haven, Connecticut, 1836–41, *d.* 18 March, 1863, and had:

I.—ALICE CLAYPOOLE GWYNNE, a member of the New York Society

of the Colonial Dames of America, who *m.*, 1870, Cornelius Vanderbilt, of New York City, *b.* 27 November, 1843, *d.* 12 September, 1899 (son of William Henry, 1821-1885, and grandson of Cornelius Vanderbilt, 1794-1877), and had: *William H., b.* 21 December, 1870, *d.* 22 May, 1892; *Cornelius, Gertrude, Alfred,* and *Gladys.*

II.—CETTIE MOORE GWYNNE, a member of the New York Society of the Colonial Dames of America, who *m.* William Edgar Shepherd, of New York City. *Issue.*

3.—SARAH CLAYPOOLE, *b.* 9 February, 1801, *d.* 31 January, 1870, who *m.*, 8 June, 1825, William David Lewis, of Philadelphia, 1792-1881, collector of the port, Philadelphia, 1851, and had:

SARAH CLAYPOOLE LEWIS, a member of the Pennsylvania Society of the Colonial Dames of America, who *m.*, 11 October, 1849, Thomas Neilson, of Philadelphia, and had:

I.—WILLIAM DELAWARE NEILSON, of Philadelphia.

II.—ROBERT HENRY NEILSON, *d.* 10 November, 1887; *m.* Emily Souder Lemiard, *d.* 22 March, 1894, and had: *Dorothy Lewis, b.* 27 April, 1892.

III.—SARAH NEILSON, *d.* 10 July, 1892.

IV.—THOMAS RUNDLE NEILSON, *m.*, 12 January, 1898, Louise Fotterall.

V.—LEWIS NEILSON, *m.*, 6 February, 1893, Clara Augusta Rosengarten, and had: *Henry Rosengarten, b.* 8 December, 1693, and *Sarah Claypoole, b.* 28 March, 1897.

VI.—EMMA FLORENCE; VII.—MARY ALICE LEWIS; VIII. FREDERICK BROOKE.

PEDIGREE XXII.

ROBERT BRUCE, King of Scotland, had by his first wife, Lady Isabel, daughter of Donald, Earl of Mar:

LADY MARJORY BRUCE, *m.* Walter, the lord high steward, and had:

ROBERT II., King of Scotland, had by his first wife, Lady Elizabeth, daughter of Sir Adam Mure, of Rowallan, Knt.:

ROBERT STUART, Duke of Albany, Regent of Scotland, who had by his first wife, Lady Marjory, Countess of Menteith:

LADY MARJORY STUART, who *m.* (his first wife) Sir Duncan Campbell, of Lochow, created Lord Campbell in 1445, *d.* 1452, and had:

SIR COLIN CAMPBELL, of Glenurchy, third son, 1400–1478. He had by his second wife, Lady Margaret Stuart, daughter of John, Lord Lorn:

SIR DUNCAN CAMPBELL, of Glenurchy, eldest son, who was slain at Flodden, in 1513, leaving issue by his second wife, Lady Margaret Moncrieffe, daughter of the laird of Moncrieffe, in Perthshire:

LADY ANNABELLA CAMPBELL, who *m.*, by dispensation obtained 9 October, 1533, Alexander Napier, laird of Merchiestoun, *b.* 1509, *k.* at battle of Pinkie, 1547, only son of Sir Alexander Napier, *k.* at Flodden, and had:

SIR ARCHIBALD NAPIER, laird of Merchiestoun and Edinballie, eldest son, *b.* before 1535, master of the Mint of Scotland in 1587, *d.* 1608, who had by his first wife, Lady Janet, *d.* 1563, daughter of Sir Francis Bothwell, a lord of Sessions, and sister of Adam Bothwell, Bishop of Orkney:

JOHN NAPIER, laird of Merchiestoun, eldest son, *b.* 1550, *d.* 1617. He was an author of many valuable books, librarian of Merchiestoun, and well known as the inventor of the table of logarithms. (*See* Playfair's "Family Antiquity," iii., 606, and "Life of John Napier," by David Stewart, Earl of Buchan, 1787.) He had by his second wife, Agnes, daughter of James Chisholme, of Cromlix, Perthshire:

ADAM NAPIER, of Blackstoun, in Renfrewshire, fifth son, half-brother of Sir Alexander Napier, created Baron Napier. He had:

A DAUGHTER (*see* Wood's Douglas's "Peerage of Scotland," ii., 282–292), who *m.* William Craik, of Arbigland, Dumfries, and had:

ADAM CRAIK, of Arbigland, who *m.* Lady Maria, daughter of Sir Colin Campbell, of Ardkinglass, created a baronet in 1679, and his wife, who was a daughter of the above Adam Napier and a sister of William Craik's wife, and had:

WILLIAM CRAIK, of Arbigland, b. 1703, who had by his first wife:

DR. JAMES CRAIK, the physician and intimate friend of President Washington, b. at Arbigland, 1730, came to Virginia in 1750, surgeon-general of the Continental Army, a member of the Maryland State Society of the Cincinnati, and d. at his home in Fairfax county, Virginia, in 1814. He m., 13 November, 1760, Marianna, b. 1740, daughter of Charles Ewell, of Prince William county, Virginia, and his wife, Sallie Ball, a cousin of President Washington, and had:

SARAH CRAIK, b. 11 November, 1764, m., 25 January, 1785, Daniel Jenifer, Jr., M.D., 1756–1809, surgeon in the Continental Army till 1782, member of the Maryland State Society of the Cincinnati, and had:

COLONEL DANIEL JENIFER, b. 15 April, 1791, d. 18 December, 1855, a member of Congress from Maryland, 1831–33, 1835–41, and United States minister to Austria. He m. Eliza Trippe Campbell, of Charles county, Maryland, and had:

NANNIE O. JENIFER, who m. William Stone Triplett, of Virginia, and had:

1.—EMILY LOUISA TRIPLETT, a member of the Virginia Society of the Colonial Dames of America, who m. Meredith F. Montague, of Richmond, Virginia, and had: *Nannie Jenifer Triplett, William Triplett, Meredith,* and *Emily Triplett.*

2.—ELIZABETH TRIPLETT, a member of the Virginia Society of the Colonial Dames of America, who m. Thomas R. Price, of New York City, and had: *Elizabeth.*

PEDIGREE XXIII.

DAVID I., King of Scotland, *m.* Lady Maud, daughter of Waltheof, Earl of Northumberland and Northampton, and had:

HENRY, Earl of Huntingdon and Northumberland, eldest son, *d. v. p.* 1152, *m.*, 1139, Lady Adeline de Warren, daughter of William, second Earl of Surrey, and his wife, Lady Isabel, daughter of Hugh the Great, son of Henry I., King of France, and had:

DAVID, Earl of Huntingdon, *m.* Lady Maud de Meschines, daughter of Hugh, Earl of Chester, and had:

LADY ISABEL DE HUNTINGDON, who *m.* Robert de Brus, or Bruce, Earl, or Lord, of Annandale, *d.* 1245, and had:

ROBERT BRUCE, Earl of Annandale, 1210–1295, a claimant to the crown of Scotland, 1290, as nearest kin to Alexander III.; *m.*, first, 1244, Lady Isabel, daughter of Gilbert de Clare, Earl of Hertford and Gloucester, and had:

ROBERT BRUCE, Earl of Annandale and Carrick, *d.* 1304, who *m.*, 1271, Marjory, Countess of Carrick, widow of Adam de Kilconcath, *d.* 1270, and daughter and heir of Neil, second Earl of Carrick, *d.* 1256, and had:

LADY MATILDA BRUCE (sister of Robert I., King of Scotland), who *m.* (his second wife) Hugh, fifth Earl of Ross, and had:

WILLIAM, sixth Earl of Ross, who had by his second wife, a daughter of Sir David Graham, of Montrose:

LADY MARGARET LESLIE, who *m.* Sir David Hamilton, of Cadyou, *d.* 1375 (*see* Riddell's "Stewardiania," p. 76), also of Royal Descent, and had:

SIR DAVID HAMILTON, of Cadyou, *d. ante* 14 May, 1392, *m.* Lady Johannetta, daughter of Sir Robert de Keith, Great Marshal of Scotland, 1324, and had:

SIR JOHN DE HAMILTON, of Cadyou, *d.* before 28 July, 1397, who *m.* Lady Janet, daughter of Sir James Douglas, Lord of Dalkeith and Liddisdale, *d.* 1420, by his first wife, Lady Agnes, daughter of Patrick Dunbar, Earl of Dunbar and Marche, also of Royal Descent, and had:

SIR JAMES HAMILTON, of Cadyou, one of the hostages for the ransom of King James I. in 1424, and a member of His Majesty's Privy Council, who *m.*, before 20 October, 1422, Lady Janet, daughter of Sir Alexander

Livingston, of Callendar, who was appointed governor to young King James II., and justice-general of Scotland in 1449, and ambassador to England, d. 145-, and his wife, a daughter of Dundas, of Dundas, and had:

GAVIN HAMILTON, fourth son, provost of the Collegiate Church of Bothwell, who m. Jean Muirhead, "the Fair Maid of Lechbrunnock," descended from the House of Lauchope (see Wood's Douglas's "Peerage of Scotland," i., pp. 311, 695), and had:

JOHN HAMILTON, of Orbiston, who m. Jean, daughter of Hamilton, of Woodhall, and had:

GAVIN HAMILTON, of Orbiston and Raplock, 1512-1540, commendator of Kilwinning, who m. Helen, daughter of Wallace, of Cairnhill, and had:

JOHN HAMILTON, of Orbiston, k. in the battle of Langsyde, who m. Margaret, daughter of Hamilton, of Haggs, and had:

MARJORY HAMILTON, who m. David Dundas, of Duddingston (see Burke's "Landed Gentry," 1858), and had:

GEORGE DUNDAS, of Manor, 1628; m. Margaret, daughter of William Livingston, of West Quarter, and had:

JOHN DUNDAS, of Manor, who m. Elizabeth, daughter of Hamilton, of Kilbrackment, and had:

RALPH DUNDAS, of Manor, who m. Helen, daughter of Sir Thomas Burnet, M.D., physician to King William and Queen Anne, of England, and had:

JOHN DUNDAS, of Manor, who had by his first wife, Anne, daughter of John Murray, of Polnaise: THOMAS, of Philadelphia, whose grandson succeeded to the estates of Manor, and

JAMES DUNDAS, b. at Manor, 1734, removed to Philadelphia, 1757, d. 1788; m. Elizabeth, d. 1787, daughter of James Moore, and had:

ELIZABETH DUNDAS, b. 28 January, 1764, d. 15 September, 1793, who m., 27 October, 1785, Henry Pratt, of "The Hills," Philadelphia, also of Royal Descent, and had:

SARAH CLEMENTINA PRATT, b. 29 December, 1791, d. 31 December, 1836; m., 14 September, 1809, Thomas McKean, Jr., of Philadelphia, b. 20 November, 1779, d. 5 May, 1852; adjutant-general of Pennsylvania, 1808-1811 (son of Thomas McKean, LL.D., member and President of the Continental Congress, from Delaware, chief justice and Governor of Pennsylvania, a signer of the Declaration of Independence, and his second wife, Sarah Armitage, of New Castle, Delaware), and had:

1.—HENRY PRATT MCKEAN, of Philadelphia and "Fernhill," b. 3 May, 1810; m., 8 July, 1841, Phœbe Elizabeth, daughter of Stephen and Martha Cornell (Mabbett) Warren, of Troy, New York, and had:

THOMAS MCKEAN, of Philadelphia and "Fernhill," b. 28 November, 1842; m., 24 September, 1863, Elizabeth Wharton, a member of the Pennsylvania Society of the Colonial Dames of America, also of Royal Descent.

2.—SARAH ANN MCKEAN, b. 10 August, 1811; m., 5 November, 1833, George Trott, of Boston and of Philadelphia, and had:

SARAH MCKEAN TROTT, b. 8 December, 1835; m., 2 December, 1857, James W. Hazlehurst, of Philadelphia, and had:

ELIZABETH BORIE HAZLEHURST, a member of the Pennsylvania Society of the Colonial Dames of America; m., 1 June, 1887, Daniel Lammot, of Philadelphia, also of Royal Descent.

3.—ELIZABETH DUNDAS MCKEAN, b. 2 March, 1815, d. s. p. 29 March, 1886; m., 23 May, 1839, Adolphe Edward Borie, of Philadelphia, Secretary of the Navy under President Grant, d. 5 February, 1880.

4.—CLEMENTINA SOPHIA MCKEAN, b. 27 May, 1829; m., 23 May, 1843, Charles Louis Borie, of Philadelphia, b. 7 January, 1819, d. 7 November, 1886, and had:

I.—ELIZABETH MCKEAN BORIE, b. 4 March, 1844, a member of the Pennsylvania Society of the Colonial Dames of America, who m., 11 December, 1872, John Thompson Lewis, of Philadelphia, and had: *Charles Borie, Phœbe Morris*, and *Elizabeth Borie*.

II.—BEAUVEAU BORIE, of Philadelphia, b. 9 May, 1846; m., 3 December, 1868, Patty Duffield Neill. *Issue.*

III.—EMILY BORIE, b. 9 April, 1851, a member of the Pennsylvania Society of the Colonial Dames of America, who m., 5 January, 1871, James Mauran-Rhodes, of Philadelphia and Ardmore, Pennsylvania, b. Providence, Rhode Island, 25 December, 1848, and had: *Clementina Borie*, m. Edward T. Hartshorne; *Mary Aborn, James Mauran, Frank Mauran, Elizabeth McKean, Emily Borie,* d. 1881; *Emily Beauveau, Charles Borie, Sophia Beauveau,* and *Lawrence Mauran*.

IV.—SARAH CLEMENTINA MCKEAN BORIE, b. 2 February, 1853, a member of the Pennsylvania Society of the Colonial Dames of America, who m., 12 October, 1886, George Champlin Mason, Jr., of Philadelphia and Ardmore, Pennsylvania, b. Newport, Rhode Island, 8 August, 1849. *No issue.*

THE ROYAL DESCENT
OF
MRS. WILLIAM E. STRONG,
OF NEW YORK CITY.

HENRY III., King of England=Lady Eleanor of Provence.
Edmund, Earl of Lancaster=Lady Blanche of Artois.
Henry, Earl of Lancaster=Lady Maud de Chaworth.
Lady Maud Plantagenet=Sir William de Burgh, Earl of Ulster.
Lady Elizabeth de Burgh=Lionel, Duke of Clarence.
Lady Philippa Plantagenet=Edmund de Mortimer, Earl of Marche.
Lady Elizabeth de Mortimer=Sir Henry de Percy, K. G., "Hotspur."
Henry, Earl of Northumberland=Lady Eleanor de Neville.
Henry, Earl of Northumberland=Lady Eleanor Poynings.
Lady Margaret de Percy=Sir William Gascoigne, of Gawthrope.
Lady Elizabeth Gascoigne=Gilbert de Talbois, of Kyme.
Sir George de Talbois, of Kyme=(Name unknown.)
Lady Anne de Talbois=Sir Edward Dymoke, of Scrivelsby, Lincolnshire.
Lady Frances Dymoke=Thomas Windebank, of Haines Hill, Berkshire.
Lady Mildred Windebank=Robert Reade, Linkenholt Manor, Southampton.
Col. George Reade, of Gloucester Co., Va.=Elizabeth Martian.
Mildred Reade=Col. Augustine Warner, Jr., of "Warner's Hall."
Mary Warner (m. 17 February, 1680)=John Smith, of "Purton," Gloucester Co., Va.
Augustine Smith, of "Purton," 1687-1756=Sarah Carver.
John Smith, of "Shooters' Hill," Va., 1715-1771—Mary Jacquelin.
Augustine Smith, of "Shooters' Hill," 1738-1774=Margaret Boyd.
Mary Jacquelin Smith, 1773-1846=John Cripps Vowell, of Alexandria, Va.
Sarah Gosnell Vowell, member of the National Society of the Colonial Dames of America, Francis Lee Smith, of Fauquier Co., Va.
Alice Corbin Smith, member of the National Society of the Colonial Dames of America | William Everard Strong, of New York City.

Francis Lee Strong. d.   Anne Massie Strong.   Alice Everard Strong.

PEDIGREE XXIV.

EDWARD I., King of England, had by his second wife, Princess Margaret, daughter of **Philip III., King of France**:

EDMUND PLANTAGENET, Earl of Kent, beheaded in 1330, who had by his wife, Lady Margaret, daughter of John, Baron de Wake, also of Royal Descent:

LADY JOAN PLANTAGENET, "the Fair Maid of Kent," divorced from William de Montacute, Earl of Salisbury. She *m.*, secondly, Sir Thomas de Holland, K.G., Earl of Kent, Captain-General of Brittany, France and Normandy, *d.* 1360 (she was the mother of King Richard II. by her third husband, Edward the Black Prince), and had:

SIR THOMAS DE HOLLAND, K.G., second Earl of Kent, marshal of England, *b.* 1397, who had by his wife, Lady Alice Fitz-Alan, daughter of Sir Richard, Earl of Arundel and Surrey, *d.* 1375, and his second wife, Lady Eleanor Plantagenet, also of Royal Descent:

LADY MARGARET DE HOLLAND, *d.* 31 December, 1440, who *m.*, first, Sir John de Beaufort, K.G., Earl of Somerset, Marquis of Dorset, lord high admiral and chamberlain, *d.* 16 March, 1410, also of Royal Descent, and had:

EDMUND DE BEAUFORT, K.G., fourth Duke of Somerset, Marquis of Dorset, Regent of France; *k.* at St. Albans, in 1455. He *m.* Lady Alianore Beauchamp, daughter of Richard, Earl of Warwick, and had:

LADY JOANE DE BEAUFORT, who *m.*, first, Sir Robert St. Lawrence, fifteenth Baron Howth, lord chancellor of Ireland, and had:

LADY ANNE ST. LAWRENCE, who *m.* Thomas Cusack, of Gerardstown, and had:

ELIZABETH CUSACK, who *m.*, 1563, Patrick Delafield, son of Sir Thomas Delafield, of Fieldstown, county Kildare (*see* Burke's "History of the Commoners," i., 544), also of Royal Descent, and had:

JOHN DELAFIELD, who *m.* Anne de la Bere, and had:

JOHN DELAFIELD, who *m.*, 1610, Elizabeth, daughter of Thomas Hampden, of Hampden, in Bucks, and had:

JOHN DELAFIELD, who *m.*, 1636, Elizabeth Brooke, and had:

JOHN DELAFIELD, *b.* 1637. For distinguished military services at the battle of Zenta, he was created a Count of the Holy Roman Empire, in 1697, with remainder of the title to his descendants, male and female, of his name. His eldest son:

JOHN DELAFIELD, b. 1656, m. Mary, daughter of James Heanage (or Headage), and had:

JOHN DELAFIELD, b. 1692, who m. Sarah, daughter of James Goodwin, and had:

JOHN DELAFIELD, eldest son, b. 1720, d. 1763; m. Martha, b. 1719, d. 1761, daughter of John Dell, of Aylesbury, in Bucks, and had:

JOHN DELAFIELD, of New York City, a Count of the Holy Roman Empire, as inherited from his great-grandfather; b. in England, 16 March, 1748. He m., 4 December, 1784, Anne, b. 24 February, 1766, d. 6 March, 1839, daughter of Joseph Hallett, of New York, and dying, 3 July, 1824, had:

1. COUNT JOHN DELAFIELD, of New York, eldest son, b. 22 January, 1786, d. 22 October, 1853. He m., first, in England, 22 January, 1817, Mary, daughter of John Roberts, of London, and had by her four children, of whom the eldest son, John, b. 1812, succeeded his father as a Count of the Holy Roman Empire, and dying, in 1866, was succeeded in the title by his eldest surviving son, Wallace Delafield, of St. Louis, Missouri, b. 1 May, 1840. He m., secondly, 27 November, 1821, Harriot Wadsworth, daughter of Benjamin Tallmadge, of Litchfield, Connecticut, and had: *Harriot, Clarence,* and

I.—MARY FLOYD DELAFIELD, b. 11 May, 1834, a member of the Maine Society of the Colonial Dames of America, who m., 4 November, 1858, Henry Adams Neely, of Portland, Maine, and had: *Harriot D.*, b. 2 January, 1862, d. 25 August, 1863, and *Albert Delafield*, b. 23 August, 1863, d. 26 December, 1890.

II.—TALLMADGE DELAFIELD, of Brooklyn, New York, who m., 2 October, 1850, Anna Andrews Lawrence, and had *Tallmadge, Harriot,* and

CORNELIA DELAFIELD, a member of the Maine Society of the Colonial Dames of America, who m., 31 October, 1877, in Aurora, New York, Theodore Clarence Woodbury, of Portland, Maine, and had: *Edith White*, b. 3 February, 1880, and *Lawrence Delafield*, b. 25 May, 1883.

2.—MAJOR JOSEPH DELAFIELD, of New York City, b. 22 August, 1790, d. 12 February, 1875; m., 12 December, 1833, Julia, b. 15 September, 1801, d. at Rhinebeck, New York, 23 June, 1882, daughter of Maturin Livingston, of Stadsburgh, New York, and his wife Margaret, daughter of Governor Morgan Lewis, a son of Francis Lewis, of New York, a signer of the Declaration of Independence, and had: *Lewis Livingston*, 1834–1883, *Maturin Livingston*, b. 1836, and

JULIA LIVINGSTON DELAFIELD, of New York City, a member of The Colonial Dames of America Society.

PEDIGREE XXV.

EDWARD I., King of England, had by his first wife, Princess Eleanor, only child of Ferdinand III., King of Castile:

PRINCESS ELIZABETH PLANTAGENET, 1282–1316, widow of John de Vere, who *m.*, secondly, 14 November, 1302, Humphrey de Bohun, fourth Earl of Hereford and Essex; lord high constable of England, *k.* at Boroughbridge 1321, and had by him:

LADY MARGARET DE BOHUN, *d.* 16 December, 1391, who *m.*, 1325, Sir Hugh de Courtenay, K.G., second Earl of Devon, *d.* 1377, also of Royal Descent, and had:

EDWARD COURTENAY, of Goderington, Devon, second son, *d. v. p.*, who *m.* Emeline, daughter and heiress of Sir John d'Auney, of Modeford Terry, Somerset, and had:

SIR HUGH COURTENAY, of Haccomb, Devon, second son, brother of Edward Courtenay, third Earl of Devon, who *m.*, thirdly, Maud, daughter of Sir John Beaumont, of Sherwill, Dorset, *d.* 1468, and had:

LADY MARGARET COURTENAY, who *m.* Sir Theobald Grenville, of Stowe, Cornwall, and had:

SIR WILLIAM GRENVILLE, of Bideford, Cornwall, *m.* Lady Philippa, daughter of Sir William Bonville, K.G., Baron Bonville, of Chuton, and had:

THOMAS GRENVILLE, of Stowe, Cornwall, sheriff of Gloucestershire, *m.* Elizabeth, sister to Sir Theobald Gorges, Knt., of Devonshire, and had:

SIR THOMAS GRENVILLE, of Stowe (*see* Edmondson's "Baronage"), *m.* Elizabeth (or Isabella), daughter of Sir Otis Gilbert, of Compton, sheriff of Devonshire, 1474, *d.* 1494, and had:

SIR ROGER GRENVILLE, of Stowe and Bideford, *m.* Margaret, daughter of Richard Whitleigh, of Efford, Devon, and had:

AMY GRENVILLE, *m.* John Drake, of Ashe, Musbury and Exmouth, sheriff of Devonshire, 1561–62, and had:

ROBERT DRAKE, of Wiscombe Park, Devon, *m.* Elizabeth, daughter of Humphrey Prideaux, of Thewborough, Devon, *d.* 1550, and had:

WILLIAM DRAKE, of Wiscombe Park, *m.* Philippa, daughter of Sir Robert Dennys, of Holcombe, Devonshire, *d.* 1592, and had:

JOHN DRAKE, *b.* at Wiscombe, 1585, came to New England 1630 and settled at Windsor, Connecticut, in 1635, *d.* 17 August, 1659; *m.* Elizabeth Rodgers, *d.* 7 October, 1681 (*see* Stiles' "History of Windsor," N. Y. His. Geneal. Record, ii., 102, and Salisbury's "Genealogies,"—this Drake pedigree is registered in the College of Heralds, London), and had:

1.—SERGEANT JOB DRAKE, of Windsor, Connecticut, *d.* 6 August, 1689, *m.*, 25 June, 1646, Mary, *d.* 11 September, 1689, daughter of Henry Wolcott, of Galdon Manor, Tolland, Somersetshire, England, and Windsor, 1578–1655, and had:

LIEUTENANT JOB DRAKE, of Windsor, 1652–1711; *m.*, 13 September, 1677, Mrs. Elizabeth Cook, 1651–1729, daughter of Daniel Clarke, of Windsor, 1623–1710, and had:

SARAH DRAKE, *b.* 10 May, 1686, *d.* 21 January, 1747, who *m.*, 3 December, 1702, Major-General Roger Wolcott, Governor of Connecticut, *etc.*, *d.* 17 May, 1767, and had:

I.—URSULA WOLCOTT, 1724–1788, who *m.* Judge Matthew Griswold, of Lyme, governor, chief justice, *etc.*, of Connecticut, 1714–1799, and had:

JOHN GRISWOLD, of Lyme, Connecticut, 1752–1812; *m.* Sarah, 1748–1802, daughter of Rev. Stephen Johnson, of Lyme, 1724–1786, and had:

URSULA GRISWOLD, 1775–1811, who *m.* Richard McCurdy, of Lyme, 1769–1857, and had:

JUDGE CHARLES JOHNSON MCCURDY, LL.D., of Lyme, who *m.* Sarah Ann, 1799–1835, daughter of Richard Lord, of Lyme, 1752–1818, also of Royal Descent, and had:

EVELYN MCCURDY, a member of the Connecticut Society of the Colonial Dames of America, who *m.* Prof. Edward Elbridge Salisbury, of New Haven, Connecticut. *No issue.*

II.—ALEXANDER WOLCOTT, M.D., *b.* 7 January, 1712, *m.*, 1745 (his third wife), Mary Richards, of New London, *d.* 25 March, 1795, and had:

ALEXANDER WOLCOTT, *b.* 15 September, 1758, *d.* 26 June, 1828, in Boston, Massachusetts; *m.*, 1 September, 1785, Frances Burbank, of Springfield, Massachusetts, and had:

FRANCES WOLCOTT, *b.* 9 August, 1786, *m.*, 1803, secondly, Arthur W. Magill, of Middletown, Connecticut, and had:

JULIETTE A. MAGILL, *b.* 11 September, 1806, *m.*, 9 August, 1829, John H. Kinzie, of Chicago, Illinois, *d.* 15 September, 1870, and had:

ELEANOR LYTLE KINZIE, president of the Georgia and second vice-president of the National Societies of the Colonial Dames of America, *b.* 18 June, 1835, who *m.*, 21 December, 1857, William Washington Gordon, of Savannah, Georgia, who graduated at Yale in 1854, served with General Lee, General Hood, General Joseph E. Johnston and General Hugh Mercer in the Civil War; was, by special appointment of President McKinley, Brigadier-General commanding 2d Brigade, 1st Division, 7th Army Corps United States Army, in the Spanish War; was appointed commissioner to Porto Rico with General Brooke and Admiral Schley, to arrange for the evacuation of that island, and had:

I.—ELEANOR KINZIE GORDON, b. 27 September, 1858, m., 2 January, 1884, Richard Wayne Parker, of Newark, New Jersey, and had: *Alice Gordon*, b. 27 January, 1885; *Eleanor Wayne*, b. 21 March, 1887; *Elizabeth Wolcott*, b. 19 November, 1889; *Wayne*, b. 29 September, 1892, d. 1 April, 1899, and *Cortlandt*, b. 5 February, 1896.

II.—JULIETTE MAGILL GORDON, b. 31 October, 1860, a member of the Georgia Society of the Colonial Dames of America, who m., 21 December, 1886, William Mackay Low, of Wellesbourne House, Warwickshire, England. *No issue.*

III.—SARAH ALICE GORDON, b. 7 August, 1863, d. 30 December, 1880.

IV.—WILLIAM WASHINGTON GORDON, JR., b. 16 April, 1866, m., 2 March, 1892, Ellen Buchanan Screven, also of Royal Descent, a member of the Georgia Society of the Colonial Dames of America, and had: *William Washington III.*, b. 4 March, 1893, and *Ellen Buchanan*, b. 1 June, 1895, d. 21 May, 1897.

V.—MABEL McLANE GORDON, b. 28 October, 1870, a member of the Georgia Society of the Colonial Dames of America, who m., 31 October, 1899, Hon. Rowland Charles Frederick Leigh, of Stoneleigh Abbey, Warwickshire, England.

VI.—GEORGE ARTHUR GORDON, b. 30 August, 1872.

2.—JOHN DRAKE, JR., of Windsor, d. 7 July, 1688–89; m., 30 November, 1648, Hannah Moore, and had:

LYDIA DRAKE, b. 26 January, 1661, d. May, 1702; m., 10 April, 1681, Joseph Loomis, of Windsor, and had:

CAPTAIN JOSEPH LOOMIS, b. 8 October, 1684, d. 30 May, 1748; m., 28 June, 1710, Mary Cooley, of Springfield, Massachusetts, and had:

MARY LOOMIS, b. 12 January, 1720–21, d. 5 May, 1744; m., 28 October, 1742, Elijah Fitch, and had:

MARY FITCH, b. 25 April, 1744, d. 11 November, 1774, m., 6 December, 1759, Ebenezer Reed, and had:

DR. ELIJAH FITCH REED, of Windsor, b. 13 May, 1767, d. South Windsor, 9 September, 1847; m., 6 June, 1792, Hannah, daughter of Alexander and Joanna (Smith) McLean, and had:

PEDIGREE XXV.—Continued.

REV. JULIUS ALEXANDER REED, D.D., *b.* at Windsor 16 January, 1809, *d.* 27 August, 1890, at Davenport, Iowa; *m.*, at Jacksonville, Illinois, 2 December, 1835, Caroline Blood, also of Royal Descent, and had:

MARY REED, *b.* Fairfield, Iowa, 9 February, 1843, a member of the Massachusetts and Iowa Societies of the Colonial Dames of America, who *m.*, 7 August, 1863, Samuel Francis Smith, of Davenport, Iowa, and had: *Anna Reed, b.* 15 September, 1870.

3.—ELIZABETH DRAKE, who *m.* first, 14 November, 1644, (*see* Stiles's "History of Windsor,"), William Gaylord, of Windsor, Connecticut, *d.* 14 December, 1656, and had:

NATHANIEL GAYLORD, *b.* September 3, 1656, who *m.*, 17 October, 1678, Abigail Bissell, *b.* 23 November, 1658, *d.* 23 September, 1723, and had:

JOSIAH GAYLORD, *b.* 24 February, 1686, who *m.*, 7 May, 1713, Naomi Burnham, *b.* 3 June, 1688, *d.* January, 1762, and had:

NEHEMIAH GAYLORD, *b.* 15 June, 1722, *d.* 1801, who *m.*, 10 May, 1748, Lucy Loomis, *b.* 5 August, 1727, *d.* 2 September, 1800, and had:

LUCY GAYLORD, *b.* 14 April, 1749, *d.* 4 July, 1837, who *m.*, 1769, Zachariah Mather, of Stockbridge, Massachusetts, *b.* 22 September, 1743, *d.* 21 August, 1816, and had:

LUCY MATHER, *b.* 2 June, 1770, *d.* 29 March, 1862, who *m.*, 4 February, 1788, John Field Fitch, of East Windsor, Connecticut, *b.* 7 February, 1766, *d.* 1819, and had:

AUGUSTUS FITCH, M.D., of Columbia, South Carolina, *b.* 30 October, 1794, *d.* 26 August, 1857, who *m.*, 1 May, 1821, Abigail Putnam, *b.* 26 April, 1797, *d.* 31 July, 1834, and had:

JULIA ANN FITCH, who *m.*, 30 January, 1851, Augustus Horatio Jones, of Charleston, South Carolina, and had:

ANNIE VANE JONES, of Savannah, Georgia, a member of the Georgia Society of the Colonial Dames of America, the Order of the Crown, *etc.*

PEDIGREE XXVI.

EDWARD I., King of England, had by his first wife, Princess Eleanor, daughter of Ferdinand III., King of Castile and Leon:

PRINCESS JOAN D'ACRE, *d.* 1307, who *m.*, first (his second wife), Gilbert de Clare, Earl of Clare, Hertford and Gloucester, *d.* 1295, also of Royal Descent, and had:

LADY MARGARET DE CLARE, widow of Piers de Gavestone, who *m.*, secondly, Hugh, second Baron d'Audley, created, in 1337, Earl of Gloucester, *d. s. p. m.*, 1347, and had:

LADY MARGARET D'AUDLEY, who *m.* Sir Ralph, second Baron Stafford, K.G., one of the founders of the Order of the Garter, created, in 1351, Earl of Stafford, *d.* 1372, and had:

LADY JOANE DE STAFFORD, who *m.* John, second Baron de Cherleton, lord of Powys, Wales, chamberlain to King Edward III., and had:

SIR EDWARD DE CHERLETON, K.G., fourth Baron de Cherleton, lord of Powys, second son, elected a Knight of the Garter, 1406-07, *d. s. p. m.*, 14 March, 1420; who *m.* Lady Eleanor de Holland, daughter of Thomas, second Earl of Kent, also of Royal Descent, and had:

LADY JOANE DE CHERLETON, who *m.* Sir John de Grey, K.G., created, in 1418, Earl of Tankerville, *k.* 22 March, 1420, also of Royal Descent, and had:

SIR HENRY DE GREY, second Earl of Tankerville, *d.* 1449, who *m.* Lady Antigone Plantagenet, daughter of Humphrey, Duke of Gloucester, and had:

LADY ELIZABETH DE GREY, *m.* Sir Roger Kynaston, Knt., *d.* 1517, also of Royal Descent, and had:

LADY MARY KYNASTON, *m.* Howell ap Ievan, of Yns-y Maen-Gwyn, and had:

HUMPHREY AP HOWELL, *m.* Anne, daughter of Sir Richard Herbert, Knt., of Colebrook, and had:

JANE VCH. HUMPHREY, *m.* Griffith ap Howell, of Nannau, Merionethshire, *temp.* 1541 (*see* Dwnn's "Visitations of Wales," ii., 226), a descendant of Bledhyn ap Cynfyn, a prince of Powys, and had:

JOHN AP GRIFFITH, of Nannau, second son, who *m.* Elizabeth, daughter of David Lloyd, of Trawsfynedd, and had:

LEWIS AP JOHN, of Dyffrydan township, 1654, m. Ellen, daughter of Howell ap Gruffydd, and had:

OWEN AP LEWIS, who m. Mary, daughter of Tudor Vaughan, of Caer y Nwch, Merionethshire, and had:

ROBERT AP OWEN, who m. Margaret, daughter of John ap Lewis, and had:

LEWIS AP ROBERT, (see P. S. P. Conner's "Lewis Pedigree," and Glenn's "Merion in the Welsh Tract"), who m. Mary, and had:

ELLIS LEWIS, b. in Wales about 1680, came from Ireland to Pennsylvania (he was a Quaker, and his "Certificate of Removal" is dated at Mt. Mellick, Queen's county, Ireland, 25 May, 1708), and settled in Kennett township, Chester county, d. 31 August, 1750, will proved 29 October, 1750. He had by his first wife, m., at Concord Meeting, Chester county, in 1713, Elizabeth, b. 3 March, 1687–88, daughter of Nathaniel Newlin, of Newlin township, Chester county, member of the Provincial Assembly, 1698; justice of the county, 1703; commissioner of property, etc., and had:

ROBERT LEWIS, of Philadelphia, b. 21 March, 1714, member of the Assembly, 1745, d. 1790; m., at Concord Meeting, 23 May, 1733, Mary, 1714–1782, daughter of William Pyle, of Chester county, a member of the Assembly and a justice, and had:

ELLIS LEWIS, of Philadelphia, 1734–1776, who m., secondly, 16 June, 1763, Mary, daughter of David Deshler, of Philadelphia, and had:

PHEBE LEWIS, 1767–1845, who m., 10 October, 1787, Robert Waln, Jr., 1765–1836, and had:

REBECCA WALN, 1802–1846, who m. Jeremiah Fisher Leaming, of Philadelphia, 1795–1888, and had:

REBECCA LEAMING, 1836–1888, who m., 1869, Charles Pendleton Tutt, M.D., 1832–1866, son of Colonel Charles P. and Ann Mason (Chichester) Tutt, and had: *Charles Leaming*, and

REBECCA WALN TUTT, a member of the Virginia Society of the Colonial Dames of America, who m., first, Edward Gray Pendleton, and had: *Maud Pendleton*, d., and m., secondly, Franc Ogilvy-Wood, of Colorado Springs, Colorado, and had: *Guy Catlin Wood*, d.

PEDIGREE XXVII.

HENRY I., King of France, had by his third wife, Anne of Russia:

HUGH THE GREAT, Count de Vermandois, Duke of France, *etc.*, *m.*, thirdly, Lady Adela, or Adelheid, 1080–1117, daughter and heiress of Herbert IV., Count de Vermandois, 1045–1080, also of Royal Descent, and had by her:

LADY ISABEL DE VERMANDOIS, *d.* 1131, who *m.*, first, 1096, Robert, Baron de Bellomonte, Earl of Mellent and Leicester, *d.* 1118, and had:

ROBERT DE BELLOMONTE, second Earl of Leicester, justice of England, *d.* 1168, who had by his wife, Lady Aurelia, or Amicia, daughter of Ralph de Waer, Earl of Norfolk, Suffolk and Cambridge, which earldoms he forfeited in 1074:

ROBERT DE BELLOMONTE, third Earl of Leicester, steward of England, *d.* 1196, who had by his wife, Lady Petronella, daughter of Hugh de Grentesmaismill:

LADY MARGARET DE BELLOMONTE, who *m.* Sairer, Baron de Quincey, of Bushby, created Earl of Winchester, one of the sureties for King John's Magna Charta, *d.* 1219, and had:

ROGER DE QUINCEY, second Earl of Winchester, constable of Scotland, *d.* 1264, who had by his second wife, Lady Helen, daughter of Alan Macdonal, lord of Galloway:

LADY ELIZABETH DE QUINCEY, who *m.* Alexander, second Baron Cumyn, first Earl of Buchan, and had:

LADY —— CUMYN (sister of Alexander, second Earl, *d.* 1289), who *m.* Sir John de Keith, great marshal of Scotland, and had:

ADAM DE KEITH, rector of Keith-Marischall, 1292, *k.* in 1336, father of:

JOHANNA KEITH, who *m.* Sir Alexander Stewart, of Derneley and Cambusnethan, Knt., third son of Sir Alan Stewart, of Dreghorn, who was *k.* at Hallidon Hill, 1333, and had:

LADY JANET STEWART, who *m.* Thomas, first Lord Somerville, *d.* 1445, and had:

LADY MARGARET DE SOMERVILLE, who *m.*, first, Sir Roger Kyrkepatrick, laird of Klyoscbern, Dumfriesshire, and had:

ALEXANDER KYRKEPATRICK, second son, laird of Kirkmichael, whose son:

WILLIAM KIRKPATRICK. of Kirkmichael, obtained, in 1565, from the vicar of the parish of Garrel, the church-lands and glebe of the parish, though, just previous to this, he was "under scandal with the Reformers for allowing mass to be celebrated within his bounds." He was summoned to Parliament in 1548, and was father of:

SIR ALEXANDER KIRKPATRICK, Knt., of Kirkmichael, eldest son, who *m.* Margaret Chateris, and had:

WILLIAM KIRKPATRICK, of Kirkmichael, eldest son, father of:

WILLIAM KIRKPATRICK, of Kirkmichael, who sold his estate, and *d.* 9 June, 1686. His eldest son (*see* Wood's Douglas's "Peerage of Scotland"):

GEORGE KIRKPATRICK, of Knock, in Kirkmichael parish, had Thomas (an ancestor of Eugenie, former Empress of France), and

ALEXANDER KIRKPATRICK, younger son, whose son

ALEXANDER KIRKPATRICK, *b.* in Watties Neach, Dumfrieshire, removed to Belfast, Ireland, about 1725, and then to America in 1736, and settled finally in Somerset county, New Jersey, where he *d.* 3 June, 1758, leaving issue by his wife, Elizabeth (*see* "Kirkpatrick Genealogy"):

DAVID KIRKPATRICK, *b.* Watties Neach, 17 February, 1724, *d.* Mine Brook, Somerset county, New Jersey, 19 March, 1814; *m.*, 31 March, 1748, Mary McEowen, and had:

ANNE KIRKPATRICK, who *m.* Captain Moses Este, of Morristown, New Jersey, and had:

JUDGE DAVID KIRKPATRICK ESTE, of Cincinnati, who *m.*, first, 1819, Lucy Singleton, daughter of General William Henry Harrison, President of the United States, also of Royal Descent, and had by her:

LUCY ANN HARRISON ESTE, who *m.* Joseph Reynolds, of Baltimore and Hagerstown, Maryland, and had:

ANNA HARRISON REYNOLDS, who *m.* John Law Crawford, and had:

LUCY ESTE CRAWFORD, a member of the Maryland Society of the Colonial Dames of America, who *m.* George C. Woodruff, of Litchfield, Connecticut. *No issue.*

PEDIGREE XXVIII.

ROBERT II., King of Scotland, had by his first wife, Lady Elizabeth, daughter of Sir A'dam Mure, of Rowallan:

PRINCESS CATHERINE STEWART, who m. Sir David Lindsay, Knt., of Glenesk, created, in 1389, Earl of Crawford, and had:

ALEXANDER LINDSAY, second Earl of Crawford, k. 13 January, 1445-46, who m. Lady Mariotta, daughter of Sir David Dunbar, of Cockburn, son of George, Earl of Dunbar and Marche, and had:

SIR WALTER LINDSAY, of Kinblethmont, Edzell and Bewfort, third son, who m. Lady Isabel, daughter of William, Lord Livingston, or Sophia, daughter of Livingston, of Saltcoats, and had:

SIR DAVID LINDSAY, Knt., of Bewfort and Edzell, d. 1527, who had by his first wife, Catherine Fotheringham, of Powrie:

WALTER LINDSAY, of Edzell, eldest son, k. v. p., at Flodden, 1513, who m. a daughter of Erskine, of Dun, and had:

SIR DAVID LINDSAY, of Edzell and Glenesk, eldest son, d. 1558. His relation, David Lindsay, seventh Earl of Crawford, "having been used by his sons with unnatural barbarity, disponed, in 1541, his estates and honors" in favor of this Sir David Lindsay, who became eighth Earl of Crawford, who subsequently conveyed back the estates and title to the grandson of the seventh Earl, reserving only during his lifetime the title of Earl of Crawford. He had by his second wife, Lady Catherine, daughter of Sir John Campbell, of Calder:

SIR DAVID LINDSAY, of Edzell, eldest son, one of the lords of Session, d. 1610; m., first, Lady Helen Lindsay, daughter of David, ninth Earl of Crawford, and had by her:

LADY MARGARET LINDSAY, who m. David Carnegy, of Kinniard, created Lord Carnegy and Earl of Southesk, d. 1658, and had:

LADY CATHERINE CARNEGY, who m. Sir John Stuart, created Lord Stuart, of Traquier, and Earl of Traquier, Lord Linton and Cabarston; lord high treasurer of Scotland in 1635, d. 1659, and had:

JOHN STUART, second Earl of Traquier, 1622–1666; m., secondly, 2 April, 1654, Lady Ann Seton, daughter of George, Earl of Winton, and had by her:

CHARLES STUART, fourth Earl of Traquier, 1659–1741; m. Lady Mary Maxwell, 1671–1759, daughter of Robert, Earl of Nithesdale, and had:

(113)

JOHN STUART, sixth Earl of Traquier, 1698–1779; *m.*, 1740, Lady Christiana, 1702–1771, daughter of Sir Peter Anstruther, Bart, and widow of Sir William Weir, Bart, and had:

LADY CHRISTINA STUART, who *m.*, at Traquier House, the seat of her father, in 1769 (*see* "Am. Historical Register," July, 1895), Judge Cyrus Griffin, of Williamsburg, Virginia, president of the last Continental Congress, *b.* 1749, *d.* 1810, and had:

MARY GRIFFIN, *m.* Major Thomas Griffin, of Yorktown, and had:

MARY BERKELEY GRIFFIN, who *m.* William Waller, of Williamsburg, Virginia, and had:

WILLIAM NEVISON WALLER, of Williamsburg, who had by his first wife, *m.*, 1 February, 1842, Elizabeth, daughter of John Tyler, President of the United States of America:

MARY STUART WALLER, a member of the Georgia Society of the Colonial Dames of America, who *m.*, 25 April, 1867, Captain Louis G. Young, of Savannah. *No issue.*

PEDIGREE XXIX.

ROBERT BRUCE, King of Scotland, had by his wife, Lady Elizabeth de Burgh, of Royal Descent:

LADY MATILDA BRUCE, who m. Thomas Isaac, Esq., and had:

JOANNA ISAAC, who m. John d'Ergadia, lord of Lorn, and had:

ISABEL D'ERGADIA, who m. Sir John Stewart, of Innermeath, and had:

SIR JAMES STEWART, "the Black Knight of Lorn," third son, who m., 1439, Lady Joan de Beaufort, also of Royal Descent, widow of James I., King of Scotland, and had:

SIR JOHN STEUART, of Balveny, lord of Lorn, created, in 1457, Earl of Athol, d. 19 September, 1512, uterine brother of King James II. He m., secondly, Lady Eleanor, daughter of William Sinclair, Earl of Orkney and Caithness, also of Royal Descent, and had:

LADY ISABEL STEWART, who m. (his second wife, see Wood's Douglas's "Peerage of Scotland," i., 141 and 549), Alexander Robertson, fifth Baron of Strowan, and had:

JOHN ROBERTSON, first laird of Muirton, in Elgin, second son, who m. Margaret Crichton (possibly a daughter of Sir James Crichton, of Fendraught, eldest son of William, third Lord Crichton, who forfeited, 24 February, 1483-84), and had:

GILBERT ROBERTSON, of Muirton, heir, who m. Janet, daughter of John Reid, of Ackenhead, and had:

DAVID ROBERTSON, of Muirton, heir, who m. —— Innes, and had:

WILLIAM ROBERTSON, of Muirton, heir, who m. Isabel Petrie, and had:

WILLIAM ROBERTSON, of Gladney, who m. —— Mitchell, and had:

REV. WILLIAM ROBERTSON, of Edinburgh, (see Burke's "Royal Families," ii., Ped. 190), who m. a daughter of Pitcairn, of Dreghorn, and had: WILLIAM ROBERTSON, Royal Historiographer (see Lord Brougham's account of the Robertsons), and:

JEAN ROBERTSON, who m. Alexander Henry, of Aberdeen, and had:

COLONEL JOHN HENRY,* who came to Virginia in 1730, and was seated at "Studley" and "The Retreat," in Hanover county. He m. Sarah, widow of Colonel Syme, and daughter of Isaac Winston, and had:

---

* MRS. WILLIAM L. ROYALL, a member of the Virginia State Society of the National Society of the Colonial Dames of America, is also of Royal Descent through John Henry.

PEDIGREE XXIX.—Continued.

1.—PATRICK HENRY, of "Red Hill," Charlotte county, Virginia, 1736–1799, first Governor of Virginia; m., first, 1754, Sarah Shelton, of Hanover, Virginia, and had by her:

ELIZABETH HENRY, who m. Philip Aylett, of Virginia, also of Royal Descent, and had:

MARY MACON AYLETT, who m. Philip Fitzhugh, and had:

LUCY FITZHUGH, who m. John Redd, and had:

LUCY REDD, a member of the Indiana Society of the Colonial Dames of America, the Order of the Crown, *etc.*, who m. William Jacqueline Holliday, of Indianapolis, Indiana, also of Royal Descent, and had:

I.—ARIANA AMBLER HOLLIDAY, a member of the Indiana Society of the Colonial Dames of America, who m. Henry W. Bennett, of Indianapolis.

II.—JAQUELINE S. HOLLIDAY, m. Florence Baker.

III.—LUCY FITZHUGH HOLLIDAY, m. George E. Hume.

GOVERNOR PATRICK HENRY, m., secondly, Dorothea Dandridge, also of Royal Descent, and had by her:

JOHN HENRY, who m. Elvira Bruce McClelland, and had:

WILLIAM WIRT HENRY, of Richmond, Virginia, who m. Lucy Gray Marshall, a member of the Virginia Society of the Colonial Dames of America, and had:

I.—LUCY GRAY HENRY, a member of the Virginia Society of the Colonial Dames of America, who m. Matthew Bland Harrison, of Richmond, Virginia.

II.—ELIZABETH HENRY, a member of the Virginia Society of the Colonial Dames of America, who m. James Lyons, of Richmond, Virginia.

2.—ANNE HENRY, m. Colonel William Christian, removed to Jefferson county, Kentucky, an officer in the Virginia Line, Continental Army, and had:

PRISCILLA CHRISTIAN, who m., October, 1785, Colonel Alexander Scott Bullitt, b. Prince William county, Virginia, 1761, d. Jefferson county, Kentucky, 13 April, 1816; member and speaker of Kentucky State Senate, and was the first lieutenant-governor of the State, 1800, and had:

WILLIAM CHRISTIAN BULLITT, of Louisville, Kentucky, m., 1819, Mildred Ann, daughter of Joshua and Reachy (Walker) Fry, and had:

JOHN CHRISTIAN BULLITT, of Philadelphia, Pennsylvania, b. 10 February, 1824, m., 1850, Therese C. Langhorne, and had:

THERESE LANGHORNE BULLITT, of Philadelphia, a member of the Pennsylvania Society of the Colonial Dames of America, who m., 1874, John W. Coles, M.D., surgeon United States Army, and had: *Therese Pauline.*

PEDIGREE XXX.

HUGH CAPET, King of France, had by his wife, Lady Adela (or Alisa), daughter of William, Duke of Aquitaine, and his wife, Princess Adelheid, daughter of Otto I. the Great, Emperor of Germany, 936–973 (and his second wife, Adelheid, widow of Lothary, King of Italy):

PRINCESS HAVIDE, or Hedewige, who *m.* Ranigerus IV., eleventh Count of Hainault, 977, and had:

LADY BEATRIX, who *m.* Eblo I., Count of Rouci and Reimes, and had:

LADY ADELA, Countess de Rouci, who *m.* Hildwin IV., Count of Montdider and Rouci, and had:

LADY MARGARET DE ROUCI, who *m.* Hugh de Clermont, Count de Beauvois, and had:

LADY ADELIZA DE CLERMONT, who *m.* Gilbert de Tonsburg, Kent, second Earl of Clare, and had:

LADY ADELIZA DE CLARE, who *m.* Alberic de Vere, the first great high chamberlain of England, *k.* 1140, and had:

LADY JULIANA DE VERE, who *m.* Hugh, third Baron Bigod, lord high steward, created in 1140 Earl of Norfolk, *d.* 1177, and had:

ROGER BIGOD, created in 1189 Earl of Norfolk, lord high steward, one of the sureties for the observance of the Magna Charta, *d.* 1220. He *m.*, first, Lady Isabel de Warren, also of Royal Descent, daughter of Hameline Plantagenet, Earl of Surrey, and had:

HUGH BIGOD, Earl of Norfolk, a surety for the Magna Charta, *d.* 1225, who *m.*. Lady Maud, daughter of William le Marshal, Earl of Pembroke, protector of England, and had:

SIR RALPH BIGOD, third son, who *m.* Lady Berta de Furnival, and had:

LADY ISABEL BIGOD, who *m.*, first, Gilbert de Lacy, and had:

LADY MAUD DE LACY, who *m.* Geoffrey, Baron de Genevill, of Trim, *d.* 1306–07, and had:

PETER DE GENEVILL, second son and heir, Baron de Genevill, *m.* Lady Joan, daughter of Hugh le Brune, Earl of Angoulême, and had:

LADY JOAN DE GENEVILL, who *m.* Sir Roger, Baron de Mortimer, of Wigmore, created Earl of Marche, executed for treason in 1330, also of Royal Descent, and had:

LADY MAUD DE MORTIMER, who m. John, second Baron de Cherlton, of Powys, chamberlain to Edward III., d. 1360 (see Jones's "Feudal Barons of Powys "), and had:

LADY JANE DE CHERLETON, who m. John, sixth Baron le Strange, of Knockyn, d. 1397 (see Lloyd's "History of Powys Fadog," iv., 118), also of Royal Descent, and had:

LADY ELIZABETH LE STRANGE, who m. Gruffydd ap Madoc Vychan, of Rhuddalt, third Baron of Glyndyfrdwy (see Burke's "Royal Families," chart pedigree, vol. ii., p. lxi.), and had:

LADY ISABEL, who m. Goronway ap Gruffith ap Madoc, and had:

TUDOR AP GRUFFITH AP GORONWAY, of Penllyn, father of:

HOWEL AP TUDOR, father of:

DAVID-LLWYD, father of:

LADY GWENHWYFAR, who m. David ap Evan-Vaughn, of Llanuwchllyn, and had:

DAVID-LLWYD AP DAVID, of Llandderfel, Penllyn, 1500, who m., first, Annesta Griffith, and had by her:

ROBERT AP DAVID-LLWYD (or Lloyd), of Nantfreur, Penllyn, d. before 1592, who had by his wife, Mary v. Reynold:

THOMAS AP ROBERT, of Gwern y Brechtwn, b. before 1520, d. May, 1612, bur. in the Church of Llandderfel, who had, by his wife Catherine Robert Griffith:

EVAN AP THOMAS, of Nant y Friar, 1555–1640, who m. Dorothea Evans, d. 1619, and had:

THOMAS AP EVAN, 1579–1649, sheriff of Merionethshire, 1623, m. Catherine, daughter of William ap David, of Llandderfel, and had:

FFOULKE AP THOMAS, bapt. 14 April, 1623, who m. Lowry, daughter of Edward ap David, of Llanvor, Merionethshire, and had:

EDWARD AP FFOULKE, b. 1651, d. 1741; m. Eleanor, d. 1733, daughter of Hugh ap Cadwalader ap Rhys, of the parish of Spytu, Denbighshire. He lived at Coed-y-foel, and left for Pennsylvania, 2 February, 1698, with his wife and nine children, where they arrived 17 June, 1698, and purchased seven hundred acres in Gwynedd township, Montgomery county, Pennsylvania (see Jenkins's "History of Gwynedd," and Glenn's "Merion in the Welsh Tract"). Their son:

THOMAS FOULKE, of Gwynedd, Pennsylvania, had:

WILLIAM FOULKE, of Gwynedd, who had:

AMOS FOULKE, of Philadelphia, 1740–1791; m., 1779, Hannah Jones, 1749–1829, also of Royal Descent, and had:

EDWARD FOULKE, of Gwynedd, 1784–1851; m., 1810, Tacy Jones, and had, besides other issue:

1.—ANN JONES FOULKE, 1811–1888; m., 1833, Hiram Corson, M.D., of Conshohocken, and had:

SUSAN FOULKE CORSON, a member of the Pennsylvania Society of the Colonial Dames of America, who m., 26 November, 1868, Jawood Lukens, of Conshohocken, Pennsylvania. *No issue.*

2.—PRISCILLA FOULKE, 1821–1882; m., 22 April, 1849, Thomas Wistar, Jr., of Philadelphia, and had:

SUSAN FOULKE WISTAR, a member of the Pennsylvania Society of the Colonial Dames of America, who m., 27 May, 1872, Howard Comfort, of Philadelphia, and had: *William Wistar, b.* 27 May, 1874.

3.—REBECCA JONES FOULKE, b. 18 May, 1829, a member of the Pennsylvania Society of the Colonial Dames of America; m., 8 October, 1857, Robert R. Corson, of New Hope, Pennsylvania. *No issue.*

THE ROYAL DESCENTS
OF
MRS. THOMAS SETTLE,
AND
MRS. TENCH C. COXE.

EDWARD I., King of England=Princess Eleanor of Castile.
- Princess Elizabeth Plantagenet=Humphrey de Bohun, Earl of Hereford.
- William de Bohun, Earl of Northampton=Lady Elizabeth de Badlesmere.
- Lady Elizabeth de Bohun=Richard Fitz-Alan, Earl of Arundel.
- Lady Elizabeth Fitz-Alan=Sir Robert Goushill, of Hault Hucknall.
- Lady Elizabeth Goushill=Sir Robert Wingfield, of Letheringham.
- Sir Henry Wingfield, of Orford=Elizabeth Rowks.
- Sir Robert Wingfield, of Upton=Margery Quarles.
- Robert Wingfield, of Upton=Elizabeth Cecil.
- Dorothea Wingfield=Adam Claypoole, of Latham, Lincolnshire.
- Sir John Claypoole, of Latham=Marie Angell.
- James Claypoole, of Philadelphia=Helen Merces.
- Joseph Claypoole, of Philadelphia=Rebecca Jennings.
- George Claypoole, of Philadelphia=Hannah ———.
- George Claypoole=Mary Parkhouse.
- William Claypole, M.D., Wilmington, N. C.=Mary Wright.
- Ann Claypole=William Henry Hill, Wilmington, N. C.
- Eliza Ann Hill=William Augustus Wright, Wilmington, N. C.
- Florence Wright=William Fotterall Potter.

Eliza Potter, member of the National Society of the Colonial Dames of America, the Order of the Crown, etc. *No issue.* = Thomas Settle, of Greensboro, N. C.

Sarah Potter, member of the National Society of the Colonial Dames of America, the Order of the Crown, etc. = Tench C. Coxe, of Asheville, N. C.
- Franklin Coxe, b. Sept, 1899.

PEDIGREE XXXI.

EDWARD I., King of England, had by his second wife, Princess Margaret, daughter of Philip III., King of France:

PRINCE EDMUND, of Woodstock, Earl of Kent, who *m.* Lady Margaret, daughter of John, Baron Wake, also of Royal Descent, and had:

PRINCESS JOAN PLANTAGENET, the Fair Maid of Kent, who *m.*, first, William de Montacute, Earl of Salisbury; *m.*, secondly, Sir Thomas de Holland, K.G., Earl of Kent, captain-general of Brittany, France and Normandy, also of Royal Descent, and *m.*, thirdly, Edward the Black Prince, son of King Edward III., and had by him King Richard II. By her second husband she had:

SIR THOMAS DE HOLLAND, K.G., second Earl of Kent, earl marshal of England, *d.* 1397, who *m.* Lady Alice, daughter of Sir Richard Fitz-Alan, K.G., Earl of Arundel and Surry, *d.* 1375, also of Royal Descent, and had:

LADY ALIANORE DE HOLLAND, widow of Roger de Mortimer, Earl of Marche, who *m.*, secondly, Sir Edward de Cherleton, K.G., fourth Lord Cherleton, of Powys, elected a Knight of the Garter, 1406-07, *d.* 14 March, 1420, also of Royal Descent, and had:

LADY JOANE DE CHERLETON, who *m.* Sir John de Grey, K.G., also of Royal Descent, created, in 1418, Earl of Tancarville, in Normandy. He was slain in the battle of Baugy Bridge, 22 March, 1420, and had by Lady Joane:

SIR HENRY DE GREY, Knt., second Earl of Tankerville, *d.* 1449, who *m.* Lady Antigone, daughter of Humphrey Plantagenet, Duke of Gloucester, regent of France, and had:

LADY ELIZABETH DE GREY, who *m.* Sir Roger Kynaston, Knt., *d.* 1517, also of Royal Descent (*see* Jones's " Feudal Barons of Powys "), and had:

HUMPHREY KYNASTON, of Morton, Salop, *d.* 1534, who *m.* Elizabeth, daughter of Meredith ap Howel, of Lansilin, Denbighshire, also of Royal Descent, and had:

MARGARET KYNASTON (*see* Burke's " Royal Families," I., Ped. 47), who *m.* John Lloyd Wynn, of Dyffryn, also of Royal Descent, and had:

HUMPHREY LLOYD WYNN, of Dyffryn, who had:

KATHERINE LLOYD, who *m.* her kinsman, John Lloyd, of Dolobran Hall, *b.* about 1575, *d.* after 1639, also of Royal Descent (*see* Glenn's

"Merion in the Welsh Tract," p. 336; Smith's " Lloyd and Carpenter Families," and Foster's " Royal Descents "), and had:

CHARLES LLOYD, of Dolobran Hall, b. 1613, bur. 17 August, 1657; a magistrate for Montgomeryshire, who m. Elizabeth, daughter of Thomas Stanley, of Knockyn, Salop, son of Sir Edward Stanley, Knt., and had:

THOMAS LLOYD,* b. Dolobran, 17 February, 1640, d. 10 September, 1694. He was educated at Jesus College, Oxon, and was William Penn's agent in Pennsylvania, and the first Deputy Governor and President of the Provincial Council of Pennsylvania, 1664–93. He m., first, 9 September, 1665, Mary, daughter of Roger Jones, of Welshpool, Montgomeryshire, and had by her, who d. 1680:

1.—DEBORAH LLOYD, 1682–172–; m., 12 September, 1704, Dr. Mordecai Moore, of Anne Arundel county, Maryland, his second wife, and had:

DEBORAH MOORE, 1705–1751; m., 9 February, 1720–21, Dr. Richard Hill, of Hill's Point, Maryland, b. 1698, d., Funchal, 1762, and had:

I.—MARGARET HILL, 1737–1816; m., 21 September, 1758, William Morris, of Philadelphia, 1732–1766, and had:

1.—JOHN MORRIS, M.D., of Philadelphia, 1759–1793; m., 16 October, 1783, Abigail Dorsey, d. 1793, and had:

MARGARET MORRIS, 1792–1832, who m., 4 October, 1810, Isaac Collins, Jr., of Philadelphia, and had:

FREDERIC COLLINS, of Philadelphia, b. 21 January, 1820, d. 27 November, 1892; m., 28 August, 1844, Laetitia P. Dawson, and had: *Annie Morrison*, b. 26 July, 1849, m., 10 April, 1890, Morris Earle, and

ELIZABETH DAWSON COLLINS, a member of the Pennsylvania Society of the Colonial Dames of America, b. 23 January, 1847, who m., 3 June, 1869, Charles F. Hulse, of Philadelphia (son of Charles Hulse, of Nottingham, England), d. 28 August, 1876, and had:

I.—LAETITIA COLLINS HULSE, a member of the Pennsylvania Society of the Colonial Dames of America, who m., 28 April, 1892, Samuel Bowman Wheeler, of Philadelphia, also of Royal Descent, and had: *Samuel B.*, b. 22 February, 1893; *Frederic C.*, b. 30 March, 1894, and *Elizabeth Dawson*, b. 7 May, 1897.

II.—MARGARET MORRIS HULSE, b. 22 April, 1873, who m. 2 November, 1898, Burnet Landreth, Jr., of Philadelphia.

---

* The following ladies, members of the National Society of the Colonial Dames of America, are also of Royal Descent, through Thomas Lloyd :

MRS. JOHN LOWELL, JR., Massachusetts State Society.

MRS. JAMES A. LOWELL, Massachusetts State Society.

PEDIGREE XXXI.—Continued.

2.—GULIELMA MARIA MORRIS, b. 18 August, 1766, d. 9 September, 1826; m., 8 April, 1784, John Smith, of Philadelphia, b. 3 November, 1791, d. 18 April, 1803, also of Royal Descent, and had:

> JOHN JAY SMITH, of "Ivy Lodge," Philadelphia, b. 16 May, 1798, d. 23 September, 1881, who m., 1821, Rachel C., daughter of Robert Pearsall, of Flushing, Long Island, and had:
>
> ELIZABETH PEARSALL SMITH, of Germantown, Philadelphia, a member of the Pennsylvania Society of the Colonial Dames of America.

3.—RICHARD HILL MORRIS, of Philadelphia, 1762–1841; m., secondly, 25 October, 1798, Mary, daughter of Richard S. Smith, of Burlington, New Jersey, and had by her, who d. 1848:

I.—EDMUND MORRIS, of Burlington, New Jersey, 1804–1874; m., 1827, Mary P., d. 1876, daughter of William Jenks, of Bucks county, Pennsylvania, and had:

> MARY ANN MORRIS, a member of the Pennsylvania Society of the Colonial Dames of America, the Order of the Crown, etc., who m., 5 November, 1863, Alexander C. Fergusson, of Philadelphia, and had:
>
> EDMUND M. FERGUSSON, m., 1898, Mary F. Huber.
>
> AGNES M. FERGUSSON, m., 1893, Charles Edwin Noblit.
>
> HENRY A. FERGUSSON, m., 1892, Jessie M. Dysart.
>
> MARY M. FERGUSSON, d. 1876.
>
> ALEXANDER C. FERGUSSON, JR., m., 1895, Linda W. Cook.
>
> HELEN FERGUSSON.

II.—CHARLES MOORE MORRIS, 1810–1883; m., 12 October, 1831, Ann Jenks, d. 1870, and had:

WILLIAM JENKS MORRIS, b. 27 August, 1832, m., 26 December, 1858, Ann W. Humphreys, 1831–1886, and had:

GERTRUDE R. MORRIS, a member of the Pennsylvania Society of the Colonial Dames of America, who m., 28 January, 1891, James Smith Merritt, of Philadelphia, and had: *Morris Hill*, b. 28 December, 1891, and *James Smith*, b. 31 May, 1896.

II.—RACHEL HILL, 1735–1796, who m., 17 April, 1759, Richard Wells, of Philadelphia, and had:

MARY WELLS, 1761–1819, who m., 24 November, 1785, Benjamin W. Morris, of Philadelphia, 1762–1825, and had:

SARAH MORRIS, who m., 5 August, 1804, Jacob Shoemaker Waln, of Philadelphia, d. 4 April, 1850, and had:

I.—EDWARD WALN, of Philadelphia, who m., Ellen, daughter of Henry Nixon, of Philadelphia, and his wife, Maria, daughter of Robert Morris, of Philadelphia, and had:

ELLEN WALN, a member of the Pennsylvania Society of the Colonial Dames of America, Society Daughters of the American Revolution, etc., who m. Charles Custis Harrison, of Philadelphia, Provost of the University of Pennsylvania, and had: *George Leib, Edward W.*, d. 1872; *Ellen Nixon, Charles Custis, Henry Waln*, and *Esther Waln.*

II.—MARY WALN, who m. Richard Vaux, recorder, 1841–47, and mayor of Philadelphia, 1856–60, member of Congress, 1872, and had:

META VAUX, of Philadelphia, a member of the Pennsylvania Society of the Colonial Dames of America.

2.—MARY LLOYD, youngest daughter, m., 1694, Judge Isaac Norris, of "Fair Hill," Germantown, Philadelphia. Isaac Norris settled in Philadelphia in 1693, and at his death, in 1735, was a member of the Colonial Assembly of Pennsylvania. He was mayor of the city, presiding judge of the Common Pleas Court, and member of the Governor's Council for over thirty years. He had by Mary Lloyd:

I.—ISAAC NORRIS, of "Fairhill," b. 1701, d. 1764. He was elected to succeed his father in the Assembly, and was almost perpetual speaker till 1759, when he resigned. He m., 1739, Sarah, daughter of James Logan, of "Stenton;" 1674–1751, chief justice of Pennsylvania, also of Royal Descent, and had:

MARY NORRIS, 1740–1803, who m., 1770, Brigadier-General John Dickinson, 1732–1808, president of the Supreme Executive Council of Pennsylvania, 1782, member of the first Continental Congress, etc., and had:

MARIA DICKINSON, 1783–1854, who m., 1808, Albanus Charles Logan, M.D., of "Stenton," 1783–1854, also of Royal Descent, and had:

GUSTAVUS GEORGE LOGAN, of "Stenton," Philadelphia, 1815–1876; m., 1846, Anna, daughter of William Armatt, of London, England, and had:

FRANCES ARMATT LOGAN, a member of the Pennsylvania Society of the Colonial Dames of America, d. 8 May, 1898.

II.—CHARLES NORRIS, of "Fairhill," Philadelphia county, Pennsylvania, 1712–1766; m., secondly, 1759, Mary, daughter of Joseph Parker, of Chester, Pennsylvania, deputy register, and had by her, who d. 1799:

JOSEPH PARKER NORRIS, of " Fairhill," *b.* 5 May, 1763, *d.* 22 June, 1841; *m.*, 20 May, 1790, Elizabeth Hill, *d.* January, 1861, daughter of Joseph Fox, of Philadelphia, speaker of Pennsylvania Assembly, and had:

I.—ISAAC NORRIS, of Philadelphia, *b.* 21 February, 1802, *d.* 1890; *m.* 18 May, 1830, Mary, daughter of George Pepper, of Philadelphia, and had:

MARY PEPPER NORRIS, *b.* 7 October, 1837, a member of the Pennsylvania Society of the Colonial Dames of America, who *m.*, 30 April, 1857, Travis Cochran, of Philadelphia, *b.* 7 March, 1830, and had: *Mary Norris, John T., d.* 23 March, 1882; *Isaac N., Elizabeth Travis, d.* 4 December, 1870, and *Fanny T.*

II.—MARY PARKER NORRIS, *b.* 19 June, 1791, who *m.*, 11 November, 1813, William Fishbourne Emlen, of Philadelphia, and had:

GEORGE EMLEN, of Philadelphia, *b.* 25 September, 1814, *d.* 7 June, 1853, who *m.*, 6 May, 1840, Ellen Markoe, and had *George*, p. 126, and

ELLEN EMLEN, of Philadelphia, *b.* 13 February, 1850, a member of the Pennsylvania Society of the Colonial Dames of America.

3.—THOMAS LLOYD, JR., *b.* 15 September, 1675, *d.* Goodmansfield, London, before 1718; *m.* Sarah Young, *b.* 2 November, 1676, *d.* in Philadelphia, and had:

THOMAS LLOYD, 3d, of Philadelphia, *d.* 14 May, 1754; *m.* Susanna, *d.* 8 April, 1740, widow of Dr. Edward Owen, and daughter of Philip Kearny, of Philadelphia, and had:

I.—SUSANNAH LLOYD, *d.* 24 October, 1772, who *m.*, 4 November, 1762 (his first wife), Thomas Wharton, Jr., of Philadelphia, member of the Pennsylvania Committee of Safety, 1775-76, president of the Council of Safety, 1776, president of the Supreme Executive Council, 1777-78, *d.* 23 May, 1778, at Lancaster, Pennsylvania, and had:

WILLIAM MOORE WHARTON, of Philadelphia, *b.* 24 June, 1768, *d.* 14 August, 1816. He had by his second wife, Deborah Shoemaker:

1.—DANIEL CLARK WHARTON, of Philadelphia, *b.* 9 July, 1808, *d.* 11 May, 1876; *m.* Ann Waln, daughter of Thomas W. and Hannah (Griffitts) Morgan, and had:

I.—MARY MORGAN WHARTON, of Philadelphia, a member of the Pennsylvania Society of the Colonial Dames of America.

II.—ANNE ROTCH WHARTON, a member of the Pennsylvania Society of the Colonial Dames of America, who *m.*

Charles J. Churchman, of Philadelphia, and had: *Mary W., Agnes, Charles W., Clark W.,* and *Waln Morgan.*

III.—HELEN ROTCH WHARTON, a member of the Pennsylvania Society of the Colonial Dames of America, who *m.*, 2 April, 1874, George Emlen, Jr., of Philadelphia, *b.* 27 November, 1843, also of Royal Descent, and had: *Annie Wharton, d.* 17 July, 1875; *Ellen Markoe,* and *Dorothea.*

2.—ELIZABETH SHOEMAKER WHARTON, *b.* 16 June, 1813, who *m.* William J. McCluney, United States Navy, and had:

ARABELLA MCCLUNEY, a member of the Pennsylvania Society of the Colonial Dames of America, who *m.*, 7 February, 1877, Stiles Huber, of Philadelphia, and had: *Wharton McC.*

II.—SARAH LLOYD, *d.* 1788, who *m.*, 1757, Judge William Moore, of Philadelphia, *d.* 1793, president of the Supreme Executive Council of Pennsylvania, 1781, and had:

ROBERT KEARNY MOORE, *d.* 1807 on his estate opposite Louisville, Kentucky; *m.*, 5 May, 1806, Catharine, *b.* 27 May, 1775, *d.* 22 March, 1863, daughter of Jonas and Catharine (Walker) Allen, of Virginia, and had:

SARAH LLOYD ROBERT MOORE, only child, *b.* Louisville, Kentucky, 24 February, 1807, *d.* 4 August, 1833; *m.*, 29 April, 1823, Urban Epenetus Ewing, M.D., of Louisville, *d.* 23 December, 1874, and had, besides other issue: *Mary L., m.* Thomas Eaches (and had: *Urban E. Eaches,* of Louisville), and

SARAH LLOYD MOORE EWING, a member of the Kentucky Society of the Colonial Dames of America, and Kentucky State Regent of the Daughters of the American Revolution Society. She *m.*, first, Nathaniel Burwell Marshall, M.D., of Louisville, Kentucky, also of Royal Descent, a grandson of Chief Justice Marshall, and had:

1.—SALLIE MOORE EWING MARSHALL, *m.* William Jarvis Hardy, Jr., of New York City, and had: *William J., Marshall Burwell,* and *Ewing Lloyd.*

2.—CLAUDIA BURWELL MARSHALL, *m.* James Bruce Morson, of Birmingham, Alabama, and had: *Sallie Marshall, Claudia Hamilton,* both accidentally drowned, 26 August, 1891, and *Thomas Seddon.*

3.—BURWELL KEITH MARSHALL, of Louisville, *m.* Lizzie Veech, and had: *Richard Veech, Elizabeth, Mary Louisa, Sallie Ewing,* and *Burwell.*

4.—EWING MARSHALL, M.D., of Louisville, *m.* Martha Snead, and had: *Alice Snead, Mary Lloyd,* and *Evelyn.*

5.—MARY LLOYD EWING MARSHALL, m. Philip Trapnill Allin, of Louisville. *No issue.*

SARAH LLOYD MOORE EWING, m., secondly, Henry Lewis Pope, of Louisville, and had:

HENRY EWING POPE, of Louisville, only child.

4.—RACHEL LLOYD, b. 20 January, 1667–68, who m., first, 6 July, 1688 (his first wife), Samuel Preston, of Philadelphia, Pennsylvania, b. Pautuxent, Maryland, 1665; mayor of Philadelphia, 1711; Colonial treasurer, 1714; Provincial councillor, 1708, etc., d. 10 September, 1743 (see Keith's "Provincial Councillors of Pennsylvania," and Glenn's "Colonial Mansions"), and had:

I.—MARGARET PRESTON, b. 1689, who m., 27 May, 1709, Dr. Richard Moore, of Anne Arundel county, Maryland (son of Dr. Mordecai Moore and his first wife), will proved in September, 1734, and had:

RICHARD MOORE, of Anne Arundel county, Maryland, d. 1760, who m. Mary West, of "The Wood Yard," on the Eastern Shore, Maryland, and had:

HANNAH MOORE, d. 22 May, 1805, who m. Hugh Roberts, b. 1744, d. 25 June, 1825, also of Royal Descent, and had:

ELIZABETH ROBERTS, who m., 10 July, 1794, John Davis, of Philadelphia, and had:

LUCELLA DAVIS, d. 30 May, 1881, who m. John Pennington, of Philadelphia, b. Monmouth county, New Jersey, 1 August, 1799, d. 18 March, 1867, and had:

ELIZABETH DAVIS PENNINGTON, a member of the Pennsylvania Society of the Colonial Dames of America, who m. Henry Carey Baird of Philadelphia, b. 10 September, 1825, son of Captain Thomas J. Baird, United States Army, and Elizabeth, daughter of Matthew Carey, of Philadelphia, and had:

HELENA LAWRENCE BAIRD, m. William Howard Gardiner, of Boston, and had: *William Howard*, b. 24 March, 1875; *John Pennington*, b. 18 June, 1876, and *Edward Carey*, b. 14 November, 1878.

II.—HANNAH PRESTON, 1693–1772, who m., 25 May, 1711, Samuel Carpenter, Jr., son of Samuel Carpenter, of Philadelphia, Provincial councillor and treasurer, and had:

1.—HANNAH CARPENTER, d. 1766, who m., 8 April, 1746 (his first wife), Samuel Shoemaker, mayor of Philadelphia, 1769–71, d. 1800, son of Samuel Shoemaker, mayor of Philadelphia, 1743, 1752 and 1760, and had:

BENJAMIN SHOEMAKER, of Philadelphia, 1746–1808, who m., 1773, Elizabeth, daughter of Edward and Anna (Coleman) Warner, and had:

ANNA SHOEMAKER, 1777-1865, who *m.*, first, 5 May, 1796, Robert Morris, Jr., of Philadelphia, son of Robert Morris, of Philadelphia, the financier of the American Revolution, and had:

ELIZABETH ANNA MORRIS, *d.* 24 December, 1870, who *m.*, first, 7 June, 1821, Sylvester Malsan, and had:

HENRY MORRIS MALSAN, *m.*, 25 September, 1848, Sarah E. White, of Whitesboro', New York, and had:

1.—ANNA LOUISE MALSAN, *b.* 4 April, 1850, a member of the New York Society of the Colonial Dames of America, who *m.* Charles E. Smith, of Whitesboro', New York, and had: *Adrian L., Claude Malsan,* and *Bertha Bulkley.*

2.—JULIA PAULINE MALSAN, *b.* 12 June, 1852, a member of the New York Society of the Colonial Dames of America, who *m.*, 8 October, 1878, M. A. C. Ludwig Wilhelmi, of New York City, and had: *Frederick William, b.* 7 September, 1879, and *Julia White, b.* 12 November, 1881, *d.* 3 March, 1888.

2.—JUDGE PRESTON CARPENTER, of Salem, New Jersey, *b.* 28 October, 1721, *d.* 20 October, 1785, had by his first wife, *m.*, 17 October, 1742, Hannah, *b.* 1723, daughter of Samuel Smith, of Salem, and had:

I.—ELIZABETH CARPENTER, who *m.*, 1767, Ezra Firth, of Salem county, New Jersey, and had:

HANNAH FIRTH, *b.* 26 September, 1778, *d.* 24 January, 1854, who *m.*, 20 April, 1797, Isaac C. Jones, of Philadelphia, *b.* 9 December, 1769, *d.* 26 January, 1865, and had:

LYDIA JONES, *b.* 24 October, 1804, *d.* 19 February, 1878, who *m.*, 8 June, 1825, Caspar Wistar, M.D., of Philadelphia, *b.* 5 June, 1801, *d.* 4 April, 1867, and had:

MARY WALN WISTAR, *b.* 8 June, 1829, who *m.*, 5 September, 1855, Moses Brown, of Germantown, Philadelphia, and had:

MARY WALN WISTAR BROWN, *b.* 23 November, 1862, a member of the Pennsylvania Society of the Colonial Dames of America, who *m.*, 9 February, 1888, Thomas S. K. Morton, M.D., of Philadelphia, and had: *Samuel George, b.* 2 December, 1888, *d.* 31 January, 1889; *Mary Waln Wistar, b.* 26 November, 1889; *Thomas George, b.* 17 October, 1891, *d.* 10 September, 1892; *Helen Kirkbride, b.* 13 May, 1893, *d.* 20 February, 1895, and *Sarah Wistar, b.* 27 November, 1895.

II.—THOMAS CARPENTER, of Carpenter's Landing, Gloucester county, New Jersey, 1742-1847; he served as adjutant of Colonel Dick's regiment of New Jersey militia, and as paymaster and quartermaster of Gloucester and Salem counties' troops in the Revolutionary War; *m.*, 13 April, 1774, Mary, daughter of Edward Tonkin, of Burlington county, New Jersey, and had:

EDWARD CARPENTER, of Glassboro', New Jersey, 1772-1813, *m.*, 5 September, 1799, Sarah, daughter of James Stratton, M.D., of Swedesboro', New Jersey, and had:

1.—MARY TONKIN CARPENTER, 1804-1893; *m.*, 1830, Richard W. Howell, of Camden, New Jersey, 1799-1859, and had:

ANNA HOWELL, a member of the Pennsylvania Society of the Colonial Dames of America, who *m.*, 1869, Malcolm Lloyd, of Philadelphia, and had: *Howell*, *b.* 1871, *m.*, 1897, Emily Innes; *Malcolm J.*, *b.* 1874; *Stacy B.*, *b.* 1876; *Francis Vernon*, *b.* 1878; *Anna Howell*, *b.* 1880; *Esther*, *b.* 1882, and *Mary Carpenter*, *b.* 1887.

2.—EDWARD CARPENTER, JR., of Philadelphia, 1813-1889, who *m.*, 16 November, 1837, Anna Maria, daughter of Benjamin M. Howey, of Gloucester county, New Jersey, and had:

SARAH CAROLINE CARPENTER, a member of the Pennsylvania Society of the Colonial Dames of America, who *m.*, 18 July, 1865, Andrew Wheeler, of Philadelphia, and had: *Andrew, Jr.*, *m.* Mary Wilcox Watson (*issue: Sophia Wilcox* and *Eleanor Ledlie*); *Annie, d.* young; *James May, d.* young; *Samuel Bowman, m.* Laetitia C. Hulse, also of Royal Descent (see p. 122); *Arthur Ledlie*, *Walter Stratton* and *Herbert*.

III.—MARGARET CARPENTER, *b.* 26 August, 1756, *d.* 3 October, 1821; *m.*, 1776, James Mason Woodnutt, of Salem, New Jersey, and had:

HANNAH WOODNUTT, *b.* 12 October, 1784, *d.* 185–, who *m.*, 1799, Clement Acton, of Salem county, New Jersey, *d.* 21 January, 1820, and had:

1.—MARGARET WOODNUTT ACTON, who *m.* John D. Griscom, M.D., of Philadelphia, and had:

CLEMENT A. GRISCOM, of Philadelphia and Haverford, who *m.* Frances Canby Biddle, a member of the Pennsylvania Society of the Colonial Dames, Society Daughters of the American Revolution, *etc.*, also of Royal Descent, and had: *Clement A.*, *Rodman E.*, *Lloyd C.*, *Francis C.*, and

HELEN BIDDLE GRISCOM, a member of the Pennsylvania Society of the Colonial Dames of America, who *m.* Samuel Bettle, of Philadelphia.

2.—CLEMENT JAMES ACTON, of Cincinnati, Ohio, *b.* 1817, *d.* 6 July, 1875, who *m.*, 1846, Mary, *b.* 24 April, 1823, daughter of Colonel John Noble, of Columbus, Ohio, and had: *Margaret W.*, wife of Augustus W. Durkee, of New York, and

ELIZA NOBLE ACTON, *b.* 26 May, 1852, a member of the Pennsylvania and the Ohio Societies of the Colonial Dames of

America, who *m.*, 1878, Frank N. Hickok, of New York, *b.* 23 October, 1847, and had: *Margaret Acton, b. 9 April, 1880.*

IV.—HANNAH CARPENTER, *b.* 1743, *d.* 1820; *m.*, first, 1768, Charles Ellet, of Salem, New Jersey (his second wife), and had by her:

JOHN ELLET, of Salem county, New Jersey, *b.* 1769, *d.* 1824; *m.*, first, 1792, Mary, daughter of William Smith, of Salem, New Jersey, and had by her:

HANNAH CARPENTER ELLET, *b.* 1793, *d.* 1862; *m.*, first, 1813, George Wishart Smith, of Princess Anne county, Virginia, *d.* Philadelphia, Pennsylvania, 1821, and had by him:

CHARLES PERRIN SMITH, of Trenton, New Jersey, *b.* 1819, *d.* 1883; *m.*, 1843, Hester A., daughter of Colonel Matthew Driver, of Caroline county, Maryland, and had: *Ellen Wishart, Charles P., Florence Burman,* and

ELIZABETH ALFORD SMITH, of Trenton, New Jersey, a member of the New Jersey Society of the Colonial Dames of America.

PEDIGREE XXXII.

HENRY III., King of England, 1206–1272; *m.*, 1236, Eleanor of Provence, *d.* 1291, and had by her:

PRINCE EDMUND, Earl of Leicester, Lancaster and Chester, high steward of England, 1245–1295. He had by his second wife, Blanche, widow of Henry I., King of Navarre, *d.* 1274, and daughter of Robert, Earl of Artois, son of **Louis VIII., King of France,** by his wife, Blanche of Castile:

HENRY PLANTAGENET, third Earl of Lancaster, *d.* 1345; *m.* Maud, *b.* 1280, daughter of Patrick de Chaworth, 1253–1282, and had:

LADY ELEANOR PLANTAGENET, widow of John, second Baron Beaumont, *d.* 1342, who *m.*, secondly (his second wife), Sir Richard Fitz-Alan, K.G., ninth Earl of Arundel and seventh Earl of Surrey, *d.* 1375, and had by her:

JOHN FITZ-ALAN, Baron Maltravers, who *m.* Lady Eleanor, the heiress and granddaughter of John, Baron Maltravers, and had:

JOHN FITZ-ALAN, Lord Maltravers, lost at sea, in 1380, who had:

LADY JOAN FITZ-ALAN, *m.* Sir William Echyngham, *d.* 1412, and had:

SIR THOMAS ECHYNGHAM, Knt., *d.* 1444, who had:

THOMAS, Baron Echingham, *d.* 1482, who had:

LADY MARGARET ECHINGHAM, who *m.* William Blount, *d. v. p.*, eldest son of Sir Walter le Blount, K.G., *d.* 1474; treasurer of Calais, 1461; created Lord Montjoy, and his wife, Lady Anne Nevill, also of Royal Descent, and had:

ELIZABETH BLOUNT, who *m.* Sir Andrews, Baron Wyndsore, of Stanwell and Bardsley Abbey, *d.* 1549, also of Royal Descent, and had:

LADY EDITH WYNDSORE, who *m.* George Ludlow, of Hill Deverill, high sheriff of Wiltshire, 1567, *d.* 1580 (*see* Keith's "Ancestry of Benjamin Harrison"), and had:

THOMAS LUDLOW, of Dinton, *d.* 1607, who *m.* Jane, daughter of Thomas Pyle, of Bopton, Wilts, and had:

GABRIEL LUDLOW, *bapt.* 10 February, 1587, called to the Bar, 1620, *d.* 1639; *m.* Phyllis ———, and had:

SARAH LUDLOW, *d.* about 1668, who *m.* (his fourth wife) Colonel John Carter, of "Carotoman," Lancaster county, Virginia, who came to Virginia about 1643, probably from Middlesex, and became a member of the Virginia House of Burgesses from Lower Norfolk county in 1643–44; county justice and a member of the Governor's Council, 1657, d. 10 June, 1669, and had:

COLONEL ROBERT CARTER,* of "Carotoman," 1663–1732, only son by Sarah Ludlow, a member and speaker of the House of Burgesses, 1695–99; treasurer of the Colony, 1704–32, etc. (see Keith's "Ancestry of Benjamin Harrison"). He m., first, 1688, Judith, d. 1699, daughter of John Armistead, of "Hesse," Gloucester county, Virginia, and m., secondly, 1701, Elizabeth, daughter of Thomas Landon, of Middlesex county, Virginia, and widow of ——— Willis. From his wealth and authority in the colony he became known as "King Carter" (see Glenn's "Some Colonial Mansions").

COLONEL ROBERT CARTER had by his first wife:

1.—ELIZABETH CARTER, 1680–1721, who m., first, Nathaniel Burwell, of Gloucester county, Virginia, also of Royal Descent, and had:

I.—LEWIS BURWELL, of "White Marsh," who m. Mary Willis, and had:

REBECCA BURWELL, who m. Jacqueline Ambler, and had:

ANNE AMBLER, who m. George Fisher, and had:

ELIZA JACQUELINE FISHER, who m. Thomas Marshall Colston, and had:

RALEIGH COLSTON, who m. Gertrude Powell, and had:

JANE COLSTON, a member of the Virginia Society of the Colonial Dames of America, who m., 12 September, 1871, Conway Robinson Howard, of Richmond, Virginia, and had: *Mary Eloise*, wife of Francis Elliott Shoup; *Gertrude, Jeanie Colston*, and *Conway Robinson*.

II.—ELIZABETH BURWELL, who m. William Nelson, of Yorktown, president of the Virginia Colony, and had:

---

* The following ladies, members of the National Society of the Colonial Dames of America, are also of Royal Descent through Colonel Robert Carter:

MRS. BENJAMIN O'FALLON, Missouri State Society.
MISS MARGARET GORDON, Maryland State Society.
MRS. R. CURZON HOFFMANN, Maryland State Society.
MRS. THOMAS C. MCLEAN, Maryland State Society.
MISS CARY ANN NICHOLAS, Maryland State Society.
MISS ELIZABETH CARY NICHOLAS, Maryland State Society.
MRS. WILLIAM C. PAGE, Maryland State Society.
MRS. ALEX. B. RANDALL, Maryland State Society.
MISS ANNIE N. SANDERS, Pennsylvania State Society.
MRS. ARTHUR E. POULTNEY, Maryland State Society.

ROBERT NELSON, *m.*, secondly, Susan Robinson, and had by her:

PEYTON RANDOLPH NELSON, *m.* Sally Berkeley Nicolson, also of Royal Descent, and had:

WILLIAM WILMER NELSON, *m.* Sally Browne Catlett, and had:

SALLY BERKELEY NELSON, of Richmond, Virginia, a member of the Virginia Society of the Colonial Dames of America, who *m.* William Todd Robins, Colonel Confederate States Army, and had: *Ruth Nelson, Elizabeth Todd, Augustine Warner, Wilmer Nelson,* and *Sally Berkeley Nicolson.*

III.—CARTER BURWELL, who *m.* Lucy Grymes, and had:

NATHANIEL BURWELL, who *m.* Mrs. Lucy (Page) Baylor, also a descendant of the aforesaid Robert Carter, 1663-1732, and had:

GEORGE H. BURWELL, who *m.* Agnes Atkinson, and had:

ISABELLA DIXON BURWELL, who *m.* Peter H. Mayo, and had:

AGNES ATKINSON MAYO, a member of the Virginia Society of the Colonial Dames of America, who *m.* Thomas Nelson Carter, of Richmond, Virginia, also a descendant of Robert Carter, 1663-1732, aforesaid, and had: *Isabelle Burwell.*

IV.—COLONEL ROBERT CARTER BURWELL, of Isle of Wight county, Virginia, *m.* Sarah Nelson, and had:

FRANCES BURWELL, who *m.* Governor John Page, of " Rosewell," also of Royal Descent, and had:

FRANCES PAGE, who *m.*, secondly, Dr. Carter Berkeley, of " Edgewood," also of Royal Descent, and had:

CATHERINE FRANCES BERKELEY, who *m.* Lucius Horatio Minor, of " Edgewood," also of Royal Descent, and had:

MARY WILLIS MINOR, of Baltimore, a member of the Maryland Society of the Colonial Dames of America.

ELIZABETH CARTER, aforesaid widow of Nathaniel Burwell, *m.*, secondly, Dr. George Nicholas, R. N., of Williamsburg, Virginia, and had:

JUDGE ROBERT CARTER NICHOLAS, of Hanover county, Virginia, 1725-1788, treasurer of Virginia and first presiding judge of the Court of Appeals of Virginia. He *m.* Ann, daughter of Colonel Wilson Cary, of " Rich Neck " and " Ceeleys," and had:

I.—JUDGE PHILIP NARBORNE NICHOLAS, of Richmond, Virginia, who *m.* Maria Carter Byrd, also of Royal Descent, and had:

ELIZABETH BYRD NICHOLAS, of Washington, a member of the District of Columbia Society of the Colonial Dames of America and national treasurer of the General Society, member of the Order of the Crown, *etc.*

II.—JUDGE GEORGE NICHOLAS, of Kentucky, who m. Margaret Smith, of Maryland, and had:

JUDGE SAMUEL SMITH NICHOLAS, of Kentucky, who m. his cousin, Mary M., daughter of General John Spear Smith, of Baltimore, Maryland, and had:

CARY ANNE NICHOLAS, a member of the Virginia Society of the Colonial Dames of America, who m. Rudolph Fink, of Crescent Hill, Jefferson county, Kentucky, a native of Germany, and had: *Albert, Mary Nicholas, Margaret Carter, Henry,* and *Cary.*

III.—WILSON CARY NICHOLAS, of Albemarle county, Virginia, Governor of Virginia and United States Senator from Virginia. He m. Margaret, daughter of General Samuel Smith, of Baltimore, Maryland, and had:

ROBERT CARTER NICHOLAS, of Louisiana, 1793–1856, United States Senator from Louisiana. He m., in 1840, Susan Vinson, of Louisiana, and had:

CAROLINE NICHOLAS, a member of the Virginia Society of the Colonial Dames of America, who m. William Gerald Müller, of "Albemarle Farm," Hammond, Louisiana, and had:

1.—GRETCHEN MÜLLER, who m. Y. L. Bayne, of Alabama, and had: *Y. L., Jr.,* and *William Müller.*

2.—SUE MÜLLER, who m. Harlie Short, of Nebraska, and had: *Harlie, Jr.,* and *Victor Burthe.*

2.—JUDITH CARTER, who m., 1718 (his second wife), Mann Page, of "Rosewell," Gloucester county, Virginia, 1690–1730, and had:

I.—MANN PAGE, b. 1719, member of Congress from Virginia in 1777; m., first, 1743, Alice, daughter of John Grymes, of Middlesex county, Virginia, and had:

JOHN PAGE, of "Rosewell," b. 17 April, 1744, d. 11 October, 1808, Governor of Virginia; m., first, 1765, Frances, daughter of Robert Carter Burwell, of the Isle of Wight county, Virginia, also of Royal Descent, and had by her, who d. 1784:

FRANCES PAGE, b. 1777 (widow of Thomas Nelson, Jr.), who m. secondly, Dr. Carter Berkeley, of "Edgewood," and had:

CATHARINE FRANCES BERKELEY, who m. Lucius Horatio Minor, of "Edgewood," also of Royal Descent, and had:

MARY WILLIS MINOR, of Baltimore, a member of the Maryland Society of the Colonial Dames of America.

II.—ROBERT PAGE, of "Broadneck," m., 20 January, 1750, Sarah Walker, and had:

1.—JOHN PAGE, of "Pagebrook," who m. Maria Horsmanden Byrd, also of Royal Descent, and had:

SARAH WALKER PAGE, who m., 1815, Major Thomas M. Nelson, United States Army, d. 1853, member of Congress from Virginia, 1816–19; a presidential elector, 1829 and 1833, and had:

MARIA BYRD NELSON, who m. William Gray Woolfolk, of Columbus, Georgia, and had:

ROSA WOOLFOLK, a member of the Maryland Society of the Colonial Dames of America, who m. Robert Ober, of Baltimore, and had: *Gustavus* and *Maria Byrd Nelson.*

2.—CATHARINE PAGE, who m. Benjamin C. Waller, and had:

WILLIAM WALLER, of Williamsburg, Virginia, m. Mary Berkeley Griffin, also of Royal Descent, and had:

WILLIAM NEVISON WALLER, of Williamsburg, who m., first, 1 February, 1842, Elizabeth, daughter of John Tyler, President of the United States, and had:

MARY STUART WALLER, a member of the Georgia Society of the Colonial Dames of America, who m., 25 April, 1867, Captain Louis G. Young, of Savannah, Georgia. *No issue.*

3.—JOHN CARTER, of "Carotoman," b. 1690, secretary of the Virginia Colony, 1722; member of the Council, 1726, *etc.*, d. 30 April, 1743, who m., 1723, Elizabeth, daughter of Colonel Edward Hill, of "Shirley," Charles City county, Virginia, and had:

I.—EDWARD CARTER, of "Blenheim," Albemarle county, Virginia, member of the House of Delegates, *etc.*, who m. Sarah, daughter of Colonel John Champe, of Fredericksburg, Virginia, and had:

1.—ROBERT CARTER, of "Redlands," who m. Mary, daughter of John Coles, of Albemarle county, and had:

ROBERT HILL CARTER, of "Redlands," who m. Margaret, daughter of General John Spear Smith, of Baltimore, Maryland, and had:

MARY COLES CARTER, of St. Timothy's, Catonsville, Baltimore county, Maryland, a member of the Maryland Society of the Colonial Dames of America.

2.—ELIZABETH CARTER, who m. William Stanard, of Roxbury, Charles City county, Virginia, and had:

VIRGINIA STANARD, who m. (his second wife) Samuel Slaughter, of Culpeper county, Virginia, and had:

COLUMBIA SLAUGHTER, who m. William Green, LL.D., of Richmond, Virginia, and had:

ELIZABETH TRAVERS GREEN, who m. James Hayes, of Richmond, Virginia, and had:

ANNE SOMERVILLE HAYES, a member of the Kentucky Society of the Colonial Dames of America, who m., 31 March, 1891, Urban Ewing Eaches, of Louisville, Kentucky, also of Royal Descent, and had: *Katharine Moore Ewing* and *Elizabeth Travers Green.*

3.—JANE CARTER, who m., first, Samuel Kellett Bradford, of Virginia, and had:

SAMUEL KELLETT BRADFORD, JR., of Culpeper county, Virginia, m., 27 July, 1816, Emily, daughter of Samuel Slaughter, of Culpeper, by his first wife, Miss Banks, and had:

LOUISA M. BRADFORD, who m., August, 1842, General Horatio G. Wright, United States Army, and had:

MARY HILL WRIGHT, of New York City, a member of the New York Society of the Colonial Dames of America, who m., 21 February, 1867, Edwin H. Wootton, of Kent county, England, and had: *Hubert Wright, Mary Isabel,* wife of Charles H. Richardson, and *Moray Nairne.*

II.—CHARLES CARTER, of "Shirley," 1732–1806, who m., first, 1756, his cousin, Mary Walker, daughter of Colonel Charles Carter, of "Cleve" (and his first wife, Mary Walker), son of Colonel Robert Carter, 1663–1732, aforesaid, and his second wife, Mrs. Elizabeth (Landon) Willis, and had:

ELIZABETH HILL CARTER, 1764–1832, who m. Colonel Robert Randolph, of "Eastern View," Fauquier county, Virginia, 1760–1825, also of Royal Descent, and had:

CAPTAIN CHARLES CARTER RANDOLPH, of "The Grove," who m. Mary Ann Fauntleroy Mortimer, of Fredericksburg, Virginia, and had:

LANDONIA RANDOLPH, who m. Robert Dabney Minor, United States Navy, of Fredericksburg, Virginia, and had:

LANDONIA RANDOLPH MINOR, a member of the Virginia Society of the Colonial Dames of America, who m. William Sparrow Dashiell, of Richmond, Virginia, and had: *Robert Minor* and *Thomas Grayson.*

PEDIGREE XXXIII.

LOUIS VIII., King of France, had by his wife, Princess Blanche of Castile, also of Royal Descent:

ROBERT, COUNT OF ARTOIS, third son, k. 1247, who m., 1237, Matilda, d. 1249, daughter of Henry, Duke of Brabant, and his wife, m., 1207, Mary, d. 1239, daughter of Philip of Swabia, Emperor of Germany, d. 1208, and had:

LADY BLANCHE, of Artois, widow of Henry, King of Navarre, d. 1274, who m., secondly, Edmund Plantagenet, Earl of Leicester, Lancaster, and Chester; lord high steward of England, son of Henry III., King of England, 1245-1295, and had:

HENRY PLANTAGENET, third Earl of Leicester, d. 1345, who m. Lady Maud, b. 1280, daughter of Sir Patrick de Chaworth, 1253-1282, and his wife, Isabel, daughter of William de Beauchamp, first Earl of Warwick, and had:

LADY ELEANOR PLANTAGENET, widow of John, second Baron Beaumont, who m., secondly (his second wife), Sir Richard Fitz-Alan, K.G., ninth Earl of Arundel and seventh Earl of Surrey, d. 1375, and had:

JOHN FITZ-ALAN, Lord Maltravers, second son, who m. Lady Eleanor, granddaughter and heiress of John, Lord Maltravers, and had:

JOHN FITZ-ALAN, eldest son, d. v. p., who had by his second wife, Katherine, widow of William Stafford, of Frome, and daughter and co-heir of Sir John Chideock, heir to the barony of Fitz-Payne:

"SIR THOMAS ARUNDEL, alias FITZ-ALAN," Knt. (brother of John, Earl of Arundel), his will, 3 October, 1485, given on p. 378, Nichols' "Testamenta Vetusta," who had by his wife, Katherine, daughter of Sir John Dynham, and sister and co-heiress of Sir John, Baron Dynham, K.G.:

LADY ELEANOR FITZ-ALAN, who m. Sir Thomas Browne, Knt., treasurer of the household to King Henry VI., and had:

SIR GEORGE BROWNE, Knt., of Beechworth Castle, county Surrey, second son, who had:

SIMON BROWNE, of Browne Hall, Lancastershire, who had:

THOMAS BROWNE, of Brandon, d. 1 May, 1608, who had by Margaret, his wife, who d. 1 May, 1605:

FRANCIS BROWNE, of Weybird Hall, Brandon, county Suffolk, d. 9 May, 1626, who had:

WILLIAM BROWNE, b. 1608, who came from London, where he was a member of the Fishmongers' Company, to Salem, Massachusetts, in 1634-5. He m., first, in London, Mary, d. 1635, sister of Rev. Mr. Young, of Long Island, New York, and m., secondly, Sarah, daughter of Samuel Smith, of Yarmouth, and d. 25 January, 1687, leaving issue by his second wife:

MAJOR WILLIAM BROWNE,* of Salem, Massachusetts, d. 1716; member of Governor Andros's council and of the council of safety (*see* Salisbury's "Genealogies," Savage's "Genealogical Dictionary," and the *American Heraldic Journal*, vol. ii). He m., first, Hannah, daughter of George Curwen, and had:

1.—COLONEL SAMUEL BROWNE, of Salem, d. 1731; justice of court of common pleas, member of His Majesty's council, who m., secondly, 1705, Abigail, daughter of John Keatch, of Bristol, England, and had:

WILLIAM BROWNE, of Beverley, Massachusetts, 1709-1763, who m., 14 November, 1737, Mary, daughter by his second wife of William Burnet (son of Rt. Rev. Bishop Gilbert Burnet), Provincial Governor of New York and Massachusetts, and had:

WILLIAM BURNET BROWNE, of "Elsing Green," King William county, Virginia, b. 7 October, 1738, who m., first, Judith Frances Carter, of "Cleve," also of Royal Descent, and had Betty Carter, Judith Walker, and

MARY BURNET BROWNE, who m. (his second wife) Herbert Claiborne, of "Chestnut Grove," New Kent county, Virginia, b. 1746, also of Royal Descent, and had:

HERBERT AUGUSTINE CLAIBORNE, 1784-1841; m. Delia, daughter of James Hayes, of Richmond, Virginia, and had:

MAJOR JOHN HAYES CLAIBORNE, of Richmond, Virginia, who m. Anna Virginia, daughter of George W. Bassett, of "Eltham," New Kent county, Virginia, son of John Bassett (also of Royal Descent) and his wife, Betty Carter, daughter of the aforesaid William Burnet Browne, and had:

DELIA CLAIBORNE, a member of the Virginia Society of the Colonial Dames of America, who m., 10 June, 1885, Simon Bolivar Buckner, of "Glen Lily," Hart county, Kentucky, Lieutenant-General Confederate States Army, Governor of Kentucky, *etc.*, and had: *Simon Bolivar*, b. 18 July, 1886.

2.—MARY BROWNE, who m., 1699, Chief Justice Benjamin Lynde, of Salem, Massachusetts, 1665-1744, also of Royal Descent, and had:

* MRS. LEWIS W. WASHINGTON (deceased), a member of the National Society of the Colonial Dames of America, was also of Royal Descent through Major William Browne.

PEDIGREE XXXIII.—Continued.

CHIEF JUSTICE BENJAMIN LYNDE, JR., of Salem, 1700–1781, who *m.* Mary Goodrich Bowles, and had:

LYDIA LYNDE, who *m.* Rev. William Walter, and had:

HARRIET LYNDE WALTER, who *m.* John Odin, and had:

ESTHER ODIN, who *m.* Rev. Benjamin Dorr, D.D., and had:

1.—MARY WARREN DORR, a member of the Pennsylvania Society of the Colonial Dames of America, who *m.* William L. Schäffer, of Philadelphia.

2.—HARRIET ODIN DORR (deceased), a member of the Pennsylvania Society of the Colonial Dames of America, who *m.* Major James Edward Carpenter, of Philadelphia, also of Royal Descent. *Issue.*

3.—ESTHER ODIN DORR, a member of the Pennsylvania Society of the Colonial Dames of America, who *m.* William Hewitt Webb, of Philadelphia, and had:

ANNE GRISCOM WEBB, a member of the Pennsylvania Society of the Colonial Dames of America, who *m.* Albert Ripley Leeds, of Hoboken, N. J.

THE ROYAL DESCENTS

OF

MRS. WILLIAM D. BETHELL,

AND

MRS. JOHN M. GRAY.

EDWARD I., King of England=Princess Eleanor of Castile.
    Princess Joan Plantagenet=Gilbert de Clare, Earl of Gloucester and Hereford.
        Lady Margaret de Clare=Hugh de Audley, Earl of Gloucester.
           Lady Margaret de Audley=Sir Ralph de Stafford, K. G., Earl of Stafford.
Sir Hugh de Stafford, K. G., Earl of Stafford=Lady Philippa de Beauchamp.
           Lady Margaret de Stafford=Sir Ralph de Neville, K. G., Earl of Westmoreland.
Ralph de Neville, of Oversley, Warwickshire=Lady Mary de Ferrers.
  John de Neville, of Wymersley, Yorkshire=Lady Elizabeth de Newmarch.
           Joan de Neville=Sir William Gascoigne, of Gawthrope, Yorkshire.
Sir William Gascoigne, of Gawthrope, York=Lady Margaret de Percy.
         Lady Elizabeth Gascoigne=Gilbert de Talboys, of Kyme.
        Sir George de Talboys, of Kyme=(Name unknown.)
          Lady Anne de Talboys=Sir Edward Dymoke, of Scrivelsby, Lincolnshire.
           Lady Frances Dymoke=Thomas Windebank, of Haines Hill, Berkshire.
            Mildred Windebank=Robert Reade, Linkenholt Manor, Southampton.
Col. George Reade, of Gloucester Co., Va.=Elizabeth Martian.
           Mildred Reade=Col. Augustine Warner, Jr., of "Warner's Hall."
          Elizabeth Warner=Col. John Lewis, Gloucester Co., Va.
        Col. Charles Lewis=Mary Howell.
          Anne Lewis=Edmund Taylor, Caroline Co., Va.
        Francis Taylor=Rev. Nathaniel Moore, Granville Co., N. C.
       Anne Lewis Moore=Edward Washington Dale, Columbia, Tenn.
         Elvira H. Dale=Jerome Bonaparte Pillow, of Tenn.

Cynthia Pillow=William Decatur Bethell,   Elvira Pillow=John Maffitt Gray,
         of Denver, Col.   of Nashville, Tenn.

Bessie=Dr. John M.   Jennie=John P.   William D.=Helen   Annie=Dr. J. W.   John M.   Rebecca
Bethell. | Foster.   Bethell. | Edrington.   Bethell. | Worden.   Gray. | Madden.   Gray. | Wilson.

Bethell Pinckney   John M.   Bethell   Cynthia   John P.   William D.   Charles W.   Annie G.   Rebecca
Foster.   Foster.   Foster.   Edrington. Edrington. Edrington.   Bethell.   Bethell.   Madden.   Gray.

PEDIGREE XXXIV.

HENRY I., King of France, *m.* Anne, daughter of Jaroslaus, Grand Duke or Czar of Russia, 1015–1051, and had:

HUGH THE GREAT, Duke of France and Burgundy, Count de Vermandois, who *m.*, thirdly, 938, Lady Adelheid, 1080–1117, daughter of Herbert, fourth Count de Vermandois and Troyes, 1045–1080, also of Royal Descent (*see* Anderson's "Royal Genealogies"), and had:

LADY ISABEL DE VERMANDOIS, *d.* 1131 (*see* Planche's "The Conqueror and His Companions" for a sketch of this lady), who *m.*, first, Robert de Beaumont, first Baron de Bellomont by tenure, and Earl of Mellent, created Earl of Leicester, and had by him, who *d.* 1118:

ROBERT-BOSSU DE BELLOMONT, second Earl of Leicester, lord justice of England, *d.* 1168, who *m.* Lady Amicia, daughter of Ralph de Waer, Earl of Norfolk, Suffolk and Cambridge, and had:

GERVASE PAGANEL, Baron of Dudley, Staffordshire, who *m.* Lady Felice, daughter and heiress of Athelstan Dodo, son of Geoffrey, son of Athelstan Dodo, who built Dudley Castle, and had:

LADY HAWYSE PAGANEL, Baroness of Dudley, heiress, who *m.* John de Someri, in Cambridge, Baron of Dudley, in right of his wife, and had:

RALPH DE SOMERI, Baron of Dudley, eldest son, *d.* 1210, who *m.* Margaret ———, and had:

WILLIAM PERCEVAL DE SOMERI, Baron of Dudley, eldest son, *d.* 1221, who had:

ROGER DE SOMERI, second son, *d.* 1272, who *m.*, secondly, Lady Amabel, daughter of Robert de Chaucumbe, and widow of Gilbert, third Baron de Segrave, who *d.* 1254, and had by her:

LADY MARGARET DE SOMERI (widow of Urian St. Pierre), who *m.*, secondly, Ralph Baron Basset, lord of Drayton, Staffordshire (a grandson of Richard Basset, justice of England, son of Ralph Basset, justice of England, *d.* 1120), and had:

RALPH, BARON BASSET, of Drayton, who *m.* either Lady Joan, daughter of John de Grey, justice of Chester, *d.* 1265 (*see* Burke), or Lady Joan, daughter of Reginald de Grey, *d.* 1308, son of John, the justice of Chester (*see* Dugdale), and had:

SIR RALPH, BARON BASSET, of Drayton, K.B., *d.* 1343, who *m.* Lady

Joan, daughter of Thomas Beauchamp, third Earl of Warwick, also of Royal Descent, and had:

LADY JANE BASSET, who m. John de Stourton, of Preston, Wilts, d. 1364, and had:

WILLIAM DE STOURTON, steward of Wales in 1402, who m. Elizabeth, daughter of John Moyne (or Moigne), of Moddenton, Wilts, and had:

SIR JOHN DE STOURTON, created Baron Stourton in 1448, d. 1462, who m. Lady Margery, daughter of Sir John Wadham, of Merrifield, Somerset, and had:

WILLIAM, SECOND BARON STOURTON, d. 1478, who m. Lady Margaret, daughter of Sir John Chidoke, or Chidiock, also of Royal Descent, and had:

LADY JOAN DE STOURTON, who m. Tristram Fauntleroy, of Mitchell's Marsh, Hants, (see Dugdale's "Baronage"), will dated 25 July, 1539, d. 1539 (son of John Fauntleroy, of The Marsh, at Alvestop, Dorset, and brother of Agnes Fauntleroy, wife of Edward, fifth Lord Stourton, d. 1536 (see Wallace's "Historical Magazine," July, 1891; Hutchin's "Dorsetshire,"), and had:

JOHN FAUNTLEROY, of Crandall, Hampshire, d. February, 1598, who m. Margaret ——, d. April, 1613, and had:

WILLIAM FAUNTLEROY, of Crandall, d. February, 1625, who m. Frances ——, bur. at Hedley, in 1638, and had:

JOHN FAUNTLEROY, of Crandall and Hedley, Hampshire, only son, bapt. at Crandall, 3 January, 1588; bur. at Hedley, 11 March, 1644; m., at Hedley, 5 September, 1609, Phœbe Wilkinson, bur. at Hedley, 29 September, 1629, and had:

COLONEL MOORE FAUNTLEROY,* second son, came to Virginia and had grant of land in Upper Norfolk in 1643. He had a confirmation of arms issued to him, 1633, by Borough, Garter King at Arms; he was an extensive land-owner in Virginia, and a burgess, 1644–1659, and justice of Rappahannock county (see an account of him and family in "Virginia Historical Magazine," July, 1891). He m., first, in England, 26 December, 1639, Dorothy, daughter of Thomas Colle, of Liss, Hampshire, and m., secondly, in Virginia, Mary Hill, marriage contract dated 1648. He d. before 1665, having issue by second wife:

---

* The following ladies, members of the National Society of the Colonial Dames of America, are also of Royal Descent through Moore Fauntleroy:

MRS. THOMAS F. SCREVEN, Georgia State Society.

MRS. WILLIAM W. GORDON, JR., Georgia State Society.

MISS FRANCES M. SCOTT, Arkansas State Society.

MISS LIZZIE C. MILLER, North Carolina State Society.

COLONEL WILLIAM FAUNTLEROY, of Rappahannock county, Virginia, a county justice, 1680-95, who *m.*, 1680, Katharine (will proved 1728), daughter of Colonel Samuel Griffin, of Northumberland county, Virginia, and had:

1.—COLONEL MOORE FAUNTLEROY, of Richmond county, Virginia, *d.* 1739, who *m.* Margaret, daughter of Paul Micou, of "Port Micou," Essex county, Virginia, and had:

I.—JUDITH FAUNTLEROY, who *m.* Landon Carter, of Pittsylvania county, Virginia, also of Royal Descent, and had:

WORMLEY CARTER, who *m.* Sarah Edwards, and had:

WORMLEY CARTER, who *m.* Lucinda Washington Alexander, and had:

JUDGE WILLIAM ALEXANDER CARTER, 1818-1881, who *m.*, 1848, Mary Eliza Hamilton, and had:

MARY ADA CARTER, a member of the Pennsylvania Society of the Colonial Dames of America, who *m.*, 1874, Joseph K. Corson, M.D., surgeon United States Army, also of Royal Descent, and had: *Mary Carter*, *b.* 1876, *d.* 1890, and *Edward Foulke*, *b.* 1883.

II.—ELIZABETH FAUNTLEROY, who *m.* Colonel William Brockenbrough, of Richmond county, and had:

JOHN BROCKENBROUGH, M.D., a signer of the Westmoreland Association, who *m.* Sarah, daughter of William Roane, and had:

JUDGE WILLIAM BROCKENBROUGH, of the Virginia Court of Appeals, who *m.* Judith, daughter of Rev. John White and his wife, Mary Braxton, also of Royal Descent, and had:

SARAH JANE BROCKENBROUGH, who *m.* Colonel Edward Colston, of Berkeley county, Virginia, and had:

ELIZABETH MARSHALL COLSTON, who *m.* R. Alfred Williams, of Richmond, Virginia, and had:

ROSALIE BELL WILLIAMS, a member of the Maryland Society of the Colonial Dames of America, who *m.* William C. Page, of Baltimore, and had: *Rosalie Braxton*, *Ellen West*, and *Virginia Dandridge*.

2.—COLONEL WILLIAM FAUNTLEROY, of "Naylor's Hole," Richmond county, Virginia, *b.* 1684, burgess, 1736-1772; *m.* Apphia, daughter of John Bushrod, of Westmoreland county, Virginia, and had:

COLONEL WILLIAM FAUNTLEROY, of "Naylor's Hole," 1713-1793, who had by his second wife, Margaret, daughter of Jeremiah Murdock, a justice in King George county, Virginia, 1728-1752:

I.—JOSEPH FAUNTLEROY, of "Greenville," Frederick (Clark) county, Virginia, 1754-1815; *m.* Elizabeth Foushee, daughter of Bushrod Fauntleroy, and had:

ROBERT HENRY FAUNTLEROY, 1807–1850, United States Coast Survey; m. Jane Dale, daughter of Robert Owen, of New Harmony, Indiana, and had:

ELEANOR FAUNTLEROY, a member of the California Society of the Colonial Dames of America, who m. Professor George Davidson, of United States Coast Survey.

II.—JOHN FAUNTLEROY, of Richmond county, Virginia, 1745–1798; a member of the House of Delegates, 1784, who m. Judith, widow of Leroy Griffin, a daughter of Colonel James and Lettice (Lee) Ball, of "Bewdley," and had:

LETTICE LEE FAUNTLEROY, d. 1820, who m. Austin Brockenbrough, M.D., of Richmond county, Virginia, and had:

COLONEL JOHN FAUNTLEROY BROCKENBROUGH, d. 1865, who m. Frances Ann Carter, and had:

ELLA BROCKENBROUGH, who m. John Watrus Beckwith, and had:

ELLA STANLEY BECKWITH, a member of the Georgia Society of the Colonial Dames of America, who m. Alexander Rudolf Lawton, of Savannah, and had: *Alexander Rudolf* and *John Beckwith.*

PEDIGREE XXXV.

EDWARD III., King of England, *m.*, 1327, Lady Philippa, daughter of William, Count of Hainault and Holland, and his wife, Joanna, daughter of Charles de Valois, younger son of **Philip III., King of France,** and had:

EDMUND PLANTAGENET, Earl of Cambridge and Duke of York, who *m.*, first, Lady Isabel, daughter of **Peter, King of Castile and Leon,** and had by her:

RICHARD PLANTAGENET, Earl of Cambridge, beheaded in 1415, who *m.* Lady Anne, daughter of Edward de Mortimer, Earl of March, and his wife, Lady Philippa, daughter of Lionel, Duke of Clarence, second son of **Edward III., King of England,** and had:

RICHARD PLANTAGENET, Earl of Cambridge and Duke of York, the Protector, starter of the War of Roses, *k.* in the final battle of Wakefield, 1460. He *m.* Lady Cecily, daughter of Ralph de Nevill, Earl of Westmoreland, also of Royal Descent, and had:

SIR GEORGE PLANTAGENET, K.G., Duke of Clarence (brother of Kings Richard III. and Edward IV., father of King Edward V. and Richard, Duke of York, both murdered in the Tower of London, and Elizabeth, consort of King Henry VII.), who *m.* Lady Isabel de Nevill, daughter of Richard, Earl of Salisbury and Warwick, also of Royal Descent (her sister, Anne, *m.*, first, Edward, only son of King Henry VII., and *m.*, secondly, King Richard III.). He was attainted of treason and drowned in a butt of Malmsey wine in the Tower of London, in 1477, and his honors were forfeited. His only daughter:

LADY MARGARET PLANTAGENET, Countess of Salisbury, beheaded for high treason, when 72 years old, 27 May, 1541 (sister of Edward, " the last of the Plantagenets," who was executed in 1499 on London Tower Hill), *m.* Sir Richard Pole, K.G., and had:

SIR HENRY POLE, first Lord Montagu, beheaded in 1539, on London Tower Hill, for high treason. He *m.* Lady Jean, daughter of George Neville, Lord Abergavenny, also of Royal Descent, and had:

LADY KATHERINE POLE, who *m.* Sir Francis Hastings, K.G., second Earl of Huntingdon, also of Royal Descent, and had:

LADY CATHERINE HASTINGS, who *m.* Sir Henry, tenth Baron Clinton, K.B., second Earl of Lincoln, also of Royal Descent, and had:

THOMAS CLINTON, third Earl of Lincoln, d. 15 January, 1619; m. Elizabeth, daughter of Henry Knyvett, of Charlton, Wilts, and had:

LADY SUSAN CLINTON, who m. " John Humfrey, Esq.," 1595-1661, a lawyer, of Dorchester, in Dorsetshire. Mr. Humfrey was one of the six gentlemen to whom the council of Plymouth, England, in March, 1627-8, sold that part of New England " between three miles north of the Merrimac and three miles south of the Charles," for the Massachusetts Bay Company, of London; John Winthrop, Governor, and John Humfrey, Deputy-Governor. Mr. Humphrey came to New England, with Lady Susan, in July, 1634, and made his home on his farm of five hundred acres at Swampscott (Lynn), Massachusetts, and entered upon his duties as assistant, and was one of the founders of Lynn. In 1640 he was a member of the Ancient and Honorable Artillery Company; in 1641 was appointed to the command of the militia with the rank of Sergeant Major-General. He and his wife, Lady Susan, returned to Sandwich, Kent, England, 26 October, 1641, having sold his farm to Lady Deborah Moody. Their daughter:

ANNE HUMPHREY, b. 1621, who m., first, at Salem, Massachusetts, William Palmer (or Palmes?), of Ardfinan, in Ireland, and had:

SUSAN PALMER, b. 1665 (" New England Historical Genealogical Register, vol. xxxi., p. 307), who m. Samuel Avery, of New London, Connecticut, d. 1 May, 1723, son of Captain James Avery, 1620-1700, from whom are descended:

1.—ALICE GERRY, a member of the Maryland Society of the Colonial Dames of America, who m. David Stewart, of Baltimore.

2.—CLARA JENNESS, a member of the Maryland Society of the Colonial Dames of America, who m. W. T. Hamilton, of Hagerstown.

ANNE HUMPHREY m., secondly, Rev. John Myles, a pioneer Baptist, who was driven away from Swansea and took refuge in New England, in 1663, and in 1670 was one of the founders of Swansea, Massachusetts, and d. in 1683, aged 62 years. Their descendant:

ESTHER SLACK DARLING, m. Captain Nathan Arnold, of Cumberland, Rhode Island, who died from wounds and exposure after the battle of Rhode Island, 29 August, 1778, also of Royal Descent, (p. 18), and had:

SETH ARNOLD, of Smithfield, Rhode Island, who m. Belinda Mason Streeter, daughter of Jonathan and Patience (Mason) Mason, and a descendant of Roger Williams, the founder of Rhode Island, and had:

FRANCES ESTHER ARNOLD, 1820-1896, who m., 1 August, 1837, William Henry Hatheway, of Dighton, Massachusetts, 1814-1875, and had:

BELINDA OLNEY HATHEWAY, a member of the Rhode Island Society of the Colonial Dames of America, the Order of the Crown, *etc.*, who m. Joshua Wilbour, of Bristol, Rhode Island, United States Consul at Dublin. *No issue.*

PEDIGREE XXXVI.

Henry I., King of France, had by his third wife, Anne of Russia:

HUGH THE GREAT, Duke of France and Burgundy, Marquis of Orleans, and Count of Paris and Vermandois, who m., thirdly, 938, Lady Adelheid, daughter of Herbert, Count of Vermandois, and had by her:

LADY ISABEL DE VERMANDOIS, who m., first, Robert, Earl of Mellent, first Baron de Bellomont, created Earl of Leicester, and had:

ROBERT DE BELLOMONT, second Earl of Leicester, justiciary of England, d. 1168, who had by his wife, Lady Amicia, daughter of Ralph de Waer, Earl of Norfolk:

ROBERT DE BELLOMONT, third Earl of Leicester, high steward of England, d. 1190, who had by his wife, Lady Petronella, daughter of Hugh Grentemaisnill, high steward of England:

LADY MARGARET DE BELLOMONT, who m. Saier de Quincey, created, 1207, Earl of Winchester, d. 1219 (see "The Magna Charta Barons and their American Descendants"), and had:

ROGER DE QUINCEY, second Earl of Winchester, constable of Scotland, d. 1264, who m. Lady Helen, daughter of Alan McDonal, Lord of Galloway, also of Royal Descent, and had:

LADY ELIZABETH DE QUINCEY, who m. Alexander, Baron Cumyn, second Earl of Buchan, d. 1289, also of Royal Descent, and had:

LADY AGNES CUMYN, who m. (see Wood's Douglas's "Peerage of Scotland," i., 62, and Dugdale's "Baronage of England," i., 504) Gilbert de Umfraville, eighth Earl of Angus, d. 1307-8, and had:

ROBERT DE UMFRAVILLE, ninth Earl of Angus, 1274-1326, who had by his second wife, Lady Alianore:

SIR THOMAS DE UMFRAVILLE, of Harbottle Castle, Northumberland, second son, who m. Joane, daughter of Adam de Rodam, of Northumberland, and had:

SIR THOMAS DE UMFRAVILLE, Lord of Riddesdale and Kyme, second son, who had by his wife, Lady Agnes:

LADY JOANE DE UMFRAVILLE (sister of Gilbert d'Umfraville, titular Earl of Kyme, k. 1422), who m. Sir William Lambert, of Owlton, Durham, and Harbottle, Northumberland (see Douglas's "Peerage of Scotland," i., 64, 456; Burke's "Dictionary of the Peerage"), also of Royal Descent, and had:

ROBERT LAMBERT, of Owlton (or Owton), father of:

HENRY LAMBERT, of Ongar, Essex, living in 1447, who had:

ELIZABETH LAMBERT, heiress, who m., about 1488, Thomas Lyman, of Navistoke, Essex, d. 1509, son of John Lyman, a London merchant, who purchased the estate of Navistoke, and had:

HENRY LYMAN, of Navistoke and High Ongar, Essex, 1517, who m. Alicia, daughter of Simon Hyde, of Westersfield, Essex, and had:

JOHN LYMAN, of High Ongar, eldest son, d. 1587, at Navistoke, who had by his wife, Margaret, daughter of William Gérard, of Beauchamp, St Paul, Essex:

HENRY LYMAN, of High Ongar, eldest son, d. 1609, who m., secondly, Phillis, daughter of John Scott, of Navistoke, and had by her, who was living, widow of Ralph Green, of High Ongar, in 1629:

RICHARD LYMAN,* bapt. 20 October, 1580, at High Ongar, came to Charlestown, Massachusetts, in 1631, and d. August, 1640, at Hartford, Connecticut, of which he was one of the original proprietors. He m., before 1617, Sarah Osborne, b. Halsted, Kent, d. Hartford, 1640, and had:

1.—RICHARD LYMAN, d. at Northampton, Massachusetts, 3 June, 1662: m. Hepzibah, daughter of Thomas Ford, and had:

JOHN LYMAN, b. 1655, d. Northampton, 13 October, 1727; m., December, 1694, Abigail, daughter of John Holton, and had:

ABNER LYMAN, of Northampton, b. 1 February, 1701, d. 25 January, 1774; m., 3 May, 1739, Sarah, b. 11 January, 1708, daughter of Ichabod Allis, and widow of Joseph Miller, and had:

SARAH LYMAN, b. 11 April, 1740; m., 7 December, 1758, Joseph Allen, b. at Northampton, 12 October, 1735, d. at Charlotte, Vermont, 17 June, 1810, and had:

EUNICE ALLEN, b. 25 February, 1775, at Pittsfield, Massachusetts, d. 19 July, 1843, at Pittsford, Vermont, who m., 1791, Remembrance Hitchcock, of Pittsford, Vermont, b. 1770, d. 17 August, 1849, and had:

---

* The following ladies, members of the National Society of the Colonial Dames of America, are also of Royal Descent through Richard Lyman:

MRS. CHARLES H. ANSON, Massachusetts State Society.
MISS AMELIA DE PAU FOWLER, Maryland State Society.
MISS BESSIE H. LYMAN, Massachusetts State Society.
MISS EMILY R. LYMAN, Pennsylvania State Society.
MRS. CHARLES H. BURBANK, New Hampshire State Society.
MRS. GEORGE W. CROCKETT, Massachusetts State Society.
MRS. ROBERT P. LISLE, Pennsylvania State Society.

HENRY HITCHCOCK, of Rutland, Vermont, b. Pittsford, 22 August, 1805, d. 28 August, 1871; m., 23 June, 1837, Hannah Lucy Hulett, also of Royal Descent, and had:

ABIGAIL JANE HITCHCOCK, b. at Clarendon Springs, Vermont, 3 May, 1843, a member of the Massachusetts Society of the Colonial Dames of America, of the Order of the Crown, etc., who m., 15 February, 1866, Horace Hoxie Dyer, of Rutland, Vermont, and had: *Horace Edward*, b. 16 April, 1870; m. 6 December, 1893.

2.—LIEUTENANT JOHN LYMAN, of Northampton, Massachusetts, b. High Ongar, 16 September, 1623, d. 20 August, 1690; m., 12 January, 1655, Dorcas, daughter of John Plum, of Branford, Connecticut, d. 1648, and had:

I.—MOSES LYMAN, of Northampton, b. 20 February, 1662-3, d. 25 February, 1701; m. Ann ——, and had:

1.—MARY LYMAN, d. 18 January, 1776, who m., 18 June, 1719, Captain Samuel Dwight ("Dwight Genealogy," i., pp. 272-288, and "Lyman Genealogy," pp. 33, 318, etc.), and had:

MARY DWIGHT, b. 2 March, 1721, d. 21 January, 1809; m., March, 1738, Daniel Hall, Jr., of Middletown, Connecticut, and had:

MARY HALL, b. 3 November 1742, d. 10 January, 1833; m., 3 December, 1765, Judge Eliphalet Terry ("Terry Genealogy," pp. 10-38), and had:

ELIPHALET TERRY, of Hartford, Connecticut, b. 26 December, 1776, d. 8 July, 1849; m., 5 June, 1817, Lydia Coit ("Coit Genealogy," p. 131), and had:

MARY HALL TERRY, b. 3 June, 1820, a member of the New York Society of the Colonial Dames of America, the Order of the Crown, etc., who m., 1 September, 1840, Charles Collins, b. 2 April, 1817, d. 30 November, 1891, also of Royal Descent (see p. 152), and had:

I.—LYDIA COIT COLLINS, a member of the New York Society of the Colonial Dames of America, who m., 8 June, 1864, William Platt Ketcham, of New York, and had:

1.—ARTHUR COLLINS KETCHAM, m., 7 April, 1890, Bruce Allen, and had: 1. *William Tredwell*, b. 27 February, 1891; *Margaret Bruce*, b. 25 February, 1892; and *Archer Collins*, b. 5 April, 1893.

2.—MARY VAN WINKLE KETCHAM, m., 1 December, 1890, Thomas Hunt Talmadge, d. 29 November, 1895, and had: *Thomas Hunt*, b. 9 December, 1894, and *Lillian*, b. 3 April, 1896.

3.—ETHEL MIRIAM KETCHAM, unm.

II.—CLARENCE LYMAN COLLINS, of New York, a member of the Society of the Colonial Wars, *etc.*, who *m.* Marie Louise, daughter of Horace F. Clark, and his wife, Marie Louise, daughter of Commodore Cornelius Vanderbilt, of New York, and had:

> EDITH LYMAN COLLINS, Comtesse Czaykowska, a member of the Order of the Crown, who *m.*, in Paris, France, 7 January, 1897, Richid Bey, Comte Czaykowska, councillor of State and first secretary to the Turkish embassy at Rome, and had:
>
>> 1.—COUNT VLADIMIR CLARENCE LADISLAS MICHEL, *b.* at Rome, 10 October, 1897.
>>
>> 2.—CHEVALIER STANISLUS MICHEL FREDERIC MARIE, *b.* at The Hague, 20 June, 1899.

III.—LOUISE TERRY COLLINS, a member of New York Society of the Colonial Dames of America, the Order of the Crown, *etc.*, who *m.*, 4 October, 1884, William Allen Butler, Jr., of New York, and had:

> 1.—WILLIAM ALLEN BUTLER, 3D, *b.* 7 January, 1886.
>
> 2.—LYMAN COLLINS BUTLER, *b.* 2 January, 1888.
>
> 3.—CHARLES TERRY BUTLER, *b.* 20 September, 1889.
>
> 4.—LYDIA COIT BUTLER, *b.* 19 November, 1891.
>
> 5.—LOUISE TRACY BUTLER, *b.* 23 October, 1894.

2.—CAPTAIN MOSES LYMAN, of Northampton, *b.* 27 February, 1689, *d.* 24 March, 1762; *m.*, 13 December, 1712, Mindwell Sheldon, 1692–1780, and had:

1.—REV. ISAAC LYMAN, of York, Maine, *b.* 25. February, 1724–25, *d.* 1810; *m.*, 24 April, 1750, Ruth Plummer, of Gloucester, Massachusetts, 1730–1824, and had:

> THEODORE LYMAN, of Boston, *b.* 8 January, 1755, *d.* Waltham, Massachusetts, 24 May, 1839; *m.*, secondly, 24 January, 1786, Lydia Williams, of Marlboro, Massachusetts, and had by her:
>
> GEORGE WILLIAM LYMAN, of Waltham, Massachusetts, *b.* 4 December, 1786. He *m.*, first, 31 May, 1810, Elizabeth Gray, 1791–1824, daughter of Harrison Gray Otis, of Boston, and had:
>
>> GEORGE THEODORE LYMAN, of Bellport, Long Island, *b.* 23 December, 1821; *m.*, 17 April, 1845, Sally, *b.* 4 October, 1825, daughter of James W. Otis, of New York, and had:
>>
>>> ALICE LYMAN, *b.* 14 January, 1852, a member of the Pennsylvania Society of the Colonial Dames of America, who *m.* William Platt Pepper, of Philadelphia.

GEORGE WILLIAMS LYMAN, m., secondly, 3 May, 1827, Anne, b. 9 May, 1798, daughter of William Pratt, of Boston, and had:

SARAH PRATT LYMAN, b. 5 February, 1835, a member of the Massachusetts Society of the Colonial Dames of America, who m., 23 April, 1862, Philip H. Sears, of Boston, and had: *Annie Lyman, Mary Pratt, Richard, Francis Philip*, and *Evelyn*.

2.—PHŒBE LYMAN, 1719-1802, who m. Caleb Strong, of Northampton, 1701-1776, and had:

MARTHA STRONG, 1749-1827, who m., 1773, Rev. Ebenezer Moseley, 1741-1825, and had:

SOPHIA MOSELEY, 1773-1821, who m. John Abbot, of Westford, Massachusetts, 1777-1854, and had:

JOHN WILLIAM PITT ABBOT, of Westford, b. 27 April, 1806, d. 16 August, 1862; m., 18 July, 1833, Catharine Abbot, b. 18 March, 1808, d. 14 April, 1891, and had:

JOHN WILLIAM ABBOT, of Westford, b. 14 April, 1834, d. 10 November, 1897; m., 21 October, 1857, Elizabeth Rowell Southwick, b. 8 September, 1838, and had:

I.—CATHARINE MABEL ABBOT, b. 28 January, 1861; m. 15 September, 1881, Abbot L. Kebler, 1856-1888, and had: *Catharine Abbot*, b. 22 June, 1885; d. 1. August, 1896, and *Elizabeth Abbot*, b. 31 October, 1888.

II.—EMMA SOUTHWICK ABBOT, b. 17 July, 1864, a member of the Massachusetts and Colorado Societies of the Colonial Dames of America, who m., 5 June, 1888, Julian A. Kebler, of Denver, Colorado.

III.—LUCY KEBLER ABBOT, b. 26 March, 1870; m. 22 June, 1893, Julian Abbot Cameron, and had: *Alexander Abbot*, b. 5 August, 1895.

IV.—JOHN CAMERON ABBOT, b. 25 February, 1872; m. 12 January, 1898, Anna M. Fletcher, and had: *John Fletcher*, b. 28 November, 1898.

3.—MOSES LYMAN, of Goshen, Connecticut, b. 13 October, 1713, d. 1768; m., 24 March, 1742, Sarah Heighton (or Hayden), and had:

COLONEL MOSES LYMAN, of Goshen, b. 20 March, 1743, d. 29 September, 1829, and had by his second wife, Mrs. Mary Buel Judd, who d. 1835:

MARY LYMAN, b. 27 June, 1787, d. 8 May, 1870; m., 30 April, 1811, Amos Morris Collins, of Hartford, and had:

I.—WILLIAM LYMAN COLLINS, of Hartford, b. 10 February, 1812, who m. Harriet Rierson Collins, and had:

ELLEN COLLINS, a member of the Connecticut Society of the Colonial Dames of America, the Order of the Crown, etc.

II.—CHARLES COLLINS, b. 2 April, 1817, d. 30 November, 1891, who m., 1 September, 1840, Mary Hall Terry, also of Royal Descent, and had issue as above.

III.—ERASTUS COLLINS, who m., 1848, Mary Sarah Atwood, and had:

CAROLINE LYMAN COLLINS, a member of the Connecticut Society of the Colonial Dames of America, the Order of the Crown, etc., who m., 1886, Charles Whitney Page, of Middletown, and had: *Atwood Collins*, b. 12 November, 1887; *Charles Whitney*, b. 27 January, 1890, and *Ruth Whitney*, b. 6 May, 1890.

II.—LIEUTENANT BENJAMIN LYMAN, of Northampton, b. 10 August, 1674, d. 14 October, 1723; m., 27 October, 1698, Thankful Pomeroy, and had:

1.—MARY LYMAN, who m., 22 November, 1750, Lieutenant Oliver Pomeroy, and had:

RACHEL LYMAN POMEROY, b. 15 September, 1754, d. 14 August, 1774; m., 27 October, 1771, Brigadier-Major Edward Bulkeley, an original member of the Society of the Cincinnati, also of Royal Descent, and had:

ROXA LYMAN BULKELEY, b. 25 October, 1772, m., 25 February, 1793, Colonel Selah Francis, and had:

ROXA BULKELEY FRANCIS, b. 4 July, 1796, d. 1868; m., 4 May, 1815, Judge Jesse Booth, quartermaster in the War of 1812, in the regiment of his father-in-law, and also held important offices in State and county. He served in the New York Legislature, and also served as judge for a number of years. Their daughter:

ELLEN C. BULKELEY BOOTH, a member of the Connecticut Society of the Colonial Dames of America, who m., 21 November, 1864, Byron Coleman Dick, of Oakland, California. *No issue.*

2.—CAPTAIN WILLIAM LYMAN, of Northampton, b. 12 December, 1715, d. 13 March, 1774; m. Jemima Sheldon, and had:

GENERAL WILLIAM LYMAN, b. Northampton, 7 December, 1755, d. Colchester, England, 22 September, 1811, *bur.* in Gloucester Cathedral, 30 September, 1811. He m., 11 June, 1803, Jerusha Welles, and had:

MARTHA LYMAN, b 29 February, 1792, d. 14 April, 1831; m., 4 August, 1818, John Cox, and had:

JAMES SITGREAVES COX, b. 13 February, 1823; m., 25 June, 1857, Mary Fullerton, b. 15 January, 1836, daughter of Erskine and Mary (Fullerton) Hazard, and had:

MARTHA LYMAN COX, *b.* 17 May, 1860, a member of the Massachusetts Society of the Colonial Dames of America, who *m.*, 1 September, 1887, William Sohier Bryant, of Longwood, Massachusetts, and had: *Mary Cleveland, Elizabeth Sohier, Alice, Julia Cox, Gladys,* and *William Sohier.*

3.—AARON LYMAN, *b.* 1 April, 1705, *d.* 12 June, 1788; *m.*, 12 December, 1733, Eunice Dwight, *d.* 28 March, 1760, and had:

SUSANNAH LYMAN, *b.* 16 November, 1734, *d.* 1 February, 1770; *m.*, 9 November, 1763, Major Elihu Kent, *b.* 1 June, 1733, *d.* 12 February, 1814, and had:

SUSAN KENT, *b.* 20 September, 1768, *d.* 29 December, 1839; *m.*, 5 October, 1788, Judge Hezekiah Huntington, *b.* 30 December, 1759, *d.* 27 May, 1842, and had:

JULIA ANN HUNTINGTON, *b.* 10 December, 1790, *d.* 24 January, 1849; *m.*, 12 October, 1814, Judge Leicester King, *b.* 1 May, 1789, *d.* 19 September, 1856, and had:

CATHERINE BRINDLEY KING, *b.* 8 July, 1832; *m.*, 19 September, 1855, William Kimbrough Pendleton, *b.* 8 September, 1817, *d.* 1 September, 1899, and had:

CLARINDA HUNTINGTON PENDLETON, *b.* 25 August, 1856, a member of the Georgia Society of the Colonial Dames of America, who *m.*, 30 January, 1879, Joseph Rucker Lamar, of Augusta, Georgia, and had: *Philip Rucker, b.* 16 June, 1880; *William Pendleton, b.* 5 October, 1882, and *Mary Lamar, b.* 15 April, *d.* 11 July, 1885.

THE ROYAL DESCENT

OF

MRS. GEORGE M. CONARROE,

OF PHILADELPHIA, PA.

EDWARD I., King of England =Princess Eleanor of Castile.
    Princess Elizabeth Plantagenet=Humphrey de Bohun, Earl of Hereford.
    William de Bohun, Earl of Northampton=Lady Elizabeth de Badlesmere.
    Lady Elizabeth de Bohun=Richard Fitz-Alan, K.G., Earl of Arundel.
    Lady Elizabeth Fitz-Alan=Sir Robert Goushill, of Hault Hucknall, Derby.
    Lady Joan Goushill=Sir Thomas Stanley, K.G., Lord Stanley.
    Lady Margaret Stanley=Sir William Troutbeck, of Prynes Castle, Cheshire.
    Lady Jane Troutbeck=Sir William Griffith, of Penrhyn Castle.
    Sir William Griffith, of Penrhyn Castle=Jane Puleston of Carnarvon.
    Lady Sibill Griffith=Owen ap Hugh, of Bodeon.
    Jane Owen=Hugh Gwyn, of Penarth.
    Sibill Gwyn=John Powell, of Llanwddyn.
    Elizabeth Powell=Humphrey ap Hugh, of Llwyn-du.
    Owen Humphrey, of Llwyn-du =Jane ———.
    Rebecca Humphrey=Robert Owen, of Fron Gôch, d. Philadelphia, 1697.
    Owen Owen, of Philadelphia=(Name unknown).
    Sarah Owen=John Biddle, of Philadelphia.
    Col. Clement Biddle, of Philadelphia=Rebekah Cornell.
    Ann Wilkinson Biddle=Thomas Dunlap, of Philadelphia.
Nannie Dunlap, a member of the National Society of the Colonial Dames of America.=George Mecum Conarroe, of Philadelphia.

PEDIGREE XXXVII.

HENRY III., King of England, had by his wife (*m.* 1236), Lady Eleanor, daughter of Raymond de Berenger, Count of Provence:

PRINCE EDMUND, 1245–1295, Earl of Leicester, Lancaster, and Chester, lord high steward of England, who had by his second wife, Blanche, widow of Henry I., King of Navarre, and daughter of Robert, Earl of Artois, son of Louis VIII., King of France:

HENRY PLANTAGENET, Earl of Lancaster and Leicester, *d.* 1345, who *m.* Lady Maud, daughter of Patrick de Chaworth, 1253–1282, and his wife, Lady Isabel, daughter of William de Beauchamp, first Earl of Warwick, also of Royal Descent, and had:

LADY ELEANOR PLANTAGENET, widow of John de Beaumont, who *m.*, 1346, secondly (his second wife), Sir Richard Fitz-Alan, K.G., Earl of Arundel and Surrey, *d.* 24 January, 1375–6, and had:

SIR RICHARD FITZ-ALAN, K.G., tenth Earl of Arundel, *b.* 1346, beheaded in 1397, who *m.*, first, Lady Elizabeth de Bohun, also of Royal Descent, and had:

LADY ELIZABETH FITZ-ALAN, who *m.*, thirdly, Sir Robert Goushill, Knt., of Hault Hucknell Manor, Derby, and had:

LADY JOAN GOUSHILL, who *m.* Sir Thomas Stanley, installed 14 May, 1457, K.G., Lord Stanley, *d.* 12 January, 1458–59, and had:

LADY MARGARET STANLEY (sister of Sir William Stanley, who crowned Henry VII.. on Bosworth Field), who *m.*, first, Sir John Butler, of Bewsey, Knt., and *m.*, secondly, Sir William Troutbeck, of Prynes Castle, Werrall, Cheshire, slain at Bloreheath, and had:

LADY JANE TROUTBECK, who *m.*, first, Sir William Boteler, and *m.*, secondly, Sir William Griffith, K.B., of Penrhyn Castle, Carnarvonshire, chamberlain of North Wales, and had:

SIR WILLIAM GRIFFITH, of Penrhyn, chamberlain of North Wales, who *m.*, secondly, Jane, daughter of John Puleston, of Carnarvon Castle, also of Royal Descent, and had by her:

LADY SIBILL GRIFFITH, who *m.* Owen ap Hugh, of Bodeon, high sheriff of Anglesea in 1563 and 1580, *d.* 1613, and had:

JANE OWEN, who *m.* Hugh Gwyn, of Penarth, high sheriff of Carnarvonshire in 1600, and had:

SIBILL GWYN, who *m.*, *ante* 20 September, 1588, John Powell (John ap Howell Gôch), of Gadfa, Llanwddwn township, Montgomeryshire, who was buried in the church at Llanwddyn, 24 July, 1636, and had:

ELIZABETH POWELL, who m. Humphrey ap Hugh ap David ap Howel ap Grono ap Einion, of Llwyn-du, Merionethshire, and had by him, who d. 1664–5:

1.—SAMUEL AP HUMPHREY, of Portheven, Merionethshire, who had by his wife, Elizabeth:

DANIEL HUMPHREYS, who removed in 1682 to Haverford township, in the "Welsh Tract," Pennsylvania (see Glenn's "Merion in the Welsh Tract," "The Humphreys Family History," etc.). He m., 1695, Hannah, daughter of Dr. Thomas Wynne, of Merion, Pennsylvania, speaker of the first three general assemblies of Pennsylvania, and had:

JOSHUA HUMPHREYS, of Darby, 1710–1793; m., at Merion Meeting House, 1742, Sarah, daughter of Edward Williams, of "Blockley," Philadelphia county, Pennsylvania, and had:

JOSHUA HUMPHREYS, of Ponte Reading, Pennsylvania, 1751–1838. He was the first naval constructor and master shipbuilder to the Government, 1774. He m. Mary Davids, of Philadelphia, 1757–1805, and had:

I.—SAMUEL HUMPHREYS, b. 1798, chief naval constructor to the Government, 1826–46; d. at Georgetown, District of Columbia, 16 August, 1846. He m., 1808, Letitia, daughter of Andrew Atkinson, of "Cavan Garden," county Donegal, Ireland, and of Florida, and his wife, Lady Jane, daughter of Sir Archibald Murray, of Black Barony, in Scotland, and had:

WILLIAM PENN HUMPHREYS, United States Navy, of San Francisco, California, m., 1870, Mary Stencon, and had:

ALICE HUMPHREYS, of San Francisco, a member of the California Society of the Colonial Dames of America, the Order of the Crown, etc.

II.—SARAH HUMPHREYS, 1780–1854, who m. Henry Hollingsworth, of Philadelphia, and had:

HANNAH HOLLINGSWORTH, 1813–1881, who m. Thomas Stewardson, M.D., of Philadelphia, 1807–1878, and had:

MARY HOLLINGSWORTH STEWARDSON, of Philadelphia, a member of the Pennsylvania Society of the Colonial Dames of America.

2.—OWEN HUMPHREY, of Llwyn-du, parish of Llangelynin, Talybont, Merionethshire, eldest son, 1625–1699, a justice under Cromwell, who had by his wife, Jane:

REBECCA HUMPHREY,* who *m.*, 1678 (marriage certificate extant), Robert Owen, of Fron Gôch, Merionethshire, *b.* 1657, *d.* Merion township, Philadelphia county, Pennsylvania, 1697. He removed to Pennsylvania in 1690, and was a justice of the peace for Merion township, and a member of the provincial assembly (*see* Glenn's "Owen of Merion," *Pennsylvania Magazine*, vol. xiii., part 2; Glenn's "Merion in the Welsh Tract," p. 112, *etc.*, for the Welsh families connected with this pedigree), and had issue:

1.—ROBERT OWEN, of Philadelphia, *m.* Susannah, daughter of Judge William Hudson, mayor of Philadelphia, and had:

HANNAH OWEN, 1720–1791, who *m.*, first, John Ogden, of Philadelphia, and *m.*, secondly, 7 June, 1752 (his second wife), Joseph Wharton, of "Walnut Grove," Philadelphia, and had by him, who *d.* 1776, aged 69 years:

RACHEL WHARTON, 1762–1836, who *m.*, 13 December, 1781, William Lewis, of Philadelphia, 1746–1801, and had:

HANNAH OWEN LEWIS, *b.* 6 June, 1795, *d.* 24 January, 1857, who *m.*, 23 June, 1824, Richard Wistar, Jr., of Philadelphia, *b.* 3 October, 1790, *d.* 3 November, 1863, and had:

FRANCES ANNA WISTAR, who *m.*, 23 June, 1857, Lewis Allaire Scott, of Philadelphia, also of Royal Descent, and had:

HANNAH LEWIS SCOTT, of Philadelphia, a member of the Pennsylvania Society of the Colonial Dames of America.

2.—OWEN OWEN, high sheriff and coroner of Philadelphia county, father of:

SARAH OWEN, who *m.*, 3 March, 1736, John Biddle, of Philadelphia, son of William Biddle, of "Mt. Hope," Burlington county, New Jersey, and had:

I.—OWEN BIDDLE, of Philadelphia, *b.* 1737, a delegate to the Provincial Congress, 1775; member of the Pennsylvania committee of safety and of the council of safety; delegate to the constitutional convention, 1776, *etc.*, who *m.*, 29 September, 1760, Sarah, daughter of Thomas Parke, Jr., of Chester county, Pennsylvania, and had:

CLEMENT BIDDLE, *b.* 6 August, 1778, *d.* 10 February, 1856; *m.*, first, 1810, Mary, daughter of William Canby, and had by her:

1.—WILLIAM CANBY BIDDLE, *b.* 25 September, 1816, *d.* 22 December, 1887; *m.*, 21 February, 1838, Rachel Miller, and had:

---

* The following ladies, members of the National Society of the Colonial Dames of America, are also of Royal Descent through Rebecca Humphrey:

MRS. EUGENE BLACKFORD, Maryland State Society.

MRS. ARTHUR E. POULTNEY, Maryland State Society.

I.—FRANCES CANBY BIDDLE, b. 11 August, 1840, a member of the Pennsylvania Society of the Colonial Dames of America, who m., 18 June, 1862, Clement Acton Griscom, of Philadelphia and Haverford, also of Royal Descent, and had: *Clement A., Rodman E., Lloyd C., Francis C.,* and

HELEN BIDDLE GRISCOM, b. 9 October, 1866, a member of the Pennsylvania Society of the Colonial Dames of America, who m., 20 June, 1889, Samuel Bettle, of Philadelphia, and had: *Griscom,* b. 19 February, 1890.

II.—MARY BIDDLE, b. 17 December, 1849, a member of the Pennsylvania Society of the Colonial Dames of America, who m., 28 January, 1869, Howard Wood, of Philadelphia, and had: *Biddle, Helen B., Alan Wood, 3d; Howard, Clement B., Owen B.,* d. 20 February, 1882; *Rachel Biddle, Marion Biddle,* and *Dorothy,* d. 9 April, 1887.

III.—HANNAH NICHOLSON BIDDLE, b. 18 April, 1855, a member of the Pennsylvania Society of the Colonial Dames of America, who m., 18 October, 1877, Charles Williams, of Philadelphia and Haverford, and had: *William Biddle, Frances Biddle,* and *Eleanor Poultney Biddle.*

2.—ROBERT BIDDLE, of Philadelphia, who m. Anna, daughter of Daniel L. and Hannah (Nicholson) Miller, and had:

HANNAH MILLER BIDDLE, b. 24 August, 1850, a member of the Pennsylvania Society of the Colonial Dames of America, who m., 5 January, 1882, John C. W. Frishmuth, of Riverton, N. J., and had: *Edna Helen, John Whitney, Robert Biddle,* and *Clarice.*

II.—COLONEL CLEMENT BIDDLE, of Philadelphia, b. 10 May, 1740, d. 14 July, 1814. He was a distinguished officer in the Continental army; m., secondly, Rebekah, daughter of Gideon Cornell, lieutenant-governor and chief justice of the Rhode Island Colony, and had by her:

1.—ANN WILKINSON BIDDLE, b. 12 June, 1791; m., 2 June, 1822, Thomas Dunlap, of Philadelphia, and had:

NANNIE DUNLAP, b. 21 November, 1830, a member of the Pennsylvania Society of the Colonial Dames of America, who m. George Mecum Conarroe, of Philadelphia.

2.—COLONEL CLEMENT CORNELL BIDDLE, Philadelphia, third son, b. 24 October, 1784, captain of the State Fencibles and colonel of First Regiment Volunteer Light Infantry of Pennsylvania in the War of 1812. He m. Mary Searle, daughter of John Barclay, mayor of Philadelphia, 1791, a native of Ballyshannon, Ireland, and had:

PEDIGREE XXXVII.—Continued.

JOHN BARCLAY BIDDLE, *b.* 3 January, 1815, who *m.*, 7 November, 1850, Caroline, daughter of William Phillips, and had:

ANNA CLIFFORD BIDDLE, a member of the Pennsylvania Society of the Colonial Dames of America, who *m.*, in 1881, Clement Stocker Phillips, of Philadelphia.

3.—THOMAS BIDDLE, of Philadelphia, *b.* 4 June, 1776, *m.*, 12 February, 1806, Christine, daughter of General Jonathan Williams, and had:

I.—COLONEL HENRY JONATHAN BIDDLE, of Philadelphia, *b.* 16 May, 1807, adjutant-general of Pennsylvania Volunteers, *d.* from wound received at New Market Cross-Roads, 30 June, 1862; *m.*, 1 June, 1854, Mary Deborah, daughter of Samuel Baird, of Philadelphia, and had:

LYDIA MCFUNN BIDDLE, *b.* 9 April, 1857, a member of the Pennsylvania Society of the Colonial Dames of America, who *m.* Moncure Robinson, Jr., of Philadelphia.

II.—ALEXANDER BIDDLE, of Philadelphia, *b.* 29 April, 1819; *m.*, 11 October, 1855, Julia Williams, a member of the Pennsylvania Society of the Colonial Dames of America, daughter of Samuel Rush, M.D., of Philadelphia, and had:

MARIANNE BIDDLE, of Philadelphia, a member of the Pennsylvania Society of the Colonial Dames of America.

4.—REBEKAH CORNELL BIDDLE, *b.* 7 November, 1782, *m.*, 1 September, 1808, Professor Nathaniel Chapman, of Philadelphia, and had:

GEORGE WILLIAM CHAPMAN, of Philadelphia, *b.* 10 December, 1816, *m.* Emily, daughter of John Markoe, of Philadelphia, and had:

I.—MARY RANDOLPH CHAPMAN, a member of the Pennsylvania Society of the Colonial Dames of America, who *m.* John Borland Thayer, of Philadelphia, and had: *George C., Henry C., John B., Walter, Mary, Sidney,* and *Farnum.*

II.—ELIZABETH CAMAC CHAPMAN, a member of the Pennsylvania Society of the Colonial Dames of America, who *m.* William Davis Winsor, of Philadelphia, and had: *Louise Brooks* and

EMILY CHAPMAN WINSOR, a member of the Pennsylvania Society of the Colonial Dames of America, who *m.* William R. Philler, of Philadelphia and Haverford.

III.—REBECCA CHAPMAN, a member of the Pennsylvania Society of the Colonial Dames of America, who *m.* James Davis Winsor, of Philadelphia and Haverford, and had: *Henry, James, Davis, Rebecca, Ellen,* and

MARY WINSOR, of Haverford, a member of the Pennsylvania Society of the Colonial Dames of America.

3.—GAINOR OWEN, b. 26 October, 1688, who m., at Merion Meeting House, 4 October, 1706, Jonathan Jones, of Merion, Pennsylvania, 1680–1770 (son of Dr. Edward Jones, of Merion, d. 1737, and his wife, Mary, daughter of Dr. Thomas Wynne, of Sussex, Delaware county, Pennsylvania, who came with William Penn, in the "Welcome"), and had:

I.—OWEN JONES, of Merion, Pennsylvania, b. 19 November, 1711, d. 10 October, 1793, the last colonial treasurer of Pennsylvania, who m., 30 May, 1740, Susannah, 1719–1801, daughter of Hugh Evans, of Merion, 1682–1772, also of Royal Descent, and had:

1.—LOWRY JONES, b. 1743, d. 15 April, 1804, who m., 5 July, 1760, Daniel Wister, Philadelphia, b. 4 April, 1738, d. 2 December, 1805, son of John and Catherine Wister, and had:

I.—CHARLES JONES WISTER, of Philadelphia, b. 12 April, 1782, d. 23 July, 1865; m., 15 December, 1803, Rebecca, daughter of Joseph Bullock, of Philadelphia, and had:

WILLIAM WYNNE WISTER, of Philadelphia, b. 25 March, 1807, d. 17 December, 1898; m. Hannah Lewis, daughter of Alexander and Rachel Wilson, and had:

RACHEL WILSON WISTER, b. 22 January, 1835, m., 12 November, 1862, William Barton Rogers, son of James B. and Rachel Rogers, and had:

MABEL ROGERS, a member of the Pennsylvania Society of the Colonial Dames of America, who m., 15 April, 1896, Edgar W. Baird (son of Matthew Baird), of Philadelphia and Merion, and had: *Edgar W.*, b. 5 April, 1897, and *Gainor Owen*, b. 27 October, 1898.

II.—JOHN WISTER, of Germantown, Philadelphia, b. 20 March, 1776, d. 10 December, 1862, who m., 1798, Elizabeth, daughter of Thomas Harvey, of Bucks county, Pennsylvania, and had:

LOUIS WISTER, of "St. Mary's," near Ardmore, Pennsylvania, m., 3 July, 1850, Elizabeth Emlen, daughter of Dr. Jacob and Sarah Emlen (Physick) Randolph, and had by her, who d. 25 December, 1891: *Sara Edythe*, and

ELIZABETH HARVEY WISTER, a member of the Pennsylvania Society of the Colonial Dames of America, who m., 18 December, 1883, Charles Penrose Keith, of Philadelphia. *No issue.*

2.—HANNAH JONES, b. 28 December, 1749, d. 1829, who m., 1779, Amos Foulke, of Philadelphia, also of Royal Descent, and had:

EDWARD FOULKE, of Gwynedd township, Montgomery county, Pennsylvania, b. 17 November, 1784, d. 17 July, 1851; m., 11 December, 1810, Tacy, daughter of Isaac and Gainor Jones, of Montgomery county, Pennsylvania, and had, besides other issue:

PEDIGREE XXXVII.—Continued.

I.—ANN JONES FOULKE, 1811–1888; *m.*, 1833, Hiram Corson, M.D., of Conshohocken, and had:

SUSAN FOULKE CORSON, a member of the Pennsylvania Society of the Colonial Dames of America, who *m.*, 26 November, 1868, Jawood Lukens, of Conshohocken. *No issue.*

II.—PRISCILLA FOULKE, 1821–1882; *m.*, 22 April, 1849, Thomas Wistar, Jr., of Philadelphia, and had:

SUSAN FOULKE WISTAR, a member of the Pennsylvania Society of the Colonial Dames of America, who *m.*, 27 May, 1872, Howard Comfort, and had: *William Wistar, b.* 27 May, 1874.

III.—REBECCA JONES FOULKE, *b.* 18 May, 1829, a member of the Pennsylvania Society of the Colonial Dames of America, who *m.*, 8 October, 1857, Robert R. Corson, of New Hope, Pennsylvania.

II.—REBECCA JONES, *b.* 20 February, 1709, *d.* 8 January, 1779. She *m.*, at Merion Meeting House, 4 June, 1733, John Roberts, *b.* 26 June, 1710, *d.* Merion 13 January, 1776, and had:

LIEUTENANT-COLONEL ALGERNON ROBERTS, *b.* 24 November, 1750, *d.* at Merion in 1815. He *m.*, 18 January, 1781, Tacy, daughter of Colonel Isaac Warner, of Blockley, Philadelphia county, Pennsylvania, and had:

1.—ALGERNON SYDNEY ROBERTS, *b.* 29 March, 1798, *d.* 14 September, 1865; *m.*, 10 April, 1823, Elizabeth, 1802–1891, daughter of Captain Anthony and Mary (Ogden) Cuthbert, of Philadelphia, and had:

I.—ALGERNON SYDNEY ROBERTS, JR., of Philadelphia, *b.* 24 October, 1827, who *m.*, 7 November, 1850, Sarah, daughter of James and Sarah Carstairs, and had:

ELIZABETH CUTHBERT ROBERTS, a member of the Pennsylvania Society of the Colonial Dames of America, who *m.*, 28 December, 1882, Walter Scott Wyatt, of Ohio, United States Army.

II.—ELIZABETH CUTHBERT ROBERTS, of Philadelphia, a member of the Pennsylvania Society of the Colonial Dames of America.

2.—EDWARD ROBERTS, of Philadelphia, *b.* 29 June, 1800, *d.* 3 November, 1872; *m.*, in May, 1825, Mary Elizabeth Reford, 1801–1862, and had:

I.—ANNA FRANCES ROBERTS, *b.* 7 November, 1827, *d.* 13 October, 1890; *m.* Edward Browning, of Philadelphia, and had:

MARY ROBERTS BROWNING, a member of the Pennsylvania Society of the Colonial Dames of America, who *m.* Arthur Vincent Meigs, M.D., of Philadelphia, also of Royal Descent, and had: *Edward Browning* and *John Forsythe.*

II.—ADELAIDE ROBERTS, a member of the Pennsylvania Society of the Colonial Dames of America, who *m.* Daniel Francis Shaw, M.D.

THE ROYAL DESCENT

OF

MRS. WILLIAM J. HOLLIDAY,

OF INDIANAPOLIS, IND.

ROBERT BRUCE, King of Scotland, had:
Margery, *m.* Walter, High Steward, and had:
Robert II., King of Scotland, who had:
Catherine, *m.* Sir David Lindsay, and had:
Alexander, 2d Earl of Crawford, who had:
Walter Lindsay, of Beaufort, who had:
Sir David Lindsay, of Edzell, who had:
Walter Lindsay, of Edzell, who had:
Alexander Lindsay, of Edzell, who had:
Rev. David Lindsay, Bishop of Ross, who had:
Rachel, *m.* Rev. Dr. John Spottiswood, and had:
Sir Robert Spottiswood, of New Abbey, who had:
Dr. Robert Spotswood, of Tangier, who had:
Gen. Alexander Spotswood, of Va., who had:
Anne, *m.* Col. Bernard Moore, of Va., and had:
Bernard Moore, of "Chelsea," Va., who had:
Elizabeth, *m.* Col. James Macon, and had:
Mary, *m.* Col. William Aylett, and had:
Col. Philip Aylett, of King William Co., Va.

ROBERT BRUCE, King of Scotland, had:
Margery, *m.* Walter, High Steward, and had:
Robert II., King of Scotland, who had:
Robert III., King of Scotland, who had:
James I., King of Scotland, who had:
James II., King of Scotland, who had:
Margery, *m.* William, Lord Crichton, and had:
Sir James Crichton, of Fendraught, who had:
Margaret, *m.* John Robertson, and had:
Gilbert Robertson, of Muirton, who had:
David Robertson, of Muirton, who had:
William Robertson, of Muirton, who had:
William Robertson, of Gladney, who had:
Rev. William Robertson, of Edinburgh, who had:
Jean, *m.* Alexander Henry, and had:
Col. John Henry, of Va., who had:
Gov. Patrick Henry, of Va., who had:
m. Elizabeth Henry, of "Red Hill," Va.

Mary Macon Aylett—Philip Fitzhugh, of Va.

Lucy Fitzhugh=John Robertson Redd, of Va.

Lucy Redd, member of the National Society of—William Jacqueline Holliday, of Indianapolis, the Colonial Dames of America | Ind., also of Royal Descent.

Ariana Ambler Holliday, member of the National Society of the Colonial Dames of America,
m.
Henry W. Bennett.
Issue.

Jaqueline S. Holliday,
m.
Florence Baker.
Issue.

Lucy Fitzhugh Holliday,
m.
George E. Hume.

PEDIGREE XXXVIII.

CHARLEMAGNE, Emperor of the West, had by his third wife, Lady Hildegarde, *d.* 783, daughter of Childebrand, Duke of Suabia:

PEPIN, KING OF LOMBARDY and Italy, who *m.* Lady Bertha, daughter of William, Count of Thoulouse, and had:

BERNARD, KING OF LOMBARDY, who had by his wife, Lady Cunegonde:

PEPIN, COUNT OF VERMANDOIS and Peronne, 840, who had:

HERBERT I., COUNT DE VERMANDOIS, *d.* 902, who had:

HERBERT II., COUNT DE VERMANDOIS, *d.* 943, who had:

ALBERT I., THE PIOUS, COUNT DE VERMANDOIS, *d.* 987, who *m.* Princess Gerberga, daughter of Louis IV., King of France, and had:

HERBERT III., COUNT DE VERMANDOIS, who had:

OTHO, COUNT DE VERMANDOIS, 1021-1045, who had:

HERBERT IV., COUNT DE VERMANDOIS, 1045-1080, who *m.* Lady Hildebrante, daughter of Raoul III., Count de Valois, and had:

ADELHEID, COUNTESS OF VERMANDOIS, who *m.* (his third wife) Hugh Magnus, Duke of France and Burgundy, Marquis of Orleans, Count of Paris, Valois and Vermandois, son of Henry I., of France, and had:

LADY ISABEL DE VERMANDOIS, who *m.*, first, Robert, first Baron de Bellomont, Earl of Mellent, created, in 1103, Earl of Leicester, and had:

ROBERT, second Earl of Leicester, justiciary of England, *d.* 1168, who had by his wife, Lady Aurelia, daughter of Ralph de Waer, Earl of Norfolk, Suffolk and Cambridge, 1066:

ROBERT, third Earl of Leicester, steward of England, *d.* 1196, who had by his wife, Petronella, daughter of Hugh de Grentemaisnill:

LADY MARGARET DE BELLOMONT, who *m.* Saier de Quincy, created, 1207, Earl of Winchester, a surety for the Magna Charta of King John, *d.* 1219 (*see* "The Magna Charta Barons and their American Descendants"), and had:

ROGER DE QUINCY, second Earl of Winchester, constable of Scotland, *d.* 1264, who had by his wife, Lady Helen, daughter of Alan McDonal, Lord of Galloway:

LADY MARGARET DE QUINCY, who *m.* (his second wife) William de Ferrers, seventh Earl of Derby, *d.* 1254, and had:

WILLIAM DE FERRERS, Lord of Groby, second son by second wife, *d.* 1287, who *m.* Lady Joan, sister of Hugh, Earl of Winchester, executed in 1336, and daughter of Hugh le Despencer, *k.* 1265, and had:

LADY ANNE DE FERRERS, who *m.* (his first wife) John, second Lord Grey de Ruthyn, *d.* 1323, and had:

LADY MAUD DE GREY, who *m.* Sir John de Norville, lord of Norton, Yorkshire, and had:

JOHN DE NORTON, of Sharpenhow, in Bedfordshire, father of:

JOHN NORTON, of Sharpenhow, who had by his second wife, Jane, daughter of John Cooper, or Cowper:

RICHARD NORTON, second son (brother of Thomas, father of Thomas Norton, the Elizabethan poet, who *d.* 1532), who *m.* Margery Wingate, of Sharpenhow, will proved in 1572, and had:

WILLIAM NORTON, of Sharpenhow, who had by his first wife, Margery, daughter of William Hawes, and widow of —— Hamon:

WILLIAM NORTON, of Storford, (*see* the Hertfordshire and Bedfordshire Visitations), who *m.* Alice, daughter of John Browest, and had:

REV. WILLIAM NORTON, of Ipswich, Massachusetts, *b.* 1610, *d.* 30 April, 1694 (*see* Mather's "Magnalia," vol. i., 286; "New England Historical Genealogical Register," xiii., 225; "American Heraldic Journal," January, 1886; "Herald and Genealogist," part xv., 276), who *m.* Lucy, sister of Sir George Downing, and daughter of Emanuel Downing and his wife, Lucy Winthrop, a sister of Governor John Winthrop, and had:

REV. JOHN NORTON, of Hingham, who *m.* Mary Mason, and had:

ELIZABETH NORTON, *m.* Colonel John Quincy, of Braintree, and had:

ELIZABETH QUINCY, *m.* Rev. William Smith, of Weymouth, and had:

ABIGAIL SMITH, *b.* 22 November, 1744, *d.* 28 October, 1818, who *m.*, 25 October, 1764, John Adams, of Quincy, Massachusetts, second President of the United States, *b.* 30 October, 1735, *d.* 4 July, 1826, and had:

JOHN QUINCY ADAMS, of Quincy, Massachusetts, sixth President of the United States, *b.* 11 July, 1767, *d.* 29 February, 1848, who *m.* in London, 27 July, 1797, Louisa Catharine, *b.* 12 February, 1775, *d.* 15 May, 1852, daughter of Joshua Johnson, of London and Nantes, a grandson of Thomas and Mary (Baker) Johnson, of Maryland, 1660, and had:

CHARLES FRANCIS ADAMS, of Quincy, Massachusetts, *b.* 18 August, 1809, *d.* 21 November, 1886; United States Minister to Great Britain, 1861-68, *etc.*, and always a prominent candidate for the Presidency of the United States. He *m.*, 3 September, 1820, Abigail Brown Brooks, of Boston, also of Royal Descent, and had:

MARY ADAMS, a member of the Massachusetts Society of the Colonial Dames of America, who *m.* Henry P. Quincy, of Boston, and had: *Dorothy* and *Eleanor*.

PEDIGREE XXXIX.

EDWARD III., King of England, had by his wife, Philippa, daughter of William, Count of Hainault and Holland:

SIR EDMUND PLANTAGENET, surnamed *de Langley*, K.G., Duke of York; Earl of Cambridge, who had by his first wife, Princess Isabel, daughter and co-heiress of Peter, King of Castile and Leon:

LADY CONSTANCE PLANTAGENET, who *m.* Thomas, second Baron le Despencer, of Glamorgan, created, 1337, Earl of Gloucester, beheaded in 1400, also of Royal Descent, and had:

LADY ISABEL LE DESPENCER, who *m.*, first, Richard Beauchamp, Lord Bergavenny; created, 1421, Earl of Worcester, and had:

LADY ELIZABETH BEAUCHAMP, 1415–1447, who *m.*, 1435, Sir Edward Nevill, K.G., Baron Bergavenny, *d.* 1476, also of Royal Descent, and had:

SIR GEORGE NEVILL, Baron Bergavenny and Latimer, 1440–1492, who had by his first wife, Margaret, *d.* 1485, daughter of Sir Hugh Fenn, sub-treasurer of England:

SIR EDWARD NEVILL, of Aldington Park, Kent, beheaded for treason 9 January, 1538, who had by his wife, Lady Eleanor, also of Royal Descent, daughter of Andrew, Lord Windsor of Stanwell:

LADY KATHERINE NEVILL, widow of —— Royden (*see* Foster's "Royal Lineages," p. 5), who *m.*, secondly, Clement Throckmorton, of Haseley, Warwick, sewer to the Queen; commander at siege of Bologne (*see* Nicolas's "Testamenta Vetusta," p. 560, and Burke's "Royal Families," ii., Ped. 124), *d.* 1594–99, and had:

KATHERINE THROCKMORTON, (*see* Burke's "Royal Families," i., Ped. 83), who *m.* Thomas Harby, of Alveston, Northamptonshire, *d.* 1592, and had:

KATHERINE HARBY, sister of Sir Job Harby, Bart. (*see* Burke's "Royal Families," ii., Ped. 116), who *m.* Dr. Daniel Oxenbridge, of Daventry, Northamptonshire, *d.* 1642, son of Rev. John Oxenbridge, of Southam (*see* Burke's "History of the Commoners," under "Beckford of Fonthill"), and had:

1.—REV. JOHN OXENBRIDGE,* pastor of the First Church, Boston,

---

* MRS. GEORGE S. HALE, a member of the Massachusetts State Society of the National Society of the Colonial Dames of America, is also of Royal Descent through Rev. John Oxenbridge.

Massachusetts, *b.* at Daventry, 30 January, 1609, *d.* 28 December, 1674. He had by his third wife, Susannah:

THEODORA OXENBRIDGE, *b.* 1659, *d.* 1697; *m.*, 21 November, 1677 (his first wife), Rev. Peter Thacher, of Milton, Massachusetts, and had:

REV. OXENBRIDGE THACHER, of Milton, *m.* Sarah Kent, and had:

BATHSHEBA THACHER, *m.*, 1769, Jeremiah Dummer Rogers, of Charlestown, Massachusetts, *d.* 1784, and had:

MARGARET ROGERS, *m.* Jonathan Chapman, and had:

JONATHAN CHAPMAN, mayor of Boston, Massachusetts, *m.* Lucinda Dwight, and had:

FLORENCE CHAPMAN, a member of the Massachusetts Society of the Colonial Dames of America, who *m.* Henry Rogers Dalton, of Boston, Massachusetts, and had: *Alice, Philip Spalding, Susan Dexter, Florence, d. 1890, and Ellen Bancroft.*

2.—ELIZABETH OXENBRIDGE, who *m.* Caleb Cockercraft (or "Cockroft"), *d.* 1644, and had:

ELIZABETH COCKERCRAFT, who *m.* Nathaniel Hering, *d.* 1678, and had:

OLIVER HERING, who *m.* Elizabeth Hughes, and had:

OLIVER HERING, JR., who *m.* Anna Maria Morris, and had:

CAPTAIN JULINES HERING, of Jamaica, who *m.*, 2 April, 1761, Mary, daughter of Captain John Inglis, of Philadelphia, and his wife, Catherine, daughter of George McCall, of Philadelphia, and had:

MARY HELEN HERING, who *m.* Henry Middleton, of Charleston, South Carolina, Governor of South Carolina, member of Congress, minister to Russia, *etc.*, son of Arthur Middleton, a signer of the Declaration of Independence, and had:

ELIZA MIDDLETON, who *m.* Joshua Francis Fisher, of Philadelphia, also of Royal Descent, 1807–1873, and had:

MARIA MIDDLETON FISHER, a member of the Society of the Colonial Dames, who *m.* Brinton Coxe, of Philadelphia. *Issue.*

PEDIGREE XL.

EDWARD I., King of England, *m.*, first, 1254, Lady Eleanor, daughter of Ferdinand III., King of Castile, and had by her:

PRINCESS JOANE OF ACRE, *m.*, first, 1290, Gilbert de Clare, third Earl of Gloucester and seventh Earl of Hertford, *d.* 1295, and had:

LADY ELIZABETH DE CLARE, widow of John de Burgh and of Theobald de Verdon, *m.*, third, Sir Roger d'Amory, *d.* 1322, and had:

LADY ELIZABETH D'AMORY, who *m.* John, third Baron Bardolf, of Wormegay, *d.* 1363, and had:

WILLIAM, fourth Baron Bardolf, *d.* 1385; *m.* Agnes, *d.* 1403, daughter of Sir Michael, second Baron Poynings (her first husband), and had:

LADY CECELIA BARDOLF, *d.* 1432; *m.* Sir Brian Stapylton, Knt., of Ingham, Norfolk, *d.* 1438, and had:

SIR MILES STAPYLTON, Knt., of Ingham, *d.* 1466; *m.*, secondly, Lady Katherine, daughter of Sir Thomas de la Pole, Knt. (first husband), son of Michael de la Pole, second Earl of Suffolk, also of Royal Descent (*see* Burke's "Royal Families," Ped. 117), and had:

LADY ELIZABETH STAPYLTON, heiress, who *m.*, first, Sir William Calthorpe, Knt., of Burnham and Ingham, Norfolk, *d.* 1494, and had:

LADY ELIZABETH CALTHORPE, *m.* Francis Hassylden, of Gilden Morden, Cambridgeshire, and Little Chesterford, Essex; sheriff of Cambridgeshire in 1509, *d.* 1522, and had:

FRANCES HASSYLDEN, heiress, *d.* 1581; *m.*, 1515, Sir Robert Peyton, Knt., of Iselham, Cambridgeshire; sheriff of Cambridgeshire and Huntingdonshire, 17 and 27 Henry VIII. and 1 Mary, *d.* 1550 (*see* Hayden's "Virginia Genealogies," p. 464), and had:

ROBERT PEYTON, of Iselham, 1523–1590, M.P., high sheriff of Cambridgeshire, *m.* Elizabeth, *d.* 1591, daughter of Richard, Lord Rich, of Letze, lord high chancellor of England, 1548, and had:

SIR JOHN PEYTON, Knt. and Baronet, of Iselham, lord of Peyton Hall, in Boxford; M.P. 1593, high sheriff of Cambridgeshire; created a Baronet and knighted by James I., *d.* 1616; *m.*, 1580, Lady Alice, *d.* 1626, daughter of Sir Edward Osborne, Knt., lord mayor of London, 1583, and had:

SIR EDWARD PEYTON, second Baronet, of Iselham, 1578–1656; knighted 4 February, 1610; *m.*, secondly, 1614, Jane, daughter of Sir James Calthorpe, of Norfolk, Knt., and widow of Sir Henry Thymelthorp, and had by her:

THOMAS PEYTON, of Wicken and Rougham, Norfolk, 1616-1687, who m., first, Elizabeth, d. 1668, daughter of Sir William Yelverton, of Rougham, second Baronet, and his wife, Lady Ursula, daughter of Sir Thomas Richardson, Knt.; speaker of House of Commons and lord chief justice of King's Bench, 1626, and had:

MAJOR ROBERT PEYTON, of Gloucester county, Virginia, "living in Virginia, 1693" (see Hayden's "Virginia Genealogies"); "left no male issue" (see Kimber's, 1771, and Betham's "Baronetage," 1800).

ELIZABETH PEYTON, his daughter, m., 168-, Colonel Peter Beverley, of Gloucester county, Virginia, d. 1728, son of Robert Beverley, of "Beverley Park," King and Queen and Caroline counties, Virginia, who d. 1687. He was clerk of Virginia House of Burgesses, 1691-96; speaker, 1700-14; surveyor-general and member of the council, 1719-28; treasurer of Virginia Colony, 1719-1723, and had by Elizabeth Peyton:

ELIZABETH BEVERLEY, 1691-1723, who m., 1709, William Randolph, of "Chatsworth," 1681-1742, and had:

PETER RANDOLPH, of "Chatsworth," surveyor of customs of North America, 1749; member of the Virginia House of Burgesses, etc., d. 1767; m. Lucy, daughter of Robert Bolling, of "Bollingbrook," a descendant of the Indian Princess Pocahontas, of Virginia, and had:

COLONEL ROBERT RANDOLPH, of "Eastern View," Fauquier county, Virginia, 1760-1825; m. Elizabeth Hill Carter, of "Shirley," d. 1832, also of Royal Descent, and had:

CAPTAIN CHARLES CARTER RANDOLPH, of "The Grove," who m. Mary Anne Fauntleroy Mortimer, of Fredericksburg, Virginia, and had:

LANDONIA RANDOLPH, who m. Robert Dabney Minor, United States Navy, of Fredericksburg, Virginia, and had:

LANDONIA RANDOLPH MINOR, a member of the Virginia Society of the Colonial Dames of America, who m. William Sparrow Dashiell, of Richmond, Virginia, and had: *Robert Minor* and *Thomas Grayson.*

PEDIGREE XLI.

DAVID I., King of Scotland, 1124, had by his wife, Lady Matilda, widow of Simon de St. Liz, Earl of Huntingdon, *d.* 1115, and daughter of Waltheof, Earl of Northumberland, beheaded in 1075:

PRINCE HENRY OF SCOTLAND, eldest son, Earl of Northumberland, eldest son, *d. v. p.* 1159; *m.*, 1139, Lady Ada, *d.* 1178, daughter of William de Warren, second Earl of Surrey, and had:

PRINCESS MARJORY (sister of King Malcolm IV., and King William I., of Scotland), who *m.* Gilchrist, Earl of Angus, and had:

LADY BEATRIX, who *m.* Walter Stewart, generally called of Dondonald, high steward and justiciary of Scotland, *d.* 1241, and had:

LADY MARGARET STEWART, who *m.* Colin Fitzgerald, who for bravery in the battle of Large, on the part of King Alexander III., in 1263, received the charter of free barony of Kintail, in Rosshire, and *d.* in 1278, at the Castle of Island Donan, and had:

KENNETH, second lord of Kintail, who *m.* Lady Morba Macdonald, daughter of Alexander, lord of Lorn, and *d.* in 1304, had:

KENNETH MACKENNETH, third lord of Kintail, *d.* 1378, who *m.* Lady Margaret, daughter of David de Strathbogie, Earl of Athol, and had:

KENNETH MACKENZIE, fourth lord of Kintail, who *m.* Fynvola, daughter of Roderick Macleod, of Lewes, and had:

MURDOCK MACKENZIE-DON, fifth lord of Kintail, *d.* 1375, who *m.* Isabel, daughter of Murdoch Macaula, of Lochbroom, and had:

MURDOCH MACKENZIE, sixth lord of Kintail, *d.* 1416, who *m.* Fynvola, daughter of Macleod, of Harris, and had:

ALEXANDER MACKENZIE, seventh lord of Kintail, *d.* 1488, who *m.*, first, Lady Agnes, daughter of Colin Campbell, first lord of Argyle, and had:

SIR KENNETH MACKENZIE, eighth lord of Kintail, *d.* 1507, who *m.*, secondly, Lady Agnes, daughter of Hugh, Lord Lovat, and had by her:

JOHN MACKENZIE, ninth lord of Kintail, *d.* 1556–57, who *m.* Elizabeth Grant, and had:

KENNETH MACKENZIE, tenth lord of Kintail, *d.* 6 June, 1568, who *m.* Lady Isabel Stewart, daughter of John, third Earl of Atholl, and had:

LADY AGNES MACKENZIE, who *m.*, 1567, Lachlan-Mohr MacIntosh, of Dunachtane and Knocknagail, the sixteenth chief of Clan Chattan (*see*

Douglas's " Peerage of Scotland," ii., 480; Buchanan's "Ancient Scottish Surnames ;" Shaw's " MacIntoshes and Clan Chattan "), and had :

WILLIAM MACINTOSH, of Essick and Borlum, second son, *d.* 1630, who *m.*, 1594, Elizabeth, daughter of Robert Innes, of Invermarkie, grandson of Robert Innes, of Innerbrakie, and his wife, Elspeth, daughter of Sir John Stewart, of Balveny, first Earl of Athol, also of Royal Descent, and had :

LACHLAN MACINTOSH, of Borlum and Bolkeskine, who *m.*, first, Anne, widow of Sir Lachlan McIntosh, of MacIntosh, and had:

CAPTAIN JOHN-MOHR MACINTOSH,* eldest son, *b.* Bolkeskine 24 March, 1700; came to America in 1733, and settled in that part of Georgia now called McIntosh county. He entered actively upon the defence of the colony against the Spaniards, and was captain of the first company of Highlanders organized in America, and at Fort Moosa was severely wounded and taken prisoner, sent to Madrid, and exchanged at the treaty of Aix la Chapelle; a delegate to the Provincial Assembly of Georgia, 1751, *etc.* He *m.*, 4 March, 1725, Marjory, *b.* 1701, daughter of John Frazer, of Garthmore, and his wife, Elizabeth Frazer, of Errogy, and *d.* at " Borlum," near Darien, Georgia, 1761, having issue:

1.—COLONEL WILLIAM MCINTOSH, of Darien, *b.* at " Borlum," 27 January, 1726, *d.* 1796. He took an active part in the Revolutionary War, and commanded the first regiment of cavalry in the Georgia Continental Line, and was a delegate to the first Provincial Congress at Savannah, July, 1775. He *m.* Jane Maccoy, and had :

MAJOR-GENERAL JOHN MCINTOSH, of " Fairhope," near Darien, Georgia, where he *d.* 12 November, 1826. He served with distinction in the Revolutionary War and the War of 1812. He *m.*, 17 June, 1781, Sarah, daughter of William Swinton, and had:

COLONEL JAMES SIMMONS MCINTOSH, United States Army, *b.* 19 June, 1787. He served in the American Army in the War of 1812; in the Seminole War and in the Mexican War, and was mortally wounded at El Molino del Rey, and died in the City of Mexico, 26 September, 1847. He *m.*, 29 December, 1815, Mrs. Eliza (Matthews) Shumate, *d.* 1833, and had :

MARY ELIZA MCINTOSH, a member of the California Society of the Colonial Dames of America, who *m.*, first, Colonel Charles Clark Keeney, M.D., United States Army, and had: *Charles McI.* and *James Ward*, and *m.*, secondly, William Alvord, of San Francisco. *No issue.*

---

* MRS. ROBERT E. BROWN, a member of the Georgia State Society of the National Society of the Colonial Dames of America, is also of Royal Descent through John MacIntosh.

2.—GEORGE MCINTOSH, a member of the Provincial Congress which met at Savannah 4 July, 1775, who had by his wife, Lady Anne, daughter of Sir Patrick Houstoun, 1735-1762, president of the King's Council in Georgia:

JOHN HOUSTON MCINTOSH, of Darien, Georgia, who *m.*, 30 April, 1791, Eliza Bayard, *d.* 1846, also of Royal Descent, and had:

I.—JOHN HOUSTON MCINTOSH, JR., 1802-1852, who *m.*, 13 September, 1832, Mary Randolph Higbee, of Trenton, New Jersey, and had:

MARY RANDOLPH MCINTOSH, a member of the Georgia Society of the Colonial Dames of America, who *m.*, 12 March, 1861, John Kilgour, of Cincinnati, Ohio, and had: *Charles, Bayard Livingston, Elizabeth, Louise,* and

1.—MARY KILGOUR, a member of the New York Society of the Colonial Dames of America, who *m.*, 16 April, 1890, Edmund E. Miller, of Cincinnati, and had: *Mary Kilgour, b.* 4 April, 1891.

2.—CHARLOTTE KILGOUR, a member of the New York Society of the Colonial Dames of America, who *m.*, 21 April, 1896, Captain Ashton B. Hyle, M.D., United States Army, and had: *John Kilgour, b.* 21 March, 1897.

II.—ELIZA BAYARD MCINTOSH, who *m.* Duncan L. Clinch, United States Army, and had:

ELIZA BAYARD CLINCH, who *m.* General Robert Anderson, United States Army, of Fort Sumter fame, and had:

ELIZA MCINTOSH CLINCH ANDERSON, a member of the New York Society of the Colonial Dames of America, who *m.* James M. Lawton, of New York City.

THE ROYAL DESCENTS

OF

MR. AND MRS. CHARLES COLLINS,

OF NEW YORK CITY.

ALFRED THE GREAT, King of England = Ethelbith, daughter of Ethelan the Great.
Edward the Elder, King of England = Edgiva, daughter of Earl Sigelline.
Edmund I., King of England = Elgiva, granddaughter of Alfred the Great.
Edgar the Peaceful, King of England = Elfrida, daughter of Ordgar, Earl of Devon.
Ethelred the Unready, King of England = Elgifa, daughter of Earl Thorad.
Edmund Ironsides, King of England = Algitha of Denmark.
Prince Edward the Exile, of England = Agatha of Germany.
Princess Margaret, of England = Malcolm Canmore, King of Scotland.
David I., King of Scotland = Lady Matilda of Northumberland.
Henry, Earl of Huntingdon = Lady Ada de Warren.
David, Earl of Huntingdon = (Name uncertain).
Lady Margaret de Huntingdon = Alan McDonald, lord of Galloway.
Lady Helen McDonald = Roger, 2d Earl of Winchester.
Lady Elizabeth de Quincey = Alexander, 2d Earl of Buchan.
Lady Agnes Cumyn = Gilbert, 8th Earl of Angus.
Robert, 9th Earl of Angus = Alianore ———.
Sir Thomas de Umfraville, of Harbottle = Joan de Rodam.
Sir Thomas de Umfraville, of Riddesdale = Agnes ———.
Lady Joan de Umfraville = Sir William Lambert, of Owlton.
Robert Lambert, of Owlton = (Name unknown).
Henry Lambert, of Ongar = (Name unknown).
Elizabeth Lambert = Thomas Lyman, of Navistoke.
Henry Lyman, of High Ongar = Alicia Hyde, of Westersfield.
John Lyman, of High Ongar = Margaret Gérard, of Beauchamp.
Henry Lyman, of High Ongar = Phillis Scott, of Navistoke.
Richard Lyman, d. Hartford, Ct., 1640 = Sarah Osborne.
Lieut. John Lyman, of Northampton, Mass. = Dorcas Plum.
Moses Lyman, of Northampton, Mass. = Anne ———.

Moses Lyman = Mindwell Sheldon.　　Mary Lyman = Samuel Dwight.
Moses Lyman = Sarah Hayden.　　Mary Dwight = Daniel Hall, Jr.
Moses Lyman = Mary Judd.　　Mary Hall = Eliphalet Terry.
Mary Lyman = Amos M. Collins.　　Eliphalet Terry = Lydia Coit.

Charles Collins, 1817–1891 = Mary Hall Terry, 1820–1900.

Lydia Coit Collins = William P. Ketcham.　　Clarence Lyman Collins = Marie Louise Clark.　　Louise Terry Collins = William Allen Butler, Jr.

Arthur Collins Ketcham = Margaret Van W. Bruce Allen.　Mary Ketcham = Thomas Hunt Talmadge.　Ethel Miriam Ketcham.　　Edith Lyman Collins = Richid Bey, Comte Czaykowski.　Wm. Allen Butler.　Lyman Collins Butler.　Charles Terry Butler.　Lydia Coit Butler.　Louise Tracy Butler.

William T. Ketcham.　Thomas H. Talmadge.　　　Vladimer.　Stanislaus.
Margaret B. Ketcham.　Lillian Talmadge.
Arthur C. Ketcham.

PEDIGREE XLII.

JAMES I., King of Scotland, had by his wife, Lady Joan de Beaufort, daughter of Sir John, Earl of Somerset, a grandson of Edward III., King of England:

PRINCESS JANET STEWART (sister of King James II.), who m. George Gordon, second Earl of Huntley, also of Royal Descent, and had:

ALEXANDER GORDON, third Earl of Huntley, who m. Lady Janet Stewart, daughter of John, Earl of Athol, also of Royal Descent, and had:

LADY JOAN GORDON, who m. Colin Campbell, third Earl of Argyle, d. 1533, also of Royal Descent, and had:

ARCHIBALD CAMPBELL, fourth Earl of Argyle, d. 1558, who m., secondly, Lady Margaret, daughter of William Græm, Earl of Monteith, also of Royal Descent, and had by her:

SIR COLIN CAMPBELL, sixth Earl of Argyle, d. 1584, who m. Lady Agnes, daughter of William Keith, marshal of Scotland, also of Royal Descent, and widow of James, Earl of Moray, the regent of Scotland, and had:

ARCHIBALD CAMPBELL, seventh Earl of Argyle, who m. Lady Anne, daughter of William Douglas, Earl of Morton, also of Royal Descent, and had:

LADY MARY CAMPBELL, who m. Robert Montgomery, Jr., of Skelmurlie, d. v. p. (see Wood's Douglas's "Peerage of Scotland," i., pp. 74, 509), also of Royal Descent, and had:

SIR ROBERT MONTGOMERY, of Skelmurlie, Bart., d. 7 February, 1684, who m. Antonia, daughter of Sir James Scott, of Rossie, Fifeshire, and had:

LADY MARGARET MONTGOMERY, who m. Godfrey Macalester, laird of Loup, and chief of Clan Alester, in Kintyre (see Gregory's "History of the Western Islands," and Burke's "Royal Families," i., Ped. 106), and had:

JOHN MACALESTER, of Ardnakill and Torrisdale Glen, d. aged 96 years, who m. Miss McNeill, of Terfergus, d. aged 98 years, and had:

MARGARET MACALESTER, b. 1712, who m., first, Charles MacQuarrie, of Campbelltown (of MacQuarrie, of Ulva family), and m., secondly, Duncan Macalester, of Tarbert, and had by her first husband:

ISABELLA MACQUARRIE, 1740–1807, who m. Charles Macalester, of Tarbert, master of Campbelltown, lost at sea in 1797, and had:

CHARLES MACALESTER, JR., b. Campbelltown, Kintyre, 1766, d. Philadelphia, Pennsylvania, 1832, who m. Anna Sampson, of Perth, and had:

EMILY MACALESTER, who m. Nicholas Hopkins, of Philadelphia, and had, besides other issue (see "Americans of Royal Descent," fourth edition, vol. ii., p. 627):

EDWARD MACALESTER HOPKINS, of Philadelphia, who m., first, Lydia, daughter of Samuel N. Lewis, of Philadelphia, and had by her:

EMILY MACALESTER HOPKINS, of Philadelphia, a member of the Pennsylvania Society of the Colonial Dames of America.

PEDIGREE XLIII.

EDWARD III., King of England, *m.*, 1327, Lady Philippa, daughter of William, Count of Hainault and Holland, and had:

SIR LIONEL PLANTAGENET, K.G., Duke of Clarence, Earl of Ulster, *etc.*, 1338-1368; *m.*, first, 1352-54, Lady Elizabeth, 1332-1363, daughter of Sir William de Burgh, third Earl of Ulster, murdered in Ireland 6 June, 1333, also of Royal Descent, and his wife, Lady Maud Plantagenet, also of Royal Descent, and had:

LADY PHILIPPA PLANTAGENET, only child, who *m.*, in 1368, when only 13 years of age, Edmund de Mortimer, third Earl of March, lord-lieutenant of Ireland, Earl of Ulster, *d.* 1381, and had:

LADY ELIZABETH DE MORTIMER, 1371-1417, who *m.*, first, Sir Henry Percy, K.G., the renowned Hotspur, *k.* at Shrewsbury in 1403, son of Henry, fourth Lord Percy, of Alnwick, created, 1377, Earl of Northumberland, also of Royal Descent, and had:

SIR HENRY PERCY, K.G., second Earl of Northumberland, *b.* 1393, *k.* at St. Albans in 1455. He *m.* Lady Eleanor Nevil (her second husband), daughter of Ralph, first Earl of Westmoreland, and Lady Joan de Beaufort, also of Royal Descent, and had:

HENRY PERCY, third Earl of Northumberland, *k.* at Towton, in 1461. He *m.* Lady Eleanor, only child of Richard Poynings, *d. v. p.* 1430, eldest son of Robert, fifth Lord Poynings, *k.* 1446, and had:

SIR HENRY PERCY, K.G., fourth Earl of Northumberland, who was murdered, 28 April, 1489, by order of King Henry VII., having issue by his wife, Lady Matilda, sister of William, second Earl of Pembroke and Huntingdon, and daughter of Sir William de Herbert, K.G., of Ragland, created Earl of Pembroke in 1468:

SIR HENRY ALGERNON PERCY, K.G., fifth Earl of Northumberland, *d.* 1527. He *m.* Lady Catherine, daughter of Sir Robert Spencer, Knt., of Spencer-Combe, Devonshire, by Eleanor, Countess of Ormond and Wiltshire, his wife, also of Royal Descent, and had:

LADY MARGARET PERCY, who *m.* Sir Henry Clifford, K.G., eleventh Baron Clifford, created, 1525, Earl of Cumberland, also of Royal Descent, and had:

LADY CATHERINE CLIFFORD, widow of John, Baron Scroope, of Bolton, who *m.*, secondly, Sir Richard Cholmoneley, Knt., of Roxby, and had by him:

SIR HENRY CHOLMONELEY, Knt., of Grandmount, Whitby, and Roxby, d. 1641, who had by his wife, Margaret, daughter of Sir William de Babthorpe:

MARY CHOLMONELEY, b. 1593, d. 1649, who m. the Hon. Rev. Henry Fairfax, of Oglethorpe, rector of Bolton-Percy, in Yorkshire, b. 1588, d. 1665 (second son of Sir Thomas, created Baron Fairfax, of Cameron, d. 1640, who purchased the title for £1500 from King James I. (see Wood's Douglas's " Peerage of Scotland," i., 560; Lodge's " Peerage of Ireland," v., 1789; Neill's " Fairfaxes of England and America," etc.), and had:

HENRY FAIRFAX, of Oglethorpe, who succeeded as fourth Lord Fairfax, of Cameron, in 1671, b. 1631, d. 1688 (see Burke's " Royal Families," ii., Ped. 147); m. Frances, daughter of Sir Robert Berwick, of Tolston, Yorkshire, and had:

HON. HENRY FAIRFAX, of Denton and Tolston, sheriff of Yorkshire, 1691, d. 1708; m. Anne, daughter of Richard Harrison, of Yorkshire, and had:

HON. WILLIAM FAIRFAX, of "Belvoir," in Virginia, fourth son, b. 1691, d. 1757; president of the Council of Virginia; m., first, Sarah, daughter of Major Walker, of the Bahamas, and had by her:

> SARAH FAIRFAX, who m. Major John Carlyle, of Alexandria, Virginia, and had:
>
> SARAH CARLYLE, who m. William Herbert, of Alexandria, Virginia, and had:
>
> WILLIAM HERBERT, who m. Maria Dulany, and had:
>
> ARTHUR HERBERT, who m. Alice Gregory, and had:
>
> MARY HERBERT, a member of the Virginia Society of the Colonial Dames of America, who m. 4 June, 1890, John D. Hooe, of Warrenton, Virginia, and had: *Bernard* (deceased).

HON. WILLIAM FAIRFAX, of "Belvoir," m., secondly, Deborah, daughter of Francis Clarke, of Salem, Massachusetts, and had by her:

HON. REV. BRYAN FAIRFAX, of Alexandria, Virginia, who succeeded as eighth Lord Fairfax, d. 1802. He m., first, Elizabeth, daughter of Wilson Cary, of Virginia, and had by her:

1.—THOMAS FAIRFAX, of "Vacluse," Fairfax county, Virginia, ninth Baron Fairfax, of Cameron, 1762–1846, who had by his third wife, Margaret, daughter of William Herbert, of Alexandria, Virginia:

> HON. ORLANDO FAIRFAX, M.D., of Richmond, Virginia, who had by his wife, Mary Randolph Cary:
>
> MONIMIA FAIRFAX, who m. George Davis, and had:
>
> I.—MARY FAIRFAX DAVIS, a member of the North Carolina Society

PEDIGREE XLIII.—Continued.

of the Colonial Dames of America, the Order of the Crown, etc., who *m.* Minor Fairfax Heiskell Gouverneur, of Wilmington, North Carolina.

II.—CARY DAVIS, who *m.* Donald MacRae, of Wilmington, North Carolina.

2.—HON. FERNANDO FAIRFAX, of Alexandria, *b.* 1763, who *m.* Elizabeth Cary, and had:

FLORETTA FAIRFAX, who *m.* Rev. Samuel Haggins, and had:

REV. JOHN HAGGINS, of Bath county, Kentucky, who *m.* Margery Mildred, daughter of Colonel William and Elizabeth (Carr) Johnson, and had:

COLONEL GEORGE WASHINGTON FAIRFAX HAGGINS, who *m.* Sarah, daughter of Cornelius and Mary (Norman) Beebe, and had:

NANCY JOHNSON HAGGINS, who *m.* Joseph Kling, of Seymour, Indiana, and had:

VIRGINIA LYNDALL KLING, of Cincinnati, Ohio, who *m.* Horace Bernard Dunbar, of Boston, Massachusetts, and had: *Dorothy, b.* 1 April, 1894.

THE ROYAL DESCENTS

OF

MRS. KELLER ANDERSON,

AND

MRS. THOMAS DAY.

EDWARD I., King of England=Princess Eleanor of Castile.
Princess Joan Plantagenet=Gilbert de Clare, Earl of Gloucester and Hertford.
Lady Margaret de Clare=Hugh de Audley, Earl of Gloucester.
Lady Margaret de Audley=Sir Ralph de Stafford, K.G., Earl of Stafford.
Sir Hugh de Stafford, K.G., Earl of Stafford=Lady Philippa de Beauchamp.
Lady Margaret de Stafford=Sir Ralph de Neville, K.G., Earl of Westmoreland.
Ralph de Neville, of Oversley, Warwickshire=Lady Mary de Ferrers.
John de Neville, of Wymersley, Yorkshire=Lady Elizabeth de Newmarch.
Joan de Neville=Sir William Gascoigne, of Gawthrope, Yorkshire.
Sir William Gascoigne, of Gawthrope, York=Lady Margaret de Percy.
Lady Elizabeth Gascoigne=Gilbert de Talboys, of Kyme.
Sir George de Talboys, of Kyme=(Name unknown.)
Lady Anne de Talboys=Sir Edward Dymoke, of Scrivelsby, Lincolnshire.
Lady Frances Dymoke=Thomas Windebank, of Haines Hill, Berkshire.
Mildred Windebank=Robert Reade, Linkenholt Manor, Southampton.
Col. George Reade, of Gloucester Co., Va.=Elizabeth Martian.
Mildred Reade=Col. Augustine Warner, Jr., of "Warner's Hall."
Elizabeth Warner=Col. John Lewis, Gloucester Co., Va.
Col. Charles Lewis=Mary Howell.
Anne Lewis=Edmund Taylor, Caroline Co., Va.
Frances Taylor=Rev. Nathaniel Moore, Granville Co., N. C.
Anne Lewis Moore=Edward Washington Dale, Columbia, Tenn.
Anne Lewis Dale=James Robertson, of Ayrshire, Scotland.

Jean Robertson=Col. Keller Anderson, United States Army. Mary Robertson=Capt. Thomas Day, of Memphis, Tenn.

Claude Desha Anderson, of Memphis, Tenn.=Mary Simmons.   Jean Keller Anderson.   Mary Louise Day.

Claude Desha Anderson, Jr.

PEDIGREE XLIV.

EDWARD III., King of England, *m.*, 1327, Lady Philippa, daughter of William, Count of Hainault and Holland, and his wife, Joanna, daughter of Charles de Valois, younger son of **Philip III., King of France,** and had:

EDMUND PLANTAGENET, Earl of Cambridge and Duke of York, who *m.*, first, Lady Isabel, daughter of **Peter, King of Castile and Leon,** and had by her:

RICHARD PLANTAGENET, Earl of Cambridge, beheaded in 1415, who *m.* Lady Anne, daughter of Edward de Mortimer, Earl of March, and his wife, Lady Philippa, daughter of Lionel, Duke of Clarence, second son of **Edward III., King of England,** and had:

RICHARD PLANTAGENET, Earl of Cambridge and Duke of York, the Protector, starter of the War of Roses, *k.* in the final battle of Wakefield, 1460. He *m.* Lady Cecily, daughter of Ralph de Nevill, Earl of Westmoreland, also of Royal Descent, and had:

SIR GEORGE PLANTAGENET, K.G., Duke of Clarence (brother of Kings Richard III. and Edward IV., father of King Edward V. and Richard, Duke of York, both murdered in the Tower of London, and Elizabeth, consort of King Henry VII.), who *m.* Lady Isabel de Nevill, daughter of Richard Earl of Salisbury and Warwick, also of Royal Descent (her sister, Anne, *m.*, first, Edward, only son of King Henry VII., and *m.*, secondly, King Richard III.). He was attainted of treason and drowned in a butt of Malmsey wine in the Tower of London, in 1477, and his honors were forfeited. His only daughter:

LADY MARGARET PLANTAGENET, Countess of Salisbury, beheaded for high treason, when 72 years old, 27 May, 1541 (sister of Edward, "the last of the Plantagenets," who was executed in 1499 on London Tower Hill), *m.* Sir Richard Pole, K.G., and had:

SIR HENRY POLE, first Lord Montagu, beheaded in 1539, on London Tower Hill, for high treason. He *m.* Lady Jean, daughter of George Neville, Lord Abergavenny, also of Royal Descent, and had:

LADY WINIFRED POLE, widow of Sir Thomas Hastings, who *m.* (his second wife) Thomas Barrington, high sheriff of Hertford and Essex, in 1562, and had:

SIR FRANCIS BARRINGTON, Bart., M.P. for Essex, 1601, *etc.*, knighted at Theobald's, 7 May, 1607, created a baronet in 1611, *d.* 3 July, 1629; *m.*, first, Lady Joan, daughter of Sir Henry Cromwell (*alias* Williams), of Hinchingbrook, and had by her:

LADY JOAN BARRINGTON, who *m*. Sir Richard Everard, of Much-Waltham, Essex, created a baronet in 1628 (see Banks's "Extinct Baronage," 1808; Brown's "Genesis of the United States," page 826; "New England His. Gen. Reg.," July, 1889; Kimber's "Baronetage," 1771; Meade's "Old Families and Churches of Virginia"), and had:

SIR HUGH EVERARD, Bart., second son, 1654–1705, who *m*. Mary, daughter of John Brown, M.D., of Salisbury, and had:

SIR RICHARD EVERARD, Bart., Governor of North Carolina, for the Proprietors, *d*. 1732, who *m*. Susannah, *d*. 1739, daughter of Rev. Richard Kidder, D.D., Bishop of Bath and Wells, accidentally *k*. in 1703, and had:

LADY SUSANNAH EVERARD, who *m*. (Kimber's "Baronetage," Vol. I.) David Meade, *b*. County Kerry, Ireland (*see* "Meade," in O'Hart's "Irish Landed Gentry"), who *d*. in Nansemond county, Virginia, and had:

1.—ANNE MEADE, who *m*. Richard Randolph, Jr., of "Curles," Virginia, a descendant of the Indian Princess Pocahontas, of Virginia, and had:

MARY RANDOLPH, who *m*. William Bolling, and had:

THOMAS BOLLING, who *m*. Louisa Morris, and had:

VIRGINIA RANDOLPH BOLLING, who *m*. Alex. Quarles Holladay, and had:

MARY STUART HOLLADAY, a member of the North Carolina Society of the Colonial Dames of America, who *m*. Rev. Peyton Harrison Hoge, of Louisville, Kentucky, and had: *Virginia Randolph Bolling, William Lacy, Mary Stuart, Peyton Harrison, Elizabeth Addison,* and *Evelyn Cary.*

2.—MARY MEADE, who *m*. George Walker, of Virginia, and had:

HELEN WALKER, who *m*. William Call, major in Virginia line, Continental Army, and had:

GENERAL RICHARD KEITH CALL, Governor of the Florida Territory and member of Congress from Florida, who *m*. Mary Kirkman, and had:

MARY CALL, who *m*. Theodore Brevard, of Tallahassee, Florida, Brigadier-General Confederate States Army, and had:

CAROLINE MAYS BREVARD, of Tallahassee, a member of the North Carolina Society of the Colonial Dames of America.

PEDIGREE XLV.

HENRY III., King of England, 1206–1272; *m.*, 1236, Eleanor of Provence, *d.* 1291, and had by her:

PRINCE EDMUND, Earl of Leicester, Lancaster and Chester, high steward of England, 1245–1295. He had by his second wife, Blanche, widow of Henry I., King of Navarre, *d.* 1274, and daughter of Robert, Earl of Artois, son of **LOUIS VIII., King of France**, by his wife, Blanche of Castile:

HENRY PLANTAGENET, third Earl of Lancaster, *d.* 1345; *m.* Maud, *b.* 1280, daughter of Patrick de Chaworth, 1253–1282, and had:

LADY ELEANOR PLANTAGENET, widow of John, second Baron Beaumont, *d.* 1342, who *m.*, secondly (his second wife), Sir Richard Fitz-Alan, K.G., ninth Earl of Arundel and seventh Earl of Surrey, *d.* 1375, and had by her:

JOHN FITZ-ALAN, Baron Maltravers, who *m.* Lady Eleanor, the heiress and granddaughter of John, Baron Maltravers, and had:

JOHN FITZ-ALAN, Lord Maltravers, lost at sea, in 1380, who had:

LADY JOAN FITZ-ALAN, *m.* Sir William Echyngham, *d.* 1412, and had:

SIR THOMAS ECHYNGHAM, Knt., *d.* 1444, who had:

THOMAS, Baron Echingham, *d.* 1482, who had:

LADY MARGARET ECHINGHAM, who *m.* William Blount, *d. v. p.*, eldest son of Sir Walter le Blount, K.G., *d.* 1474; treasurer of Calais, 1461; created Lord Montjoy, and his wife, Lady Anne Nevill, also of Royal Descent, and had:

ELIZABETH BLOUNT, who *m.* Sir Andrews, Baron Wyndsore, of Stanwell and Bardsley Abbey, *d.* 1549, also of Royal Descent, and had:

LADY EDITH WYNDSORE, who *m.* George Ludlow, of Hill Deverill, high sheriff of Wiltshire, 1567, *d.* 1580 (*see* Keith's "Ancestry of Benjamin Harrison"), and had:

THOMAS LUDLOW, of Dinton, *d.* 1607, who *m.* Jane, daughter of Thomas Pyle, of Bopton, Wilts, and had:

GABRIEL LUDLOW, *bapt.* 10 February, 1587, called to the Bar, 1620, *d.* 1639; *m.* Phyllis ———, and had:

SARAH LUDLOW, *d.* about 1668, who *m.* (his fourth wife) Colonel John Carter, of "Carotoman," Lancaster county, Virginia, who came to Vir-

(181)

ginia about 1643, probably from Middlesex, and became a member of the Virginia House of Burgesses from Lower Norfolk county in 1643-44; county justice and a member of the Governor's Council, 1657, d. 10 June, 1669, and had:

COLONEL ROBERT CARTER,* of "Carotoman," 1663-1732, only son by Sarah Ludlow, a member and speaker of the House of Burgesses, 1695-99; treasurer of the Colony, 1704-32, etc. (see Keith's "Ancestry of Benjamin Harrison"). He m., first, 1688, Judith, d. 1699, daughter of John Armistead, of "Hesse," Gloucester county, Virginia, and m., secondly, 1701, Elizabeth, daughter of Thomas Landon, of Middlesex county, Virginia, and widow of ———— Willis. From his wealth and authority in the colony he became known as "King Carter" (see Glenn's "Some Colonial Mansions").

COLONEL ROBERT CARTER had by his second wife:

1.—COLONEL CHARLES CARTER, of "Cleve," King George county, Virginia, 1707-1764, who m., first, Mary Walke, and had by her:

I.—ELIZABETH CARTER, who m. William Churchill, of "Wilton," Middlesex county, Virginia, and had:

HANNAH CHURCHILL, m. Benjamin Robinson, and had:

WILLIAM ROBINSON, m. Martha Stubbs, and had:

BENJAMIN NEEDLES ROBINSON, who m. Lucy Heabred Moore, also of Royal Descent, and had:

ELIZABETH TAYLOR ROBINSON, m. John Daniel Turner, M.D., and had:

LOUISE BEVERLEY TURNER, a member of the Virginia Society of the Colonial Dames of America, who m. Isaac N. Jones, of Richmond, Virginia, and had: *Bernard Moore.*

II.—JUDITH FRANCES CARTER, who m. William Burnet Browne, of "Elsing Green," King William county, Virginia, also of Royal Descent, and had:

MARY BURNET BROWNE, who m. Herbert Claiborne, of "Chestnut Grove," New Kent county, Virginia, also of Royal Descent, and had:

HERBERT AUGUSTINE CLAIBORNE, 1784-1841; m. Delia, daughter of John Hayes, of Richmond, Virginia, and had:

MAJOR JOHN HAYES CLAIBORNE, of Richmond, Virginia; m. Anna

---

* The following ladies, members of the National Society of the Colonial Dames of America, are also of Royal Descent, through Colonel Robert Carter:

MRS. EDWARD C. ANDERSON, Georgia State Society.

MRS. ALEXANDER R. LAWTON, Georgia State Society.

Virginia, daughter of George Washington Bassett, of "Eltham," New Kent county, Virginia, also of Royal Descent, and had:

DELIA CLAIBORNE, a member of the Virginia Society of the Colonial Dames of America, who m., 10 June, 1885, General Simon Bolivar Buckner, of "Glen Lily," Hart county, Kentucky, and had: *Simon B.*, b. 18 July, 1886.

COLONEL CHARLES CARTER, of "Cleve," had by his second wife, Ann Byrd, also of Royal Descent:

I.—MARIA CARTER, who m. William Armistead, of "Hesse," Gloucester county, Virginia, and had:

ELEANOR BOWLES ARMISTEAD, who m. Judge William McMechen, of Baltimore, Maryland, and had:

SIDNEY JANE MCMECHEN, who m. John Charles Van Wyck, of Baltimore, and had:

SIDNEY MCMECHEN VAN WYCK, b. 6 April, 1830, d. at San Francisco, California, 27 April, 1887, who m. Nannie Churchill Crittenden, also of Royal Descent, and had:

LAURA SANCHEZ VAN WYCK, of San Francisco, a member of the California Society of the Colonial Dames of America.

II.—LANDON CARTER, of "Cleve," 1751–1811, m., first, Mildred Willis, also of Royal Descent, and had:

LUCY LANDON CARTER, m. General John Minor, of Fredericksburg, Virginia, and had:

LUCIUS HORATIO MINOR, of "Edgewood," m. Catherine Frances Berkeley, also of Royal Descent (see p. 188), and had:

MARY WILLIS MINOR, of Baltimore, a member of the Maryland Society of the Colonial Dames of America.

2.—MARY CARTER, b. 1712, d. 17 September, 1736, who m. George Braxton, of "Newington," King and Queen county, Virginia, and had:

CARTER BRAXTON, of "Elsing Green," b. 10 September, 1736, d. 10 October, 1797, a member of the Continental Congress and a signer of the Declaration of Independence. He m., first, 16 July, 1755, Judith, daughter of Christopher Robinson, 3d, and his wife, Judith Wormeley, and had by her, who d. 1757:

I.—MARY BRAXTON, b. 1756, d. about 1782, who m., 1779, Robert Page, Jr., of "Broad Neck," b. 15 June, 1752, d. 1794, and had:

SARAH WALKER PAGE, b. about 1784, d. 1833, who m., about 1800, Humphrey Brooke, of Spottsylvania county, Virginia, b. about 1757, d. 1843-4, and had:

ANNA AYLETTE BROOKE, b. 16 January, 1808, d. 2 June, 1845, who m., 27 December, 1825, Oliver Abbott Shaw, of Lexington,

Massachusetts, also of Royal Descent, *b.* May, 1799, *d.* March, 1855, and had:

1.—SARAH COLUMBIA BRAXTON SHAW, *b.* 4 July, 1837, *d.* May, 1872; *m.*, 1 January, 1869, Albert Henry Rose, and had:

> ANNA BROOKE ROSE, of Alameda, California, a member of the Virginia and California Societies of the Colonial Dames of America.

2.—JOANNA MAYNARD SHAW, *b.* 26 May, 1830, a member of the Virginia and California Societies of the Colonial Dames of America, who *m.*, 15 October, 1846, Selden Stuart Wright, of Essex county, Virginia, 1822–1893, and had:

I.—MARY STUART WRIGHT, 1847–1878; *m.*, 1867, William B. Hooper, and had, besides other issue:

> MARY STUART HOOPER, a member of the Virginia and California Societies of the Colonial Dames of America, who *m.*, 1889, Cavalier Hamilton Jouett, of San Francisco. *Issue.*

II.—COLONEL STUART SELDEN WRIGHT, of Fresno, California, who *m.*, 1873, Maria Byrd Hopkins, also of Royal Descent, a member of the Virginia and California Societies of the Colonial Dames of America, and had:

> LOUISE KIMBALL WRIGHT, a member of the Virginia and California Societies of the Colonial Dames of America, who *m.*, 1895, John M. McClure, of Oakland, California. *Issue.*

III.—ANN AYLETTE BROOKE WRIGHT, a member of the Virginia and California Societies of the Colonial Dames of America.

IV.—ELIZA SHAW WRIGHT, a member of the Virginia and California Societies of the Colonial Dames of America, who *m.*, 1881, John D. Tallant, of San Francisco. *Issue.*

II.—JUDITH BRAXTON, who *m.* John White, and had:

MARY PAGE WHITE, who *m.* (his first wife) Andrew Stevenson, of Blenheim, Albemarle county, Virginia, member and Speaker of the House of Representatives and United States Minister to England, and had:

JOHN WHITE STEVENSON, of Covington, Kentucky, former Governor of Kentucky and United States Senator, who *m.* Sibella Winston, and had:

JUDITH WHITE STEVENSON, a member of the Virginia Society of the Colonial Dames of America, who *m.* John Flack Winslow, of Cincinnati, Ohio, and had: *John W. Stevenson, b.* Covington, Kentucky, 3 April, 1893.

3.—ANNE CARTER, who m., 1722, Benjamin Harrison, of "Berkeley," Charles City county, Virginia, a member of the House of Burgesses, d. 1745, also of Royal Descent (p. 34), and had:

I.—BENJAMIN HARRISON, of "Berkeley," member of the Continental Congress, a signer of the Declaration of Independence, Governor of Virginia, b. 1726, d. 24 April, 1791, who m., 13 December, 1730, Elizabeth Bassett, also of Royal Descent, and had:

GENERAL WILLIAM HENRY HARRISON, of Ohio, the ninth President of the United States, b. 9 February, 1773, d. Washington City, 4 April, 1841. He m., 22 November, 1795, Ann, d. 25 February, 1864, aged 88 years, daughter of John Cleves Symmes, of Ohio, 1742–1814, associate justice of the Supreme Court of New Jersey, United States district judge for the Northwest Territory, one of the founders of the city of Cincinnati, and had:

1.—JOHN SCOTT HARRISON, of Cleves, Ohio, b. 4 October, at Vincennes, 1804, d. 1878, a member of Congress. He m., secondly, 12 August, 1831, Elizabeth Irwin, and had by her:

GENERAL BENJAMIN HARRISON, of Indianapolis, Indiana, b. 20 August, 1833, the twenty-third President of the United States. He m., first, Caroline, daughter of Rev. John Witherspoon Scott, of Ohio, and his wife, Mary, daughter of John Neal, of Philadelphia, Pennsylvania, and had by her, who d. 25 October, 1892:

MARY SCOTT HARRISON, a member of the Virginia Society of the Colonial Dames of America, who m., 5 November, 1884, James Robert McKee, of Indianapolis, Indiana, and had issue: *Benjamin H.* and *Mary Lodge.*

2.—LUCY SINGLETON HARRISON, 1800–1826, who m., 1819 (his first wife), Judge David K. Este, of Cincinnati, also of Royal Descent, and had:

LUCY ANNE HARRISON ESTE, who m. Joseph F. Reynolds, of Baltimore, Maryland, and had:

ANNA HARRISON REYNOLDS, who m. John Law Crawford, and had:

LUCY CRAWFORD, a member of the Maryland Society of the Colonial Dames of America, who m. George C. Woodruff, of Litchfield, Connecticut. *No issue.*

II.—NATHANIEL HARRISON, a member of the Virginia State Senate, 1780, who m. Mary, daughter of Edmund Ruffin, of Prince George county, Virginia, and had:

EDMUND HARRISON, of Amelia county, Virginia, 1761-1826, member of the House of Delegates, member of the Council, 1793, *etc.*, who *m.* Martha Wayles Skipwith, also of Royal Descent, and had:

WILLIAM HENRY HARRISON, of Amelia county, Virginia, 1812-1884, who *m.* Lucy A. Powers, and had:

PROFESSOR EDMUND HARRISON, A.M., *b.* 17 February, 1843, president of Bethel Female College, Kentucky; *m.* Kate Steger, and had:

1.—LULIE HARRISON, a member of the Virginia Society of the Colonial Dames of America, who *m.* Dana Henry Rucker, of Richmond, Virginia, and had: *Edmund Harrison, b.* 18 February, 1898.

2.—JENNIE HARRISON, a member of the Virginia Society of the Colonial Dames of America, who *m.* Charles H. Chalkley, of Hopkinsville, Kentucky.

3.—LELIA SKIPWITH HARRISON, a member of the Virginia Society of the Colonial Dames of America, who *m.* Howard D. Hoge, of Richmond.

III.—CARTER HENRY HARRISON, of "Clifton," who *m.* Susan, daughter of Isham Randolph, of "Dungeness," who *d.* 1742, and had:

ROBERT CARTER HARRISON, who had by his first wife, Ann Cabell:

1.—MARY HOPKINS HARRISON, who *m.* Samuel Q. Richardson, and had:

ROBERT CARTER RICHARDSON, who *m.* Marie Louise Harris, and had:

MARY CABELL RICHARDSON, of Covington, Kentucky, a member of the Virginia Society of the Colonial Dames of America, a founder of the Order of Colonial Governors, *etc.*

2.—VIRGINIA HARRISON, who *m.* David Castleman, and had:

HUMPHREYS CASTLEMAN, of Columbus, Georgia, who *m.* Eva Garrard, a member of the Georgia Society of the Colonial Dames of America, and had:

ISABEL GARRARD CASTLEMAN, a member of the Georgia Society of the Colonial Dames of America (also of Royal Descent through Elizabeth Burwell, p. 34), who *m.* Samuel Harrison McAfee.

4.—COLONEL LANDON CARTER, of "Sabine Hall," Richmond county, Virginia, who had by his second wife, Maria Byrd, also of Royal Descent:

I.—MARIA BYRD CARTER, who *m.* Robert Beverley, of "Wakefield," Culpeper county, Virginia, *d.* 1800, also of Royal Descent, and had:

EVELYN BYRD BEVERLEY, widow of George Lee, who *m.*, secondly, Patrick Hume Douglas, M.D., of Loudoun county, Virginia, *d.* 1837, and had:

WILLIAM BYRD DOUGLAS, *b.* 1815, *d.* Nashville, Tennessee, 13 December, 1882; *m.*, first, Martha Rebecca Bright, and had:

MARY MARGARET DOUGLAS, a member of the Virginia Society of the Colonial Dames of America, who *m.*, first, James R. Buckner, and had: *James R.*, and *m.*, secondly, Edward D. Richards, and had: *Evelyn B.* (see p. 58), all of Nashville, Tennessee.

II.—LANDON CARTER, of Pittsylvania county, Virginia; *m.* Judith Fauntleroy, also of Royal Descent, and had:

WORMELEY CARTER, who *m.* Sarah Edwards, and had:

WORMELEY CARTER, who *m.* Lucinda Washington Alexander, and had:

JUDGE WILLIAM ALEXANDER CARTER, who *m.* Mary Eliza Hamilton, and had:

MARY ADA CARTER, a member of the Pennsylvania Society of the Colonial Dames of America, who *m.*, 1874, Joseph K. Corson, M.D., surgeon United States Army, also of Royal Descent, and had: *Mary Carter*, *b.* 1876, *d.* 1890, and *Edward Foulke*, *b.* 1883.

LANDON CARTER, of "Sabine Hall;" *m.*, thirdly, Elizabeth Wormeley, and had by her:

1.—ROBERT CARTER, of "Sabine Hall;" *m.* Winifred Beale, and had:

I.—LANDON CARTER, of "Sabine Hall," 1756–1820; *m.*, secondly, Mary, daughter of John Armistead, and had by her:

FRANCES CARTER, who *m.* Major Rozier Dulany, United States Army, also of Royal Descent, and had:

REBECCA DULANY, who *m.* Colonel Richard H. Dulany, of "Welborne," Virginia, also of Royal Descent, and had:

FRANCES ADDISON CARTER DULANY, a member of the Maryland Society of the Colonial Dames of America, who *m.* J. Southgate Lemmon, of Baltimore.

II.—FRANCES CARTER, who *m.* Thomas Ludlow Lee, and had:

WINIFRED BEALE LEE, who *m.* William Brent, of "Richland," and had:

THOMAS LEE BRENT, *m.* Jane Duncan Wilkins, and had:

WINIFRED LEE BRENT, a member of the Maryland Society of the Colonial Dames of America, who m. Henry F. Le H. Lyster, of Detroit, Michigan, and had: 1. *Dr. William J.*, United States Army; 2. *Eleanor Carroll*, wife of Edward H. Parker, of Detroit; 3. *Henry Lawrence;* 4. *Florence Murray;* 5. *Thomas Lee Brent.*

2.—ELIZABETH WORMELEY CARTER, m. Nelson Berkeley, of "Airwell," Hanover county, Virginia, and had:

DR. CARTER BERKELEY, of "Edgewood;" m. Mrs. Frances (Page) Nelson, also of Royal Descent (see pp. 34, 133 and 134), and had:

CATHERINE FRANCES BERKELEY, m. Lucius Horatio Minor, of "Edgewood," also of Royal Descent (see p. 183), and had:

MARY WILLIS MINOR, of Baltimore, a member of the Maryland Society of the Colonial Dames of America.

THE ROYAL DESCENTS
OF
MRS. THOMAS LEE ALFRIEND,
AND
MRS. HERBERT DALE LAFFERTY.

	ALFRED THE GREAT, of England, had:
ALFRED THE GREAT, of England, had:	Ethelwida, *m.* Baldwin II., of Flanders, and had:
Edward the Elder, King of England, who had:	Arnolph the Great, Count of Flanders, who had:
Edmund I., King of England, who had:	Baldwin III., Count of Flanders, who had:
Edgar the Peaceful, King of England, who had:	Arnolph II., Count of Flanders, who had:
Ethelred II., King of England, who had:	Baldwin IV., Count of Flanders, who had:
Edmund II., King of England, who had:	Baldwin V., Count of Flanders, who had:
Edward the Exile, Prince of England, who had:	Maud, *m.* William the Conqueror, and had:
Margaret, *m.* Malcolm III., of Scotland, and had:	Henry I., King of England, who had:
David I., King of Scotland, who had:	Maud, *m.* Geoffrey, Count of Anjou, and had:
Prince Henry of Scotland, who had:	Henry II., King of England, who had:
David, Earl of Huntingdon, who had:	John, King of England, who had:
Isabella, *m.* Robert, Earl of Annandale, and had:	Henry III., King of England, who had:
Robert Bruce, Earl of Annandale, who had:	Edmund, Earl of Lancaster, who had:
Robert Bruce, Earl of Carrick, who had:	Henry, Earl of Lancaster, who had:
Robert Bruce, King of Scotland, who had:	Joan, *m.* John de Mowbray, and had:
Margery, *m.* Walter, High Steward, and had.	John, 4th Baron de Mowbray, who had:
Robert II., King of Scotland, who had:	Eleanor, *m.* Roger de la Warr, and had:
Catherine, *m.* Sir David Lindsay, and had:	Joan, *m.* Sir Thomas de West, and had:
Alexander, Earl of Crawford, who had:	Sir Reginald, Baron de la Warr, who had:
Walter Lindsay, of Beaufort, who had:	Sir Richard, Baron de la Warr, who had:
Sir David Lindsay, of Edzell, who had:	Sir Thomas, Baron de la Warr, who had:
Walter Lindsay, of Edzell, who had:	Sir George West, Knt., who had:
Alexander Lindsay, of Edzell, who had:	Sir William, Baron de la Warr, who had:
Rev. David Lindsay, Bishop of Ross, who had.	Sir Thomas, Baron de la Warr, who had:
Rachel, *m.* Rev. Dr. John Spottiswood, and had:	Gov. John West, of Va., who had:
Sir Robert Spottiswood, of New Abbey, who had:	Col. John West, of "West Point," Va., who had:
Surgeon Robert Spottiswood, who had:	Capt. Nathaniel West, of Va., who had:
Gen. Alexander Spotswood, of Va., who had:	Unity, *m.* William Dandridge, R. N., and had:

John Spotswood, of Virginia, *m.* Mary Dandridge, of "Elsing Green," Va.

Anne Spotswood = Lewis Burwell.

Spotswood Burwell = Mary Marshall.

Mary Ann Spotswood Burwell = Otis F. Manson, M.D.

Eliza Sanger Manson, member of the National = Thomas Lee Alfriend, of Richmond, Va.
Society of the Colonial Dames of America.

| Mary Burwell Alfriend, member of the National Society of the Colonial Dames of America. *No issue.* = Herbert Dale Lafferty. | Otis Manson Alfriend. | Sally Spotswood Alfriend. | Maria Lee Alfriend. |

PEDIGREE XLVI.

EDWARD I., King of England, had by his first wife, Princess Eleanor, daughter of Ferdinand III., King of Castile and Leon:

PRINCESS ELEANOR PLANTAGENET, who m. Henri, Count de Barr, and had:

LADY ELEANOR DE BARR, who m. Llewelyn ap Owen ap Merededd, of Royal Descent from Rhys ap Tudor, Prince of South Wales, and had:

THOMAS AP LLEWELYN, who m. Lady Eleanor, also of Royal Descent, daughter of Philip ap Iver ap Cadivor, and had:

ELEANOR V. PHILIP, who m. Griffith Vychan, lord of Glyndyfrdwy, and had:

LOWRY VAUGHN (sister of Owen Glendower), who m. Robert Puleston, of Emral, and had:

JOHN PULESTON, of Emral, who m. Angharad, daughter of Griffith Hanmer, of Hanmer, and had:

MARGARET PULESTON (see Dwnn's "Visitations of Wales"), m. David ap Ievan ap Einion, constable of Harlech Castle, 1468, and had:

EINION AP DAVID, of Cryniarth, in Edermon, who had:

LLEWELYN AP EINION, who had:

GRIFFITH AP LLEWELYN, who m. Mary, daughter of Howell ap Harry, and had:

CATHERINE VCH GRIFFITH, who m. Edward ap Ievan, of Llanwddyn parish, Montgomeryshire, and had:

ELLEN VCH EDWARD, who m. Lewis ap Griffith, of Yshute (Ysputty-Ievan) Denbighshire, 1525–1600, also of Royal Descent, and had:

ROBERT AP LEWIS, of Rhiwlas, near Bala, Merionethshire, 1555–1645, who m. Gwyrryl (Gwervyl), daughter of Hewelyn (Llewelyn) ap David, of Llan Rwst, Denbighshire, and had:

EVAN AP ROBERT AP LEWIS,* of Rhiwlás and Vron Gôch, Merionethshire, 1585–1662 (see Glenn's "Merion in the Welsh Tract"), m. Jane ———, and had:

1.—OWEN AP EVAN, of Fron Gôch farm, near Bala, d. 1669; m. Gainor John, d. 14 December, 1678, and had:

---

* MRS. HENRY SHIPPEN HUIDEKOPER, a member of the Pennsylvania Society of the National Society of the Colonial Dames of America, is also of Royal Descent through Evan Robert Lewis.

JANE OWEN, b. at Fron Gôch, 1653–54, d. Merion, Pennsylvania, 1 September, 1686; m. in Wales, 1672–73, Hugh Roberts, of Kiltalgarth township, Merionethshire, a minister among the Friends, d. 1702. They removed to Chester county, Pennsylvania, in 1683, and in 1692 he was a member of the Provincial Council, and had:

ROBERT ROBERTS, b. 7 January, 1673, who had by his second wife, Priscilla Jones:

ELIZABETH ROBERTS, who m. Isaac Parrish, and had:

ISAAC PARRISH, who m. Sarah Mitchell, and had:

JOSEPH PARRISH, who m. Susanna Cox, and had:

WILLIAM DILLWYN PARRISH, who m. Elizabeth W. Miller, and had:

MARY PARRISH, a member of the Pennsylvania Society of the Colonial Dames of America, who m. Louis Starr, M.D., of Philadelphia, and had: *Louis,* b. 5 June, 1882; *Dillwyn P.,* b. 3 October, 1883, and *Elizabeth Parrish,* b. 29 April, 1889.

2.—EVAN AP EVAN, of Vron Gôch, who m. twice, and had:

THOMAS AP EVAN, *alias* THOMAS EVANS, b. at Vron Gôch, 1651, came to Pennsylvania 1698, lived in Gwynedd, and d. at Goshen in 1738. He had by his first wife, Ann, d. at Gwynedd, 26 March, 1716:

HUGH EVANS, of Merion, Pennsylvania, d. Philadelphia, 6 April, 1772, aged 90 years, a member of the Provincial Assembly, 1722, 1746–54. He m., thirdly, 13 February, 1716, Lowry, widow of Robert Lloyd, and daughter of Reese John William, also of Royal Descent, and had (*see* Jenkins's " History of Gwynedd," p. 152):

SUSANNA EVANS, 1719–1801, who m., 30 May, 1740, Owen Jones, Sr., of Merion, 1711–1793, the last Provincial treasurer of Pennsylvania, also of Royal Descent (p. 160), and had:

1.—HANNAH JONES, 1749–1829, who m., 1779, Amos Foulke, of Philadelphia, 1740–1791, also of Royal Descent, and had:

EDWARD FOULKE, of Gwynedd, 1784–1851; m., 1810, Tacy, daughter of Isaac and Gainor Jones, and had, besides other issue:

I.—ANNE JONES FOULKE, 1811–1888, m., 1833, Hiram Corson, M.D., of Conshohocken, and had:

SUSAN FOULKE CORSON, a member of the Pennsylvania Society of the Colonial Dames of America, who m., 26 November, 1868, Jawood Lukens, of Conshohocken. *No issue.*

II.—PRISCILLA FOULKE, 1821–1882, m., 22 November, 1849, Thomas Wistar, Jr., of Philadelphia, and had:

SUSAN FOULKE WISTAR, a member of the Pennsylvania Society of the Colonial Dames of America, who m., 27 May, 1872,

Howard Comfort, of Philadelphia, and had: *William Wistar, b* 27 May, 1874.

III.—REBECCA JONES FOULKE, *b.* 18 May, 1829, a member of the Pennsylvania Society of the Colonial Dames of America, who *m.*, 8 October, 1857, Robert R. Corson, of New Hope, Pennsylvania. *No issue.*

2.—LOWRY JONES, who *m.*, 5 July, 1760, Daniel Wister, of Philadelphia, 1738–1805, and had:

I.—JOHN WISTER, of Philadelphia, 1776–1862; *m.* Elizabeth Harvey, and had:

LOUIS WISTER, of Ardmore, Pennsylvania, *m.* Elizabeth Emlen Randolph, and had: *Sara Edythe,* and

ELIZABETH HARVEY WISTER, a member of the Pennsylvania Society of the Colonial Dames of America, who *m.* Charles Penrose Keith, of Philadelphia, author of "The Provincial Councillors of Pennsylvania and their Descendants," "Ancestry of Benjamin Harrison," *etc. No issue.*

II.—CHARLES JONES WISTER, of Philadelphia, 1782–1865, who *m.* Rebecca Bullock, and had:

WILLIAM WYNNE WISTER, of Philadelphia, *m.* Hannah Lewis Wilson, and had:

RACHAEL WILSON WISTER, who *m.*, 12 November, 1862, William Barton Rogers, and had:

MABEL ROGERS, a member of the Pennsylvania Society of the Colonial Dames of America, who *m.* Edgar W. Baird, of Philadelphia, and had: *Edgar W.* and *Gainor Owen.*

THE ROYAL DESCENT

OF

MRS. BYRON COLEMAN DICK,

OF OAKLAND, CAL.

HUGH CAPET, King of France, had:
Robert the Pious, King of France, who had:
Henry I., King of France, who had:
Hugh Magnus, Duke of France, who had:
Isabel, *m.* Robert, Earl of Mellent, and had:
Robert, second Earl of Leicester, who had:
Robert, third Earl of Leicester, who had:
Margaret, *m.* Saier de Quincey, and had:
Roger, Earl of Winchester, who had:
Elizabeth, *m.* Alexander Cumyn, and had:
Agnes, *m.* Gilbert de Umfraville, and had:
Robert, second Earl of Angus, who had:
Thomas de Umfraville, of Harbottle, who had:
Sir Thomas de Umfraville, of Kyme, who had:
Joan, *m.* Sir William Lambert, and had:
Robert Lambert, of Owlton, who had:
Henry Lambert, of Ongar, who had:
Elizabeth, *m.* Thomas Lyman, and had:
Henry Lyman, of Navistoke, who had:
John Lyman, of High Ongar, who had:
Henry Lyman, of High Ongar, who had:
Richard Lyman, of Hartford, Conn., who had:
John Lyman, of Northampton, Mass., who had:
Benjamin Lyman, of Northampton, who had:
Mary, *m.* Oliver Pomeroy, and had:

HUGH CAPET, King of France, had:
Robert the Pious, King of France, who had:
Henry I., King of France, who had:
Hugh Magnus, Duke of France, who had:
Isabel, *m.* William, Earl of Surrey, and had:
William, Earl of Warren and Surrey, who had:
Isabel, *m.* Hameline Plantagenet, and had:
Isabel, *m.* Roger, Earl of Norfolk, and had:
Hugh Bigod, Earl of Norfolk, who had:
Sir Hugh Bigod, Knt., who had:
Sir John Bigod, Knt., who had:
Roger Bigod, of Settington, who had:
Joan, *m.* Sir William de Chauncy, and had:
John Chauncy, of Stepney, who had:
John Chauncy, of Sawbridgeworth, who had:
John Chauncy, of Sawbridgeworth, who had:
John Chauncy, of Pishobury, who had:
Henry Chauncy, of New Place, who had:
George Chauncy, of Yardleybury, who had:
Rev. Charles Chauncy, D.D., who had:
Sarah, *m.* Rev. Gershom Bulkeley, and had:
Edward Bulkeley, of Wethersfield, who had:

Rachel Lyman Pomeroy *m.* Brig.-Major Edward Bulkeley.

Col. Selah Francis═Roxa Lyman Bulkeley.

Judge Jesse Booth, of New York═Roxa Bulkeley Francis.

Byron Coleman Dick, of Oakland, Cal.═Ellen Cordelia Bulkeley Booth, member of the Conn Society of the Colonial Dames of America.
No issue.

PEDIGREE XLVII.

DAVID I., King of Scotland, had by his wife, Lady Matilda, daughter of Waltheof, Earl of Northumberland:

HENRY, Prince of Scotland, eldest son, Earl of Northumberland, *d. v. p.*, 1152, who *m.*, 1139, Lady Ada de Warren, *d.* 1178, daughter of William, second Earl of Warren and Surrey, and had:

PRINCESS MARGARET, widow of Conan le Petit, Earl of Brittany and Richmond, *d.* 20 February, 1171, who *m.*, secondly, Humphrey, fourth Baron de Bohun, constable of England, and had:

LADY —— DE BOHUN, who *m.* (his first wife) Reginald, sixth Baron de Mohun, of Dunster, *d.* 1256, and had:

JOHN DE MOHUN, Baron de Mohun, of Dunster, *d.* 1278; *m.* Joan, daughter of Sir Reginald Fitz-Piers, of Blewleveny, and had:

SIR JOHN DE MOHUN, first Lord Mohun of Dunster Castle, by writ, *d.* 1330; *m.* Auda, daughter of Sir Richard Tibetot, Knt., and had:

LADY MARGARET DE MOHUN, who *m.* Sir John Cantilupe, Knt., grandson of John Cantilupe, of Smithfield, and had:

ELEANOR CANTILUPE, who *m.* Sir Thomas de West, Knt., of Roughcombe, Wiltshire, Governor of Christ Church Castle; summoned to Parliament, 1333, for Warwickshire as Baron West, *d.* 1344, and had:

SIR THOMAS DE WEST, Knt., second Baron West, of Hampston-Cantilupe, and Great Torrington, Devonshire; *m.* Lady Alice, daughter of Reginald Fitz-Piers, Baron of Wolverly, and had:

SIR THOMAS DE WEST, third Baron West, Knt., *d.* in 1405; *m.* Lady Joan, half-sister and heiress of Thomas, Lord de la Warr, and daughter of Roger de la Warr, *d.* 1371, and his second wife, Lady Eleanor de Mowbray, also of Royal Descent, and had:

SIR REGINALD DE WEST, second son, who, on the death of Lord de la Warr, had livery of the lands of his mother's inheritance, and was summoned to Parliament as Lord de la Warr (*see* Doyle's "Official Baronage"). He *d.* 27 August, 1451, possessed of vast estates, having had issue by his wife, Margaret, daughter of Robert Thorley:

RICHARD DE WEST, Lord de la Warr, *d.* 10 March, 1475; *m.* Catherine, daughter of Robert, Baron de Hungerford, and had:

SIR THOMAS DE WEST, K.B., K.G., Lord de la Warr, *d.* 1524; *m.*, first, Elizabeth, daughter of Hugh Mortimer, of Mortimer Hall, Hants, and *m.*, secondly, Alianor, daughter of Sir Roger Copley, of Gatton, and had:

SIR GEORGE WEST, Knt., second son, *d.* 1538; *m.* Lady Elizabeth, daughter of Sir Anthony Moreton, of Lechdale, Gloucestershire, and had:

SIR WILLIAM WEST, *b. ante* 1520, *d.* 30 December, 1595, created Baron de la Warr, 5 February, 1570 (*see* Foster's " Peerage "); *m.*, 1554, Elizabeth, daughter of Thomas Strange, of Chesterton, Gloucestershire, and had:

SIR THOMAS WEST, only son, second Lord de la Warr (*see* Dugdale's " Baronage " of 1676; Brown's " Genesis of the United States," p. 1045), *d.* April, 1602; *m.* Anne Knowles, and had:

LADY PENELOPE WEST, *b.* 9 September, 1582, who *m.*, 1599, Herbert Pelham, of Boston, Lincolnshire, *d.* July, 1624 (*see* " American Heraldic Journal," iii., p. 84; Berry's "Sussex Pedigrees "), and had:

HERBERT PELHAM,* of Boston, Lincolnshire, eldest son, *b.* 1600, *d.* in July, 1674. He removed with some of his children, his wife being dead, to Cambridge, Massachusetts, in 1638, and was treasurer of Harvard College in 1643, and was chosen an assistant in 1645. In 1647 he returned to England, and became a member of Parliament in 1654 (*see* " Mass. His. Col.," third ser., iii.). He *m.*, first, 1626, Jemima, daughter of Thomas Waldegrave, of Bures, Essex, and *m.*, secondly, Elizabeth, daughter of Godfrey Bosville, of Gunthwaite, Yorkshire, and widow of Roger Harlakenden, who *d.* in New England, in 1638, and had by her:

PENELOPE PELHAM, *bapt.* at Bures, in 1633, *d.* 7 December, 1703; *m.*, 1657, in New England, Josiah Winslow, of Marshfield, who was *b.* at Plymouth, 1629, and *d.* at Careswell, 18 December, 1680; was commander of the military of Plymouth Colony and of that of the United Colonies in the King Philip War, 1675, and Governor of Plymouth Colony, 1673–80. He was son of Edward Winslow, of Droitwich, Worcestershire, one of the Pilgrims to New England, and Governor of Plymouth Colony. Governor Winslow and Penelope had:

JUDGE ISAAC WINSLOW, of Marshfield, *b.* 1670, *d.* 6 December, 1738. Commander of the Colony's militia; member of the council twenty years; chief justice of Court of Common Pleas and judge of probate; *m.*, 11 July, 1700, Sarah, *d.* 1753, aged 80, daughter of John Wensley, of Boston, and had:

PENELOPE WINSLOW, *b.* 27 December, 1704, *d.* 1737; *m.*, June 30, 1724,

---

* MRS. GEORGE S. HALE, a member of the Massachusetts State Society of the National Society of the Colonial Dames of America, is of Royal Descent through Herbert Pelham.

PEDIGREE XLVII.—Continued.

James, b. 14 April, 1700, d. July, 1757, son of James (of Nathaniel of Richard the Pilgrim) and Sarah (Doty) Warren, and had:

SARAH WARREN, b. 13 May, 1730; d. 15 March, 1797; m., 2 December, 1755, William, b. 12 October, 1729, d. 15 June, 1809, son of Nicholas and Sarah (Warren) Sever, and had:

WILLIAM SEVER, b. 23 June, 1759, d. 27 October, 1798; m., 29 October, 1785, Mary, b. 21 December, 1759, d. 15 January, 1821, daughter of John and Mary (Church) Chandler, and had:

PENELOPE WINSLOW SEVER, b. 21 July, 1786, d. 2 April, 1872; m., 6 September, 1807, Levi, b. 25 October, 1782, d. 29 May, 1868, son of Levi and Martha (Waldo) Lincoln, and had:

DANIEL WALDO LINCOLN, b. 19 January, 1813, d. 1 July, 1880, who m., 30 November, 1841, Frances Fiske, b. 15 October, 1819, d. 8 April, 1873, daughter of Francis Taliaferro Merrick, 1792–1863, and had:

1.—FRANCES MERRICK LINCOLN, of Worcester, Massachusetts, a member of the Massachusetts Society of the Colonial Dames of America.

2.—MARY WALDO LINCOLN, a member of the Massachusetts Society of the Colonial Dames of America, who m. Joseph Estabrook Davis, of Boston, and had: *Lincoln*, b. 31 March, 1872, and *Mabel*, b. 25 March, 1875.

3.—WALDO LINCOLN, of Worcester, Massachusetts, m., 24 June, 1873, Fanny Chandler (daughter of George and Josephine Rose Chandler, of Worcester), a member of the Massachusetts Society of the Colonial Dames of America, and had: *Merrrick*, b. 25 May, 1875; *Josephine Rose*, b. 28 February, 1878; *Daniel Waldo*, b. 2 September, 1882; *George Chandler*, b. 6 August, 1884, and *Dorothy*, b. 4 March, 1890.

PEDIGREE XLVIII.

HENRY I., King of France, had by his wife, Anne of Russia:

HUGH THE GREAT, Duke of France and Burgundy, Marquis of Orleans, Count of Paris, Valois and Vermandois, who had by his third wife, Lady Adelheid, daughter of Herbert IV., Count de Vermandois, also of Royal Descent:

LADY ISABEL DE VERMANDOIS, d. 1131, who m., first, Robert de Beaumont, or Bellomont, Earl of Mellent, created, in 1103, Earl of Leicester, d. 1118 (see " L'Art de Verifier les Dates," xii.), and had:

LADY ELIZABETH DE BELLOMONT, who m. Gilbert Fitz-Gilbert de Clare, created, in 1138, Earl of Pembroke, d. 1149, and had:

RICHARD DE CLARE, "the Strongbow," second Earl of Pembroke, lord justice of Ireland, d. s. p. m. 1176, who m. Lady Eva, daughter of Dermot MacMurcha, the last King of Leinster, and had:

LADY ISABEL DE CLARE, who m., 1189 (his first wife), William le Marshal, Earl of Pembroke, Protector of England during the nonage of Henry III., d. 1219, and had:

LADY ISABEL MARSHALL, who m., first, Gilbert de Clare, Earl of Clare, Hertford and Gloucester, a surety for the Magna Charta, d. 1229, and had:

LADY ISABEL DE CLARE, who m. Robert Bruce, fifth Earl of Annandale, 1210–1295, and had:

ROBERT BRUCE, Earl of Annandale and Carrick, 1245–1304 ; m., 1271, Margaret, Countess of Carrick, widow of Adam Kilconcath, d. 1270, and daughter and heiress of Neil, second Earl of Carrick, d. 1256, and had:

LADY MARY BRUCE (sister of Robert Bruce, King of Scotland), widow of Sir Neil Campbell, who m., secondly, Sir Alexander Fraser, lord chamberlain of Scotland, 1323, k. 1332, and had:

SIR JOHN FRASER, of Aberbothnot, eldest son, whose only child:

LADY MARGARET FRASER, m. Sir William Keith, great marshal of Scotland, d. 1406-8, and had:

LADY ELIZABETH KEITH, who m. Sir Adam de Gordon, of Huntley, k. at Homildon, and had:

LADY ELIZABETH DE GORDON, only child, who m., before 27 March, 1408, Alexander de Seton, and had:

ALEXANDER DE SETON, of Gordon and Huntly, created, in 1445, Earl of Huntly, *d.* 1470, who had by his fourth wife, "The Fair Maid of Moray," a daughter of Comyn of Altyre:

LADY MARGARET DE GORDON, *b. ante* 1460, *d.* 1506, who *m.* (the obligation for the marriage of his half-sister signed by George de Gordon, Earl of Huntly, 26 June, 1484) Hugh Rose, eighth laird of Kilravock and Geddes (his second wife), *d.* 17 March, 1517 (*see* " Rose of Kilravock," 1683, reprint by the Spalding Club, Edinburgh, 1848), and had:

JOHN ROSE, of Bellivat, second son, who *m.* (contract dated "at Elgin the penult daye of Aprill in y⁸ yeir of God I^{M}V^C and xxvj yeirs ") Marjory, daughter of James Dunbar, of Cunzie, also of Royal Descent, and had:

JOHN ROSE, of Bellivat, who *m.* a daughter of Alexander Urquhart, of Burdsyards, and had:

JOHN ROSE, of Bellivat, who *m.*, first, a daughter of —— Falconar, of Hawkerton, and had:

HUGH ROSE, second son, who *m.* Katherine, daughter of —— Ord, of Finachty, and had:

PATRICK ROSE, of Lochihills, eldest son, *d.* 31 March, 1727, who *m.* Isabel Falloch, of Bogtown, and had:

JOHN ROSE, of Wester Alves, *d. v. p.*, 13 April, 1724, who *m., ante* 1704, Margaret Grant, of Whitetree, *d.* 1774, and had (*see* W. G. Stanard's " Rose Chart-Pedigree," 1895):

REV. ROBERT ROSE, third son, *b.* at Wester Alves, 12 February, 1704; came to Virginia in 1725, was rector of St. Anne's parish, Essex county, 1728–1747, and of Albemarle parish, 1747–1751; *d.* at Richmond, 30 June, 1751. He had by his second wife, *m.* 6 November, 1740, Anne, daughter of Henry Fitzhugh, of " Bedford," King George county, Virginia, 1720–1789:

COLONEL HUGH ROSE, of " Geddes," Amherst county, Virginia, 1743–1797, a member of the Amherst county committee of safety; county lieutenant; member of the House of Delegates; high sheriff of Amherst county, 1775; *m.* Caroline, daughter of Colonel Samuel Jordan, of " Seven Islands," Buckingham county, Virginia, *d.* 1789, and had:

1.—ROBERT H. ROSE, M.D., *d.* 1835; *m.* Frances Taylor, daughter of Colonel James and Nelly (Conway) Madison, of " Montpelier," Virginia, and sister of President Madison, and had:

NELLY CONWAY ROSE, *m.* John Francis Newman, and had:

I.—ELLEN ROSE NEWMAN, *d.* 1869, who *m.* Rev. John Ambrose Wheelock, *d.* 1866, and had:

ELIZABETH JOSEPHINE WHEELOCK, of Grand Rapids, Michigan, a member of the Order of the Crown, *etc.*

II.—MARY FRANCES NEWMAN, m. James Rose, and had:
NELLIE CONWAY ROSE, a member of the Order of the Crown, who m. William T. Baggett, of San Francisco, and had *Nellie Rose.*

2.—GUSTAVUS ADOLPHUS ROSE, M.D., of Lynchburg, Virginia, b. Nelson county, Virginia, 13 March, 1789, d. at La Porte, Indiana, 20 January, 1860; m., 4 January, 1816, Ann Shepherd, b. 9 September, 1797, d. 5 July, 1856, daughter of Hon. David S. Garland, member of Congress, of Lynchburg, Virginia, and had:

I.—JUDITH CABELL ROSE, of Richmond, Virginia, a member of the Virginia Society of the Colonial Dames of America, who m., at La Porte, Indiana, 21 July, 1846, Benjamin Powell Walker, b. Hartford, Indiana, 30 January, 1817, d. New York, 14 February, 1887, and had:

1.—JOHN GARLAND; 2. GUSTAVUS A.; 3. FREDERICK, d. inf., 1862.

4.—WILLIAM JAMES WALKER, of Richmond, Virginia, m., first, Josephine Irvine, daughter of Dr. R. T. Coleman, of Richmond, and had: *Robert C.;* and m., secondly, Columbia Stanard Hayes, a member of the Virginia Society of the Colonial Dames of America.

5.—BENJAMIN POWELL WALKER, m. Lillie Mackie, of New Bedford, Massachusetts, and had: *Bradford Mackie.*

6.—FRANCES MARIA, m. Clarendon Harris, of Cambridge, Massachusetts, and had: *Clarendon, Edward Doubleday* and *Katherine Holbrook.*

7.—LANDON ROSE WALKER, of Richmond, Virginia.

8.—ANNIE FITZHUGH ROSE WALKER, of Richmond, a member of the Virginia Society of the Colonial Dames of America, the Order of the Crown, *etc.*

II.—DAVID GARLAND ROSE, who m. Maria Louisa, daughter of John and Frances (Allen) Walker, and had:

MARIA LOUISA ROSE, a member of the Virginia Society of the Colonial Dames of America, who m. Samuel J. Filer, of Springfield, Massachusetts.

III.—CAROLINE MATILDA ROSE, of Chicago, a member of the Virginia and Illinois Societies of the Colonial Dames of America, b. Lynchburg, Virginia, m. William James Walker, of La Porte, Indiana, and had:

1.—MARTHA GARLAND WALKER, member of the Virginia and Illinois Societies of the Colonial Dames of America, who m. Sylvanus Landor Trippe, of New York, and had: *Carolyn Rose Walker.*

2.—JOHN CRAWFORD; 3. WILLIAM JAMES; 4. FRANCES M.

5.—CAROLINE M. WALKER, who m. George Fisher, of Harrisburg, Pennsylvania, and had: *Carolyn* and

ROSE FISHER, a member of the Virginia Society of the Colonial Dames of America, who m. Madison B. Kennedy, of New York.

THE ROYAL DESCENTS
OF
MR. AND MRS. WM. J. HOLLIDAY,
OF INDIANAPOLIS, IND.

ALFRED THE GREAT, of England, had:	ALFRED THE GREAT, of England, had:
Ethelwida, m. Baldwin II., of Flanders, and had:	Edward the Elder, King of England, who had:
Arnolph, Count of Flanders, who had:	Edmund I., King of England, who had:
Baldwin III., Count of Flanders, who had:	Edgar, King of England, who had:
Arnolph II., Count of Flanders, who had:	Ethelred, King of England, who had:
Baldwin IV., Count of Flanders, who had:	Edmund Ironsides, King of England, who had:
Baldwin V., Count of Flanders, who had:	Edward, the Exile, Prince of England, who had:
Matilda, m. William the Conqueror, and had:	Margaret, m. Malcolm, King of Scots, and had:
Henry I., King of England, who had:	Matilda, m. Henry I., King of England, and had:
Maud, m. Geoffrey, of Anjou, and had:	Maud, m. Geoffrey, Count of Anjou, and had:
Henry II., King of England, who had:	Henry II., King of England, who had:
John, King of England, who had:	John, King of England, who had:
Henry III., King of England, who had:	Henry III., King of England, who had:
Edward I., King of England, who had:	Edmund, Earl of Lancaster, who had:
Edward II., King of England, who had:	Henry, Earl of Lancaster, who had:
Edward III., King of England, who had:	Joan, m. John de Mowbray, and had:
Lionel, Duke of Clarence, who had:	John, Baron de Mowbray, who had:
Philippa, m. Edmund de Mortimer, and had:	Eleanor, m. Roger de la Warr, and had:
Elizabeth, m. Sir Henry Percy, K.G., and had:	Joan, m. Sir Thomas de West, and had:
Henry, Earl of Northumberland, who had:	Sir Reginald, Lord de la Warr, who had:
Henry, Earl of Northumberland, who had:	Sir Richard, Lord de la Warr, who had:
Margaret, m. Sir William Gascoigne, and had:	Sir Thomas, Lord de la Warr, who had:
Elizabeth, m. Gilbert de Talboys, and had:	Sir George West, Knt., who had:
Sir George de Talboys, Knt., who had:	Sir William, Lord de la Warr, who had:
Anne, m. Sir Edward Dymoke, and had:	Sir Thomas, Lord de la Warr, who had:
Frances, m. Sir Thomas Windebank, and had:	Col. John West, of Va., who had:
Mildred, m. Robert Reade, and had:	Col. John West, Jr., of Va., who had:
Col. George Reade, of Va., who had:	Nathaniel West, of Va., who had:
Mildred, m. Augustine Warner, and had:	Unity, m. William Dandridge, of Va., and had:
Mary, m. John Smith, of "Purton," and had:	Martha, m. Philip Aylett, of Va., and had:
Augustine Smith, of Va., who had:	Col. William Aylett, of Va., who had:
John Smith, of "Shooter's Hill," who had:	Col. Philip Aylett, of Va., who had:
Edward Smith, of Va., who had:	Mary, m. Philip Fitzhugh, of Va., and had:
Ariana, m. William D. Holliday, and had:	Lucy, m. John Robertson Redd, and had:

William Jaquelin Holliday m. Lucy Redd.

Ariana Ambler=Henry W. Holliday	Bennett.	Jaquelin S. Holliday	=Florence Baker.	Lucy Fitzhugh Holliday, m. George E. Hume.
Edward Jaquelin Bennett.	Louise Bennett.	William Jaquelin Holliday.	Frederick Taylor Holliday.	

THE ROYAL DESCENT

OF

MRS. BRITTON DAVIS,

OF EL PASO, TEXAS.

HUGH CAPET, King of France, 987, had by his wife, Lady Adela (or Alisa), daughter of William, Duke of Aquitaine, by his wife, Lady Adelheid, daughter of Otto I., Emperor of Saxony:

PRINCESS HEDEWIGE (or Havide), sister of King Robert the Pious, who *m.* Rynerius (or Raginerus) IV., eleventh Count of Hainault, and had:

LADY BEATRIX, *m.* Eblo I., Count de Rouci and de Reimes, and had:

LADY ADELA (or Alexandria), Countess de Rouci, who *m.* Hildwin IV., Count de Montdidier and de Rouci, and had:

LADY MARGARET DE ROUCI, who *m.* Hugh, first Count de Clermont (*see* "L'Art de Verifier les Dates," xii., 282), and had:

LADY ADELIZA DE CLERMONT, who *m.* Gilbert de Tonsburg, in Kent, second Earl of Clare, and had:

GILBERT DE CLARE, created, in 1138, Earl of Pembroke, *d.* 1149, who *m.* Lady Elizabeth de Bellomont, daughter of Robert, Earl of Mellent and Leicester, and had:

RICHARD DE CLARE, "the Strongbow," second Earl of Pembroke, lord justice of Ireland, *d.* 1176, who had by his wife, Lady Eva, daughter of Dermot Mac Murcha, King of Leinster:

LADY ISABEL DE CLARE, who *m.*, 1189 (his first wife), William le Marshal, Earl of Pembroke, protector of England during the nonage of Henry III., *d.* 1219, and had:

LADY MAUD MARSHALL, who *m.*, first, Hugh Bigod, third Earl of Norfolk, one of the sureties for the Magna Charta of King John, *d.* 1225, and had:

SIR RALPH BIGOD, Knt., third son, who *m.* Lady Berta de Furnival, and had:

LADY ISABEL BIGOD, who *m.*, first, Gilbert 'de Lacy, *d. v. p.*, son of Walter, sixth Baron de Lacy, of Trim, *d.* 1241, and had:

LADY MARGARET DE LACY, who *m.* (his first wife) John, sixth Baron de Verdon, *k.* 1274, and had:

PEDIGREE XLIX.—Continued.

Sir Theobald de Verdon, seventh Baron, lord high constable of Ireland, *d.* 1309; *m.* Lady Maud, daughter of Sir Edmund, seventh Baron de Mortimer, of Wigmore, *k.* 1303, and had:

Lady Elizabeth de Verdon, who *m.* Bartholomew, second Baron Burghersh, and had:

Sir Bartholomew Burghersh, third Baron, *d.* 1369, whose daughter:

Lady Elizabeth Burghersh, *m.* Maurice Fitz-Gerald, fourth Earl of Kildare, *d.* 1390, and had:

Gerald Fitz-Gerald, fifth Earl of Kildare, lord justice of Ireland in 1405, *d.* 1410, who *m.* Lady Margery, daughter of Sir John de Rocheford, Knt., lord of Thistledown, and had:

John-cam Fitz-Gerald, sixth Earl of Kildare, *d.* 1427, who had by his wife, Margaret de la Herne:

Thomas Fitz-Gerald, seventh Earl of Kildare, lord deputy of Ireland in 1454, and in 1493, lord chancellor, who, dying 25 March, 1478, left issue by his wife, Lady Joan, who *d.* 1486, daughter of James Fitz-Gerald, seventh Earl of Desmond, also of Royal Descent:

Gerald Fitz-Gerald, eighth Earl of Kildare, lord deputy of Ireland, who *m.* Lady Allison, daughter of Sir Rowland Eustace, Baron of Portlester, lord chancellor and treasurer of Ireland, and had:

Lady Eleanor Fitz-Gerald, who *m.*, first, Donnel Mac Fineere Mac Carthy-Reagh, prince of Carberry, in Ireland, and had:

Lady Julia Mac Carthy, who *m.* Dermod O'Sullivan, eleventh Lord Beare and Bantry, who was *k.*, 1549, by an accident, at his castle of Dunboy, and had:

Sir Philip O'Sullivan-Beare, who as tanist to his brother Sir Owen's son, Dermond, held the Castle of Ardea, county Kerry. He *m.* a daughter of Cormack O'Brien, Earl of Thomond, also of Royal Descent, and had:

Daniel O'Sullivan-Beare, of Ardea Castle, who *m.* Lady Margaret, daughter of the Earl of Clancarthy, by his wife, Lady Margaret, daughter of Donogh O'Brien, fourth Earl of Thomond, and had:

Philip O'Sullivan-Beare, of Ardea, who *m.* Lady Honora, daughter of Donogh, Earl of Clancarthy, *d.* 1666, and his wife, Lady Ellen, daughter of Thomas Butler, Lord Thurles, governor of Kilkenny, *d.* 1619, also of Royal Descent, and had:

Daniel O'Sullivan-Beare, of Ardea, who *m.* Lady Ellen, daughter of Daniel O'Sullivan-Mor, tenth lord of Dunkerron, who *d.* 1699, also of Royal Descent, and had:

Owen O'Sullivan, of Ardea, who *m.* Mary, daughter of Colonel Owen Mac Sweeney, of Muskerry, and had:

MAJOR PHILIP O'SULLIVAN, of Ardea, who *m.* Joanna, daughter of Dermod McCarthy-Mor, of Killoween, county Kerry, and had:

JOHN SULLIVAN, *b.* Ardea, county Kerry, 17 June, 1690, came to America in 1723, and *d.* at South Berwick, Maine, 20 June, 1795, aged 105 years (*see* "N. E. Historical and Genealogical Register," October, 1865), and had by his wife, Margaret Browne, a native of County Kerry, who *d.* in 1801, aged 87 years:

MARY SULLIVAN, 1752–1827; *m.* Theophilus Hardy, of Durham, New Hampshire, and had:

MARGERY HARDY, who *m.* Edward Wells, of Durham, and had:

CHARLES WELLS, of New York City, who *m.* Mary Wiggin, and had:

MARIE ANTOINETTE WELLS, who *m.* Levi Steele, and had:

ANTOINETTE WELLS STEELE, a member of the New York and Texas Societies of the Colonial Dames of America, who *m.* Britton Davis, of El Paso, Texas, and had: *Newton, b.* New York, 22 March, 1890; *Antoinette, b.* Orange, N. J., 13 November, 1892; and *Britton, b.* El Paso, 5 October, 1896.

THE ROYAL DESCENT
OF
MRS. LOUIS C. WASHBURN,
OF ROCHESTER, NEW YORK.

EDWARD III., King of England=Lady Philippa of Hainault.
    Lionel, Duke of Clarence=Lady Elizabeth de Burgh.
    Lady Philippa Plantagenet=Edmund Mortimer, Earl of Marche.
    Lady Elizabeth Mortimer=Sir Henry Percy, "Hotspur."
    Henry, Earl of Northumberland=Lady Eleanor Neville.
    Henry, Earl of Northumberland=Lady Eleanor Poynings.
    Lady Margaret Percy=Sir William Gascoigne.
    Lady Dorothy Gascoigne=Sir Ninian Markenfield.
    Lady Alice Markenfield=Robert Mauleverer.
    Dorothy Mauleverer=John Kaye, of Woodsome.
    Robert Kaye, of Woodsome=Ann Flower, of Whitewell.
    Grace Kaye=Sir Richard Saltonstall, of Huntwick.
    Richard Saltonstall, of Ipswich, Mass.=Muriel Gurdon.
    Nathaniel Saltonstall, of Haverhill, Mass.=Elizabeth Ward.
    Gurdon Saltonstall, Governor of Connecticut=Elizabeth Rosewell.
    General Gurdon Saltonstall=Rebecca Winthrop.
    Rebecca Saltonstall=David Mumford, New London, Ct.
    Thomas Mumford=Mary Sheldon Smith.
    George Huntington Mumford=Anne Elizabeth Hart.
Henrietta Saltonstall Mumford, a member of=Louis Cope Washburn, Rochester, N. Y.
the National Society of the Colonial Dames
of America,

| Henrietta Mumford Washburn. | Helen Carpenter Washburn. | Louis Mumford Washburn. |

PEDIGREE L.

EDWARD III., King of England, had by his wife, Lady Philippa, daughter of William, Count of Hainault, also of Royal Descent:

SIR LIONEL PLANTAGENET, K.G., Duke of Clarence, Earl of Ulster, who m., first, Lady Elizabeth de Burgh, daughter of William, Earl of Ulster, also of Royal Descent, and had:

LADY PHILIPPA PLANTAGENET, who m. Edmund de Mortimer, third Earl of Marche, also of Royal Descent, and had:

LADY ELIZABETH DE MORTIMER, who m. Sir Henry de Percy, the renowned " Hotspur," also of Royal Descent, and had:

HENRY DE PERCY, second Earl of Northumberland, k. at St. Albans, 1455; m. Lady Eleanor Neville, daughter of Ralph, first Earl of Westmoreland, by his second wife, both of Royal Descent, and had:

HENRY DE PERCY, third Earl of Northumberland, k. at Towton, 1461; m. Lady Eleanor, daughter of Richard, Baron Poynings, and had:

LADY MARGARET DE PERCY, who m. Sir William Gascoigne, of Gawthrope, Yorkshire, also of Royal Descent, and had:

LADY DOROTHY GASCOIGNE, who m. Sir Ninian de Markenfield, also of Royal Descent, and had:

LADY ALICE MARKENFIELD, who m. Robert Mauleverer, second son of Sir William Mauleverer, of Wothersome, Yorkshire, also of Royal Descent (see " Magna Charta Barons and their Descendants "), and had:

DOROTHY MAULEVERER, who m. John Kaye, of Woodsome, Yorkshire, also of Royal Descent, and had:

ROBERT KAYE, of Woodsome, *temp.* 1612, who m. Ann, daughter of John Flower, of Whitewell, and had:

GRACE KAYE,* who m. Sir Richard Saltonstall, of Huntwick, b. 1586, lord of the manor of Ledsham, near Leeds, England. He was one of the first-named associates of the original patentees of Massachusetts Bay in charter granted 4 May, 1628, also first named among the assist-

---

* The following ladies, members of the National Society of the Colonial Dames of America, are also of Royal Descent, through Grace Kaye :

MRS. FLEMING G. BAILEY, Georgia State Society.
MRS. ROBERT RANTOUL, Minnesota State Society.
MRS. NEAL RANTOUL, Massachusetts State Society.
MRS. EDMUND M. WHEELRIGHT, Massachusetts State Society.

ants appointed thereby, and also one of the original patentees of Connecticut, and came to America in April, 1630, and was founder of Watertown, Massachusetts. He returned to England, and was appointed ambassador to Holland, and was also a member of the high court of justice held to try the Duke of Hamilton and others for high treason. His eldest son by Grace Kaye:

RICHARD SALTONSTALL, of Ipswich, Massachusetts, b. at Woodsome, Yorkshire, 1610, d. at Hulme, England, 29 April, 1694; graduate of Emmanuel College, Cambridge; came to New England in 1630 with his father; was deputy to general court, 1635-7; assistant, 1637-49-64-80-82; was appointed by the general court sergeant-major in Colonel Endicott's Regiment, October, 1641. He m. Muriel, daughter of Brampton Gurdon, of Assington, County Suffolk, England; member of Parliament from Sudbury, 1620; high sheriff, 1629; and Muriel Sedley, his wife, also of Royal Descent, and had:

COLONEL NATHANIEL SALTONSTALL, of Haverhill, Massachusetts, eldest son, b. Ipswich, 1639, d. Haverhill, Massachusetts, 21 May, 1707; Colonel of the Essex Regiment; was assistant 1679-92; member of council under Sir Edmund Andros, also member of their Majesties' council under charter of William and Mary, 1689; judge of oyer and terminer court, 1692, but resigned, refusing to serve in witchcraft trials. He m., 28 December, 1663, Elizabeth, daughter of Rev. John and Alice Ward, of Haverhill, and had:

1.—GOVERNOR GURDON SALTONSTALL, eldest son, b. 27 March, 1666, d. 20 September, 1724. He was ordained to the ministry and settled at New London, Connecticut, and was the governor of the Connecticut colony, 1707-24. He had by his first wife ("Early Connecticut Marriages," ii., 1), Jerusha, d. Boston, 25 July, 1697, daughter of James Richards, of Hartford:

    I.—ELIZABETH SALTONSTALL, b. 1 May, 1690, who m. Richard Christophers, and had:

        RICHARD CHRISTOPHERS, who m. Lucretia Bradley, and had:

        ELIZABETH CHRISTOPHERS, who m. Captain Joseph Hurlburt and had:

        HANNAH HURLBURT, b. 12 December, 1769, d. 1855, who m. Rev. William Patten, and had:

        WILLIAM SAMUEL PATTEN, who m. Eliza Williams Bridgham, and had:

        ELIZABETH BRIDGHAM PATTEN, b. 1831, who m., 1860, Arthur Fenner Dexter, 1830-1886, and had:

        ELIZABETH BRIDGHAM DEXTER, of Providence, a member of the Rhode Island Society of the Colonial Dames of America.

II.—SARAH SALTONSTALL, *b.* 8 April, 1694, who *m.*, first, John Gardiner, Jr., of New London, Connecticut (son of John Gardiner, third lord of Gardiner's Island manor), *d.* 15 January, 1725, and had:

JERUSHA GARDINER, who *m.*, 7 March, 1742, John Christophers, of New London ("Early Connecticut Marriages," ii., 19), and had:

LUCRETIA CHRISTOPHERS, who *m.* John Mumford, Jr., of New London, and had:

CATHERINE MUMFORD, who *m.*, 5 January, 1800, Isaac Thompson, M.D., of Stratford and New London, Connecticut, and had:

ELLEN DOUGLAS THOMPSON, who *m.*, 16 April, 1833, Frederick Lennig, of Philadelphia, Pennsylvania, *b.* in Germany, only son of John Frederick and Margaret Antoinette (Geyger) Lennig, and had:

1.—MARGARET ANTOINETTE LENNIG, a member of the Pennsylvania Society of the Colonial Dames of America, Daughters of the American Revolution Society, Society of the Colonial Governors, the Mary Washington Memorial Association, Society of Mayflower Descendants, Society Daughters of the Cincinnati, who *m.*, 30 May, 1878, Joseph Henry Oglesby (son of Joseph Henry and Elizabeth (Hite) Oglesby, of Louisville, Kentucky), and had: *Joseph Henry*, *b.* 1 July, 1881.

2.—LUCRETIA CHRISTOPHERS LENNIG, of Philadelphia, a member of the Pennsylvania Society of the Colonial Dames of America.

GOVERNOR GURDON SALTONSTALL, 1666–1724, had by his second wife, Elizabeth, daughter of William Rosewell:

GENERAL GURDON SALTONSTALL, JR., of New London, fourth son, *b.* 22 December, 1708. He served as delegate to several colonial conventions; was a member of several committees of New London conducting Revolutionary affairs, and was appointed a brigadier general in 1776. He *m.*, 15 March, 1732, Rebecca, daughter of John Winthrop, F.R.S., *d.* London, 1747 (a son of Chief Justice Waite Still Winthrop, son of John Winthrop, governor of the Connecticut and New Haven Colonies, 1657–1676, son of John Winthrop, the "Father of the Massachusetts Colony," governor of Massachusetts Bay Colony, 1629–1649), and his wife, Anne, daughter of Joseph Dudley, president of the Colony of Massachusetts, New Hampshire and Maine, 1686, governor of Massachusetts Colony, *etc.*, son of Major-General Thomas Dudley, governor of Massachusetts Colony, 1634–1650, *etc.*, and had:

REBECCA SALTONSTALL, *b.* 31 December, 1734, who *m.*, 1 January, 1758, David Mumford, of New London, and had:

THOMAS MUMFORD, *b.* 13 July, 1770, *m.*, 20 January, 1795, Mary Sheldon Smith, of Litchfield, Connecticut, and had:

PEDIGREE L.—Continued.

GEORGE HUNTINGTON MUMFORD, b. 21 July, 1805, m., 24 May, 1836, Anne Elizabeth, daughter of Truman Hart, of Palmyra, New York, and had:

I.—HENRIETTA SALTONSTALL MUMFORD, a member of the New York Society of the Colonial Dames of America, who m., April, 1890, Louis Cope Washburn, of Rochester, New York, and had: *Henrietta Mumford, Helen Carpenter*, and *Louis Mumford*.

II.—HELEN ELIZABETH MUMFORD, a member of the New York Society of the Colonial Dames of America, who m., 10 November, 1870, William L. Halsey, of Rochester, New York. *No issue.*

III.—GEORGE HART MUMFORD, m., 10 December, 1867, Sarah Dana, and had: *Gurdon S.* and *George Dana Mumford*, who m., 25 April, 1894, Ethel Watts, and had: *George Hart*, b. January, 1895.

IV.—MARY LOUISE MUMFORD, who m., 2 January, 1873, Edward Payson Fowler, M.D., of New York, and had: *Edward M.* and *Louise Mumford*, who m. Robert Miles Gignoux, and had: *Louise M.* and *Mildred*.

2.—ELIZABETH SALTONSTALL, d. 1726, m., secondly, 1692, Rev. Roland Cotton, of Sandwich, Massachusetts, 1667-1721-2, and had:

I.—REV. JOHN COTTON, D.D., the founder of Newton, Massachusetts, m., 19 February, 1719, Mary Gibbs, and had:

MARY COTTON (widow of Rev. Mr. Cheny), who m., secondly, 13 October, 1748, Rev. Dr. Joseph Pynchon, of Boston, 1705-1756, and had:

MARGARET PYNCHON, who m., 28 April, 1779, Stephen Keeler, of Norwalk, Connecticut, and had:

I.—MATHERS KEELER, who m., 20 August, 1832, Serena Howard, and had:

EUGENIA MARY KEELER, who m., 19 September, 1866, Julius Frank Caulkins, and had:

EDITH SERENA CAULKINS, a member of the Order of the Crown, who m. Lyman Francis Gray, of Buffalo, New York:

II.—MARGARET KEELER, who m. Dr. Erastus Sergeant, Jr., of Lee and Stockbridge, Massachusetts, and had:

MARY ANN SERGEANT, who m. Rev. Samuel Newbury, of Middlebury, Vermont, and had: *Samuel Sergeant, Katherine Sedgwick* (Mrs. Robb), *Egbert*, and

1.—MARY ANN NEWBURY, a member of the Massachusetts and Iowa Societies of the Colonial Dames of America, the Order of the Crown, *etc.*, who m. Judge Austin Adams, of Dubuque, Iowa, and had: *Annabel, Eugene, Herbert*, and *Cecilia*.

PEDIGREE L.—Continued.

2.—FRANCES E. NEWBURY, a member of the Massachusetts and Michigan Societies of the Colonial Dames of America, who m. John J. Bagley, of Detroit, Michigan.

II.—JOANNA COTTON, 1694–1772, m. Rev. John Brown, d. 1742, and had:

ABIGAIL BROWN, m. Rev. Edward Brooks, 174—-1781, and had:

1.—PETER CHARDON BROOKS, of Boston, who m. Ann Gorham, and had:

ABIGAIL BROWN BROOKS, d. 6 January, 1889, who m., 3 September, 1829, Charles Francis Adams, of Quincy, Massachusetts, b. 18 August, 1809, d. 21 November, 1886, United States Minister to Great Britain, 1861–68, etc., also of Royal Descent, son of John Quincy Adams, President of the United States, and a grandson of John Adams, President of the United States (p. 164), and had:

MARY ADAMS, a member of the Massachusetts Society of the Colonial Dames of America, who m. Henry Parker Quincy, of Boston, and had *Dorothy* and *Elinor*.

2.—JOANNA COTTON BROOKS, m. Nathaniel Hall, of Medford, Massachusetts, b. 1761, and had:

CAROLINE HALL, m. (his second wife) Rev. Francis Parkman, D.D., of Boston, 1788–1852, and had:

I.—FRANCIS PARKMAN, of Boston, 1823–1893, the historian, who m. Catherine Scollay, daughter of Dr. Jacob and Mary (Scollay) Bigelow, of Boston, and had:

GRACE PARKMAN, a member of the Massachusetts Society of the Colonial Dames of America, who m. Charles P. Coffin, of Longwood, Massachusetts, and had: *Francis Parkman, Miriam,* and *Mary Bigelow.*

II.—CAROLINE HALL PARKMAN, b. 30 June, 1825, who m. Rev. John Cordner, LL.D., of Boston, 1816–1894, and had:

CAROLINE PARKMAN CORDNER, of Boston, a member of the Massachusetts Society of the Colonial Dames of America.

THE ROYAL DESCENT

OF

MRS. ERASTUS GAYLORD PUTNAM,

OF ELIZABETH, NEW JERSEY.

CHARLEMAGNE, Emperor of the West=Lady Hildegarde of Savoy.

Louis I., King of France=Lady Judith of Bavaria.

Charles II., King of France=Lady Richildis (second wife).

Princess Judith of France=Baldwin I., Count of Flanders.

Baldwin II., Count of Flanders=Ethelwida, dau. Alfred the Great of England.

Arnoul, Count of Flanders=Lady Alix of Vermandois.

Baldwin III., Count of Flanders=Lady Matilda of Saxony.

Arnoul II., Count of Flanders=Lady Susanna d'Inree of Italy.

Baldwin IV., Count of Flanders=Lady Agiva of Luxemberg.

Baldwin V., Count of Flanders=Adela, gr. dau. of Hugh Capet.

Lady Matilda of Flanders=William I., King of England.

Henry I., King of England=Matilda, dau. Malcolm III., of Scotland.

Maud, Empress of Germany=Geoffroi, Count of Anjou.

Henry II., King of England=Eleanor, Duchess of Aquitaine.

John, King of England=Lady Isabel de Taillefer.

Henry III., King of England=Lady Eleanor of Provence.

Edward I., King of England=Eleanor, dau. of Ferdinand III., of Castile.

Princess Joan Plantagenet=Ralph, Earl of Gloucester.

Thomas de Monthermer=(Name unknown.)

Lady Margaret de Monthermer=Sir John, Baron de Montacute.

John, Earl of Salisbury=Lady Maud Buxhull.

Thomas, Earl of Salisbury=Lady Eleanor de Holland.

Lady Alice de Montacute=Richard, Earl of Salisbury.

Lady Alice de Neville=Henry, Lord Fitzhugh.

Lady Elizabeth Fitzhugh=Sir William Parr, K.G.

William, Lord Parr, of Horton=Lady Mary Salisbury.

Lady Elizabeth Parr=Sir Nicholas de Woodhull, Bedfordshire.

Fulke Woodhull, of Thenford=Alice Coles.

Lawrence Woodhull, of Thenford=(Name unknown.)

Mary Woodhull=William Nicolls, of Islippe.

John Nicolls, of Islippe=Joane Grafton.

Rev. Matthias Nicolls, of Islippe=Martha Oakes.

Judge Matthias Nicolls, of New York=Abigail Johns.

William Nicoll, of Islip, L. I., N. Y.=Anne Van Rensselaer.

Benjamin Nicoll, of Islip, L. I., N. Y.=Charity Floyd.

Benjamin Nicoll, Jr., of N. York=Mary Magdelen Holland.

Prof. Samuel Nicoll, M.D., of N. York=Anne Fargie.

Frances Mary Nicoll=George Bloom Evertson, of Poughkeepsie.

Frances Mary Evertson, member of the National Society of the Colonial Dames of America,=William Amos Woodward, of New York.

Mary Nicoll Woodward, member of the National Society of the Colonial Dames of America. (Issue d. young.)=Erastus Gaylord Putnam, of Elizabeth, N. J.

PEDIGREE LI.

HENRY III., King of England, had by his wife, Lady Eleanor, daughter of Raymond de Berenger, Count of Provence:

EDMUND PLANTAGENET, Earl of Leicester, Lancaster, and Chester, lord high steward, who had by his second wife, Lady Blanche, granddaughter of Louis VIII., King of France:

HENRY PLANTAGENET, Earl of Lancaster and Leicester, who m. Lady Maud, also of Royal Descent, daughter of Patrick de Chaworth, 1253–1282, and had:

LADY ELEANOR PLANTAGENET, who m., secondly (his second wife), Sir Richard Fitz-Alan, K.G., Earl of Arundel and Surrey, and had:

LADY ALICE FITZ-ALAN, who m. Sir Thomas de Holland, K.G., second Earl of Kent, marshal of England, also of Royal Descent, and had:

LADY ELEANOR DE HOLLAND, who m. (his first wife) Thomas de Montacute, last Earl of Salisbury, also of Royal Descent, and had:

LADY ALICE DE MONTACUTE, who m. Sir Richard de Nevill, K.G., created Earl of Salisbury, 4 May, 1442; lord great chamberlain of England, who was beheaded for siding with the Yorkists in 1461, and his head was fixed upon a gate of the city of York, also of Royal Descent, and had:

LADY ALICE DE NEVILLE (sister of Richard Neville, K.G., Earl of Salisbury and Warwick, the renowned "king maker"), who m. Henry, fifth Baron Fitzhugh, of Ravensworth, steward of the honor of Richmond and Lancaster, also of Royal Descent, d. 1472, and had:

LADY ELIZABETH FITZ-HUGH, who m. Sir William Parr, K.G., constable of England, also of Royal Descent, and had:

WILLIAM, LORD PARR, of Horton, Northampton, d. 1546, who was uncle of Katherine Parr, last wife of Henry VIII., of England. He was chamberlain to her Majesty, and was advanced to the peerage 23 December, 1543. He m. Lady Mary, daughter of Sir William Salisbury, and had:

LADY ELIZABETH PARR (she is also called Alice), who m. (his second wife) Sir Nicholas Woodhull, lord of Woodhull, county Bedford, d. 1532, and had by her (see the Northamptonshire Visitations, 1564 and 1618; the Yorkshire Visitations, 1584, and Dugdale's "Baronage"):

FULKE WOODHULL, of Thenford Manor, Northamptonshire, second son and heir, and eldest son by his father's second wife, who m. Alice, daughter of William Coles, or Colles, of Lye, or Leigh, county Worcester, and had:

LAWRENCE WOODHULL, younger son (brother of Nicholas, eldest son and heir apparent in 1618, who had five sons then living, his apparent heir being son Gyles, *b.* 1582, *see* "Miscellanæ Geneal. et Heraldica," iv., 417), father of:

1.—MARY WOODHULL, who *m.* (his second wife) William Nicolls, of Islippe, Northamptonshire, and had:

JOHN NICOLLS, who *m.* Joane, daughter and heir of George Grafton, and had:

REV. MATTHIAS NICOLLS, who *m.*, 1630, Martha Oakes, of Leicestershire, and had:

MATTHIAS NICOLLS, *b.* at Islippe, Northamptonshire, 1621, was a graduate of Cambridge University and a lawyer of the Inner Temple. He was appointed secretary of the commission "to visit the colonies and plantations known as New England," and commissioned captain of the military force, before leaving England, 1664; was secretary of the province of New York, 1664–87; member of the King's council, 1667–80; speaker of Provincial Assembly, 1683–4; judge of the court of admiralty, 1686; mayor of New York, 1672, and *d.* 22 December, 1687, and was buried at Cow Neck, Long Island. He *m.* Abigail Johns, who administered on his estate 22 July, 1693, and had:

WILLIAM NICOLL, commonly called "the Patentee," *b.* 1657, at Islippe, Northamptonshire, and educated for the bar. He came to America with his father in 1664, and was a lawyer of great prominence at New York. He was member of the Governor's council, New York, 1691–8; attorney-general of the province, 1687; member of the Provincial Assembly, 1701–23, and speaker, 1702–18. He purchased, 29 November, 1683, from Winnequaheagh, Sachem of Connectquut, a tract of land on Long Island, embracing originally one hundred square miles, but in consequence of sales made the quantity now owned by the family does not exceed forty thousand acres, comprising the Nicoll Manor, at Islip, Long Island. He also owned one-half of Shelter Island. He was vestryman of Trinity Church, New York, 1698–1702, and *d.* at Nicoll Manor in May, 1723. He *m.*, 1693, Anne, daughter of Jeremias Van Rensselaer, and widow of her cousin, Kiliaen Van Rensselaer, of Watervliet, New York, patroon of the lordship and manor of Rensselaerswyck, and had:

BENJAMIN NICOLL, *b.* at Islip, Long Island, 1694, who inherited from his father the Islip estate, known as Nicoll Manor, and devoted himself to its care, and *d.* in 1724. He *m.*, 1714, Charity, his first cousin, daughter of his aunt, Margaret Nicoll, and Richard Floyd, of Setaulket, Long Island (who *m.*, secondly, September 26, 1725, Rev. Dr. Samuel Johnson, first president of King's, afterwards Columbia, College, New York, and their son, Dr. William Samuel Johnson, was first president of Columbia College, New York), and had:

BENJAMIN NICOLL, JR., *b.* at Islip, Long Island, 17 March, 1718, graduated at Yale College in 1734. He was a lawyer, and successively incorporator, trustee, and governor of King's College, New York, a founder and trustee of the Society Library, New York, 1754, and a vestryman of Trinity Church, New York, 1751–60, and *d.* 15 April, 1760. He *m.* Mary Magdalen, daughter of Edward Holland, mayor of the city of New York, and had:

DR. SAMUEL NICOLL, *b.* 19 August, 1754, *d.* 2 February, 1796. He was a graduate of the Edinburgh University, 1776, and completed his medical studies in Paris, and was professor of chemistry in Columbia College, 1792–96. He *m.*, first, 1 June, 1782, Anne, his second cousin, daughter of Captain Winter Fargie, of the British army, and Eve, his wife, daughter of Henry Holland and his wife, Alida Beeckman, and had by her:

FRANCES MARY NICOLL, *b.* at Stratford, Connecticut, 17 December, 1785, *d.* 24 March, 1861; *m.*, 13 April, 1809 (his second wife), George Bloom Evertson, son of Jacob Evertson (descended from Admiral John Evertson, lieutenant-admiral of Zeeland, *k.* in battle against the English, 1666), and his wife, Margaret, daughter of George Bloom, and had:

FRANCES MARY EVERTSON, a member of the New Jersey Society of the Colonial Dames of America, Daughters of the American Revolution, Daughters of Holland Dames of New York, and hereditary life member of the National Mary Washington Memorial Association, *b.* at Poughkeepsie, New York, 26 April, 1811, *d.* in New York City, 15 March, 1899; *m.*, 4 December, 1828, William Amos Woodward, *b.* in New London, Connecticut, 21 March, 1801, *d.* at Keewaydin, Orange county, New York, 19 September, 1883, and had:

I.—GEORGE EVERTSON WOODWARD, *m.* Eliza Bethia Deodata Mortimer. *Issue.*

II.—FRANCIS WILLIAM WOODWARD, a member of the Society of Colonial Wars, who *m.*, 1 October, 1862, Anne Jay (daughter of General George Patton Delaplaine, of Madison, Wisconsin), a member of the New Jersey Society of the Colonial Dames of America, a descendant of Governor William Livingston, of New Jersey, and had:

HARRIET B. WOODWARD, a member of the New Jersey Society of the Colonial Dames of America, who *m.*, at Eau Claire, Wisconsin, 18 October, 1899, Caleb Forbes Davis, of Keokuk, Iowa.

III.—MARY NICOLL WOODWARD, a member of the New Jersey Society of the Colonial Dames of America, Society Daughters of the American Revolution, Huguenot Society of America, Daughters of Holland Dames, and hereditary life member of the National Mary Washington Memorial Association, who *m.*, 30 January, 1867, Erastus Gaylord Putnam, of Elizabeth, New Jersey, descended from John and Priscilla Putnam, who settled in Salem, Massachusetts, in 1634, and had four children, who died young.

IV.—HARRIET BOWEN WOODWARD, *m.* John Wylie Barrow. *Issue.*

2.—RICHARD WOODHULL, *b.* at Thenford, 13 September, 1620, removed to Long Island, New York, about 1647, and purchased, in 1665, 108,000 acres, now the site of Brookhaven. (*See* Thompson's "History of Long Island," iii., 399; "N. Y. Geneal. and Biog. Record," iii., 10; iv., 54–8.) He was made justice of the Court of Assizes in 1666, and dying in October, 1690, left issue by his wife Deborah:

RICHARD WOODHULL, of Setauket, *b.* 9 October, 1649, *d.* 18 October, 1699, a justice of the Court of Assizes in 1678. He *m.*, 19 August, 1680, Temperance, daughter of Rev. Jonah Fordham, of Southampton, Long Island (*see* Pelletreau's "Early Long Island Wills," his wife, "Temperance Topping," was executrix to his will, proved 28 May, 1700), and had:

NATHANIEL WOODHULL, of Mastic, Long Island, second son, *d.* 9 March, 1760; *m.*, 1716, Sarah, daughter of Richard Smith, of Smithtown, Long Island, and had: *Hannah* (who *m.*, 7 October, 1740, Selah Strong, of Brookhaven, Long Island, and had: *Major Nathaniel Strong*, *m.* Amy Brewster, and had: *Selah*), and

1.—CAPTAIN EBENEZER WOODHULL, *d.* 4 October, 1803, who *m.* Abigail, *d.* 21 November, 1829, daughter of Hezekiah Howell, and had:

RUTH WOODHULL, 1770–1810, who *m.* Selah Strong, aforesaid, and had:

SCHUYLER STRONG, who *m.* Frances Cruger, and had:

RUTH WOODHULL STRONG, a member of the Pennsylvania Society of the Colonial Dames of America, who *m.* Benjamin Dorrance, of Dorrancetown, Luzerne county, Pennsylvania, and had: *Anne, Frances,* and *Ruth, d.* 13 February, 1895.

2.—GENERAL NATHANIEL WOODHULL, of Mastic, eldest son, *b.* 30 December, 1722, *d.* in a prison-ship, 20 September, 1776. Prior to the Revolution he had served under both Amherst and Abercrombie during the war with France. At the breaking out of the American Revolution he was chosen president of the Provincial Congress of New York, and was twice re-elected. After the battle of Long Island he was made a prisoner, and was assassinated because he refused to say "God save the King." He m., 1761, Ruth, d. 1822, daughter of Nicoll Floyd, of Mastic (and sister of General William Floyd, a signer of the Declaration of Independence), and had:

ELIZABETH WOODHULL, only child, b. 30 November, 1762, d. 14 September, 1839, who m., first, Henry Nicoll, of New York, and had:

ELIZA WILLETTS NICOLL, who m. Richard Smith, 5th, and had:

JOHN LAWRENCE SMITH, who m. Mary Nicoll Clinch, and had:

1.—CORNELIA STEWART SMITH, a member of the New York Society of the Colonial Dames of America, who m. Prescott Hall Butler, of New York City, and had: *Lawrence Smith, Charles Stewart*, and *Susan Louisa*.

2.—LOUISA NICOLL SMITH, who m. F. S. Osborne.

3.—KATE ANNETTE SMITH, who m. J. B. Wetherill.

4.—ELLA BATAVIA SMITH, a member of the New York Society of the Colonial Dames of America, who m. Devereux Emmet, of New York.

5.—BESSIE SMITH, a member of the New York Society of the Colonial Dames of America, who m. Stanford White, of St. James, Long Island, New York, and had: *Lawrence Grant*.

ELIZABETH WOODHULL, 1762–1839; m., secondly, General John Smith, of St. George's Manor, Suffolk, Long Island, New York, member of Congress, United States Senator, *etc.*, and had:

SARAH AUGUSTA TANGIER SMITH, only daughter, b. May 19, 1794, d. 13 November, 1877; m., 2 June, 1816, John L. Lawrence, member of the New York State Senate, comptroller of New York City, minister to Sweden, *etc.*, and had:

1.—JUDGE ABRAHAM R. LAWRENCE, of New York City, fifth son, a justice of the Supreme Court of the State of New York for over twenty-five years. He m. Eliza, only daughter of William Miner, M.D., of New York City, and had:

RUTH LAWRENCE, of New York City, only daughter, a member of the New York Society of the Colonial Dames of America.

2.—ELIZABETH LAWRENCE, who m., 1837, Alfred Newbold Lawrence, of New York, b. 1813, also of Royal Descent, and had:

HANNAH NEWBOLD LAWRENCE, of New York City, a member of the New York Society of the Colonial Dames of America.

3.—LYDIA LAWRENCE, who m. William Thurston Horn, of New York, and had:

ANNIE L. HORN, of New York City, a member of the New York Society of the Colonial Dames of America.

THE ROYAL DESCENT

OF

MRS. SELDEN STUART WRIGHT,

OF SAN FRANCISCO, CAL.

EDWARD I., King of England=Princess Eleanor of Castile.
Princess Elizabeth Plantagenet=Humphrey de Bohun, Earl of Hereford.
Lady Margaret de Bohun=Hugh de Courtenay, Earl of Devon.
Lady Elizabeth de Courtenay=Sir Andrew Luttrell, of Chilton.
Lady Elizabeth Luttrell=John Stratton, of Weston.
Elizabeth Stratton=John Andrews, of Stoke.
Elizabeth Andrews=Thomas Wyndsore.
Sir Andrews Wyndsore, of Stanwell=Lady Elizabeth Blount.
Lady Edith Wyndsore=George Ludowe, of Hill Deverill.
Thomas Ludlow, of Dinton=Jane Pyle, of Bopton, Wilts.
Gabriel Ludlow, 1587-1639=Phyllis ———.
Sarah Ludlow (fourth wife)=John Carter, of Gloucester Co., Va.
Robert Carter, of "Carotoman"=Elizabeth (Landon) Willis.
Mary Carter=George Braxton, of King and Queen Co., Va.
Carter Braxton, of "Elsing Green," Va.=Judith Robinson.
Mary Braxton=Robert Page, of "Broad Neck," Va.
Sarah Walker Page=Humphrey Brooke, of Spottsylvania Co., Va.
Anne Aylett Brooke=Oliver Abbott Shaw, Lexington, Mass.

Joanna Maynard Shaw, member of the National Society of the Colonial Dames of America, the Order of the Crown, etc. *Issue* (see pp. 184, 219).— Selden Stuart Wright, of Essex Co., Va.

PEDIGREE LII.

HENRY I., King of France, had by his third wife, Anne of Russia, of Royal Descent:

HUGH THE GREAT, Duke of France and Burgundy, *etc.*, who had by his wife, Lady Adelheid de Vermandois, also of Royal Descent:

LADY ISABEL DE VERMANDOIS, *d.* 1131, widow of Robert de Beaumont, Earl of Mellent and Leicester, *d.* 1118, who *m.*, secondly, William de Warren, second Earl of Surrey, and had:

LADY GUNDREDA DE WARREN, who *m.*, first, Roger de Bellomont de Newburg, second Earl of Warwick, *d.* 1153, and had:

WALERAN DE NEWBURG, fourth Earl of Warwick, *d.* 1205, who *m.*, secondly, Lady Alice, daughter of John d'Harcourt, Knt., and widow of John de Limsey, and had by her:

LADY ALICE DE NEWBURG, *m.* William, Baron de Mauduit, of Hanslape, heritable chamberlain of the Exchequer, *d.* 1256, and had:

LADY ISABEL DE MAUDUIT, who *m.* William, fifth baron of Beauchamp of Elmly, *d.* 1268, and had:

WALTER DE BEAUCHAMP, first baron of Alcester and Powyke, third son (brother of William, created Earl of Warwick), steward to the household of King Edward I., *d.* 1306. He *m.* Lady Alice, daughter of Ralph, Baron de Toni, of Flamsted, Herts, and his wife, Lady Alice de Bohun, also of Royal Descent, and had:

GILES DE BEAUCHAMP, fourth baron of Alcester, in Warwickshire and Powyke, in Gloucestershire, *temp.* 14 Edward III., third son, who had:

ROGER DE BEAUCHAMP, second son, first Baron Beauchamp, of Bletsho, chamberlain to the household of King Edward III., *d.* 1379, who had by his first wife, Sybil, daughter of Sir William de Patshull:

ROGER, second Baron Beauchamp, of Bletsho and Lydiard-Tregoze, who had:

SIR JOHN, third Baron Beauchamp, of Bletsho, *d.* 1413, who had:

LADY MARGARET DE BEAUCHAMP, who *m.*, first, Sir Oliver de St. John, Knt., of Penmark, in Glamorganshire. (Her second husband was John de Beaufort, Duke of Somerset, by whom she had: Lady Margaret, who *m.* Edward Tudor, Earl of Richmond, and had: Henry VII., King of England.) By her first husband, Lady Margaret had:

PEDIGREE LII.—Continued.

SIR JOHN DE ST. JOHN, K.B., of Penmark, eldest son, who m. Lady Alice, daughter of Sir Thomas Bradshaw, and had:

SIR JOHN DE ST. JOHN, of Bletsho, Bedfordshire, who m. Lady Sybil, daughter of Morgan ap Jenkyns ap Philip, and had:

SIR JOHN DE ST. JOHN, Knt., who m. Lady Margaret, daughter of Sir William Walgrave, Knt., and had by her:

OLIVER ST. JOHN, created, in January, 1559, Lord St. John, of Bletsho, who had by his wife, Agnes Fisher:

THOMAS ST. JOHN, of Bletsho, younger son, who had:

SIR OLIVER ST. JOHN, Knt., member of Parliament, of Caysho, Bedfordshire, who m. Sarah, daughter of Edward Bulkley, of Odell, Bedfordshire, and had:

LADY ELIZABETH ST. JOHN,* b. 1605, d. at Lyme, Connecticut, 3 March, 1677, who m., 6 August, 1629 (his second wife), Rev. Samuel Whiting, D.D., b. 20 November, 1597, at Boston, Lincolnshire (see Thompson's "History of Boston"). They came to America in 1636, and settled at Lynn, Massachusetts, where he d. 11 December, 1679 (see "Memoir of Rev. Samuel Whiting, D.D.," by William Whiting, of Boston; "American Heraldic Journal," i., 58, and Drake's "History of Boston"). Rev. Samuel Whiting had by Elizabeth, his wife:

1.—REV. SAMUEL WHITING, of Billerica, Massachusetts, b. Shirbeck, England, 1630, d. 1713; m., 12 November, 1656, Dorcas, b. 1 November, 1637, daughter of Leonard Chester, of Wethersfield, and had:

   I.—OLIVER WHITING, b. 1665, d. 1736; m., 1690, Anne Danforth, b. 8 March, 1668, d. 13 August, 1737, and had:

      DORCAS WHITING, d. 21 May, 1763, m., 17 March, 1720 (his third wife), Joshua Abbott, b. 16 June, 1685, d. 11 February, 1769, and had:

      OLIVER ABBOTT, b. 26 March, 1727, d. 10 April, 1796; m., 13 February, 1752, Joanna French, and had:

      JOANNA ABBOTT, b. 24 July, 1755, m. 21 May, 1776, Simon Winship, b. 2 November, 1749, d. 4 January, 1813, and had:

      JOANNA WINSHIP, b. 5 May, 1777, d. 10 March, 1848; m., about 1798, Darius Shaw, and had:

      OLIVER ABBOTT SHAW, b. May, 1799, d. March, 1855; m., 27 De-

---

* The following ladies, members of the National Society of the Colonial Dames of America, are also of Royal Descent, through Elizabeth St. John:

MRS. MANNING F. FORCE, Ohio State Society.

MRS. JOHN C. GRAY, Massachusetts State Society.

MISS JULIA LOUISE ROBINSON, Pennsylvania State Society.

cember, 1825, Ann Aylett Brooke, also of Royal Descent, *b.* 16 January, 1808, *d.* 2 June, 1845, and had:

1.—SARAH COLUMBIA BRAXTON SHAW, *b.* 4 July, 1837, *d.* May, 1872; *m.*, 1 January, 1869, Albert Henry Rose, and had:

ANNA BROOKE ROSE, of Alameda, California, a member of the Virginia and California Societies of the Colonial Dames of America.

2.—JOANNA MAYNARD SHAW, of San Francisco, *b.* 26 May, 1830, member of the Virginia and California Societies of the Colonial Dames of America, who *m.*, 15 October, 1846, Selden Stuart Wright, of Essex county, Virginia, *b.* 7 March, 1822, *d.* 26 February, 1893, and had:

I.—MARY STUART WRIGHT, *b.* Lexington, Holmes county, Mississippi, 17 August, 1847, *d.* San Rafael, California, 7 September, 1878; *m.*, 21 November, 1867, William B. Hooper, *b.* 1835, and had:

1.—MARY STUART HOOPER, *b.* 15 August, 1868, a member of the Virginia and California Societies of the Colonial Dames of America, who *m.*, March, 1889, Cavalier Hamilton Jouett, of San Francisco, *d.* 9 October, 1898, and had: *William Hooper, b.* 9 December, 1889, and *John Hamilton, b.* 14 May, 1892.

2.—CATHERINE BURCHELL HOOPER, *b.* 26 November, 1869, *d.* April, 1888.

3.—GEORGE KENT HOOPER, *b.* 22 April, 1871.

4.—EULALIE HOOPER, *b.* 1873, *d.* 1877.

5.—SELDEN STUART, *b.* 6 November, 1874; 6. ROSA, *b.* 19 July, 1876.

II.—ROBERT WALKER WRIGHT, *b.* 27 September, 1848, Lexington, Mississippi, *d.* 11 July, 1850.

III.—COLONEL STUART SELDEN WRIGHT, of Fresno, California, *b.* Yazoo City, Mississippi, 5 November, 1850; *m.*, 30 April, 1873, Maria Byrd Hopkins, a member of the Virginia and California Societies of the Colonial Dames of America, also of Royal Descent (p. 57), and had:

LOUISE KIMBALL WRIGHT, *b.* 6 December, 1874, a member of the Virginia and California Societies of the Colonial Dames of America, who *m.*, 7 June, 1895, John Mannen McClure, of Oakland, California, and had: *Wright Mannen, b.* 7 April, 1896.

IV.—ANN AYLETTE BROOKE WRIGHT, of Haywards, Alameda county, California, *b.* 9 January, 1853, Yazoo City, Mississippi, a member of the Virginia and California Societies of the Colonial Dames of America.

V.—GEORGE THOMAS WRIGHT, of San Francisco, California, b. Yazoo county, Mississippi, 22 March, 1855; m. Sophie Landsburger, and had: *Cedrie*, b. 9 April, 1889.

VI.—SARAH MAYNARD WRIGHT, b. Carroll county, Mississippi, 26 May, 1857, d. in San Francisco, California, 10 August, 1860.

VII.—ELIZA SHAW WRIGHT, b. Carroll county, Mississippi, 12 June, 1859, a member of the Virginia and California Societies of the Colonial Dames of America, who m., in San Francisco, in April, 1881, John Drury Tallant, of San Francisco, and had:

    1.—ELISE, b. 15 April, 1883; 2. DRURY, b. November, 1885; 3. SELDEN S., b. 1 March, 1887, d. 20 January, 1897; 4. JOHN D., b. 17 April, 1888.

VIII.—PAGE BRAXTON WRIGHT, b. San Francisco, 27 January, 1863, d. 12 May, 1864.

IX.—RALPH KIRKHAM WRIGHT, b. San Francisco, 24 April, 1865.

X.—ROBERTA EVELYN LEE WRIGHT, b. 30 January, 1868, m., 26 November, 1892, George H. Hillmann, of Alameda, California, and had:

    1.—MARY SELDEN, b. 6 December, 1893; 2. KATHERINE, b. March, 1897.

XI.—WILLIAM HAMMOND WRIGHT, b. 4 November, 1871.

XII.—BROOKE MAYNARD WRIGHT, b. Geneva, Switzerland, 30 January, 1877.

II.—SAMUEL WHITING, who had by his wife, Elizabeth:

ELIZABETH WHITING, who m. Rev. Samuel Ruggles, of Billerica, and had:

ELIZABETH RUGGLES (widow of Samuel Dummer, of Wilmington), b. 21 June, 1707, who m., secondly, 29 May, 1739 (*see* "N. E. His. Geneal. Reg.," xii., 339), Rev. Daniel Rogers, of Littleton, Massachusetts, b. at Ipswich, Massachusetts, 17 October, 1706, d. 22 November, 1782, a descendant of Governor Thomas Dudley, Major-General Daniel Dennison, Rev. Dr. John Rogers, president of Harvard College, 1676, etc., and had:

1.—JEREMIAH DUMMER ROGERS, of Charlestown, 1743–1784, who m., 25 December, 1769, Bathsheba Thatcher, also of Royal Descent, and had:

    MARGARET ROGERS, 1778–1858, who m., 1804, Jonathan Chapman, of Boston, d. 1832, and had:

JONATHAN CHAPMAN, 1807-1848, mayor of the city of Boston, 1840-42, who m., 25 April, 1832, Lucinda, daughter of Jonathan Dwight, and had:

FLORENCE CHAPMAN, b. 1847, a member of the Massachusetts Society of the Colonial Dames of America, who m., 1872, Henry Rogers Dalton, of Boston, and had: *Alice, Philip Spalding, Susan Dexter, Florence, d. 1890, and Ellen Bancroft.*

2.—SARAH ROGERS, b. February, 1755, d. 5 July, 1835, who m., 8 May, 1784 (his second wife), Samuel Parkman, of Boston, b. 22 August, 1751, d. 11 June, 1824, and had:

I.—REV. FRANCIS PARKMAN, D.D., of Boston, b. 3 June, 1788, d. 12 November, 1852, who m., secondly, Caroline Hall, d. August, 1871, also of Royal Descent, and had by her:

  1.—FRANCIS PARKMAN, of Boston, 1823-1893, the historian, who m. Catherine Bigelow, and had: *Francis, Katherine S.,* and

    GRACE PARKMAN, a member of the Massachusetts Society of the Colonial Dames of America, who m. Charles P. Coffin, of Longwood, Massachusetts. *Issue.*

  2.—CAROLINE HALL PARKMAN, b. 30 June, 1825, who m. Rev. John Cordner, LL.D., of Boston, 1816-1894, and had: *Mary Agnes, Elizabeth P.,* and

    CAROLINE PARKMAN CORDNER, of Boston, a member of the Massachusetts Society of the Colonial Dames of America.

II.—ELIZABETH WILLARD PARKMAN, b. 31 March, 1785, d. 14 April, 1853, who m., 2 February, 1809, Robert Gould Shaw, d. 3 May, 1853, and had:

SAMUEL PARKMAN SHAW, b. 19 November, 1813, d. 7 December, 1869, who m. Hannah Buck, and had eleven children, of whom:

I.—HANNAH BLAKE SHAW, a member of the Massachusetts Society of the Colonial Dames of America.

II.—MRS. GRANT WALKER, of Boston, Massachusetts, a member of the Order of the Crown.

2.—ELIZABETH WHITING, 1645-1733, who m. Rev. Jeremiah Hobart, of Haddam, Connecticut, b. Haverhill, England, 6 April, 1630, d. 1715-16, son of Rev. Peter Hobart, 1604-1679, and had:

DOROTHY HOBART, 1679-1733, who m., first, 19 April, 1704, Daniel Mason, of Norwich, Connecticut, d. ante 1707, and had:

JEREMIAH MASON, of Norwich, Connecticut, 1705-1779; m., 1727, Mary, 1704-1799, daughter of Thomas Clark, of Haddam, and had:

COLONEL JEREMIAH MASON, of Lebanon, 1730-1813; m., 1754, his cousin, Elizabeth, daugther of James and Anna Fitch, and had:

ELIZABETH MASON, *m.*, 1786, her cousin, Judge John Griswold Hillhouse, of Montville, Connecticut, *d.* 1806, and had:

MARIAN HILLHOUSE, who *m.* Elias W. Williams, and had:

MARY ELIZABETH WILLIAMS, *b.* 23 January, 1825, *d.* 12 July, 1897, who *m.*, 14 October, 1857, William Fitch, of Fitchville, Connecticut, and had:

SARAH GRISWOLD FITCH, a member of the New York Society of the Colonial Dames of America, who *m.*, 14 July, 1897, Francis Hillhouse, of New Haven, Connecticut, and had: *Mary Fitch, b.* 15 April 1898.

DOROTHY HOBART, 1679–1733, *m.*, secondly, 1 October, 1707, Hezekiah Brainerd, of Haddam, *b.* 24 May, 1680, *d.* 24 May, 1727, a member of the governor's council of Connecticut, 1723, *etc.*, and had: *Rev. Nehemiah Brainerd*, 1712–1744 (*m.* Elizabeth Fiske), and

I.—DOROTHY BRAINERD, *b.* 23 February, 1710, who *m.* Lieutenant David Smith, and had:

JERUSHA SMITH, *m.* Ezra Brainerd, of Haddam, Connecticut, *b.* 17 August, 1744, a member of the general assembly, 1777–1818, and had:

CALVIN BRAINERD, of Haddam, *b.* 23 September, 1778, *m.* Sarah, daughter of Captain Nehemiah Brainerd (son of the aforesaid Rev. Nehemiah Brainerd), *b.* 1741, a member of the general assembly, and Sarah Brainerd, his wife, and had:

CORDELIA BRAINERD, *b.* 30 March, 1814, *m.* Rev. Eleazar Cady Thomas, D.D., and had:

MARY HALSEY THOMAS, *b.* Gates, Monroe county, New York, 29 August, 1842, a member of the California Society of the Colonial Dames of America, who *m.*, in San Francisco, 25 October, 1880, John R. Jarboe, of Santa Cruz, California.

II.—MARTHA BRAINERD, *b.* Haddam, 1 September, 1716, *d.* 11 October, 1754, who *m.*, 2 August, 1738, Major-General Joseph Spencer, *b.* 3 October, 1714, *d.* 13 January, 1789, and had:

JOSEPH SPENCER, *d.* Vienna, West Virginia, 11 May, 1824; *m.*, 1777, Deborah Selden, *b.* Lynn, Connecticut, 29 December, 1753, *d.* Vienna, 25 August, 1825, and had:

ELIZABETH SPENCER, *b.* Vienna, 17 September, 1786, *d.* Detroit, Michigan, 31 March, 1853; *m.* Lewis Cass, Governor of Michigan, *etc.*, *b.* Exeter, New Hampshire, 9 October, 1782, *d.* Detroit, 17 June, 1866, and had:

MATILDA FRANCES CASS, *b.* Detroit, 11 July, 1818, *d.* London, England, 16 November, 1898, who *m.*, 19 September, 1839, Henry Ledyard, *b.* New York, 5 March, 1812, *d.* London, England, 7 June, 1880, son of Benjamin Ledyard, 1779–1811, and his wife, Susan French, daughter of Henry Brockholst Livingston, of New York, 1757–1823, and had:

ELIZABETH CASS LEDYARD, of Colorado Springs, Colorado, a member of the Rhode Island Society of the Colonial Dames of America, *b.* 1 October, 1840, who *m.*, 9 April, 1862, Francis Wayland Goddard, *b.* 5 May, 1833, *d.* 16 May, 1889, who was also of Royal Descent, as follows: *William Arnold,* of Rhode Island, 1587–1676 (see p. 13) had *Joanna Arnold,* who *m.* Zachariah Rhodes (see p. 15), and had: *Rebecca Rhodes,* who *m.*, first, 3 February, 1672, Nicholas Power, *d.* Providence, 19 December, 1675, and had: *Nicholas Power, Jr., d.* Providence, 18 May, 1734; *m.* Mary Tillinghast, *d.* 13 November, 1769, and had: *Hope Power, b.* 4 January, 1701, *d.* 8 June, 1792; *m.* James Brown, *d.* Providence, 27 April, 1739, and had: *Nicholas Brown,* of Providence, *b.* 28 July, 1729, *d.* 29 May, 1791; *m.* 2 May, 1762, Rhoda Jenckes, *d.* 16 December, 1783, and had: *Hope Brown, b.* 22 February, 1773, *d.* 21 August, 1855; *m.* Thomas Pointer Ives, *d.* Providence, 30 April, 1835, and had: *Charlotte Rhoda Ives,* who *m.*, 22 May, 1821, William Giles Goddard, *d.* Providence, 16 February. 1846, and had: *Francis Wayland Goddard,* 1833–89, who had by his wife, Elizabeth Cass Ledyard, aforesaid:

1.—CHARLOTTE IVES GODDARD, *b.* 1 March, 1863, a member of the Rhode Island Society of the Colonial Dames of America, who *m.*, 12 October, 1887, Amos Lockwood Danielson, of Providence, Rhode Island, and had: *Henry Ledyard, b.* 21 July, 1888.

2.—HENRY LEDYARD GODDARD, *b.* at Providence, Rhode Island, 23 November, 1866, *d.* at Colorado Springs, Colorado, 30 August, 1893.

3.—REV. JOSEPH WHITING, of Southampton, Long Island, New York, *b.* Lynn, 6 April, 1641, *d.* 7 April, 1723. He *m.*, first, 11 November, 1646, Sarah, daughter of Judge Thomas Danforth, deputy governor of Massachusetts, 1678–84, and president of Maine, 1692, and had by her:

I.—REV. JOHN WHITING, of Concord, Massachusetts, *b.* 20 January, 1681, *d.* 4 May, 1752. He *m.*, 1712, Mary, *d.* at Concord, 29 May, 1731, aged 42 years, daughter of Rev. John Cotton, of Hampton, New Hampshire, *d.* 1710 son of Rev. Seaborn Cotton, and grandson of Rev. John Cotton, of Boston, Mass., and his wife, Anne, daughter of Captain Thomas Lake, of Boston, and a descendant of Governor Simeon Bradstreet and Governor Thomas Dudley, of Massachusetts, and had:

JUDGE THOMAS WHITING, of Concord, Massachusetts, *b.* 25 June, 1717, *d.* 1776; *m.*, 25 March, 1742, Lydia, daughter of Rev. Thomas and Lydia (Richardson) Parker, of Dracut, Massachusetts, and had:

1.—MARY WHITING, b. 5 July, 1748, who m., first, 17 April, 1766, Captain William Barron, of Concord, who served under General Amherst in Canada, and in the Northeast Provinces, 1755–63, d. at Petersham, Massachusetts, and had:

MARY AUGUSTA BARRON, who m., 27 February, 1800, Stalham Williams, of Dalton, Massachusetts, and Utica, New York, and had:

1.—FRANCES LUCRETIA WILLIAMS, d. 29 February, 1884, m., 3 January, 1821, Captain Richard Winslow Sherman, of Vergennes, Vermont, d. 22 March, 1868, and had:

CORNELIA FRANKLIN SHERMAN, a member of the New York Society of the Colonial Dames of America, who m., first, 2 January, 1853, William Thomas Mumford, of Rochester, New York, d. 10 April, 1856, and m., secondly, 29 January, 1877, William Bennett Jackson, of Utica, New York, d. 28 December, 1890.

2.—SARAH TILESTON NEWTON WILLIAMS, who m., first, 22 February, 1846, David Scoville, of Rochester, New York, d. 1847, and m., secondly, June, 1852, Thomas H. Wood, of Utica, d. Paris, France, 1874, and had:

SARAH ELIZABETH SCOVILLE, a member of the New York Society of the Colonial Dames of America, who m., 30 November, 1875, Wallace Clarke, M.D., of Montreal, Canada, and Utica, New York, and had: *Wallace Roxburgh* and *Thomas Wood*.

2.—JOHN LAKE WHITING, b. Concord, 22 July, 1755, d. Lancaster, Massachusetts; m., 1782, Olive, 1762–1842, daughter of Ross Wyman, and had:

RELIEF WHITING, b. Shrewsbury, Massachusetts, 11 July, 1783, d. 7 December, 1851; m., 24 February, 1805, at Carlisle, Massachusetts, Reuben Foster Blood, and had:

CAROLINE BLOOD, b. Carlisle, 4 December, 1805, d. Davenport, Iowa, 1 October, 1890; m., 2 December, 1835, Rev. Julius Alexander Reed, D.D., b. Windsor, Connecticut, 16 January, 1809, d. Davenport, Iowa, 27 August, 1890, and had:

1. ANNA REED, b. Wyeth, Illinois, 30 August, 1836, member of the Society of the Mayflower Descendants, the Order of the Crown, *etc.*, who m., at Grinnell, Iowa, 16 December, 1861, Henry Washington Wilkinson, of Providence, Rhode Island, b. Manville, Rhode Island, 20 August, 1835, d. Franklin, Massachusetts, 6 May, 1898, and had: I. *Henry Lawrence*, b. 10 August, 1865, m., 4 June, 1896, Bertha Sandfred, of Bridgeport, Connecticut; II. *Alfred Hall*, b. 29 May, 1868,

m., 19 November, 1895, Elizabeth Burrows Kenyon, of Providence, Rhode Island; III. *Anna Reed, b.* 10 January, 1870, *m.*, 9 October, 1895, Edward Harris Rathburn, of Woonsocket, Rhode Island, and had: *Rachel Harris, b.* 13 September, 1897.

2.—ROSANNA REED, *b.* 11 August, 1839, *d.* 24 April, 1840.

3. MARY REED, *b.* Fairfield, Iowa, 9 February, 1843, a member of the Massachusetts and Iowa Societies of the Colonial Dames of America, Society of Mayflower Descendants, *etc.*, who *m.*, 17 August, 1863, Samuel Francis Smith, Jr., of Davenport, Iowa, *b.* Waterville, Maine, 5 September, 1836, son of Rev. Samuel Francis Smith, D.D., of Boston, Massachusetts, the author of the national anthem, " America," and had: *Anna Reed, b.* Davenport, 15 September, 1870.

II.—BENJAMIN WHITING, *b.* 1694, *d.* at Wallingford, Connecticut, 2 October, 1773; *m.*, 30 May, 1723, Rebecca, daughter of John and Mary (Mason) Parmlee, and had:

ABIGAIL WHITING, *b.* 7 September, 1736, who *m.*, 11 May, 1757, Dringon Andrews, *b.* Meriden, Connecticut, 27 August, 1730, *d.* 1 June, 1807, and had:

WHITING ANDREWS, *b.* Meriden, 23 March, 1764, *d.* Claramount, New Hampshire, 18 December, 1811; *m.* Lucy, daughter of Benjamin Curtis, of Meriden, and had:

ABIGAIL ANDREWS, *b.* 25 January, 1792, *d.* at Hampton, New York, 26 July, 1856, who *m.*, 1816, Mason Hulett, Jr., *b.* Belcherstown, Massachusetts, 19 February, 1775, *d.* Hampton, New York, 5 October, 1847, also of Royal Descent, and had:

HANNAH LUCY HULETT, *b.* at Hampton, 4 July, 1817; *d.* at Rutland, 28 January, 1892, who *m.*, 23 June, 1837, Henry Hitchcock, of Rutland, Vermont, 1805-71, also of Royal Descent, and had:

ABIGAIL JANE HITCHCOCK, *b.* Clarendon Springs, Vermont, 3 May, 1843, a member of the Massachusetts Society of the Colonial Dames of America, the Order of the Crown, *etc.*, who *m.*, 15 February, 1866, Horace Hoxie Dyer, of Rutland, Vermont, and had: *Captain Horace Edward*, a member of the Order of Runnemede, *etc.*, *b.* 16 April, 1870.

THE ROYAL DESCENT
OF
MRS. WILLIAM ALVORD,
OF SAN FRANCISCO, CAL.

PHILIP III., King of France =Princess Isabella of Arragon.

EDWARD I., King of England = Princess Margaret of France.

Edmund, Earl of Kent = Margaret de Wake.   ROBERT BRUCE, King of Scots = Elizabeth de Burgh.

Lady Joan Plantagenet = Thomas, Earl of Kent.   Matilda of Scotland = Thomas Isaac, Esq.

Thomas, Earl of Kent = Alice Fitzalan.   Joanna Isaac = John, Lord of Lorn.

Margaret de Holland = John, Earl of Somerset.   Isabel d'Ergadia = Sir John Stewart.

Joan, widow of King James I. = James Stewart, the "Black Knight of Lorn."

Sir John Stewart, Earl of Athol = Eleanor, dau. William, Earl of Orkney.

Sir John Stewart, Earl of Athol = Mary, dau. Archibald, Earl of Argyle.

Lady Isabel Stewart = Kenneth Mackenzie, Lord of Kintail.

Lady Agnes Mackenzie = Lachlan MacIntosh, Chief of Clan Chattan.

William MacIntosh, of Essick and Borlum = Elizabeth Innes.

Lachlan MacIntosh, of Borlum = Ann, widow of Sir Lachlan McIntosh.

Capt. John MacIntosh, of "Borlum," Ga. = Marjory Frazer, of Garthmore.

Col. William McIntosh, of Darien, Ga. = Jane Maccoy.

Gen. John McIntosh, of "Fairhope," Ga. = Sarah Swinton.

Col. James S. McIntosh, U. S. Army = Mrs. Eliza (Matthews) Shumate.

Col. Charles C. Keeney, M.D., U. S. Army, — Mary Eliza McIntosh, member of the California Society of the Colonial Dames of America.   William Alvord, of San Francisco, (second husband). *No issue.*

Charles McIntosh Keeney.   James Ward Keeney.

PEDIGREE LIII.

HENRY I., King of France, had by his wife, Lady Anne, daughter of Jaroslaus, Grand Duke, or Czar, of Russia:

HUGH THE GREAT, Duke of France and Burgundy, Count de Vermandois, who *m.*, thirdly, Adela, Countess de Vermandois, and had by her:

LADY ISABEL DE VERMANDOIS, *d.* 1131, who *m.*, first, in 1096, Robert, Baron de Bellomont, Earl of Mellent and Leicester, and had:

ROBERT DE BELLOMONT, second Earl of Leicester, justiciary of England, *d.* 1168, who *m.* Lady Amicia de Waer, daughter of Ralph, Earl of Norfolk, Suffolk and Cambridge, and had:

ROBERT DE BELLOMONT, third Earl of Leicester, lord high steward of England, *d.* 1196, who *m.*, 1167, Lady Petronella, daughter of Hugh, Baron de Grentesmaismil, and had:

LADY MARGARET DE BELLOMONT, who *m.* Saher de Quincey, one of the twenty-five trustees of the Magna Charta, created, 1207, Earl of Winchester, *d.* 1219, and had:

LADY HAWISE DE QUINCEY, who *m.* Hugh de Vere, fourth Earl of Oxford, great high chamberlain, *d.* 1263, and had:

ROBERT DE VERE, fifth Earl of Oxford, *d.* 1296; *m.* Alice, daughter of Gilbert de Saundford, chamberlain in fee to Queen Eleanor, 1250, and had:

ALPHONSUS DE VERE, second son, *d. v. p.*, who *m.* Jane, daughter of Sir Richard Foliot, and had:

JOHN DE VERE, seventh Earl of Oxford, who fought at Cressy, commanded at Poictiers, and was *k.* at Rheims, 14 June, 1360. He *m.* Lady Maud, widow of Robert Fitzpayne and daughter of Bartholomew, Baron de Badlesmere, executed in 1322, and his wife, Lady Margaret de Clare, also of Royal Descent, and had:

LADY MARGARET DE VERE, widow of Henry de Beaumont, *d.* 1369, who *m.*, secondly, Sir John Devereux, and had:

SIR WILLIAM DEVEREUX, who *m.* Anne, daughter of Sir John Barre, and had:

SIR WALTER DEVEREUX, *k.* 1402, who *m.* Agnes Crophull, and had:

ELIZABETH DEVEREUX, who *m.* Sir John Milbourne, and had:

SIMON MILBOURNE, who *m.* Jane, daughter of Sir Ralph Baskerville, of Erdisley, Hereford, also of Royal Descent, and had:

PEDIGREE LIII.—Continued.

BLANCHE MILBOURNE, who m. James Whitney, of Newport in the Marches, and had:

SIR ROBERT WHITNEY, K.B., a Gloucestershire magistrate, who m. Margaret Wye, and had:

SIR ROBERT WHITNEY, knighted 2 October, 1553, d. 5 August, 1567; m. Sybil, daughter of Sir James Baskerville, also of Royal Descent, and had:

ROBERT WHITNEY, who m. Elizabeth Morgan, and had:

THOMAS WHITNEY, of Lambeth Marsh, London, d. April, 1637, m., 12 May, 1583, Mary, buried 25 September, 1629, daughter of John Bray, and had:

JOHN WHITNEY, b. 1589, bapt. 20 July, 1592, came from Islesworth parish, near London, with his wife Elinor and five sons, to New England in June, 1635, and d. at Watertown, Massachusetts, 1 June, 1673. He m., first, in London, Elinor ———, who d. at Watertown, 11 May, 1659, aged 60 years (see Pierce's "John Whitney of Watertown," W. L. Whitney's "Whitney Family," Henry Melville's "Ancestry of John Whitney," "Magna Charta Barons and Their American Descendants," p. 181, etc.), and had by her:

1.—JOHN WHITNEY, b. 1620, bapt. Islesworth parish, 14 September, 1621, came with his parents to New England, d. at Watertown, Massachusetts, 12 October, 1692. In 1642 he m. Ruth, daughter of Robert and Mary Reynolds, of Wethersfield, and had:

I.—BENJAMIN WHITNEY, b. Watertown, 28 June, 1660, d. 1736; m., first, 30 March, 1687, Abigail, daughter of William and Mary (Bemis) Hagar, and m., secondly, Elizabeth ———, and had:

ENSIGN DANIEL WHITNEY, b. Watertown, 17 July, 1700, d. Watertown, 1775; m. Dorothy, b. 1706, daughter of Simon and Joanna (Stone) Taintor, and had by her, who d. 7 August, 1788:

MARY WHITNEY, b. 10 September, 1731, d. August, 1805; who m., 10 June, 1762, Major John Woodbridge, of Continental Army, b. Windsor, Connecticut, 24 July, 1732, d. South Hadley, Massachusetts, 27 December, 1782, son of Rev. John, 1702–1783; son of Rev. John, 1678–1718; son of Rev. John, 1644–1691; son of Rev. John, b. 1613 at Stenton, England, d. at Newbury, Massachusetts, 1695, and had:

MARTHA WOODBRIDGE, b. 8 January, 1771, d. 12 July, 1830, who m., 1794, John Dunlap, of Huntingdon, Massachusetts, and had:

SAMUEL DUNLAP, b. 6 March, 1801, d. Amherst, Massachusetts,

29 July, 1872; *m.*, 1 November, 1836, Sarah Electa, daughter of Roswell and Peace (Cook) Field, and had:

SARAH ALMIRA DUNLAP, a member of the New Hampshire Society of the Colonial Dames of America, the Order of the Crown, *etc.*, who *m.*, 1 May, 1876, Professor David Pearce Penhallow, of Montreal, Canada, and had: *Dunlap Pearce, b.* 9 August, 1880.

II.—NATHANIEL WHITNEY, of Weston, Massachusetts, 1646–1732; *m.*, 1673, Sarah Hagar, and had:

NATHANIEL WHITNEY, of Watertown, Massachusetts, 1675–1730; *m.*, 1695, Mary Robinson, and had:

ISRAEL WHITNEY, of Killingby, Connecticut, 1710–1746; *m.* Hannah ———, and had:

SYBIL WHITNEY, 1733–1812, who *m.* Captain Oliver Cummings, of Dunstable, Massachusetts, *d.* 1810, and had:

CAPTAIN JOSIAH CUMMINGS, of Dunstable, 1763–1834; *m.*, 1785, Sarah Taylor, and had:

SALLY CUMMINGS, who *m.*, 1806, John Cummings, of Tyngsboro, Massachusetts, 1779–1886, also of Royal Descent (*see* "Magna Charta Barons and Their American Descendants"), and had:

WILLARD CUMMINGS, of Tyngsboro, *b.* 1811, who *m.*, 1835, Mary Ann Pollard, and had:

ELLEN MARIA CUMMINGS, who *m.*, 1853, Joshua Flagg Davis, of Chalmsford, Massachusetts, *b.* 1822, and had:

ANNA MARIA DAVIS, *b.* 20 March, 1856, a member of the Order of the Crown, *etc.*, who *m.*, 30 June, 1886, Lord Karl von Rydingsvärd, of Sweden and Boston, Massachusetts.

2.—RICHARD WHITNEY, *bapt.* Islesworth parish, 6 January, 1623–24, who *m.*, 7 May, 1651, Martha Credam, and had:

RICHARD WHITNEY, who *m.* Elizabeth Sawtell, and had:

RICHARD WHITNEY, who *m.*, at Lancaster, Massachusetts, Hannah Whitcomb, and had:

DANIEL WHITNEY, who *m.*, at Lancaster, 9 February, 1744, Dorothy Goss, and had:

SILAS WHITNEY, who *m.*, at Stow, Massachusetts, 3 September, 1780, Patience Goodnow, and had:

JOHN WHITNEY, who *m.*, at Waltham, Massachusetts, 1 July, 1804, Susannah Piles, and had:

GEORGE H. WHITNEY, of Ithaca, New York, who *m.*, at Providence, Rhode Island, 13 April, 1852, Priscilla Gallup, and had:

ISABEL WHITNEY, a member of the New York Society of the Colonial Dames of America, who *m.*, 9 April, 1898, William H. Sage, of "Uplands," Albany, New York.

3.—BENJAMIN WHITNEY, *b.* Watertown, 6 June, 1643, *d.* 1723; *m.*, first, at York, Maine, Jane ———, *d.* 14 November, 1690, and had:

JONATHAN WHITNEY, of Sherborn, Milford, *etc.*, Massachusetts, *b.* 1680, *d.* January, 1754; *m.*, about 1700, Susanna ———, and had:

MARY WHITNEY, *b.* 28 May, 1710, *d.* 9 July, 1788; *m.* Joseph Jones, of Milford, Massachusetts, *b.* 27 December, 1709, *d.* 3 April, 1796, and had:

JOSEPH JONES, JR., of Milford, *b.* 29 September, 1737, *d.* 22 August, 1799; *m.* Ruth, *b.* 10 November, 1743, *d.* 1825, daughter of Nehemiah Nelson, and had:

ALEXANDER JONES, *b.* 8 August, 1764, *d.* 19 March, 1840; *m.*, in Charleston, South Carolina, 28 January, 1790, Mary, *b.* Milledgeville, Georgia, 24 December, 1773, *d.* Providence, Rhode Island, 5 September, 1835, daughter of George Farquhar, 1745–1779, and had:

REV. ALEXANDER JONES, *b.* Charleston, South Carolina, 8 November, 1796, *d.* Perth Amboy, New Jersey, in 1874; *m.* Anne Northey, daughter of Captain Benjamin King Churchill, of Bristol, Rhode Island, and had:

CLARA CHURCHILL JONES, *b.* 31 May, 1820, *d.* 29 December, 1881; *m.* Alexander Parker Crittenden, *b.* 14 January, 1816, *d.* at San Francisco, California, 5 November, 1870, son of Thomas Turpin and Mary Howard (Parker) Crittenden, of Kentucky, and had:

NANNIE CHURCHILL CRITTENDEN, *b.* Brazoria, Texas, 19 January, 1843, who *m.* Sidney McMechen Van Wyck, *b.* Baltimore, Maryland, 6 April, 1830, *d.* San Francisco, California, 27 April, 1887, also of Royal Descent, and had:

I.—LAURA SANCHEZ VAN WYCK, of San Francisco, *b.* Oakland, California, 5 September, 1879, a member of the California Society of the Colonial Dames of America, the Order of the Crown, *etc.*

II.—SIDNEY MCMECHAN VAN WYCK, JR., of San Francisco.

THE ROYAL DESCENT
OF
MRS. VIRGINIA LYNDALL DUNBAR,
OF CINCINNATI, OHIO.

EDWARD III., King of England=Lady Philippa of Hainault.
Lionel, Duke of Clarence=Lady Elizabeth de Burgh.
Lady Philippa Plantagenet=Edmund de Mortimer, Earl of Marche.
Lady Elizabeth de Mortimer=Sir Henry de Percy, called "Hotspur."
Henry de Percy, Earl of Northumberland=Lady Eleanor de Neville.
Henry de Percy, Earl of Northumberland=Lady Eleanor de Poynings.
Henry de Percy, Earl of Northumberland=Lady Matilda de Herbert.
Henry de Percy, Earl of Northumberland=Lady Catherine Spencer.
Lady Margaret de Percy=Henry de Clifford, Earl of Cumberland.
Lady Catherine de Clifford=Sir Richard Cholmoneley, of Roxby.
Sir Henry Cholmoneley, of Roxby=Lady Margaret de Babthorpe.
Lady Mary Cholmoneley=Rev. Henry Fairfax, of Bolton-Percy.
Henry, Lord Fairfax, of Cameron=Lady Frances Berwick.
Henry Fairfax, of Denton=Anne Harrison, of Yorkshire.
William Fairfax, of "Belvoir," Va.=Deborah Clarke.
Rev. Bryan, Lord Fairfax of Cameron=Elizabeth Cary.
Fernando Fairfax, of Alexandria, Va.=Elizabeth Cary.
Mercy Floretta Fairfax=Rev. Samuel Haggins.
Rev. John Haggins, of Bath Co., Ky.=Margery Mildred Johnson.
Col. George Washington Fairfax Haggins=Sarah Ann Beebe.
Nancy Johnson Haggins=Joseph Kling, of Seymour, Indiana.
Virginia Lyndall Kling=Horace Bernard Dunbar, of Boston, Mass.
Dorothy Dunbar, b. 1 April, 1894.

PEDIGREE LIV.

HENRY III., King of England, had by his wife, Lady Eleanor, daughter of Raymond, Count of Provence, also of Royal Descent:

EDMUND PLANTAGENET, 1245-1295, Earl of Leicester. He m., secondly, Blanche, widow of Henry, King of Navarre, and daughter of Robert, Earl of Artois, son of Louis VIII., King of France, and had by her:

HENRY PLANTAGENET, Earl of Leicester and Lancaster, d. 1345. He m. Lady Maud, daughter of Patrick de Chaworth and Lady Isabel de Beauchamp, also of Royal Descent, and had:

LADY JOAN PLANTAGENET, who m., first, John, third Baron de Mowbray, of Axholme, d. 1361, also of Royal Descent, and had:

JOHN DE MOWBRAY, fourth Baron Mowbray, of Axholme, d. 1368. He m. Lady Elizabeth, only child of John, third Lord Segrave, by his wife, Lady Margaret Plantagenet, also of Royal Descent, and had:

LADY MARGERY DE MOWBRAY, who m. John, second Baron de Welles, d. 1422, also of Royal Descent, and had:

EUDO DE WELLES, eldest son, d. v. p., who m. Lady Maud, daughter of Ralph, Baron de Greystock, also of Royal Descent, and had:

SIR LIONEL DE WELLES, Baron Welles, of Gainsby, lord lieutenant of Ireland, k. in the battle of Towton Field, 1461. He had by his first wife, Lady Joan, daughter of Sir Robert Waterton, Knt.:

LADY MARGARET DE WELLES, who m. Sir Thomas Dymoke, Knt., of Scrivelsby, Lincolnshire, and had:

SIR LIONEL DYMOKE, Knt., of Scrivelsby, high sheriff of Lincolnshire, d. 1519; m. Joan, daughter of Richard Griffith, of Stockford, and had:

LADY ALICE DYMOKE, who m. (his second wife) Sir William Skipwith, Knt., of Ormsby, sheriff of Lincolnshire, also of Royal Descent (*see* Burke's "Royal Families," Ped. cii.), and had:

SIR WILLIAM HENRY SKIPWITH, Knt., of Ormsby and Prestwould, Leicestershire, only son, who had by his wife, Anne, daughter of John Tothby (or his wife Jane, daughter of Francis Hall, of Grantham):

SIR WILLIAM SKIPWITH, Knt., of Prestwould, who m. Margaret, daughter of Roger Cave, of Stamford, and had:

SIR WILLIAM SKIPWITH, Bart., of Prestwould, eldest son, who sold Prestwould in 1653, and was created, 20 December, 1622, a baronet, and had issue by his wife, a daughter of Sir Thomas Kempe:

SIR GREY SKIPWITH, of Virginia, third Bart., brother of Sir Henry, second Bart., who *d. s. p.* He had by his wife, Bridget:

SIR WILLIAM SKIPWITH, of Virginia, fourth Bart., who *m.* Sarah, daughter of John Peyton, of Virginia, and had:

SIR WILLIAM SKIPWITH, of "Prestwould," Mecklenburg county, Virginia (brother of Sir Grey, of Virginia, fifth Bart., *b.* 2 August, 1705), who succeeded as sixth Bart., *b.* 1707, *d.* 1764; *m.*, 1733, Elizabeth, only daughter of John Smith, sheriff of Middlesex county, and had:

1.—SIR PEYTON SKIPWITH, of "Prestwould," seventh Bart., *d.* 1805; *m.*, first, Ann, and *m.*, secondly, Jean, both daughters of Hugh Miller, of Blandford, Virginia, *d.* London, 13 February, 1762, and had by Ann:

PEYTON SKIPWITH, second son, brother of Sir Grey Skipwith, of "Prestwould," Warwickshire, England, eighth Bart., 1771–1852, in whose line the baronetcy is continued. He removed from "Prestwould" to Maury county, Tennessee, where he *m.* Cornelia, daughter of Major-General Nathaniel Greene, of the Continental Army, and dying at his seat "Coates," in Georgia, had:

GEORGE GREENE SKIPWITH, *b.* at "Prestwould," *d.* at "Estoteville," Hinds county, Mississippi, 24 December, 1853. He *m.* Mary Ann, daughter of William Newsum and his wife, Sallie, daughter of Wilson Cary and Jean B., daughter of Dabney Carr, and his wife, a sister of President Jefferson, and had:

MARY SKIPWITH, a member of the Virginia Society of the Colonial Dames of America, who *m.*, in December, 1860, Percy Roberts, of New Orleans. *No issue.*

2.—COLONEL HENRY SKIPWITH, of Williamsburg, Virginia, 1751–1815, an officer in the Virginia Line, Continental Army, who *m.*, 1772, a daughter of John Wayles, of "The Forest," Charles City county, Virginia, and his wife, Martha, daughter of Francis Eppes, and had:

MARTHA WAYLES SKIPWITH, who *m.* Edmund Harrison, of Amelia county, Virginia, 1761–1826, member of the House of Delegates and of the Council, 1793, also of Royal Descent (pp. 35, 186), and had:

WILLIAM HENRY HARRISON, of Amelia county, Virginia, 1812–1884, who *m.* Lucy A. Powers, and had:

PROFESSOR EDMUND HARRISON, of Louisville, *m.* Kate Steger, and had:

1.—LULIE HARRISON, a member of the Virginia Society of the Colonial Dames of America, who *m.* Dana Henry Rucker, of Richmond, Virginia, and had: *Edmund Harrison, b.* 18 February, 1898.

2.—JEANIE HARRISON, a member of the Virginia Society of the Colonial Dames of America, who *m.* Charles H. Chalkley, of Hopkinsville.

3.—LELIA SKIPWITH HARRISON, a member of the Virginia Society of the Colonial Dames of America, who *m.* Howard D. Hoge, of Richmond.

PEDIGREE LV.

JAMES II., King of Scotland, had by his wife, Lady Mary, daughter of Arnold of Egmond, Duke of Guelders:

PRINCESS MARY STEWART, who had by her second husband, Sir James, first Lord Hamilton, of Cadyou:

JAMES HAMILTON, second Lord Hamilton, created Earl of Arran, who had by his third wife, Lady Janet, daughter of Sir David Betoun, of Creich:

JAMES HAMILTON, second Earl of Arran, created Duke of Chatelherault, who had by his wife, Lady Margaret, daughter of James Douglas, third Earl of Morton:

SIR CLAUD HAMILTON, third son, created Lord Hamilton, of Paisley, who had by his wife, Lady Margaret, daughter of George, sixth Lord Seton:

JAMES HAMILTON, created, 10 July, 1606, Earl of Abercorn, eldest son, *d. v. p.* 16 March, 1617, who had by his wife, Lady Marion, daughter of Sir Thomas, fifth Lord Boyd:

SIR GEORGE HAMILTON, Bart., of Donalong, county Tyrone, Ireland fourth son, who *m.*, in 1629, Lady Mary Butler, daughter of Walter, Viscount Thurles, and had:

LADY MARGARET HAMILTON, who *m.*, in 1688, Matthew Forde, M.P., of Coolgreany, county Wexford, Ireland, *d.* 1713 (*see* Wood's Douglas's "Peerage of Scotland," ii., 8), son of Nicholas Forde, of Killyleagh, county Down, and had:

MATTHEW FORDE, M.P., of Seaforde, county Down, *d.* 1729, who *m.*, in 1698, Anne (will probated at Dublin, 12 March, 1768), daughter of Rev. William Brownlowe, rector of Lurgan parish, county Armagh, and had:

STANDISH FORDE, fourth son (refer to his sister Margaret Forde's will, probated at Dublin, May, 1773), who came to Maryland in 1730, and settled in Philadelphia in 1734, where he *d.* in 1766. He *m.*, first, Hannah ———, and *m.*, secondly, Parthenia ——— (*see* "Phila. Adm.," 1766, Lib. H., fo. 15, and "Phila. Wills," 1766, Lib. N., fo. 506), and had by the latter, who *d.* in 1766:

STANDISH FORDE, JR., *b.* Philadelphia, 8 April, 1759; *d.* 28 April, 1806 (*see* "Philadelphia Wills," Lib. 1, fo. 487). He *m.*, at Christ Church,

Philadelphia, 5 December, 1795, Sarah, b. 16 January, 1775, daughter of John and Eleanor (Waters) Britton, of Philadelphia, and had, besides others:

1.—ELINOR FORDE, b. 9 October, 1796, d. 19 February, 1868; m., 14 October, 1812, William Sutton Hansell, b. 9 November, 1787, d. 22 December, 1872, and had: *Mary Sutton, William Forde, Henry Holcombe, Sarah Forde, Standish F., Barnett, John Forde, Theophilus Brantley, Robert, Edward, Susan Budd, Samuel Robb, George* and

    I.—ANNE SUTTON HANSELL, who m., 8 June, 1852, Alexander Thomas Lane, of Philadelphia, and had:

        ANNE HANSELL LANE, who m., 30 April, 1883, John Scollay, of Philadelphia, and had: *Edith Anne* (deceased), *Anna Lane*, and *Elinor Gertrude*.

    II.—ELLEN FORDE HANSELL, who m., 16 October, 1845, Joseph French Page, of Philadelphia, and had: *Joseph French, Edward Delano, Henry Hansell, William Hansell, Louise Rodman, Robert Hansell*, and

        1.—ELLEN HANSELL PAGE, a member of the Pennsylvania Society of the Colonial Dames of America, who m. Henry C. Butcher, of Philadelphia, and had:

            I.—LAURA PAGE BUTCHER, a member of the Pennsylvania Society of the Colonial Dames of America.

            II.—HENRY C. BUTCHER, JR., of Philadelphia.

            III.—ALICE TYSON, wife of George Brinton Roberts, of Philadelphia.

            IV.—ELEANOR PAGE BUTCHER.

        2.—FRANCES PAGE, a member of the New York Society of the Colonial Dames of America, who m. Winthrop Burr, of Boston.

2.—MARGARET LAMB FORDE, b. 3 February, 1799, who m., 8 September, 1820, Benjamin Poultney Smith, and had, besides others:

JOHN JAMES SMITH, who m., 17 September, 1844, Mary Ann Atkinson, and had:

SARAH FORDE SMITH, a member of the Pennsylvania Society of the Colonial Dames of America, who m. Charles Benjamin Wilkinson, and had: *Mary Elizabeth* and *J. Atkinson*.

THE ROYAL DESCENT

OF

MRS. FREDERICK C. POISSON,
OF LONDON, ENGLAND.

EDWARD I., King of England=Princess Eleanor of Castile.
  Princess Joan Plantagenet=Gilbert de Clare, Earl of Gloucester and Hertford.
    Lady Margaret de Clare=Hugh de Audley, Earl of Gloucester.
      Lady Margaret de Audley=Sir Ralph de Stafford, K.G., Earl of Stafford.
Sir Hugh de Stafford, K.G., Earl of Stafford=Lady Philippa de Beauchamp.
      Lady Margaret de Stafford=Sir Ralph de Neville, K.G., Earl of Westmoreland.
Ralph de Neville, of Oversley, Warwickshire=Lady Mary de Ferrers.
  John de Neville, of Wymersley, Yorkshire=Lady Elizabeth de Newmarch.
        Joan de Neville=Sir William Gascoigne, of Gawthrope, Yorkshire.
Sir William Gascoigne, of Gawthrope, York=Lady Margaret de Percy.
      Lady Elizabeth Gascoigne=Gilbert de Talboys, of Kyme.
        Sir George de Talboys, of Kyme=(Name unknown.)
        Lady Anne de Talboys=Sir Edward Dymoke, of Scrivelsby, Lincolnshire.
          Lady Frances Dymoke=Thomas Windebank, of Haines Hill, Berkshire.
            Mildred Windebank=Robert Reade, Linkenholt Manor, Southampton.
    Col. George Reade, of Gloucester Co., Va.=Elizabeth Martian.
            Mildred Reade=Col. Augustine Warner, Jr., of "Warner's Hall."
            Mildred Warner=Lawrence Washington, Westmoreland Co., Va.
      Augustine Washington, Stafford Co., Va.=Mary Ball, of "Epping Forest," Va.
            Betty Washington=Col. Fielding Lewis, of "Kenmore," Va.
        Howell Lewis, Kanawha Co., W. Va.=Ellen Pollard.
            Frances Fielding Lewis=Humphrey B. Gwathmey, of Richmond, Va.
  Virginia Gwathmey, member of the National=Adam Empie, of Wilmington, N. C.
    Society of the Colonial Dames of America.

Herbert Russell Latimer, died in 1887.	Frances Fielding Lewis Empie, member of the Order of the Crown, National Society of the Colonial Dames of America, etc.	Frederick C. Poisson, of Hyde Park Gate, London, England. *No issue.*	Annie Empie, member of the Order of the Crown, Society of the Colonial Dames of America, etc.	=Edward Bailey.
Herbert Russell Latimer.	Empie Latimer.			Edward. Virginia. Karin D. Frances F. L.

PEDIGREE LVI.

ROBERT III., King of Scotland, had by his wife, Lady Annabella, daughter of Sir John Drummond:

PRINCESS MARY STEWART, second daughter, who m. George Douglas, Earl of Angus, also of Royal Descent, and had:

LADY ELIZABETH DOUGLAS, who m. Sir Alexander Forbes, first Lord Forbes, and had:

JAMES, second Lord Forbes, d. 1460, who m. Lady Egidia, or Geiles Keith, also of Royal Descent, daughter of Sir William de Keith, created 4 July, 1458, the first earl marshal of Scotland, and had:

DUNCAN FORBES, second son, who m. Lady Christiana Mercer, daughter of the laird of Ballar, and had:

WILLIAM FORBES, of Corsindae, who m. Margaret, daughter of Lumsden of Cullon, and widow of the laird of Caskieben, and had:

DUNCAN FORBES, of Monymusk, who m. Agnes, daughter of William Gray, and had:

WILLIAM FORBES, of Monymusk, who m. Lady Margaret Douglas, daughter of the ninth Earl of Angus, and had:

JOHN FORBES, of Leslie, who m., secondly, Lady Margaret, daughter of the laird of Skeene, and had:

ALEXANDER FORBES, of Auchinhamper and Auchorties, who m. Anne, daughter of William Seaton, of Minnues, and had:

JOHN FORBES, of Auchorties, Aberdeenshire, who m. Barbara, daughter of William Johnstoun, of Aberdeenshire, and had:

ALEXANDER FORBES, of Auchorties, and afterwards of London (see Playfair's "British Family Antiquity," "The Barclays of Ury," and Jaffray's Diary), who m. Jean, youngest daughter of Robert Barclay, of Ury, the celebrated Apologist for the Quakers, 1648–1690, also of Royal Descent, and had:

CHRISTIANA FORBES, b. 6 February, 1714–15, d. 9 March, 1733–4, who m., 10 September, 1732, William Penn, the third, of London, b. 21 March, 1702–3, d. February, 1746, son of William Penn, Jr., and grandson of William Penn, the founder of Pennsylvania, and had:

CHRISTIANA GULIELMA PENN, b. 22 October, 1733, d. 1803, heiress of the Penn estates in England and Ireland, and of the Springetts, in Sussex, who m., 1761, Peter Gaskell, of Bath, England, d. 1785, and had:

PETER PENN-GASKELL, of Shaunagary and of "Ashwood," b. 9 May, 1763, d. 16 July, 1831, who m., 5 November, 1793, Elizabeth, daughter of Nathan Edwards, of Montgomery county, Pennsylvania, and had:

CHRISTIANA GULIELMA PENN-GASKELL, b. 27 May, 1805, d. 1830, who m., 2 January, 1827, William Swabric Hall, of Laventhorpe Hall and London, b. 1799, d. 26 September, 1862, and had:

COLONEL PETER PENN-GASKELL HALL, of Philadelphia, paymaster United States Army (retired), b. 16 March, 1830, who m., first, 24 December, 1861, Anne, daughter of Philip Mixsell, of Easton, Pennsylvania, and had:

1.—CHRISTIANA GULIELMA PENN-GASKELL HALL, of Philadelphia, a member of the Society of Colonial Dames.

2.—ELIZA PENN-GASKELL HALL, a member of the Society of Colonial Dames, who m., 1 June, 1892, Henry James Hancock, of Philadelphia, also of Royal Descent, a member of the Order of Runnemede, and had: *Jean Barclay Penn-Gaskell, b. 24 March, 1893.*

COLONEL HALL, m., secondly, November, 1871, Amelia, sister of his first wife, and had by her: *William, Peter Penn-Gaskell, Amelia,* and *Philip M.*

PEDIGREE LVII.

ROBERT II., King of Scotland, had by his first wife, Lady Elizabeth, daughter of Sir Adam Mure, of Rowallan:

ROBERT STEWART, 1399–1419, Duke of Albany, regent of Scotland, who *m.*, first, Margaret, Countess of Monteith, and had by her:

LADY MARJORY STEWART, who *m.* (his first wife) Sir Duncan Campbell, of Lochow, created, in 1445, Lord Campbell, *d.* 1453, also of Royal Descent, and had:

ARCHIBALD CAMPBELL, second son, *d. v. p.*, who *m.* Lady Elizabeth, daughter of Sir John Somerville, of Carnwarth, and had:

SIR COLIN CAMPBELL, second Lord Campbell, of Lochow, created, in 1457, Earl of Argyle, lord high chancellor of Scotland, 1483, *d.* 1493, who *m.* Lady Isabel Stewart, daughter of John, second Lord Lorn, and had:

LADY HELEN CAMPBELL, who *m.* Hugh, third Lord Montgomery, created, 1507, Earl of Eglington, also of Royal Descent, and had:

SIR NEIL MONTGOMERY, of Lainshaw, Knt., third son, *k.* 1547; *m.* Margaret, daughter of Quintin Mure, laird of Skeldon, and had:

SIR NEIL MONTGOMERY, of Lainshaw, Knt., second son, *m.* Lady Jean, daughter of John, fourth and last Lord of Lyle, and had:

SIR NEIL MONTGOMERY, of Lainshaw, Knt., *d. ante* 1613; *m.* Elizabeth, daughter of John Cunningham, of Aiket, and had:

WILLIAM MONTGOMERY, second son, *d.* 16 November, 1659; *m.*, 1602, Jean, daughter and heiress of John Montgomery, of Brigend, and had:

JOHN MONTGOMERY, of Brigend, *d. ante* 7 December, 1647; *m.*, 1626, Elizabeth, daughter of Thomas Baxter, of Shirnston, and had:

HUGH MONTGOMERY, of Brigend, *d.*, Glasgow, 6 May, 1710, aged 80 years. He *m.*, 1653, Lady Katherine, daughter of Sir William Scott, of Clerkington, a senator of the College of Justice, and had:

WILLIAM MONTGOMERY, who disposed of his interest in the manor of Brigend, in 1692, and removed with his family, in 1701, to America, and purchased a farm, in 1706, called "Eglington," in Monmouth county, New Jersey. He *m.*, 8 January, 1684, in Edinburgh, Isabel, daughter of Robert Burnet, of Lethintie, one of the original proprietors of East, or New Jersey, and had:

1.—ROBERT MONTGOMERY, of "Eglington," Monmouth county, New

Jersey, 1687–1766; *m.*, 1710, Sarah Stacy, of Burlington, New Jersey, and had:

JAMES MONTGOMERY, of "Eglington," 1720–1760; *m.*, 1746, Esther, daughter of John Wood, of Burlington county, New Jersey, and had:

WILLIAM MONTGOMERY, of Philadelphia, 1752–1831; *m.*, 1781, Rachel, daughter of Sampson Henry, of Philadelphia, and had:

MARY MONTGOMERY, *b.* 1794, who *m.*, 1815, Professor Charles Delucena Meigs, M.D., of Philadelphia, and had:

EMILY MEIGS, who *m.* J. Williams Biddle, of Philadelphia, and had:

CHRISTINE BIDDLE, a member of the Society of the Colonial Dames of America, who *m.* Richard M. Cadwalader, of Philadelphia, also of Royal Descent. *Issue.*

2.—JAMES MONTGOMERY, of Upper Freehold, Monmouth county, New Jersey, third son, who *m.* Mary ——, and had:

ALEXANDER MONTGOMERY, of Allentown, Pennsylvania, second son, 1735–1798, who *m.* Eunia West, of Eatonton, New Jersey, 1733–1796, and had:

THOMAS WEST MONTGOMERY, M.D., of New York, 1764–1820; *m.*, 1788, Mary, daughter of Judge John Berrien, of Rocky Hill, a justice of the Supreme Court of New Jersey, and had:

JULIA MONTGOMERY, *b.* 1797, *d.* 1882, who *m.*, 1825, William M. Biddle, of Philadelphia, *d.* 1855, and had:

JULIA MONTGOMERY BIDDLE, *b.* 1840, a member of the Pennsylvania Society of the Colonial Dames of America, who *m.*, 1863, Charles Stuart Huntington, of New York, *d.* 1890, and had:

FLORENCE HUNTINGTON, *b.* New York, 1864, who *m.*, first, William M. Biddle, and *m.*, secondly, Owen A. Conner, *d.* 1897.

PEDIGREE LVIII.

HENRY III., King of England, *m.*, 1236, Lady Eleanor Berenger, daughter of Raymond, Count de Provence, and had:

EDMUND PLANTAGENET, Earl of Lancaster, who *m.*, secondly, Lady Blanche, widow of Henry, King of Navarre, and daughter of Robert, Earl of Artois, *k.* 1247, son of Louis VIII., King of France, and had by her:

HENRY PLANTAGENET, Earl of Lancaster and Leicester, who *m.* Lady Maud, daughter of Sir Patrick de Chaworth, Knt., and his wife, Lady Isabel de Beauchamp, also of Royal Descent, and had:

LADY JOAN PLANTAGENET, who *m.* John, third Baron Mowbray, also of Royal Descent, and had:

JOHN, fourth Baron Mowbray, who *m.* Lady Elizabeth Segrave, also of Royal Descent, and had:

LADY ELEANOR MOWBRAY, *m.* Roger, Baron de la Warr, and had:

LADY JOAN DE LA WARR, who *m.* Sir Thomas, third Baron West, *d.* 1405, also of Royal Descent, and had:

SIR REGINALD DE WEST, second son, Baron de la Warr, *d.* 27 August, 1451, *m.* Margaret, daughter of Robert Thorley, and had:

SIR RICHARD WEST, second Baron de la Warr, 1432–1476, *m.* Lady Catherine, daughter of Robert, Baron de Hungerford, and had:

SIR THOMAS WEST, K.G., third Baron de la Warr, *d.* 1524, who *m.*, secondly, Eleanor, daughter of Sir Roger Copley, of Gatton, and had:

SIR GEORGE WEST, second son, *d.* 1538, who *m.* Lady Elizabeth, daughter of Sir Anthony Moreton, of Lechdale, and had:

SIR WILLIAM WEST, who was disabled from all honors in 1549, but restored in the blood in 1563, and was created, 5 February, 1570, Lord de la Warr, and *d.* 30 December, 1595. He *m.*, 1554, Elizabeth, daughter of Thomas Strange, of Chesterton, Gloucestershire, and had:

SIR THOMAS WEST, only son, second Lord de la Warr, knighted in Dublin, 12 July, 1599, by the Earl of Essex, *d.* April, 1602; *m.* Anne Knowles, and had:

PEDIGREE LVIII.—Continued.

HON. COLONEL JOHN WEST,* b. 14 December, 1590; B.A., Oxford, 1 December, 1613; brother of Tnomas West, third Lord de la Warr, and Francis West, both Governors of Virginia. He came to Virginia, and was a member of the House of Burgesses and the Council, 1631-59, and Governor of the Virginia Colony, 1635-37, Muster-Master General of Virginia, 1641, and dying in 1659, he left issue by his wife, Anne ——— (see "Virginia Historical Magazine," vol. i., p. 423):

HON. COLONEL JOHN WEST, JR., of "West Point," King William county, only child, 1632-1689, a member of the Virginia House of Burgesses, 1685, and colonel under Berkeley in Bacon's rebellion. He m. Unity, daughter of Joseph Croshaw, of York county, member of the House of Burgesses, 1658, and had:

1.—ANNE WEST, who m. Henry Fox, of King William county, Virginia, and had:

ANNE FOX, b. 20 May, 1684, d. 4 May, 1733, who m. (his third wife) Captain Thomas Claiborne, of "Sweet Hall," King William county, 1680-1732, also of Royal Descent, and had:

I.—NATHANIEL CLAIBORNE, m. Jane Cole, and had:

WILLIAM CLAIBORNE, of Manchester, Virginia, d. 1809; m. Mary, daughter of Ferdinand Leigh, of King William county, and had:

NATHANIEL HERBERT CLAIBORNE, 1777-1859, m., 1815, Elizabeth Archer Binford, and had:

ELIZABETH HERBERT CLAIBORNE, 1829-1855, who m., 1851, James Coleman Otey, of Bedford county, and had:

LULIE LEIGH OTEY, a member of the Virginia Society of the Colonial Dames of America, who m., 1870, Hervey Darneal, of Alameda, California, and had: *Susan Cole, Herbert Claiborne,* and *Hervey Otey.*

II.—DANIEL CLAIBORNE, of King William county, who had:

MARY ANN CLAIBORNE, who m. John Butts, and had:

GENERAL DANIEL CLAIBORNE BUTTS, who m. Elizabeth Randolph Harrison, also of Royal Descent, and had:

DANIEL CLAIBORNE BUTTS, who m. Ariadne Smith, and had:

MARIE ELOISE BUTTS, who m. Robert Dunlop, and had:

---

* The following ladies, members of the National Society of the Colonial Dames of America, are also of Royal Descent, through John West:

MISS MARY M. LYONS, Virginia State Society.

MRS. WILLIAM L. ROYALL, Virginia State Society.

MISS ANNA S. DANDRIDGE, Maryland State Society.

1. AGNES DUNLOP, a member of the Virginia Society of the Colonial Dames of America, who m. William H. Wight, of Cockeysville, Maryland, and had: *Robert D.*

2.—MARIE DUNLOP, a member of the Virginia Society of the Colonial Dames of America, who m. Warner Moore, of Richmond, Virginia, and had: *Marie Jean* and *Warner.*

III.—COLONEL AUGUSTINE CLAIBORNE, of "Windsor," King William county, 1721–1787, m. Mary Herbert, of "Puddlecock," Dinwiddie county, Virginia, and had:

HERBERT CLAIBORNE, of "Chestnut Grove," New Kent county, Virginia, b. 7 August, 1746, who had by his wife, Mary Burnet Browne, also of Royal Descent:

HERBERT AUGUSTINE CLAIBORNE, of Richmond, Virginia, 1784–1841, m. Delia, daughter of James Hayes, of Richmond, and had:

MAJOR JOHN HAYES CLAIBORNE, of Richmond, Virginia, m. Anna Virginia Bassett, of "Eltham," also of Royal Descent, and had:

DELIA CLAIBORNE, a member of the Virginia Society of the Colonial Dames of America, who m., 10 June, 1885, General Simon B. Buckner, of Hart county, Kentucky, and had: *Simon Bolivar*, b. 18 July, 1886.

2.—CAPTAIN NATHANIEL WEST, of King William county, Virginia, a member of the House of Burgesses, 1702, who had:

UNITY WEST, only child, who m., 1719, Captain William Dandridge, of "Elsing Green," King William county, a member of the Governor's council, 1727, Captain Royal Navy, 1737–41, d. 1743, and had:

I.—COLONEL NATHANIEL WEST DANDRIDGE, of King and Queen county, Virginia, b. 7 September, 1729, d. 16 January, 1789, who m., 1747, Dorothea, daughter of Major-General Alexander Spotswood, also of Royal Descent, and had:

1.—DOROTHEA DANDRIDGE, who m. (his second wife) Patrick Henry, first Governor of Virginia, also of Royal Descent, and had:

JOHN HENRY, who m. Elvira Bruce McClelland, and had:

WILLIAM WIRT HENRY, of Richmond, Virginia, who m. Lucy Gray Marshall, a member of the Virginia Society of the Colonial Dames of America, and had:

1.—LUCY GRAY HENRY, a member of the Virginia Society of the Colonial Dames of America, who m. Matthew Bland Harrison, of Richmond, Virginia.

2.—ELIZABETH HENRY, a member of the Virginia Society of the Colonial Dames of America, who m. James Lyons, of Richmond, Virginia.

2.—MAJOR ALEXANDER, SPOTSWOOD DANDRIDGE, of "The Bower," Jefferson county, Virginia, *b.* 1753, an aide-de-camp to General Washington, *m.* Ann, daughter of Major-General Adam Stephen, of the Virginia Line, and had:

ADAM STEPHEN DANDRIDGE, of "The Bower," *b.* 5 December, 1782, *d.* 20 November, 1821, *m.*, 1 January, 1805, Sarah, daughter of Philip Pendleton, and had:

ALEXANDER SPOTSWOOD DANDRIDGE, M.D., of Cincinnati, Ohio, *b.* 2 November, 1819, *d.* 29 April, 1889; *m.*, 4 May, 1843, Martha, daughter of Colonel Nathaniel Pendleton, of Cincinnati, member of Congress, and had:

1.—SUSAN BOWLER DANDRIDGE, a member of the New York Society of the Colonial Dames of America, who *m.* John M. Bowers, of New York City.

2.—MARY EVELYN DANDRIDGE, of Cincinnati, a member of the Virginia Society of the Colonial Dames of America.

II.—MARTHA DANDRIDGE, who *m.* Philip Aylett, of Virginia, and had:

COLONEL WILLIAM AYLETT, *m.* Mary, daughter of Colonel James Macon and his wife, Elizabeth Moore, also of Royal Descent, and had:

1.—COLONEL PHILIP AYLETT, *m.* Elizabeth, daughter of Governor Patrick Henry, of Virginia, also of Royal Descent, and had:

MARY MACON AYLETT, *m.* Philip Fitzhugh, and had:

LUCY FITZHUGH, *m.* John Robertson Redd, and had:

LUCY REDD, a member of the Indiana Society of the Colonial Dames of America, who *m.* William J. Holliday, of Indianapolis, Indiana, also of Royal Descent, and had:

1.—ARIANA AMBLER HOLLIDAY, a member of the Indiana Society of the Colonial Dames of America, who *m.* Henry W. Bennett, of Indianapolis.

2.—JAQUELIN S. HOLLIDAY, *m.* Florence Baker.

3.—LUCY FITZHUGH HOLLIDAY, *m.* George E. Hume.

2.—ELIZABETH AYLETT, *b.* 1769, who *m.*, 17 July, 1787, Alexander Spotswood Moore, of King William county, also of Royal Descent, and had:

MILDRED WALKER MOORE, *b.* 1788, *m.*, 1806, Rev. John Wilson Campbell, of Virginia, and had:

ELIZABETH CAMPBELL, who *m.* John Maben, of Richmond, Virginia, and had:

1.—MARY MABEN, a member of the Maryland Society of the Colonial Dames of America, who m. Frank Peyton Clark, of Baltimore, and had: *Bessie Campbell* and *William Lawrence.*

2.—JANE MABEN, who m. J. Dorsey Cullen, of Richmond, and had:

ELIZABETH CAMPBELL CULLEN, a member of the Virginia Society of the Colonial Dames of America, who m. John F. T. Anderson, of Ashland, Virginia.

III.—ELIZABETH DANDRIDGE, m. Philip Whitehead Claiborne, also of Royal Descent, and had:

PHILADELPHIA CLAIBORNE, m. Abner Waugh, and had:

SARAH SPOTSWOOD WAUGH, m. James Lyons, and had:

LUCY LYONS, m. John Hopkins, and had:

JOHN HOPKINS, m. Abby Byrd Page, also of Royal Descent, and had:

WILLIAM EVELYN HOPKINS, 1821-1894, Commodore United States Navy, who m. Louise Kimball, and had:

MARIA BYRD HOPKINS, a member of the California Society of the Colonial Dames of America, who m. Colonel Stuart Selden Wright, of Fresno, California, also of Royal Descent, and had:

LOUISE KIMBALL WRIGHT, a member of the Virginia Society of the Colonial Dames of America, who m., 7 June, 1895, John M. McClure, of Oakland, California, and had: *Mannen Wright*, b. 7 April, 1896.

IV.—MARY DANDRIDGE, who m., 1745, John Spotswood, d. 1759, also of Royal Descent, and had:

1.—CAPTAIN JOHN SPOTSWOOD, who m. Sallie Rowsee, and had:

ROBERT SPOTSWOOD, who m. Louisa Bott, and had:

REV. JOHN SPOTSWOOD, D.D., of Petersburg, Virginia, who m. Sarah Peters, daughter of William Shippen Willing, of Philadelphia, and had:

LUCY SPOTSWOOD, a member of the Pennsylvania Society of the Colonial Dames of America, who m. George Peirce, of Philadelphia.

2.—ANN SPOTSWOOD, who m. Lewis Burwell, and had:

SPOTSWOOD BURWELL, who m. Mary Marshall, and had:

MARY ANN SPOTSWOOD BURWELL, who m. Dr. Otis F. Manson, and had:

ELIZA SANGER MANSON, a member of the Virginia Society of the Colonial Dames of America, who m. Thomas Lee Alfriend, of Richmond, Virginia, and had: *Sallie Spotswood, Anna Lee, Otis Manson,* and

MARY BURWELL ALFRIEND, a member of the Virginia Society of the Colonial Dames of America, who m. Herbert Dale Lafferty, of Richmond, Virginia. *No issue.*

THE ROYAL DESCENT

OF

MISS ISA GARTEREY URQUHART GLENN,

OF ATLANTA, GA.

ALFRED THE GREAT, of England, had:
Edward the Elder, King of England, who had.
Edmund I., King of England, who had:
Edgar the Peaceful, King of England, who had:
Ethelred II., King of England, who had:
Edmund II., King of England, who had:
Prince Edward the Exile, of England, who had:
Margaret, *m.* Malcolm III., of Scotland, and had:
Matilda, *m.* Henry I., of England, and had:
Maud, *m.* Geoffrey, Count of Anjou, and had.
Henry II., King of England, who had:
John, King of England, who had:
Henry III., King of England, who had:
Edward I., King of England, who had:
Joan, *m.* Gilbert, Earl of Clare, and had:
Margaret, *m.* Hugh, Lord d'Audley, and had:
Margaret, *m.* Sir Ralph Stafford, K.G., and had:
Hugh, Earl of Stafford, K.G., who had:
Margaret, *m.* Sir Ralph Neville, K.G., and had:
Margaret, *m.* Richard, Lord le Scrope, and had:
Sir Henry, Lord le Scrope, of Bolton, who had:
Margaret, *m.* John Bernard, and had:
John Bernard, of Abingdon, who had:
John Bernard, of Abingdon, who had:
Francis Bernard, of Abingdon, who had:
Francis Bernard, of Kingsthorpe, who had:
Col. William Bernard, of Va., who had:
Lucy, *m.* Dr. Edmund Gwynne, and had:

THE EMPEROR CHARLEMAGNE, had:
Louis I., King of France, who had:
Charles II., King of France, who had:
Judith, *m.* Baldwin I., of Flanders, and had:
Baldwin II., Count of Flanders, who had:
Arnoul the Great, Count of Flanders, who had
Baldwin III., Count of Flanders, who had:
Arnoul II., Count of Flanders, who had ·
Baldwin IV., Count of Flanders, who had:
Baldwin V., Count of Flanders, who had:
Maud, *m.* William the Conqueror, and had ·
Henry I., King of England, who had:
Maud, *m.* Geoffrey, Count of Anjou, and had:
Henry II., King of England, who had:
John, King of England, who had:
Henry III., King of England, who had:
Edward I., King of England, who had:
Thomas, Earl of Norfolk, who had:
Margaret, *m.* John de Segrave, and had:
Elizabeth, *m.* John de Mowbray, and had:
Margery, *m.* Sir John de Welles, and had:
Eudo de Welles, heir, *d. v. p.*, who had:
Sir Lionel, Baron Welles of Gainsby, who had:
Margaret, *m.* Sir Thomas Dymoke, and had:
Sir Robert Dymoke, of Scrivelsby, who had:
Sir Edward Dymoke, of Scrivelsby, who had:
Frances, *m.* Sir Thomas Windebank, and had:
Mildred, *m.* Robert Reade, and had:
George Reade, of Va.—Elizabeth Martian.

Lucy Gwynne, of Gloucester Co., Va.—Thomas Reade. Augustine Warner, Jr.,—Mildred Reade.

John Smith—Mary Warner. John Lewis—Elizabeth Warner.

Augustine Smith—Sarah Carver. Charles Lewis—Mary Howell.

Mildred Reade—Philip Rootes. John Smith—Mary Jacquelin. Howell Lewis—Mary Willis.

Thomas Reade Rootes—Maria Smith. Mildred Lewis—John Cobbs.

Thomas Reade Rootes, Jr.—Sarah Ryng Battaile.

Sarah Robinson Rootes—John Addison Cobb.

Mildred Lewis Rootes Cobb—Luther Judson Glenn.

John Thomas Glenn—Helen Augusta Garrard.

Isa Garterey Urquhart Glenn, of Atlanta, member of the National Society of the Colonial Dames of America.

PEDIGREE LIX.

EDWARD III., King of England, had by his wife, Lady Philippa, daughter of William, Count of Hainault and Holland:

SIR LIONEL PLANTAGENET, K.G., Duke of Clarence, Earl of Ulster, *etc.*, who had by his first wife, Lady Elizabeth, daughter of Sir William de Burgh, Earl of Ulster, murdered in Ireland 6 June, 1333, and his wife, Lady Maud Plantagenet, both of Royal Descent:

LADY PHILIPPA PLANTAGENET, only child, who *m.*, in 1368, when she was only 13 years of age, Edmund de Mortimer, third Earl of Marche, lord-lieutenant of Ireland, Earl of Ulster, *d.* at Cork, 26 December, 1381, and had:

LADY ELIZABETH DE MORTIMER, *b.* 12 February, 1371, *d.* 20 April, 1417, who *m.*, in 1380, first, Sir Henry de Percy, K.G., the renowned "Hotspur," *k.* at Shrewsbury in 1403, son of Henry, Baron Percy, of Alnwick, created, 1377, Earl of Northumberland, also of Royal Descent, and had:

SIR HENRY DE PERCY, K.G., second Earl of Northumberland, *b.* 3 February, 1393, *k.* at St. Albans in 1455. He *m.* Lady Eleanor Neville (her second husband), daughter of Sir Ralph, first Earl of Westmoreland, K.G., and his second wife, Lady Joan de Beaufort, both of Royal Descent, and had:

HENRY DE PERCY, third Earl of Northumberland, *k.* at Towton in 1461, who *m.* Lady Eleanor, only child of Richard Poynings, *d. v. p.* 1430, eldest son of Robert, fifth Lord Poynings, *k.* 1446, and had:

LADY MARGARET DE PERCY, who *m.* Sir William Gascoigne, of Gawthrope, Yorkshire, also of Royal descent, and had:

LADY ELIZABETH GASCOIGNE, who *m.* Gilbert, Baron de Talboys, of Kyme, *d.* 1566, and had:

SIR GEORGE DE TALBOYS, Knt., son and heir, whose daughter:

LADY ANNE DE TALBOYS, who *m.* Sir Edward Dymoke, of Scrivelsby, Lincolnshire, hereditary champion of England, high sheriff of Lincolnshire, officiated as "champion" at the coronations of Edward VI., Queen Mary, and Queen Elizabeth, also of Royal Descent, and had:

LADY FRANCES DYMOKE, who *m.* Sir Thomas Windebank, of Haines Hill, Hurst parish, Berkshire, clerk of the signet to Queen Elizabeth and King James I., *d.* 24 October, 1607, and had:

PEDIGREE LIX.—Continued.

LADY MILDRED WINDEBANK, who m., in 1600 (his third wife), Robert Reade, of Linkenholt Manor, Southamptonshire, will dated 10 December, 1626, and had:

COLONEL GEORGE READE,* named in the will of his grandfather, Andrew Reade, 1619. He came to the Virginia Colony about 1637, and was burgess for James City county, 1644-49, and Gloucester county, 1656; secretary of the colony *pro tem.*, in 1640; a member of the council, 1657 till decease; will proved 20 November, 1671. He m., before 1657, Elizabeth, daughter of Captain Nicholas Martian, of York county, Virginia, a justice, 1633-1657, will probated 24 April, 1657, and had:

1.—THOMAS READE, of Gloucester county, Virginia, will executed 4 January, 1694; m. Lucy, daughter of Dr. Edmund Gwynne, and his wife, Lucy Bernard, also of Royal Descent (*see* p. 38), and had:

   I.—MILDRED READE, who m. Major Philip Rootes, of "Rosewell," Virginia, and had:

      1.—THOMAS READE ROOTES, who had by his wife, Maria Smith, also of Royal Descent (*see* p. 251).

         THOMAS READE ROOTES, JR., of "Whitemarsh," who had by his wife, Sarah Ryng Battaile:

         SARAH ROBINSON ROOTES, who m. John Addison Cobb, son of John Cobbs, of "The Sand Hills," Augusta, and his wife, Mildred Lewis, also of Royal Descent (*see* p. 257), and had:

         I.—MARY WILLIS COBB, who m. first (his second wife), Colonel Frank H. Erwin, and had:

            LUCY COBB ERWIN, a member of the Georgia Society of the Colonial Dames of America, who m. Abner Welborn Hill, of Atlanta, and had: *Lamar*, *Ashby*, *Abner W.*, and *Thomas Cobb*.

         MARY WILLIS COBB m., secondly, John A. Johnson, M.D., and had:

            SARAH COBB JOHNSON, a member of the Georgia Society of the Colonial Dames of America, who m. Hugh Hagan, M.D., of Atlanta, and had: *Hugh* and *Willis Cobb*.

---

* The following ladies, members of the National Society of the Colonial Dames of America, are also of Royal Descent, through George Reade:

MRS. DANIEL H. BUELL, Maryland State Society.

MISS EVELYN BYRD MCCANDLISH, Maryland State Society.

MISS SUSETTE G. STEWART, Kentucky State Society.

MRS. HAMPTON L. FERRILL, Georgia State Society.

PEDIGREE LIX.—Continued.

II.—MILDRED LEWIS ROOTES COBB, who m. Luther Judson Glenn, descended from Dr. John Glenn, of Dublin, N. C., son of Andrew Glenn, of Longcroft, Linlithgow, and had:

JOHN THOMAS GLENN, of Atlanta, who m. Helen Augusta, a member of the Georgia Society of the Colonial Dames of America, daughter of William Waters Garrard and his wife, Frances Isabella Garterey Urquhart, also of Royal Descent, and had: *Garrard, Helen Mildred Lewis, William Louis,* and

ISA GARTEREY URQUHART GLENN, of Atlanta, a member of the Georgia Society of the Colonial Dames of America.

III.—SARAH MARTHA COBB, who m. Major John Charles Whitner, of Atlanta, and had:

1.—SARAH ROOTES WHITNER, a member of the Georgia Society of the Colonial Dames of America, who m. Warren Howard, of Atlanta, and had: *Martha Cobb, Whitner,* and *Mary Ann.*

2.—MARY ANN WHITNER, a member of the Georgia Society of the Colonial Dames of America, who m. Benjamin Charles Milner, Jr., of Atlanta, and had: *Charles Whitner, Benjamin Charles, 3d, Jean Shepard,* and *John Cobb.*

3.—ELIZA SPANN WHITNER, of Atlanta, a member of the Georgia Society of the Colonial Dames of America.

4.—MARTHA MILDRED WHITNER, a member of the Georgia Society of the Colonial Dames of America, who m. Willis J. Milner, of Atlanta, and had: *Willis J., Spann Whitner* and *Benjamin C.*

IV.—GENERAL THOMAS READE ROOTES COBB, who m. Marian Lumpkin, and had:

MARIAN THOMAS COBB, a member of the Georgia Society of the Colonial Dames of America, who m. Hoke Smith, of Atlanta, and had: *Marion, Mary Brent, Lucy,* and *Callie.*

2.—ELIZABETH ROOTES, who m. (his second wife) Rev. John Thompson, of Culpeper county, Virginia, d. 1772, and had:

PHILIP ROOTES THOMPSON, of Culpeper, who had by his second wife, Sally Slaughter, of Culpeper:

JUDGE ROBERT AUGUSTINE THOMPSON, of San Francisco, who had by his first wife:

SARAH ELIZABETH THOMPSON, a member of the Virginia Society of the Colonial Dames of America, who m. G. W. Huie, of San Francisco, and had:

SALLIE HELENA HUIE, a member of the Virginia Society of the Colonial Dames of America, who m., 1899, her cousin, William Thompson.

JUDGE ROBERT AUGUSTINE THOMPSON had by his second wife, Elizabeth Jane Early:

1.—RUTH HAIRSTON THOMPSON, a member of the Virginia and California Societies of the Colonial Dames of America, who m. William Craig, of San Francisco, California.

2.—ROBERTA THOMPSON, of San Francisco, a member of the Virginia and California Societies of the Colonial Dames of America.

II.—MARY READE, who m. Captain Mordecai Throckmorton, 1696-1768, also of Royal Descent, and had:

LUCY THROCKMORTON, m. Robert Throckmorton, and had:

FRANCES THROCKMORTON, m. General William Madison, and had:

REBECCA CONWAY MADISON, m. Reynolds Chapman, and had:

JUDGE JOHN MADISON CHAPMAN, m. Susannah Digges Cole, also of Royal Descent, and had:

I.—SUSIE ASHTON CHAPMAN, a member of the Tennessee Society of the Colonial Dames of America, the Order of the Crown, *etc.*, who m. Calvin Perkins, of Memphis, Tennessee. *Issue.*

II.—BELLE CHAPMAN, a member of the Virginia Society of the Colonial Dames of America, the Order of the Crown, *etc.*, who m. William Moncure, of Richmond, Virginia. *Issue.*

III.—ASHTON ALEXANDER CHAPMAN.

2.—JOHN READE, who m. Mary Lilly, and had:

MARGARET READE, m. Thomas Nelson, of Yorktown, Virginia, and had:

MARY NELSON, who m. Edmund Berkeley, of "Barn Elms," and had:

NELSON BERKELEY, of "Airwell," who m. Elizabeth Wormeley Carter, also of Royal Descent, and had:

DR. CARTER BERKELEY, of "Edgewood," who m. Mrs. Frances (Page) Nelson, also of Royal Descent, and had:

CATHERINE FRANCES BERKELEY, who m. Lucius Horatio Minor, of "Edgewood," also of Royal Descent, (*see* pp. 56, 183, 255), and had:

MARY WILLIS MINOR, of Baltimore, a member of the Maryland Society of the Colonial Dames of America.

3.—MILDRED READE, who m., before 1671, Colonel Augustine Warner, Jr., of Warner's Hall, Gloucester county, Virginia, b. 3 July, 1642, d. 19 June, 1681, a member and speaker of the Virginia House of Burgesses, 1658–77, a member of the Council from 10 May, 1680 (son of Captain Augustine Warner, of Warner's Hall, 1610–1674, a burgess for York county, 1652, Gloucester county, 1655, a member of the Council, 1659–74, etc.), and had:

I.—MARY WARNER, who m., 17 February, 1688, John Smith, of "Purton," Gloucester county, Virginia, son of Major John Smith, of Warwick county, Virginia, and had:

AUGUSTINE SMITH, b. 16 June, 1687, d. 30 December, 1756; m., 9 November, 1711, Sarah, daughter of Captain William Carver, a justice for Lower Norfolk county, 1665; high sheriff, 1670; a member of the House of Burgesses, 1665–72; general surveyor of highways, who took a prominent part in Bacon's rebellion, and was executed, and had by her:

JOHN SMITH, of "Shooter's Hill," Middlesex county, Virginia, b. 13 November, 1715, d. 19 November, 1771, a member of the House of Burgesses; m., 17 November, 1737, Mary, daughter of Edward and Martha (Cary) Jacquelin, of Jamestown, Virginia, and had: *Maria*, wife of Thomas Reade Rootes (*see* p. 248), and

1.—MARY SMITH, who m. Rev. Thomas Smith, and had:

SARAH SMITH, who m. Benjamin Dabney, and had:

THOMAS SMITH GREGORY DABNEY, who m. Sophia Hill, and had:

SOPHIA DABNEY (Mrs. Thurmond, of Sewanee, Tennessee), a member of the Virginia Society of the Colonial Dames of America. Issue: *Sophia Dabney*.

2.—EDWARD SMITH, who m. Elizabeth Bush, and had:

ARIANA AMBLER SMITH, who m. William D. Holliday, and had:

WILLIAM JAQUELIN HOLLIDAY, of Indianapolis, who m. Lucy Redd, also of Royal Descent, a member of the Virginia and Indiana Societies of the Colonial Dames of America, and had:

1.—ARIANA AMBLER HOLLIDAY, a member of the Virginia and Indiana Societies of the Colonial Dames of America, who m. Henry W. Bennett, of Indianapolis, and had: *Edward Jaquelin* and *Louise*.

2.—JAQUELIN S. HOLLIDAY, who m. Florence Baker, and had: *William J.* and *Frederick Taylor*.

3.—LUCY FITZHUGH HOLLIDAY, who m. George E. Hume, and had: *William Manser*.

PEDIGREE LIX.—Continued.

3.—AUGUSTINE SMITH, of "Shooter's Hill," b. 3 August, 1738, d. 1774, m. (his second wife) Margaret, daughter of David Boyd, of Northumberland county, Virginia, and had:

MARY JACQUELIN SMITH, b. 12 February, 1773, d. 31 October, 1846; m. John Cripps Vowell, of Alexandria, Virginia, and had:

SARAH GOSNELLE VOWELL, b. 6 October, 1813, a member of the Virginia Society of the Colonial Dames of America, who m. Francis Lee Smith, of Fauquier county, Virginia, and had:

1.—L. JACQUELIN SMITH, b. 2 October, 1837, d. Morristown, New Jersey, 19 February, 1895. He served four years in the Confederate army, was aide-de-camp to General R. E. Lee, and was lieutenant-colonel of artillery at the end of the Civil War. He m. Mary, daughter of John and Sarah Poythress (Smith) Campbell, of New York City, and had: *John Campbell, Augustine Jacquelin, Sarah Poythress,* and *Gladys.*

2.—MARGARET VOWELL SMITH, of Alexandria, Virginia, b. 2 March, 1839, a member of the Virginia Society of the Colonial Dames of America, the Order of the Crown, *etc.*, author of "Governors of Virginia."

3.—CLIFTON HEWITT SMITH, of New York City, b. 19 August, 1841. He served four years in the Confederate army, was captain and assistant adjutant-general on General Beauregard's staff, was taken prisoner at Fort Morgan and confined in Fort Lafayette.

4.—MARY JACQUELIN SMITH, b. 4 October, 1843, d. 7 September, 1884.

5.—FRANCIS LEE SMITH, JR., of Alexandria, Virginia, b. 6 October, 1845. When a cadet at the Virginia Military Institute he took part with the cadet corps in the battle at New Market, 15 May, 1864, where he was twice severely wounded; a member of the Virginia Senate, 1879–83; was captain of the Alexandria Light Infantry, and lieutenant-colonel Third Regiment Virginia Volunteers. He m. Jannie L., daughter of Major W. T. Sutherlin, of Danville, Virginia, and had: *Jannie S.* and *Sarah Vowell, d.*

6.—ALICE CORBIN SMITH, a member of the Virginia Society of the Colonial Dames of America, b. 15 June, 1848, m. William E. Strong, of New York City, and had: *Francis Lee, d., Annie Massie,* and *Alice Everard.*

7.—MAJOR COURTLAND HAWKINS SMITH, of Alexandria, Virginia, b. 29 August, 1850, d. 22 July, 1892; was mayor of Alexandria, 1879, assistant adjutant-general of Virginia, and an aide-de-camp and chief of staff to Governor Fitzhugh Lee. He m., 15 December, 1875, Charlotte E. Rossiter, of New York City, and had: *Francis Lee, d.,* and *Cortland H., b.* 21 January, 1878.

8.—SARAH VOWELL SMITH, b. 23 March, 1853; m. Edward L. Daingerfield, of Alexandria, Virginia, and had: *Sarah Vowell, John Bathurst, d., Mary Helen, Francis Lee,* and *Edward Lonsdale, d.*

9.—ROBERT WOODLEIGH SMITH, b. 2 November, 1856, d. 6 August, 1857.

II.—MILDRED WARNER, who m., first, 1690, Lawrence Washington (eldest son of Colonel John Washington, 1627–1677, by his second wife, Anne Pope, of Charles county, Maryland, m. 1660), b. Bridge's Creek, Westmoreland county, Virginia, 166–, d. at Bridge's Creek in 1697, and had:

1.—JOHN WASHINGTON (uncle of President Washington), b. Bridge's Creek, 1692, d. in Gloucester county, Virginia, m. Catherine Whiting, and had:

WARNER WASHINGTON, b. Bridge's Creek, 1717, d. Frederick county, Virginia, 1791, m., first, Elizabeth, daughter of Colonel William Macon, of New Kent county, Virginia, and had by her:

WARNER WASHINGTON, JR., b. Gloucester county, Virginia, 15 April, 1751, d. Clark county, Virginia. He m., secondly, at Elmington, Gloucester county, Virginia, 13 June, 1795, Sarah Warner Rootes, and had by her:

READE WASHINGTON, b. at "Audley," in Virginia, 18 May, 1796, d. at Pittsburgh, Pennsylvania. He m., in 182–, Elizabeth Crawford, of Chambersburg, Pennsylvania, and had:

AUGUSTUS WASHINGTON, b. about 1823, who m., April 6, 1852, Susan T. Fulton, of Pittsburgh, Pennsylvania, and had:

1.—WILLIAM HERBERT WASHINGTON, Philadelphia, d. 14 July, 1900, aged 45; m., November 14, 1885, Constance L. Bowden, of New York, and had: *Bowden,* b. 16 July, 1892.

2.—ELIZABETH CRAWFORD WASHINGTON, a member of the Pennsylvania Society of the Colonial Dames of America.

2.—AUGUSTINE WASHINGTON, of Stafford county, Virginia, d. 12 April, 1743, aged about 50 years, who m., 6 March, 1730–1 (his second wife), Mary, d. at "Mt. Vernon," 25 August, 1789, aged about 80 years (see Hayden's "Virginia Genealogies," p. 81), daughter of Colonel Joseph Ball, of "Epping Forest," Lancaster county, Virginia, and had:

I.—COLONEL CHARLES WASHINGTON (brother of President Washington), b. 2 May, 1738; m. Mildred, daughter of Colonel Francis Thornton, and had:

COLONEL GEORGE AUGUSTINE WASHINGTON, m. Frances Bassett, and had:

ANNA MARIA WASHINGTON, *m.* Rubin Thornton, and had:

CHARLES AUGUSTINE THORNTON, *m.* Cornelia Randolph, and had:

ANNA MARIA WASHINGTON THORNTON, a member of the North Carolina Society of the Coloniel Dames of America, who *m.* Philip Barton Key, of Statesville, North Carolina.

II.—BETTY WASHINGTON (sister of President Washington), *b.* at "Wakefield," Westmoreland county, Virginia, 20 June, 1733, who *m.*, in May, 1750 (his second wife), Colonel Fielding Lewis, of "Kenmore," Spottsylvania county, Virginia, and had:

1.—HOWELL LEWIS, of Kanawha county, West Virginia, who *m.* Ellen Pollard, and had:

FRANCES FIELDING LEWIS, who *m.* Humphrey Brooke Gwathmey, of Richmond, Virginia, and had:

VIRGINIA GWATHMEY, a member of the North Carolina Society of the Colonial Dames of America, who *m.* Adam Empie, of Wilmington, North Carolina, and had: *Swift Miller, Brooke Gwathmey, Virginia* (deceased); *Adam* (deceased); *Ellen* (deceased); *Theodore Gwathmey* (who *m.* Evelyn Pearson); *Adam,* and

I.—ANNIE EMPIE, a member of the North Carolina Society of the Colonial Dames of America, the Order of the Crown, *etc.*, who *m.* Edward Bailey, and had: *Edward, Virginia, Karin Dohlstrome,* and *Frances Fielding Lewis.*

II.—FRANCES FIELDING LEWIS EMPIE, a member of the North Carolina Society of the Colonial Dames of America, the Order of the Crown, *etc.*, who *m.*, first, Herbert Russell Latimer, *d.* 1887, and had: *Herbert Russell* and *Empie,* and *m.*, secondly, in 1890, Frederick C. Poisson, of London, England. *No issue.*

2.—ROBERT LEWIS, private secretary to his uncle, General George Washington, who *m.* Judith Walker Browne, also of Royal Descent, and had:

ELIZABETH BURNET LEWIS, who *m.* George Washington Bassett, of "Eltham," New Kent county, Virginia, 1800–1878, also of Royal Descent, and had:

I.—ANNA VIRGINIA BASSETT, who *m.* Major John Hayes Claiborne, of Richmond, Virginia, also of Royal Descent, and had:

DELIA CLAIBORNE, a member of the Virginia Society of the Colonial Dames of America, who *m.* General Simon B. Buckner, of Hart county, Kentucky, and had: *Simon B.*

II.—ELLA BASSETT, a member of the Virginia Society of the Colonial Dames of America, d. 1898, who m. Lewis William Washington. *Issue.*

3.—MILDRED WASHINGTON, widow of Roger Gregory, who m., secondly (his third wife), Colonel Henry Willis, and had:

COLONEL LEWIS WILLIS, who m. Mary Champe, and had:

MILDRED WILLIS, who m. Landon Carter, of "Cleve," also of Royal Descent, and had:

LUCY LANDON CARTER, m. General John Minor, of "Hazel Hill," and had:

LUCIUS HORATIO MINOR, of "Edgewood," m. Catherine Frances Berkeley, also of Royal Descent (p. 250), and had:

MARY WILLIS MINOR, of Baltimore, a member of the Maryland Society of the Colonial Dames of America.

III.—ELIZABETH WARNER, b. 24 November, 1672, d. 5 February, 1720, who m. at "Cheesecake," before 1692, Colonel John Lewis, of "Warner Hall," of Gloucester county, Virginia, b. 30 November, 1669, d. 14 November, 1725, colonel of county militia; a councillor in 1715; member and speaker of the House of Burgesses, and had:

1.—COLONEL CHARLES LEWIS, of "The Byrd," Gloucester county, will proved 20 December, 1779; colonel of county militia, commissioned 20 March, 1753, and 18 August, 1761. He m., 17 May, 1717, Mary, 1700–1779, daughter of John Howell, and had:

I.—ANNE LEWIS, b. 2 March, 1732, d. 1809 or 1810, who m. Edmund Taylor, of Caroline county, Virginia, b. 5 July, 1723, d. 1808, will dated 10 January, 1807, son of John Taylor (and Catherine, daughter of Philip Pendleton, 1650–1721), son of James Taylor, d. 1698, and had:

FRANCES TAYLOR, d. 26 January, 1815, aged 62, who m., 15 January, 1789, Rev. Nathaniel Moore, b. in Granville county, North Carolina, 10 December, 1757, d. at Columbia, Tennessee, 23 June, 1829, and had:

1.—MARY MOORE, b. 18 August, 1794, d. 28 June, 1884; m., 26 July, 1814, William Porter, d. 28 December, 1843, aged 70, and had:

WILLIAM TAYLOR PORTER, b. 21 April, 1828, d. 21 March, 1864; m., 17 February, 1857, Mary Pillow, b. 6 March, 1838, and had:

LOUISE PORTER, b. 30 January, 1858, a member of the Tennessee Society of the Colonial Dames of America, the Order of the Crown, *etc.*, who m., 11 December, 1880, William Keeling Phillips, of Nashville, b. 20 January, 1854.

2.—ANNE LEWIS MOORE, b. 3 November, 1796, d. 13 February, 1828; m., 22 May, 1815, Edward Washington Dale, b. 11 November, 1790, in Worcester county, Maryland, d. 7 July, 1840, at Columbia, and had: *Mary F.*, wife of Archibald Williams; *Thomas, Nathaniel,* and

I.—ELVIRA H. DALE, who m. Jerome Bonaparte Pillow, of Tennessee, son of Gideon Pillow, and his wife, Anne, daughter of Josias Payne, Jr., and had: *Mrs. Anne Lewis Ridley, Mrs. Martha Woodson Long, Mrs. Frances Parker, Edward Dale, Jerome B.,* and

    1.—ELVIRA DALE PILLOW, a member of the Virginia Society of the Colonial Dames of America, the Order of the Crown, *etc.*, who m. John Maffitt Gray, of Nashville, and had:

        I.—ANNIE PAYNE GRAY, m. J. W. Madden, M.D., of Nashville, and had: *Annie Gray.*

        II.—JOHN M. GRAY, JR., of Nashville, m. Rebecca Wilson, and had: *Rebecca.*

    2.—CYNTHIA SAUNDERS PILLOW, a member of the Virginia Society of the Colonial Dames of America, the Order of the Crown, *etc.*, who m. Captain William Decatur Bethell, of Memphis, Tennessee, and Denver, Colorado, and had:

        I.—BESSIE BETHELL, m. John M. Foster, M.D., of Denver, and had: *Bethell, Pinckney,* and *John M.*

        II.—JEROME PILLOW BETHELL, d. s. p., who m. Lucy Watts.

        III.—CHARLES C. PINCKNEY BETHELL, d. unm.

        IV.—HATTIE BETHELL, d. young.

        V.—JENNIE BETHELL, m. John P. Edrington, of Memphis, and had: *William Bethell, Cynthia,* and *John Price, Jr.*

        VI.—WILLIAM DECATUR BETHELL, JR., of Memphis, m. Helen Worden, of Denver, and had: *William Decatur, 3d,* and *Charles Worden.*

II.—ANNE LEWIS DALE, b. 14 May, 1821, d. 17 February, 1888; m., 9 October, 1845, James Robertson, b. Ayrshire, Scotland, 8 December, 1816, d. at Memphis, Tennessee, 26 May, 1898, and had: *Mrs. Elvira Gray, Edward H., John Nathaniel, Edward Dale, James T., Jerome Pillow,* and

    1.—JEAN ROBERTSON, b. Maury county, Tennessee, 1 September, 1846, a member of the Virginia Society of the Colonial Dames of America, the Order of the Crown, *etc.*, who m., 11 February, 1869, Colonel Keller Anderson, United States Army, of Memphis, b. Cynthiana, Kentucky, 21 September, 1842, and had:

I.—CLAUDE DESHA ANDERSON, of Memphis, b. 1871; m., 1896, Mary Simmons, and had: *Claude Desha*, b. 11 August, 1897.

II.—JEAN KELLER ANDERSON, of Memphis.

2.—MARY ROBERTSON, a member of the Virginia Society of the Colonial Dames of America, the Order of the Crown, *etc.*, who m. Captain Thomas Day, of Memphis, and had: *Mary Louise*.

II.—JOHN LEWIS, 1720–1794, who m., 1741, Jane Lewis, b. 1727, and had:

MARY LEWIS, d. 1813, who m. Captain William Williams, d. 1813, and had:

FIELDING LEWIS WILLIAMS, 1794–1845, who m., 1827, Frances P. Boyd, d. 1833, and had:

FIELDING LEWIS WILLIAMS, JR., 1832–1898, who m., 1863, Abby Louisa Miller, of Bristol, Rhode Island, b. 1842, and had:

1.—LOUISE MILLER WILLIAMS, a member of the Rhode Island Society of the Colonial Dames of America, who m. John Taylor Lewis, of Virginia, also of Royal Descent.

2.—MILDRED LEWIS WILLIAMS, a member of the Rhode Island Society of the Colonial Dames of America, who m., 1891, William Frederick Williams, of Bristol, Rhode Island, and had: *William Frederick*, b. 3 April, 1896.

III.—HOWELL LEWIS, of "The Byrd," who m. Mary, daughter of Colonel Henry Willis and his first wife, Mrs. Mildred (Howell) Brown, and had:

MILDRED LEWIS, who m. John Cobbs, of the "Sand Hills," Augusta, Georgia, and had: *John Addison Cobb* (p. 248), and

I.—MARY WILLIS COBBS, who m. Colonel Robert W. Flournoy, and had:

MARY MILDRED FLOURNOY, who m. Nathaniel Alexander Adams, and had:

MARY WILLIS ADAMS, who m. William Bullock Jackson, and had:

MARY VIRGINIA JACKSON, a member of the Georgia Society of the Colonial Dames of America, who m. Richard Wylly Thiot, of Savannah, and had: *Florence King, Richard Wylly, Edith Nowlan,* and *Mary Mildred Bryan.*

II.—MILDRED COBBS, m. William H. Jackson, and had:

MILDRED LEWIS COBB JACKSON, m. Colonel John D. Grant, and had:

WILLIAM DANIEL GRANT, m. Sarah Francis Reid, and had:

SARAH FRANCES GRANT, a member of the Georgia Society of the Colonial Dames of America, who *m.* John Marshall Slaton, of Atlanta.

2.—COLONEL ROBERT LEWIS, of "Belvoir," Albemarle county, Virginia, *d.* 1757, who *m.* Jane, daughter of Nicholas and Mildred (Thompson) Meriwether, and had [besides other issue, from whom is descended MRS. JOHN B. GORDON (*nee* Frances R. Haralson), of "Kirkwood," Atlanta, a member of the Georgia Society of the Colonial Dames of America, mother of MRS. BURTON-SMITH (*nee* Frances Gordon) and CAROLINE LEWIS GORDON, of Atlanta, both members of the Georgia Society of the Colonial Dames of America]:

I.—JANE LEWIS, who *m.*, first, Major Thomas Meriwether, and had:

MARY MERIWETHER, who *m.* Captain Richard P. White, and had:

MALINDA LEWIS WHITE, who *m.* Pleasant Moore Benning, and had:

JUDGE HENRY LEWIS BENNING, of Muscogee county, Georgia, brigadier-general Confederate States Army, *m.* Mary Howard Jones, and had:

1.—LOUISE VIVIAN BENNING, a member of the Georgia Society of the Colonial Dames of America, who *m.* Samuel Spencer, of New York City.

2.—ANNA CAROLINE BENNING, of Columbus, Georgia, a member of the Georgia Society of the Colonial Dames of America, a member of the Order of the Crown, *etc.*

II.—NICHOLAS LEWIS, *b.* 1742, who *m.* Mary, daughter of Dr. Thomas and Mildred Thornton (Meriwether) Walker, of "Castle Hill," Virginia, and had:

NICHOLAS MERIWETHER LEWIS, *b.* 1767, who *m.* his cousin, Mildred, daughter of Joseph Hornby, and his wife, Mildred, daughter of Dr. Thomas Walker, of "Castle Hill," and had:

ANNAH HORNSBY LEWIS, who *m.*, 31 August, 1814 (his second wife), Hancock Taylor, *b.* 29 January, 1781, *d.* 29 March, 1841, and had:

MARY LOUISE TAYLOR, *b.* 20 May, 1824, who *m.*, 2 May, 1843, Archibald Magill Robinson, of Louisville, Kentucky, and had:

ANNAH WALKER ROBINSON, *b.* 5 November, 1848, a member of the Mississippi Society of the Colonial Dames of America, who *m.*, 5 October, 1870, James Henry Watson, of Memphis, Tennessee, *b.* 3 January, 1848, and had: *John William Clark, b.* 5 October, 1871, *d.* 27 June, 1872; *Archibald R., b.* 27 December,

1872; *James Henry*, b. 5 July, 1874; *Louise Taylor*, b. 23 December, 1875, d. 3 September, 1876; *Catherine Davis*, b. 25 November, 1877, and *Elizabeth Lee*, b. 8 October, 1880.

3.—JOHN LEWIS, of "Warner's Hall," 1644-1754, had by his wife, Frances Fielding:

COLONEL CHARLES LEWIS, who had by his wife, Lucy Taliaferro:

MARY WARNER LEWIS, who *m.*, first, Philip Lightfoot, and had:

PHILIP LIGHTFOOT, *m.* Sallie Savigne Bernard, and had:

WILLIAM BERNARD LIGHTFOOT, *m.* Sarah Bee Ross, and had:

I.—NORA MEADE LIGHTFOOT, a member of the Maryland Society of the Colonial Dames of America, who *m.* William Reynolds, of Baltimore, and had: *Eleanor Tarleton* and *Nora Lightfoot*.

II.—SALLIE BERNARD LIGHTFOOT, a member of the Maryland Society of the Colonial Dames of America, who *m.* Robert Tarleton, of Baltimore, and had:

1.—SARAH LIGHTFOOT TARLETON, a member of the Maryland Society of the Colonial Dames of America, who *m.* Alexander B. Colvin, M.D., of Canada.

2.—ROBERT MELVIN TARLETON, of Baltimore, *unm.*

3.—MARGARET, wife of Marshall Winchester, of Baltimore.

THE ROYAL DESCENT

OF

MRS. FRANKLIN R. CARPENTER,

OF DENVER, COLORADO.

Princess Eleanor of Castile=EDWARD I., King of England=Princess Margaret of France.

Humphrey, Earl of Here-=Elizabeth Plantag- Thomas, Earl of Norfolk=Alice Halys.
ford   enet.

Eleanor de Bohun=James, Earl of Ormond. Margaret Plantagenet=John de Segrave.

Petronella Butler=Gilbert de Talbot. Elizabeth de Segrave=John de Mowbray.

Richard de Talbot=Ankeretta le Strange. Jane de Mowbray=Thomas de Grey.

John, Earl of Shrewsbury=Maud de Neville. Thomas de Grey=Alice de Neville.

Thomas de Talbot=(Name unknown.) Elizabeth de Grey=Philip d'Arcy.

Elizabeth de Talbot=Henry de Grey.

Lady Margaret de Grey=John, Baron d'Arcy.

Philip, Baron d'Arcy=Lady Eleanor Fitz-Hugh.

Lady Margaret d'Arcy=Sir John Conyers, of Hornby, Yorkshire.

Richard Conyers, of Horden=Lady Elizabeth Claxton, of Horden, Durham.

Robert Conyers, of Horden=Margaret Bamforth, of Seham, Durham.

Christopher Conyers, of Horden=Elizabeth Jackson, of Bedale, Durham.

Richard Conyers, of Horden=Mabel Lumley, of Ludworth, Durham.

Christopher Conyers, of Horden=Anne Hedsworth, of Harraton, Durham.

Mary Conyers=William Wilkinson, of Lanchester, Durham.

Lawrence Wilkinson, Providence, R. I.=Susannah Smith, of Providence, R. I.

Samuel Wilkinson, Providence, R. I.=Plain Wickenden, of Providence, R. I.

Joseph Wilkinson, of Scituate, R. I.=Martha Pray, of Smithfield, R. I.

Prudence Wilkinson=Isaiah Angell.

Prudence Angell=Gideon Austin.

Ruth Austin=James Cranston.

Martha Cranston=Silas Bingham, Jr.

Hannah Bingham=James Fuller Howe, M.D.

Annette Howe=Franklin R. Carpenter, M.A., Ph.D., F.G.S.A., etc.,
of Denver, Colorado.

| Arthur Howe Carpenter, b. Oct. 19, 1877. | Harold Howe Carpenter, b. Jan. 26, 1881; d. Oct. 20, 1890. | Cranston Howe Carpenter, b. Oct. 10, 1882. | Malcolm Howe Carpenter, b. Aug. 7, 1884. | Grace Howe Carpenter, b. Oct. 21, 1887; d. Aug. 27, 1899. | Annette Howe Carpenter, b. Aug. 15, 1892. | Talbot Howe Carpenter, b. Jan. 19, 1896. |

PEDIGREE LX.

ETHELRED II., King of England, called the Unready, *d.* 1016, had by his first wife, Lady Elgiva, *d.* 1003, daughter of Earl Thorad:

PRINCESS ELGIVA, who *m.* Uthrea, Earl of Northumbria, and had:

LADY AGATHA, or Aldigitha, who *m.* Maldred, son of Crynan, lord of the Isles, and grandson of Malcolm II., King of Scotland, and had:

COSPATRICK, Earl of Northumberland and Dunbar, who had:

COSPATRICK, first Earl of Dunbar, *d.* 1139, who had:

COSPATRICK, second Earl of Dunbar, *d.* 1147, who had:

COSPATRICK, third Earl of Dunbar, *d.* 1166, who had:

WALDEVE, fourth Earl of Dunbar, *d.* 1182, who had:

PATRICK, fifth Earl of Dunbar, who had:

PATRICK, sixth Earl of Dunbar, who *m.* Lady Euphemia, daughter of Walter Stewart, the fifth hereditary high steward of Scotland, and had:

LADY —— DUNBAR, who *m.* her cousin, James Stewart, the seventh hereditary lord high steward of Scotland, and had:

WALTER STEWART, the eighth hereditary lord high steward of Scotland, 1293–1326, who had by his third wife, Lady Isabel, daughter of Sir John Graham, of Abercorn:

LADY EGIDIA STEWART, half-sister of King Robert II., of Scotland, and widow of James Lindsay, Earl of Crawford, who *m.*, secondly, Sir Hugh de Eglintoun, of that Ilk, justiciary of Lothian, 1361, lord of Ardrossan, *d.* 1376, and had:

LADY ELIZABETH DE EGLINTOUN, sole heiress, who *m.* John de Montgomery, laird of Eglintoun and Ardrossan, in right of his wife, who signalized himself in the battle of Otterburn by capturing Henry de Percy, whose ransom built the Castle of Polnone, *d.* after 8 October, 1392, and had:

SIR JOHN DE MONTGOMERY, laird of Eglisham, Eglintoun and Ardrossan, a hostage for the Earl of Douglas in 1408; one of the jury which tried the Duke of Albany in 1425, *d. ante* 10 August, 1430. He *m.* Lady Margaret, daughter of Robert Maxwell, laird of Caerlaverock, and had:

LADY ANNE DE MONTGOMERY, who *m.* (contract dated 16 June, 1425) Sir Robert Cunyngham, laird of Kilmures, one of the hostages for James I., and knighted by him (the eldest son of Sir William, *d.* 1418, the

PEDIGREE LX.—*Continued.*

second son of Sir William Cunyngham, by his first wife, name unknown, *see* Paterson's " His. of Ayr and Wigton," viii., 470, and Douglas's " Peerage," i., 321), and had:

ALEXANDER CUNYNGHAM, created Lord Kilmures in 1450, and Earl of Glencairn in 1488, *k.* at Bannockburn, who *m.* Lady Margaret, daughter of Sir Adam Hepburn, second lord of Hales, and had:

WILLIAM CUNYNGHAM, laird of Craigends, second son, *m.* Elizabeth, daughter of Walter Stewart, of Arthurly and Wester-Patrick, and had:

WILLIAM CUNYNGHAM, laird of Craigends, *m.* Egidia, daughter of John Campbell, of Killoch, and had:

GILBERT CUNYNGHAM, third laird of Craigends, *k.* 1547, who *m.* Margaret (or Elizabeth), daughter of William Livingston, fourth laird of Kilsyth, *d.* 1540, and had:

JAMES CUNYNGHAM, of Ashenyeard, second son, who *m.* Margaret Fleming, daughter of the laird of Barrochan, and had:

WILLIAM CUNYNGHAM, of Glengarnock, second son, who *m.* Rebecca Muirland, daughter of the laird of Lenhouse, and had:

RICHARD CUNYNGHAM, of Glengarnock, who *m.*, 3 October, 1654, Elizabeth, daughter of James Heriot, of Trabroun, and had:

ROBERT CUNYNGHAM, *b.* 24 March, 1669; removed to the Island of St. Christopher, and *d.* 1749; *m.*, 26 September, 1693, Judith Elizabeth, daughter of Daniel de Bonneson, of Morlais, France, and had:

MARY CUNYNGHAM, *b.* 4 April, 1699, *d.* 13 March, 1771, who *m.*, 1723 Isaac Roberdeau, who removed from Rochelle, France, to the Island of St. Christopher, in 1685, and *d.* before 1743, and had:

DANIEL ROBERDEAU, of Philadelphia, only son, *b.* St. Christopher, 1727. He was a member of the Pennsylvania Assembly, 1756–60; of the Council of Safety, 1775–76; general commanding the Pennsylvania troops in the Revolutionary War; member of the Continental Congress, 1777–79, and signer of the Articles of Confederation. He *m.*, first, 3 October, 1761, Mary Bostwick, and had:

MARY ROBERDEAU, *b.* Philadelphia, May, 1774, who *m.* Thomas Patten, of Alexandria, Virginia, and had:

SELINA BLAIR PATTEN, *b.* Alexandria, 12 September, 1805, who *m.* Rev. John T. Wheat, D.D., of Virginia, and had:

JOSEPHINE MAY WHEAT, *b.* 22 February, 1833, who *m.* Francis E. Shober, sometime member of Congress from North Carolina, and had:

MAY SHOBER, a member of the North Carolina Society of the Colonial Dames of America, the Order of the Crown, *etc.*, who *m.* Archibald Boyden, of Salisbury, and had: *May Wheat* and *Jane Henderson*.

THE ROYAL DESCENT

OF

MRS. HOMER HINE STUART,

OF NEW YORK CITY.

HUGH CAPET, King of France=Adela, dau. William, Duke of Aquitaine.

Robert I., the Pious,=Lady Constance of Provence.
King of France

Princess Havide=Rynerius IV., Count of Hainault.
or Hedewige

Henry I., King of=Lady Anne of Russia.
France

Lady Beatrix=Eblo de Rouci.

Hugh Magnus,=Lady Adelheid of Vermandois.
Duke of France

Countess Adela=Hildwin de Montdider.

Lady Margaret de Rouci=Hugh de Clermont.

William de Warren,=Lady Isabel de Vermandois. Robert de Bellomont, Earl of Leicester.   Lady Adeliza=Gilbert de Tonsburg, Earl of Clare.
Earl of Surrey   de Clermont

William de Warren,=Lady Alice de Talvas, also of Royal Descent.   Lady Elizabeth de Bellomont=Gilbert de Clare, Earl of Pembroke.
Earl of Surrey

Lady Isabella de=Hameline Plantagenet, Earl of Surrey.   Richard "the Strongbow,"=Eva, dau. Dermot, King of Leinster.
Warren   2d Earl of Pembroke

Lady Isabella de=Roger Bigod, Earl of Norfolk.   Lady Isabel de Clare=William le Marshal, Protector of England.
Warren

Hugh Bigod, second Earl of Norfolk=Lady Maud Marshall.

Sir Hugh Bigod, Justiciary of England=Joan, dau. of Robert Burnet.

Sir John Bigod, Knt.=(Name unknown.)

Sir Roger Bigod, of Settington=(Name unknown.)

Lady Joan Bigod=Sir William de Chauncy, of Skirpenbeck.

John Chauncy, of Stepney=Margaret Gifford, of Gedleston.

John Chauncy, of Sawbridgeworth=Anne Leventhorp, of Shingey.

John Chauncy, of Sawbridgeworth=Daughter of Thomas Boyce.

John Chauncy, of Pishobury=Elizabeth (Proffit) Mansfield.

Henry Chauncy, of Newplace Giffords=Lucy ——.

George Chauncy, of Yardleybury=Anne Welsh, of Great Wymondley.

Rev. Charles Chauncy, D.D., 1592-1671, second=Catherine Eyre, of New Sarum.
President of Harvard College

Rev. Nathaniel Chauncy, of Hatfield, Mass.=Abigail Strong, of Northampton, Mass.

Rev. Nathaniel Chauncy, of Durham, Ct.=Sarah Judson, of Stratford, Conn.

Col. Elihu Chauncy, of Durham, Mass.=Mary Griswold, of Killingworth.

Catherine Chauncy=Rev. Elizur Goodrich, D.D., of Durham, Mass.

Rev. Samuel Goodrich, of Ridgefield, Conn.=Elizabeth Ely, of Pachog.

Catherine Chauncy Goodrich=David Dunbar, of Berlin, Conn.

Margaret Elizabeth Dunbar, member of the So-—Homer Hine Stuart, of New York, b. 1 April, 1810,
ciety of Colonial Dames of the State of New | d. 5 October, 1885.
York

Katharine Dunbar Stuart,=John G. Dunscomb, of New York.
member of the Society of the Colonial Dames of the State of New York

Homer Hine Stuart,=Margaret Inglis Stuart,
Jr., of Philadel- | Beck-   of New York
phia, Penna. | with   City. Unm.
                  Kenny.

Margaret Stuart Dunscomb, b. Jan. 26, 1886.

Cecil Dunscomb, b. Sept. 20, 1887.

John Carol Dunscomb, b. Oct. 27, 1889.

Godefroi Dunscomb, b. Jan. 23, 1893.

Homer Howland Stuart, b. July 5, 1890.

PEDIGREE LXI.

EDWARD I., King of England, *m.*, secondly, 1299, Margaret, daughter of Philip III., King of France, and had by her:

EDMOND, Earl of Kent, beheaded in 1329. He *m.* Lady Margaret, daughter of John, Baron de Wake, also of Royal Descent, and had:

LADY JOAN PLANTAGENET, "the Fair Maid of Kent" (divorced wife of William de Montacute, Earl of Salisbury), who *m.*, secondly, Sir Thomas de Holland, K.G., Earl of Kent, *d.* 1360, also of Royal Descent (she *m.*, third, Edward, "the Black Prince," son of King Edward III., and by him was the mother of King Richard II.), and had:

SIR THOMAS DE HOLLAND, K.G., 1350–1397, second Earl of Kent, marshal of England, who *m.* Lady Alice Fitz-Alan, daughter of Richard, K.G., Earl of Arundel and Surrey, and his wife, Lady Eleanor Plantagenet, also of Royal Descent, and had:

LADY MARGARET HOLLAND, *d.* 31 December, 1440, who *m.*, first, Sir John de Beaufort, K.G., Marquis of Dorset, Earl of Somerset, *d.* 1418, also of Royal Descent, and had:

LADY JOAN DE BEAUFORT, who *m.*, first, James I., King of Scotland, and had James II., King of Scotland, and *m.*, secondly, in 1439, Sir James Stewart, "the Black Knight of Lorn," also of Royal Descent, and had:

SIR JOHN STEWART, created, in 1457, Earl of Athol, *d.* 1512, who *m.*, secondly, Lady Eleanor, daughter of William Sinclair, Earl of Orkney and Caithness, also of Royal Descent, and had:

LADY ELIZABETH STEWART, who *m.* (his second wife) Andrew, third Lord Gray (*see* Playfair's "British Family Antiquity," iii.), and had:

LADY JEAN GRAY, who *m.*, first, Sir Alexander Blair, of Balthyock (*see* Wood's Douglas's "Peerage of Scotland," i., 669, ii., 156), and had:

SIR THOMAS BLAIR, Knt., of Balthyock, Perthshire, who had:

LADY EUPHAME BLAIR, *m.* Andrew Scott, the second son of Sir William Scott, of Balweary and Innertiel, by his wife, Lady Isabel Lindsay, the daughter of Patrick, fourth Lord Lindsay, of the Byres, also of Royal Descent (*see* Douglas's "Peerage of Scotland," i., 384), and had:

ANDREW SCOTT, of Kirkstyle, who *m.* Lady Margaret, daughter of Sir Patrick Ogilvie, of Inchmartin, and had by her an only son:

GEORGE SCOTT, of Kirkstyle, who *m.* Catherine, daughter of Hugh Montcrief, of Rind, and had:

PATRICK SCOTT, who sold the lands of Kirkstyle, and acquired the lands and Barony of Ancrum, in Roxburghshire. He m., first, Elizabeth, daughter of Simson, of Monturpie, in Fife, and had by her:

SIR JOHN SCOTT, Bart., of Ancrum, created a baronet of Nova Scotia 27 October, 1671, d. 1712 (see Playfair's "British Family Antiquity," viii., App. 308), who m., first, Elizabeth, daughter of Francis Scott, of Mangerton, and had by her:

JOHN SCOTT, third son, who came to New York about 1702, and was appointed commandant of Fort Hunter, on the Mohawk. He m., 1702, Magdalen, daughter of John Vincent, of New York, and had:

JOHN SCOTT, of New York, b. 1702, d. 30 April, 1733, eldest son, who m. Marian Morin, who d. 5 September, 1755, and had:

BRIGADIER-GENERAL JOHN MORIN SCOTT, 1730-1784, only son; secretary of State of New York, member of the Provincial and of the Continental Congress, and a member of the Society of the Cincinnati. He m. Helena Rutgers, of New York, and had:

LEWIS ALLAIRE SCOTT, only son, secretary of State of New York, b. 11 February, 1759, d. 17 March, 1798. He m., 18 January, 1785, Juliana, daughter of William Sitgreaves, of Easton, Pennsylvania, and had:

JOHN MORIN SCOTT, of Philadelphia, Pennsylvania, only son, elected mayor of Philadelphia in 1841, and twice re-elected, b. in New York City, 25 October, 1789. He m., 15 May, 1817, Mary, daughter of George Emlen, of Philadelphia, and dying 3 April, 1858, had issue:

1.—SARAH EMLEN SCOTT, who m. Joseph Dennie Meredith, of Philadelphia, and had:

MARY EMLEN MEREDITH, a member of the New York Society of the Colonial Dames of America, who m. J. Montgomery Hare, of New York City. *Issue.*

2.—LEWIS ALLAIRE SCOTT, of Philadelphia, b. 10 August, 1819, who m., 27 June, 1857, Frances Anna, daughter of Richard Wistar, Jr., of Philadelphia, 1790-1863, also of Royal Descent, had, besides other children:

HANNAH LEWIS SCOTT, of Philadelphia, a member of the Pennsylvania Society of the Colonial Dames of America.

3.—JULIA SCOTT, a member of the Pennsylvania Society of the Colonial Dames of America, who m. Robert Waln Leaming, of Philadelphia, d. 1884, and had, besides other children:

I.—MARY EMLEN LEAMING, a member of the Pennsylvania Society of the Colonial Dames of America, who m. Richard Francis Wood, of Philadelphia. *Issue.*

II.—JULIA LEAMING, a member of the Pennsylvania Society of the Colonial Dames of America, who m. Nicholas Lennig, of Philadelphia, also of Royal Descent.

PEDIGREE LXII.

EDWARD I., King of England, had by his first wife, Princess Eleanor of Castile:

PRINCESS JOAN D'ACRE, who *m.*, first, Gilbert de Clare, Earl of Hertford and Gloucester, and had:

LADY MARGARET DE CLARE, widow of Piers de Gavestone, Earl of Cornwall, who *m.*, secondly, Hugh, second Baron d'Audley, created, 1337, Earl of Gloucester, *d.* 1347, and had:

LADY MARGARET D'AUDLEY, who *m.* Sir Ralph Stafford, K.G., second Baron Stafford, created, 1351, Earl of Stafford, *d.* 1372, also of Royal Descent, and had:

SIR HUGH DE STAFFORD, K.G., second Earl of Stafford, *d.* 1268, who *m.* Lady Philippa de Beauchamp, daughter of Sir Thomas, Earl of Warwick, also of Royal Descent, and had:

LADY MARGARET DE STAFFORD, who *m.* Sir Ralph de Neville, K.G., created, 1397, Earl of Westmoreland, earl marshal of England, also of Royal Descent, and had:

LADY PHILIPPA DE NEVILLE, who *m.* Thomas de Dacre, sixth Baron de Dacre, of Gillesland, who *d.* 1457, and had:

THOMAS DE DACRE, of Gillesland *d. v. p.*, who *m.* Elizabeth, daughter of Sir Richard Bowet, *d.* 1423, and his wife, Amy d'Ufford, also of Royal Descent, and had:

LADY JOAN DE DACRE, heiress, will proved 14 July, 1486, who *m.*, *ante* 1457, Sir Richard Fienes, also of Royal Descent, constable of the Tower of London; lord chamberlain to the household of King Edward IV., and Baron Dacre, of the South, in right of his wife, 1459–84, *d.* 1484, and had:

SIR JOHN FIENES, eldest son, *d. v. p. ante* 1484, who *m.* Lady Alice, daughter of Henry, Baron Fitzhugh, of Ravensworth, *d.* 1472, and Lady Alice de Neville, also of Royal Descent, and had:

SIR THOMAS FIENES, heir to his grandfather, Sir Richard, Baron Dacre, of the South, made a Knight of the Bath by Henry VII.; will proved in 1534. He *m.* Anne, daughter of Sir Humphrey Bouchier, *k. v. p.* at Barnetfield fighting under the royal banner, also of Royal Descent, and had:

LADY CATHERINE DE FIENES, sister of Thomas, heir, *d. v. p.* before

1531, father of Thomas, who succeeded to the title, and was hanged for treason in 1541, aged 24 years. Her sister Mary m. Henry, Lord Norreys, who was hanged in 1537. She m. (see Horsfield's "History of Sussex," ii., p. 484, and the "Sussex Arch. Coll.," viii., pp. 214 and 233; Sussex "Visitations," 1634, and the Haynes chart pedigree, prepared in 1860 by Judge Nathaniel Chauncey, of Philadelphia, and Rev. Henry Jones of Bridgeport, Connecticut) Richard Loudenoys, of Briade, Sussex, and had:

MARY LOUDENOYS, heiress, who m. (see Kent "Visitations," 1574; Berry's "Kent Pedigrees," Essex "Visitations," 1612 and 1634, and Nichol's "Topographer," i., p. 228) Thomas Harlakenden, of Worthon, Kent, will dated 1562, proved in 1564, and had:

ROGER HARLAKENDEN, of Earl's Colne, Essex, and Kenardiston and Woodchurch, Kent, third son, 1535-1603. He signed the Harlakenden-Loudenoys pedigree in the Herald's "Visitation of Kent," 1574, and was the steward to the Earl de Vere, from whom he purchased the manor of Earl's Colne in 1583 (see Brayley's "History of Essex"). He had by his first wife, Elizabeth, daughter of Thomas Hardres, and widow of George Harlakenden, of Woodchurch:

RICHARD HARLAKENDEN, of Earl's Colne, heir, d. 24 August, 1631, aged 66 years (see Nichol's "Topog. et Geneal.," i., 25). He m. Margaret (or Mary), daughter of Edward Hubbart (or Hobart), of Stanstead-Montifichet, and had:

MABEL HARLAKENDEN,* b. Earl's Colne, 27 September, 1614, d. 1655. She came to New England in 1635 with her brother Roger, brother of Richard, the heir (see "N. E. His. Geneal. Reg.," x., 129; xiv., 319; xv., 327, and xvi., 167, 194. Morant's "His. of Essex," Porter's "Historical Notices," etc.). She m., first (his second wife), in 1636, Colonel John

---

* The following ladies, members of the National Society of the Colonial Dames of America, are also of Royal Descent, through Mabel Harlakenden:

MISS MELISSA D. ATTERBURY, New York State Society.
MRS. CHARLES DEERING, Pennsylvania State Society.
MRS. HENRY S. HOWE, Massachusetts State Society.
MRS. JOHN F. MAYNARD, New York State Society.
MRS. ALFRED P. ROCKWELL, Massachusetts State Society.
MRS. DANIEL STIMSON, New York State Society.
MRS. KILIAEN VAN RENSSELAER, New York State Society.
MISS JULIA C. WELLS, New York State Society.
MRS. ALEXANDER D. JONES, South Carolina State Society.
MISS CORNELIA L. NEVINS, New York State Society.
MISS LOUISE E. NEVINS, New York State Society.

Haynes, b. Coddicot, Hertfordshire, 1597, Governor of the Massachusetts colony, 1635, and first Governor of the Connecticut Colony, 1639, d. at Hartford, 1 March, 1653–54, and had:

RUTH HAYNES, 1639–1688, who m., 1654–55, Samuel Wyllys, of Hartford, 1632–1709 (son of George Wyllys, Governor of the Connecticut Colony, 1645, see Talcott's "Wyllys Family"), and had:

1.—RUTH WYLLYS, 1656–1729, m., 1692 (his second wife), Rev. Edward Taylor, b. at Sketchley, Leicestershire, 1642, arrived in New England 26 April, 1668, d. 24 June, 1729, at Westfield, Massachusetts, and had:

ELDAD TAYLOR, b. Westfield, 10 April, 1708, d. 21 May, 1777, at Boston; was a Representative, 1762–64, and member of the Governor's Council; he had by his second wife, Thankful Day, d. 1803:

I.—ELIZABETH TAYLOR, who m. Andrew Perkins, of Norwich, Connecticut, and had:

CHARLES PERKINS, of Norwich, who m. Clarissa Deming, and had:

LUCRETIA DEMING PERKINS, who m. (his second wife) John Williams Quincy, Jr., of New York, and had:

MARY PERKINS QUINCY, of New Haven, a member of the Connecticut Society of the Colonial Dames of America.

II.—MAJOR EDWARD TAYLOR, of the Massachusetts Line, Continental Army, who m. Sarah, daughter of Jonathan Ingersoll, a captain in the Hampshire regiment, in the Crown Point expedition, 1755, k. in battle, and his wife, Eunice Mosely, and had:

PAMELIA TAYLOR, who m., 1800, Archippus Morgan, of West Springfield, and had:

FRANCIS MORGAN, of New York, who m. Semphronia Antoinette Converse, and had:

FRANCES WEBB MORGAN, who m. George Anson Starkweather, of New York, and had:

ANTOINETTE CONVERSE STARKWEATHER, b. New York City, 10 March, 1864, a member of the Massachusetts Society of the Colonial Dames of America, who m. John K. Burgess, of Dedham, Massachusetts. *No issue.*

2.—HEZEKIAH WYLLYS, b. 3 April, 1672, d. 24 December, 1741. He held many municipal offices in Hartford, and was secretary of the Connecticut colony, 1712–34. He m., 2 May, 1704, Elizabeth, d. 1762, daughter of Rev. Jonathan Hobart, of East Haddam, Connecticut, and his wife, Elizabeth Whiting, also of Royal Descent, and had:

COLONEL GEORGE WYLLYS, of Hartford, 1710–1796, secretary of the

Connecticut colony for 66 years; *m.* his cousin, Mary, 1715–1774, daughter of Rev. Timothy Woodbridge, of Simsbury, and had:

MARY WYLLYS, *b.* 1742, *m.*, 8 March, 1764, Eleazer Pomeroy, of Middletown, Connecticut, *d.* 1783, and had:

SAMUEL WYLLYS POMEROY, of Pomeroy, Ohio, 1764–1841; *m.*, 1793, Clarissa, daughter of Richard and Mary (Wright) Alsop, of Middletown, Connecticut, and had:

CLARA ALSOP POMEROY, who *m.*, 1833, Valentine B. Horton, of Pomeroy, Ohio, and had:

FRANCES DABNEY HORTON, of Sandusky, Ohio, a member of the Ohio Society of the Colonial Dames of America, who *m.* Brigadier-General and Judge Manning F. Force, LL.D., of Cincinnati, Ohio.

3.—MEHITABLE WYLLYS, 1658–1697, who *m.*, first, 1676, Rev. Daniel Russell, of Charlestown, Massachusetts, 1658–1680 (son of Richard Russell, treasurer of the Massachusetts colony, 1644–74), and had:

MABEL RUSSELL, 1677–1722, who *m.*, first, 12 June, 1701, Rev. John Hubbard, *b.* 1679, *d.*, Jamaica, Long Island, 1705, and had:

1.—COLONEL JOHN HUBBARD, of New Haven, who *m.*, 30 August, 1724, Elizabeth Stevens, and had:

COLONEL LEVERETT HUBBARD, M.D., of New Haven, who *m.*, 22 May, 1746, Sarah Whitehead, and had:

SARAH HUBBARD, who *m.*, 1776, Judge John Trumbull, LL.D., of Hartford, and had:

JULIANA TRUMBULL, who *m.*, 29 June, 1806, William Woodbridge, of Detroit, 1780–1861, first Governor of Michigan, and had:

DUDLEY B. WOODBRIDGE, of Detroit, who *m.*, 28 October, 1861, Martha J. Lee, and had:

MATTIE WOODBRIDGE, a member of the Michigan Society of the Colonial Dames of America, the Order of the Crown, *etc.*, who *m.*, 27 October, 1886, Charles Horton Metcalf, of Detroit, and had: *Woodbridge, b.* 23 June, 1888; *Marjorie Woodbridge, b.* 9 February, 1891; *Elizabeth Woodbridge, b.* 27 May, 1893, and *Marian Woodbridge, b.* 18 September, 1895.

2.—DANIEL HUBBARD, of New Haven, Connecticut, *b.* 3 April, 1706, *d.* 24 March, 1741; *m.* Martha Coit, of New London, Connecticut, *b.* 1706, and had:

I.—RUSSELL HUBBARD, *b.* 1732, *m.*, 1755, Mary Gray, of Wyndham, Connecticut, and had:

PEDIGREE LXII.—*Continued.*

MARY HUBBARD, who *m.*, 1777, Lieutenant David Nevins, of Norwich, Connecticut, *b.* 1747, *d.*, New York, 21 January, 1838, and had:

JAMES NEVINS, of Philadelphia, *b.* 1 August, 1790, *d.* 11 March, 1866; *m.* Achsah Willis, *b.* 27 May, 1792, *d.* 23 August, 1847, and had:

1.—JONATHAN WILLIS NEVINS, of Philadelphia, *b.* 26 March, 1826, *d.* 21 August, 1861; *m.*, April, 1848, Adaline Tichenor, *b.* 2 May, 1824, and had:

> KATHERINE NEVINS, a member of the Pennsylvania Society of the Colonial Dames of America, who *m.*, 30 September, 1885, Thomas Hewson Bradford, M.D., of Philadelphia, and had: *Mary Hewson, b.* 26 July, 1886; *Katherine Nevins, b.* 12 May, 1888, and *William, b.* 19 January, 1890.

2.—ISABELLA NEVINS, who *m.*, 26 April, 1838, Edward Siddons Whelen, of Philadelphia, also of Royal Descent (*see* "Americans of Royal Descent," ped. ii.), *b.* 22 August, 1813, and had:

> ISABELLA NEVINS WHELEN, a member of the Pennsylvania Society of the Colonial Dames of America, who *m.*, 2 September, 1871, Prof. Persifor Frazer, M.D., of Philadelphia, and had: *Persifor, m.* Mary, daughter of John Lowber Welsh, of Philadelphia; *Lawrence* (deceased), *John* and *Charlotte.*

3.—CORNELIA NEVINS, who *m.* Joseph Reese Fry, and had:

> ELIZABETH FRY, a member of the Pennsylvania Society of the Colonial Dames of America, who *m.*, 14 November, 1867, John Jacob Ridgway, of Philadelphia, and had: *Thomas, Mabel*, wife of Edward F. Coward, of New York, and *Violet*.

II.—DANIEL HUBBARD, JR., *m.* Mary Greene, and had:

HENRY HUBBARD, *m.* Mary Chadwell, and had:

MARY GREENE HUBBARD, *m.* William Scollay Whitwell, and had:

ELIZABETH WHITWELL, a member of the Massachusetts Society of the Colonial Dames of America, who *m.* William Tudor, of Boston (a grandson of Colonel William Tudor, Judge Advocate General, Continental Army), and had: *Henry D., b.* Paris, 30 October, 1874; *William, b.* Boston, 14 June, 1876, who served with the "Rough-Riders" regiment during the American-Spanish war; *Elizabeth, b.* Boston, 27 November, 1878; *Delia*

Aimée, b. Marietta, Georgia, 22 April, 1880, and *Mary*, b. Paris, 30 July, 1886.

MABEL RUSSELL, 1677-1722, *m.*, secondly, 1707 (his first wife), Rev. Samuel Woodbridge (son of Rev. Benjamin, d. 1710, son of Rev. John, 1634-1695, and his wife Mercy, daughter of Thomas Dudley, Governor of Massachusetts Colony), b. about 1683, d. at East Hartford, Connecticut, 1746, and had:

1.—RUSSELL WOODBRIDGE, b. 8 May, 1719, d. East Hartford, 1782; *m.*, 1741, Anna Olmsted, and had:

DEODATUS WOODBRIDGE, b. 6 September, 1757, d. East Hartford, 1836; *m.*, first, 1780, Esther Willis, and had by her:

ELECTA WOODBRIDGE, b. 2 January, 1781, d. 1858; *m.*, 1798, George Cheney, of Manchester, Connecticut, b. 20 December, 1771, d. 1829, and had:

CHARLES CHENEY, b. South Manchester, Connecticut, 26 December, 1803, d. 20 June, 1874; *m.*, at Providence, Rhode Island, 21 October, 1829, Waitstill Dexter Shaw, b. Providence, Rhode Island, October 17, 1809, d. Mt. Pleasant, Ohio, April 6, 1841, and had:

KNIGHT DEXTER CHENEY, b. Mt. Pleasant, Ohio, 9 October, 1837, *m.*, at Exeter, New Hampshire, 4 June, 1862, Ednah Dow Smith, b. at South Berwick, Maine, 12 May, 1841, and had:

EDNAH PARKER CHENEY, of South Manchester, Connecticut, a member of the Connecticut Society of the Colonial Dames of America.

2.—ELIZABETH WOODBRIDGE, 1714-1754, who *m.*, 1737, Rev. Ephraim Little, 1707-1787, and had:

FAITH LITTLE, b. 1754, who *m.*, 1781, Rev. Lemuel Parsons, 1753-1791, and had:

NANCY WOODBRIDGE PARSONS, 1787-1882, who *m.*, 1807, Quartus Knight, 1783-1827, and had:

LEMUEL PARTRIDGE KNIGHT, 1815-1891, who *m.*, 1845, Julia Jane Judson, 1822-1897, and had:

FANNY JUDSON KNIGHT, a member of the Michigan Society of the Colonial Dames of America, the Order of the Crown, *etc.*, who *m.*, 1876, William Addison Butler, of Detroit, and had: *Edith Knight*, b. 1877, and *Lawrence Knight*, b. 1879.

MEHITABLE WYLLYS, 1658-1697, had by her third husband, *m.* in 1676, Rev. Timothy Woodbridge, of Hartford, d. 30 April, 1732:

MARY WOODBRIDGE, b. 19 June, 1692, d. 17 February, 1766, who *m.*, 7 May, 1724, Judge William Pitkin, of East Hartford, Connecticut, judge of the superior court and Governor of the Connecticut Colony, *b.* 30 April, 1694, *d.* 1 October, 1769, and had:

Rev. Timothy Pitkin, of Farmington, Connecticut, *b.* 13 January, 1727, *d.* 8 July, 1812; *m.*, 9 August, 1753, Temperance, *b.* 29 April, 1732, *d.* 19 May, 1772, daughter of Rev. Thomas Clap, D.D., of Windham, Connecticut, president of Yale College, *d.* 1767, and his first wife, Mary Whiting, daughter of Rev. Samuel and Elizabeth (Adams) Whiting, and had:

I.—Timothy Pitkin, *m.*, 6 June, 1801, Elizabeth Hubbard, and had:

Rev. Thomas Clap Pitkin, *m.*, 19 May, 1841, Harriet Louisa Starr, and had: *Mary Caswell, Louisa Burr,* and

Anna Denio Pitkin, a member of the Michigan Society of the Colonial Dames of America.

II.—Catherine Pitkin, *b.* 22 February, 1757, *d.* 13 September, 1837, *m.*, 17 November, 1774, Rev. Nathan Perkins, D.D., of West Hartford, Connecticut, *b.* 12 May, 1748, *d.* 18 January, 1838, and had:

Catherine Perkins, *b.* 20 January, 1782, *d.* 19 February, 1848, who *m.*, 20 December, 1803, Charles Seymour, of Hartford, Connecticut, *b.* January 17, 1777, *d.* 21 January, 1852, and had:

Mary Seymour, *b.* 1 November, 1820, *d.* 18 April, 1883, who *m.*, 28 October, 1846, Russell Goodrich Talcott, of Hartford, Connecticut, *b.* 15 August, 1818, *d.* March 3, 1863, and had:

Mary Kingsbury Talcott, of Hartford, a member of the Connecticut Society of the Colonial Dames of America, the Order of the Crown, *etc.*

4.—Mary Wyllys, 1656–1729, who *m.*, 1684 (his second wife), Rev. Joseph Eliot, of Guilford, Connecticut, 1638–1694 (son of Rev. John Eliot, the apostle to the Indians), and had:

I.—Rev. Jared Eliot, M.D., of Killingworth, Connecticut, 1685–1763, who *m.*, 1710, Elizabeth, daughter of Samuel Smithson, and had:

Aaron Eliot, of Killingworth (Clinton), 1718–1785, who *m.* Mary, daughter of Rev. William Worthington, and had:

Benjamin Eliot, 1762–1848, *m.*, in Virginia, Frances Panca, and had:

Mary Worthington Watkins Eliot, 1798–1865, who *m.*, 1821, Chester Ashley, of Little Rock, Ark., *b.* Amherst, Massachusetts; was United States Senator from Arkansas when he *d.*, in Washington City, in 1878, also of Royal Descent, and had:

1.—William Eliot Ashley, of Little Rock, Arkansas, *d.* 1868, who *m.* at Little Rock, in 1846, Frances E. Grafton, also of Royal Descent, and had:

FRANCES ANN ASHLEY, a member of the Massachusetts and Arkansas Societies of the Colonial Dames of America, who *m.* Clifton Sidney Gray, M.D., of Little Rock, *d. s. p.* 14 February, 1899.

2.—FRANCES ANN ASHLEY, 1825–1851, who *m.* at Little Rock, 1850, Rev. Andrew Fields Freeman, of Little Rock, *b.* Warrenton, North Carolina, and had:

MARY ASHLEY FREEMAN, a member of the Massachusetts and Arkansas Societies of the Colonial Dames of America, the Order of the Crown, *etc.*, who *m.*, 1872, Judge Sterling R. Cockrill, of Little Rock, chief justice of the supreme court of Arkansas, also of Royal Descent, and had: *Ashley, Ann McDonald, Sterling R., Mary Freeman, Emmet, Garland,* and *Freeman.*

II.—ABIAL ELIOT, who *m.* Mary Leete, and had:

NATHANIEL ELIOT, who *m.* Beulah Parmalee, and had:

WILLIAM ELIOT, who *m.* Ruth Rossiter, and had:

WILLIAM HORACE ELIOT, who *m.* Mary Law, and had:

WILLIAM HORACE ELIOT, who *m.* Sarah Sawyer, and had:

WILLEMENA ELIOT, a member of the Massachusetts and Michigan Societies of the Colonial Dames of America, who *m.*, 26 December, 1877, Dr. Justin Edwards Emerson, of Detroit, Michigan, and had: *Paul Eliot, Filip Law,* and *Ralf de Pomeroy.*

THE ROYAL DESCENT

OF

MISS ANNIE FITZHUGH ROSE WALKER,

OF RICHMOND, VA.

ALFRED THE GREAT, of England, had:	THE EMPEROR CHARLEMAGNE, had:
Edward the Elder, King of England, who had:	Pepin, King of Italy, who had:
Edmund I., King of England, who had:	Bernard, King of Italy, who had:
Edgar the Peaceful, King of England, who had:	Pepin, Count de Vermandois, who had:
Ethelred II., King of England, who had:	Herbert I., Count de Vermandois, who had:
Edmund II., King of England, who had:	Herbert II., Count de Vermandois, who had:
Prince Edward the Exile, of England, who had:	Albert I., Count de Vermandois, who had:
Margaret, *m.* Malcolm III., of Scotland, and had:	Herbert III., Count de Vermandois, who had:
St. David, King of Scotland, who had:	Otho, Count de Vermandois, who had:
Henry, Prince of Scotland, who had:	Herbert IV., Count de Vermandois, who had:
David, Earl of Huntingdon, who had:	Adelheid, *m.* Hugh, Count de Vermandois, and had:
Isabel, *m.* Robert, Earl of Annandale, and had:	Isabel, *m.* William, Earl of Surrey, and had:
Robert Bruce, Lord of Annandale, who had:	Ada, *m.* Henry, Prince of Scotland, and had:
Robert Bruce, Earl of Carrick, who had:	David, Earl of Huntingdon, who had:
Robert Bruce, King of Scotland, who had:	Isabel, *m.* Robert, Lord of Annandale, and had.
Margery, *m.* Walter, High Steward, and had:	Robert Bruce, Lord of Annandale, who had:
Robert II., King of Scotland, who had:	Robert Bruce, Earl of Carrick, who had:
Egidia, *m.* William Douglas, and had:	Mary, *m.* Sir Alexander Fraser, and had:
Egidia, *m.* Henry, Earl of Orkney, and had:	Sir John Fraser, of Aberbothnot, who had:
William, Earl of Orkney and Caithness, who had:	Margaret, *m.* Sir William de Keith, and had.
Eleanor, *m.* John Stewart, Earl of Athol, and had:	Elizabeth, *m.* Sir Adam de Gordon, and had:
Isabel, *m.* Alexander Robertson, and had:	Elizabeth, *m.* Alexander de Seton, and had:
John Robertson, of Muirton, who had:	Alexander Seton, Earl of Huntley, who had:
Gilbert Robertson, of Muirton, who had.	Margaret, *m.* Hugh Rose, of Kilravock, and had:
David Robertson, of Muirton, who had:	John Rose, of Bellivat, who had:
William Robertson, of Muirton, who had:	John Rose, of Bellivat, who had:
William Robertson, of Gladney, who had:	John Rose, of Bellivat, who had:
Rev. William Robertson, of Edinburgh, who had:	Hugh Rose, who had:
Jean, *m.* Alexander Henry, of Aberdeen, and had:	Patrick Rose, of Lochihills, who had:
Col. John Henry, of Hanover Co., Va., who had:	John Rose, of Wester Alves, who had:
Jane, *m.* Col. Samuel Meredith, and had:	Rev. Robert Rose, d. Richmond, Va., who had:
Jane, *m.* David S. Garland, and had:	Col. Hugh Rose, of Amherst Co., Va., who had.

Ann Shepherd Garland *m.* Dr. Gustavus A. Rose, of Lynchburg, Va.

Judith Cabell Rose, of Richmond, Va., member of the Virginia Society of the Colonial Dames of America. = Benjamin Powell Walker, of Hartford, Indiana, d. New York City, 14 Feb., 1887.

Annie Fitzhugh Rose Walker, of Richmond, Va., member of the Virginia Society of the Colonial Dames of America, the Order of the Crown, etc.

PEDIGREE LXIII.

EDWARD I., King of England, had by his first wife, Princess Eleanor of Castile:

PRINCESS ELIZABETH PLANTAGENET, widow of John de Vere, who m., secondly, 1306, Humphrey de Bohun, fourth Earl of Hereford and Essex, and had:

LADY ELEANOR DE BOHUN, who m., first, 1327, James Butler, second Earl of Carrick, created Earl of Ormond, 1328, and had:

LADY PETRONELLA BUTLER, who m. (his first wife) Gilbert, third Baron Talbot, of Goodrich Castle, 1332–1387, and had:

RICHARD, fourth Baron Talbot, of Goodrich Castle, and, in the right of his wife, sixth Baron le Strange, d. 1396. He m. Lady Ankeretta, daughter of John, fourth Baron le Strange, of Blackmere, and had:

GENERAL SIR JOHN DE TALBOT, K.G., lord of Furnival, second son, created, 1448, Earl of Shrewsbury, lord-lieutenant of Ireland, Earl of Waterford and Wexford, in Irish Peerage, lord chancellor of Ireland, k. in battle in France in 1453, aged 80 years. He m., first, 1408, Lady Maud, daughter of Thomas de Neville, baron of Furnival, d. 1406, also of Royal Descent, and had:

LORD THOMAS DE TALBOT, eldest son, d. v. p. in France, 145-, who had:

LADY ELIZABETH TALBOT, who m. Sir Henry de Grey, of Wilton, and had:

LADY MARGARET DE GREY, d. 144-, who m., first, John D'Arcy, fifth Baron D'Arcy, b. 1377, d. 1411, and had:

PHILIP, sixth Baron D'Arcy, d. 1418, who had by his wife, Lady Eleanor, daughter of Henry, third Baron Fitz-Hugh:

LADY MARGARET D'ARCY, who m. Sir John Conyers, of Hornby Castle, Yorkshire, and had:

RICHARD CONYERS, of Horden, Durham, who m. Lady Elizabeth, daughter of Sir Robert Claxton, Knt., of Horden, and had:

ROBERT CONYERS, of Horden, who m. Margaret Bamforth, of Seham, Durham, and had:

CHRISTOPHER CONYERS, of Horden, who m. Elizabeth, daughter of John Jackson, of Bedale, and had:

RICHARD CONYERS, of Horden, who m. Isabel, daughter of Robert Lumley, of Ludworth, and had:

CHRISTOPHER CONYERS, of Horden, who *m.*, secondly, 1586, Lady Anne, daughter of Sir John Hedsworth, Knt., of Harraton, Durham (*see* Durham "Visitations," 1575), and had:

MARY CONYERS, who *m.* William Wilkinson, of Lanchester, Durham, son of Lawrence Wilkinson, of Harperley House, Durham, and had:

LAWRENCE WILKINSON,* a lieutenant in the army of Charles I.; taken prisoner at the surrender of Newcastle, 22 October, 1644; his estates having been sequestered and sold by Parliament, 1645, he came, with his wife and a son to Providence, Rhode Island, in 1646; was a commissioner, 1659, 1667; deputy, 1667, 1673, *etc.; d.* 9 August, 1692. He *m.* Susannah, *d.* 1692, daughter of Christopher and Alice Smith, of Providence, and had:

1.—JOHN WILKINSON, of Providence, *b.* Smithfield, 2 March, 1654, *d.* 10 April, 1708; *m.*, 16 April, 1689, Deborah Whipple, *b.* 1 August, 1670, *d.* 24 June, 1748, and had:

JOHN WILKINSON, of Providence, *b.* 16 March, 1690, *d.* 25 September, 1756; *m.*, 20 March, 1718, Rebecca Scott, of Smithfield, *b.* 11 February, 1699, *d.* after 1756, and had:

JOHN WILKINSON, of Smithfield, *b.* 20 March, 1724, *d.* 23 June, 1804; *m.* Ruth Angell, of Providence, and had:

OZIEL WILKINSON, of Pawtucket, *b.* 30 January, 1744, *d.* 22 October, 1815; *m.*, 8 April, 1766, Lydia Smith, of Smithfield, *b.* 11 February, 1747, and had:

ISAAC WILKINSON, of Pawtucket, *b.* 10 October, 1768, *d.* 2 March, 1843; *m.* Lois Marsh, of Pawtucket, and had:

MARY WILKINSON, *b.* 11 October, 1804, *d.* 27 February, 1883; *m.*, 13 December, 1821, Benjamin Fessenden, of Pawtucket, *b.* 13 June, 1797, *d.* 6 January, 1881, and had:

MARY WILKINSON FESSENDEN, *b.* 24 October, 1827, *d.* 20 September, 1886; *m.*, 30 October, 1849, William Francis Sayles, of Pawtucket, *b.* 20 September, 1824, *d.* 7 May, 1894, also of Royal Descent, and had:

MARY FESSENDEN SAYLES, a member of the Rhode Island Society of the Colonial Dames of America, *b.* 29 September, 1850, who *m.*, 21 May, 1872, Roscoe Stetson Washburn, of Providence, and had: *Maurice King, Roscoe Clifton, William F. S.* (deceased), and *John Fessenden* (deceased).

2.—CAPTAIN SAMUEL WILKINSON, of Providence, Rhode Island, eldest

---

* MRS. EDWIN A. DAMON, a member of the Pennsylvania State Society in the National Society of the Colonial Dames of America, is also of Royal Descent through Lawrence Wilkinson.

son, a justice of the peace, *d.* 27 August, 1727; *m.*, 1672, Plain, daughter of Rev. William Wilkenden, of Providence, and had:

I.—JOSEPH WILKINSON, *m.* Martha Pray, and had:

PRUDENCE WILKINSON, *m.* Isaiah Angell, and had:

PRUDENCE ANGELL, *m.* Gideon Austin, and had:

RUTH AUSTIN, *m.* James Cranston, and had:

MARTHA CRANSTON, *m.* Silas Bingham, Jr., and had:

HANNAH BINGHAM, *m.* Dr. James Fuller Howe, and had:

ANNETTE HOWE, who *m.* Franklin R. Carpenter, Ph.D., of Denver, Colorado. *Issue,* see p. 260.

II.—RUTH WILKINSON, 1685–86–1738, who *m.* William Hopkins, of Providence, Rhode Island, and had:

STEPHEN HOPKINS, of Providence, Rhode Island, *b.* 7 March, 1707, *d.* 13 July, 1785; member of the Continental Congress, a signer of the Declaration of Independence, Governor of Rhode Island, *etc.* He *m.*, 9 October, 1726, Sarah, 1707–1753, daughter of Sylvanus Scott, of Providence, and had:

LYDIA HOPKINS, 1733–1793, who *m.*, 1763, Colonel Daniel Tillinghast, of Providence, 1732–1803, and had:

JOHN TILLINGHAST, of Uxbridge, Massachusetts, *b.* 1766, at Providence, *d.* 1839, at Newport, Indiana; *m.*, 1803, Hannah (Sherman) Russell, 1769–1837, and had:

SARAH SCOTT TILLINGHAST, 1806–1880, who *m.*, 1832, Griffin Clark, of Norwich and Hampton, Connecticut, and Oregon, Wisconsin, 1801–1876, and had:

ANNAH RUSSELL CLARK, a member of the Rhode Island Society of the Colonial Dames of America, who *m.*, 6 May, 1868, Shepard Leach Sheldon, of Madison, Wisconsin, and had: *Georgiana Russell* and *Henry Tillinghast.*

THE ROYAL DESCENT

OF

MRS. GEORGE INNES, JR.,

OF NEW YORK CITY.

HUGH CAPET, King of France=Adela, dau. William, Duke of Aquitaine.

Robert I., the Pious,=Lady Constance of Provence.
King of France

Princess Havide=Rynerius IV., Count of Hainault.
or Hedewige

Henry I., King of France=Lady Anne of Russia.

Lady Beatrix=Eblo de Rouci.

Countess Adela=Hildwin de Montdider.

Hugh Magnus,=Lady Adelheid of Vermandois.
Duke of France

Lady Margaret de Rouci.=Hugh de Clermont.

William de Warren,=Lady Isabel de Vermandois.
Earl of Surrey

Robert de Bellomont, Earl of Leicester.

Lady Adeliza=Gilbert de Tonsburg, Earl of Clare.
de Clermont

William de Warren,=Lady Alice de Talvas, also of Royal Descent.
Earl of Surrey

Lady Elizabeth de Bellomont=Gilbert de Clare, Earl of Pembroke.

Lady Isabella de Warren=Hameline Plantagenet, Earl of Surrey.

Richard "the Strongbow,"=Eva, dau. Dermot, King of Leinster.
2d Earl of Pembroke

Lady Isabella de Warren=Roger Bigod, Earl of Norfolk.

Lady Isabel de Clare=William le Marshal, Protector of England.

Hugh Bigod, second Earl of Norfolk=Lady Maud Marshall.

Sir Hugh Bigod, Justiciary of England=Joan, dau. of Robert Burnet.

Sir John Bigod, Knt.=(Name unknown.)

Sir Roger Bigod, of Settington=(Name unknown.)

Lady Joan Bigod=Sir William de Chauncy, of Skirpenbeck.

John Chauncy, of Stepney=Margaret Gifford, of Gedleston.

John Chauncy, of Sawbridgeworth=Anne Leventhorp, of Shingey.

John Chauncy, of Sawbridgeworth=Daughter of Thomas Boyce.

John Chauncy, of Pishobury=Elizabeth (Proffit) Mansfield.

Henry Chauncy, of Newplace Giffords=Lucy ———.

George Chauncy, of Yardleybury=Anne Welsh, of Great Wymondley.

Rev. Charles Chauncy, D.D., 1592-1671, second=Catherine Eyre, of New Sarum.
President of Harvard College

Rev. Nathaniel Chauncy, of Hatfield, Mass.=Abigail Strong, of Northampton, Mass.

Rev. Nathaniel Chauncy, of Durham, Ct.=Sarah Judson, of Stratford, Conn.

Col. Elihu Chauncy, of Durham, Mass.=Mary Griswold, of Killingworth.

Catherine Chauncy=Rev. Elizur Goodrich, D.D., of Durham, Mass.

Judge Elizur Goodrich, LL.D., of New Haven, Ct.=Anne Willard Allen.

Nancy Goodrich, 1793-1847=Henry Leavitt Ellsworth, of Hartford, son of Oliver Ellsworth, Chief Justice of the United States Supreme Court.

Annie Goodrich Ellsworth. She was a member of the Society of the Colonial Dames of the State of New York. When her father was Chief of the U. S. Patent Office she had the honor of sending the first telegram, May 24, 1844, at the request of Mr. Morse, which read, " What hath God wrought." She d. in New York, 21 January, 1900, aged 73 years.=Roswell Smith, b. Lebanon, Ct., 30 March, 1829 ; d. New York, 19 April, 1892.

Julia Goodrich Smith, m. 23 April, 1879=George Innes, Jr., of New York City.

Elizabeth Innes, b. New York, 22 March, 1880.

Juliet Innes, b. Montclair, N. Y., 17 June, 1881.

George Ellsworth Innes, b. Montclair, N. Y., 10 October, 1882.

PEDIGREE LXIV.

EDWARD III., King of England, had by his wife, Lady Philippa, daughter of William, Count of Hainault and Holland:

THOMAS PLANTAGENET, Duke of Gloucester, who had by his wife, Lady Alianore, daughter of Humphrey de Bohun, last Earl of Hereford and Essex, Earl of Northampton, also of Royal Descent:

LADY ANNE PLANTAGENET (widow of Thomas and Edmund, Earls of Stafford), who *m.*, thirdly, William de Bouchier, Earl of Ewe, and had:

SIR JOHN DE BOUCHIER, K.G., fourth son, *d.* 1474, *m.* Lady Margery, daughter and heiress of Richard de Berners, of West Horsley, Surry, and had:

SIR HUMPHREY DE BOUCHIER, eldest son, *k. v. p.* at Barnetfield, whose daughter:

LADY ANNE DE BOUCHIER, *m.* Sir Thomas Fienes, K.B., Baron Dacre of the South, 1470–1534, and had:

LADY CATHERINE FIENES (*see* p. 267), who *m.* Richard Loudenoys, of Briade, Sussex, and had:

MARY LOUDENOYS, sole heir, who *m.* Thomas Harlakenden, of Warhorn, Kent (*see* "Visitations of Essex," 1612 and 1634, and Berry's "Kent Pedigrees"), *d.* 1564, and had:

ROGER HARLAKENDEN, of Kenardiston, Kent, 1535–1603 (*see* "Visitations of Kent," 1574), who *m.*, first, Elizabeth, daughter of Thomas Hardres, and widow of George Harlakenden, of Woodchurch, Kent (*see* Braley's "History of Essex"), and had:

THOMAS HARLAKENDEN, of Earl's Colne, Essex, third son, who *m.* Dorothy Cheney, of Drayton, Berks, and had:

DOROTHY HARLAKENDEN,* *bapt.* 12 December, 1596, *bur.* Toppesfield, 3 August, 1636; *m.*, 2 April, 1617 (his first wife), Samuel Symonds, *b.* at Great Yeildham, Essex, *bapt.* 9 June, 1595; came to New England in 1637, and was provincial councillor and deputy-governor of the Massa-

---

* The following ladies, members of the National Society of the Colonial Dames of America, are also of Royal Descent through Dorothy Harlakenden:

MRS. CHARLES DEERING, Pennsylvania State Society.
MRS. DANIEL STIMSON, New York State Society.
MISS MARIAN F. HARRIS, Pennsylvania State Society.
MISS ELIZABETH W. WHITE, New Hampshire State Society.

chusetts Bay Colony, 1673–78, d. at Ipswich, in October, 1678 (see "The Ancestry of Priscilla Baker," "The Ancestry of Ebenezer Greenough," Symonds "Heraldic Collection of Essex," in the Camden Society Publications, and the "American Heraldic Journal," January, 1865), and had:

I.—WILLIAM SYMONDS, of Ipswich, Massachusetts, m. Mary, daughter of Jonathan Wade, of Ipswich, and had:

DOROTHY SYMONDS, b. 21 October, 1670, m., 19 December, 1695, Cyprian, b. 17 January, 1671, son of John Whipple, of Ipswich, 1632–1695, and had:

SAMUEL WHIPPLE, of Stonington, Connecticut, b. 13 September, 1702, m., 20 June, 1726, Bethiah Patch, and had:

AMOS WHIPPLE, of Stonington, b. 16 March, 1739, m., 26 January, 1769, Ann Hewitt, b. 26 May, 1746, and had:

MALACHI WHIPPLE, of Albany, New York, b. 20 June, 1770, d. 12 December, 1836; m. Priscilla Brown, 1777–1860, and had:

LUCY WHIPPLE, b. 21 November, 1817, d. 26 May, 1884; m., 7 August, 1834, at Berne, New York, Chauncy Hulburt, of Philadelphia, b. 15 August, 1813, d. 31 August, 1896, and had:

1.—JOANNA CROMBIE HULBURT, deceased.

2.—HELEN AMELIA HULBURT, a member of the New York Society of the Colonial Dames of America, Society of "Mayflower" Descendants, etc., who m. Elijah Warrington Murphey, of Albany, New York, and had: *Harriet Louise*, wife of Henry Otis Chapman, of New York; *Lucy Whipple, d.; Helen Virginia, d.; Martha, Virginia Hulburt, Chauncy Hulburt*, and *Elijah Warrington*.

3.—DAYTON WHIPPLE HULBURT, of Philadelphia, who m. Elizabeth Gundaker, of Philadelphia.

4.—HARRIET LOUISE HULBURT, who m. Thomas Fraley Baker, of Philadelphia.

5.—ISABELLA VIRGINIA HULBURT, who m. Ellis Hughes Hanson, of Philadelphia.

6.—LUCY MATILDA HULBURT, who m., first, Ferdinand Heiskill, of Philadelphia, and had: *Florence M.*, wife of John Mickle Okie, of Berwyn, and m., secondly, Edward Hughes Hanson, of Bala, Pennsylvania, and had: *Richard Edward* and *Helen Louise*.

7.—MARY VINCENT HULBURT, deceased.

8.—LEWIS CHEESMAN HULBURT, of Los Angeles, California, who m. Charlotte Smith, of Orange, New Jersey.

9.—ANNA BARNET HULBURT, who m. Henry W. Peacock of Philadelphia.

II.—ELIZABETH SYMONDS, *b.* Topperfield, 1624, *d.* Salem, 7 May, 1685; *m.*, at Ipswich, 24 May, 1644, Daniel Epes, of Salem, *d.* 8 January, 1693 (*see* Platt's " Ancestry of Ebenezer Greenough ") and had:

MARTHA EPES, 1654–1686; *m.*, 1679 (his first wife), Robert Greenough, of Rowley, Massachusetts, *d.* 30 March, 1718, and had:

DANIEL GREENOUGH, *b.* 22 February, 1686, *d.* Bradford, Massachusetts, 25 April, 1746; *m.*, first, 25 January, 1722, Elizabeth Hatch, of Portsmouth, New Hampshire, and had:

SYMONDS GREENOUGH, *b.* New Castle, New Hampshire, 1724, *d.* at Haverhill, Massachusetts; *m.* Abigail, *b.* 24 November, 1725, daughter of John Chadwick, of Watertown, and had:

EBENEZER GREENOUGH, *b.* Haverhill, 18 February, 1753, *d.* Chester, New Hampshire, 15 December, 1827; *m.* Mary, 1759–1842, daughter of Rev. Ebenezer Flagg, of Chester, 1704–1796, and had:

EBENEZER GREENOUGH, JR., of Sunbury, Pennsylvania, *b.* 11 December, 1783, *d.* 1847; *m.*, 5 March, 1814, Abigail, *b.* 12 December, 1791, *d.* 14 August, 1868, daughter of Joseph and Susanna (Pusey) Israel, of New Castle county, Delaware, and had:

1.—MARY GREENOUGH, *b.* 26 April, 1816, *d.* 23 August, 1854; *m.*, 28 November, 1838, George Lippincott, of Philadelphia, and had:

EMILY ABIGAIL LIPPINCOTT, of Philadelphia, a member of the Pennsylvania Society of the Colonial Dames of America, *d. unm.*, 23 July, 1898.

2.—CLARA ANN GREENOUGH, *b.* 16 December, 1817, who *m.* Franklin Platt, of Philadelphia, and had:

CLARA GREENOUGH PLATT, a member of the Pennsylvania Society of the Colonial Dames of America, who *m.* James B. Canby, of Wilmington, Delaware, and Philadelphia, and had: *Clara G. Franklin P.*, and *James Benjamin.*

3.—MARIAN GREENOUGH, *b.* 13 April, 1829, widow of William Taylor Dilworth, who *m.*, secondly, James Seguin de Benneville, M.D., of Philadelphia, and had:

MARIE MATHILDE DE BENNEVILLE, of Philadelphia, a member of the Pennsylvania Society of the Colonial Dames of America.

THE ROYAL DESCENT

OF

MRS. EDWARD HUGHES HANSON,

OF BALA, PENNA.

ALFRED THE GREAT, King of England=Ethelbith, daughter of Ethelan the Great.
Edward the Elder, King of England,·Edgiva, daughter of Earl Sigelline.
Edmund I., King of England—Elgiva, gr. dau. of Alfred the Great.
Edgar the Peaceful, King of England, Elfrida, daughter of Ordgar, Earl of Devon.
Ethelred the Unready, King of England=Elgifa, daughter of Earl Thorad.
Edmund Ironsides, King of England, Lady Algitha of Denmark.
Prince Edward the Exile, of England, Lady Agatha of Germany.
Princess Margaret, of England, Malcolm III., King of Scotland.
Princess Matilda, of Scotland, Henry I., King of England.
Empress Maud, of Germany, Geoffrey-Plantagenet, Count of Anjou.
Henry II., King of England, Lady Eleanor of Aquitaine.
John, King of England, Lady Isabel de Taillefer.
Henry III., King of England, Lady Eleanor of Provence.
Edward I., King of England, Princess Eleanor of Castile.
Edward II., King of England, Princess Isabella of France.
Edward III , King of England,=Lady Philippa of Hainault.
Thomas, Duke of Gloucester, Lady Alianore de Bohun.
Lady Anne Plantagenet—William de Bouchier, Earl of Eu.
Sir John de Bouchier, K.G.=, Lady Margery de Berners.
Sir Humphrey de Bouchier, Knt.=(Name unknown)
Lady Anne de Bouchier,·Sir Thomas Fienes, K.B., Baron Dacre.
Lady Catherine Fienes=Richard Loudenoys, of Briade, Sussex.
Mary Loudenoys, Thomas Harlakenden, of Warborn, Kent.
Roger Harlakenden, of Kenardiston, Kent, Elizabeth Hardres, of Woodchurch, Kent.
Thomas Harlakenden, of Earl's Colne, Essex, Dorothy Chency, of Drayton, Berks.
Dorothy Harlakenden, Samuel Symonds, Gov. of Mass. Colony, 1673-8.
William Symonds, of Ipswich, Mass., Mary Wade, of Ipswich, Mass.
Dorothy Symonds=Cyprian Whipple, of Ipswich, Mass.
Samuel Whipple, of Stonington, Conn., Bethia Patch.
Amos Whipple, of Stonington, Conn.=Ann Hewitt.
Malachi Whipple, of Albany, N. Y., ·Priscilla Brown.
Lucy Whipple, Chauncy Hulburt, of Philadelphia, Pa.

Ferdinand Heiskill,--Lucy Matilda Hulburt, Edward Hughes Hanson,
of Philadelphia | of Philadelphia and
(first husband), | Bala, Pa.

Florence M. Heiskill · John M. Okie, Richard Edward   Helen Louise
                      of Berwyn, Pa.   Hanson.   Hanson.

PEDIGREE LXV.

ROBERT II., King of Scotland, had by his first wife, Lady Elizabeth, daughter of Sir Adam Mure, of Rowallan:

LADY MARGARET STEWART, who *m*. (his second wife) Eoin-Mor, or John MacDonald, lord of the Isles, and had:

DONALD MACDONALD, lord of the Isles, who *m*. Lady Margaret, daughter of Sir Walter Leslie and his wife, Euphemia, Countess of Ross, and had:

ALEXANDER MACDONALD, lord of the Isles and Earl of Ross, *d*. 1448–9, who *m*. Lady Elizabeth, daughter of Alexander de Seton, lord of Gordon and Huntley, and had:

HUGH MACDONALD, lord of the Isles, second son, *d*. 1498, who had by his second wife, Lady Mary, daughter of the chieftain of clan Gun:

DONALD-GALLOCH MACDONALD, lord of the Isles, *d*. 1506, who had by his wife, a daughter of the MacDonalds in Ireland:

DONALD-GRAMMACH MACDONALD, lord of the Isles, *d*. 1534, who *m*. Margaret, daughter of MacDonald of Moydert, and had:

DONALD-GORME MACDONALD. As eldest son of his father he claimed the title of lord of the Isles, but King James V. opposed him, and in the war which ensued Donald was slain, in 1537, leaving issue by his wife, Margaret, daughter of John Roderick McLeod, of Lewis:

DONALD-GORME MACDONALD, of Slate, who was restored in his honors by Queen Mary, in 1567, and *d*. 1585. His second son:

ARCHIBALD MACDONALD, had by his wife, Margaret, daughter of Angus MacDonald, of Dunivaig and Glynnis, in Argyle:

SIR DONALD MACDONALD, of Slate, created a baronet of Nova Scotia, 14 July, 1625, *d*. 1643–4. He *m*. Lady Janet, daughter of Kenneth, first Lord Mackenzie, of Kintail, and sister of the second Earl of Seaforth, and had:

SIR JAMES MACDONALD, of Slate, 2d Bart., *d*. 8 December, 1678, in the Isle of Skye. He fought under Montrose in 1645, and had by his second wife, Mary, daughter of John MacLeod, of that Ilk:

LADY MARIAN MACDONALD, who *m*. Patrick MacGregor, who commanded his clansmen under Montrose in support of the royal cause, 1644–5, and was outlawed, and had John, his heir, who changed his name to "John Murray," and was the ancestor of Sir John Murray, Bart., 1795, and

JAMES MACGREGOR, second son, who changed his name to "Thomas MacGehee" when his clan was outlawed, and was an officer in the English army. He removed to Virginia, and resided in St. John's parish, King William county, where his will, dated 27 July, 1727, was probated, and had issue:

EDWARD MACGEHEE, who *m*. Katherine de Jarnette, and had:

DANIEL MACGEHEE, who *m*. Jane Brooke Hodnet, and had:

KATHERINE BROOKE GARTEREY MACGEHEE, who *m*. David Urquhart, and had: 1. *Katherine Louisa Banks*, who *m*. Jesse Ansley, *issue;* 2. *Jane Eliza Brooks*, who *m*. William Weeden, of Alabama, *issue;* 3. *Dr. John A.*, no *issue;* 4. *Sarah Ann*, who *m*. John Garner, *issue;* 5. *David W.*, d. *unm.;* 6. *Mary Matilda*, who *m*. (his first wife) William Waters Garrard, *issue;* 7. *Caroline Lucy*, who *m*. Lemuel Tyler Downing, *issue;* and

FRANCES ISABELLA GARTEREY URQUHART, 1818–1890, who *m*., 1843 (his second wife) William Waters Garrard, of "Hilton," Muscogee county, Georgia, 1818–1866, also of Royal Descent, and had:

1.—WILLIAM URQUHART GARRARD, *m*. Mary Lawton, and had: *William, Guilielma, Emily,* and *Cecilia.*

2.—EVA MATILDA GARRARD, a member of the Georgia Society of the Colonial Dames of America, who *m*. Humphreys Castleman, of Columbus, also of Royal Descent (see p. 186), and had: *Louis* and

MARY ISABELLA GARRARD CASTLEMAN, a member of the Georgia Society of the Colonial Dames of America, who *m*. Samuel Harrison McAfee, of West Point, Georgia.

3.—LOUIS FORD GARRARD, *m*. Anna Leonard, and had: *Louis Ford, Francis Urquhart, Anna Leonard, Guy Castleman, Van de Van, Helen Glenn,* and *Isabel.*

4.—HELEN AUGUSTA GARRARD, *b*. 28 August, 1850, a member of the Georgia Society of the Colonial Dames of America, who *m*., 23 April, 1873, John Thomas Glenn, of Atlanta, captain in Confederate States Army, *d*. 14 March, 1899, also of Royal Descent, and had: *Garrard, Helen Mildred Lewis, William Louis, John Thomas* (deceased), *Luther Judson* (deceased), and

ISA GARTEREY URQUHART GLENN, a member of the Georgia Society of the Colonial Dames of America, the Order of the Crown, *etc.*

5.—GERTRUDE KATE GARRARD, a member of the Georgia Society of the Colonial Dames of America, who *m*. James Watson Harris, of Meriden, Mississippi, and had: *Garrard, Isabel* (wife of William H. Hall), *Helen Glenn, Eva Castleman,* and *David Urquhart.*

PEDIGREE LXVI.

ROBERT II., King of Scotland, had by his second wife, Lady Euphemia, Countess of Moray, daughter of Hugh, Earl of Ross:

DAVID, Earl of Caithness and Strathern, who had by his wife, Lady Euphemia:

LADY EUPHEMIA STEWART, Countess of Strathern, who *m.* (his second wife) Sir Patrick Graham, Earl of Strathern, *jure uxoris*, and had:

LADY EUPHEMIA GRAHAM, who *m.* Archibald, Earl of Douglas and second Duke of Touraine, son of Archibald, Earl of Douglas and his wife, Princess Margaret, daughter of Robert III., King of Scotland, by his wife, Lady Annabella Drummond, and had:

LADY MARGARET DOUGLAS, "the Fair Maid of Galloway," who *m.* John Stewart, first Earl of Athol, uterine brother of King James II., and son of Sir James Stewart, "the Black Knight of Lorn," by his wife, Lady Joan, widow of King James I., and daughter of Sir John de Beaufort, K.G., Marquis of Dorset, *etc.*, and his wife, Lady Margaret de Holland, both descendants of kings of England and France, and had:

LADY CATHERINE STEWART, who *m.* John, sixth Lord Forbes, son of Lord William, son of Lord James Forbes (son of Sir Alexander Forbes and his wife, Lady Elizabeth, daughter of George Douglas, first Earl of Angus and his wife, Princess Mary, daughter of Robert III., King of Scotland, by his wife, Lady Annabella Drummond) and his wife, Lady Egidia, daughter of William de Keith, Earl Marshal of Scotland, and his wife, Lady Mary, daughter of James, Lord Hamilton, and his wife, Princess Mary, daughter of James II., King of Scotland, by his wife, Lady Mary, daughter of Arnold, Duke of Guilders, and had:

LADY ELIZABETH FORBES, who *m.* (*see* Douglas's "Baronage," p. 341, and Wood's Douglas's "Peerage," i., 592) John Grant, of Grant and Freuchie, and had:

JAMES DE GRANT, of Freuchie, heir, baillie of Kinloss Abbey, 1539, who had by his second wife, Lady Barbara Erskine:

ARCHIBALD GRANT, second son, who *m.* Lady Isabella Comyn, of Erneside, and had:

HELEN GRANT, *d.* 1694, who *m.* Alexander MacDuff, of Keithmore, *d.* 1700, and had:

ELEANOR DUFF, who *m.* William Green, of the bodyguard to William of Orange, and had:

ROBERT GREEN, of Orange (Culpeper) county, Virginia (*see* Slaughter's "St. Mark's Parish"), member of the House of Burgesses, 1695-1747, who *m*. Eleanor Dunn, and had:

NICHOLAS GREEN, of Kentucky, who *m*. Elizabeth, daughter of Ajalon and Joyce (Barbour) Price, of Culpeper, and had:

NICHOLAS GREEN, who had by his wife, Lucy:

ELIZABETH GREEN, who *m*., 1777, Anthony Garrard, of Stafford county, Virginia, *bapt*. 12 February, 1756, in Overwharton parish, *d*. 1807, and had:

JACOB GARRARD, of Wilkes county, Georgia, who *m*., 1813, Martha Newsom Hardin, and had:

WILLIAM WATERS GARRARD, of "Hilton," near Columbus, Georgia, 1818-1866, who *m*., 1843, Frances Isabella Garterey Urquhart, also of Royal Descent, and had, besides other issue:

1.—HELEN AUGUSTA GARRARD, of Atlanta, *b*. 28 August, 1850, a member of the Georgia Society of the Colonial Dames of America, who *m*., 23 April, 1873, Captain John Thomas Glenn, *b*. 21 March, 1844, *d*. 14 March, 1899, also of Royal Descent, an aide-de-camp to his uncle, General Howell Cobb, Confederate States Army, son of Luther J. Glenn. Colonel Confederate States Army, and had, besides other issue:

> ISA GARTEREY URQUHART GLENN, of Atlanta, a member of the Georgia Society of the Colonial Dames of America, the Order of the Crown, the Society Daughters of the American Revolution, *etc*.

2.—EVA MATILDA GARRARD, a member of the Georgia Society of the Colonial Dames of America, who *m*. Humphreys Castleman, of Columbus, also of Royal Descent, and had: *Louis*, and

> MARY ISABELLA GARRARD CASTLEMAN, a member of the Georgia Society of the Colonial Dames of America, who *m*. Samuel Harrison McAfee, of West Point, Georgia.

3.—GERTRUDE KATE GARRARD, a member of the Georgia Society of the Colonial Dames of America, who *m*. James Watson Harris, of Jackson, Mississippi. *Issue*.

PEDIGREE LXVII.

HENRY III., King of England, had by his wife, Lady Eleanor, daughter of Raymond de Berenger, Count of Provence:

EDMUND PLANTAGENET, Earl of Lancaster, *etc.*, lord high steward of England, who had by his second wife, Lady Blanche, widow of Henry I., King of Navarre, and daughter of Robert, Count of Artois, son of Louis VIII., King of France:

HENRY PLANTAGENET, Earl of Lancaster, who *m.* Lady Maud, also of Royal Descent, daughter of Patrick de Chaworth, and had:

LADY JOAN PLANTAGENET, who *m.* John, third Baron de Mowbray, of Axholm, also of Royal Descent, and had:

JOHN DE MOWBRAY, fourth Baron, who had by his wife, Lady Elizabeth, daughter of John, third Baron de Segrave, and his wife, Margaret Plantagenet, Duchess of York, also of Royal Descent:

LADY MARGERY DE MOWBRAY (sister of Thomas, Duke of Norfolk), who *m.* John, second Baron de Welles, and had:

EUDO DE WELLES, eldest son, *d. v. p.*, who *m.* Lady Maud, also of Royal Descent, daughter of Ralph, fifth Baron de Greystock, and had:

SIR LIONEL DE WELLES, sixth Baron, Governor of Ireland, *k.* 1461, whose daughter

LADY CICELY DE WELLES, *m.* Sir Robert Willoughby, a grandson of Sir William, Baron Willoughby de Eresby, and his wife, Lady Lucy le Strange, also of Royal Descent, and had:

SIR CHRISTOPHER WILLOUGHBY, K.B., 1453–1499, who *m.* Lady Margaret, daughter of Sir William Jenney, of Knottishall, Suffolk, and had:

CHIEF JUSTICE SIR THOMAS WILLOUGHBY, will proved 5 November, 1545, who *m.* Lady Bridget, daughter of Sir Robert Reade, of Bore Place, Kent, chief justice, *etc.*, and had:

CHRISTOPHER WILLOUGHBY, will proved 11 January, 1586; *m.* Margery Tottishurst, and had:

CHRISTOPHER WILLOUGHBY, of Chiddingstone, Kent, *d. ante* 1633, who had by his wife, Martha ———:

COLONEL WILLIAM WILLOUGHBY, of London and Portsmouth, an officer in the Parliamentary Army, in the Civil War; commissioner of the Royal Navy, *etc.*, *d.* 1651, who had by his wife, Elizabeth (her will dated in 1662), "who was an Eaton" (*see* "N. E. His. Gen. Reg.," October, 1899):

FRANCIS WILLOUGHBY, who came to New England in 1638; returned to England and was commissioner of the Royal Navy, 1652; member of Parliament, 1659; came to New England again in 1662, and was deputy-governor of Massachusetts Colony, 1665–71 (*see* Salisbury's "Family Histories"). He *m.*, thirdly, about 1659, Mrs. Margaret Taylor, daughter of William Locke, of Merton, county Surry, England, and had by her:

SUSANNAH WILLOUGHBY, 1664–1710, who *m.* (his first wife) Judge Nathaniel Lynde, of Saybrook, Connecticut, 1659–1729, also of Royal Descent, and had:

ELIZABETH LYNDE, 1688–1778, who *m.* Judge Richard Lord, of Lyme, Connecticut, 1690–1776, and had:

CAPTAIN ENOCH LORD, of Lyme, 1726–1814; *m.* Hepzibah Mervin, and had:

RICHARD LORD, of Lyme, 1752–1818; *m.* Ann Mitchell, and had:

SARAH ANN LORD, 1799–1835, who *m.* Judge Charles Johnson McCurdy, LL.D., of Lyme, also of Royal Descent, and had:

EVELYN MCCURDY, only child, a member of the Connecticut Society of the Colonial Dames of America, who *m.* Professor Edward Elbridge Salisbury, of New Haven, Connecticut. *No issue.*

THE ROYAL DESCENT

OF

MRS. WILLIAM WASHINGTON GORDON,

OF SAVANNAH, GA.

EMPEROR CHARLEMAGNE=Hildegarde de Suabia.

Louis I., King of France. — Pepin, King of Italy.

Charles II. **ALFRED THE GREAT.** Bernard, King of Italy.

Louis II. Edward the Elder. Pepin de Peronne.

Charles III.=Egiva, of England. Herbert I. de Vermandois.

Louis IV., King of France. Herbert II. de Vermandois.

Gerberga, Princess of France=Albert I. de Vermandois.

Herbert III. de Vermandois. **HUGH CAPET**, of France.

Otho de Vermandois. Robert I., King of France.

Herbert IV. de Vermandois. Henry I., King of France.

Adelheid de Vermandois=Hugh Magnus, of France.

William, Earl of Surrey=Isabel. **WILLIAM THE CONQUEROR.**

Henry, Earl of Northumberland=Ada. Henry I., King of England.

Humphrey, Earl of Hereford=Margaret. Maud, Empress of Germany.

Henry, Earl of Hereford and Essex. Henry II., King of England.

Humphrey, Earl of Hereford and Essex. John, King of England.

Humphrey de Bohun. Henry III., King of England.

Humphrey, Earl of Hereford and Essex. Edward I., King of England.

Humphrey, Earl of Hereford and Essex=Elizabeth Plantagenet.

Lady Margaret de Bohun=Sir Hugh, Earl of Devon.

Edward Courtenay, of Goderington=Emeline d'Auney, of Modeford.

Sir Hugh Courtenay, of Haccomb=Maud Beaumont, of Shirwill.

Lady Margaret Courtenay=Sir Theobald Grenville, of Stowe.

Sir William Grenville, of Bideford=Philippa Bonville, of Chuton.

Thomas Grenville, of Stowe=Elizabeth Gorges.

Sir Thomas Grenville, of Stowe=Elizabeth Gilbert, of Compton.

Sir Roger Grenville, of Stowe=Margaret Whitleigh, of Efford.

Lady Amy Grenville=John Drake, of Ashe, Devon.

Robert Drake, of Wiscombe, Devon=Elizabeth Prideaux, of Thewboro.

William Drake, of Wiscombe Park=Philippa Dennys, of Holcombe.

John Drake, d. Windsor, Ct., 1659.=Elizabeth Rodgers.

Job Drake, d. Windsor, Ct., 1689=Mary Wolcott.

Job Drake, d. Windsor, Ct., 1171=Elizabeth (Clarke) Cook.

Sarah Drake, 1686-1747=Gen. Roger Wolcott, Gov. of Conn., d. 1767.

Alexander Wolcott, M.D., of New London=Mary Richards (third wife).

Alexander Wolcott, d. Boston, 1828=Frances Burbank.

Frances Wolcott=Arthur W. Magill, of Middletown, Ct.

Juliette A. Magill=John H. Kinzie, d. Chicago, 1870.

Eleanor Lytle Kinzie, vice-president of the National, and president of the Georgia Society of the Colonial Dames of America.=Gen. William Washington Gordon, of Savannah, Georgia. *Issue (see* p. 107).

PEDIGREE LXVIII.

ROBERT II., King of Scotland, had by his first wife, Lady Elizabeth, daughter of Sir Adam Mure, of Rowallan:

LADY CATHERINE STEWART, who m. Sir David Lindsay, of Glenesk, created Earl of Crawford, and had:

ALEXANDER LINDSAY, second Earl of Crawford, who m. Lady Mariotta, only child of Sir David Dunbar, of Cockburn, also of Royal Descent, and had:

SIR WALTER LINDSAY, of Beaufort, third son, who m. (see " Wood's Douglas's Peerage of Scotland," I., 164, 376) Sophia, or Isabella, Livingston, and had:

SIR DAVID LINDSAY, of Edzell and Beaufort, d. 1527, who had by his first wife, Catherine Fotheringham, of Powrie:

WALTER LINDSAY, of Edzell, eldest son, k. v. p. at Flodden, 9 September, 1513, who m. a daughter of Erskine, of Dun, and had:

ALEXANDER LINDSAY (younger brother of Sir David Lindsay, of Edzell, eighth Earl of Crawford), who m. a daughter of Barclay, of Mathers, and had:

RIGHT REV. DAVID LINDSAY, D.D., of Leith, 1531–1613, Bishop of Ross in 1600, Chaplain to King James I., who had by his wife, whose name has not been preserved:

RACHEL LINDSAY, who m. the Most Rev. John Spottiswood, of that Ilk, b. 1565, Archbishop of St. Andrews, in 1615; Lord High Chancellor of Scotland, in 1635. He crowned King Charles I., at Holyrood, in 1639, and dying in London, 2 December, 1639, was buried by the King's command in Westminster Abbey (see Playfair's "British Family Antiquity," VIII., 305). Archbishop Spottiswood had by Rachel, his wife:

SIR ROBERT SPOTTISWOOD, Knt., of New Abbey, Kent, second son, b. 1596 (see the "Spottiswood Miscellany," 1844, Vol. I.). He was a member of the Privy Council to James VI., of Scotland, and was appointed by King Charles I. lord president of the college of justice and secretary for Scotland in 1636. He m., 1629, Lady Bethia, eldest daughter of Sir Alexander Morrison, of Preston Grange, a senator in the college of justice, and his wife, Eleanor Maule, also of Royal Descent, and was executed for political reasons by the Covenanters, 20 January, 1646, having had issue:

ROBERT SPOTTISWOOD, surgeon to the Governor and garrison of Tangier (*see* Campbell's "Spottiswood Genealogy," 1868, and Fontaine's "Spottiswood Genealogy," 1881). He *m.* Catharine Elliott, widow, and dying at Tangier, in 1680, had by her:

MAJOR-GENERAL ALEXANDER SPOTSWOOD,* of "Porto Bello," James City county, Virginia, only son, *b.* at Tangier, 1676, *d.* 7 June, 1740; aide-de-camp to the Duke of Marlborough; arrived in Virginia 20 June, 1710, in the man-o'-war *Deptford;* lieutenant-governor and commander-in-chief of the Virginia colony, *etc.* (*see* Douglas's "Baronage of Scotland," 1798). He *m.*, 1724, —— Butler, daughter of Richard and Ann Brayne, of Westminster (*see* "Virginia Historical Magazine," II., 340), and had:

1.—JOHN SPOTSWOOD, of Virginia, eldest son, *d.* 1759; *m.*, 1745, Mary Dandridge, of "Elsing Green," also of Royal Descent, and had:

    I.—ANN SPOTSWOOD, who *m.* Lewis Burwell, and had:

    SPOTSWOOD BURWELL, who *m.* Mary Marshall, and had:

    MARY ANN SPOTSWOOD BURWELL, who *m.* Otis F. Manson, M.D., and had:

    ELIZA SANGER MANSON, a member of the Virginia Society of the Colonial Dames of America, who *m.* Thomas Lee Alfriend, of Richmond, Virginia, and had:

    1.—MARY BURWELL ALFRIEND, a member of the Virginia Society of the Colonial Dames of America, who *m.* Herbert Dale Lafferty, of Richmond. *No issue.*

    2. OTIS MANSON; 3. SALLY SPOTSWOOD; 4. ANNA LEE.

    II.—CAPTAIN JOHN SPOTSWOOD, who *m.* Sallie Rouze, and had:

    ROBERT SPOTSWOOD, who *m.* Louisa Bott, and had:

    REV. JOHN SPOTSWOOD, D.D., of Petersburg, Virginia, who *m.* Sarah Peters, daughter of William Shippen Willing, of Philadelphia, and had:

    LUCY SPOTSWOOD, *b.* New Castle, Delaware, a member of the Pennsylvania Society of the Colonial Dames of America, who *m.* George Peirce, of Philadelphia.

2.—DOROTHEA SPOTSWOOD, who *m.*, 1747, Colonel Nathaniel West Dandridge, of Virginia, also of Royal Descent, and had:

    I.—MAJOR ALEXANDER SPOTSWOOD DANDRIDGE, of "The Bower," Jefferson county, Virginia, *m.* Ann Stephen, and had:

    ADAM STEPHEN DANDRIDGE, of "The Bower," 1782–1821, *m.*, 1805, Sarah Pendleton, and had:

---

* MISS ANNA SPOTSWOOD DANDRIDGE, a member of the Maryland Society Colonial Dames of America, is also of Royal Descent through Alexander Spotswood.

ALEXANDER SPOTSWOOD DANDRIDGE, M.D., of Cincinnati, Ohio, 1819–1889; *m.*, 1843, Martha, daughter of Colonel Nathaniel Pendleton, of Cincinnati, and had, besides other children:

1.—SUSAN BOWLER DANDRIDGE, a member of the New York Society of the Colonial Dames of America, who *m.* John M. Bowers, of New York City.

2.—MARY EVELYN DANDRIDGE, of Cincinnati, a member of the Virginia Society of the Colonial Dames of America.

II.—DOROTHEA DANDRIDGE, who *m.* (his second wife) Patrick Henry, of "Red Hill," Virginia, first Governor of Virginia, also of Royal Descent, and had:

JOHN HENRY, who *m.* Elvira Bruce McClelland, and had:

WILLIAM WIRT HENRY, of Richmond, Virginia, who *m.* Lucy Gray Marshall, a member of the Virginia Society of the Colonial Dames of America, and had:

1.—LUCY GRAY HENRY, a member of the Virginia Society of the Colonial Dames of America, who *m.* Matthew Bland Harrison, of Richmond, Virginia.

2.—ELIZABETH HENRY, a member of the Virginia Society of the Colonial Dames of America, who *m.* James Lyons, of Richmond, Virginia.

3.—ANN CATHERINE SPOTSWOOD, 1726–1802, who *m.*, 1745, Colonel Bernard Moore, of "Chelsea," King William county, Virginia, and had:

I.—ALEXANDER SPOTSWOOD MOORE, *b.* 1763, who *m.*, 19 July, 1787, Elizabeth, *b.* 1769, daughter of Colonel William Aylett, of "Fairfield," also of Royal Descent, and had:

MILDRED WALKER MOORE, *b.* 17 June, 1788, who *m.*, 17 June, 1806, Rev. John Wilson Campbell, of Virginia, and had:

ELIZABETH CAMPBELL, who *m.* John Maben, of Richmond, and had:

1.—MARY MABEN, a member of the Maryland Society of the Colonial Dames of America, who *m.* Frank Peyton Clark, of Baltimore, and had: *Bessie Campbell* and *William Lawrence*.

2.—JANE MABEN, who *m.* J. Dorsey Cullen, of Richmond, and had:

ELIZABETH CAMPBELL CULLEN, a member of the Virginia Society of the Colonial Dames of America, who *m.* John F. T. Anderson, of Ashland, Hanover county, Virginia.

II.—LUCY MOORE, who *m.*, 1774, Rev. Henry Skyren, of Hampton, Virginia, *b.* at White Haven, England, and had:

ELIZABETH SKYREN, who m. Robert Temple, of "Ampthill" and Fredericksburg, Virginia, and had:

MARY TEMPLE, who m. Thomas Crouch, of Richmond, and had:

ELIZABETH SKYREN CROUCH, who m., 7 July, 1857, Howson Hooe Wallace, of Richmond, Virginia, b. 1 April, 1830, and had:

BESSIE BROWN WALLACE, b. Fredericksburg, 19 February, 1860, a member of the Virginia Society of the Colonial Dames of America, who m. Charles Armistead Blanton, M.D., of Richmond, Virginia, and had: *Wyndham Bolling, Howson Wallace,* and *Elizabeth Skyren.*

III.—BERNARD MOORE, of "Chelsea," m., first, Lucy Ann Heabred Leiper, of Chester county, Pennsylvania, and had by her:

1.—ELIZABETH MOORE, m. Colonel James Macon, and had:

MARY MACON, m. Colonel William Aylett, and had:

COLONEL PHILIP AYLETT, who m. Elizabeth, daughter of Governor Patrick Henry, of Virginia, also of Royal Descent, and had:

MARY MACON AYLETT, who m. Philip Fitzhugh, and had:

LUCY FITZHUGH, who m. John Robertson Redd, of Virginia, and had:

LUCY REDD, a member of the Indiana Society of the Colonial Dames of America, who m. William J. Holliday, of Indianapolis, and had:

I.—ARIANA AMBLER HOLLIDAY, a member of the Indiana Society of the Colonial Dames of America, who m. Henry W. Bennett, of Indianapolis. *Issue.*

II.—JAQUELIN S. HOLLIDAY, m. Florence Baker. *Issue.*

III.—LUCY FITZHUGH HOLLIDAY, m. George E. Hume. *Issue.*

2.—ANDREW LEIPER MOORE, m. Ann Fitzhugh, sister of Governor Thomas Nelson and daughter of Robert Nelson, son of William Nelson and his wife, Elizabeth Burwell, also of Royal Descent, and had:

LUCY HEABRED MOORE, who m. Benjamin Needles Robinson, also of Royal Descent, and had:

ELIZABETH TAYLOR ROBINSON, who m. John Daniel Turner, M.D., and had:

LOUISE BEVERLEY TURNER, a member of the Virginia Society of the Colonial Dames of America, who m. Isaac N. Jones, of Richmond, Virginia, and had: *Bernard Moore.*

PEDIGREE LXIX.

JOHN, King of England, who had by his second wife (*m.* 1200), Lady Isabel, daughter of Aymer de Taillefer, Count of Angueleme:

PRINCESS ELEANOR PLANTAGENET, who *m.* Simon de Montfort, second Earl of Leicester, *k.* 1264, also of Royal Descent, and had:

LADY ELEANOR DE MONTFORT, who *m.* Llewelyn ap Gryffth, Prince of North Wales, and had:

LADY CATHERINE, who *m.* Philip ap Ivor ap Cadivor, and had:

LADY ELEANOR, who *m.* Thomas ap Llewelyn, of Trefgarned, lord of South Wales, also of Royal Descent, and had:

LADY ELEANOR, who *m.* Griffith Vychan IV., lord of Glyndyfrdwy, also of Royal Descent, and had:

TUDOR, lord of Gwyddelwern (brother of the celebrated Owen Glendower), *b.* 1345, *k.* 15 May, 1405, who *m.* Maud v. Ieuf ap Howell ap Adar, and had:

LADY LOWRY, heiress, who *m.* Gruffydd ap Einion, of Cors-y-Gedol, Merionethshire, and had:

ELLISSAU AP GRUFFYDD, *m.* Margaret v. Jenkin ap Ievan, also of Royal Descent, and had:

LOWRY, *m.* Reinaullt ap Gruffydd ap Rhys, of Branas Uchaf, and had:

MARY, *m.* Robert Lloyd ap David Lloyd, of Gwern y Brychdwyn, and had:

THOMAS LLOYD, *b.* 1515–20, *d.* 1612; *m.* Catherine v. Robert ap Griffith, and had:

MARY LLOYD, *m.* Richard, of Tyddyn Tyfod, and had:

RHYS AP RICHARD, who had:

GRIFFYTH AP RHYS, *alias* Griffith Price, who had:

RICHARD PRICE, of Glanlloidiogin, Llanfawr parish, Merionethshire, will dated 26 January, 1685–86, proved in 1686, who had:

HANNAH PRICE, 1656–1741, who *m.* Rees ap John ap William, *d.* 26 May, 1697 (*see* Glenn's "Merion in the Welsh Tract," p. 73). They came from Iscregenan, Merionethshire, bearing a certificate of removal from the Society of Friends, dated 4 April, 1684, to Pennsylvania, and took up land in the "Welsh Tract," near Philadelphia, and had:

LOWRY JONES, 1680–1762, widow of Robert Lloyd, d. at Merion, Pennsylvania, 1714, who m., secondly, 13 February, 1716, at Merion Meeting House (his third wife), Hugh Evans, of Philadelphia, 1682–1772, and had:

SUSANNAH EVANS, b. 25 January, 1719–20, d. 4 July, 1801; m., 30 July, 1740, Owen Jones, b. 19 November, 1711, d. 9 October, 1793, the last provincial treasurer of Pennsylvania, also of Royal Descent, and had:

HANNAH JONES, 1749–1829; m., 1779, Amos Foulke, of Philadelphia, 1740–1791, also of Royal Descent (p. 118), and had:

EDWARD FOULKE, of Gwynedd, Pennsylvania, 1784–1851; m., 1810, Tacy Jones, and had, besides other issue:

1.—ANNE JONES FOULKE, 1811–1888; m., 1833, Hiram Corson, M.D., of Conshohocken, and had:

SUSAN FOULKE CORSON, a member of the Pennsylvania, Society of the Colonial Dames of America, who m., 26 November, 1868, Jawood Lukens, of Conshohocken. *No issue.*

2.—PRISCILLA FOULKE, 1821–1882; m., 1849, Thomas Wistar, Jr., of Philadelphia, and had:

SUSAN FOULKE WISTAR, a member of the Pennsylvania Society of the Colonial Dames of America, who m., 27 May, 1872, Howard Comfort, of Philadelphia, and had: *William Wistar, b.* 27 May, 1874.

3.—REBECCA JONES FOULKE, b. 18 May, 1829, a member of the Pennsylvania Society of the Colonial Dames of America, who m., 8 October, 1857, Robert R. Corson, of New Hope, Pennsylvania. *No issue.*

PEDIGREE LXX.

EDWARD I., King of England, had by his first wife, Princess Eleanor, daughter of Ferdinand III., King of Castile and Leon:

PRINCESS JOAN PLANTAGENET, who had by her first husband, Gilbert de Clare, Earl of Hertford and Gloucester:

LADY MARGARET DE CLARE, who had by her second husband, Hugh d'Audley, first Earl of Gloucester:

LADY MARGARET D'AUDLEY, who *m.* Sir Ralph, second Baron de Stafford, K.G., first Earl of Stafford, and had:

SIR HUGH DE STAFFORD, K.G., second Earl of Stafford, who *m.* Lady Philippa, daughter of Sir Thomas de Beauchamp, K.G., Earl of Warwick, also of Royal Descent, and had:

LADY MARGARET DE STAFFORD, who *m.* (his first wife) Sir Ralph Neville, K.G., first Earl of Westmoreland, earl marshal of England, also of Royal Descent, and had:

LADY ALICE DE NEVILLE, who *m.* Sir Thomas de Grey, of Heton, beheaded 5 August, 1415, also of Royal Descent, and had:

LADY ELIZABETH DE GREY, who *m.* Sir Philip d'Arcy, fourth Baron d'Arcy, Admiral of the Royal Navy, also of Royal Descent, and had:

JOHN D'ARCY, fifth Baron d'Arcy, who *m.* Lady Margaret, daughter of Sir Henry, fifth Baron de Grey, of Wilton, also of Royal Descent, and had:

PHILIP D'ARCY, sixth Baron d'Arcy, *m.* Lady Eleanor, daughter of Henry, fourth Baron Fitzhugh, also of Royal Descent, and had:

LADY MARGERY D'ARCY, who *m.* Sir John Coniers, K.G., of Hornby, and had:

LADY ELEANOR CONIERS, who *m.* Sir Thomas de Markenfield, will dated 8 April, 1497, and had:

SIR NYAN MARKENFIELD, who *m.* Lady Dorothy, daughter of Sir William Gascoigne, *d.* 4 March, 1486, also of Royal Descent, and had:

LADY ALICE MARKENFIELD, who *m.*, 16 October, 1524, Robert Mauleverer, of Worthersome, York, also of Royal Descent, and had:

DOROTHY MAULEVERER, who *m.*, 1542, John Kaye, of Woodersome, Yorkshire, and had:

EDWARD KAYE, of Woodersome, *m.* Anne, daughter of Robert Tirwhitt, of Ketelby, Lincolnshire, and had:

PEDIGREE LXX.—Continued.

LUCIA KAYE, who m. John Pickering, of Techmersh, Northamptonshire, and had:

ELIZABETH PICKERING, who m. Robert Throckmorton, of Ellington, Huntingdonshire (see "The Magna Charta Barons and their American Descendants," p. 199), and had:

GABRIEL THROCKMORTON, of Ellington, 1577–1626, m. Alice, daughter of William Bedles, of Bedfordshire, and had:

ROBERT THROCKMORTON, of Ellington, 1608–1662, will proved at London, 21 June, 1664; m. Judith Bromsall, and had:

JOHN THROCKMORTON, of Ellington, 1633–1678, m. ―――― Mason, and had:

GABRIEL THROCKMORTON, second son, b. 1665. He came to Virginia before 1684, and inherited under will of his brother Robert, of Peyton Pawa, Huntingdonshire, proved 3 May, 1699, a plantation in New Kent County, Virginia. He was the presiding justice of Gloucester county, Virginia, and dying in January, 1737, had by his wife, m. in 1690, Frances, daughter of Mordecai Cooke, of "Mordecai's Mount," Gloucester county, Virginia:

MAJOR ROBERT THROCKMORTON, of Ware parish, Gloucester county, Virginia, who m., first, 14 August, 1730, Mary Lewis, also of Royal Descent, and had:

ROBERT THROCKMORTON, of Culpeper county, Virginia, b. 20 November, 1736, who m., 16 June, 175–, Lucy, daughter of Captain Mordecai Throckmorton (brother of the aforesaid Major Robert Throckmorton), 1696–1767, high sheriff of King and Queen county, Virginia, 1740, and his wife, Mary Reade, also of Royal Descent, and had:

FRANCES THROCKMORTON, m. General William Madison, and had:

REBECCA CONWAY MADISON, m. Reynolds Chapman, and had:

JUDGE JOHN MADISON CHAPMAN, m. Susannah Digges Cole, also of Royal Descent, and had:

1.—SUSIE ASHTON CHAPMAN, a member of the Tennessee Society of the Colonial Dames of America, who m. Calvin Perkins, of Memphis. *Issue.*

2.—BELLE CHAPMAN, a member of the Virginia Society of the Colonial Dames of America, who m. William Moncure, of Richmond, Virginia. *Issue.*

3.—ASHTON ALEXANDER CHAPMAN.

PEDIGREE LXXI.

RHYS AP TEWDWR, Prince of South Wales, who was defeated and slain by the Normans, *temp.* William Rufus, had by his wife, Lady Gwenllian, daughter of **Gruffydd ap Cynan, Prince of North Wales**:

PRINCESS ELIZABETH, who *m.* Edmund, Baron Carew, and had:

SIR EDGAR DE CAREW, Baron of Carew, or Cayrowe, who had:

JOHN (ST. ANDREW) DE CAREW, Baron of Carew, who had:

ANNE (NESTA) DE CAREW, who *m.* Thomas Awbrey, son of William Awbrey, of Aberkynfrig and Slough, Brecknockshire, a descendant of Stiant Awbrey, brother of Baron de Awbrey, Earl of Bullen and Earl Marshal of France, 1066, and had:

THOMAS AWBREY, of Aberkynfrig, constable and ranger of the forest of Brecon, who *m.* Johan, daughter of Trahaerne ap Einion, lord of Comond, and had:

THOMAS AWBREY-GÔCH, of Aberkynfrig, who *m.* Nesta, daughter of Owen Gethyn, of Glyn Taway, and had:

RICHARD AWBREY, of Aberkynfrig, who *m.* Creislie, daughter of Philip ap Elidor (or Phe ap Eledr), and had:

GWALTER (WALTER) AWBREY, of Aberkynfrig, who *m.* Johan, daughter of Rees Morgan ap Einion, of Carmarthen, and had:

MORGAN AWBREY, of Aberkynfrig, who *m.* Alice, daughter of Watkin Thomas ap David Lloyd, and had:

JENKIN AWBREY, of Aberkynfrig, who *m.* Gwenlliam, daughter of Owain ap Griffith, of Tal y Llyn, and had:

HOPKIN AWBREY, of Aberkynfrig, who *m.* Anne, daughter of John ap Griffith, of Gwyn, and had:

WILLIAM AWBREY, of Aberkynfrig, *d.* 27 June, 1547; *m.*, secondly, Jane, widow of Thomas Lloyd, and daughter of Sir Richard Herbert, Knt., of Montgomery Castle, a gentleman usher to Henry VIII., by his second wife, Jane, daughter of Gwilim ap Rees Phillip, of Llwynhowell, and had by her:

RICHARD AWBREY, of Aberkynfrig, eldest son, *d.* 1580, who sold his paternal estate. He *m.* Margaret, daughter of Thomas Gunter, of Gileston, and had:

RICHARD AWBREY, of Llanelyw, *d.* 23 September, 1646, buried in the church of Llanelyw; a stone recites his wife's parentage and children; he m. Anne, daughter of William Vaughan, of Llanelyw, and had:

THOMAS AWBREY, third son, who had:

WILLIAM AWBREY, of Llanelyw, Brecknock, b. 1626, d. 16 December, 1716, buried in the church; a stone recites his parentage, marriage and issue. He m., 1646, his cousin, Elizabeth, daughter of William, eldest son of Richard Awbrey, d. 1646, aforesaid, and obtained the Llanelyw estate, and had:

MARTHA AWBREY,* b. ante 1662, d. 7 February, 1726-7, who joined the Society of Friends, and, "being engaged to be married to one Rees Thomas, who had gone to Pennsylvania, accompanied by her relatives, John and Barbara Bevan, of Treverigg, Glamorganshire, to Philadelphia," was m., 18 April, 1692, at Haverford Meeting, Pennsylvania, to the said Rees Thomas, who became a justice of the peace and member of the assembly; will proved 12 February, 1742-3 (see Glenn's "Merion in the Welsh Tract," p. 305, etc.), and had:

WILLIAM THOMAS, m., 12 May, 1724, Elizabeth Harry, and had:

REES THOMAS, m., 13 November, 1758, Priscilla Jerman, and had:

WILLIAM THOMAS, m., 5 April, 1786, Naomi Walker, and had:

REES THOMAS, m., 29 March, 1810, Rebecca Brooke, and had:

WILLIAM B. THOMAS, m., 22 January, 1836, Emily W. Holstein, and had:

1.—ANNA ELIZABETH THOMAS, a member of the Pennsylvania Society of the Colonial Dames of America, who m., 3 February, 1858, Nathan Brooke, of Media, Pennsylvania, d. 1888, and had:

    I.—WILLIAM THOMAS BROOKE, m., 11 May, 1881, Rebecca Chapman, and had: *Ida Lewis, Josephine Atmore,* and *Gertrude Chapman.*

    II.—IDA LONGMIRE BROOKE, m., 14 December, 1881, J. Howard Lewis, Jr., and had: *John Crozer, Sarah Fallon, Helen Brooke, Emily Thomas,* and *Mildred Irwin.*

    III.—HUGH JONES BROOKE, m., 25 April, 1893, Harriet Boyer Weand.

    IV.—HUNTER, JR.; V. EMILY THOMAS.

2.—MARY A. THOMAS, a member of the Pennsylvania Society of the Colonial Dames of America, who m., 25 February, 1874, Hunter Brooke, of Philadelphia, and had: *Helen* and *Marie Thomas.*

---

* * The following ladies, members of the National Society of the Colonial Dames of America, are also of Royal Descent through Martha Awbrey:

MRS. CHARLES RICHARDSON, Pennsylvania State Society.
MRS. GEORGE B. ROBERTS, Pennsylvania State Society.
MRS. HENRY K. DILLARD, Pennsylvania State Society.
MISS MARY WILLIAM PEROT, Pennsylvania State Society.

3.—REBECCA BROOKE THOMAS, a member of the Pennsylvania Society of the Colonial Dames of America, who m., 20 November, 1867, George Hamilton Colket, of St. Davids, Pennsylvania, and had:

I.—EMILY THOMAS COLKET, m., 30 October, 1889, Harrison Koons Caner, and had: *Harrison Koons, George Colket, William John,* and *Gerald Wayne.*

II.—MARY WALKER; III. TRISTRAM COFFIN; IV. GEORGE H.

PEDIGREE LXXII.

ROBERT BRUCE, King of Scotland, had by his second wife, Lady Elizabeth de Burgh, of Royal Descent:

LADY MATILDA BRUCE, who m. Thomas Isaac, Esquire, and had:

JOANNA ISAAC, who m. John d' Ergadia, lord of Lorn, and had:

ISABEL D' ERGADIA, who m. Sir John Stewart, lord of Innermeth, and had:

ROBERT STEWART, created, in 1439, Lord Lorn and Innermeth, who m. Lady Margaret, daughter of Robert Stewart, Duke of Albany, son of **Robert II., King of Scotland,** and had:

LADY MARGARET STEWART, who m. Robert, eighth Lord Erskine, d. 1453, also of Royal Descent, and had:

LADY MARGARET ERSKINE, who m., *ante* 1457, James Rutherford, of Edgarston, son of James Rutherford, of Lethbertshiels, and had:

THOMAS RUTHERFORD, of Edgarston, who had:

ROBERT RUTHERFORD, of Edgarston, who had:

THOMAS RUTHERFORD, of Edgarston, who had:

RICHARD RUTHERFORD, of Edgarston, who had by his wife, a granddaughter of the laird of Buccleugh:

ROBERT RUTHERFORD, of Edgarston, who m. Margaret, daughter of Andrew Riddle, of that Ilk, and his wife Violet, daughter of William Douglas, of Pompherston (*see* Douglas's " Baronage of Scotland "), and had by her:

JOHN RUTHERFORD, of Edgarston, who m. Barbara Abernethy, daughter of the Bishop of Caithness, and had by her:

THOMAS RUTHERFORD, of Edgarston, who, dying in 1720, had issue by his wife, Susannah, daughter of Riddle, of Minto:

SIR JOHN RUTHERFORD, Knt., who m., 1710, Elizabeth Cairncross, of Colmslie, and had by her nineteen children, of whom:

WALTER RUTHERFURD, captain in 62d Foot, English Army, who m., first, Catherine, daughter of James Alexander, of New York, also of Royal Descent, and had:

JOHN RUTHERFURD, of Edgarston, New Jersey, b. 1760, d. 23 February, 1840; Presidential elector and United States Senator from New Jersey, 1791-98. He m., 1781, Magdalena, daughter of General Lewis Morris, chief justice and Governor of New Jersey, a member of the Continental Congress, and a signer of the Declaration of Independence, and had:

ROBERT WALTER RUTHERFURD, of New York, 1778–1851, who *m.* his cousin, Sabina E., daughter of Colonel Lewis Morris, Jr., and had:

JOHN RUTHERFURD, of New York, *d.* 1871; *m.* Charlotte, daughter of James Kane Livingston, of New York, and had:

1. HELENA RUTHERFURD, a member of the New York Society of the Colonial Dames of America, who *m.* Alfred Ely, of Newton, Massachusetts, and New York City.

2. LIVINGSTON RUTHERFURD.

3. ARTHUR ELLIOTT RUTHERFURD.

4. MORRIS RUTHERFURD.

PEDIGREE LXXIII.

CONN CEADCATHA ("Conn of the Hundred Battles"), **King of all Ireland**, A.D., 123–157, had:

LADY SABINA, who m., secondly, Olioll Olum, first king of United Munster, and had:

CIAN, third son, founder of Clan Cian in Ormond, the chief family of the Sept being O'Cearbhaill, anglicized O'Carroll. Cian's descendant (see O'Hart's "Irish Pedigrees," third edition, 107):

EILE RIGH DHEARG, or "Eile the red," after whom the territory possessed by the O'Carrolls in Leinster was called Duiche Eiligh, or Ele, "the estates of Ely," whereof his posterity were styled kings, then princes, and finally chiefs and barons. The fourteenth son and heir from him was:

MONACH O'CARROLL, who was the first to use this surname. His descendant and heir in the eighth generation was:

FIONN II., "King of Ely," k. in 1205, who had:

TEIGE O'CARROLL, chief of Ely, who had:

DONAL, who had:

DONOUGH DHEARG, d. 1306, who had:

WILLIAM ALAINN, who had:

DONOUGH, d. 1377 (these were chieftains of Ely), who had:

RODERIC, of Ely, who had:

DANIEL [who had: *Roderic*, who had: *Donough*], who had (according to O'Clery's "Linea Antiqua"):

TEIGE COACH, of Litterlouna, created "lord baron of Ely" in 1552, d. 1554, who had:

DONOUGH (whose brother Roger succeeded to Ely), who had:

DANIEL, of Litterlouna, who had:

ANTHONY, of Litterlouna, who had:

DANIEL O'CARROLL, of Litterlouna, Kings county, who had (besides possibly *Anthony*, of Lishlenboy, County Tipperary, will proved 1724, to whose son, Captain James Carroll, of Lord Dongan's Regiment of Dragoons, Daniel Carroll, of Rock Creek, wrote an interesting genealogical letter about their relations in America, 20 December, 1762, preserved in the Catholic archives at Notre Dame, Indiana):

CHARLES CARROLL,* of Litterlouna and the Inner Temple, London, who arrived in Maryland, 1 October, 1688, and received large grants of land in the Province, was a magistrate, register of the land office, agent and receiver general of rents, for the Calverts. He was commissioned attorney-general 18 July, 1688. He m. Mary Darnall, and had:

1.—DANIEL CARROLL, of "Duddington," who had by his wife, Anne Rosier:

I.—ELIZABETH CARROLL, m. Daniel Carroll, of Rock Creek, Upper Marlboro, Maryland, 1762, also of Royal Descent, and had:

DANIEL CARROLL, b. 1752, m. Eleanor Digges, and had:

WILLIAM CARROLL, m. Henrietta Maria Williamson, and had:

DAVID WILLIAMSON CARROLL, m. Melanie Scull, and had:

MELANIE CARROLL, a member of the Maryland Society of the Colonial Dames of America, who m. Daniel A. Boone, of Baltimore, and had: *Carroll J., d.; William C., R. Sanchez, Charles Louis, Melanie,* wife of Ferdinand C. Dugan; *Clara,* and *Ellen Theresa.*

II.—CHARLES CARROLL, who had by his second wife, Ann Sprigg:

WILLIAM THOMAS CARROLL, who m., 14 October, 1828, Sally Sprigg, and had:

ALIDA CATHERINE CARROLL, who m., in Washington, District of Columbia, 18 December, 1866, John Marshall Brown, of Portland, Maine, and had:

SALLY CARROLL BROWN, a member of the Maryland Society of the Colonial Dames of America, who m., 5 April, 1893, Herbert Payson, of Portland, Maine, and had: *Alida,* b. 27 January, 1895; *Anne Carroll,* b. 14 October, 1896; *John Brown,* b. 1 October, 1897, and *Charles Shipman,* b. 16 October, 1898.

2.—CHARLES CARROLL, of "Doughoregan Manor," Howard county, Maryland, 1702–1782, attorney-general of Maryland, m. Elizabeth Brooke, and had:

CHARLES CARROLL of "Carrollton," 1737–1832, a member of the Continental Congress and a signer of the Declaration of Independence, United States Senator, *etc.; m.,* 1768, Mary, daughter of Henry Darnall, Jr., and had:

COLONEL CHARLES CARROLL of "Carrollton," only son, d. 1861, who m., 1799, Harriet, d. 1861, daughter of Benjamin Chew, of Philadelphia, chief justice of Pennsylvania, and had:

---

* The following ladies, members of the National Society of the Colonial Dames of America, are also of Royal Descent through Charles Carroll:

MRS. OUTERBRIDGE HORSEY (deceased), Maryland State Society.

MRS. RICHARD S. HILL, Maryland State Society.

MARY SOPHIA CARROLL, 1804–1886, who *m.* Richard Henry Bayard, *d.*, Philadelphia, 1868, United States Senator from Delaware, son of James A. Bayard, United States Senator from Delaware, and his wife Ann, daughter of Richard Bassett, Governor of Delaware, and brother of James A. Bayard, Jr., United States Senator from Delaware, and had :

I.—CAROLINE BAYARD, who *m.* Henry Baring Powel, of Philadelphia, *d.* 1852, and had :

MARY DE VAUX POWEL, a member of the Society of the Colonial Dames of America, who *m.* Rev. George Woolsey Hodge, of Philadelphia. *Issue.*

II.—RICHARD BASSETT BAYARD, of Baltimore, *d.* 1878, *m.*, 1860, his cousin, Ellen Gilmor Howard, and had : *Richard H.*, and

ELLEN HOWARD BAYARD, of Baltimore, a member of the Maryland Society of the Colonial Dames of America.

THE ROYAL DESCENT

OF

MRS. PHILIP H. COOPER,

OF MORRISTOWN, NEW JERSEY.

HUGH CAPET, King of France = Adela, dau. William, Duke of Aquitaine.

Robert I., the Pious, King of France = Lady Constance of Provence.

Princess Havide or Hedewige = Rynerius IV., Count of Hainault.

Henry I., King of France = Lady Anne of Russia.

Lady Beatrix = Eblo de Rouci.

Hugh Magnus, Duke of France = Lady Adelheid of Vermandois.

Countess Adela = Hildwin de Montdider.

Lady Margaret de Rouci = Hugh de Clermont.

William de Warren, Earl of Surrey = Lady Isabel de Vermandois = Robert de Bellomont, Earl of Leicester.

Lady Adeliza de Clermont = Gilbert de Tonsburg, Earl of Clare.

William de Warren, Earl of Surrey = Lady Alice de Talvas, also of Royal Descent.

Lady Elizabeth de Bellomont = Gilbert de Clare, Earl of Pembroke.

Lady Isabella de Warren = Hameline Plantagenet, Earl of Surrey.

Richard "the Strongbow," 2d Earl of Pembroke = Eva, dau. Dermot, King of Leinster.

Lady Isabella de Warren = Roger Bigod, Earl of Norfolk.

Lady Isabel de Clare = William le Marshal, Protector of England.

Hugh Bigod, second Earl of Norfolk = Lady Maud Marshall.

Sir Hugh Bigod, Justiciary of England = Joan, dau. of Robert Burnet.

Sir John Bigod, Knt. = (Name unknown.)

Sir Roger Bigod, of Settington = (Name unknown.)

Lady Joan Bigod = Sir William de Chauncy, of Skirpenbeck.

John Chauncy, of Stepney = Margaret Gifford, of Gedleston.

John Chauncy, of Sawbridgeworth = Anne Leventhorp, of Shingey.

John Chauncy, of Sawbridgeworth = Daughter of Thomas Boyce.

John Chauncy, of Pishobury = Elizabeth (Proffit) Mansfield.

Henry Chauncy, of Newplace Giffords = Lucy ———.

George Chauncy, of Yardleybury = Anne Welsh, of Great Wymondley.

Rev. Charles Chauncy, D.D., 1592-1671, second President of Harvard College = Catherine Eyre, of New Sarum.

Sarah Chauncy, 1631-1699 = Rev. Gershom Bulkeley, 1636-1713.

Rev. John Bulkeley, of Colchester, Conn. = Patience Prentice, of New London, Conn.

Gershom Bulkeley = Abigail Robbins.

Patience Bulkeley = Ichabod Lord.

Sarah Bulkeley = John Taintor.

Abigail Lord = Enos Hosford.

John Taintor, of Windham, Conn. = Sarah Hosford.

Sarah Taintor, 1787-1827 = Israel Foote, of New York, 1783-1871.

John Taintor Foote, of Morristown, N. J. = Jordena Cannon Harris.

Katharine Jordena Foote, member of the National Society of the Colonial Dames of America = Philip H. Cooper, Captain in the United States Navy.

Dorothy B. Cooper, b. 9 March, 1889.

Leslie B. Cooper, b. 24 March, 1894.

PEDIGREE LXXIV.

ALFRED THE GREAT, King of England, had by his wife, Lady Elswitha, daughter of Ethelan the Great, Earl of Mercia:

EDWARD THE ELDER, King of England, who had by his third wife, Lady Egiva, daughter of the Saxon Earl, Sigelline:

PRINCESS EGIVA, who *m.*, first (his second wife), Charles III., King of France, a lineal descendant of the Emperor Charlemagne, and had:

LOUIS IV., King of France, who *m.* Lady Gerberga de Saxe, daughter of Henry I., Emperor of Germany, and widow of Giselbert I., Duke of Lorraine, and had:

PRINCESS MATHILDE (or "Mahaut de France"), who *m.* Conrad le Pacifique, King of Arles, and had:

LADY BERTHA, who *m.* Eudes I., second Count of Blois, son of Thibaut I., Count of Blois, and his wife, Lady Leutgarde (widow of William, *Lougue Epee*, Duke of Normandy (*see* "L'Art," xiii., p. 6), daughter of Herbert II., Count de Vermandois, a lineal descendant of the Emperor Charlemagne (*see* p. 163), and had:

EUDES II., fourth Count de Blois and Champagne, second son, who had by his second wife, Lady Ermengarde, daughter of Robert, first Count d'Auvergne:

LADY BERTHE DE BLOIS, who *m.*, first, Alain III., Duke of Bretagne, *d.* 1 October, 1040, eldest son of Geoffroi I., Duke of Bretagne, *d.* 1008, and his wife, Lady Havois, or Hawiga, daughter of Richard I., Duke of Normandy, and his second wife, Lady Gonnor (*see* Anderson's "Royal Genealogies"), and had:

LADY HAVOIS DE BRETAGNE, who *m.* ("L'Art," xiii., 202), Hoel V., Duke of Bretagne, *d.* 13 April, 1084, and had:

ALAIN, Duke of Bretagne, *d.* 13 October, 1119, who had by his second wife (*see* "L'Art," xiii., 62), Lady Ermengarde, the divorced wife of William IX., Duke of Aquitaine, and daughter of Foulques IV., Count d'Anjou:

CONAN III., Duke of Bretagne, Prince of Rennes and Nantes, *d.* 17 September, 1148, who had by his wife, Lady Mathilde (*see* "L'Art," xiii., 203):

LADY BERTHA DE BRETAGNE, only child, who *m.*, first (*see* "L'Art," xiii., 249), Alain II., Count de Penthievre, Duke of Bretagne, and fourth

Earl of Richmond (*see* Dugdale's "Baronage," and "L'Art," xiii., 205, 247), and had:

LADY CONSTANCE DE BRETAGNE (sister of Conan IV., Duke of Bretagne and Earl of Richmond, *d.* 1171, who *m.* Margaret, sister of William, King of Scots, and had *Constance*, only child, who *m.*, first, Geoffroi, son of Henry II., of England, who *m.*, after 1160, Alain III., Viscount de Rohan (*see* "L'Art," xiii., 206, 273, and "Dictionnaire de la Noblesse"), and had:

ALAIN IV., Viscount de Rohan, Count of Brittainy, feudal Baron le Zouche, of Ashby, who *m.* (*see* "L'Art," xiii., 274) Lady Mabilla, daughter of Raoul II., lord of Fougeres, a crusader, *d.* 1196 (*see* the authorities and particulars for this genealogy cited in "L'Art de Verifier les Dates des Faits Historiques"), and had:

ROGER LE ZOUCHE, feudal Baron le Zouche, of Ashby (*see* Nicolas's "Historic Peerage"), father of

ROGER LE ZOUCHE, feudal Baron le Zouche, of Ashby (brother of Williom, Baron le Zouche, *d.* 1199, who in confirming grants made by his father to the Abbey of St. Segius, in Anjou, in a deed to the monks of Swaverey, in Cambridgeshire, calls Roger le Zonche his father, and Alan le Zouche, Earl of Brittany, his grandfather (Burke's "Extinct Peerages"). Roger le Zouche was an adherent of King John, and for his fidelity received the gift of many manors of the rebel barons, and was sheriff of Devonshire in 1229. He had by his wife, Lady Margaret:

LADY ALICE LE ZOUCHE, who *m.* (*see* Dugdale's "Baronage," 1675) Sir William Harcourt, of Stanton-Harcourt, Oxford, and had:

LADY ARABELLA HARCOURT (widow of Sir Fluke Pembrugge), who *m.*, secondly, Sir John de Digby, *d.* 1267, both buried at Tilton (*see* Nichol's "Leicestershire," iii., Pt. I., 471–72, and Salisbury's "Genealogies"), and had:

JOHN DE DIGBY, of Tilton, Leicestershire (*see* Leland's "Itinerary," iii., Pt. I., 462), eldest son, had by his wife, Margaret (Wake?):

JOHN DE DIGBY, second son, who *m.* Elizabeth, daughter of William d'Oseville, and had:

ROBERT DE DIGBY, of Tilton, only son, *d.* before 1412; *m.* Catherine, daughter of Simon de Pakeman, in Leicestershire, and had:

SIMON DE DIGBY, of Tilton and of Drystoke, Rutlandshire, eldest son, *d.* before 1440; *m.* Jean, daughter of Sir James Beler, or Bellaire, of Kirby Bellers, Leicestershire, and had:

SIR EVERARD DE DIGBY, of Drystroke, eldest son, high sheriff of Rutlandshire, 1459; member of Parliament, 1446; *k.* at Towton, with his three brothers, 29 March, 1461 (*see* Nichol's "Leicestershire," iii., Pt. I., p. 463, and Hutchins' "Dorsetshire," iii. 475); *m.* Anne, daughter of Sir Francis Clarke, of Whyssendom, Rutland, and had:

EVERARD DE DIGBY, of Tilton, eldest son, high sheriff of Rutland, 1459, *etc.*; member of Parliament for Rutland; buried at Tilton; will proved 12 February, 1508-9. He *m*. Jacquetta, *d*. 29 June, 1496, buried at Drystoke, daughter of Sir John Elys (*see* Nichols' "Topog. et Geneal.," iii., 284), and had:

SIR JOHN DE DIGBY, of Eye Kettleby, Leicestershire, third son, high sheriff of Rutland, 1491, *etc.*, and Warwick and Leicestershire, 1515; knighted on Bosworth Field by Henry VII., and appointed knight-marshal to the King and captain of Calais (*see* Leland's "Itinerary," iv., 19); will dated 1 August, 1529, was proved 30 October, 1546, but his epitaph at Melton states he *d*. in 1533 (*see* Hutchins' "Dorset," iv., 475). He *m*., first, Catherine, daughter of Nicholas (or John) Griffin, of Brabrooke, Northamptonshire (*see* Warwickshire "Visitations," 1619), and had by her, who *d*. before 1517:

WILLIAM DIGBY, of Kettleby, eldest son, *d. ante* 1 August, 1529, who had by his first wife, Rose, daughter of William Perwich, or Prestwith, of Luffenham (*see* Leicestershire "Visitations," 1619, and Salisbury's "Genealogies," vol. i., Pt. 2, pp. 438-445, and authorities there cited):

SIMON DIGBY, of Beadale, Rutland, who was attainted and executed for being a rebel in March, 1570 (*see* "Calendar of Eng. State Papers," Dom. ser., addenda). He *m*. Anne, daughter of Reginald Grey, and had:

EVERARD DIGBY, second son, who *m*. Catherine, daughter of Magistri Stockbridge de van der Shaff, Theodor de Newkirk, and had:

ELIZABETH DIGBY,* only child, 1584-1669. She was educated a Protestant in Holland in her mother's family, and *m*., at St. John's, Hackney, London, 25 October, 1614, Enoch Lynde, of St. Andrew's parish, Hubbard, London, *d*. 23 April, 1636 (letters to administer his estate granted to his widow, 7 October, 1637), and had:

JUDGE SIMON LYNDE, of Boston, Massachusetts, third son, *bapt*. at St. Andrew's, June, 1624, *d*. 22 November, 1687; came to Boston in 1650 (*see* Salisbury's "Genealogies" and the "Lynde Diaries"), and *m*., February, 1652-53, Hannah, *b*. 28 June, 1635, *d*. 20 December, 1684,

---

* The genealogy of "the renowned family of Digby," preserved at Sherbourne Castle, Dorsetshire, was prepared from the Digby archives by the order Sir Kenelm Digby, at a cost of $6000. It is a folio volume of 589 vellum leaves, the first 165 ornamented with the illuminated coats of arms, and crests of the family and its allies. It contains also sketches of family monuments, and memorial windows and portraits, besides transcripts of family wills, grants, patents, deeds, *etc.*; funeral entries, marriage and baptismal records, *etc.*; to illustrate and prove the history of this distinguished family. The genealogy of the Lynde and allied families was compiled and printed in seven large volumes, by Professor and Mrs. Salisbury, of New Haven, at a cost of $22,000.

daughter of John Newgate, or Newdigate, *d.* 4 September, 1665, aged 84 years, and had:

I.—JUDGE SAMUEL LYNDE, of Boston, Massachusetts, *b.* 1 December, 1653, *d.* October, 1721; *m.*, 20 October, 1674, Mary, 1657–1697, daughter of Jarvis Ballord, of Boston, and had:

MARY LYNDE, *b.* 16 November, 1680, *d.* 26 March, 1732; *m.*, 6 April, 1702, John Valentine, of Boston, *d.* 1742, advocate-general of the province of Massachusetts Bay and New Hampshire and Rhode Island, and had:

THOMAS VALENTINE, of Hopkinton, Massachusetts, *b.* 3 August, 1713, *d.* 17 April, 1783; *m.*, 17 July, 1735, Elizabeth, daughter of James Gooche and his wife Elizabeth, daughter of Sir Charles Hobby, Knt., of Boston, and had:

I.—ELIZABETH VALENTINE, *b.* 18 May, 1739, *d.* 26 March, 1807; *m.* Zaccheus Ballord, *b.* 21 March, 1731, *d.*, at Thompson, Connecticut, 1800, and had:

LYNDE BALLORD, of Thompson, *b.* 15 May, 1774, *d.* 7 June, 1825; *m.*, 4 December, 1794, Polly, 1777–1816, daughter of John and Chloe (Fuller) Bates, and had:

REV. JOHN BATES BALLORD, *b.* 25 October, 1795, *d.* New York, 29 January, 1856; *m.*, 28 May, 1824, Augusta Maria Gilman, *b.* Gilmanton, New Hampshire, 26 June, 1804, *d.* 17 May, 1890, at Colchester, Connecticut, and had:

ESEK STEERE BALLORD, of Davenport, Iowa, *b.* Bloomfield, Connecticut, 26 July, 1830, a founder of the Order of Runnemede; *m.*, 4 September, 1862, Frances A. Webb, and had, besides other issue (*see* " The Magna Charta Barons and Their American Descendants "):

KATHARINE AUGUSTA BALLORD, *b.* 5 August, 1864, a member of the Iowa Society of the Colonial Dames of America, who *m.*, 26 June, 1888, Leon M. Allen, of Davenport, Iowa, and had: *Leon Ballord, b.* 9 January, 1891; *Frances Priscilla, b.* 17 April, 1894, and *Allerton, b.* 6 February, 1898.

II.—SAMUEL VALENTINE, of Hopkinton, *b.* 7 December, 1745, *d.* 10 March, 1834; *m.*, 17 December, 1771, Elizabeth, daughter of Colonel John and Hannah (Simpson) Jones, and had:

1.—SAMUEL VALENTINE, JR., of Hopkinton, *b.* 14 February, 1773, *d.* 19 February, 1823; *m.*, secondly, January 1, 1809, Mary, *b.* 29 January, 1783, *d.* 13 August 1861, daughter of Captain Richard Fiske, of Framingham, Massachusetts, *b.* 25 February, 1750, *d.* 9 January, 1824, and had by her:

ELIZA FISKE VALENTINE, b. Hopkinton, 10 November, 1813, a member of the Massachusetts and Michigan Societies of the Colonial Dames of America, the Order of the Crown, *etc.*, who *m.* Benjamin Stow Farnsworth, of Boston, Massachusetts, b. 9 August, 1804, d. at Detroit, 30 November, 1893, and had:

I.—HARRIET ELIZA PRESCOTT FARNSWORTH, of Detroit, a member of the Massachusetts and Michigan Societies of the Colonial Dames of America, the Order of the Crown, *etc.*

II.—HENRIETTA LYNDE FARNSWORTH, of Detroit, a member of the Massachusetts and Michigan Societies of the Colonial Dames of America, *etc.*, and founder of the Order of the Crown.

III.—MARY SUSAN FARNSWORTH, a member of the Order of the Crown, *m.* 14 February, 1867, William Wirt Smith, of Chicago, and had:

EDNA VALENTINE SMITH, a member of the Order of the Crown.

2.—COLONEL JOSEPH VALENTINE, of Hopkinton, b. 18 November, 1776, d. 26 March, 1845; *m.*, first, Fanny Haven, d. 1841, and had:

HARRIET JONES VALENTINE, 1800–1870; *m.*, first, 1806, Abraham Harrington, of Hopkinton, 1792–1828, and had:

FRANCES A. HARRINGTON, b. 26 May, 1817, d. 22 October, 1886; *m.*, 1838, Norman Cutter, of St. Louis, Missouri, and had:

MARY WEBBER CUTTER, a member of the Massachusetts and Missouri Societies of the Colonial Dames of America, who *m.*, 24 January, 1859, Hugh McKittrick, of St. Louis, Missouri, and had:

1.—THOMAS HARRINGTON McKITTRICK, b. 17 April, 1864; *m.*, 9 May, 1888, Hildegarde Sterling, and had: *Thomas H., Jr.*, b. 14 March, 1889; *Margaret*, b. 8 January, 1891, and *Edward Sterling*, b. 3 November, 1897.

2.—MARTHA McKITTRICK, b. 12 January, 1866, d. 5 November, 1892; *m.*, 6 November, 1889, William C. Stribling, and had: *Mildred Clarkson*, b. 23 August, 1890, and *William C., Jr.*, b. 27 January, 1892.

3.—HUGH McKITTRICK, JR., b. 16 August, 1868; *m.*, 9 May, 1895, Grace Kennett, and had: *Hugh*, b. 27 March, 1896, d. 7 February, 1899; *William Kennett*, b. 1 August, 1897, and *Mary*, b. 3 September, 1898.

4.—ALAN, b. 17 July, 1871, d. 5 December, 1886; 5. WALTER, b. 19 March, 1873; 6. MARY, b. 22 February, 1875; 7. RALPH, b. 17 August, 1877.

II.—NATHANIEL LYNDE, b. 22 November, 1659, d., Saybrook, Connecticut, 5 October, 1729, the first treasurer of Yale College; *m.*, in Boston,

1683, Susannah, 1664–1709, daughter of Francis Willoughby, deputy-governor of Massachusetts Colony, 1665–71, and had:

I.—HANNAH LYNDE, b. 2 December, 1694, d. before 1736; m., 22 June, 1725, Rev. George Griswold, b. 13 August, 1692, d. Lyme, Connecticut, 14 October, 1761, and had:

ELIZABETH GRISWOLD, b. 16 July, 1729, d. 16 January, 1779; m., 1747, John Raymond, b. 18 January, 1725, d., Montville, Connecticut, 7 May, 1789; second lieutenant in Captain Chapman's Company at the battle of Bunker's Hill, and had:

ANNA RAYMOND, b. 13 December, 1758, d., Salem, Connecticut, 28 July, 1842; m., 24 May, 1787, Stephen Billings, b. 8 December, 1750, d. Salem, 29 January, 1798; captain in 7th Regiment Connecticut Line; a member of the Society of the Cincinnati, and had:

NANCY BILLINGS, b. 23 December, 1792, d. 2 January, 1858, at Berlin, Ohio; m., 13 March, 1815, Joseph Otis, b. 24 September, 1792, d., at Berlin, 16 April, 1844, and had:

JOSEPH EDWARD OTIS, of Chicago, b. 30 April, 1830; m., 3 May, 1859, Ellen Maria Taylor, b. 30 August, 1837, and had:

MARY TAYLOR OTIS, a member of the Massachusetts and Illinois Societies of the Colonial Dames of America, b. 24 November, 1860, who m., 19 November, 1885, John Elias Jenkins, of Chicago, Illinois, b. 18 October, 1849, and had: *John Elliott*, b. 30 December, 1890.

II.—ELIZABETH LYNDE, 1684–1778, who m. Judge Richard Lord, of Lyme, Connecticut, 1690–1776, and had:

1.—ELIZABETH LORD, b. 1735, who m., 1760, Jared Eliot, Jr., of Killingworth, Connecticut, 1728–1811, also of Royal Descent, and had:

JARED ELIOT, of Killingworth, 1761–1841, who m., 1785, Clarissa, daughter of John Lewis, and had:

MARY ELIOT, 1792–1838 (widow of Henry Eliot), who m., secondly, Joseph Dana Grafton, of St. Genevieve, Missouri, and had:

FRANCES E. GRAFTON, 1829–1898, who m., at Little Rock, in 1846, William Eliot Ashley, of Little Rock, Arkansas, d. 1868, also of Royal Descent, and had: *Chester Grafton, Francis Freeman, Harriet Eliza, William Eliot,* and

FRANCES ANNE ASHLEY, a member of the Massachusetts and Arkansas Societies of the Colonial Dames of America, who m. Clifton Sidney Gray, M.D., b. Missouri, and d. s. p., Little Rock, Arkansas, 14 February, 1899.

2.—CAPTAIN ENOCH LORD, of Lyme, 1726–1814, who m. Hepzibah, daughter of Joseph Mervin, of Lyme, and had:

RICHARD LORD, of Lyme, 1752–1818, who m. Anne, daughter of Captain William Mitchell, and had:

SARAH ANN LORD, 1799–1835, who m. Judge Charles Johnson McCurdy, LL.D., of Lyme, also of Royal Descent (p. 106), and had:

EVELYN McCURDY, only child, a member of the Connecticut Society of the Colonial Dames of America, who m. Professor Edward Elbridge Salisbury, of New Haven, Connecticut. *No issue.*

III.—ELIZABETH LYNDE, b. 25 March, 1662, d. June, 1746, who m. George Pordage, of Boston, and had:

HANNAH PORDAGE, who m., secondly, 1714, James Bowdoin, of Boston, 1676–1747, member of the Colonial Council, and had:

ELIZABETH BOWDOIN, 1717–1771 (sister of Governor James Bowdoin), who m., 26 October, 1732, James Pitts, of Boston, 1710–1776, member of the Colonial Council, and had:

SAMUEL PITTS, 1745–1805; m., 1776, Johanna Davis, and had:

THOMAS PITTS, 1779–1836; m., 9 November, 1802, Elizabeth Mountfort, and had:

I.—EMELINE PITTS, 1812–1893, who m. Benjamin Sanborn, M.D., 1800–1846, and had:

NANCY MERRILL SANBORN, of Detroit, a member of the Massachusetts and Michigan Societies of the Colonial Dames of America, the Order of the Crown, *etc.*

II.—SAMUEL MOUNTFORT PITTS, 1810–1886, who m., 24 June, 1836, Sarah Bradford Merrill, and had:

1.—FRANCES PITTS, a member of the Massachusetts and Michigan Societies of the Colonial Dames of America, the Order of the Crown, *etc.*, who m. General Henry M. Duffield, of Detroit, and had: *Henry Martyn, Pitts, Divie Bethune, Dr. Francis, Morse Stewart,* and *Graham.*

2.—THOMAS PITTS, of Detroit, who m. Louise Strong Chapin, and had: *Samuel Lendall,* and

HELEN STRONG PITTS, a member of the Massachusetts and Michigan Societies of the Colonial Dames of America, who m., 19 June, 1900, Arthur M. Parker, of Detroit.

3.—JULIA PITTS, a member of the Massachusetts and Michigan Societies of the Colonial Dames of America, the Order of the Crown, *etc.*, who m. Thomas Cranage, of Bay City, Michigan, and had: *Samuel Pitts,* and

PEDIGREE LXXIV.—Continued.

MARY HILL CRANAGE, a member of the Massachusetts and Michigan Societies of the Colonial Dames of America, the Order of the Crown, *etc.*

IV.—CHIEF JUSTICE BENJAMIN LYNDE, of Salem, who *m.*, 27 April, 1699, Mary Browne, also of Royal Descent (p. 138), and had:

CHIEF JUSTICE BENJAMIN LYNDE, JR., of Salem, who *m.*, 1 November, 1731, Mary Goodrich, daughter of Major John Bowles, of Roxbury, and had:

LYDIA LYNDE, who *m.* Rev. William Walter, of Boston, and had:

HARRIOT TYNGE WALTER, who *m.* John Odin, and had:

ESTHER ODIN, who *m.* Rev. Benjamin Dorr, D.D., and had:

I.—ESTHER ODIN DORR, a member of the Pennsylvania Society of the Colonial Dames of America, who *m.* William Hewitt Webb, of Philadelphia, and had:

ANNIE GRISCOM WEBB, a member of the Pennsylvania Society of the Colonial Dames of America, who *m.* Albert Ripley Leeds, of Hoboken, New Jersey.

II.—MARY WARREN DORR, a member of the Pennsylvania Society of the Colonial Dames of America, who *m.* William L. Schäffer, of Philadelphia.

III.—HARRIOT ODIN DORR, a member of the Pennsylvania Society of the Colonial Dames of America, who *m.*, 17 October, 1867, Major James Edward Carpenter, of Philadelphia, also of Royal Descent (*see* "Americans of Royal Descent," ii., 639), and had: *Edward, Helen, Grace, d. young; William Dorr,* and *Lloyd Preston.*

PEDIGREE LXXV.

EDWARD I., King of England, had by his first wife, *m.*, 1254, Eleanor, *d.* 1290, daughter of Ferdinand III., King of Castile and Leon:

PRINCESS ELIZABETH PLANTAGENET, 1282–1316, widow of Sir John de Vere, who *m.*, secondly, 14 November, 1302, Humphrey de Bohun, Earl of Hereford and Essex, lord high constable, *k.* at Boroughbridge in 1321, also of Royal Descent, and had:

SIR WILLIAM DE BOHUN, K.G., fifth son, created, 1337, Earl of Northampton, *d.* 1360, who *m.* Lady Elizabeth, *d.* 1356, daughter of Bartholomew, first Baron de Badlesmere, executed in 1322, and his wife, Lady Margaret de Clare, also of Royal Descent, and had:

LADY ELIZABETH DE BOHUN, who *m.* (his first wife) Sir Richard Fitz-Alan, K.G., tenth Earl of Arundel, beheaded in 1398, also of Royal Descent, and had:

LADY ELIZABETH FITZ-ALAN, *d.* 8 July, 1425, who had by her third husband, Sir Robert Goushill, of Hault Hucknall, county Derby (*see* Glover's "History of Derby," ii., 78):

LADY JOAN GOUSHILL, who *m.* Sir Thomas Stanley, K.G., Baron Stanley, *d.* 12 January, 1458, and had:

LADY ELIZABETH STANLEY (a sister of Sir William Stanley, who crowned Henry VII. on Bosworth Field), who *m.* Sir Richard Molineux, of Sefton, county Lancaster, *k.* at Bloreheath in 1459, and had:

SIR THOMAS MOLINEUX, of Sefton, knight-banneret, who *m.* Lady Anne, daughter of Thomas de Dutton, and had:

SIR WILLIAM MOLINEUX, of Sefton, *d.* 1548; *m.* Lady Jane, daughter of Sir Richard Rigge, and had:

SIR RICHARD MOLINEUX, of Sefton, *d.* 1568; *m.* Lady Eleanor, daughter of Sir Alexander Ratcliffe, of Ordsall, and had:

LADY MARGARET MOLINEUX, *d.* 1617, who *m.* John Warren, Esqr., of Poynton, Baron of Stockport, high sheriff of Cheshire, *d.* 1588, second son, and appointed heir of Sir Edward Warren, of Poynton, Baron of Stockport, *d.* 1568 (*see* Watson's "Ancient Earls of Warren and Surrey," and Ormerod's "History of Cheshire"), and had:

SIR EDWARD WARREN, Knt., of Poynton, heir, Baron of Stockport, *bapt.* at Prestbury, 9 April, 1563, high sheriff of Cheshire; knighted while serving with the army in Ireland; *bur.* at Stockport, 14 November,

1609. He *m.*, secondly, at Prestbury, 16 October, 1581, Anne, daughter of Sir William Davenport, of Bramall, Cheshire, and had by her, who was *bur.* at Stockport, 13 July, 1597:

JOHN WARREN, of Poynton, heir, admitted to Gray's Inn, London, 4 March, 1609–10, *d.* 20 June, 1621 (Inqui. P. M. at Chester, 30 April, 1622). He *m.* (covenant dated 11 February, 1593; contract, 28 October, 1594), Anne Ognal, of Bylkesley, Warwickshire, *bur.* at Stockport, May, 1652, and had:

EDWARD WARREN, of Poynton, heir, *b.* 10 May, *bapt.* 19 May, 1605, *bur.* at Stockport, 10 September, 1687, will dated 26 January, 1683, proved at Chester in 1687. He was a royalist, and his estates were sequestered, but was pardoned in 1647. He gave the Herald his pedigree for the "Visitation," 17 September, 1663. He had by his first wife, Margaret Arderne, *bur.* at Stockport, 20 April, 1644, ten children, of whom:

HUMPHREY WARREN, of Charles county, Maryland, third child, *b.* at Poynton, 7 July, 1632. "He was reared as a merchant" (*see* Herald's Cheshire "Visitations," 1663; Watson's "Ancient Earls of Warren and Surrey and their Descendants," and Ormerod's "History of Cheshire"), and came to Maryland as a "merchant" with his young son Humphrey, one of his head-rights (Maryland Land Records, lib. v., fo. 235), and was granted, 12 February, 1662–3, a tract of 300 acres of land, called "Frailty," in Charles county, surveyed for him 22 June, 1663, and patented to him 4 August, 1664. He was an active Protestant, and was appointed a commissioner of the peace, 16 September, 1670. He *d.* intestate in 1673, at his seat, "Halton's Point," Charles county, and 9 May, 1673, his estate was administered and committed to Thomas Howell, who *m.* his widow (Maryland Testa. Proc., v., 439). He was twice married in England, and had by his first wife, *d. ante* 1652, whose name has not been found:

COLONEL HUMPHREY WARREN, of Charles county, Maryland, *b.* about 1652. He was appointed a commissioner of the peace, 2 March, 1675, and was an active Protestant in 1689, and 4 September, 1689, was appointed colonel of foot in Charles county. He was one of the committee of seven of the Protestant freemen which seized the government of Maryland from the representative of the Proprietary, 1 August, 1689, and was a justice of the quorum and a coroner for Charles county, 1689. By his will, dated 14 August, 1689, proved Charles county, 25 February, 1694–5, he devised a large estate. He was twice married, and had by his second wife, Margery, *m. ante* 1681, whose surname is unknown, who survived him:

JOHN WARREN, of Charles county, third son, *b.* 18 June, 1687, will dated 12 August, 1713, proved 13 February, 1713–14.

He left a large estate. He had by his wife, Judith, whose surname is unknown, who survived him:

ANN WARREN, who m. William Dent, of Charles county, and had:

ANN DENT, who m. Samuel Briscoe, and had:

WILLIAM DENT BRISCOE, who m. Sarah Stone, and had:

WALTER HANSON STONE BRISCOE, who m. Emeline Wellmore Dallam, and had:

JEANNETTE ELEANOR BRISCOE, who m. James Richard Thomas, and had:

JEANNETTE BRISCOE THOMAS, a member of the Maryland Society of the Colonial Dames of America, who m. James Bourne Parran, of Baltimore, and had: *Jeannette Briscoe.*

HUMPHREY WARREN, of Charles county, Md., 1632–1673, had by his second wife, Eleanor, whose surname is unknown:

THOMAS WARREN, of Charles county, Maryland (*see* Testa. Proc., Md. Archives, xvii., 122), who was brought to Maryland in 1663 (*see* " Maryland Immigrants," Land Office, Annapolis). He received from his father's estate the farm called " Frailty " (*see* Calvert's Rent Roll), where he resided at the time of his decease, and which he devised to his second wife, Jane, by his will dated 6 January, 1705-6; proved 23 November, 1710. He *m.*, first, before 13 June, 1688 (at this date his father-in-law conveyed a farm called " Strife," in Charles county, to his daughter Mary and her husband, Thomas Warren), Mary, a daughter of Capt. William Barton, Jr., of Port Tobacco parish, Charles county, who was appointed, 4 September, 1689, Captain of Foot, in Charles county, and for several terms was a Commissioner for the Peace, and was recommended by Lord Baltimore, October, 1691, for a seat in the Council, and had by her *Thomas*, a minor in 1705, living in 1757, *Sarah, Elizabeth*, and:

BARTON WARREN, of Charles county, Maryland, a minor in 1705. He inherited from his father's estate the farms " Frailty " and " Strife " (*see* Calvert's Rent Roll, 13 June, 1736), which he devised by will, dated 3 February, proved 9 March, 1757, to his sons and his wife Elizabeth ———, by whom he had (all named in his will), *Notley, John, Edward*, of Georgia; *Robert, b.* 6 September, 1742, *d.* in Tennessee, 26 October, 1826, having nineteen married children alive; *Susannah, Mrs. Jane Hungerford,* and

1.—WILLIAM BARTON WARREN, who removed to Lancaster county, Virginia, and then to Woodford county, Kentucky, and *d.* at Georgetown in 1809, aged 71 years. He *m.*, at Port Tobacco, Maryland, Mary Jane Yates, and had, besides other issue:

WILLIAM MONROE WARREN, of Georgetown, Kentucky, *b.* 1 July, 1775, *d.* 22 February, 1824; *m.*, at Georgetown, Maria F. Fauntleroy, *b.* 17 July, 1780, also of Royal Descent, and had: *Anne E.* (who *m.* E. L. Johnson, *issue*), *Margaret L.* (who *m.* Thornton F. Johnson, *issue*), *John F., Maria,* and

WILLIAM BARTON WARREN, of Jacksonville, Illinois, *b.* 1 March, 1802, *m.* Ann Dorsey Price, and had, besides others who *d.* young:

I.—WILLIAM MONROE WARREN, *m.* Priscilla Hitt, and had: *Maria, William Barton, Sarah Hitt, Robert, Samuel, Mary, Annie, Margaret.*

II.—PHIL WARREN, of Springfield, Illinois, *m.* Cordelia Birchal, and had: *Caleb Birchal, Phil Barton, Adele, Louise,* wife of J. E. T. Butler, *Lillian,* wife of O. B. Caldwell, *Cordelia, Maria,* and *Florence.*

III.—MARIA WARREN, who *m.* William A. Turney, and had: *Annie,* wife of T. J. Baird; *William, John A., Maria,* and *Maud,* wife of J. A. Kimber.

IV.—MARY LOUISA WARREN, a member of the Order of the Crown, *etc.*, who *m.* Thomas Booth, of St. Louis. *Issue d.* young.

V.—AGNES WARREN, who *m.* V. M. Kenney, of Berlin, Illinois, and had: *Dr. Joseph B.,* of Colorado Springs; *Dr. W. Warren,* of St. Louis; *Annie,* wife of C. W. Nelson, of St. Louis; *Lou Booth,* and *Sallie Warren.*

2.—MARY WARREN (she removed in 1779 to Pittsylvania county, Virginia, with her children), who *m.*, first, Harrison Musgrave, of Charles county, Maryland, who *d. ante* 29 April, 1760, intestate (the date of her bond, filed in Charles county, 14 June, by his widow, as administratrix, with her brothers, Notley and John Warren, as securities; *see* "Testamentary Proceedings," vol. xxxvii., fo. 377, and "Inventories," vol. lxx., Register of Wills office, Annapolis). She *m.*, secondly (his second wife), John Stone, of Port Tobacco, Maryland, will dated 6 August, probated in Charles county by his widow, 12 September, 1775, and had by him: *John, Matthew, Elizabeth* and *Warren,* and

REV. BARTON WARREN STONE, youngest child, "*b.* near Port Tobacco, 24 December, 1772," *d.* at Hannibal, Missouri, 6 November, 1844. He was a Christian minister (*see* his "Biography," published in 1847). He *m.*, first, 2 July, 1801, Elizabeth, daughter of Colonel William Campbell, of Muhlenburg county, Kentucky, and his wife, Tabitha, daughter of General William Russell, Jr., of Culpeper county, Virginia (*see* "Americans of Royal Descent," pp. 862–863), and had by her, who *d.* May 30, 1810:

MARY ANNE HARRISON STONE, *b.* Bourbon county, Kentucky, 21 September, 1805, *d.* 31 August, 1872, who *m.*, 5 September, 1821, Captain

Charles Chilton Moore, of "Forest Retreat," Fayette county, Kentucky, who served in the army in the War of 1812, b. Culpeper county, Virginia, 1 December, 1789, d. 8 August, 1860, and had:

HANNAH A. RANSDELL MOORE, b. 25 April, 1825, d. 11 May, 1890, who m., 25 October, 1845, John de Lafayette Grissim, M.D., of Georgetown, Kentucky, b. Tennessee, 27 January, 1818, d 16 April, 1869, and had:

1.—MARY GRISSIM, m. Charles Oscar Kenney, of Georgetown. *No issue.*

2.—LIDA CAMPBELL GRISSIM, a member of the Virginia Society of the Colonial Dames of America, the Order of the Crown, *etc.*, who m., 15 December, 1874, Judge Samuel Franklin Leib, of "Liebheim," San José, California, and had: *Lida Campbell*, a member of the Order of the Crown, *etc.*, *Elna Warren, Franklin Allen, Roy Chilton,* and *Earl Warren.*

3.—BARTON WARREN, *d. inf.* 4. CHARLES CHILTON, drowned, aged 13.

5. ANNAH WARREN GRISSIM, of Georgetown, *unm.*

6.—JEANETTE DE LAFAYETTE GRISSIM, a member of the Order of the Crown, *etc.*, m. William B. Gano, of Dallas, Texas. *Issue: Allene Stone, Marcus D., d. inf.; Vera, d. inf.; Richard Chilton, Annette Warren,* and *Martha Moore.*

7.—EVELYN MOORE GRISSIM, m. Paul Fürst, of Dallas, Texas, and had: *Hannah Moore, Elise Campbell,* and *Franklin Leib.*

8.—JOHN DE LAFAYETTE GRISSIM, M.D., of San José, California, *unm.*, a member of the Order of Runnemede, *etc.*

THE ROYAL DESCENT
OF
MRS. MARY NEWBURY ADAMS,
OF DUBUQUE, IOWA.

WILLIAM I., King of England, had:	HUGH CAPET, King of France, had:
Henry I., King of England, who had:	Robert the Pious, King of France, who had:
Maud, m. Geoffrey, Count of Anjou, and had:	Henry I., King of France, who had:
Henry II., King of England, who had:	Philip I., King of France, who had:
John, King of England, who had:	Louis VI., King of France, who had:
Henry III., King of England, who had:	Louis VII., King of France, who had:
Edward I., King of England, who had:	Philip II., King of France, who had:
Thomas, Earl of Norfolk, etc., who had:	Louis VIII., King of France, who had:
Margaret, m. John de Segrave, and had:	Louis IX., King of France, who had:
Elizabeth, m. John de Mowbray, and had:	Philip III., King of France, who had:
Margery, m. John de Welles, and had:	Philip IV., King of France, who had:
Margery, m. Sir Stephen le Scrope, and had:	Isabel, m. Edward II., King of England, and had:
Sir Henry, Baron le Scrope, of Marham, who had:	Edward III., King of England, who had:
Joan, m. Henry, Baron Fitzhugh, and had:	Thomas, Duke of Gloucester, who had:
Henry, third Baron Fitzhugh, who had:	Anne, m. Sir William, Earl of Ewe, and had:
Eleanor, m. Philip, Baron d'Arcy, and had:	Sir John Bouchier, K.G., Baron Berners, who had:
Margery, m. Sir John Conyers, K.G., and had:	Sir Humphrey Bouchier, Knt., who had:
Eleanor, m. Sir Thomas Markenfield, and had:	Sir John Bouchier, Baron Berners, who had:
Sir Nyan de Markenfield, Knt., who had:	Jane, m. Edmund Knyvett, and had:
Alice, m. Robert Mauleverer, and had:	John Knyvett, of Plumstead, Norfolk, who had:
Dorothy, m. John Kaye, of Woodsome, and had:	Sir Thomas Knyvett, of Plumstead, who had:
Robert Kaye, of Woodsome, Yorkshire, who had:	Abigail, m. Sir Martin Sedley, and had:
Grace, m. Sir Richard Saltonstall, Knt., and had:	Muriel, m. Brampton Gurdon, M.P., and had:

Richard Saltonstall, of Ipswich, Mass., m. Muriel Gurdon, of Assington, Suffolk.

Col. Nathaniel Saltonstall, of Haverhill=Elizabeth Ward, of Haverhill, Mass.

Elizabeth Saltonstall=Rev. Roland Cotton, of Sandwich, Mass.

Rev. John Cotton, D.D., of Newton, Mass.=Mary Gibbs.

Mary Cotton=Rev. Joseph Pynchon, D.D., of Boston, Mass.

Margaret Pynchon=Stephen Keeler, of Norwalk, Conn.

Margaret Keeler=Dr. Erastus Sergeant, Jr., of Lee, Mass.

Mary Ann Sergeant=Rev. Samuel Newbury, of Middlebury, Vt.

Mary Keeler Newbury, member of the Conn. and Mich. Societies of the Colonial Dames of America, the Order of the Crown, etc. = Judge Austin Adams, of Dubuque, Iowa.

Annabel=O. S. Goan.   Eugene=Anna   Cecilia   Herbert=Elsie
Adams   Adams Plaister. Adams.   Adams Payne.
                                         Unm.

Adelaide Emily Percival Elizabeth Donald, Adele   Waldo   Olive   Harlon Philip
Goan.   Goan. Goan.   Goan.   d. inf. Adams. Adams. Adams. Adams. Adams.

PEDIGREE LXXVI.

ROBERT THE PIOUS, King of France, had by his second wife, Lady Constance, daughter of William, Count of Provence:

ROBERT, DUKE OF BURGUNDY, *d.* 1075, whose eldest son

HENRY OF BURGUNDY, *d. v. p.*, was the father of

EUDES, DUKE OF BURGUNDY, *d.* 1102, whose daughter:

LADY ALIX (widow of Bertrand, Count of Tripoli), *m.*, secondly, William de Talvas III., Count of Alençon and Ponthieu, and had:

LADY ADELA DE TALVAS, *d.* 1174, who *m.*, first, William de Warren, third Earl of Surrey, *d.* 1148, also of Royal Descent (*see* pp. 11-12), and had:

LADY ISABELLA DE WARREN, who *m.*, secondly, Hameline Plantagenet, fifth Earl of Warren and Surrey, and had:

LADY ISABELLA DE WARREN, who *m.* (his first wife) Roger Bigod, created Earl of Norfolk, also of Royal Descent, and had:

HUGH BIGOD, second Earl of Norfolk, *m.* Lady Maud Marshall, daughter of William, Earl of Pembroke, protector of England, and had:

SIR RALPH BIGOD, third son, who *m.* Berta de Furnival, and had:

LADY ISABEL BIGOD, who *m.*, secondly, John Fitzgeoffrey, of Barkhampstead, justiciary of Ireland in 1246, and had:

JOHN FITZJOHN, justiciary of Ireland, *d.* in 1258, father of:

MAUD FITZJOHN, who *m.*, secondly, William de Beauchamp, created Earl of Warwick, *d.* 1298, also of Royal Descent, and had:

LADY SARAH DE BEAUCHAMP, who *m.* Richard, sixth Baron de Talbot, of Goodrich, *d.* 1306, also of Royal Descent, and had:

LADY GWENTHELLEAN DE TALBOT, who *m.* Sir Payne de Turberville, custos of Glamorganshire, 134-, and had:

LADY SARAH DE TURBERVILLE, who *m.* William de Gamage, sheriff of Gloucestershire in 1325, and had:

GILBERT DE GAMAGE, of Rogiad, who *m.* Lettice, daughter of Sir William Seymour, of Penhow, and had:

SIR WILLIAM GAMAGE, of Rogiad and Coyty, who *m.* Mary, daughter of Sir Thomas de Rodburg, and had:

SIR THOMAS GAMAGE, of Rogiad and Coyty, who *m.* Matilda, daughter of Sir John Dennis, and had:

LADY JANE GAMAGE, who m. Roger ap Arnold ap Arnholt-Vychan, of Llanthony Manor, in Monmouthshire, also of Royal Descent, and had:

THOMAS ARNOLD, eldest son, succeeded to Llanthony Manor. He m. Agnes, daughter of Sir Richard Wairnstead, and had:

RICHARD ARNOLD, second son, of Street parish, Somersetshire, m. Emmote, daughter of Pearce Young, of Damerham, Wilts, and had:

RICHARD ARNOLD, eldest son, of Bagbere Manor, Dorsetshire; will dated 15 May, 1593, was proved 9 July, 1595; buried in July, 1595, in the Milton Church. He had by his first wife, whose name has not been preserved:

THOMAS ARNOLD, of Melcombe Horsey and Cheselbourne Manors, Dorsetshire. He m., first, Alice Gully (see p. 13). He had by his second wife (whose name has not been preserved) an only son (see Austin's "Genealogical Dictionary of Rhode Island," "Ralph Earle and His Descendants," the "N. E. His. Geneal. Reg.," vol. xxxiii., p. 432):

THOMAS ARNOLD, bapt. 18 April, 1599. He m., first, in England, about 1623-4, came to New England, and m., secondly, about 1638-9, Phebe, daughter of George Parkhurst, of Watertown, Massachusetts. He removed to Providence, Rhode Island, from Watertown, in 1654, and was a deputy in 1666-67, 1670-72, and town councillor, 1672; d. September, 1674, and had by his second wife, who d. in 1688:

1.—ELIZABETH ARNOLD, d. 20 October, 1747, who m., 22 November, 1678, Captain Samuel Comstock, d. 27 May, 1727, and had: *Hassadiah* (see below) and:

JOHN COMSTOCK, b. 26 March, 1693, d. 12 June, 1750; m. Esther Jenks, and had:

SAMUEL COMSTOCK, d. 16 January, 1765, m., 1 January, 1738, Anna Brown, d. 16 November, 1776, and had:

BENJAMIN COMSTOCK, b. 7 March, 1747, d. 30 September, 1828; m., 28 January, 1776, Mary Winsor, b. 2 April, 1755, d. 9 November, 1825, and had:

WILLIAM COMSTOCK, b. 20 January, 1786, d. 27 October, 1873; m., 19 September, 1824, Harriet Pearson, b. 16 October, 1803, d. 26 August, 1882, and had:

ANNA LOUISE COMSTOCK, b. 20 April, 1836, m., 13 May, 1853, Edward Augustus Balch, b. 2 April, 1833, d. 14 January, 1871, and had:

ANNA AUGUSTA BALCH, b. 29 October, 1858, a member of the Rhode Island Society of the Colonial Dames of America, who m., 6 May, 1886, Charles Value Chapin, of Providence, Rhode Island, and had: *Howard Miller*, b. 11 May, 1887.

2.—ELEAZER ARNOLD, of Providence, Rhode Island, b. 17 June, 1651, *d.* 29 August, 1722; *m.* Eleanor, *d.* 1722, daughter of John and Elizabeth Smith, of Providence, and had:

JOSEPH ARNOLD, of Smithfield, Rhode Island, *d.* 4 November, 1746, who *m.*, 20 June, 1716, Mercy Stafford, *b.* 27 September, 1694, *d.* 175-, and had:

I.—CALEB ARNOLD, of Gloucester, Rhode Island, *m.*, 26 January, 1746, Patience Brown, and had:

NEHEMIAH ARNOLD, of Providence, *b.* 15 March, 1748, *d.* 12 March, 1835; *m.*, 1774, Alice Brown, *b.* 12 August, 1754, *d.* 18 May, 1822, and had:

AMY ARNOLD, who *m.*, 19 September, 1796, Governor Caleb Earle, of Providence, and had:

MARY ANN EARLE, who *m.*, 1828, William Robinson Watson, of Providence, and had:

WILLIAM H. WATSON, *b.* 8 November, 1829, *m.*, 1 May, 1854, Sarah Thompson Carlile, of Providence, and had:

LUCY CARLILE WATSON, of Utica, New York, *b.* 10 February, 1855, a member of the New York Society of the Colonial Dames of America.

II.—SAMUEL ARNOLD, *b.* 12 July, 1736, *m.* Elizabeth ———, and had: *Israel*, and

ELIZABETH ARNOLD, *b.* 29 March, 1775, who *m.* Christopher Brown, *b.* 26 December, 1769, and had:

NABBY BROWN, *b.* 7 September, 1799, *d.* 24 July, 1877; *m.* Israel Arnold, Jr., *b.* 8 May, 1792, *d.* 16 November, 1864 (son of the aforesaid Israel Arnold, 1755-1840, and his wife Deborah Olney), and had:

CHARLOTTE B. ARNOLD, *b.* 22 May, 1833, who *m.* 1 January, 1856, William Bibby, *b.* 10 June, 1829, and had:

MAUD BELLE BIBBY, a member of the New Hampshire Society of the Colonial Dames of America, the Order of the Crown, *etc.*, who *m.*, 4 June, 1890, Samuel de Wolf Lewis, of Newport, New Hampshire.

3.—RICHARD ARNOLD, of Providence, *b.* 22 March, 1642, *d.* 22 April, 1710; will probated 10 May; member of the Town Council, 1700, and speaker of the House of Deputies, 1707-8. He *m.*, first, Mary Angell, and had by her, who *d.* in 1695:

I.—MARY ARNOLD, who *m.* Thomas Steere, *d.* 27 August, 1735, and had:

PHEBE STEERE, *b.* 26 October, 1699, *d.* 1 August, 1767; *m.* John Matthewson, *b.* 6 October, 1699, and had:

PEDIGREE LXXVI.—Continued.

ELIZABETH MATTHEWSON, b. 4 November, 1742, d. 9 April, 1822; m., first, 23 October, 1763, Mason Hulett, of Belcherstown, Massachusetts, and had:

MASON HULETT, JR., of Hampton, New York, 1775–1847; m. Abigail Andrews, also of Royal Descent, and had:

HANNAH LUCY HULETT, b. 4 July, 1817, d. 28 January, 1893; m., 23 June, 1837, Henry Hitchcock, of Rutland, Vermont, also of Royal Descent (p. 149), and had:

ABIGAIL JANE HITCHCOCK, b. 3 May, 1843, a member of the Massachusetts Society of the Colonial Dames of America, etc., who m., 15 February, 1866, Horace Hoxie Dyer, of "Dyer Place," Rutland, Vermont, b. 2 April, 1820, and had: *Captain Horace Edward*.

II.—THOMAS ARNOLD, b. 24 March, 1675, d. 3 February, 1727; m., 6 December, 1706, Elizabeth Burlingame, b. 9 January, 1684, d. 5 May, 1752, and had:

JONATHAN ARNOLD, b. 18 November, 1708, d. 29 December, 1796; m. Abigail Smith, b. 10 June, 1714, d. 29 June, 1801, and had:

WELCOME ARNOLD, b. 25 March, 1745, d. 30 September, 1797; m., 11 February, 1773, Patience Greene, b. 13 May, 1754, d. 2 November, 1809, and had:

RICHARD JAMES ARNOLD, b. 5 October, 1796, d. 10 March, 1873; m. Louisa Caroline Gindrat, b. 8 April, 1804, d. 15 October, 1871, and had:

MARY CORNELIA ARNOLD, b. 22 January, 1841, a member of the Rhode Island Society of the Colonial Dames of America, who m., 27 June, 1861, William Richmond Talbot, of Providence, Rhode Island, and had: *Mary Cornelia*, b. 9 November, 1862; *Charlotte Richmond*, b. 16 September, 1864, d. 28 February, 1865; *Arnold Gindrat*, b. 19 December, 1865; *Helen*, b. 1 June, 1872; *Harriet*, b. 28 August, 1873, and *William de Peyster*, b. 27 April, 1877, d. 28 October, 1878.

III.—CAPTAIN RICHARD ARNOLD, of Smithfield, Rhode Island, 1668–1745, who m., first, Mary, daughter of Joseph and Mary (Pray) Woodward, and had by her:

1.—RICHARD ARNOLD, who m., 19 May, 1722, Ruth Aldrich, and had:

RUTH ARNOLD, who m., 3 March, 1738–9, Gideon Comstock, son of Hassadiah (and his first wife, Catherine Pray), son of Captain Samuel Comstock and his wife Elizabeth, a daughter of the aforesaid Thomas Arnold, 1599–1674, and had:

COLONEL ADAM COMSTOCK, of the Rhode Island Line, Continental Army, b. Smithfield, January, 1740, d. Saratoga, New

York, 10 April, 1819. After the war was a New York judge, assemblyman, and State senator. He *m.*, 10 April, 1763, Margaret McGregor, *b.* 8 September, 1745, *d.* Saratoga, 3 March, 1807, and had:

RUTH COMSTOCK, *b.* 31 December, 1763, *d.* 16 August, 1800, who *m.*, at Schenectady, 11 February, 1787, Rev. Nicholas Van Vranken, of Fishkill, New York, *b.* 24 May, 1762, *d.* 20 May, 1804, and had:

MARGARET MATILDA VAN VRANKEN, *b.* 23 November, 1795, *d.* 12 September, 1850, who *m.*, at Schenectady, 29 September, 1819, Phinehas Prouty, a captain in the War of 1812, *b.* Langdon, New Hampshire, 14 January, 1788, *d.* Geneva, New York, 21 February, 1862, and had:

I.—HARRIET PROUTY, *b.* Geneva, 28 May, 1823, a member of the New York Society of the Colonial Dames of America, who *m.*, at Geneva, 11 December, 1844, General Thomas Hillhouse, *b.* Watervliet, Albany county, New York, 10 March, 1816, *d.* Yonkers, 31 July, 1897, and had:

    1.—MARGARET PROUTY HILLHOUSE, of New York City, *b.* at "Walnut Grove," Watervliet, 5 January, 1846, a member of the New York Society of the Colonial Dames of America, the Society of Daughters of the Cincinnati, the Society of Daughters of the Holland Dames, the Mary Washington Association, the Daughters of the American Revolution Society, *etc.*

    2.—HARRIET AUGUSTA HILLHOUSE, a member of the New York Society of the Colonial Dames of America, the Society of Daughters of the Cincinnati, *etc.*, who *m.* Walter Wood Adams, of Dobb's Ferry-on-Hudson, New York.

    3.—ADELAIDE HILLHOUSE, of New York.

II.—SARAH AUGUSTA PROUTY, who *m.* Alexander de Lafayette Chew, of Geneva, New York, also of Royal Descent, and had:

    CATHERINE ALEXANDER CHEW, a member of the New Jersey Society of the Colonial Dames of America, who *m.* Samuel Winship, of Morristown, New Jersey. *Issue.*

III.—PHINEHAS PROUTY, JR., *m.* Adelaide Cobleigh, and had:

    ADELAIDE ALEXANDER PROUTY, of Geneva, New York, a member of the Pennsylvania Society of the Colonial Dames of America, who *m.* Walter Chrystie, of High Bridge, New Jersey, and had: *Phinehas Prouty, Margaret Harlan,* and *Walter.*

2.—THOMAS ARNOLD, of Smithfield, d. 11 December, 1765, m., thirdly, Patience Cook, and had by her:

LYDIA ARNOLD, b. 16 October, 1749, d. 10 July, 1828, who m. William Buffum, of Smithfield, b. 20 December, 1741, d. 27 August, 1829, and had:

PATIENCE BUFFUM, who m. Pliny Earle, of Leicester, Massachusetts, and had:

THOMAS EARLE, of Philadelphia, who m. Mary Hussey, of Nantucket, Massachusetts, and had:

1.—GEORGE H. EARLE, of Philadelphia, who m. Ellen Frances Von Leer, and had:

FLORENCE EARLE, a member of the Pennsylvania Society of the Colonial Dames of America, who m. Edward Hornor Coates, of Philadelphia.

2.—CAROLINE EARLE, a member of the Pennsylvania Society of the Colonial Dames of America, who m. Richard P. White, of Philadelphia. *Issue.*

3.—FRANCES EARLE, a member of the Pennsylvania Society of the Colonial Dames of America, who m. Edward Hine Johnson, of Philadelphia.

CAPTAIN RICHARD ARNOLD, of Smithfield, 1668–1745; m., secondly, 14 November, 1715, Dinah, daughter of John and Dinah (Steere) Thornton, and had by her:

JOSIAH ARNOLD, 1717–1745; m. Amy Phillips, and had:

JONATHAN ARNOLD, b. 3 December, 1741, d. 1 February, 1793; m., first, 19 January, 1763, Molly Burr, b. 23 November, 1743, d. 18 October, 1781, and had:

SALLY ARNOLD, b. 22 November, 1777, d. 17 July, 1814; m., 8 October, 1797, James Burrill, b. 25 April, 1772, d. 25 December, 1820, and had:

SARAH PERKINS BURRILL, b. 8 February, 1812, d. 4 January, 1852; m., 16 November, 1829, William Sedley Fearing, b. 12 October, 1802, d. 8 April, 1843, and had:

KATE SEDLEY FEARING, b. 25 December, 1842, a member of the Massachusetts Society of the Colonial Dames of America, who m., first, 18 January, 1872, Alexander Carter, of The Spring, Kenilworth, England, and m., secondly, 12 October, 1880, Edwin Cely Trevilian, of Midelney Place, Curry Rivel, Somerset, England, and had: *Maurice Fearing Cely Trevilian*, b. 22 October, 1881.

PEDIGREE LXXVII.

ROBERT BRUCE, King of Scotland, had by his second wife, Lady Elizabeth, daughter of Richard de Burgh, Earl of Ulster, of Royal Descent:

LADY MARGARET BRUCE, who *m.*, 1344 (his first wife), William, Earl of Sutherland, *d.* 1370, and had:

WILLIAM, EARL OF SUTHERLAND, *d.* 1389 (his wife's name unknown), who had:

ROBERT, EARL OF SUTHERLAND, *d.* 1442, who had by his wife, Lady Mabilla, daughter of John Dunbar, Earl of Moray, son of Patrick, Earl of Dunbar and March, and his first wife, Lady Agnes Randolph, both of Royal Descent:

ALEXANDER SUTHERLAND, of Dunbeath, third son, will executed 12 November, 1456, who *m.* Lady Mariot McDonnell, daughter of Donald, lord of the Isles, *d.* 1427, and his wife, Margaret, Countess of Ross (*see* Wood's Douglas's "Peerage of Scotland," vol. ii., 8, 339, 573), and had:

LADY MARJORY SUTHERLAND, Countess of Caithness, who *m.*, November, 1456 (his second wife), William Sinclair, of Roslyn, third Earl of Orkney and Earl of Caithness (in right of his second wife), chancellor of Scotland, also of Royal Descent, and had:

LADY ELEANOR SINCLAIR, who *m.* (his second wife) Sir John Stewart, of Balveny and Lorn, first Earl of Athol, *d.* 1512, also of Royal Descent, and had:

LADY ISABEL STEWART, who *m.* (his second wife, *see* Wood's Douglas's "Peerage of Scotland," i., 141 and 549) Alexander Robertson, fifth baron of Strowan, and had:

JOHN ROBERTSON, first laird of Muirton, in Elgin, second son, who *m.* Margaret, daughter of Sir James Crichton, of Fendraught, eldest son of William, third Lord Chrichton (*see* Wood's Douglas's "Peerage," i., 610; ii., 716), and had:

GILBERT ROBERTSON, of Muirton, who *m.* Janet, daughter of John Reid, of Ackenhead, and had:

DAVID ROBERTSON, of Muirton, who *m.* —— Innes, and had:

WILLIAM ROBERTSON, of Muirton, who *m.* Isabel Petrie, and had:

WILLIAM ROBERTSON, of Gladney, who *m.* —— Mitchell, and had:

REV. WILLIAM ROBERTSON, of Edinburgh (*see* Burke's "Royal Families," ii., ped. 190), who m. a daughter of Pitcairn, of Dreghorn, and had :

JEAN ROBERTSON, who m. Alexander Henry, of Aberdeen, and had:

COLONEL JOHN HENRY, of Hanover county, Virginia, who m. Sarah, widow of John Syme, and daughter of Isaac Winston, of Hanover county, d. 1760, and had, besides other issue (see p. 116):

JANE HENRY, who m. Colonel Samuel Meredith, and had :

JANE HENRY MEREDITH, who m. David S. Garland, of Lynchburg, Virginia, member of Congress, and had :

ANN SHEPHERD GARLAND, 1797–1856, who m., 4 January, 1816, Gustavus Adolphus Rose, M.D.. of Lynchburg, 1789–1860, also of Royal Descent, and had:

1.—JUDITH CABELL ROSE, of Richmond, Virginia, a member of the Virginia Society of the Colonial Dames of America, who m., 21 July, 1846, Benjamin Powell Walker, d., New York, 14 February, 1887, son of John, of Hartford, Indiana, 1787–1844, son of Benjamin, 1758–1846, son of John Walker, who was slain by Indians, in Northumberland county, Pennsylvania, in August, 1782, and had, besides other issue (see p. 199) :

ANNIE FITZHUGH ROSE WALKER, a member of the Virginia Society of the Colonial Dames of America, the Order of the Crown, *etc.*

2.—DAVID GARLAND ROSE, who m. Maria Louisa, daughter of John Walker, 1787–1844, aforesaid, and had :

MARIA LOUISA ROSE, a member of the Virginia Society of the Colonial Dames of America, who m. Samuel J. Filer, of Springfield, Massachusetts, and had : *Rose, Helen,* and *Edith.*

3.—CAROLINE MATILDA ROSE, of Chicago, a member of the Illinois Society of the Colonial Dames of America, who m. William James Walker, of La Porte, Indiana, son of John Walker, 1787–1844, aforesaid, and had :

I.—MARTHA GARLAND WALKER, of Chicago, a member of the Illinois Society of the Colonial Dames of America, who m. Sylvanus L. Trippe, of New York, and had: *Carolyn Rose Walker.*

II.—CAROLINE M. WALKER, a member of the Illinois Society of the Colonial Dames of America, who m. George Fisher, of Harrisburg, Pennsylvania, and had : *Carolyn,* and

ROSE FISHER, a member of the Virginia Society of the Colonial Dames of America, who m. Madison B. Kennedy, of New York, and had : *Jane.*

PEDIGREE LXXVIII.

ROBERT III., King of Scotland, had by his wife, Lady Annabella, daughter of Sir John Drummond, of Stobhall:

PRINCESS ELIZABETH STEWART, who *m.* Sir James Douglas, Lord of Dalkeith and Morton, and had:

SIR JAMES DOUGLAS, third Lord of Dalkeith, who *m.* Lady Agnes Keith, daughter of the earl marshal of Scotland, and had:

SIR JOHN DOUGLAS, second son (brother of James, first Earl of Morton), who *m.* the heiress of Hawthornden, of Abernethy, and had:

DAVID DOUGLAS, of Tilquhille, or Tiliwhilly, 1479, who *m.* Janet, daughter of Thomas Ogston, and had:

JAMES DOUGLAS, of Tiliwhilly, who *m.* Christian Forbes, of Tolquhoun, and had:

ARTHUR DOUGLAS, of Tiliwhilly, 1535, who *m.* Janet, daughter of Auchenleck of Balmanno, and had:

JOHN DOUGLAS, of Tiliwhilly, 1576, who *m.* Giles, daughter of Robert Erskine, of Dun, and had:

JOHN DOUGLAS, of Tiliwhilly, 1594, who *m.* Mary, daughter of Sir Peter Young, and had:

JAMES DOUGLAS, of Tiliwhilly and Inchmarlo, fourth son and eventually heir, *d.* 1672, who *m.* Isabel, a granddaughter of Sir John Ramsay, Lord Bothwell, of Balmain, and had:

JOHN DOUGLAS, of Inchmarlo and Tiliwhilly, who *m.* Grizel, daughter of Thomas Forbes, of Watertown, and his wife Jean, daughter of David Ramsay, of Balmain, and had:

JOHN DOUGLAS, of Tiliwhilly, 1723-1749, who *m.* Agnes, daughter of Rev. James Horn, of Westhall, minister of Elgin, and his wife Isabel, daughter of David Ramsey, of Balmain, and had:

EUPHEMIA DOUGLAS, *d.* 21 December, 1766, aged 55, who *m.*, 1733, Charles Irvine, of Cults, near Aberdeen, *d.* 28 March, 1779, aged 83, both buried at Cults (*see* "American Historical Register," p. 308, November, 1895, for his ancestry), and had:

JOHN IRVINE, M.D., *b.* 15 September, 1742. He came to Georgia about 1765, and was a member of the last royal assembly of 1780; went to England and was physician to the Admiralty, and subsequently returned to Georgia and *d.* at Savannah, 15 October, 1808. He *m.*, first, at

Sunbury, Georgia, 5 September, 1765, Ann Elizabeth, daughter of Colonel Kenneth Baillie, ensign in the Darien Rangers 1735, *d.* July, 1766 (*see* "Am. His. Register," vol. iii., p. 311, for an account of his family), and had:

ANNE IRVINE, *b.* 14 January, 1770, who *m.*, first, 13 April, 1786, Captain James Bulloch (son of Archibald Bulloch, 1750-1777, president of Georgia, 1776, and Mary, daughter of Judge James de Veaux, of Georgia, 1750-1785), and had:

JOHN IRVINE BULLOCH, M.D., clerk of the federal court, *d.*, Cedar Hill, Liberty county, Georgia, 1827, who *m.*, 1 January, 1814, Charlotte, daughter of John Glenn, Chief Justice of Georgia, 1776-78, and had:

WILLIAM GASTON BULLOCH, M.D., *b.* 3 August, 1815, deceased; *m.*, 6 November, 1851, Mary Eliza Adams, a member of the Georgia Society of the Colonial Dames of America, daughter of John Lewis, of Cobb county, Georgia, and had:

1.—JOSEPH GASTON BULLOCH, M.D., of the United States Indian service, a member of the Aryan Order of St. George, etc., *m.* Eunice Helena Bailey, and had: *Archibald Irvine de Veaux, William Gaston Glenn,* and *Douglas Eugene St. Cloud.*

2.—ROBERT HUTCHINSON BULLOCH, of Savannah.

3.—EMMA HAMILTON BULLOCH, of Savannah, a member of the Georgia Society of the Colonial Dames of America.

PEDIGREE LXXIX.

ALFRED THE GREAT, King of England, had by his wife, Lady Alswitha, daughter of Ethelan the Great, Earl of Mercia, lineally descended from Crida, first king of Marcia, *d*. A.D. 594 (*see* Dr. James Anderson's "Royal Genealogies," 1732; and Betham's "Genealogical Tables"):

LADY ETHELFLEDA, *d*. 15 June, 919, who *m*. Ethelred, Earl of Mercia, 895, *d*. 912, son of Hugh the Great, Earl of Mercia, and had:

LADY ELFWINA, co-heiress of Mercia (sister of Algiva, queen consort of Edmund I.), who *m*. Edulf (son of Ordgar, Earl of Devon), brother of Lady Alfrida, wife of King Edgar, and had:

LEOFWINE, appointed by Ethelred II. Earl of Mercia, 1005, who *m*. Lady Alward, daughter of Athelstan, the Danish Duke of the East Angles, and had:

LEOFRIC THE GREAT, Earl of Mercia, or Chester and Leicester, 1016, *d*. 31 August, 1027, who *m*. the celebrated Lady Godiva, of Coventrytown, daughter of the Earl of Lincoln, and had:

ALGAR, Earl of Mercia, 1053, who *m*. Lady Alversa Malet, and had:

EDWYN, the last Saxon Earl of Mercia, *k*. 1071, brother-in-law of Harold, King of England. His son:

EDWYN DE TEMPLE, a feudal baron, sometimes styled Earl of Leicester and Coventry, took his surname from his manor, in Sparkenhoe Hundred, Leicestershire (*see* Barton's "Leicestershire," and Lodge's "Irish Peerages," 1754, under Palmertson). His presumed descendant:

HENRY DE TEMPLE, feudal Baron of Temple Manor and Little-Shepey, Leicestershire, *temp*. 3 Edward I., *m*. Lady Maud, or Matilda, daughter of Sir John Ribbesford, Knt., and had:

RICHARD DE TEMPLE, Baron of Temple-Manor, 24 Edward I., who *m*. Catherine, daughter of Thomas de Langley, and had:

NICHOLAS DE TEMPLE,* 16 Edward II., who *m*. Lady Margery, daughter

---

* NICHOLAS DE TEMPLE, 16 Edward II. (according to a pedigree in the Leicestershire "Visitations"), had: NICHOLAS DE TEMPLE, who *m*. Maria, daughter of Robert Dabernon, and had: THOMAS DE TEMPLE, who *m*. Joan, daughter of John Brasbridge, and had: ROBERT DE TEMPLE, who *m*. Maria, daughter of William Ringescote, and had: THOMAS TEMPLE, of Witney, Oxfordshire.

See also Nicholl's "Herald and Genealogist," vol. viii.; "American Heraldic Journal," January, 1865, and October, 1866, and Baker's "Northamptonshire," vol. i.

of Sir Roger Corbet, of Sibton (or Isabella, daughter of William Barwell), and had:

RICHARD DE TEMPLE, of Shepey, 20 Edward III., who m. Lady Agnes, daughter of Sir Ralph Stanley, Knt., and had:

NICHOLAS DE TEMPLE, 46 Edward III., who m. Maud, daughter of John Burguillon, of Newton, in Leicestershire, and had:

RICHARD DE TEMPLE, buried in All Saint's, Shepey Magna, who m. Joan, daughter of William de Shepey, of Shepey Magna, Leicestershire, and had:

THOMAS TEMPLE, of Whitney, Oxfordshire (either third son of Richard aforesaid, or second son of Robert, see Note, p. 331), who m. Maria, or Mary, daughter of Thomas Gedney, and had:

WILLIAM TEMPLE, of Witney, who m. Isabel, daughter and heiress of Henry Everton, and had:

THOMAS TEMPLE, of Witney, who m. Alice, daughter and heiress to John Heritage, of Burton-Dorset, Warwickshire, and had:

PETER TEMPLE, of Stowe, Buckinghamshire and Burton-Dorset, who had a grant of the Manor of Marston-Boteler, in Warwickshire, second son, d. 28 May, 1577. He m. Millicent, daughter of William Jykett, or Jekyle, of Newington, in Middlesex, and had:

JOHN TEMPLE, of Stowe, eldest son, 1542–1603; m. Susan, daughter of Thomas Spencer, of Everton, in Northampton, and had:

SIR THOMAS TEMPLE, of Stowe, created a baronet, 29 June, 1611, d. 1637. He m. Esther, daughter of Miles Sandys, of Latimers (or Eaton), Bucks, and had: SIR PETER TEMPLE, second Bart., b. 1592, and:

SIR JOHN TEMPLE, Knt., of Biddleson and Stanton-Bury (see "The National Cyclo. of Useful Knowledge," xi., 938; Nicholl's "Herald and Genealogist," viii.; Burke's; Kimber's, etc., "Baronetages;" Lodge's "Peerage of Ireland," 1754; Baker's "Northamptonshire," i.; the "American Heraldic Journal," January, 1865, October, 1866). He m., first, Dorothy, daughter of Edmund Lee, of Stanton-Bury, and had:

DOROTHY TEMPLE,* who m., at Odell, 4 January, 1634, John Alston,

---

* The following ladies, members of the National Society of the Colonial Dames of America, are also of Royal Descent through Dorothy Temple:

MRS. FRANK GAINES, Alabama State Society.
MISS MARY MCGAW FISKE, Massachusetts State Society.
MRS. JAMES J. MAYFIELD, Alabama State Society.
MRS. FREDERICK G. MARTIN, Arkansas State Society.
MRS. GEORGE W. VAN HOOSE, Alabama State Society.
MRS. WARREN B. WATKINS, Alabama State Society.
MRS. SAMUEL G. WOOLF, Alabama State Society.
MRS. ANNIE J. WARING, Georgia State Society.
MRS. JOSEPH B. SOLOMON, North Carolina State Society.
MISS MARY E. FITTS, Alabama State Society.

of Parvenham, Bedfordshire; entered at the Inner Temple; buried at Parvenham, 15 August, 1687 (his mother was the second wife of Sir John Temple, his father-in-law; *see* Kimber and Johnson's "Baronetages," 1771, i., 457), and had:

JOHN ALSTON, of Parvenham, fourth son, *d*. 1704, who *m*. Anne Willis, and had:

MAJOR JOHN ALSTON, *bapt*. at Filmersham, Bedfordshire, 5 December, 1673, came to North Carolina before 1720, and was associate justice of the colony, 1724–30; *d*. in Chowan county, North Carolina, 1758, having issue by his wife, Mary Clark, who survived him:

MAJOR JAMES ALSTON, of New Berne, North Carolina, *d*. 1761, *m*. Christine, daughter of Colonel George Lillington, of North Carolina, and had:

1.—COLONEL JAMES ALSTON, *d*. 1815, *m*., 1774, Grizeal Yancey, 1752–1845, and had:

I.—SARAH ALSTON, 1779–1861, who *m*. Joseph Groves, 1768–1850, and had:

REV. JOHN JOSEPH GROVES, 1800–1885; *m*. Mary Louisa Harvie, and had:

JOSEPH ASBURY GROVES, M.D., of Selma, Alabama, *b*. 1830, *m*. Elizabeth Royall Robertson, and had:

ELIZABETH ROYALL GROVES, a member of the North Carolina and Alabama Societies of the Colonial Dames of America, the Order of the Crown, *etc*.

II.—NATHANIAL ALSTON, 1775–1852; *m*., 1800, Mary Grey Jeffreys, and had:

JUDGE WILLIAM JEFFREYS ALSTON, *b*. 31 December, 1800, *d*. June, 1876; member United States Congress and Alabama State Senate; *m*., 26 August, 1824, Martha Cade, of Marengo county, Alabama, and had:

MARY GREY ALSTON, *b*. 26 August, 1837, who *m*., 1 March, 1855, James Kent, M.D., of Petersburg, Virginia, *b*. 8 January, 1830, *d*. 22 May, 1881, colonel of the Forty-fourth Regiment of Alabama, Confederate States Army, during the Civil War, and had:

MARY ROSALINE KENT, *b*. 1 March, 1856, a member of the North Carolina and Alabama Societies of the Colonial Dames of America, the Order of the Crown, *etc*., who *m*., 8 September, 1875, Edward Taylor Fowlkes, of Selma, Alabama, *b*. 19 May, 1848, *d*. 3 June, 1886, and had: *Grace Byrd*, *b*. 17 August, 1876, *d*. 22 August, 1876, and *Ethel Edward*, *b*. 2 November, 1879.

2.—WILLIAM ALSTON, lieutenant-colonel North Carolina Line, Continental Army, member of the Provincial Congress, *etc.*, who *m.* his cousin, Charity Alston, and had:

MAJOR JAMES ALSTON, of Abbeville, South Carolina, an officer under General Jackson in the Florida war, *m.* Catherine, daughter of Major Andrew Hamilton, of Abbeville, who served under General Pickens in the Revolutionary war; a member of the South Carolina Assembly, *etc.*, and had:

JANE ALSTON, who *m.* Colonel Henry Coalter Cabell, of Richmond, Virginia (son of Governor William H. Cabell, of Virginia), chief of artillery in the Confederate States army of the peninsula, and of McLaw's Division, Confederate States army of Northern Virginia, and had:

KATHERINE HAMILTON CABELL, a member and the president of the Virginia Society of the Colonial Dames of America, who *m.* Herbert A. Claiborne, Jr., of Richmond, Virginia, also of Royal Descent (*see* "Americans of Royal Descent," ii., 689), and had: *Jennie Alston.*

PEDIGREE LXXX.

EDWARD I., King of England, had by his first wife, Princess Eleanor of Castile:

PRINCESS JOAN, who *m.*, first, Gilbert de Clare, Earl of Clare, Hertford and Gloucester, *d.* 1295, and had:

LADY MARGARET DE CLARE, who *m.*, secondly, Hugh, Baron d'Audley, created, 1337, Earl of Gloucester, *d. s. p., m.*, 1347, and had:

LADY MARGARET D'AUDLEY, who *m.* Sir Ralph de Stafford, K.G., second Baron Stafford, created, 1351, Earl of Stafford, *d.* 1372, and had:

HUGH DE STAFFORD, second Earl of Stafford, *d.* 1386, who *m.* Lady Phillippa de Beauchamp, daughter of Sir Henry, third Earl of Warwick, one of the original Knights of the Garter, *d.* 1369, and had:

LADY MARGARET DE STAFFORD, who *m.* (his first wife) Sir Ralph, K.G., fourth Baron Nevill, of Raby, earl marshal of England, created, 1399, Earl of Westmoreland, *d.* 1425, and had:

LADY MARGARET DE NEVILL, who *m.* Sir Richard le Scrope, of Bolton, *d.* 1420, and had:

SIR HENRY LE SCROPE, of Bolton, *d.* 1459, *m.* Elizabeth, daughter of John le Scrope, of Masham and Upsal, and had:

RICHARD LE SCROPE, second son, who *m.* Eleanor Washburne, and had:

ELEANOR LE SCROPE, who *m.* Sir Thomas Wyndham, *d.* 1522, and had:

MARY WYNDHAM, who *m.* Erasmus Paston, *d.* 1540, and had:

SIR WILLIAM PASTON, *d.* 1610, who *m.* Frances Clere, and had:

GERTRUDE PASTON, who *m.* Sir William Reade, son of William Reade, of London, *d.* 1522, and had:

SIR THOMAS READE, who *m.* Mildred, daughter of Sir Thomas Cecil, first Earl of Exeter, and had:

THOMAS READE, of Barton, *m.* Ann, daughter of Thomas Hooe, and had:

THOMAS READE, who *m.* Mary Stoneham, and had:

SIR THOMAS READE, Bart., *m.* Mary, daughter of John Brockett, and had:

SIR THOMAS READE, *m.* Mary, daughter of Sir Thomas Cornwall, of Burford, Sulop, and had:

WILLIAM READE, of Woburn, Massachusetts, *d.*, at New-Castle-on-Tyne, 1656. He *m.* Mabel Kendall, *d.* 5 June, 1690, and had:

RALPH READE, of Woburn, 1630–1711; *m.* Mary Peirce, 1636–1701, and had:

JOSEPH READ, of Woburn, *m.*, 1692, Phœbe Walker, and had:

NATHANIEL REED, *b.* 28 March, 1704, *m.*, 3 October, 1778, Hannah, *b.* 1 October, 1716, daughter of Ebenezer Flagg, 1678–1700, and had:

CAPTAIN JOSHUA REED, 1739–1805; *m.*, 28 November, 1759, Rachel, 1737–1818, daughter of Joshua Wyman, of Woburn, 1639–177–, and had:

MARY REED, 1760–1796, who *m.*, 1779, Eleaser Flagg Poole, of Woburn, 1761–1790, also of Royal Descent (*see* Browning's "Magna Charta Barons," p. 184), and had:

MARY POOLE, 1780–1857, who *m.*, 1798, Joshua Davis, of Springfield, Vermont, and had:

JOSHUA DAVIS, of Boston, Massachusetts, 1805–1873, who *m.*, 1827, Catherine Parkhurst, and had:

JOSHUA FLAGG DAVIS, of Boston and Chelmsford, Massachusetts, *m.*, 1853, Ellen Maria Cummings, also of Royal Descent (*see* p. 351), and had:

ANNA MARIA DAVIS, a member of the Vermont Society of the Colonial Dames of America, the Order of the Crown, *etc.*, who *m.*, 30 June, 1886, Lord Karl von Rydingsvård, of Sweden and Boston, Massachusetts.

PEDIGREE LXXXI.

ROBERT II., King of Scotland, had by his wife, Lady Elizabeth, daughter of Sir Adam Muir, of Rowallan:

ROBERT STUART, Duke of Albany, Regent of Scotland, who m. Lady Margaret, daughter of Murdoch, Earl of Monteith, and had:

LADY MARGARET STUART, who m. Sir Duncan Campbell, of Lochow, first Lord Campbell of Argyll, and had:

SIR COLIN CAMPBELL, of Glenurchy, d. 1478, who had by his fourth wife, Margaret, daughter of Luke Stirling, of Keir:

HELEN CAMPBELL, who m. William Stuart, of Balendivan (Baldowran) and Balquhidder, and had:

JOHN STUART, of Glenbucky, second son, who m. a daughter of Buchanan of MacCorthe, and had:

DUNCAN STUART, of Glenbucky, who m. a daughter of McLarin of Achleskin, and had:

ALEXANDER STUART, of Glenbucky, "who m. a second cousin" (a Stuart), and had:

PATRICK STUART, eldest son, who sold the right and title of Glenbucky to his brother Duncan. He m. Christian, daughter of Sir John Drummond, of Niganer, and had:

WILLIAM STUART, of Ledcreich and Translarry, who m. Mary, daughter of Duncan Macgregor, and had:

PATRICK STUART, of Ledcreich, an officer in the army of Charles I., and suffered greatly on account of his loyalty. He m. Margaret, daughter of Robert Buchanan, of Drumlain, and had:

ALEXANDER STUART, of Ledcreich, who m. Catherine, daughter of Alexander Stewart, "brother of Robert Stewart, of Glenogle," and had:

PATRICK STUART, eldest son and heir, laird of Ledcreich, in Balgheider, Perthshire, a staunch supporter of Prince Charles Edward. "He came, in company with six Argylshire gentlemen and his brother William, and above three hundred common people, from Scotland to Cape Fear, in North Carolina, in 1739" (*see* "American Historical Register," i., 441), and d. about 1772 at Cheraws, South Carolina. He m., in Perthshire, Elizabeth, daughter of Dr. Duncan Menzies, and had:

CATHERINE STUART, who m., first, 25 December, 1764, William Little,

Jr., of Cheraws (son of Chief Justice Little, of Edenton, North Carolina), b. 27 September, 1728, d. October, 1766, and had:

ELIZABETH LITTLE, b. 24 November, 1765, d. 26 April, 1829, who m., at Cheraws, 22 January, 1784, Morgan Brown, 4th, b. on Grassy Island, Pee Dee river, South Carolina, in January, 1758, d. in Tennessee, 23 February, 1840, and had:

ELIZABETH LITTLE BROWN, b. 6 February, 1792, d. 10 December, 1854, who m., first, in 1807, Samuel Vance, of Clarksville, Tennessee, 1784–1823, and had:

ELIZABETH LITTLE VANCE, b. 18 June, 1818, who m., 27 April, 1837, Robertson Topp, of Memphis, b. 20 April, 1807, d. June, 1876, and had:

FLORENCE TOPP, a member of the Tennessee Society of the Colonial Dames of America, who m., 8 August, 1867, William Martin Farrington, of Memphis, and had: *Florence*, d. 27 April, 1875; *William M.*, and *Valerie*.

PEDIGREE LXXXII.

HENRY I., King of France, had by his wife, Anne of Russia:

HUGH THE GREAT, Count of Vermandois, who had by his third wife, Lady Adelheid, daughter of Herbert IV., Count of Vermandois, also of Royal Descent:

LADY ISABEL DE VERMANDOIS, who *m.*, first, Robert de Bellomont, Earl of Mellent, created, in 1103, Earl of Leicester, and had:

LADY ELIZABETH DE BELLOMONT, who *m.* Gilbert Fitz-Gilbert de Clare, created, in 1138, Earl of Pembroke, *d.* 1149, and had:

RICHARD DE CLARE, "the Strongbow," second Earl of Pembroke, lord justice of Ireland, *d. s. p. m.* 1176, who *m.* Lady Eva, daughter of Dermot MacMurcha, the last King of Leinster, Ireland, and had:

LADY ISABEL DE CLARE, who *m.*, 1189 (his first wife), William le Marshal, Earl of Pembroke, protector of England, *d.* 1219, and had:

LADY SYBIL MARSHALL, who *m.* William de Ferrers, Earl of Derby and Nottingham, *d.* 1191, and had:

LADY MAUD DE FERRERS, widow of William de Kyme, who *m.*, secondly, William de Vyvon, son of Hugh de Vivonia and Mabel, daughter of William Malet, a surety for the Magna Charta, and had:

LADY CICELY DE VYVON, who *m.* John, Baron de Beauchamp, of Hache, Somerset, *d.* 1283, and had:

JOHN DE BEAUCHAMP, of Hache, first baron by writ, *d.* 1336, who *m.* Lady Joan d'Audley, and had:

JOHN DE BEAUCHAMP, of Hache, second Baron, *d.* 1343, who had by his wife, Lady Margaret:

LADY CICELY DE BEAUCHAMP, *m.* Sir Roger de St. Maur, and had:

SIR WILLIAM DE SEYMOUR, *m.* Margaret de Brockburn, and had:

ROGER DE SEYMOUR, *m.* Maud d'Esturmê, and had:

SIR JOHN DE SEYMOUR, *m.* Isabel MacWilliams, and had:

JOHN DE SEYMOUR, *m.* Elizabeth Coker, and had:

JOHN DE SEYMOUR, *m.* Elizabeth Darrell, and had:

SIR JOHN SEYMOUR, Knight banneret, of Wolf Hall, Wilts, *d.* 21 December, 1536, who *m.* Lady Margaret, *d.* 1550, daughter of Sir Henry Wentworth, of Nettlested, Suffolk, also of Royal Descent, and had:

SIR HENRY SEYMOUR, of Marvel, Hants, second son, made a Knight of the Bath at the coronation of his nephew, Edward VI. He was a brother of Edmund Seymour, first Duke of Somerset; Lady Jane Seymour, a queen consort of Henry VIII.; and Thomas, Lord Seymour, who m. Queen Catherine Parr, widow of Henry VIII. He m. Barbara, daughter of Thomas Morgan, Esq'r, and had *Sir John* and

LADY JANE SEYMOUR, who m. (*see* Collins's "Peerage") Sir John Rodney, of Stoke-Rodney and Pilton, Somerset, b. 1557, d. 6 August, 1612, and had sixteen children (*see* Thomas Sadler's pedigree of their descendants, 1765), of whom:

WILLIAM RODNEY, b. 1610, who d. at Hantsfield, Somersetshire, 12 June, 1699; m. Lady Alice, daughter of Sir Thomas Cæsar, a baron of the Exchequer, and had:

WILLIAM RODNEY, who came to Pennsylvania with Penn, in 1682, and became a member and first Speaker of the Assembly of Delaware; sheriff of Sussex county, and a member of Penn's Council in 1698, d. 8 April, 1708, aged 56. He m., first, in Philadelphia, 1688, Mary, daughter of Thomas and Sarah Hollyman, and had by her, who d. 20 December, 1692:

WILLIAM RODNEY, b. 27 October, 1689, d. 26 June, 1732; sheriff of Kent county, Delaware; m. Ruth, daughter of John Curtis, of New Castle, Delaware, and had:

JOHN RODNEY, of Lewes, Delaware, b. 7 September, 1725, b. 23 November, 1792; m., 1752, Ruth Hunn, and had:

JUDGE DANIEL RODNEY, of Lewes, b. 10 September, 1764, d. 2 September, 1846; Governor of Delaware, 1814–17; United States Senator from Delaware, 1826–27; m., 1788, Sarah, daughter of Major Henry Fisher, of Lewes, and had:

REV. JOHN RODNEY, of Germantown, Philadelphia, b. 20 August, 1796, d. 188–, who m. Sarah, daughter of James S. Duval, of Philadelphia, and had:

JOHN DUVAL RODNEY, of Philadelphia, who had:

LOUISE CHASZOURNE RODNEY, of Philadelphia, a member of the Pennsylvania Society of the Colonial Dames of America.

THE ROYAL DESCENT

OF

MRS. JOHN J. BAGLEY,

OF DETROIT, MICH.

WILLIAM I., King of England, had:
Henry I., King of England, who had:
Maud, *m.* Geoffrey, Count of Anjou, and had:
Henry II., King of England, who had:
John, King of England, who had:
Henry III., King of England, who had:
Edward I., King of England, who had:
Thomas, Earl of Norfolk., *etc.*, who had:
Margaret, *m.* John de Segrave, and had:
Elizabeth, *m.* John de Mowbray, and had:
Margery, *m.* John de Welles, and had:
Margery, *m.* Sir Stephen le Scrope, and had:
Sir Henry, Baron le Scrope, of Marham, who had:
Joan, *m.* Henry, Baron Fitzhugh, and had:
Henry, third Baron Fitzhugh, who had:
Eleanor, *m.* Philip, Baron d'Arcy, and had:
Margery, *m.* Sir John Conyers, K.G., and had:
Eleanor, *m.* Sir Thomas Markenfield, and had:
Sir Nyan de Markenfield, Knt., who had:
Alice, *m.* Robert Mauleverer, and had:
Dorothy, *m.* John Kaye, of Woodsome, and had:
Robert Kaye, of Woodsome, Yorkshire, who had:
Grace, *m.* Sir Richard Saltonstall, Knt., and had:

HUGH CAPET, King of France, had:
Robert the Pious, King of France, who had:
Henry I., King of France, who had:
Philip I., King of France, who had:
Louis VI., King of France, who had:
Louis VII., King of France, who had:
Philip II., King of France, who had:
Louis VIII., King of France, who had:
Louis IX., King of France, who had:
Philip III., King of France, who had:
Philip IV., King of France, who had:
Isabel, *m.* Edward II., King of England, and had:
Edward III., King of England, who had:
Thomas, Duke of Gloucester, who had:
Anne, *m.* Sir William, Earl of Ewe, and had:
Sir John Bouchier, K.G., Baron Berners, who had:
Sir Humphrey Bouchier, Knt., who had:
Sir John Bouchier, Baron Berners, who had:
Jane, *m.* Edmund Knyvett, and had:
John Knyvett, of Plumstead, Norfolk, who had:
Sir Thomas Knyvett, of Plumstead, who had:
Abigail, *m.* Sir Martin Sedley, and had:
Muriel, *m.* Brampton Gurdon, M.P., and had:

Richard Saltonstall, of Ipswich, Mass., *m.* Muriel Gurdon, of Assington, Suffolk.
Col. Nathaniel Saltonstall, of Haverhill=Elizabeth Ward, of Haverhill, Mass.
Elizabeth Saltonstall=Rev. Roland Cotton, of Sandwich, Mass.
Rev. John Cotton, D.D., of Newton, Mass.=Mary Gibbs.
Mary Cotton=Rev. Joseph Pynchon, D.D., of Boston, Mass.
Margaret Pynchon=Stephen Keeler, of Norwalk, Conn.
Margaret Keeler=Dr. Erastus Sergeant, Jr., of Lee, Mass.
Mary Ann Sergeant=Rev. Samuel Newbury, of Middlebury, Vt.
Frances E. Newbury, member of the Mass.=Gov. John Judson Bagley, of Detroit, Mich.
and Mich. Societies of the Colonial Dames
of America, *etc.*

Florence=R. M.	Katherine	John=Esther	Frances=Dr. F.	Margaret=George	Olive=Stedman
Bagley. Sherman.	Bagley, *d. unm.*	Newbury Bagley	Cutler. Bagley	Brown. Bagley	Hosmer. Bagley	Butterick.

Mary	Harold	Mary	John	Dwight	Philip	Marjorie	Dorothy	Margaret	Frances	Helen
Sherman.	Sherman.	Bagley.	Bagley.	Bagley.	Bagley.	Brown.	Brown.	Hosmer.	Butterick.	Butterick.

Paul Bagley, *unm.* Helen Bagley=James Anderson.
Helen Anderson.

PEDIGREE LXXXIII.

DAVID I., King of Scotland, had by his wife, Lady Matilda, widow of Simon de St. Liz, *d.* 1115, and daughter of Waltheof, Earl of Northumberland, beheaded in 1075:

HENRY, Earl of Northumberland, eldest son, *d. v. p.*, 1152, who *m.*, 1139, Lady Ada de Warren, *d.* 1178, daughter of William, second Earl of Warren and Surry, and had:

DAVID, Earl of Huntingdon (brother of King William the Lion), who *m.* Lady Maud, daughter of Hugh, Earl of Chester, and had:

LADY ISABEL DE HUNTINGDON, who *m.* Robert de Bruce, Earl of Annandale, and had:

ROBERT DE BRUCE, Earl of Annandale, a claimant to the crown of Scotland, who *m.* Lady Isabel de Clare, daughter of Gilbert, Earl of Clare and Gloucester, also of Royal Descent, and had:

ROBERT DE BRUCE, Earl of Annandale and Carrick, 1245–1304, who *m.*, 1271, Margaret, Countess of Carrick, and had:

LADY ISABEL BRUCE (sister of King Robert I., of Scotland), who *m.*, first, Sir Thomas Randolph, of Strathwith, high chamberlain of Scotland, 1296, and had:

THOMAS RANDOLPH, created, in 1314, Earl of Moray; regent of Scotland; *m.* Lady Isabel, daughter of Sir John Stewart, of Bonkyl, and had:

LADY AGNES RANDOLPH, known as "Black Agnes." During the absence of her husband she defended the castle of Dunbar for nineteen weeks against the English, in 1337–8. She *m.* Patrick, ninth Earl of Dunbar and Marche, and Earl of Moray, 1285–1369, also of Royal Descent, and had:

LADY AGNES DUNBAR, who *m.*, about 1372 (his first wife), Sir James Douglas, lord of Dalkeith and Liddesdale, *d.* 1420, and had:

LADY JANET DOUGLAS, who *m.* Sir John Hamilton, of Cadyow, *d.* before 28 July, 1397, and had:

SIR JAMES HAMILTON, of Cadyow, one of the hostages for the ransom of King James I. in 1424, and a member of His Majesty's Privy Council, who *m.*, before 20 October, 1422, Lady Janet, daughter of Sir Alexander Livingston, of Callendar, governor to young King James II., justice-general of Scotland in 1449, and ambassador to England, d. 145-, and his wife, a daughter of Dundas, of Dundas, and had:

GAVIN HAMILTON, provost of the Collegiate Church of Bothwell (see Wood's Douglas's "Peerage of Scotland," i., 311, 695), who m. Jean Muirhead, "the Fair Maid of Lechbrunnock," and had:

JOHN HAMILTON, of Orbiston, who m. Jean, daughter of Hamilton, of Woodhall, and had:

GAVIN HAMILTON, of Orbiston and Raplock, 1512–1540, commendator of Kilwinning, who m. Helen, daughter of Wallace, of Cairnhill, and had:

JOHN HAMILTON, of Orbiston, killed in the battle of Langsyde, who m. Margaret, daughter of Hamilton, of Haggs, and had:

MARJORY HAMILTON, who m. David Dundas, of Duddingston, and had:

JAMES DUNDAS, of Duddingston, eldest son (see Burke's "Landed Gentry," 1858), who had:

BETHIA DUNDAS, who m. James Hume, manager of the estates of James, Earl of Moray (son of Sir Patrick Hume, of Fastcastle, and his wife Elizabeth, daughter of Sir Neil Montgomery, of Lainshaw, k. 1547, also of Royal Descent, and sister of Isabel, wife of Robert Logan, of Restalrig), and had:

ISABEL HUME, who m. Patrick Logan, b. Ormiston, East Lothian, about 1630, a member of the Society of Friends, "an apt schoolmaster," employed in Ireland and in Bristol, England, by the Friends, after 1690 (see "Early History of the Society of Friends in Bristol," by William Tanner), who, it is believed, was a son of Robert Logan, aforesaid, eldest son of Sir Robert Logan, of Fastcastle, the last laird of Restalrig, d. 1602 (see "Americans of Royal Descent," vol. i., p. 226), and had:

JAMES LOGAN,* of "Stenton," Philadelphia county, Pennsylvania, b. Lurgan, County Armagh, Ireland, 20 October, 1674, d. 31 December, 1751. He succeeded his father as the schoolmaster at Bristol till 1699, when he came to Pennsylvania with William Penn as his secretary, and became chief justice of Pennsylvania and president of the Provincial Council, etc. He m., 1714, Sarah, daughter of Charles Read, of Philadelphia, a Provincial assemblyman and alderman, and had:

1.—WILLIAM LOGAN, of "Stenton," Philadelphia county, Pennsylvania, 1718–1776, a Provincial councillor (see Keith's "Provincial Councillors of Pennsylvania"), who m., 24 March, 1740, Hannah, 1722–1777, daughter of George Emlen, of Philadelphia, and had:

---

* MISS HETTY SMITH, a member of the Pennsylvania State Society of the National Society of the Colonial Dames of America, is of Royal Descent through James Logan.

I.—SARAH LOGAN, 1751–1796, who *m.*, 17 March, 1772, Thomas Fisher, of Philadelphia, 1741–1810 (*see* p. 16, Keith's "Provincial Councillors of Pennsylvania"), and had:

1.—WILLIAM LOGAN FISHER, of "Wakefield," Philadelphia county, Pennsylvania, 1781–1862; *m.*, first, 25 November, 1802, Mary, daughter of Samuel Rodman, of New Bedford, Massachusetts, and had:

THOMAS RODMAN FISHER, of Philadelphia, who *m.*, 18 November, 1829, Letitia, daughter of Jonathan Ellicott, of Ellicott's Mills, Maryland, and had:

MARY RODMAN FISHER, a member of the Pennsylvania Society of the Colonial Dames of America, who *m.*, 1 February, 1860, George W. Carpenter, of Germantown, Philadelphia, and had:

1.—LETITIA E. CARPENTER, *m.*, 18 April, 1881, William Redwood Wright, of Philadelphia.

2.—ELIZABETH RODMAN FISHER CARPENTER, a member of the Pennsylvania Society of the Colonial Dames of America, who *m.* Robert E. Glendinning, of Philadelphia.

2.—JOSHUA FISHER, of "Wakefield," Philadelphia, 1775–1806; *m.*, 1807, Elizabeth Powell, daughter of Tench and Ann (Willing) Francis, and had:

JOSHUA FRANCIS FISHER, of "Alverthorpe," Philadelphia, 1806–1873; *m.* Eliza Middleton, *d.* 1890, also of Royal Descent, and had:

MARIA MIDDLETON FISHER, a member of the Society of the Colonial Dames of America, who *m.* Brinton Coxe, of Philadelphia, and had: *Charlotte, Eliza, Marie,* and *Edmund.*

II.—CHARLES LOGAN, M.D., of "Belle Mead," Powhatan county, Virginia, *d.* 1794, *m.*, in 1779, by Friends' ceremony in Philadelphia, Mary Pleasants, and had:

SARAH PLEASANTS LOGAN, *b.* Philadelphia, 23 November, 1781, *m.*, at the residence of Samuel Pleasants, "Fine Creek," Powhatan county, 28 June, 1800, James Carter, M.D., of Prince Edwards county, Virginia, *b.* 3 May, 1769, and had:

MARY PLEASANTS CARTER, *b.* 16 August, 1807, *d.* 8 August, 1877; *m.*, 15 September, 1818, Thomas Radford Bolling, of Petersburg, Virginia, and had:

SALLY LOGAN BOLLING, *b.* 9 June, 1839, *d.* 25 April, 1892; *m.*, 7 April, 1858, Thomas Cowles Shearer, of Mobile, Alabama, and had:

MARTHA COWLES SHEARER, a member of the Pennsylvania and Texas Societies of the Colonial Dames of America, who m. George F. Pendexter, of Austin, Texas, son of George W. and Clara (Drew) Pendexter, of Dover, New Hampshire, and had: *George.*

III.—DR. GEORGE LOGAN, of "Stenton," 1753–1821; United States Senator, 1801–07; m., 1781, Deborah, daughter of Charles Norris, of "Fairhill," Philadelphia county, Pennsylvania, and had:

DR. ALBANUS CHARLES LOGAN, of "Stenton," m. Maria Dickinson, also of Royal Descent, and had:

GUSTAVUS GEORGE LOGAN, of "Stenton," m. Anna Armatt, and had:

FRANCES ARMATT LOGAN, a member of the Pennsylvania Society of the Colonial Dames of America, d. 8 May, 1898.

2.—HANNAH LOGAN, 1719–1761; m., 7 October, 1748, John Smith, of "Franklin Park," Burlington county, New Jersey, 1722–1771, a member of the Pennsylvania Assembly, and of the Governor's Council in New Jersey, and had:

I.—JOHN SMITH, of "Green Hill," Burlington county, New Jersey, 1761–1803; m., 8 April, 1784, Gulielma Maria Morris, 1766–1826, also of Royal Descent, and had:

JOHN JAY SMITH, of "Ivy Lodge," Philadelphia county, Pennsylvania, 1798–1881; m., 1821, Rachel C. Pearsall, and had:

ELIZABETH PEARSALL SMITH, of Germantown, Philadelphia, a member of the Pennsylvania Society of the Colonial Dames of America.

II.—JAMES SMITH, of Burlington county, New Jersey, 1750–1833; m., 13 January, 1772, Esther, daughter of William Heulings, of Burlington, New Jersey, and had:

1.—HANNAH SMITH, 1773–1830, who m. 11 December, 1794, Henry S. Drinker, of Philadelphia, d. 1824, and had:

ESTHER DRINKER, b. 1 November, 1798, who m. Israel Pemberton Pleasants, and had:

NANCY PEMBERTON PLEASANTS, a member of the Pennsylvania Society of the Colonial Dames of America, who m. Samuel S. Hollingsworth, of Philadelphia, and had: *Esther D. P., Samuel S., Mary E.,* d. 1883; *Israel P. P., Roger P., John V. P.,* and *Nancy P.*

2.—JAMES LOGAN SMITH, of Chambersburg, Pennsylvania, b. 14 September, 1793, d. 6 March, 1843; m., secondly, 11 September, 1838, Mary daughter of James Couper, M.D., and had:

ANNIE COUPER SMITH, who m. Rev. Alexander Proudfit, and had:

MARY COUPER PROUDFIT, of Springfield, Ohio, a member of the Maryland and Ohio Societies of the Colonial Dames of America.

PEDIGREE LXXXIV.

ROBERT THE PIOUS, King of France, had by his second wife, Lady Constance, daughter of William, Count of Provence:

LADY ADELA, who *m.*, first, Richard III., Duke of Normandy, (she *m.*, secondly, Baldwin V., of Flanders, and by him was the mother of Maud, queen consort of William the Conqueror), and had:

LADY ALIX, who *m.* Ranulf, viscount of Bayeux, and had:

RANULF DE MESCHINES, viscount of Bayeux, created, 1119, Earl Palatine of Chester; *m.* Lady Maud, daughter of Rubard, Viscount de Auveranches, created, 1086, Earl of Chester, and had:

RANULF DE MESCHINES, Earl Palatine of Chester, *d.* 1153; *m.* Lady Maud, daughter of Robert, Earl of Mellent and Gloucester, and had:

HUGH DE MESCHINES, Earl Palatine of Chester, *d.* 1181, who had by his wife, Lady Bartred, daughter of Simon, Earl of Evereux:

LADY ―――― DE MESCHINES, who *m.* Reginald Bacon (*see* pp. 30–31), and had:

RICHARD BACON, who *m.* Alice de Multon, and had:

SIR ROBERT BACON, of Baconsthorp, Norfolk, who *m.* the daughter of Sir Richard d'Ingham, and had:

SIR THOMAS BACON, who *m.* Elizabeth ――――, living 1249, and had:

SIR HENRY BACON, 1270, who had:

SIR HENRY BACON, who *m.* Margaret Ludham, and had:

SIR ROGER BACON, who *m.* Felicia Kirton, and had:

BEATRICE BACON, heiress, who *m.* Sir William Thorpe, and had:

WILLIAM THORPE, *m.* Margery, daughter of John Quadlop, and had:

JOHN THORPE, whose daughter and heiress:

MARGERY THORPE, *m.* John Bacon, of Drinkstone, and had:

EDMUND BACON, of Drinkstone, who *m.* Elizabeth Crofts, and had:

JOHN BACON, of Drinkstone, who *m.* Agnes Cockfield, and had:

ROBERT BACON, of Drinkstone, who *m.* Isabel Cage, and had:

ALDERMAN JAMES BACON, of London, *d.* 15 June, 1573, *bur.* St. Dunstan's (a brother of Sir Nicholas Bacon, lord keeper of the Great Seal, 1509–1579, whose son was the celebrated Sir Francis, Lord Verulam), who had by his second wife, Margaret, daughter of William Rawlings, of London, and widow of Richard Gouldston:

SIR JAMES BACON, of Friston Hall, Suffolk, knighted in 1604 at White Hall, d. 17 January, 1618; m. Elizabeth, daughter of Francis Bacon, of Hessett, d. 14 December, 1580, and had: *Rev. James* (see p. 32 and "Va. His. Mag.," ii., 125), and:

NATHANIEL BACON, of Friston Hall, eldest son, b. 15 May, 1593, bur. 7 August, 1644, at Friston Church; m. Anne, daughter of Sir Thomas le Grosse, of Crostwick, Norfolk, and had:

THOMAS BACON, of Friston (see "Va. His. Mag.," i., 430), who had by his first wife, Elizabeth, d. 2 January, 1647, aged 25 years, daughter of Sir Robert Brooke, of Cockfield Hall, Suffolk:

MAJOR-GENERAL NATHANIEL BACON,* the younger, "the Rebel Patriot of 1676" (see "Va. His. Mag.," i., p. 170), only son, b. 2 January, 1647, d. in Gloucester county, Virginia, 26 October, 1666 (see "N. E. His. Geneal. Reg.," vol. xxxvii.; Keith's "Ancestry of Benjamin Harrison," and Brown's "Genesis of the United States"). He m. Elizabeth, bapt. 17 December, 1650, daughter of Sir Edward Duke, Bart., of Burhall Lodge, Suffolk (see Suckling's "His. of Suffolk," ii., 186; Burke's "Extinct Baronetages"), and had: *Elizabeth* (called also Mary) bapt. Friston parish, 12 April, 1674, m. Dr. Hugh Chamberlain, physician to Queen Anne, and (according to pedigrees accepted by the Georgia Society of the Colonial Dames):

NATHANIEL BACON (called also "John"), b. in Virginia 1675-6. After his father's death he was adopted in the family of Mrs. Frances Izard. In 1725 he petitioned the Virginia Council for confirmation to him of the grant of 1030 acres of land in Henrico county, which he inherited from Mrs. Izard. His will, dated in 1743, probated in Henrico county, mentions his children by his wife Elizabeth Parke, of whom:

1.—NATHANIEL PARKE BACON, of Henrico county, Virginia, father of:

CAPTAIN JOHN BACON, of Georgia, m. Agnes Hobson, and had:

I.—JOHN BACON, of Savannah, Georgia, d. April, 1812, aged 46; m.

---

* The following ladies, members of the National Society of the Colonial Dames of America, are also of Royal Descent, through General Nathaniel Bacon:

MRS. ANN BARRETT PHINIZY, Georgia State Society.
MRS. MARY E. WARE CHARBONNIER (deceased), Georgia State Society.
MRS. FRANK H. MILLER, JR., Georgia State Society.
MRS. JAMES F. MCGOWAN, Georgia State Society.
MRS. SAMUEL H. MCAFEE, Georgia State Society.
MRS. MARY K. ADAMS BULKLEY, Georgia State Society.
MRS. PLEASANT A. STOVALL, Georgia State Society.
MRS. ALEXANDER J. PERRY, Georgia State Society.
MRS. SARAH D. ADAMS MCWHORTER, Georgia State Society.

PEDIGREE LXXXIV.—*Continued.*

Eliza Ruffin, daughter of Nathaniel Cocke, of Fauquier county, Virginia, and had:

JOHN EDMUND BACON, *b.* Augusta, Georgia, 1812, *d.* Columbus, Georgia, 1882; *m.*, first, Clementina, daughter of Robert West Alston, of Halifax county, North Carolina, and had by her:

1.—ROBERT ALSTON BACON, of Graysville, Georgia, *unm.*

2.—HENRIETTA ALSTON BACON, of Alexander City, Alabama, who *m.*, 1858, Joseph Bibb McDonald, and had:

I.—JOHN BACON MCDONALD, a graduate of the United States Military Academy, Captain in the 3d Cavalry, United States Army, *b.* 1859; *m.*, 1888, Kate Murphy, and had: *Joseph Robert, d. inf.; Joseph Edmund, b.* 1890; *Robert Dyer, b.* 1892; *Lila Mary, b.* 1894; and *John Bacon, b.* 1897.

II.—MARY MALONE MCDONALD, *b.* 1860; *m.*,1885, Hiram Donald Barr, M.D., of Anniston, Alabama, and had: *Roberta Bacon, d. inf.*, and *Henrie Lynn, b.* 1889.

III.—JOSEPH STERLING MCDONALD, 1862–1898; *m.*, 1888, Lula Penny, *d.* 1897.

IV.—CLEMENTINA ALSTON MCDONALD, *b.* 1865; *m.*, 1887, James Elbert Pearson, M.D., of Sylacauga, Alabama, and had: *Katie May, b.* 1889; *Leslie Alston, b.* 1891, and *McDonald, b.* 1893.

V.—ROBERTA BACON MCDONALD, *b.* 1878; *m.*, 1899, Benjamin Russell.

II.—EDMUND BACON, *m.* Elizabeth Cocke, and had:

SARAH BACON, *m.* Sherwood Bugg, and had:

OBEDIENCE BUGG, *m.* Colonel James Maitier, and had:

KEZIA PARIS MAITIER, *m.* Major George Golphin Yoville McMurphy, and had:

SARAH SUSANNAH MCMURPHY, *m.* John Marsh Adams, and had:

ELIZABETH BACON ADAMS, a member of the Georgia and Michigan Societies of the Colonial Dames of America, who *m.* Joshua Henry Rathbone, M.D., of Ann Arbor, Michigan.

2.—NATHANIEL BACON, of Henrico county, 1705–1779, who had:

I.—AGNES BACON, *m.* Matthew Hobson, of Virginia, and had:

AGNES HOBSON, *m.* John Langston Bacon, and had:

MARY BACON, *m.* General Thomas Glascock, of Richmond county, Georgia, and had:

GENERAL THOMAS GLASCOCK, JR., *m.* Harriet Hatcher Hayes, and had:

MARY SAVANNAH GLASCOCK, *m.* Thomas Barrett, and had:

HARRIET GLASCOCK BARRETT, m. James Gardner Gould, son of Judge William Tracy Gould, son of Judge James Gould, of Litchfield, Connecticut, and Sally McCurdy, a daughter of Major-General Uriah Tracy, a descendant of Deputy-Governor William Bradford, son of Governor William Bradford, and had:

HARRIET GOULD, of Augusta, a member of the Georgia Society of the Colonial Dames of America, Society of "Mayflower" Descendants, Society of Descendants of Colonial Governors, *etc.*, who m. Richard Sims Jefferies (deceased), and had: *James Gould.*

II.—SARA BACON, *d.* 26 January, 1816, aged 76, who *m.*, before 1760, Charles Edwin Crenshaw, of Hanover county, Virginia, and had:

MARY TEMPERANCE CRENSHAW, *d.* 26 March, 1807, who *m.* William Rice, M.D., of Charlotte, Virginia, and had:

SAMUEL BLAIR RICE, of Halifax, Virginia, who *m.* Lucinda Walton, daughter of Rev. William Leftwich, of Bedford, Virginia, and had:

SARA AGNES RICE, a member of the Virginia Society of the Colonial Dames of America, who *m.* Roger A. Pryor, LL.D., judge of supreme court, New York City, Brigadier-General Confederate States Army; *b.* Dinwiddie county, Virginia, 19 July, 1828, and had:

1.—MARIE GORDON PRYOR, a member of the Virginia Society of the Colonial Dames of America, *m.* Henry Crenshaw Rice, of Charlotte, Virginia, and had: *Mary Blair, Henry Izard Bacon, Roger Pryor* and *Theodorick Bland.*

2.—THEODORICK BLAND PRYOR, *unm.* 1871.

3.—ROGER A. PRYOR, JR., of New York.

4.—MARY BLAIR PRYOR, a member of the Virginia Society of the Colonial Dames of America, who *m.* Francis T. Walker of Charlottesville, Virginia, and had: *Roger Pryor, Lindsay Howell, Frances Theodora Bland, Francis Thomas* and *Mary Blair.*

5.—WILLIAM RICE PRYOR, M.D., of New York, *m.* Louise Gabrielle, daughter of John Allan, of Richmond, Virginia, and had: *Hoffman Allan* and *Louise Gabrielle.*

6.—LUCY ATKINSON PRYOR, a member of the Virginia Society of the Colonial Dames of America, who *m.* Arthur Page Brown, of San Francisco, California, and had: *Katrina Trask, Agnes,* and *Lucy.*

7.—FRANCES THEODORA BLAND PRYOR, of New York, a member of the Virginia Society of the Colonial Dames of America, *m.* William de Leftwich Dodge, of Paris, France, and had: *Roger Pryor.*

THE ROYAL DESCENT
OF
MRS. JOHN FLICK WINSLOW,
OF CINCINNATI, OHIO.

EDWARD I., King of England=Princess Eleanor of Castile.
Princess Elizabeth Plantagenet=Humphrey de Bohun, Earl of Hereford.
Lady Margaret de Bohun=Hugh de Courtenay, Earl of Devon.
Lady Elizabeth de Courtenay=Sir Andrew Luttrell, of Chilton.
Lady Elizabeth Luttrell=John Stratton, of Weston.
Elizabeth Stratton=John Andrews, of Stoke.
Elizabeth Andrews=Thomas Wyndsore.
Sir Andrews Wyndsore, of Stanwell=Lady Elizabeth Blount.
Lady Edith Wyndsore=George Ludowe, of Hill Deverill.
Thomas Ludlow, of Dinton=Jane Pyle, of Bopton, Wilts.
Gabriel Ludlow, 1587-1639=Phyllis ———.
Sarah Ludlow (fourth wife)=John Carter, of Gloucester Co., Va.
Robert Carter, of "Carotoman"=Elizabeth (Landon) Willis.
Mary Carter=George Braxton, of King and Queen Co., Va.
Carter Braxton, of "Elsing Green," Va.=Judith Robinson.
Judith Braxton=John White, of Va.
Mary Page White=Andrew Stevenson, of "Blenheim," Va.
John W. Stevenson, of Covington, Ky.=Sibella Winston.
Judith White Stevenson=John F. Winslow, of Cincinnati.
John W. S. Winslow, b. 3 April, 1893.

PEDIGREE LXXXV.

EDWARD III., King of England, had by his wife, Lady Philippa, daughter of William, Count of Hainault and Holland:

SIR LIONEL PLANTAGENET, K.G., Duke of Clarence, who *m.*, first, Lady Elizabeth, daughter of Sir William de Burgh, third Earl of Ulster, and his wife, Lady Maud, daughter of Henry Plantagenet, Earl of Lancaster, both of Royal Descent, and had:

LADY PHILIPPA PLANTAGENET, who *m.* Edmund de Mortimer, Earl of Marche, *d.* 1381, also of Royal Descent, and had:

LADY ELIZABETH DE MORTIMER, who *m.* Sir Henry Percy, called Hotspur, *k.* 1403, also of Royal Descent, and had:

LADY ELIZABETH PERCY, who *m.* John de Clifford, Baron Clifford, *d.* 1432, also of Royal Descent, and had:

THOMAS DE CLIFFORD, Baron Clifford, *k.* 1454, *m.* Lady Joan, daughter of Thomas de Dacre, first Baron Dacre, also of Royal Descent, and had:

JOHN DE CLIFFORD, Baron Clifford, *k.* 1461, father of

JOHN DE CLIFFORD, Baron Clifford, *d.* 1485, *m.* Lady Margaret, daughter of Sir Henry de Bromflete, of Vesci, Yorkshire, also of Royal Descent, and had:

LADY MARY DE CLIFFORD, who *m.* Sir Philip Wentworth, of Nettlested, Suffolk, and had:

SIR HENRY WENTWORTH, of Nettlested, who *m.* Lady Anne, daughter of Sir John de Say, and had:

LADY ELIZABETH WENTWORTH, who *m.* Sir John Seymour, of Wolf Hall, Wilts, *d.* 1536, also of Royal Descent, and had:

SIR EDWARD DE SEYMOUR, K.G., first Duke of Somerset, beheaded in 1552; *m.*, first, Lady Catherine, daughter of Sir William Fillol, of Woodlands, Dorset, and his wife Elizabeth Wingfield, also of Royal Descent, and had:

SIR EDWARD DE SEYMOUR, Lord Seymour, *d.* 1593, *m.* Mary, or Margaret, daughter of Judge John Welsh, and had:

SIR EDWARD SEYMOUR, Bart., of Berry-Pomeroy, who *m.* Elizabeth, daughter of Sir Arthur Champernon, of Darlington, Devon, also of Royal Descent, and had:

LADY MARY SEYMOUR, *m.* Sir George Farwell, of Hill-Bishop, Somerset, *d.* 1647, and had:

PEDIGREE LXXXV.—Continued.

JOHN FARWELL, of Hill-Bishop, who m. Dorothy, daughter of Sir John Routh, and had:

HENRY FARWELL, d., at Chelmsford, Massachusetts, 1 August, 1670, m. Olive ——, d. 1 March, 1691-2, and had:

JOSEPH FARWELL, of Dunstable, Massachusetts, 1642-1722; m., 25 December, 1666, Hannah Learned, of Woburn, and had:

SARAH FARWELL, m., 5 September, 1707, Jonathan Howard, of Chelmsford, 1675-1758, and had:

JACOB HOWARD, of Chelmsford, Massachusetts, 1719-1798; m., 1745, Rachel Fletcher, and had:

SARAH HOWARD, m., 1776, John Cummings, of Tyngsboro, Massachusetts, 1753-1837, and had:

JOHN CUMMINGS, of Tyngsboro, who m., 1806, Salla Cummings, also of Royal Descent (see p. 229), and had:

WILLARD CUMMINGS, who m. Mary Anne Pollard, and had:

ELLEN MARIA CUMMINGS, who m. Joshua Flagg Davis, of Boston and Chelmsford, also of Royal Descent (see p. 336), and had:

ANNA MARIA DAVIS, a member of the Vermont Society of the Colonial Dames of America, the Order of the Crown, etc., who m., 30 June, 1886, Lord Karl von Rydingsvärd, of Sweden and Boston, Massachusetts.

THE ROYAL DESCENT

OF

MRS. SAMUEL F. LEIB,

OF "LIEBHEIM," SAN JOSÉ, CAL.

ALFRED THE GREAT, King of England=Lady Ethelbith.
　Edward the Elder, King of England=Lady Edgiva.
　　Edmund I., King of England=Lady Elgiva.
　　　Edgar the Peaceful, King of England=Lady Elfrida.
　　Ethelred the Unready, King of England=Lady Elgifa.
　　　Edmund Ironsides, King of England=Lady Algita.
　　　Prince Edward the Exile, of England=Lady Agatha.
　　　　Princess Margaret, of England=Malcolm III., King of Scotland.
　　　　Princess Matilda, of Scotland=Henry I., King of England.
　　　　　Maud, Empress of Germany=Geoffrey, Count of Anjou.
　　　　Henry II., King of England=Lady Eleanor of Aquitaine.
　　　　　John, King of England=Lady Isabel de Taillefer.
　　　Henry III., King of England=Lady Eleanor of Provence.
　　　　Edward I., King of England=Lady Eleanor of Castile.
　　　　Princess Elizabeth of England=Humphrey, Earl of Hereford and Essex.
　Sir William, Earl of Northampton, K. G.=Lady Elizabeth de Badlesmere.
　　　Lady Elizabeth de Bohun=Sir Richard, Earl of Arundel, K. G.
　　　　Lady Elizabeth Fitzalan=Sir Robert Goushill, of Hault Hucknall.
　　　　　Lady Joan Goushill=Sir Thomas, Baron Stanley, K. G.
　　　　Lady Elizabeth Stanley=Sir Richard Molineux, of Sefton.
　　　Sir Thomas Molineux, of Sefton=Lady Anne Dutton.
　　　Sir William Molineux, of Sefton=Lady Jane Rigge.
　　　Sir Richard Molineux, of Sefton=Lady Eleanor Ratcliffe.
　　　　Lady Margaret Molineux=John Warren, of Pointon, Cheshire.
　　　Sir Edward Warren, of Pointon=Lady Anne Davenport.
　　　　John Warren, of Pointon=Anne Ognal.
　　　　　Edward Warren, of Pointon=Margaret Arderne.
Humphrey Warren, of "Frailty," Charles Co., Md.=Eleanor (second wife).
Thomas Warren, of "Frailty," Charles Co., Md.=Mary Barton (first wife).
Barton Warren, of "Frailty," Charles Co., Md.=Elizabeth ———.
Mary Warren (widow of Harrison Musgrave)=John Stone, of Charles Co., Md.
　　Rev. Barton Warren Stone, 1772-1844=Elizabeth Campbell (first wife).
　　　　Mary Ann Harrison Stone=Charles Chilton Moore, of Fayette Co., Ky.
　　　　　Hannah A. Ransdell Moore=John de Lafayette Grissim, M.D., Georgetown, Ky.

Lida Campbell Grissim, a member of the Va. and Cal. Societies of the Colonial Dames of America, Society of Daughters of the American Revolution, the Order of the Crown, etc. (See p. 319.) = Judge Samuel Franklin Leib, of "Liebheim," San José, Cal.

| Lida Campbell Leib, member of the Order of the Crown. | Elna Warren Leib. | Franklin Allen Leib. | Roy Chilton Leib. | Earl Warren Leib. |

THE ROYAL DESCENT
OF
MRS. WILLIAM J. STONE, JR.
OF WASHINGTON, D. C.

ALFRED THE GREAT, of England, had:
Edward the Elder, King of England, who had:
Edmund I., King of England, who had:
Edgar, King of England, who had:
Ethelred II., King of England, who had:
Elgiva, *m.* Ulthred of Northumberland, and had:
Eldigitha, *m.* Maldred, Lord of Isles, and had:
Cospatrick, Earl of Northumberland, who had:
Gunilda, *m.* Orme, Lord of Seaton, and had:
Cospatrick, 1st Lord of Workington, who had:
Thomas de Workington, *d.* 1152, who had:
Patrick Curwen, of Workington Hall, who had:
Gilbert Curwen, of Workington Hall, who had:
Gilbert Curwen, of Workington Hall, who had:
Gilbert Curwen, of Workington Hall, who had:
Gilbert Curwen, of Workington Hall, who had:
William Curwen, of Workington Hall, who had:
Christopher Curwen, of Workington Hall, who had:
Sir Thomas Curwen, of Workington, who had:
Elizabeth, *m.* John Cleburne, *d.* 1489, and had:
Thomas Cleburne, of Cleburne Hall, who had:
Robert Cleburne, of Cleburne Hall, who had:
Edmund Cleburne, of Cleburne Hall, who had:
Richard Cleburne, of Cleburne Hall, who had:
Edmund Claiborne, of Cleburne Hall, who had:
William Claiborne, of "Romancock," who had:
William Claiborne, of "Romancock," who had:
William Claiborne, of Virginia, who had:
William Claiborne, of Virginia, who had:

ALFRED THE GREAT, of England, had:
Edward the Elder, King of England, who had:
Edmund I., King of England, who had:
Edgar, King of England, who had:
Ethelred II., King of England, who had:
Edmund Ironsides, King of England, who had:
Prince Edward the Exile, of England, who had:
Margaret, *m.* Malcolm, King of Scots, and had:
Matilda, *m.* Henry I., of England, and had:
Maud, *m.* Geoffrey, Count of Anjou, and had:
Henry II., King of England, who had:
John, King of England, who had:
Henry III., King of England, who had:
Edmund Plantagenet, Earl Lancaster, who had:
Henry Plantagenet, Earl Lancaster, who had:
Joan, *m.* John, Baron de Mowbray, and had:
John, 4th Baron de Mowbray, who had:
Eleanor, *m.* Roger, Baron de la Warr, and had:
Joan, *m.* Sir Thomas, Baron de West, and had:
Sir Reginald, Lord de la Warr, who had:
Sir Richard West, Lord de la Warr, who had:
Thomas West, K. G., Lord de la Warr, who had:
Sir George West, 2d son, *d.* 1538, who had:
Sir William West, Lord de la Warr, who had:
Sir Thomas West, Lord de la Warr, who had:
Col. John West, Gov. of Va., 1635, who had:
Col. John West, "West Point," Va., who had:
Nathaniel West, of "West Point," who had:
Unity, *m.* William Dandridge, R. N., and had:

Philip W. Claiborne, of "Liberty Hall," Va. *m.* Elizabeth Dandridge.

Philadelphia Claiborne=Rev. Abner Waugh, of Caroline Co., Va.

Sarah Spotswood Waugh=James Lyons, M. D., of Richmond, Va.

Lucy Watkins Lyons=Thomas Green, of Richmond, Va., and Washington, D. C.

Mary Frances Green, *m.* at the Van Ness=William J. Stone, Jr., of Washington, D. C.
Mansion, Washington City, 4 Dec., 1849.

Thomas=Elizabeth	George=Minerva	W'lliam Isabella	Mary=Hobart	Bessie	Roberta=Abram H.
Green | Putnam.	Blagdon | Winston	Lenthall Green	Lyons|Hutton.	Pinkney	King | Witmer,
Stone.	Stone. | Payne.	Stone. Stone.	Stone.	Stone.	Stone. | M. D.

Thomas	Isabella	John	Lucy	Robert	Isabella	Mary	Anne	William	George
Green	Green	Payne	Lyons	King	Green	Frances	Gordon	Stone	Stone
Stone.	Stone.	Stone.	Stone.	Stone.	Stone.	Stone.	Hutton.		Witmer.

PEDIGREE LXXXVI.

The Sureties for the Observance of the Magna Carta.

William d'Albini.
Hugh le Bigod.
Roger le Bigod.
Henry de Bohun.
Gilbert de Clare.
Richard de Clare.
John Fitz Robert.
Robert Fitz Walter.
William de Fortibus, d. s. p.
William Hardell, d. s. p.
William de Huntingfield.
John de Lacie.

William de Lanvallei.
William de Malet.
Geoffrey de Mandeville, d. s. p.
William le Marshal, d. s. p.
Richard de Montfichet, d. s. p.
Roger de Mowbray, d. s. p.
William de Mowbray.
Richard de Percy, d. s. p.
Saher de Quincey.
Robert de Roos.
Geoffrey de Say.
Robert de Vere.
Eustace de Vesci.

SAHER DE QUINCEY had Robert, who had Margaret, m. JOHN DE LACIE and had Maud, m. Richard de Clare (son of GILBERT DE CLARE, son of RICHARD DE CLARE, whose cousin was the mother of RICHARD DE PERCY), and had Gilbert, who had Margaret, who had Margaret d'Audley, who had Hugh de Stafford, who had Margaret, who had Alice de Neville, who m. Thomas de Grey,* and had:

Elizabeth, m. Philip d'Arcy,† and had John d'Arcy, who had:

ROGER LE BIGOD had HUGH LE BIGOD, who m. a sister of WILLIAM MARSHALL (whose wife was sister to WILLIAM FORTIBUS, brother-in-law to RICHARD DE MONTFICHET), and had Ralph, who had Isabel, who had John Fitzjohn, who had Maud, m. William de Beauchamp (son of Isabel de Mauduit, dau. of Alice de Newburgh, dau. of Margery, dau. of HENRY DE BOHUN, whose wife was sister to GEOFFREY DE MANDEVILLE), and had Isabel, who had Maud de Chaworth, who had Joan Plantagenet, m. John de Mowbray (son of John, son of Roger, son of Roger, son of WILLIAM DE MOWBRAY, brother to ROGER DE MOWBRAY), and had John, m. Elizabeth (dau. of John de Segrave, son of Alice Fitzalan, dau. of Alice de Warren, dau. of Joan de Vere, dau. of Hugh, son of ROBERT DE VERE), and had Jane, who was the mother of this Thomas de Grey.*

ROBERT DE ROOS, had William, who had Robert, m. Isabel (dau. of William, son of WILLIAM D'ALBINI), and had William, who had Alice, who had Elizabeth de Meinill, who was the mother of this Philip d'Arcy.†

EUSTACE DE VESCI, had William, who had William, who had Isabel, who had Adam de Welles, who had Adam, who had John, who had John, who had Margery, m. Stephen le Scrope (son of Blanche de Norwich, dau. of Alice, dau. of William, son of Roger, son of William, son of Roger, son of WILLIAM DE HUNTINGFIELD), and had Henry, who had Joan, who had Henry Fitzhugh, m. Elizabeth (dau. of Robert de Marmyon, son of John de Grey, son of Margaret Odingsells, dau. of Ela, dau. of

PEDIGREE LXXXVI.—Continued.

Philip d'Arcy, *m.* Eleanor Fitzhugh,** and had:

Margaret, who had Eleanor Coniers, who had Nyan de Markenfield, who *m.* Dorothy Gascoigne††, and had:

Walter Fitzrobert, son of ROBERT FITZ-WALTER), and had this Eleanor Fitzhugh.**

GEOFFREY DE SAYE, had William, who had William, whose daughter had John de Sudley, who had Joan, who had Elizabeth le Boteler, *m.* Robert de Ferrers (son of Hawise, dau. of Robert, son of John de Muscegros, son of Hawise, dau. of WILLIAM MALET), and had Robert, who had Mary, *m.* Ralph de Neville (son of Ralph, son of John, son of Ralph de Neville, son of Euphemia, dau. of Robert, son of Roger, son of JOHN FITZROBERT), and had John, who had Joan, who had William de Gascoigne, *m.* Margaret (dau. of Henry, son of Henry de Percy, son of Elizabeth de Mortimer, dau. Philippa Plantagenet, dau. of Elizabeth, dau. of William, son of John son of Margaret, dau. of John de Burgh, son of Hawise, dau. of WILLIAM DE LANVALLEI), and had this Dorothy Gascoigne.††

LADY ALICE DE MARKENFIELD, who was, as above, lineally descended from eighteen of the twenty-five Sureties for the Magna Carta of King John, and was related to six of the others. Of descendants, if any, of the other Surety, William Hardell, nothing is known. (See Browning's "Magna Carta Barons and their American Descendants"). She *m.* Robert Mauleverer, of Wothersome, Yorks. Their marriage settlement was made 16 October, 1524, and on December 1st, following, Cardinal Wolsey granted them a dispensation for marriage, as they were related. He was a son of Sir William Mauleverer, of Arncliffe Hall, sheriff of Yorks in 1521, buried at Bardsey church, 12 August, 1551. See William Brown's "Ingleby Arncliffe and its Owners." Robert Mauleverer's will, dated 5 December, 1540, was proved by his widow, 22 June following. Her will, dated 4 March, 1552-3, was proved 7 March. Both were buried at Bardsey. Thay had four sons and two daughters. Of these:

1.—DOROTHY MAULEVERER, *m.* John Kaye, (see pp. 205, 296, 358.)

2.—SIR EDMUND MAULEVERER, of Arncliffe Hall, Yorkshire, heir, a Roman Catholic, as had been his ancestors. He was knighted in 1553, (Metcalf's "Book of Knights," 109), and was appointed "captenne and conductor of C fotemen in the king and quene's maties ceruices northewardes." He was buried in Bardsey church, 27 April, 1571. His will, dated 26 April, 1571, describes him as "of Woodersome, Knighte," proved 28 July by his relict and executrix, Mary. He *m.* (covenant dated 30 September, 1541), Mary, a daughter of Sir Christopher Danby, of Thorp Perrow, Yorks, who was knighted by the Earl of Surrey, after the battle of Flodden, with Nyan de Markenfield and William Mauleverer, aforesaid, and had:

WILLIAM MAULEVERER, of Arncliffe Hall, heir, *bapt.* 1 May, 1557, at Bardsey. He became a Protestant; compiled several genealogies of his family, still preserved; was a magistrate in the North Riding, and declined to be knighted. He was buried at Arncliffe, in April, 1618. His will, dated 14 April, proved 1 October, 1618. He *m.* (covenant dated April, 1571), Eleanor, 1553-1642, a daughter of his guardian, Richard Aldburgh, of Humburton, and had fifteen children, of whom

JAMES MAULEVERER, of Arncliffe Hall, second son and heir, *b.* 1 February, 1590-1. His father devised him "my tente, drummes, and armour, and the rest of my plate not bequeathed." He declined knighthood, because he was a "patriot," and opposed to the Stewarts, and also refused to pay a composition to Charles I., and was fined £2,000 and costs. The payment of this fine, and the depreciation of his estates, owing to enforced absence and borrowing money on hard terms, placed him in very poor circumstances at the outbreak of the Civil War. He petitioned and got some relief from the Long Parliament, being voted £3,509 as a *solatium,* and was appointed a colonel of Horse under Cromwell. Before the war he had contracted for the purchase of Ayton Manor, in Pickering Lythe, and this and other expensive ventures, among them the attempt to get possession of the Markenfield and the Strangeway estates, claiming to be the rightful heir, ruined him completely, and in 1651 he became a bankrupt, and very poor. Finally he was imprisoned for debt, in York Castle, where he died, leaving no assets, and was buried in St. Mary's Church, Castlegate, York city, 25 April, 1664. His eldest surviving son, Timothy, took charge of the family estates, and in 1651, when his father became bankrupt, supported and educated the younger children, and made allowances to his father. The surviving children were the said Timothy,* 1627-1687, of Ingleby Arncliffe Hall; James, 1628-1703, Governor of Windsor, 1685; Edmund, (see below), and Elizabeth Blakiston, Eleanor Nowers, and Beatrice Wright.

JAMES MAULEVERER, 1591-1664, *m.* at Richmond Church, 27 November, 1613, Beatrice Hutton, *bapt.* at St. Olave's, York, 24 June, 1569, *d.* in 1640-42, daughter of Sir Timothy Hutton, of Marske, Yorks, (see Yorks. Arch. Jour., VII., 238), and had:

---

*From him is descended the brothers, WILLIAM BROWN, F. S. A., author of "Ingleby Arncliffe and Its Owners," and ROBERT BROWN, of Seattle, Wash., who *m.* first, at Sioux City, 28 December, 1888, Grace Clark, of Waverly, Iowa, *d.* 1890, and had PHILIP DOUGLAS, *b.* at Hastington, Neb., and *m.* secondly, at Seattle, 21 January, 1893, Caroline Schuyler Woodruff, and had HELEN GEORGIANA and LAWRENCE ABERCROMBY.

EDMUND MAULEVERER, youngest child, *d.* at West Ayton, Hutton Bushell parish, near Scarborough, 27 November 1679. His birth is recorded in his father's Bible, with the other ten children, and entered as this James's son in Dugdale's Yorks Visitation, and he was frequently mentioned in his brother Timothy's account books, 1651-55, (see pp. 63-4, "Ingleby Arncliffe"). Edmund was *m.* by the Friends's ceremony, at Kirkby Grindalythe, 1 May, 1676, (Hull Monthly Meeting Record), to Ann Peirson, of Mowthorpe, Yorks. He was buried 28 November, 1679, being then a member of the Pickering Monthly Meeting. His widow, Ann, *m,* secondly, 7 September, 1681, Matthew Watson, of Scarborough, a chemist, and came to West New Jersey, in 1682, with him, bringing her daughter Ann, the only child of Edmund Mauleverer, and settled in Chesterfield township, Burlington Co. This daughter,

ANNE MAULEVERER, *b.* 26 April, 1678, at Scarborough, who *m.* (recorded at the Chesterfield Friends's Monthly Meeting, Burlington Co., N. J.), 26 May, 1696, John Abbott, "husbandman," who had removed from Farnsfield, Nottinghamshire, in 1684, (see "Ingleby Arncliffe," p. 133). Ann *d.* 19 April, 1754, and her husband *d.* 16 October, 1739, having had ten children, of whom,

1.—JANE ABBOTT, *b.* 9 May, 1701, *d.* 3 March, 1780. She *m.* 16 February, 1726, Joseph Burr, of Burlington Co., N. J., 1694-1780, and had ten children, of whom,

HENRY BURR, of Burlington Co., *b.* 12 July, 1731, *m.* 14 July, 1753, Elizabeth Foster, *b.* 1 December, 1731, and had:

HANNAH BURR, *b.* 25 May, 1754, *m.* 5 February, 1774, Henry Ridgway, of Chesterfield Tp., Burlington Co., N. J., *b.* 26 December, 1749, and had:

JOSEPH RIDGWAY, of Philadelphia, *b.* 11 September, 1781, *m.* 21 November, 1803, Esther Coates, of Coatesville, Pa., *b.* 25 September, 1780, and had:

REBECCA RIDGWAY, *b.* 18 October, 1813, *m.* 29 June, 1842, Wallace Marshall, of Philadelphia, *b.* 16 September, 1814, and had:

I.—CHARLES MARSHALL, of Philadelphia, *m.* 24 November, 1870, Julia A. Herring, and had CHARLES, *b.* 30 December, 1873.

II.—FRANCIS RIDGWAY MARSHALL, deceased, *m.* Mary J. Chadwick.

III.—MARY ANN MARSHALL, *unm.*

2.—TIMOTHY ABBOTT, of Burlington Co., N. J. eighth child, 1717-

1776, m. 27 November, 1746, Ann Satterthwaite, d. 15 November, 1777, and had ten children, of whom:

SAMUEL ABBOTT, of Burlington Co., 1749-1828, m. 9 May, 1775, Lucy Laurie, and had:

WILLIAM ABBOTT, of Burlington Co., b. 1778, m. Sarah Field, and had:

ANN ABBOTT, 1780-1831, who m. 3 January, 1798, John Pancoast, of Plattsburg, N. J., and had:

SARAH PANCOAST, who m. Thomas Ridgway, of Philadelphia, 1797-1887, and had:

THOMAS EDWIN RIDGWAY, M. D., of Washington, D. C., a member of the Order of Runnemede. He m. Mary Josephine, daughter of Com. Dominick Lynch, U. S. Navy, and had SARAH TONITA.

DOROTHY MAULEVERER, (see p. 355), m. at Bardsey, 21 January, 1542-3, John Kaye, of Woodersome, near Huddersfield, Yorks, "being both XV. years olde." "Dorothe Kay" is named in her mother's will, 1552, of which John Kaye was an executor. He was the son of Arthur Kaye, of Woodersome, and his wife, Beatrice, daughter of Matthew Wentworth, of Bretton. See Browning's "Magna Carta Barons and their American Descendants," p. 309. Of their children,

1.—EDWARD KAYE, see below.

2.—ROBERT KAYE, see pp. 205, 359.

EDWARD KAYE, of Woodersome, m. Anna, daughter of Robert Tirwhitt, of Ketelby, Lincolnshire, and had:

I.—MARGARET KAYE, m., his second wife, William Lawrence, who removed from Ramsey, about 1539, to St. Ives, Huntingtonshire, where he was buried, 20 December, 1572. (See pp. 407, 414.)

II.—LUCIA KAYE, m. John Pickering, of Techmersh, Northants, and had:

ELIZABETH PICKERING, who m. Robert Throckmorton, of Ellington, Hunts, and had:

GABRIEL THROCKMORTON, of Ellington, 1577-1626, who m. Alice, daughter of William Bedles, and had:

ROBERT THROCKMORTON, of Ellington, 1608-1662, who m. Judith Bromsall, and had:

JOHN THROCKMORTON, of Ellington, 1633-1678, who had by his wife, ———— Mason:

PEDIGREE LXXXVI.—Continued.

GABRIEL THROCKMORTON, second son 1665-1737, (see p. 297, and the Virginia His. Mag., VI., 407). He m. Frances, daughter of Mordecai Cooke, of Gloucester Co., Va., and had:

1.—MORDECAI THROCKMORTON, sheriff of King and Queen Co., 1740, d. 1767. He m. Mary, daughter of Thomas, son of Col. George Reade, d 1671, (see p. 248), and had:

THOMAS THROCKMORTON, of Nicholas Co., Ky., 1739-1826. He had by his second wife, Mary, daughter of John Hooe:

MORDECAI THROCKMORTON, of Loudon Co., Va., 1777-1838, who had by his second wife, m. 6 February, 1812, Sarah McCarty Hooe:

JOHN ARIS THROCKMORTON, of Culpeper Co., Va., 1815-1891, major in Sixth Cavalry, C. S. A. He m. 13 March, 1839, Mary Tutt, and had:

CHARLES B. THROCKMORTON, of New York, major U. S. A. (retired), b. 27 May, 1842. He m. 8 October, 1863, Fanny Hall, daughter of Robert L. Wicliffe, of Bardstown, Ky., and had:

CHARLES WICKLIFFE THROCKMORTON, of New York, a founder and member of the Order of Runnemede. (See pp. 189-203, "The Magna Carta Barons and their American Descendants").

2.—MAJOR ROBERT THROCKMORTON, of Gloucester Co., Va., who m. 1730, Mary Lewis, also of Royal Descent, (See Ped. LIX.), and had:

ROBERT THROCKMORTON, of Culpeper Co., Va., who m. 175--, Lucy Throckmorton, also of Royal Descent, (see p. 250), and had:

FRANCES THROCKMORTON, who m. Gen. William Madison, and had:

REBECCA CONWAY MADISON, who m. Reynolds Chapman, and had:

JUDGE JOHN MADISON CHAPMAN, who m. Susannah Digges, also of Royal Descent, (see p. 78), and had:

ASHTON ALEXANDER CHAPMAN, of Franklin, W. V., a member of the Order of Runnemede.

ROBERT KAYE, of Woodersome (see p. 358), m. Anne, daughter of John Flower, of Whitewell, and had:

GRACE KAYE, (see Waters's "Gleanings in English Wills," pp. 939-969), who m. Sir Richard Saltonstall, of Huntwick. He was one of the original patentees of Massachusetts and Connecticut, and came to New England in 1630. Their eldest son,

RICHARD SALTONSTALL, of Ipswich, Mass., 1610-1694 (see p. 206). He had by his wife, Muriel Gurdon, also of Royal Descent:

PEDIGREE LXXXVI.—Continued.

JUDGE NATHANIEL SALTONSTALL, of Haverhill, Mass., 1639-1707, member of the Governor's Council. He *m.* Elizabeth, daughter of Rev. John Ward, and had:

1.—GURDON SALTONSTALL, of New London, Conn., 1666-1724. He was Governor of Connecticut, 1708-1724. He had by his second wife, Elizabeth, daughter of William Rosewell:

GURDON SALTONSTALL, of New London, who had by his wife, Rebecca Winthrop, (see p. 207):

ROSEWELL SALTONSTALL, 1741-1804, who had by his wife, Elizabeth, daughter of Matthew Stewart, of New London:

WILLIAM SALTONSTALL, of New York, *d.* 1842. He *m.* in England, Maria Hudson, and had:

MARY SUSAN SALTONSTALL, who *m.* Thomas Marston Beare, of New York, and had:

ISABEL BEARE, who *m.* George B. Mickle, of Bayside, L. I., N. Y., and had:

ANDREW H. M. SALTONSTALL, (who, in conformity with legal requirements, assumed the surname Saltonstall). A founder and member of the Order of Runnemede, etc., (see "The Magna Carta Barons and their American Descendants"). He *m.* 9 June, 1892, Susan Summers, daughter of Dr. John Harrison Hunter, of Berkeley Springs, W. Va., and had: SOPHIE FORREST, and MURIEL WINTHROP.

2.—ELIZABETH SALTONSTALL, 1668-1726, who *m.* secondly, 22 September, 1692, Rev. Roland Cotton, of Sandwich, Mass., 1667-1721, and had:

JOANNA COTTON, 1694-1772, who *m.* Rev. John Brown, 1696-1742, and had:

I.—ELIZABETH BROWN, who *m.* John Chipman, 1722-1768, and had:

ELIZABETH CHIPMAN, 1756-1823, who *m.* William Gray, 1750-1825, and had:

HENRY GRAY, 1784-1854, who *m.* Frances Peirce, 1794-1830, and had:

ELLEN CORDIS GRAY, 1830-1901, who *m.* Rev. W. Henry Brooks, S. T. D., 1831-1900, and had:

WILLIAM GRAY BROOKS, of Philadelphia.

II.—ABIGAIL BROWN, 1732-1800, who *m.* 23 September, 1764, Rev. Edward Brooks, 1733-1781, and had:

PETER CHARDON BROOKS, of Boston, 1767-1849, who *m.* 26 November, 1792, Ann Gorham, 1771-1830, and had:

1.—GORHAM BROOKS, 1795-1855, see below.

2.—ABIGAIL BROWN BROOKS, *d.* 6 January, 1889, who *m.* 3 September, 1829, Charles Francis Adams, of Quincy, Mass., 1809-1886, U. S. Minister to Great Britain, 1861-1868, also of Royal Descent (see Pedigree XXXVIII,), son of John Quincy Adams, President of the United States, and grandson of John Adams, President of the United States, and had, besides others, (see p. 69, A. R. D., 3d ed., and p. 209, ante):

CHARLES FRANCIS ADAMS, of Lincoln, Mass., *b.* 27 May; 1835, a member of the Order of Runnemede. He *m.* 8 November, 1865, Mary, daughter of Edward Ogden, of Newport, R. I., also of Royal Descent (see Ped. CCI., A. R. D., 4th edition), and had: MARY, LOUISA CATHARINE, ELIZABETH OGDEN, JOHN and HENRY.

3.—COL. RICHARD SALTONSTALL, 1672-1714, *m.* 25 March, 1702, Mehitabel Wainwright, and had:

JUDGE RICHARD SALTONSTALL, 1703-1756, *m.* Mary Cooke, and had:

NATHANIEL SALTONSTALL, M. D., 1746-1815, *m.* 21 October, 1780, Anna White, 1752-1841, and had:

LEVERETT SALTONSTALL, 1783-1845, *m.* 7 March, 1811, Mary Elizabeth Sanders, 1788-1858, and had:

LEVERETT SALTONSTALL, 1825-1895, *m.* 19 October, 1854, Rose S. Lee, 1835-1903, and had:

RICHARD MIDDLECOTT SALTONSTALL, of Boston, *b.* 28 October, 1859, who *m.* 17 October, 1891, Eleanor, *b.* 18 September, 1867, daughter of Peter Chardon Brooks, 3d, *b.* 8 May, 1831, (and his wife, Sarah Lawrence, *b.* 5 July, 1845, *m.* 4 October, 1866), son of Gorham Brooks, aforesaid, and his wife, *m.* 20 April, 1829; Ellen Shepherd, 1809-1884, and had: LEVERETT, *b.* 1 September, 1892; ELEANOR, *b.* 10 October, 1894; MURIEL GURDON, *b.* 26 March, 1896, and RICHARD, *b.* 23 July, 1897.

THE ROYAL DESCENTS
OF
MR. AND MRS. ASA G. PETTIBONE,
OF NEW YORK MILLS, NEW YORK

THE EMPEROR CHARLEMAGNE, had:	**THE EMPEROR CHARLEMAGNE**, had:
Louis I., King of France, who had:	Louis I., King of France, who had:
Gisela, *m.* Everard, Duke of Friaul, and had:	Charles II., King of France, who had:
Hedwige, *m.* Ludolph, Duke of Saxony, and had:	Louis II., King of France, who had:
Otto the Great, Duke of Saxony, who had:	Charles III., King of France, who had.
Henry I., Emperor of Germany, who had:	Louis IV., King of France, who had:
Hedwige, *m*, Hugh, Duke of France, and had:	Charles, Duke of Nether Lorraine, who had:
Hugh, Capet, King of France, who had:	Gerberga, *m.* Lambert I. de Mous, and had:
Hedwige, *m.* Rainier IV., de Hainault, and had:	Matilda, *m.* Eustace I. de Boulogne, and had:
Beatrix, *m.* Ebles I. Rouci, and had:	Eustace II., Count de Boulogne, who had:
Alix, *m.* Hilduin IV., de Montdidier, and had:	Geoffrey de Boulogne, living 1093, who had:
Marguerite, *m.* Hugh de Clermont, and had:	William de Boulogne, who had:
Adeliza, *m* Gilbert de Tonebruge, and had:	Pharamon de Boulogne de Tingry, who had:
Richard de Clare, Earl of Hertford, who had:	Sybilla, *m.* Ingelram de Fienes, and had:
Roger de Clare, Earl of Hertford, and had:	William de Fienes, of Mertock, who had:
Daughter, *m.* William de Braose, and had:	Daughter, *m.* Bartholomew de Hampden, and had
John-tatody de Braose, of Gower, who had:	Sir Reginald de Hampden, *d*, 1220, who had:
Sir Richard de Brose, of Stainton, who had:	Sir Alexander de Hampden, Sheriff, who had:
Margaret, *m.* Roger de Coleville, and had:	Sir Reginald de Hampden, *d.* 1332, who had:
Alice, *m.* Sir John de Gernon, and had:	Sir John de Hampden, Sheriff, who had:
Sir John de Gernon, of Lexton, who had:	Sir Edmund de Hampden, Sheriff, who had:
Margaret, *m.* Sir John de Peyton, and had:	Sir John de Hampden, Sheriff, who had:
John Peyton, of Peyton Hall, Suffolk, who had:	Anne, *m.* William de Puttenham, and had:
John Peyton, of Peyton Hall, Suffolk, who had:	Nicholas Putnam, of Penn, Bucks, who had:
Sir Thomas Peyton, of Iselham Hall, who had:	Henry de Putnam, of Penn, Bucks, who had:
Rose, *m.* Robert Freville, of Shelford, and had:	Richard Putnam, of Woughton, Bucks, who had
Thomasine, *m.* Christopher Burgoyne, and had:	John Putnam, *d.* Salem, Mass., 1662, who had:
Thomasine, *m.* Judge Robert Shute, and had:	Nicholas Putnam, of Stewkeley, Bucks, who had
Anne, *m.* John Leete, of Doddington, and had:	John Putnam, *d* Salem, Mass. 1662, who had:
William Leete, Gov. of Conn., 1676-83, who had:	Thomas Putnam, *d.* Salem, Mass., 1686, who had:
Abigail, *m.* Rev. John Woodbridge, and had:	Deliverance, *m.* Jonathan Walcott, and had:
Mercy, *m.* Rev. Benjamin Ruggles, and had:	William Walcott, of Attleboro, Mass., who had:
Mercy, *m.* Jonathan Humphrey, and had:	Benjamin Walcott, of Attleboro, Mass., who had
Mercy, *m.* Michael Humphrey, and had:	Benj. Stuart Walcott, Cumberland, R.I., who had
Phoebe, *m* Dr. Ephriam Guiteau, and had:	Benj. Stuart Walcott, N. Y. Mills, N.Y., who had
Louisa, *m.* Dr. Benjamin Welch, and had:	Wm. Dexter Walcott. N. Y. Mills. N.Y. who had
Louisa, *m.* Rev. Ira Pettibone, and had:	
Asa G. Pettibone, of New York Mills, N. Y. *m*	Elizabeth Hamilton Walcott, of N. Y. Mills, N.
(See Pedigree LXXXVII.)	No issue. (See Pedigree XCVII.)

PEDIGREE LXXXVII

HUGH CAPET, King of France, 987, had by his first wife Adela, daughter of William I., Count of Poitiers and Auvergne, Duke of Aquitaine:

LADY HAVIDE, who *m.* Rainier IV., Count of Hainault, and had:

LADY BEATRIX, who *m.* Ebles I., Count of Reimes and Rouci, and had:

LADY ALIX, who *m.* Hilduin IV., Count of Montdidier, and had:

LADY MARGUERITE, who *m.* Hugh de Monchi, Count of Clermont, and had:

LADY ADELIZA, who *m.* Gilbert, second "Earl of Clare," and had:

RICHARD DE CLARE, created Earl of Hertford; *m.* Lady Adeliza, daughter of Ralph, Viscount of Bayeaux, created Earl of Chester, and had:

ROGER, third Earl of Hertford, *m.* Maud St. Hilliary, and had:

LADY ———— DE CLARE, *m.* (Patent Rolls, 17 John), William de Braose, who, with his mother, was starved to death in Windsor Castle, in 1210, according to the Chronicle of Matthew de Westminster (see Dugdale's "Baronage," 1675, vol. I., pp. 418-20), son and heir of William, third Baron Braose, lord of Brecknock, Gower, etc., in Wales, of whose troubles with King John there are several versions, *d.* in France, in 1212. William de Braose "had by the daughter to R., Earl of Clare, with whom he had taken the town of Buckingham, in frank marriage":

JOHN-TADODY DE BRAOSE, the heir, a minor when his father died, who was reared at Gower Castle, his uncles, Giles, Bishop of Hereford, and Reginald de Braose, being his guardians, (see Mon. Andglie, vol. II., 557). He having no inheritance from his father, the king granted him, patent dated 25 April, 1228, certain Welsh lordships and castles, and the Manor of Bremine, in Sussex, where he was accidentally killed in 1232, (see D. Powell's His. of Wales, p. 288). On the death of John de Braose, the King siezed his lordship of Buckingham, the dowry of his wife, as security from her for the proper care of her two sons, William, the heir, and Richard, till they became of age. John de Braose *m.* the Princess Margaret, daughter of Llwellyn the Great, Prince of North Wales, and had, William, eldest son, guardian of the Welsh marches for Henry III, *d*. 1291, called "lord of Gower," who married his niece Margaret, to his ward, and

SIR RICHARD DE BRAOSE, called "Richard Brewes, of Stinton," or Stainten, [in Norfolk (Waters), or in Lincolnshire (Dugdale)], 1288-9, (see Waters's "Chesters of Chicheley," vol. I., p. 197). His daughter,

MARGARET DE BRAOSE, *d*. 1335 (Esch., 9 Edw. III., 8). She *m*. Roger de Coleville, of Bytham Castle, Lincolnshire. (Mr. Waters says that Dugdale, in his "Baronage,"—also Burke— "strangely confuses him with a much older man, of a different family," namely, Roger Coleville, sheriff of Co., Norfolk, 51 Hen. III.). Roger de Coleville was not summoned to Parl. On his father's death, in 1277, William de Brewes, or Braose, "lord of Gower," aforesaid, was his guardian. He *d*. in April, 1288 (Esch. 16 Edw. I., 37). Roger, second Baron de Coleville, by tenure, and Margaret de Braose, had three children, Edmond, third Baron, *bapt*. at St. James's, Bytham, 25 January, 1287-8, *d*. 1316, the wardship of the lands of his inheritance was given to William de Breus, or Braose, of Gower, aforesaid, during his minority, and their custody was transferred by him to his brother, Richard de Braose, grandfather of the infant, (Parl. Rolls, I., 345), but his marriage was reserved to the Crown, and was purchased by Robert de Ufford, former Justiciary of Ireland, for his daughter Margaret, and they were married by royal license, 10 February, 1291-2, when Edmond was only four years old. (Margaret was the sister of Robert, first Lord Ufford, whose daughter, Eva, was the wife of Sir John de Brews, or Braose, of Topcroft and Stinton, Norfolk). Edmond's line ended with his greatgrandson, when the descendants of Edmond's sisters became the heirs (Dugdale, I., 626), namely, Elizabeth, a co-heir in her issue; (she *m*. Ralph Basset, of Sapcote), and

ALICE COLEVILLE, a co-heir in her issue of her brother Edmond; (a cousin of Sir Peter de Braose, Sr. and Sir John de Brews, who testified in court that Sir John Gernon was the son of Alice). She *m*. Guy Gobaud, of Ripplegate, Lincolnshire, *d*. 1314, (Waters's "Chesters of Chicheley," p. 197), and *m*. secondly, (he *m*. first, Isabella Bygot, *d. s. p*. 1311), Sir John de Gernon, of Lexton, aged 30, in 1327, *d*. 1334, son of William Gernon, of Bakewell, East Thorp, Essex, aged 24 in 1274, *d*. 1327, (Esch. 1 Edw, III., 35, see "Chesters of Chicheley, 194), and had:

SIR JOHN DE GERNON, heir to his father, and co-heir to Robert, Lord Coleville in 1369. He *d*. 13 January, 1383-4, aged 69, (Esch. 7 Ric. II. 43). He *m*. first ———— (his relict was Joan), in 1332, Alice, widow of John Bygot, and had:

MARGARET GERNON, co-heiress to her father, and aged 34 at his death, and was living as the widow of Sir John Peyton, in June, 1413. She *m.* Sir John de Peyton, of Peyton Hall, Suffolk, and *jure ux.* of East Thorpe and Wicken (see "Chesters of Chicheley," and Hayden's "Virginia Genealogies"), buried at Stoke Neyland, in 1397, and had: .

JOHN DE PEYTON, of Peyton Hall, and Wicken, in Cambridge; his will, dated 1404. He *m.* Lady Joan, daughter and heiress of Sir Hamon Sutton, of Wirkshow, or Wixoe, Suffolk, and had:

JOHN DE PEYTON, of Peyton Hall, heir, *d. v. p.* 6 October, 1416, aged 24. He *m.* Grace, daughter of John Burgoyne, of Drayton, Cambridge, and had by her, who *d.* 6 May, 1439:

SIR THOMAS DE PEYTON, of Peyton Hall, and Iselham Hall, Cambridge, posthumous child, *bapt.* 14 February, 1416-17, at Dry Drayton, Camb., high sheriff of Cambridge and Huntingdon, 1443 and 1453, *d.* 30 July, 1484, buried at Iselham. He had, by his second wife, Lady Margaret, *d.* 12 December, 1458, daughter and co-heiress of Sir Hugh Francis, of Gifford Hall, Suffolk, and widow of Thomas Garneys, *d.* 12 December, 1458: Christopher, exec. to father's will, high sheriff of Cambridge, 1496, will proved in 1507, names his nephews, Sir Robert and Edmond Peyton, Francis (heir to his brother, who *d. s. p*), *d.* 1529, and

ROSE PEYTON, will dated 20 April, proved 31 May, 1529. She *m.* Robert Freville, of Little Shelford, Cambridge, will dated 7 April, proved 2 May, 1521, to be buried in the parish church of "Little Shatford," Ely, amongst ancestors; names his daughter, "Thomasine," and other children; names Sir Robert Peyton, "kinsman of my wife Rose," and appoints her executrix; printed in Nicolas's "Testamenta Vetusta," p. 574. Robert and Rose Freville had:

THOMASINE FREVILLE, (sister to George Freville, second baron of the exchequer, 1558), who *m.* Christopher Burgoyne, of Long Stanton, Cambridge, (Cambridge Visitations, 1575, 1619), and had:

THOMASINE BURGOYNE, who *m.* Judge Robert Shute, of Holington, or Hockington, Cambridge, educated at Christ's College, Cambridge, of Barnard's Inn, and Gray's Inn, 1552, recorder of Cambridge, 1558, M. P. for Cambridge, 1572, sergeant at law, 1577, second baron of the exchequer, 1579, succeeding Judge Freville, justice of the Queen's Bench, 1586, *d.* 1590, and had:

ANNE SHUTE, who *m.* John Leete, of Doddington, Huntingdon, 1613, *d.* about 1654 (see Hunts. Visitations, 1613, and Waters's "Genealogical Gleanings," p. 254,) and had:

PEDIGREE LXXXVII.—Continued.

WILLIAM LEETE, b. at Keystone, Hunts., in 1611, removed to Guilford Conn., in 1639, held many offices of trust, and was governor of Conn., 1676, until his decease, 16 April, 1683. (See Mather's "Magnalia," Trumbull's "Connecticut," Joseph Leete's "The Family of Leete," the Report of the American Historical Asso., 1891, p. 209, etc). He was thrice married. By his third wife, Anne, d. 1 September, 1668, daughter of Rev. John Payne, of Southhoe, Hunts., he had:

1.—ABIGAIL LEETE, d. 9 February, 1711, m. 29 October, 1671, Rev. John Woodbridge, of Killingworth, Conn., d. 1690 (see p. 317, 4th edition), and had:

MERCY WOODBRIDGE, b. 27 September, 1672, d. 28 June, 1707; (sister of Rev. John, Rev. Dudley, and Rev. Ephraim; for their descendants, see Ped. LXXXII., 4th edition); m. 19 November, 1696, Rev. Benjamin Ruggles, b. 11 August, 1676, d. Suffield, Conn., 5 September, 1708, and had:

I.—MERCY RUGGLES, m. Jonathan Humphrey, and had:

MERCY HUMPHREY, m. Michael Humphrey, and had:

PHOEBE HUMPHREY, m. Dr. Ephraim Guiteau, and had:

LOUISA GUITEAU, m. Dr. Benjamin Welch, and had:

LOUISA WELCH, m. Dr. Ira Pettibone, and had:

ASA G. PETTIBONE, of New York Mills, N. Y., a member of the Order of Runnemede, who m. 15 June, 1859, Elizabeth Hamilton Walcott, also of Royal Descent. (See Pedigree XCVII. and p. 362). No issue.

II.—CAPT. JOSEPH RUGGLES, b. Suffield, 30 January, 1701, d. Brookfield, Conn., 1791; m. at New Haven, 15 November, 1722, Rachel Tolle, d. ante 1747, and had:

I.—CAPT. LAZARUS RUGGLES, of New Milford, Conn., b. 29 October, 1730, d. 6 September, 1797; m. 3 September, 1764, Hannah, daughter of Ebenezer Bostwick, of New Milford, and had:

1.—JOSEPH RUGGLES, of New Milford, b. 2 March, 1757, m. Mercy Warner, and had:

DAVID RUGGLES, of Newburgh, N. Y., b. June, 1783, d. 19 December, 1837; m. Sarah, daughter of David Colden, of Coldenham, N. Y., and had:

GEN. GEORGE DAVID RUGGLES, Adj. Gen. U. S. Army, deceased. He m. in 1868, Alma Hammond, daughter of S. S. L'Hommedieu, of Cincinnati, and had:

I.—COLDEN L'HOMMEDIEU RUGGLES, b. 18 March, 1869.

II.—CHARLES HERMAN RUGGLES, of Milwaukee, a member of the Order of Runnemede, b. 1 December, 1870, m. Virginia Catherine, daughter of Dr. Robert Henry Cabell, of Richmond, Va., and had *Anna Christie,* and *Alma L'Hommedieu.*

III.—GEORGE DAVID, d. inf., 1874; IV.—ALMA HAMMOND, b. 20 December, 1874.

V.—FRANCIS AUGUSTUS RUGGLES, b. 1 March, 1880.

2.—OLIVER RUGGLES, of New Milford, Conn., New York and Philadelphia, b. 8 June, 1767, d. 3 April, 1850. He m. Phoebe Moore, and had:

HARRIETTE PHOEBE RUGGLES, b. 15 November, 1810, who m. 10 November, 1830, William Evans Rogers, of Philadelphia, and had, among other children:

1.—CORNELIA ROGERS, b. 24 March, 1837, d. 10 April, 1896, who m. 28 May, 1863, Samuel Emlen Meigs, of Philadelphia, also of Royal Descent, (see Pedigree XXXII., and p. 126, 4th edition, and Pedigree LVII., *ante*), and had:

I.—HARRIETTE RUGGLES MEIGS, b. 12 May, 1865, who m. Robert Coleman Drayton, of Philadelphia, and had: *Emlen Meigs, Robert C.,* d. 1893; *Frederick Rogers,* and *Robert G.*

II.—FREDERICK ROGERS MEIGS, b. 11 May, 1869.

2.—MONTEZUMA EDWARD ROGERS, Capt. 1st Troop, Philadelphia City Cavalry, b. 29 January, 1839, d. 24 May, 1884. He m. 25 October, 1866, Nancy Craig Wadsworth, and had:

I.—JAMES WADSWORTH ROGERS, of Paris, b. 28 May, 1868.

II.—HARRIETTE ROGERS, d. unm. April, 1892.

3.—WILLIAM EVANS ROGERS, 2d, of "Beverly," Garrison's-on-Hudson, New York, member of the Order of Runnemede, b. Philadelphia, 11 April, 1846. (See the University Magazine, January, 1894, for sketch.) He was educated in France and at the University of Pennsylvania, served in the Civil War, in the 1st Troop, Philadelphia City Cavalry; graduated as an Engineer at the U. S. Military Academy, in 1867; resigned from the Army in 1869; and, after serving as railroad commissioner for nine years, was admitted to the New York Bar, in 1892. He m. 13 February, 1868, Susan LeRoy, daughter of

Hon. Hamilton Fish, of New York, Secretary of State in President Grant's Cabinet, and his wife, Julia Kean, a descendant of James Alexander (father of Gen. William Alexander, titular Earl of Stirling), of Royal Descent, (see Pedigrees XXXI. and CCXII., 4th edition, and Pedigree III., *ante*), and from Philip Livingston, second lord of Livingston Manor, New York (see Pedigreees LXXII. and CLXVI, 3d edition), and had:

I.—JULIA FISH ROGERS, *b*. 14 November, 1868, who *m*. 27 November, 1894, Kenneth Frazier, of South Bethlehem, and New York, and had:

    1.—JULIA VERONICA FRAZIER, *b*. 5 September, 1895.

    2.—SUSAN ALICE FRAZIER, *b*. 25 April, 1899.

    3.—HARRIETTE CORNELIA FRAZIER, *b*. 8 March, 1902.

II.—HARRIETTE RUGGLES ROGERS, *b*. 21 March, 1870.

III.—CORNELIA MEIGS ROGERS, *b* 27 January, 1872.

IV.—HAMILTON FISH ROGERS, *b*. 14 August, 1873, *d*. 16 March, 1880.

V.—WILLIAM BEVERLY ROGERS, *b*. 9 June, 1880.

VI.—VIOLET MABEL ROGERS, *b*. 7 March, 1883, *d*. 31 January, 1885.

II.—MERCY RUGGLES, *b*. 10 March, 1732, *d*. 21 June, 1822, at Rootstown, Ohio, *m*. 3 September, 1754, Edmund Bostwick, *b*. September, 1732, *d*. at New Milford, Conn., 2 February, 1826, and had:

EBENEZER BOSTWICK, *b*. New Milford, 22 June, 1755, *d*. at Rootstown, Ohio, 16 March, 1840, a captain in the Revolutionary War; *m*. 10 June, 1777, Rebecca Northrop, of Brookfield, Conn, and had:

ANDREW BOSTWICK, *b*. New Milford, 3 November, 1778, *d*. at Berrien Springs, Mich., 21 October, 1838; *m*. at Sheldon, Vt., 26 September, 1808, Lucretia, *b*. 7 October, 1784, *d*. at Niles, Mich, 2 March, 1874, daughter of Judge David Sanderson, of Worcester, Mich., and had:

CATHERINE TILLINGHAST BOSTWICK, *b*. Albany, N. Y., 15 December, 1824. She *m*. at Niles, Mich., 2 March, 1841, Andrew Murray, M. D., *b*. Harrisburg, Pa., 1813, graduated at Yale 1835, *d*. at Niles, Mich., 13 October, 1854, and had:

I.—MARIA MURRAY, *b*. at St. Joseph's, Mich., January, 1848, a member of the Michigan Society of Colonial Dames. She *m*. 16 May, 1867, William C. Williams, of Detroit, and had:

1.—MAURICE OWEN WILLIAMS, *b.* 14 August, 1871, *m.* 6 June, 1900, Ethel, daughter of Henry Sanford Gregory, of Detroit.

2.—CLARA WILLIAMS, *b.* 11 November, 1874, *m.* 3 November, 1897, Ford Archer Hinchman, and had: *Ford Archer, Jr., b.* 28 August, 1896, and *William Williams, b.* 27 January, 1903.

II.—KATE MURRAY, *b.* 26 February, 1850, a member of the Michigan Society of Colonial Dames of America. She *m.* 4 February, 1896, Elijah W. Meddaugh, of Detroit.

2.—ANDREW LEETE, of Guilford, a son of Gov. Leete, an assistant in Conn. colony, 1677-1702, *m.* 1 June, 1669, Elizabeth, *d.* 4 March, 1701, daughter of Thomas Jordan, of Guilford, and had:

I.—MERCY LEETE, 1685-1751, *m.* 1711, Samuel Hooker, 3d, of Kensington, Conn., and had:

MERCY HOOKER, 1719-1800, *m.* 1750, Jedediah Goodrich, of New Britain, Conn., 1717-1803, and had:

ABIGAIL GOODRICH, 1754-1811, *m.* 1773, Isaac Lee, 3d, of New Britain, 1752-1828, and had:

POLLY LEE, 1783-1838, *m.* 1802, Joseph Shipman, of New Britain, 1779-1859, and had:

MARY LEE SHIPMAN, 1805-1891, *m.* 1824, second wife, Alfred Andrews, of New Britain, 1797-1876, and had:

ALFRED HINSDALE ANDREWS, of Chicago, and Lombard, Ill., *b.* 1836, member of the Society of Colonial Wars, *m.* 1872, Ella Cornelia, *b.* 1851, daughter of Newell Matson, of Milwaukee and Chicago, and had:

1.—BERTHA MATSON ANDREWS, *b.* 1874, *m.* 1903, Arthur Tenney Holbrook, M. D., of Milwaukee.

2.—HERBERT CORNELIUS ANDREWS, a member of the Order of Runnemede, *d.* 31 May, 1905, aged 22.

II.—WILLIAM LEETE, *b.* 24 March, 1671, who *m.* 12 February, 1699, Hannah, daughter of William and Hannah (Woulf) Stone, of Guilford, and had:

SOLOMON LEETE, *b.* September, 1722, who *m.* Zipporah, daughter of Lemuel and Mercy (Fowlee) Stone, of Guilford, and had:

ABIGAIL LEETE, *b.* 14 February, 1762, who *m.* 18 March, 1798, Calvin Crittenden, of Guilford, and had:

ANNA CRITTENDEN, *b.* 18 December, 1799, who *m.* 28 March, 1824, Sylvester Tracy, of Richmond, Mass., and had:

PEDIGREE LXXXVII.—Continued.

ROBERT SYLVESTER TRACY, of Sturgis, Mich., b. 10 July, 1842, a member of the Society of Colonial Wars, etc., who m. 5 October, 1863, Lydia Jane, daughter of Alanson and Nancy (Smith) Griggs, of Montezuma, N. Y., and had:

SARAH LOUISA TRACY, b. 13 July, 1865, who m. 22 October, 1890, Rev. James M. Patterson, and had: MARGUERITE TRACY, b. 17 November, 1891.

3.—WILLIAM LEETE, a son of Gov. Leete, had: MARY, m. James Hooker, and had: SARAH, m. John Bartlett, and had: HOOKER, who had JOHN, who had: DR. HUBBARD, who had: HARRY HUBBARD, who had: KATHERINE, m. Henry Christopher Yergason, of Cincinnati, and had: *Henry Bingham Bartlett,* only child.

4.—JOHN LEETE, eldest son of Gov. Leete, b. 1639, d. 25 November, 1692, m. 4 October, 1670, Mary, b. 1647, d. 9 March, 1712, daughter of William and Joanne (Sheafe) Chittenden, of Guilford, Conn., and had:

1.—JOHN LEETE, m. Mehitabel (or Sarah) Allen, d. 8 March, 1712, aged 47, and had:

MARY LEETE, b. 18 February, 1701, d. 12 January, 1778, m. 1726, Abial Eliot, d. 28 October, 1776, aged 90 years, (see "The Magna Carta Barons and their American Descendants," pp. 228-237), and had:

WYLLYS ELIOT, 1731-1777, who m. Abigail, daughter of Col. Andrew Ward, and had:

SARAH ELIOT, 1772-1852, m. John Scoville, 1770-1816, and had:

MARY WARD SCOVILLE, 1812-1868, who m. Judge Frederic J. Betts, of New York, and Campbell Co., Va., 1803-1879, and had:

FREDERIC H. BETTS, of New York, b. 8 March, 1843, a member of the Order of Runnemede, Society of Colonial Wars, etc., m. 16 October, 1867, Mary Louise Holbrook, and had:

I.—LOUIS FREDERIC HOLBROOK, BETTS, b. 21 May, 1870.

II.—MARY ELIOT BETTS, b. 19 October, 1871, m. 28 January, 1892, Russell H. Hoadley, and had, *Sheldon Eliot,* b. 20 November, 1894; *Louise Russell,* b. 20 March, 1896, and *Helen,* b. 20 May, 1897.

III.—WYLLYS ROSSETER BETTS, b. 12 May, 1875, m. 4 April, 1899, and had *Wyllys Rosseter,* b. 4 December, 1900.

2.—PELATIA LEETE, who had DANIEL, who had AMBROSE, who had AMBROSE, JR., who had SIDNEY WASHINGTON, who had CHARLES SIDNEY LEETE, of New Haven, a member of the Society of Colonial Wars. Issue: *Ida Louise,* and *Jeremiah Bishop.*

3.—ANNE LEETE, eldest daughter of Gov. Leete, b. 5 August, 1671, d. 1724, m. 23 July, 1691, John Collins, of Guilford, 1665-1751, and had:

1.—AVIS COLLINS, m. Peter Buell, and had: LUCRETIA, m. Benjamin Webster, and had: ELIJAH, who had: URI, who had: SOPHIA, m. Nelson M. Lloyd, and had: JOHN URI LLOYD, of Cincinnati, member of the Society of Colonial Wars.

2.—REV. TIMOTHY COLLINS, of Litchfield, Conn., fifth child, b. 13 April, 1699, d. 7 February, 1777, m. 16 January, 1723, Elizabeth, *bapt.* at Lebanon, Conn., 12 December, 1703, daughter of Samuel and Elizabeth Hyde, and had:

CYPRIAN COLLINS, b. 4 March, 1733, m. 9 January, 1756, Azuba, b. 13 December, 1734, daughter of Benjamin and Dinah Gibbs, of Litchfield, and had:

TRIPHENA COLLINS, b. 21 August, 1757, m. 15 January, 1778, Abraham Wadhams, of Goshen, Conn., b. 24 September, 1756, and had:

LUMAN WADHAMS, b. 17 September, 1781, d. Wadham's Mills, New York, 19 April, 1832; m. in 1803, Lucy Prindle, a widow, b. 5 March, 1772, d. 11 February, 1858, daughter of Edmund and Mercy (Ruggles) Bostwick, of New Milford, Conn., and had:

WILLIAM LUMAN WADHAMS, of Wadham's Mills, b. at Charlotte, Vt., 15 February, 1809, d. 18 May, 1865, m. at Westport, N. Y., 9 July, 1830, Emeline Loretta, b. at Panton, Vt., 3 November, 1808, d. at Albany, N. Y., 5 January, 1889, daughter of Samuel and Rachel (Curtis) Cole, and had:

1.—FREDERICK EUGENE WADHAMS, of Albany, N. Y., b. 27 September, 1848, a member of the Society of Colonial Wars, etc. He m. 9 October, 1878, Emma Louise, daughter of E. Darwin Jones, M. D., of Albany, and had: *Elizabeth Jones,* b. 16 September, 1879.

2.—MRS. GEORGE T. STEVENS, New York city.

THE ROYAL DESCENTS

OF

MR. THERON ROYAL WOODWARD AND WIFE,

OF CHICAGO, ILLINOIS.

THE EMPEROR CHARLEMAGNE, had:
Pepin, King of Italy, who had:
Bernard, King of Lombardy, who had:
Pepin, Count of Vermandois, who had:
Hubert I., Count of Vermandois, who had:
Hubert II., Count of Vermandois, who had:
Robert, Count of Champagne, who had:
Adeliza, *m.* Geoffrey d'Anjou, and had:
Ermengarde, *m.* Conan of Brittany, and had:
Juetta, *m.* Richard II., Duke of Normandy, and had:

Robert I., Duke of Normandy, who had:
King William the Conqueror, who had:
Henry I., King of England, who had:
Maud, *m.* Geoffrey Plantagenet, and had:
Henry II., King of England, who had:
John, King of England, who had:
Henry III., King of England, who had:
Edward I., King of England, who had:
Edward II., King of England, who had:
Edward III., King of England, who had:
Thomas, Duke of Gloucester, who had:
Anne, *m.* Sir William, Count d'Eu., and had:
Sir John Bouchier, K.G., Lord Berners, who had:
Sir Humphrey Bouchier, who had:
Sir John Bouchier, Lord Berners, who had:
Joan, *m.* Edmund Knyvett, and had:
Anne, *m.* Richard Sayer, of Colchester, and had:
John Sayre, of Amsterdam, who had:
John Bourchier Sayers, of Amsterdam, who had:
Richard Sears, of Plymouth, Mass., who had:
Deborah, *m.* Zachariah Paddock, and had:
Zachariah Paddock, of Yarmouth, who had:
Ichabod Paddock, of Middleboro, who had:
Patience, *m.* John Perkins, and had:
John Perkins, of Stockbridge, Vt., who had:
John Perkins, of Woodstock, Vt., who had:
Hannah, *m.* Zelotes H. Woodward, and had:
John P. Woodward, of Kingston, Wis., who had:

Richard III., Duke of Normandy, who had:
Alice, *m.* Radulfe, of Bayeaux, and had:
Randle, Viscount, of Bayeaux, who had:
Randle, Earl of Chester, who had:
Hugh, Earl of Chester, who had:
Agnes, *m.* William, Earl of Derby, and had:
Joan, *m.* Thomas, Baron Berkley, and had:
Margaret, *m.* Sir Anseleme Bassett, and had:
Isabel, *m.* ———— Pynchard, and had:
Symond Pynchard, who had:
Sir Edmund Pynchard-Bassett, who had:
Sir Symon Bassett, of Uley, who had:
Robert Bassett, of Uley, who had:
Giles Bassett, of Uley, who had:
Robert Bassett, of Uley, who had:
William Bassett, of Uley, who had:
Edward Bassett, of Uley, who had:
Jane, *m.* Dr. John Deighton, and had:
Frances *m.* Richard Williams, and had:
Samuel Williams, of Taunton, Mass., who had:
Judge Seth Williams, of Taunton, who had:
Sarah, *m.* Jonathan Clapp, of Norton, and had:
Lt. David Clapp, of Norton, who had:
Jonathan Clapp, of Norton, Mass., who had:
Fanny, *m.* Anson Clark, Hubbardston, and had:
Emory A. Clark, of Chicago, who had:

Theron Royal Woodward, of Chicago, Ill., who *m.* 26 Sept., 1894, Estelle Caroline Clark. (p. 387).

Najah Estelle Woodward.
b. 16 Oct., 1895.

Theron Royal Woodward.
b. 29 July, 1897.
d. 8 June 1898.

Emory Clark Woodward.
b. 27 Feb., 1900.

PEDIGREE LXXXVIII.

LOUIS VI., King of France, had by his second wife, Lady Adelaide, daughter of Humbert II., Count de Maurienne, and de Piedmont:

PIERRE DE COURTNAY, fifth son, called also Flores. He m. Lady Alice, daughter of Sir Rainaud de Courtnay, in Gastinois, first Baron, by tenure, of Oakhampton, in Devonshire, d. 1194, and had:

LADY ALICE DE COURTNAY, d. 1218, sister to Peter II., Emperor of Constantinople, and widow of William, Count de Joigni, who m. secondly, Aymer Taillefer, Count d'Anguelême, d. 1219, and had:

LADY ISABEL TAILLEFER, d. 1246, who m. first, John, King of England, and was the mother of Henry III., and m. secondly, in 1217, Hugh le Brune, Count de la Marche, in Poictou, d. 1249, and had:

LADY ISABEL LE BRUNE, sister to William de Valence, Earl of Pembroke, 1264, who m. Maurice de Berkeley, eighth baron by tenure, d. 1281, and had:

THOMAS DE BERKELEY, first Baron de Berkeley by writ, d. 1321, who m. Lady Joan, daughter of William de Ferrers, sixth Earl of Derby, d. 1246, by his wife, Lady Agnes de Meschines, daughter of Hugh, fifth Earl-palatine of Chester, of Royal Descent, d. 1181, and had:

LADY MARGARET DE BERKELEY, (sister to Maurice, second Baron). She received in her marriage portion from her father, to her and the heirs of her body, the manor of Ewley, or Uly, in Gloucestershire. She m. Sir Anseleme Bassett, Kt. (see the Glouc. Visit., 1569 and 1623), and had:

LADY ISABEL BASSETT, heiress, who m. ———— Pynchard, and had:

SYMOND PYNCHARD, who had by his second wife, Maud:

SIR EDMOND PYNCHARD, alias Bassett, who inherited Uley Manor. See "The Ancestor," October, 1904. He had by his wife, Margery:

SIR SYMOND BASSETT, Kt,. of Yewley, Ewley, or Uley Manor, "a gentleman as remarkable in his tyme as any that lived in his country," (see Smythe's "Lives of the Berkeleys"), who m. Lady Maud, daughter of Sir John de Bytton, and had:

ROBERT BASSETT, of Uley Manor, who m. Margaret Harwell, and had:

GILES BASSETT, of Uley Manor, who m. Jane Davis, and had:

ROBERT BASSETT, of Uley Manor, who *m.* Anne, widow of George Shepard, and daughter of ——— Spycer, and had:

WILLIAM BASSETT, of Uley Manor, who *m.* Jane, daughter of John Ashe, of Somersetshire, and had:

EDWARD BASSETT, of Uley Manor, who *m.* Elizabeth, daughter of Henry Lygon (*see* Glouc. Visit., 1623. The Harl. MS. No. 1534, says this Edward's wife was Mary, daughter of Richard Calthrop, and sister to Sir Martyn Calthrop, Lord Mayor of London), and had (according to the Glouc. Visit., of 1682, collated with that of 1569), only Barnard, heir, and three daughters, Elizabeth Pointz, Margaret Shillowe and Susan Dorney. The editor's note to Glouc. Visit., 1623 (printed) p. 206, quoting from MS. of Smythe's "Berkeleys" (fo. 144 and fo. 628), says that this Edward Bassett had, besides above children, William, Edward, Giles, and "Jane that is maryed to John Deighton, of Gloucester, surgeon, who have John and five others, anno 1624." Edward Bassett's daughter,

JANE BASSETT, *m.* John Deighton, M. D., of Gloucester city. They were buried in St. Nicholas's Church, Gloucester, with the following inscription: "Here lies interred the Bodies of John Deighton, of this city, Gent. and Jane, his wife, daughter of Edward Bassett, Uley, by whom he had issue, three sons and four daughters. He spent all his time in the study of chirurgery, and attained to great knowledge therein. He died 10 May, 1640, and she 23 April, 1631." The will of Dr. Deighton, dated 31 January, 1638-9, proved 21 May, 1640, mentions his eldest son, John, eldest daughter, Jane, and daughters, FRANCES WILLIAMS, and KATHERINE HAIGHBURNE. See as to "Dighton" the Me. His. Gen. Recorder, April, 1889, p. 326, by Mr. Josiah H. Drummond, of Portland, Me., a descendant, who collected this information. See also Waters's "Genealogical Gleanings," and "Notes and Queries (English), Vol. V., p. 135, September, 1891. Of the children of Dr. John Deighton and his wife, Joan, or Jane Bassett:

1.—FRANCES DEIGHTON, *bapt.* at St. Nicholas's, Gloucester city, 1 March, 1611, *m.* in the parish of Witcomb Magna, Gloucester, 11 February, 1632, Richard Williams. They had two children, *bapt.* in Gloucester, John, 27 March, 1634, and Elizabeth, 7 February, 1635. Both died young. Richard Williams, with his wife, Frances and other children, came to New England, and were among the first settlers at Taunton, Mass. See article by his descendant, Gov. Joseph H. Williams, of Augusta, Me., in the Me. His. Gen. Recorder, January, 1889, p. 255. Also "Williams," in "Notes and Queries," (Eng.) July, 1891, vol. V. p. 92.

PEDIGREE LXXXVIII.—Continued.

Richard Williams was *bapt.* at St. Mary's, Wotton-under-edge, Gloucester, 28 January, 1606. His father, William Williams, of Synwell, was buried here, 29 September, 1618. In his will, dated 26 September, 1618, he mentions his sons, Richard, and Samuel, and daughters, Ann (Mrs. Hall), Jane and Elizabeth. The daughter of Jane Williams, *bapt.* at St. Mary's, 19 March, 1608, died unmarried, and in her will, dated 31 May, 1650, proved 30 June, 1655, describes herself as of Whetenhurst, Glouc., and mentions "my brother, Richard Williams, and my sister, Elizabeth Williams, that are in New England," and Benjamin and Nathaniel, minors, "sons of my brother, Samuel Williams." The will of the said Benjamin Williams, nephew of Richard, of Massachusetts, dated 2 July, 1695, proved by his brother, Nathaniel, 22 September, 1698, describes him "of Stoake, near Guldeford, Surrey, schoolmaster." He mentions "cousins Samuel, Thomas and Benjamin Williams, in New England," "my cousin, Elizabeth Bird, of Dorchester, (children of Richard, the immigrant), in New England" (*see* "Bird," N. E. His. Gen. Reg. XXV., p. 21), "to eldest child of my cousin Williams, of New England, deceased." Will of Samuel Williams, brother of Richard, the immigrant, dated 26 September, 1668, mentions his brother Richard, and sister, Elizabeth Williams, and the children of his sister, Ann, wife of John Hall, who are also named in the will of Jane Williams, aforesaid. For descendants, see p. 376.

2.—KATHARINE DEIGHTON, *bapt.* at St. Nicholas's, in Gloucester city, 16 January, 1614. She *m.* Samuel Haighburne, or Hagburne, of Gloucester. They removed to Massachusetts, and settled at Roxbury, where Mr. Hagburne died, 24 January, 1643; will in N. E. His. Gen. Reg., Vol II., p. 261.

She *m.* secondly, 14 April, 1644, Thomas Dudley, of Roxbury, Governor of Massachusetts Colony, 1634, 1640-50, a widower, his first wife, Dorothy Yorke, having died 27 December, 1643. Governor Dudley *d.* 31 July, 1653, and his widow *m.* thirdly, 8 November, 1653, Rev. John Allin, of Dedham, Mass. Katharine *d.* 29 August, 1671, having had issue by each of her husbands.

Governor Thomas Dudley had by his wife, Katharine Deighton:

I.—DEBORAH DUDLEY, *b.* 27 February, 1645, *d.* 1 November, 1683. She *m.* Jonathan Wade, of Medford, Mass.

II.—JOSEPH DUDLEY, *b.* 23 September, 1647, *d.* 2 April, 1729. He was President of New England, an M. P. in England, Governor of Mass. and N. H., etc. He *m.* Rebecca, *d.* 21 September, 1722, daughter of Judge Edward Tyng. Issue.*

III.—PAUL DUDLEY, *bapt.* 8 September, 1650, *d.* 1 December, 1681; *m.* Mary, daughter of John Leverett, Governor of Massachusetts.

3.—JANE DEIGHTON, who *m.* John Lugg, resided near Gloucester city, and removed to Boston, Mass., where Jane was admitted a member of First Church, 10 February, 1638-9. She *m.* secondly, before 27 October, 1647, Jonathan Negus. John Lugg was mentioned as "my brother Lugg," in will of Samuel Hagburn, 1643, first husband of Jane's sister, Katharine. John and Jane Lugg had JOHN, ELIZABETH, MARY, *b.* in Boston, 1638-1644, and

ESTHER LUGG, *b.* in England, about 163--, (in a deed, Bristol Co., Mass., by her, "Easter Marshall," 11 February, 1713-14, she was upwards of four score years of age, and residing at Norton). She *m.* first, James Bell, slain by Indians at Taunton, in 1676, and *m.* secondly, 11 February, 1677, Richard Marshall, and had issue by both husbands. (*See* N. E. His. Reg. XVI., 236; Me. His. Gen. Rec., VII., 352; Waters's "Genealogical Gleanings").

Frances Deighton and Richard Williams (p. 375), had:

1.—NATHANIEL WILLIAMS, *bapt.* Taunton, Mass., 7 February, 1641, who *m.* 17 November, 1668, Elizabeth Rogers, of Taunton, and had:

ELIZABETH WILLIAMS, *b.* Taunton, 18 April, 1686, *d.* 2 May, 1732. who *m.* 17 March, 1707, John Macomber, *b.* 18 March, 1681, *d.* Taunton, 14 December, 1747, and had:

ELIJAH MACOMBER, of Taunton, who *m.* Sarah Pitts, and had:

ELIZABETH MACOMBER, *b.* Taunton, 10 September, 1756, *d.* 7 September, 1849, who *m.* 2 June, 1785, Philip Padelford, of Taunton, *b.* 13 October, 1753, *d.* 27 August, 1815, and had:

EDWARD PADELFORD, *b.* Taunton, 30 April, 1799, *d.* at Savannah, Ga., 27 June, 1870, who *m.* at Savannah, 11 November, 1823, Elizabeth Louisa Farnum, *b.* at Providence, 26 January, 1803, *d.* at Savannah, 17 November, 1869, and had:

---

*The following ladies, members of the National Society of Colonial Dames, are of Royal Descent, through Joseph Dudley:

MRS. LOUIS COPE WASHBURN, Rochester, N. Y., pp. 204, 208.
MRS. WILLIAM L. HALSEY, Rochester, N. Y., p. 208.
MRS. LYMAN F. GRAY, Buffalo, N. Y., p. 208.
MRS. AUSTIN ADAMS (Deceased), pp. 208, 320.
MRS. JOHN J. BAGLEY (Deceased), pp. 209, 341.
MRS. HENRY P. QUINCY, Boston, Mass., pp. 209, 164.
MRS. CHARLES P. COFFIN, Longwood, Mass., pp. 209, 221.
MISS CAROLINE P. CORDNER, Boston, Mass., pp. 209, 221.

MARION PADELFORD, *b.* 1 January, 1833, who *m.* at Savannah, 24 November, 1857, Francis Charles Foster, of Cambridge, Mass., *b.* Boston, 17 March, 1829, and had:

FRANCIS APTHORP FOSTER, of Cambridge, *b.* 21 September, 1872.

2.—HANNAH WILLIAMS, *m.* John Parmenter, and had:

HANNAH PARMENTER, *m.* John Emmes, and had:

HANNAH EMMES, *m.* Samuel Colesworthy, and had:

SAMUEL COLESWORTHY, *m.* Mary Gibson, and had:

DANIEL P. COLESWORTHY, *m.* Anna Collins, and had:

DANIEL C. COLESWORTHY, *m.* Mary Bowers, and had:

WILLIAM G. COLESWORTHY, of Boston, Mass., who *m.* Eugenia I. McIntyre, and had DANIEL C.

3.—SAMUEL WILLIAMS, of Taunton, *b.* 1638-9, who *m.* Mary Gilbert, and had:

I.—SARAH WILLIAMS, who *m.* 6 June, 1680, Benjamin Deane, *d.* 172--, and had:

MEHITABLE DEANE, *b.* 6 June, 1679, *m.* Josiah Richmond, 1697-1763 (*see* the "Richmond Genealogy"), and had:

LEMUEL RICHMOND, *d.* 2 April, 1802, aged 69, who *m.* Molly Richmond, *d.* at Barnard, Vt., 8 April, 1820, aged 89, and had:

POLLY RICHMOND, *b.* at Taunton, Mass., 13 April, 1766, *d.* at Barnard, 15 October, 1857, who *m.* George Townsend, *b.* 3 July, 1769, *d.* 28 July, 1843, and had:

PHOEBE RICHMOND TOWNSEND, *b.* 18 June, 1801, at Taunton, *d.* at Rockford, Ill., 12 September, 1882, who *m.* at Barnard, Vt., 1 March, 1822, Hiram Blackmer, *b.* 4 October, 1801, at Barnard, *d.* at Rockford, Ill., 1 October, 1885, and had:

LAURA J. BLACKMER, *b.* 30 August, 1832, at Barnard, who *m.* at Barnard, 24 September, 1853, Norman Cornelius Thompson, *b.* at Knoxville, Ga., 15 May, 1828, *d.* at Rockford, Ill., 4 July, 1898, and had:

NORMAN FREDERICK THOMPSON, of Rockford, Ill., *b.* at Perry, Ga., 27 June, 1856, a member of the Order of Runnemede. He *m.* at Rockford, 10 January, 1883, Adaline E., *b.* at Rockford, 13 August, 1859, daughter of Ralph and Adaline E. (Talcott) Emerson, and had: NORMAN F., *b.* Rockford, 14 March, 1884; RALPH E., *b.* Rockford, 1 July, 1888, and ADALYN, *b.* at East Orange, N. J., 4 December, 1889.

PEDIGREE LXXXVIII.—Continued.

II.—SAMUEL WILLIAMS, of Taunton, Mass., who m. Mary, daughter of Thomas Gilbert, of Taunton (*see* Emery's "Taunton," pp. 46, 82. Supp., p. 7), and had:

SETH WILLIAMS, of Taunton, Judge of C. P. Court, Ensign in 1711, b. 1676, d. 13 May, 1761 (*see* Emery's "Ministry," I. pp. 44, 51), who m. Mary Deane, of Taunton, b. 15 July, 1680, and had:

SARAH WILLIAMS, d. 29 October, 1756, who m. Jonathan Clapp, of Norton, Mass., b. 1 October, 1714, d. 9 September, 1800 (*see* Supplement, by J. H. Drummond, to "Clapp Gen," at N. E. His. Gen. Soc., Boston), and had:

LIEUT. DAVID CLAPP, of Norton, b. 30 August, 1744, d. 5 September, 1823, who m. 18 August, 1767, Hannah King, of Norton, b. 24 September, 1748, d. 18 March, 1839, and had:

JONATHAN CLAPP, of Norton, who m. 14 August, 1788, Peggy Wood, of Norton, b. 20 March, 1771, d. 30 June, 1824, and had:

FANNY CLAPP, b. 24 April, 1805, d. 3 July, 1896, who m. 8 April, 1830, Anson Clark, of Hubbardston, Mass., b. 2 December, 1809, d. 24 May, 1854, and had:

EMORY AUGUSTUS CLARK, of Chicago, b. 8 March, 1839, d. 11 February, 1905, who m. Caroline Elizabeth Haskins, b. 28 September, 1841, and had:

ESTELLE CAROLINE CLARK, (*see* p. 372), b. Barre, Mass., 31 May, 1864, who m. first, Dewelle J. King, d. 30 May, 1892, and m. secondly, at Oconomowoc, Wis., 26 September, 1894 (his second wife), Theron Royal Woodward, of Chicago, b. at Clarendon, Vt., 25 May, 1848, a member of the Societies of Mayflower Descendants, Colonial Wars, etc., also of Royal Descent (*see* p. 372), and had:

1.—NAJAH ESTELLE WOODWARD, b. Chicago, 16 October, 1895.

3.—THERON ROYAL WOODWARD, d. 8 June, 1898.

2.—EMORY CLARK WOODWARD, b. Chicago, 27 February, 1900.

THE ROYAL DESCENT
OF
MRS. CHARLES ERNEST CAMERON,
OF SYRACUSE, N. Y.

WILLIAM THE CONQUEROR, of England=Lady Maud, of Flanders, descended from Hugh Capet and Charlemagne.

Henry I., King of England=Princess Matilda, daughter of Malcolm III., King of Scotland.

Maud, Empress of Germany=Geoffrey, Count of Anjou, descended from the Emperor Charlemagne.

Henry II., King of England=Lady Eleanor, of Aquitaine, descended from the Emperor Charlemagne.

John, King of England=Lady Isabella Tailefer, descended from Hugh Capet and Charlemagne.

Henry III., King of England=Lady Eleanor, of Provence, descended from Kings of Aragon.

Edward I., King of England=Princess Eleanor, daughter of Ferdinand III., King of Castile and Leon.

Princess Elizabeth Plantagenet=Humphrey, Earl of Hereford and Essex, descended from Charlemagne, Alfred the Great, Hugh Capet, etc.

Lady Margaret de Bohun=Sir Hugh Courtnay, Earl of Devon.

Edward Courtnay of Goderington, Devon=Lady Emeline d'Auney.

Sir Hugh Courtnay, of Haccomb, Devon=Lady Maud Beaumont.

Lady Margaret Courtnay=Sir Theobald Grenville, of Stowe.

Sir William Grenville, of Bideford=Lady Philippa Bonville.

Thomas Grenville, of Stowe, Cornwall=Lady Elizabeth Gorges.

Sir Thomas Grenville, of Stowe=Lady Elizabeth Gilbert.

Sir Roger Grenville, of Stowe=Margaret Whitleigh, of Efford.

Lady Amy Grenville=John Drake, of Ashe, Devon.

Robert Drake, of Wiscombe, Devon=Elizabeth Prideaux, of Thewboro.

William Drake, of Wiscombe Park=Philippa Dennys, of Holcombe.

John Drake, 1585-1659, of Conn.=Elizabeth Rodgers. See Ped. XXV.

Elizabeth Drake, m. 14 Nov., 1644=William Gaylord, Jr., of Windsor, Conn.

Nathaniel Gaylord, m. 17 Oct., 1678=Abigail Bissell, 1658-1723.

Abigail Gaylord, m. 22 Nov., 1705=Sergeant John Griswold, of Windsor, Conn.

Abigail Griswold, b. 21 May, 1727=Capt. Noah Griswold, of Bloomfield, Conn.

Sergeant Noah Griswold, Jr., 1746-1785=Azubah Strong.

Fred. Griswold, of Bloomfield, 1767-1829=Zerviah Griswold, 1774-1863.

Electa Griswold, 1797-1871, m. 16 Nov., 1826=James Bidwell, Jr., b. 13 May, 1803, d. Hartford, 11 Jan., 1835.

Delia Bidwell, 1831-1901, m. 15 Nov., 1853=Austin Merrills Ward, of Middletown, Conn., b. 25 Oct., 1831, d. at Hartford, 17 Sept., 1875.

Mabel Ward, born in Chicago, m. 19 June, 1888.	= Charles E. Cameron, M. D., of Montreal, Syracuse, N. Y., Westbrook, Ct.	Edith Ward, born in Albany, N. Y., m. 25 June, 1896.	= Henry Cecil Dwight, Jr., of Hartford.	James Austin Ward, b. in Hartford, m. 22 July, 1897.	= Edith Wiley Rice.
Ward Griswold Cameron, born in Montreal, 13 April, 1889.	Elizabeth Ward Dwight, born 20 June, 1897.	Cecilia Brintnall Dwight, born 30 May, 1899.	Hubbard Beach Ward, born 29 April, 1898.	Constance Ward, b. 17 Sept. 1899.	

THE ROYAL DESCENTS
OF
MR. AND MRS. ALFRED PRESSON,
OF GLOUCESTER, MASS.

THE EMPEROR CHARLEMAGNE, had:
Louis I., King of France, who had:
Charles II., King of France, who had:
Louis II., King of France, who had:
Charles III., King of France, who had:
Louis IV., King of France, who had:
Charles, Duke of Nether Lorraine, who had:
Ermengard, *m.* Albert de Namur, and had:
Robert II., Count de Namur, who had:
Albert II., Count de Namur, who had:
Albert III., Count de Namur, who had:
Godefroi, Count de Namur, who had:
Henry III., Count de Namur, who had:
Ermansette, *m.* Waleron de Limburg, and had:
Henry, Marquis d'Arlon, who had:
Philippa, *m.* John de Hainault, and had:
William III., Count de Hainault, who had:
Phillippa, *m* Edward III., of England, and had:
Prince John, Duke of Lancaster, who had:
John, Marquis of Dorset, who had:
Edmund, Duke of Somerset, who had:
Henry, Duke of Somerset, who had:
Charles, Earl of Worcester, who had:
Henry, Earl of Worcester, who had:
William, Earl of Worcester, who had:
Edward, Earl of Worcester, who had:
Henry, Marquis of Worcester, who had:

THE EMPEROR CHARLEMAGNE, had:
Louis I., King of France, who had:
Gisela, *m.* Everard, Duke of Friaul, and had:
Hedwige, *m.* Ludolph, Duke Saxony, and had:
Otto the Great, Duke of Saxony, who had:
Henry I., Emperor of Germany, who had:
Hedwige, *m.* Hugh, Duke of France, and had:
Hugh Capet, King of France, who had:
Robert I., the Pious, King of France, who had:
Henry I., King of France, who had:
Philip I., King of France, who had:
Louis VI., King of France, who had:
Louis VII., King of France, who had:
Philip II., King of France, who had:
Louis VIII., King of France, who had:
Louis IX., King of France, who had :
Philip III., King of France, who had:
Margaret, *m.* Edward I., King of England, and had
Thomas Earl, of Norfolk, who had:
Margaret, *m.* John Lord Segrave, and had:
Elizabeth, *m.* John, Lord Mowbray, and had:
Thomas, K. G., Duke of Norfolk, who had:
Margaret, *m.* Sir Robert Howard, and had:
Sir John, K. G., Duke of Norfolk, who had:
Sir Thomas, K. G., Duke of Norfolk, who had:
Edmund, Lord Howard, 3d son, who had:
Margaret, *m.* Thomas Arundel, K. B., and had:
Sir Matthew Arundel, of Wardour, who had:
Thomas, Lord Arundel, of Wardour, who had:

Sir John, Lord Somerset, 2d son═Mary Arundel, of Wardour Castle, *d.* 1630.
Sir Charles Somerset, of Ross═Catherine, daughter of Walter Baskerville.
Lady Mary Johanna Somerset, *d.* 1697═Richard Smith, Jr., Calvert Co., Md., *d.* 1714.
Charles Somerset Smith, of Calvert Co., 1697-1738═Margaret———
Ann Smith, 1724-1775═Samuel Parran, 1717-1794. Elizabeth Smith.═2dly, Young Parran, 1711-1772.
of Calvert Co., Md. *d.* after 1772. of Calvert Co., *m.* 1739-41.
Alexander Parran, 1740-79═Elizabeth Eveleth, Alexander Parran, Calvert Co., Md.═Mollie King,
of Gloucester, Mass. *d.* 1824. 1757-1805. 1761-1818.
Sarah Eveleth Parran,═William Presson, Charles S. S. Parran,═Sarah I. Somerville,
1774-1859. of Gloucester, 1775-1830. 1800-1828, *m.* 1825. 1808-1875.
Alfred Presson,═Mary Ann Moore, William A. Parran═Ann H. Sollers,
of Gloucester, 1807-1873. 1815-1866. Prince Fredericktown, Md., 1826-1902.
Alfred Presson, of Gloucester, Mass., *m* Sarah Elizabeth Parran, of Prince Fredericktown, Md.
b. 29 March 1838, *m.* 12 April 1898, No issue. See p. 383.

PEDIGREE LXXXIX.

EDWARD III, King of England, had:
JOHN Duke of Lancaster, who had:
JOHN, Earl of Somerset, who had:
EDMUND, Duke of Somerset, who had:
HENRY, Duke of Somerset, who had:
CHARLES, Earl of Worcester, who had:
HENRY, Earl of Worcester, who had:
WILLIAM, Earl of Worcester, who had:
EDWARD, Earl of Worcester, who had:
HENRY, Marquis of Worcester, who had:

SIR JOHN, LORD SOMERSET, second son, brother to Edward, 2d Marquis, father of Henry, first Duke of Beaufort. He had three sons by his wife, Lady Mary Arundel, of Wardour castle, *d.* 1630, also of royal descent: HENRY, of Pently Court, Gloucestershire, who *m.* Anne, daughter of Walter, Lord Ashton, (and had Edward-Maria Somerset, *m.* Ladies Clare and Anne Calvert, daughters of Charles, Lord Baltimore, and *d. s. p.* 1711); Thomas, *d. unm.*, 1671, and

SIR CHARLES SOMERSET, of Ross, Herefordshire, (see Collins's "Peerage," 1812 ed., vol. I. p. 233). He married three times, and had by his second wife, Catherine, daughter of Walter Baskerville, and widow of George Sawier, of the Inner Temple, London, two sons and two daughters, Charles, Henry, Elizabeth, and (see Collins's "Peerage," 1779, vol. I.)

LADY MARY JOANNA SOMERSET, *d.* Calvert Co., Md., 1697, in giving birth to her only child. She eloped with Mr. Lowther, an officer in the King's Guards, and sailed with him to Maryland, to join the colony of her relative, Lord Baltimore, whose second wife, Lady Anne, was a sister to Lady Mary Arundel, aforesaid, and whose daughter, Lady Maria Calvert, had married first, Lord Edward Somerset, an uncle of Lady Mary Joanna Somerset, and married secondly, Robert Lowther Smith, a brother to Col. Walter Smith, of Calvert Co., *d.* 1711, and to Capt. Richard Smith, Jr. When Lord Baltimore erected the new county in Maryland, 22 Aug. 1666, he declared it named Somerset, "in honor of our

Deare Sister the Lady Mary Somerset." (Proceedings Md. Council, 1661-1675), she being sister to his wife, "Anne Arundel," for whom he named another county in Maryland.

Mr. Lowther died on the voyage, and Lady Mary Joanna Somerset *m.* in Maryland, about 1695, Capt. Richard Smith, Jr., of Calvert Co, surveyor-general of the Province, 1693, his third wife, son of Lieut. Richard Smith, 1628-1685, the first attorney-general of Maryland, 1655-1660; burgess, Calvert Co., 1660-67. See Davis's "Day Star of American Freedom," p. 90, for "Narrative of Barbara, (widow of John Rousby, and daughter of Henry Morgan), the second wife of Richard Smith, Jr., of Puttexent," dated 30 Dec, 1689, given in London, before the commission investigating the troubles between the Protestants and Catholics, in Maryland, and the rebellion against Lord Baltimore, in 1689. She told of the arrest and imprisonment of her husband, he being a Catholic, "for fear he should go for England to give an account of their proceedings." He was released when it was made impossible for him to sail; but was again imprisoned, because he opposed the irregular election of burgesses by the Protestants in arms, and was in jail when his wife, Barbara, went to London to complain of his treatment, and to get his release. She accompanied Col. Darnall, in the *Everard,* Sept. 26th, who went to explain the "troubles," taking with her a letter from the sheriff of Calvert Co., Michael Taney, dated 14 Sept. 1689, telling of the arrest of himself and Richard Smith, by the rebels, which she delivered to the Lords, 16 Dec. 1689, according to endorsement in the British State Paper Office.

Richard Smith, Jr., a vestryman, Christ Church parish, Calvert Co., who *d.* in 1714, leaving a will, on file at Annapolis, had by his third wife, (his first wife was Elizabeth, *b.* 28 Nov., 1655, daughter of Rev. Robert Brooke, see Ped. XCII., by whom he had Richard, Elizabeth, and Anne), Lady Mary Joanna Somerset, who was eventually sole heiress to her father:

CHARLES SOMERSET SMITH, of Calvert Co., who was accidentally drowned in St. Leonard's creek, in 1738. He was heir by his father's will to about 8,000 acres of land, and "the silver punch bowl, that hath engraved on it the arms of the Somerset family." He had by his wife, Margaret, whose surname is unknown, two sons, twins, and five daughters; of these, Richard, *d. s. p.* in London, in 1757; Charles Somerset, *m.* ——— Sothern; Elizabeth, *d.* after 1772, *m.* first, *ante* 1737, Francis Wilkinson, and *m.* secondly, 1739-41, Young Parran, 1711-1772, of Calvert Co.; Jane *m.* Col. Reeder, of St. Mary's Co.; Dicandia, *m.* and had issue; Mary, and

PEDIGREE LXXXIX.—Continued.

ANN SMITH, 1724-1775, who *m.* Samuel Parran, 1717-1749, (brother to Young Parran, aforesaid), son of Alexander Parran, 1677-1729, and his wife, Mary Young, and had:

ALEXANDER PARRAN, 1740-1779, who removed to Gloucester, Mass., in 1769, where he *m.* Elizabeth Eveleth, *d.* 1824, (great-great granddaughter of Sylvester Eveleth, of Gloucester, 1689). He was a sergeant of militia at the battle of Bunker Hill, where he was wounded, and who was subsequently in service on the American Privateer, "Fair Play," when she was sunk, in 1779, by shots from the fort at Guadaloupe, and was drowned. He left five daughters, one of whom,

SARAH EVELETH PARRAN, 1774-1859, *m.* 1803, William Presson, of Gloucester, 1775-1830, (great-grandson of William Presson, of Beverly, died 1718, who was son of John Presson, sometimes called Praeston, and Presburg, of Saco, 1674, *d.* 1684). Their second son,

ALFRED PRESTON, 1807-1873, of Gloucester, *m.* 1837, Mary Ann Moore, 1816-1866, granddaughter of Thomas Moore, of Gloucester, 1776, and had:

1.—WALTER PRESSON, Malden, Mass., 1835-1899, *m.* first, Ella McEachern, *d. s. p.,* and *m.* second, Jennie le Seur, and had HERBERT PARRAN, *b.* 1896, and WALTER SOMERSET, *b.* 1900.

2.—ALFRED PRESSON, of Gloucester, *b.* 29 Mar., 1838, who *m.* 12 Apr., 1898, Sarah Elizabeth, *b.* 1851 daughter of William Alexander Parran, of Prince Fredericktown, Md., *b.* 5 Feb., 1826, *d.* 14 Feb., 1902, son of Charles Somerset Smith Parran, 1800-1828, son of Alexander, 1757-1805, of Calvert Co., a son of the aforesaid Young Parran, by his wife, Elizabeth Smith. See p. 380. No issue.

3.—WILLIAM PRESSON, 1841-1895, *m.* Amelia Shephard, and had, ALFRED EVELETH, and WILLIAM HERBERT, both of Gloucester, Mass.

4.—HERBERT PRESSON, of Gloucster, *b.* 1849, unmarried.

THE ROYAL DESCENT
OF
MR. ORVILLE DWIGHT BALDWIN.

EMPEROR CHARLEMAGNE=Hildegarde de Suabia.

Louis I., King of France. — Pepin, King of Italy.
Charles II. — ALFRED THE GREAT. — Bernard, King of Lombardy.
Louis II. — Edward the Elder. — Pepin de Peronne.
Charles III.=Egiva, of England. — Herbert I. de Vermandois.
Louis IV., King of France. — Herbert II. de Vermandois.
Gerberga, Princess of France=Albert I. de Vermandois.
Herbert III. de Vermandois. — HUGH CAPET, King of France.
Otto de Vermandois. — Robert I., King of France.
Herbert IV. de Vermandois. — Henry I., King of France.
Adelheid de Vermandois=Hugh Magnus, de Vermandois.
Isabel de Vermandois=William de Warren, 2d Earl of Surrey.
Gundred de Warren=Roger de Newburgh, Earl of Warwick.
Waleran de Newburgh, Earl of Warwick=Alice de Harcourt.
Alice de Newburgh=William de Mauduit, Lord of Hanslape.
Isabel de Mauduit=William de Beauchamp, Lord of Elmley.
William de Beauchamp, Earl of Warwick=Maud Fitzjohn.
Guy de Beauchamp, Earl of Warwick=Alice de Toni.
Matilda de Beauchamp=Admiral Geoffery de Say, 2d Baron.
Idonae de Say=Sir John de Clinton, 3d Baron.
Margaret de Clinton=Sir Baldwin de Montfort, Knt.
Sir William de Montfort, Knt.=Margaret de Peche.
Sir Baldwin de Montfort, Knt.=Joanna de Vernon.
Robert Montfort, of Bescote, Staff.=(Name unknown.)
Katharine Montfort, heiress=Sir George Booth, of Dunham-Massie.
Sir William Booth, of Dunham-Massie.=Ellen Montgomery, of Thornley.
Jane Booth (widow)=Sir Thomas Holford, of Holford, Cheshire.
Dorothy Holford (2d wife)=John Bruen, of Bruen-Stapleford, Cheshire.
John Bruen, of Bruen-Stapleford=Margaret . . . . . . (3d wife).
Marie Bruen (See Pedigree V.)=John Baldwin, d. 1681, at Milford, Conn.
Abigail Baldwin b. 1658=Samuel Baldwin, of Fairfield, Ct., 1665-1696.
Nathaniel Baldwin, of Guilford, Conn., 1693-1760=Elizabeth Parmalee, of Guilford, 1690-1786.
Samuel Baldwin, of Guilford, Conn., 1725-1804=Mercy Stanley, m. 26 Nov. 1744, d. 1768.
Samuel Baldwin, of Goshen, N. Y., 1755-1838=Lucina Hill, of Goshen.
Harvey Baldwin, of Lexington, N. Y., 1784-1852=Nellie Calkins (1st wife).
Orin Calkins Baldwin, of Rensselaerville, N. Y.=Jane Wightman Luce, b. Middleburg, N. Y.
Orville Dwight Baldwin, of San Francisco,=Millie Eva, daughter of Charles and Catharine (Rohé) Wehn, of Philadelphia, Pa.
Member of the Order of Runnemede.

Blanche Evelyn, of the Society of Colonial Dames.=John McGaw, of Brentford, England. Orville Raymond Baldwin, of Lake Co., Cal.=Anna, dau. Eugene Deuprey.

Baldwin.   Evelyn Victoria.   Doris.   Orville Dwight.   Drusilla.   Dalthea.

PEDIGREE XC.

HENRY DE BOHUN	ROGER BIGOD		
Margery de Newburg.	HUGH BIGOD		
Alice de Mauduit.	Ralph Bigod.		
Isabel de Beauchamp.	Isabel Fitzpiers.	GEOFFREY DE SAY	ROBERT FITZWALTER
William de Beauchamp, m.	John Fitzjohn.	William de Say.	Walter Fitzrobert.
	Maud Fitzjohn.	William de Say.	Ela Odingsells.
	Guy de Beauchamp.	Geoffrey de Say.	Ida de Clinton.
	Maud de Beauchamp, m.	Geoffrey de Say.	John de Clinton.
		Idonae de Say, m. John de Clinton.	

SIR BALDWIN DE MONTFORT, who *m.* Lady Margaret de Clinton, descended from the aforesaid five Sureties for the Magna Carta, and had:

SIR WILLIAM DE MONTFORT, *d.* 1453, a descendant of Charlemange, Alfred the Great, and William the Conqueror (see p. 28), and had:

SIR BALDWIN DE MONTFORT, 1445-1475, who had:

ROBERT MONTFORT, of Bescote, Straffordshire, who had:

KATHARINE, who *m.* George Bothe, of Dunham Massie, *d.* 1483, and had:

SIR WILLIAM BOTHE, of Dunham Massie, Cheshire, 1473-1519, who had:

1.—EDWARD BOOTH, of Twemlowe, Cheshire, second son, *b.* 149—, who had:

WILLIAM BOOTH, of Temlowe, *temp.* 1597, who had:

EDWARD BOOTH, of Great Budworth parish, Cheshire, who had:

RICHARD BOOTH, *bapt.* August, 1608, at Gt. Budworth; of Stratford, Conn., 1640, *d.* there, 1687, who had by his wife, *m.* 1640, sister of Joseph Hawley:

BETHIA BOOTH, *m.* 1676, Joseph Curtiss, of Stratford, and had:

EPHRIAM CURTISS, of Stratford, Conn., 1684-1775, who had:

STILES CURTISS, of Stratford, Conn., 1708-1785, who had:

EPHRIAM CURTISS, of Stratford, Conn., 1739-1794, who had:

REBECCA CURTISS, *m.* David Birdseye, of Huntington, Conn., *d.* 1872, and had:

JOSEPH BIRDSEYE, of Huntington, Conn., 1804-1847, who had:

ISAAC W. BIRDSEYE, of Bridgeport, Conn., a member of the Order of Runnemede, Society of Colonial Wars, Society of Foreign Wars, Treasurer General of Society Sons of the American Revolution, etc., *b.* Huntington, 18 June, 1845, *m.* 4 May, 1880, Elizabeth Josephine Sherwood, of Bridgeport, also of Royal Descent (see pp. 390, 395), and had:

ELIZABETH JOSEPHINE BIRDSEYE, (only child), *b.* June 29, 1892.

2.—JANE BOOTH, who *m.* Thomas Holford, of Holford, Cheshire, and had:

DOROTHY HOLFORD, who *m.* John Bruen, of Bruen Stapleford, and had:

JOHN BRUEN, of Bruen Stapleford, Cheshire, *d.* 1625. (See below and p. 29). He was *m.* three times. By his second wife, Ann Fox, he had:

OBADIAH BRUEN, *bapt.* 25 December, 1606, a founder of New London, Conn., and of Newark, N. J., *d.* 168—. Of his issue by his wife, Sarah:

I.—CALEB BRUEN had MATTHIAS, who had HERMAN, of Perth Amboy, who had:

HERMAN WASHINGTON BRUEN, of New York, 1840-1884, who had:

HERMAN BRUEN, of New York, *b.* 30 September, 1873, a member of the Order of Runnemede.

II.—JOHN BRUEN, of Newark, 1646-169—, *m.* Esther, daughter of Richard Lawrence, of New Haven, Conn., and had:

I.—REBECCA BRUEN, *m.* Thomas Montagne, of New York, and had:

HANNAH MONTAGNE, *m.* 8 February, 1755, Morris Earle of New York, and had:

WILLIAM EARLE, *b.* Watertown, Mass., 22 April, 1775; *m.* Martha Pinto, and had:

WILLIAM PITT EARLE, *b.* Worcester, Mass., 14 June, 1812; *m.* 13 April, 1836, Elizabeth, *b.* 25 December. 1817 daughter of Judge Benjamin Pinney, of Ellington, Conn., and had:

GEN. FERDINAND PINNEY EARLE, *b.* Hartford, Conn., 11 September, 1839, *d.* New York, 3 January, 1903. A member of the Order of Runnemede. Issue.

II.—JOHN BRUEN, 1690-1767, *m.* Mary, daughter of Seth Tompkins. (N. J. His. Coll. VI. Supp., p. 134), and had:

REBECCA BRUEN, *m.* Samuel Headley, (N. J. His. Coll. VI. Supp., 113), and had:

RHODA HEADLEY, 1756-1837, *m.* Jonas Wade, (Wade Gen.), and had:

PHOEBE WADE, 1782-1867, *m.* Daniel Wurts, of Philadelphia, (Wurts Gen.), and had:

MARIA WURTS, 1807-1900, *m.* John Muir,("Muir Family"),and had:

WILLIAM MUIR, of Philadelphia, *b.* Louisville, Ky., who *m.* Augusta Elizabeth, *b.* Havre, France, daughter of Rev. Dr. E. N. Sawtell, and had:

1.—AUGUSTA ELIZABETH MUIR, *b.* Harrisburg, Pa., *m.* John H. Lippincott, and had: Augusta Elizabeth, *b.* Germantown, Philadelphia, 15 May, 1904.

2.—JOHN WALLINGFORD MUIR, of Philadelphia, *b.* Saratoga Springs.

3.—OPHELIA MUIR, of Philadelphia, *b.* Louisville, Ky.

4.—WILLIAM SAWTELL MUIR, of Philadelphia, *b.* in Chicago, *m.* Lydia Chichester, of Maryland.

5.—MARIA WURTS MUIR, of Philadelphia, *b.* Louisville, Ky.

JOHN BRUEN, of Bruen Stapleford, aforesaid, *d.* 1625, had by his third wife, Margaret:

MARIE BRUEN, (see Ped. V.), who *m.* 1653, John Baldwin, of Milford, Conn., *d.* 1681, and had:

ABIGAIL BALDWIN, *b.* 1658, who *m.* Samuel Baldwin, of Fairfield, Conn., 1665-1696, son of Nathaniel Baldwin, of Cholesburg, England, and had:

CAPT. NATHANIEL BALDWIN, of Guilford, Conn., 1693-1760, who *m.* Elizabeth Parmlee, of Guilford, 1690-1786, and had:

SAMUEL BALDWIN, of Guilford, 1725-1804, who *m.* 26 November, 1744, Mercy Stanley, *d.* 1768, and had:

SAMUEL BALDWIN, of Goshen, N. Y., 1755-1838, who *m.* Lucinda Hill, of Goshen, and had:

HARVEY BALDWIN, M. D., of Lexington, N. Y., 1784-1852, who *m.* first, Nellie Calkins, *b.* 1784, and had:

ORIN CALKINS BALDWIN, of Rensselaersville, N. Y., 1809-1861, who *m.* Jane Wightman Luce, 1815-1867, *b.* Middleburg, N. Y., and had:

ORVILLE DWIGHT BALDWIN, of San Francisco, Cal., b. 8 August, 1843, a member of the Order of Runnemede, who m. Millie Eva, b. Philadelphia, 18 January, 1853, daughter of Charles Frederick Wehn, (son of Charles and Dorothea Von Glöde Wehn), and his wife, Eva Catherine Rohé (see p. 384), and had:

1.—BLANCHE EVELYN BALDWIN, b. 18 March, 1874, a member of the National Society of Colonial Dames of America, the Order of the Crown in America, etc., who m. John McGaw, of Brentford, England, and San Francisco, b. 3 July, 1865, and had: BALDWIN, b. 27 January, 1900, and EVELYN VICTORIA, b. 13 February, 1901.

2.—ORVILLE RAYMOND BALDWIN, of "Middletown," Lake Co., Cal., who m. Anna, b. June, 1878, daughter of Eugene Deuprey, and his wife, Florence, daughter of Judge Hillyer, Governor of Alaska, and had: DORIS, b. 24 December, 1897; ORVILLE DWIGHT, b. 19 January, 1899; DRUSILLA, b. 19 January, 1900, and DALTHEA, b. in 1904.

THE ROYAL DESCENT
OF
MRS. WALTER DAMON MANSFIELD,
OF SAN FRANCISCO, CALIFORNIA.

THE EMPEROR CHARLEMANGE had:
Louis I., the Pious, King of France, who had:
Gisela, *m.* Everhard, Duke of Frioul, and had:
Hedwige, *m.* Ludolph, Duke of Saxony, and had:
Otto the Great, Duke of Saxony, who had:
Henry I., Emperor of Germany, who had:
Hedwige, *m.* Hugh, Duke of France, and had:
Hugh Capet, King of France, who had:
Hedwige, *m.* Rainier, Count Hainault, and had:
Beatrix, *m.* Ebles I., Count of Rouci, and had:
Alix, *m.* Hilduin, Count Montdidier, and had:
Marguerite, *m.* Hugh, Count Clermont, and had:
Adeliza, *m.* Gilbert, Earl of Clare, and had:
Adeliza, *m.* Aubrey, Lord de Vere, and had:
Julianna, *m.* Hugh, Earl Norfolk, and had:

THE EMPEROR CHARLEMANGE had:
Pepin, King of Italy, who had:
Bernard, King of Lombardy, who had:
Pepin, Count of Vermandois, who had:
Hubert I., Count of Vermandois, who had:
Hubert II., Count of Vermandois, who had:
Robert, Count of Champagne, who had:
Adeliza, *m.* Geoffrey, Count d'Anjou, and had:
Ermengarde, *m.* Conan, of Brittany, and had:
Juetta, *m.* Richard II., of Normandy, and had:
Robert I., Duke of Normandy, who had:
William the Conqueror, of England, who had:
Gundreda, *m.* William, Earl of Surrey, and had:
William, Earl of Warren and Surrey, who had:
Isabella, *m.* Hameline Plantagenet, and had:

Roger Bigod, Earl of Norfolk=Isabella de Warren.

Hugh Bigod, Earl of Norfolk, who had:
Sir Ralph Bigod, Knt., who had:
Isabel, *m.* Gilbert de Lacy, of Trim, and had:
Maud, *m.* Geoffrey, Lord Geneville, and had:
Peter, Lord Geneville, of Trim Castle, who had:

LLEWELYN THE GREAT, of Wales, had:
Gladuse, *m.* Ralph, Lord Mortimer, and had:
Roger, Lord Mortimer, of Wigmore, who had:
Sir Edmund, Lord Mortimer.

Lady Joan de Geneville=Sir Roger, Earl of Marche.

Maud de Mortimer=John, Lord Cherlton, of Powys Castle.

Lady Jane=John, Baron le Strange, of Knockyn Castle.

Lady Elizabeth=Gruffydd ap Madoc Vychan, Lord of Glyn-dyfrdwy.

Lady Isabel=Goronway ap Griffith, Lord of Penllyn.

Tudor ap Goronway, Lord of Penllyn=(Name unknown.)

Howel ap Tudor ap Goronway=(Name unknown.)

David-Llwyd ap Howel ap Tudor=(Name unknown.)

Lady Gwenhwyfar=David ap Evan Vaughn, of Llanuwchllyn.

David-Llwyd ap David, of Llandderfel, Penlynn.=Annesta vch. Griffith.

Robert ap David Lloyd, of Nantfreur,=Mary vch. Reynold.

Thomas ap Robert, of Gwern y Brechtwn,=Catherine vch. Robert.

Evan ap Thomas Robert, of Nant y Friar,=Dorothea Evans, *d.* 1619.

Thomas ap Evan, 1579-1649; sheriff of Merion,=Catherine v. William.

Ffoulke ap Thomas Evan, bapt. 1623=Lowry v. Edward David, of Llanvor.

Edward Ffoulke, 1651-1741, of Coed y Foel,=Eleanor, *d.* 1733, dau. Hugh ap Cadwalader, Came to Pa. in June, 1698. (See Ped. XXX.) of Spytu, Denbigh.

Jane Foulke, *d.* 8 mo. 7, 1766=4 mo. 5, 1713. Ellis Hugh, or Hughes, 1688-1764, *d.* at Exeter, Pa.

William Hughes, 1716-1760, of Exeter, Pa.,=4 mo. 1, 1738, Amy, 1712-1760, dau. Thomas and Westbury, Willetts, of Westbury, L. I., N. Y.

Ellis Hughes, 1738-1785, of Catawissa, Pa.=1 mo. 1, 1764, Hannah, dau. Francis Yarnall, Chester Co., Pa. She *d.* Baltimore, 4 mo. 1, 1816.

Phebe Hughes, 1765-1833=2 mo. 29, 1788, John Skelton, of Chester Co., Pa., 1765-1793-4.

Elizabeth Skelton, 1788-1858=12 mo. 20, 1801, at Old Town, Baltimore, Md., Thomas Stansbury, 1788-1867, of Cincinnati, Ohio, and Houston, Texas.

John Skelton Stansbury, 1813-1879, *b.* Cin-=1 mo. 1, 1857, at Sacramento, Mary Ann cinnati, *d.* Napa City, Cal. Monaghan, third wife.

May Monelle=Walter Damon Stansbury, Mansfield, of San Francisco.

Joseph Ellis Stansbury, 1859-1890.

Warren M.=Minnie Stansbury, Cooper. of Tonopah, Nevada.

Ella Elizabeth Stansbury, of Honolulu.

THE ROYAL DESCENT
OF
MRS. ISAAC W. BIRDSEYE,
OF BRIDGEPORT, CONN.

EDWARD III., King of England,=Lady Philippa of Hainault.
John, Duke of Lancaster, etc.=Lady Katherine Roet, of Hainault.
Lady Joan de Beaufort=Sir Ralph, K. G., Earl of Westmoreland.
Sir Richard, K. G., Earl of Salisbury=Lady Alice de Montacute.
Lady Alice de Neville=Henry, Baron Fitzhugh, of Ravensworth.
Lady Elizabeth Fitzhugh=Sir William Parr, K. G., of Kendal.
Sir William, Lord Parr, of Horton=Lady Mary Salisbury, of Horton.
Lady Elizabeth Parr=Sir Nicholas Woodhull, of Wodehull.
Fulke Woodhull, of Thenford=Alice Coles, of Lye.
Nicholas Woodhull, of Wodehull=Mary Rowleigh, of Farnburn.
Anthony Woodhull, of Wodehull=Anne Smyth, of London.
Agnes Woodhull=Richard Chetwood, of Warkworth.
Sir Richard Chetwood, of Wodehull=Dorothea Needham, of Shavington.
Grace Chetwood=Rev. Peter Bulkley, D.D., of Concord, Mass.
Dr. Peter Bulkley, of Fairfield, Ct.=Margaret Foxcraft.
Peter Bulkley, of Fairfield, Ct.=Hannah Bulkley.
Sarah Bulkley=Joseph Perry, of Fairfield, Ct.
Mary Perry=Gershom Banks, of Fairfield, Ct.
Gershom Banks, of Fairfield, Ct.=Ruth Banks.
Huldah Banks=Joseph Sherwood, of Greenfield, Ct.
Aaron Banks Sherwood, of Greenfield, Ct.=Elizabeth Curtiss.
Elizabeth Josephine Sherwood=Isaac W. Birdseye, of Bridgeport, Ct.
Also of Royal Descent. See Ped. XC.

Elizabeth Josephine Birdseye, only child, b. 28 June, 1892. See pp. 386, 395.

PEDIGREE XCI.

HENRY III., King of England, had by his first wife, Lady Eleanor daughter of Raymond de Berenger, Count of Provence:

EDMUND PLANTAGENET, Earl of Leicester, Lancaster, and Chester, lord high steward, who had by his second wife, Lady Blanche, granddaughter of Louis VIII., King of France.

HENRY PLANTAGENET, Earl of Lancaster and Leicester, who *m.* Lady Maud, of Royal Descent, daughter of Patrick de Chaworth, and had:

LADY ELEANOR PLANTAGENET, who *m.* secondly (his second wife), Sir Richard Fitz-Alan, K.G., Earl of Arundel and Surrey, and had:

LADY ALICE FITZ-ALAN, who *m.* Sir Thomas de Holland, K.G., second Earl of Kent, Marshal of England, also of Royal Descent, and had:

LADY ELEANOR DE HOLLAND, who *m.* (his first wife) Thomas de Montacute, last Earl of Salisbury, also of Royal Descent, and had:

LADY ALICE DE MONTACUTE, who *m.* Sir Richard de Nevill, K.G., created Earl of Salisbury, 1442; lord great chamberlain of England, who was beheaded, for siding with the Yorkists, in 1461, and his head was fixed upon a gate of York. His sister, Lady Cicely, wife of Richard, third Duke of York, was the mother of Kings Edward IV. and Richard III., the former being ancestor of all the rulers of England since Henry VII.

Lady Alice had by the Earl of Salisbury:

LADY ALICE DE NEVILLE (sister of Richard Neville, K. G., Earl of Salisbury and Warwick, the renowned "king maker"), who *m.* Henry, fifth Baron Fitzhugh, of Ravensworth, *d.* 1472, and had:

LADY ELIZABETH FITZHUGH, who *m.* Sir William Parr, K.G., constable of England, also of Royal Descent, and had:

WILLIAM LORD PARR, of Horton, Northants, *d.* 1546, who was uncle of Katherine Parr, last wife of Henry VIII., of England. He was chamberlain to Her Majesty, and was advanced to the peerage 23 December, 1543. He *m.* Lady Mary, daughter of Sir William Salisbury, and had:

LADY ELIZABETH PARR (she is also called Alice). Her sister, Lady Maud Parr, *m.* Sir Ralph Lane, of Orlingbury, and had Ralph Lane, governor of the first Virginia colony, 1585-6. She *m.* (his second wife) Sir Nicholas Woodhull, Lord Woodhull, of county Bedford, *d.*

1532. His will, 25 March, 1531, given in full in Nichols' "Collec. Topo. et Geneal.," Vol. V., 309; buried in Warkworth Church, Northants, and had (*see* the Northamptonshire Visitations, 1564 and 1618; the Yorkshire Visitations, 1584, and Dugdale's "Baronage"):

FULKE WOODHULL, of Thenford Manor, Northamptonshire, second son and heir, and eldest son by his second wife. He was a minor in 1531, according to father's will. He *m.* Alice, daughter of William Coles, or Colles, of Lye, or Leigh county, Worcester, and had (*see* p. 212):

1.—LAWRENCE WOODHULL, a younger son, who had:

RICHARD WOODHULL, of Long Island, N. Y., 1620-1690, who had:

RICHARD WOODHULL, of Setauket, 1649-1699, who had:

NATHANIEL WOODHULL, of Mastic, L. I., who had:

GEN. NATHANIEL WOODHULL, of Mastic, 1722-1776, who had:

ELIZABETH WOODHULL, 1762-1839, who *m.* first, Henry Nicholl, of New York, 1756-1790, and had:

HENRY WOODHULL NICOLL, 1789-1829, who *m.* Louisa Anna Ireland, 1800-1842, and had:

MARY LOUISE NICOLL, who *m.* Henry G. Wayne, 1815-1883, and had:

REV. HENRY NICOLL WAYNE, a member of the Order of Runnemede, father of *Henry T., Elizabeth C.*, wife of James E. Cooper, of New Britain, Conn.; *Edith D.* and *Glenn Hytton.*

2.—NICHOLAS WOODHULL, eldest son, lord of Wodehull, Bedford, *d.* 1532. He *m.* (Mary) daughter of Edward Rowleigh, of Farmburg, Warwickshire, and had:

ANTHONY WOODHULL, lord of Wodehull, *d.* 1543. He *m.* Ann, daughter of Sir John Smyth, or Smith, Baron of the Exchequer, and had:

LADY AGNES WOODHULL, heiress, who *m.* Richard Chetwoode, or Chitwoode, of Warkworth, Northants, and had:

SIR RICHARD CHETWOODE, Kt. of Woodhull, Bedford, 1618 (*see* Visitations of Northants and Bedford, 1564, 1618, 1634). He *m.* Dorothea Nodham, or Needham, of Shavington, Salop, and had:

GRACE CHETWOODE, *d.* 21 April, 1669, at New London, Conn. She *m.* (his second wife) Rev. Peter Bulkley, D. D., 1583-1659, of Concord, Mass., son of Rev. Edward Bulkley, D. D. (*see* Waters's "Gleanings in English Wills," pp. 416-17), and had:

1.—REV. GERSHOM BULKLEY,* b. Concord, Mass., 6 December, 1636, d. at Glastonbury, Conn., 2 December, 1713, m. 26 October, 1659, Sarah Chauncey, 1631-1699 (see Ped. XIX.), and had:

  I.—EDWARD BULKELEY, who m. Dorothy Prescott, and had:

    CHARLES BULKELEY, who m. Mary Sage, and had:

    1.—JOHN BULKELEY, who m. Honor Francis, and had:

      JOHN BULKELEY, who m. Sarah Wright, and had:

        ELIZABETH BULKELEY, d. 1864, who m. James Goodrich, d. at New Haven, Conn., 17 October, 1858, and had:

          WILLIAM GOODRICH, b. 29 March, 1809, at New Haven, d. at Philadelphia, 4 July, 1888. He m. at Knoxville, Tenn., 22 December, 1840, Sarah Ann, daughter of Marcus D. Bearden, and granddaughter of Maj.-Gen. John Cooke, and had:

            1.—WILLIAM GOODRICH, of Chestnut Hill, Philadelphia, b. New Haven, 12 January, 1845, a member of the military order of the Loyal Legion, the Society of Colonial Wars, etc. He m. 29 September, 1875, Helen, daughter of Anthony Groves, Jr., of Chestnut Hill. No issue.

            2.—CASPAR FREDERICK GOODRICH, Captain United States Navy, who m. Eleanor, daughter of Charles E. Milnor, of New York, and had:

              I.—ELEANOR GOODRICH, m. 1 June, 1901, Douglas Campbell, of N. Y.

              II.—CASPAR GOODRICH, b. 4 May, 1881, Ensign, United States Navy.

              III.—GLADYS GOODRICH, b. 14 June, 1886.

---

*The following ladies, members of the National Society of the Colonial Dames of America are also of Royal Descent, through Rev. Gershom Bulkley:
MISS MARY A. GRANGER, Providence, R. I., p. 85.
MRS. BYRON C. DICK, Oakland, Cal., p. 85.
MRS. HARRISON ALLEN, Philadelphia, p. 86.
MRS. WILLIAM C. SKINNER, Hartford, Conn., p. 86.
MRS. SAMUEL A. LYNDE, Chicago, p. 87.
MRS. GEORGE N. BRADY, Detroit, Mich., p. 87.
MRS. ROBERT M. BERRY, Detroit, Mich., p. 87
MRS. RICHARD H. MACAULEY, Detroit, Mich., p. 87.
MRS. ASA R. BRUNDAGE, Wilkesbarre, Pa., p. 87.
MISS MARY G. BRUNDAGE, Wilkesbarre, Pa., p. 87.
MISS LOUISE W. MCALLISTER, New York, p. 88.
MRS. PHILIP H. COOPER, Morristown, N. J., p. 88.

3.—SARAH ANNE GOODRICH, *b.* Philadelphia, 8 June, 1852, *m.* 26 September, 1871, William Earp, and had:
ELLEN FOBES, *b* 25 February, 1873.

2.—BENJAMIN BULKELEY, who *m.* Susannah Kirby, and had:
THOMAS BULKELEY, who *m.* Bathsheba Sage, and had:
SOPHIA BULKELEY, who *m.* Francis Wilcox, and had:
FREDERICK P. WILCOX, who *m.* Anna M. Clarke, and had:
ELIZABETH CLARKE WILCOX, a member of the Iowa Society of the Colonial Dames of America (*see* p. 84), who *m.* Willard B. Walworth, of Worcester, Mass.

II.—REV. JOHN BULKLEY, 1679-1733, *m.* Patience Prentice, and had:

1.—PATIENCE BULKELEY, *b.* 21 March, 1714, *m.* Ichabod Lord, and had:

JERUSHA LORD, *b.* 7 February, 1755, *m.* Rev. David Perry, and had:

FREDERICK PERRY, *b.* 21 November, 1778, *m.* Zerujah Sherrill, and had:

ELIZA SHERRILL PERRY, *b.* June, 1812, *m.* Edward M. Teall, and had:

EDWARD MCKINSTRY TEALL, of Chicago, a member of the Society of Colonial Wars, etc., *b.* 27 July, 1839.

2.—JOHN BULKLEY, 1705-1753, *m.* 29 October, 1738, Mrs. Mary (Adams) Gardiner, and Abigail Hastings.

JOHN BULKLEY had by his wife Mary:

ELIPHALET BULKLEY, *b.* 1746, *m.* Anna Bulkley, and had:
JOHN CHARLES BULKELEY, *b.* 1772, *m.* Sally Taintor, and had:
ELIPHALET ADAMS BULKELEY, *b.* 1803, *m.* Lydia S. Morgan, and had:
MORGAN GARDNER BULKELEY, of Hartford, *b.* 26 December, 1837, former Mayor of Hartford, and Governor of Conn., U. S. Senator from Conn., a founder of the Order of Runnemede, a member of the Military Order of the Loyal Legion, the Societies of Mayflower Descendants, Colonial Wars, etc. He *m.* Fannie Briggs Houghton, of San Francisco, and had:
MORGAN GARDNER, ELINOR HOUGHTON, and HOUGHTON.

JOHN BULKLEY had by his wife Abigail:

CHARLES BULKLEY, *b.* 22 May, 1752, *m.* Betsey Taintor, and had:

PEDIGREE XCI.—Continued.

GERSHOM TAINTOR BULKELEY, *d.* 22 October, 1862, aged 81, *m.* Julia Kellogg Bulkeley, *d.* 19 April, 1869, aged 75, and had:

JULIETTE E. BULKELEY, *b.* 5 January, 1828, *d.* 14 June, 1876, *m.* Lyman Hubbell, *b.* 16 September, 1827, *d.* 7 October, 1890, and had:

CHARLES BULKELEY HUBBELL, of New York, *b.* 20 July, 1853, a member of the Society of Colonial Wars, *m.* 5 June, 1879, Emily A., daughter of William H, Chandler, of Thompson, Conn., and had: JULIETTE EMILY, *b.* 7 March, 1880, MARGARET LAWRIE, *b.* 4 August, 1881, and RUTH ROSITER, *b.* 13 January, 1886.

2.—DR. PETER BULKLEY, of Fairfield, Conn., *b.* Concord, 12 June, 1643. His will dated 25 March, 1691. He had by his wife, Margaret Foxcroft:

PETER BULKLEY, named in his father's will, *b.* 25 December, 1683, will proved 31 December, 1771. He had by his wife, Hannah, daughter of John and Sarah (Whelpley) Bulkley:

SARAH BULKLEY, who *m.* Joseph Perry, of Fairfield, Conn., and had: MARY PERRY, *d.* 3 January, 1807, aged 82 years. She *m* Gershom Banks, of Fairfield, *b.* 1 May, 1712, and had:

GERSHOM BANKS, *b.* 31 August, 1752, *d.* 11 June, 1805. He *m.* his cousin, Ruth, daughter of Benjamin Banks, Jr., brother of Gershom, aforesaid, and had:

HULDAH BANKS, *b.* 5 August, 1777, *d.* 25 February, 1839, who *m.* Joseph Sherwood, of Greenfield, Conn., *b.* 13 October, 1775, *d.* 23 May, 1859, and had:

AARON BANKS SHERWOOD, of Greenfield, *b.* 15 December, 1816, He *m.* 28 September, 1843, Elizabeth Curtiss, *b.* 22 July, 1822, *d.* 1 March, 1891, and had:

ELIZABETH JOSEPHINE SHERWOOD, (*see* p. 390), who *m.* 4 May, 1880, Isaac W. Birdseye, of Bridgeport, Conn., also of Royal Descent (*see* pp. 386, 411), and had ELIZABETH JOSEPHINE, only child, *b.* 28 June, 1892.

THE ROYAL DESCENT
OF
MR. THOMAS MASON THOMSON RABORG,
OF NEW YORK CITY.

THE EMPEROR CHARLEMAGNE = Hildegarde de Suabia.

Louis I., King of France. — Pepin, King of Italy.

Charles II. ALFRED THE GREAT. — Bernard, King of Italy.

Louis II. Edward the Elder. — Pepin de Peronne.

Charles III. = Egiva, of England. — Herbert I. de Vermandois.

Louis IV., King of France. — Herbert II. de Vermandois.

Gerberga, Princess of France. = Albert I. de Vermandois.

Herbert III. de Vermandois. — HUGH CAPET, King of France.

Otho de Vermandois. — Robert I. King of France.

Herbert IV. de Vermandois. — Henry I. King of France.

Adelheid de Vermandois = Hugh de Vermandois.

Isabel de Vermandois = Robert, Count of Meulent, Earl of Leicester. pp. 11, 163.

Robert de Bellomont, Earl of Leicester = Aurelia, dau. Ralph de Guader, Earl of Norfolk, Suffolk and Cambridge.

Robert de Bellomont, Earl of Leicester = Petronella de Grentemaisnil. p. 147.

Margaret de Bellomont = Sairer de Quincey, Earl of Winchester.

Roger, Earl of Winchester = Helen, dau. Alan McDonal, Lord of Galloway. p. 397.

Lady Elizabeth de Quincey = Alexander Cumyn, Earl of Buchan. p. 147.

Lady Agnes Cumyn = Gilbert d'Umfraville, Earl of Angus. p. 147.

Robert d'Umfraville, Earl of Augus = Lady Alianore.

Sir Thomas d'Umfraville, Lord of Holmaid = Joan, daughter of Adam de Rodam.

Sir Thomas d'Umfraville, Lord of Kyme = Lady Agnes. p. 147.

Lady Elizabeth d'Umfraville = Sir William d'Elmedon, Northumberland.

Lady Joan d'Elmedon = Thomas Forster, of Bucton. p. 397.

Thomas Forster, of Bucton = Elizabeth d'Etherstone.

Thomas Forster, of Etherstone = Elizabeth Featherstonehaugh, of Stanhope Hall.

Roger Forster, second son = ——— Hussey.

Thomas Forster, of Hunsdon, Herts = Margaret Browning, of Clemsford, Essex.

Sir Thomas Forster, Justice C. P. Court = Susan Forster, of Iden, Sussex.

Susan Forster = Thomas Brooke, M. P., White Church, Southants.

Gov. Robert Brooke (see Ped. XCII.), removed to St. Mary's Co., Md., 1650. = Mary, dau. of Thomas Baker, of Battel, Sussex.

Baker Brooke, of De la Brooke Manor, 1628-1680 = Anne, granddau. of Gov. Leonard Calvert.

Leonard Brooke, d. 1718 = Anne, dau. Major William Boarman.

Mary Brooke = John Boarman, of St. Mary's Co., Md.

Catherine Boarman, d. June, 1813 = Major William Thomas, Jr., of St. Mary's Co., d. Jan,, 1813.

Anne Thomas, 1798-1862 = Hon. Thomas Mason, of Loudon Co., Va.

Matilda Brent Mason, 1839-1884 = Samuel A. Raborg, M. D., of Baltimore, Md., 1842-1889, Surgeon in 1st Md. Reg., C. S. Army.

H. Mason Raborg, of New York, Member of the Society of Colonial Wars, Metropolitan Club, N. Y., Maryland Club, Baltimore.

Anita Raborg.

Thomas Mason Thomson Raborg, of New York, Member of Order of Runnemede, Society of Colonial Wars, Metropolitan, and St. Anthony Clubs, N. Y., Society Sons of the Revolution, etc.

PEDIGREE XCII.

DAVID I., King of Scotland, had by his wife, Lady Matilda:
PRINCE HENRY, Earl of Huntingdon, *d. v. p.* 1152, who had:
DAVID, Earl of Huntingdon, whose daughter,
MARGARET, *m.* Alan McDonal, constable of Scotland, and had:
HELEN MCDONAL, who *m.* Roger, Earl of Winchester and had:
ELIZABETH DE QUINCEY, *m.* Alexander, Earl of Buchan, and had:
AGNES CUMYN, who *m.* Gilbert, Earl of Angus, and had:
ROBERT, second Earl of Angus, who had, by his second wife:
SIR THOMAS D'UMFRAVILLE, lord of Holmaid and Whitley, governor of Harbotel, *m.* Joan, daughter of Adam Rodam, and had:
SIR THOMAS D'UMFRAVILLE, lord of Riddesdale and Kyme, second son and heir, *d.* 14 February, 1390-1, aged 23, who had:
ELIZABETH D'UMFRAVILLE, who *m.* Sir William d'Elmedon, Northumberland, county palatine knight, in 1447, and had:
JOAN D'ELMEDON, *m.* Thomas Forster, of Bucton, and had:
THOMAS FORSTER, of Bucton. *m.* Elizabeth d'Etherstone, and had:
THOMAS FORSTER, of Etherstone, who *m.* Elizabeth Featherstonehaugh, of Stanhope Hall, in Durham, and had:
ROGER FORSTER (see "Foster-Barham Genealogy"), who had:
THOMAS FORSTER, of Hunsdon, an officer in the household of Queen Elizabeth, *m.* Margaret Browning, of Clemsford, and had:
SIR THOMAS FORSTER, counsel to Queen Anne, of Denmark, justice C. P., *d.* 18 May, 1612, aged 64, buried in Egham church, Surrey, *m.* Susan, daughter of Thomas Forster, of Iden, Sussex, and had:
SUSAN FORSTER, sister to Richard Forster, chief justice of the King's Bench. She *m.* Thomas Brooke, of White Church, Southants, M. P., 1604-11, *d.* 13 September, 1612, aged 52, and had:
REV. ROBERT BROOKE, *b.* London, 3 June, 1602. He was educated at Oxford University, and received his A. M. degree from Wadham College,

in 1618, and was admitted to Holy Orders, 25 February, 1626-7. He *m.* first, 25 February, 1627-8, Mary, daughter and heiress of Thomas Baker, of Battel, Sussex (see his father's will, Waters's "Gleanings in English Wills," p. 1345), by his wife, Lady Mary, daughter of Sir Thomas Engham, of Goodelstone, Kent, and had by her, who *d.* 1634, four children: BAKER, (p. 399), MARY, *b.* Battel, 16 February, 1630, *d. unm.;* THOMAS. (p. 400), and BARBARA, *b.* Wickham, *d. unm.* He *m.* secondly, 11 May, 1635, Mary, *b.* St. Giles-in-the-Field, London, daughter of Rev. Roger Mainwaring, D. D., Bishop of St. David's, 1636, and Dean of Worcester, and had by her, who *d.* in Md., 29 November, 1663, eleven children: CHARLES (p. 403), ROGER (p. 404), ROBERT (p. 404), JOHN, *b.* Battel, 20 September, 1640; MARY, *b.* Battel, 14 April, 1642; WILLIAM, *b.* Battel, 1 December, 1643; ANN, *b.* at Bretnock College, 22 January, 1645, and FRANCIS, *b.* Horwell, Hants, 30 May, 1648. Mr. Brooke* removed with his wife and children, and twenty-one men and seven women to St. Mary's Co., Md., and arrived 30 June, 1650,

---

*The following members of the Societies of Colonial Wars and Colonial Dames of America are also of royal descent through Rev Robert Brooke:
Thomas Marsh Smith, of Baltimore.
Mrs. Franklin H. Beckwith (Nannie Lawrence Kerfoot), deceased.
Miss Rosa Steele (resigned from Md. S. C. D.).
Mrs. Daniel C. Woods (Maria Louisa Crane). See p. 70, 4th Edition.
Miss Florence Phenix, deceased.
Miss Clementine Smith, of Washington, D. C.
Miss Sallie Cox Smith, of Washington, D. C.
Miss Elizabeth Young Thompson, of Baltimore.
Mrs. Albert L. Gorter (Mary Rebecca Thompson).
Mrs. Felix R. Sullivan (Elizabeth Tayloe Buchanan).
Mrs. Samuel H. Kerfoot (Annie Warfield Lawrence).
Miss Margaret Dobbin Leakin, of Baltimore.
Mrs. Albert Sioussat (Annie M. Leakin).
Mrs. Julius H. Kimball (Emily Nelson Maulsby).
Mrs. John Ritchie (Betty H. Maulsby), deceased.
Mrs. Allan R. Boyd (Jane Hall Maulsby Ritchie).
Mrs. George D. Penniman (Harriet Wilson Dushane). See Ped. XXXIX.
Mrs. L. Tyson Manly (Lily Tyson).
Mrs. James B. Parran. See p. 317.
Mrs. George Alphonzo Jones. See p. 76.
Mrs. Edward S. Beall (Eliza R. Winn). See pp. 44, 60.
Miss Laura Ogle Beall. See pp. 44, 60.
Mrs. H. B. Denman (Mary B. Young), deceased.
Miss Mary Dennison Philpot, deceased.

(see Md. Land Records, Lib. I., fo. 165; or Md. Archives, III., 256, which record gives the names of his party, also list of his children in Tyler's "Memoir of R. B. Taney," p. 22). He received a grant of 2,000 acres of land on the Patuxent river, and a creek named by him Battel, and here settled his Protestant colony. Part of this grant he called "De la Brooke," and resided here till 1652; (his son BAZIL, *d. inf.*, was *b.* here). He removed to another part of his grant, called "Brooke Place," where his last children, twins, HENRY and ELIZABETH, (first wife of Richard Smith, Jr., Calvert Co., see p. 382), were *b.* 28 November, 1655, and where he died 20 July, 1655, and was buried. Subsequently to the planting of his colony, his settlement was erected into a county under the name of Charles. He and his sons, Baker and Thomas, took the oath of fidelity, 22 July, 1650. Under commission from the proprietary, Mr. Brooke was the first commander of the new county, and was a member of the Governor's privy council from 22 July, 1650, and was its president in 1652, and acting governor in 1653, but, deserting the Calverts for the Cromwellians, he was deposed. (See Davis's "Day Star of American Freedom," p. 74.) Of his children,

1.—BAKER BROOKE, *b.* Battel, 16 November, 1628, lord of De la Brooke manor, Md.—the brick manor-house was destroyed in 184—. He was a member of the Provincial court held in October, 1658, and of that held in February, 1659, and was the surveyor general of the Province, 1673. His will, dated 19 March, 1678, proved 28 March, 1680, names his wife, Anne, and children, *Charles, Leonard* (see below), *Baker,* and *Mary,* his brother, Col. Thomas, and the latter's daughter, Mary.

He *m.*, in 1664, Anne, a granddaughter of Leonard Calvert, 1608-1647 (and his wife, Anne Brent), keeper of the rolls at Connaught, Ireland, 1621-25, first Governor of the Provence of Maryland, with Hawley and Cornwallis, 1633, and daughter of Judge William Calvert, member of the Governor's Council, secretary of the Province, etc., drowned in 1682, and his wife, Elizabeth, daughter of William Stone, the first Protestant Governor of Maryland. Of their children,

LEONARD BROOKE, will proved 2 April, 1718. He *m.* Anne, daughter of Maj. William Boarman, of St. Mary's Co., and had: *Jane* and *Mary*:—

I.—JANE BROOKE, *m.* John Smith of Calvert Co., and had:

BENJAMIN SMITH, *m.* Mary Neale, and had:

ANN SMITH, who *m.* Baker Jameson, and had:

MARY JANE JAMESON, a member of the Maryland Society of

Colonial Dames of America, also of Royal Descent, in Ped. XVII., who *m.* John W. Baughman, of Frederick, Md., and had:

1.—COURINE FRANCES BAUGHMAN, who *m.* Carlos Guillermo de Garmendia y de Cordoba, and had, *Gonzalo de Cordoba de Garmendia.*

2.—GEN. LOUIS VICTOR BAUGHMAN, of Frederick, *m.* Helen Abel, and had, *E. Austin* and *Helen Abel.*

3.—JOHN WILLIAM; 4. MARY LOUISE.

5.—CHARLES HENRY STONESTREET BAUGHMAN, *m.* Annette Hurd, and had: *Charles Francis.*

II.—MARY BROOKE, *m.* John Boarman, of St. Mary's Co., and had:

CATHERINE BOARMAN, *d.* in June, 1813, who *m.* Major William Thomas, of St. Mary's Co., *d.* in January, 1813, and had:

ANNE THOMAS, 1798-1862, who *m.* Thomas Mason, of Loudon Co., Va., and had:

MATILDA BRENT MASON, *d.* 14 August, 1884, aged 45, who *m.* Samuel A. Raborg, M. D., of Baltimore, Surgeon in 1st Maryland Regiment, C. S. Army, *b.* 15 March, 1842, *d.* 6 January, 1889, and had:

I.—H. MASON RABORG, of New York city.

II.—ANITA RABORG.

III.—THOMAS MASON THOMSON RABORG, of New York city (see p. 396), a member of the Order of Runnemede, etc.

2.—MAJOR THOMAS BROOKE, of "Brookfield Manor," Calvert Co., *b.* at Battel, 23 June, 1632, second son by his first wife. He was commissioned captain 3 June, 1658, and major of Maryland Troops, 11 February, 1660; served against Indians in 1667. He was a burgess and member of the Assembly, 1663-76, and sheriff of Calvert Co., 1667-73. His will, dated 25 October, 1676, proved 29 December, 1676, names his wife, Eleanor, and sons, *Thomas,* eldest (see below), *Robert, Ignatius, Matthew* and *Clement* (see below), and daughters, *Eleanor* (who *m.* first, John Tasker, and *m.* second, Charles Sewall), and *Mary,* and Baker Brooke, Jr., and "brother Clement Hill," executors with his wife, brother Baker, and half-brother Roger Brooke. He *m.* Eleanor Hatton, probably niece of Thomas Hatton, secretary of the Province, a privy councilor, 1648, attorney general, 1652, and daughter of Richard Hatton, of London, whose widow, Margaret, and children came to Maryland in 1649, (see Davis's "Day Star," pp. 200, 206). Of the children of Major Thomas Brooke:

THE ROYAL DESCENT
OF
GEORGE NORBURY MACKENZIE, 2d, ESQ.
OF BALTIMORE MD.

THE EMPEROR CHARLEMAGNE = Hildegarde de Suabia.

- Louis I., King of France.
  - Charles II. ALFRED THE GREAT.
    - Louis II. Edward the Elder.
      - Charles III. = Egiva, of England.
        - Louis IV., King of France.
          - Gerberga, Princess of France. = Albert I. de Vermandois.
- Pepin, King of Italy.
  - Bernard, King of Italy.
    - Pepin de Peronne.
      - Herbert I. de Vermandois.
        - Herbert II. de Vermandois.
          - Albert I. de Vermandois.
            - Herbert III. de Vermandois.
              - Otho de Vermandois.
                - Herbert IV. de Vermandois.
                  - Adelheid de Vermandois = Hugh de Vermandois.
- HUGH CAPET, King of France.
  - Robert I. King of France.
    - Henry I. King of France.
      - Hugh de Vermandois.

Isabel de Vermandois = Robert, Count of Meulent, Earl of Leicester. pp. 11, 163.

Robert de Bellomont, Earl of Leicester = Aurelia, dau. Ralph de Guader, Earl of Norfolk, Suffolk and Cambridge.

Robert de Bellomont, Earl of Leicester = Petronella de Grentemaisnil. p. 147.

Margaret de Bellomont = Sairer de Quincey, Earl of Winchester.

Roger, Earl of Winchester = Helen, dau. Alan McDonal, Lord of Galloway. p. 397.

Lady Elizabeth de Quincey = Alexander Cumyn, Earl of Buchan. p. 147.

Lady Agnes Cumyn = Gilbert d'Umfraville, Earl of Angus. p. 147.

Robert d'Umfraville, Earl of Augus = Lady Alianore.

Sir Thomas d'Umfraville, Lord of Holmaid = Joan, daughter of Adam de Rodam.

Sir Thomas d'Umfraville, Lord of Kyme = Lady Agnes. p. 147.

Lady Elizabeth d'Umfraville = Sir William d'Elmedon, Northumberland.

Lady Joan d'Elmedon = Thomas Forster, of Bucton. p. 397.

Thomas Forster, of Bucton = Elizabeth d'Etherstone.

Thomas Forster, of Etherstone = Elizabeth Featherstonehaugh, of Stanhope Hall.

Roger Forster, second son = ——— Hussey.

Thomas Forster, of Hunsdon, Herts. = Margaret Browning, of Clemsford, Essex.

Sir Thomas Forster, Justice C. P. Court = Susan Forster, of Iden, Sussex.

Susan Forster = Thomas Brooke, M. P., White Church, Southants.

Gov. Robert Brooke (see Ped. XCII.), removed to St. Mary's Co., Md., 1650. = Mary, dau. of Rt. Rev. Roger Mainwaring D. D., Bishop of St. David's.

Roger Brooke, of Calvert Co., Md., 1637-1700 = Dorothy, dau of Capt. James Neale, of Wallaston Manor, Md.

Anne Brooke, d. 1733 = James Mackall, of Calvert Co., 1677-1717.

John Mackall, of Calvert Co., 1710-1750 = Martha, dau. of James Duke, Calvert Co.

Benjamin Mackall, Calvert Co., 1745-1807 = Mary Taylor, b. 1 July, 1744; d. ———.

Sarah Taylor Mackall, 1771-1816 = Cosmo Mackenzie, Calvert Co., 1770-1807

Thomas Mackenzie, Baltimore, 1794-1866 = Tacy Burges Norbury, 1790-1837.

George Norbury Mackenzie, Baltimore, 1824-1887 = Martha Anna Downing, 1829-1894.

George Norbury Mackenzie, 2d, of Baltimore (See p. 405). = Lucy Tennille Emory, first wife. Mary Elizabeth Forwood, second wife; no issue.

Children:
- George Norbury Mackenzie, 3d
- Sara Roberta Maynadier
- Mary Gertrude Mackall Mackenzie
- Louis William Jenkins
- Anna Vernon Mackenzie
- Katherine T. Mackenzie, d. unm.
- Colin W. Mackenzie, d. unm.

Grandchildren:
- George Norbury Mackenzie, 4th.
- John Moores Maynadier Mackenzie.
- Colin Fitzgerald William Mackenzie.
- Louis Kenneth Jenkins.
- George Mackenzie Jenkins.

1.—COL. THOMAS BROOKE, of "Brookfield," Prince George Co., Md., b. 1660, d. 7 January, 1730, will proved 25 January. He was a member of the Maryland Provincial Council, 1691-1724, and president and deputy governor of the Province in 1720. He m. first, Anne, surname unknown, she joined him in deed, 1 February, 1689, and m. secondly, before 4 January, 1700, Barbara, posthumous daughter of Thomas Dent, of St. Mary's Co. She was b. in 1675-6, and survived him. He had a son Thomas by each wife. The son by the second wife, was of "The Vineyard," and named in his father's will, and d. unm. His other son,

    THOMAS BROOKE, JR., of "Brookefield," 1662-1745, m. Lucy, d. 1770 daughter of Walter Smith, will proved 4 June, 1711, (and Rachel Hall, his wife), son of Richard Smith, attorney general of Maryland, 1655-1660, will proved 19 March, 1714. Of his issue,

    I.—ELEANOR BROOKE, b. 7 March, 1716, m. Samuel Beall, colonel of 2d Frederick Co. regiment, member of the constitutional convention of Md., J. P., will proved 10 July, 1775, and had:

        BROOKE BEALL, of Georgetown, Md., alderman, 1759. He m. Margaret Johns, and had:

        CHRISTINA BEALL, 1772-1849, who m. Benjamin Mackall, Jr., of "Mattaponi," (originally a part of "Brookefield"), Calvert Co., 1763-1822, and had:

        LOUIS MACKALL, M. D., of Georgetown, D. C., b. 31 January, 1803, who m. Sarah Somervell, daughter of John Graham Mackall, 1737-1828, and had:

        LOUIS MACKALL, M. D., of Georgetown, who m. Margaret Whann McVean, and had:

        1.—SALLY SOMERVELL MACKALL, a member of the Md. Society of the Colonial Dames of America, author of "Early days of Washington City."

        2.—LOUIS MACKALL, 3d, M. D., of Washington, D. C., m. Lucy H., daughter of Charles M. Matthews, and had *Emily, Louis* 4th, and *Charles M.*

        3.—MARGARET MACKALL, m. Edward J. Weld, of Meyersdale, Pa., and had, *Louis M.*

        4.—JAMES MCVEAN MACKALL, M. D., of Washington.

        5.—UPTON BEALL MACKALL, of Montgomery Co., Md.,

    II.—MARY BROOKE, who m. Patrick Sim, M. D., and had:

        BARBARA SIM, who m. Clement Smith, M. D., and had:

PEDIGREE XCII.—*Continued.*

1.—WALTER SMITH, M. D., who *m.* Esther Belt, and had:
ELIZABETH SMITH, *m.* Richard Ringgold, and had:
ESTHER RINGGOLD, who *m.* John Spencer, and had:
JOHN THOMPSON SPENCER, of Philadelphia, who *m.* Rebecca Blackwell Willing, (see Pedigree CXXX., 3d edition), and had *Willing Harrison* and *Arthur Ringgold.*

2.—JOSEPH SIM SMITH, *m.* Elizabeth, daughter of Thomas Price, Colonel of 2d Md. Regiment, Md. Line, 1777, and had:
REBECCA PRICE SMITH, who *m.* Reuben Worthington, and had:
MARY SMITH WORTHINGTON, who *m.* Judge George Alexander Pearre, of Cumberland, Md., and had:

1.—ELIZABETH PRICE SMITH PEARRE, member of Society of Colonial Dames of America, who *m.* 1874, A. Hooton Blackiston, of "Brighthelmston," Kent Co., Md., and had: *A. Hooton* and *George Pearre.*

2.—MARY SMITH WORTHINGTON PEARRE, of Washington, D. C., a member of the Society of Colonial Dames.

3.—COL. GEORGE A. PEARRE, of Cumberland, Md., M. C.

III.—JANE BROOKE, who *m.* Alexander Contee, and had:
JANE CONTEE, who *m.* John Hanson, and had:
JANE CONTEE HANSON, who *m.* Philip Thomas, M. D., and had:
JOHN HANSON THOMAS, who *m.* Mary Isham Colston, and had:
JOHN HANSON THOMAS, M. D., who *m.* Annie Campbell Gordon, and had:

1.—BASIL GORDON THOMAS, *unm.*

2.—JOHN HANSON THOMAS, *m.* Mary Howard Beirne.

3.—RALEIGH COLSTON THOMAS, *m.* Mary McDonald.

4.—DOUGLAS H. THOMAS, of Baltimore, a member of the Society of Colonial Wars, the Order of Runnemede, etc., who *m.* Alice Lee Whitridge, and had, *Douglas H., John H.,* and *Alice L. W.*

5.—ANNIE G., wife of H. R. Duval.

6.—MARY RANDOLPH, wife of John Carroll, of "The Caves."

7.—JOHN MARSHALL THOMAS, *m.* Annie Gregg.

IV.—MAJOR THOMAS BROOKE, of "Chickamuxen," Charles Co., Md., who *m.* Sarah Mason, and had WALTER BROOKE, a captain in the Va. navy, August, 1776, appointed commodore and commander in chief of the Va. naval forces, 8 April, 1777, resigned 30 September, 1778, and d. at his seat, "Retirement," in Fairfax Co., Va., in January, 1798. (See Va. His. Mag., I., pp. 65, 331). He m. Ann Darrell, of Fairfax Co., and had, WALTER DARRELL BROOKE, (who m. 6 October, 1799, Lucy Triplett, of Fairfax Co., and had, BENJAMIN E., captain U. S. M. C., d. s. p., 1858), BENJAMIN MOODY BROOKE, MARY CORNELIA (who m. Jabez Berry Rooker, and had, HARRIET R., of Charles Town, W. Va.), and ANN, wife of John Graeff, of Lancaster, Pa.

2.—CLEMENT BROOKE, 1676-1737 (son of Major Thomas Brooke), m. Jane Sewall, d. 1761, and had:

SUSANNA BROOKE, d. 1767, m. Walter Smith, d. 1738, and had:

I.—RACHEL SMITH, 1720-1786, m. Richard Harrison, d. 1761, and had:

MARGARET HARRISON, 1753-1794, m. 15 April, 1777, David Weems, 1751-1820, and had:

GEORGE WEEMS, 1784-1853, m. Sarah Sutton, and had:

MASON LOCK WEEMS, 1814-1874, m. 11 June, 1844, Matilda Sparrow, 1823-1861, and had:

GEORGANNA WEEMS, b. 27 May, 1845, m. 11 June, 1863, Henry Williams, of Baltimore, b. 9 October 1840, and had:

1.—MASON LOCKE WEEMS; 2.—HENRY;

3.—ELIZABETH CHEW WILLIAMS, a member of the Maryland Society of Colonial Dames of America;

4.—GEORGE WEEMS; 5.—JOHN HAMILTON CHEW; 6.—MATILDA WEEMS.

II.—DOROTHY SMITH, m. Alexander Lawson, d. 1760, and had:

SUSAN LAWSON, 1743-1798, m. 30 July, 1760, Andrew Buchanan, 1734-1786, and had:

GEORGE BUCHANAN, 1763-1808, m. 10 January, 1789, Laetitia McKean, 1769-1845, and had:

MARY ANNE BUCHANAN, 1792-1866, m. 18 April, 1815, Edward Johnson Coale, 1776-1832, and had, GEORGE BUCHANAN, (see p. 406).

3.—CHARLES BROOKE, of "Brooke Place Manor," Calvert County, the eldest son by the second wife of Rev. Robert Brooke, b. St. Giles-in-the-Field, London, 3 April, 1636 (? d. s. p.). His will, dated 29 May, 1671, proved 15 December, 1671, names his brothers, John, Roger, and Henry, his sisters, Anne and Elizabeth, and his nephews, Robert Brook (son of Robert), Baker Brooke (son of Baker), and William Brooke, (son of Robert), his niece, Mary Brooke.

4.—ROBERT BROOKE, *b.* St. Bride's parish, London, 21 April, 1639, third child, by his second wife, of Rev. Robert Brooke. He settled in Essex County, Va., where he was a justice. He *m.* Katherine, daughter of Humphrey Booth, of Lancaster County, Va., and had, RICHARD, of Smithfield, Spotsylvania County, whose grandson, Humphrey Brooke, 1767-1843, *m.* 1800, Sarah Page (see p. 183), and

> HUMPHREY BROOKE, of King William County, Va., who *m.* Elizabeth, daughter of George Braxton, the elder, of King William Co., and had:
>
> COL. GEORGE BROOKE, of "Mantipike" (or Pampatike), King William County, a J. P., will dated in 1871, proved 13 May, 1782, "teste, Richard Tunstall, clerk." His daughter,
>
> CATHERINE BROOKE, named in her father's will, *m.* Richard Tunstall, 3d, clerk of King and Queen County, Va., 1782, and had issue. (See Pedigree CI.):

5.—ROGER BROOKE, of Calvert Co., *b.* at Bretnock College, 20 September, 1637, *d.* 8 April, 1700. He *m.* Dorothy, daughter of Capt. James Neale, of Wollaston Manor, Md., a member of the Maryland Council, and had:

1.—DOROTHY BROOKE, 1678-1730, who *m.* Michael Taney, Jr., *d.* 1702, son of Michael Taney, sheriff of Calvert Co., *d.* 1692, and had:

> MICHAEL TANEY, 3d, of Calvert Co., *d.* 1743. He *m.* first, (name unknown), and had *Michael Taney,* 4th, father of Chief Justice *Roger Brooke Taney, b.* 17 March, 1777. He *m.* secondly, Sarah (surname unknown), and had:
>
> SARAH TANEY, who *m.* 1761-2, Capt. Ignatius Fenwick, 3d, of "Wallington," and had:
>
> COL. JAMES FENWICK, of "Pomonky," Charles Co., 1763-1823, *m.* Henrietta Maria, *d.* 1792, daughter of John Lancaster, of Charles Co., and had:
>
> MARIA FENWICK, 1792-1836, who *m.* 4 April, 1809, Col. William Leigh Brent, 1784-1848, of "Brentland," Charles Co., and had:
>
> ROBERT JAMES BRENT, 1811-1872, Atty-Gen. of Maryland, 1852, *m.* Matilda, *d.* 4 October, 1894, daughter of Upton S. Lawrence, of Hagerstown, and had:

PEDIGREE XCII.—Continued.

I.—ROBERT FENWICK BRENT, of Baltimore.

II.—MARY HOKE BRENT, member of the Maryland Society of the Colonial Dames of America, who *m.* William Keyser, of Baltimore.

III.—LEILA LAWRENCE BRENT, a member of the Maryland Society of Colonial Dames of America, who *m.* Dunbar Hunt, of "Huntley Grange," Hempstead, L. I., N. Y., and had:

> ANITA DUNBAR HUNT, a member of the Maryland Society of the Colonial Dames of America.

IV.—IDA S. BRENT, member of the Maryland Society of Colonial Dames of America.

2.—ANN BROOKE, *m.* James Mackall, and had:

JOHN MACKALL, *m.* Martha Duke, and had:

BENJAMIN MACKALL *m.* Mary Taylor, and had:

SARAH TAYLOR MACKALL, *m.* Cosmo Mackenzie, and had:

GEORGE NORBURY MACKENZIE, I., *m.* Martha Ann Downing, and had:

GEORGE NORBURY MACKENZIE, II., of Baltimore, a member of the Order of Runnemede, Society of Colonial Wars, etc., who *m.* first, Lucy Tennie Emory, and *m.* secondly, Mary Elizabeth Forwood, no issue. By his first wife he had:

I.—GEORGE NORBURY MACKENZIE, III., of Baltimore, a member of the Society of Colonial Wars, who *m.* Sara Roberta Maynadier, and had:

> 1.—GEORGE NORBURY MACKENZIE, IV., of Baltimore.
>
> 2.—MOORES MAYNADIER MACKENZIE.

II.—MARY GERTRUDE MACKALL MACKENZIE, a member of the National Society of Colonial Dames of America, who *m.* Louis William Jenkins.

III.—ANNA VERNON; IV.—KATHERINE T., *d. unm.*; V.—COLIN W., *d. unm.*

3.—ROGER BROOKE, JR., *b.* 12 April, 1673, *m.* 23 February, 1703, Elizabeth Hutchins (or Hutchings), and had:

1.—BENNET BROOKE, of Essex Co., Va., who *m.* Mary Hill, and had:

SARAH BROWNE BROOKE, widow of ——— Tomlin, who *m.* Capt. William Fleete, of "Goshen," King and Queen Co., Va., 1757-1833, also of Royal Descent (see Pedigree CII.), sheriff, member of the Buchanan Coale (see p. 403), and had:

I.—COL. ALEXANDER FLEETE, *b.* at "Rural Felicity," King and Queen Co., 23 April, 1798, a justice and legislator. *Issue.*

II.—BENJAMIN FLEETE, M. D., of King and Queen Co., 1818-1865. *Issue.*

2.—JAMES BROOKE. 1705-1784, *m.* 1 January, 1725, Deborah Snowden, *d.* 1758, and had:

RICHARD BROOKE, 1736-1788, *m.* 1758, Jane Lynn, 1737-1774, and had:

ANNE BROOKE, 1773-1802, *m.* William Hammond Dorsey, and had:

ROBERT EDWARD DORSEY, 1796-1876, *m.* 19 July, 1825, Sarah Anne Duval, 1805-1882, and had:

CAROLINE DONALDSON DORSEY, who *m.* 9 October, 1855, George Buchanan Coale (see p. 403), and had:

MARY BUCHANAN COALE, a member of the National Society of the Colonial Dames of America, who *m.* Frances Tazewell Redwood, of Baltimore, and had, *George Buchanan.*

3.—PRISCILLA BROOKE, *b.* 16 November, 1717, *d.* August, 1785, *m.* about 1740, Charles Browne, of Queen Anne Co., Md., and had:

ROBERT BROWNE, of Queen Anne Co., *b.* about 1746, *d.* August 1794, *m.* about 1770, Sarah (surname unknown), and had:

CHARLES COCHRANE BROWNE, of Queen Anne Co., *b.* 1777, *d.* 21 March, 1826, *m.* 12 October, 1802, Martha T., daughter of Dr. Thomas Bennet Willson, and had:

CHARLES COCHRANE BROWNE, JR., of "Wheatlands," Queen Anne Co., Md., and of Howard Co., Md. He *m.* Mary Elizabeth, daughter of Dr. Thomas Willson, of "Trumpington," Kent Co., Md., and had:

BENNET BERNARD BROWNE, M. D., of Baltimore, *b.* at "Wheatlands," 16 June, 1842, a member of the Order of Runnemede, Society of Colonial Wars, etc. He *m.* in 1872, Jennie R. Nicholson, and had:

1.—JENNIE NICHOLSON BROWNE, B. A. (Bryn Mawr), M. D. (Johns Hopkins).

2.—BENNET BERNARD BROWNE, JR., M. D. (Johns Hopkins).

3.—MARY NICHOLSON BROWNE, B. A. (Bryn Mawr), M. D. (Johns Hopkins).

4.—DE COURCY BROWNE.

5.—ETHEL NICHOLSON BROWNE.

THE ROYAL DESCENT
OF
MR. NIXON GROSVENOR NORRIS.

THE EMPEROR CHARLEMAGNE had:
Louis I., the Pious, King of France, who had:
Charles II., the Bald, King of France, who had:
Louis II., King of France; who had:
    Charles III., King of France = Egiva, of England.

ALFRED THE GREAT, of England, had:
Edward, the Elder, King of England, who had:

Louis IV., King of England, who had:
Gerberga, *m.* Albert de Vermandois, and had:
Hubert III., Count of Vermandois, who had:
Otto, Count of Vermandois, who had:
Hubert IV., Count of Vermandois, who had:
    Adelheid de Vermandois = Hugh Magnus, Count of Vermandois.

HUGH CAPET, King of France, had:
Robert, the Pious, King of France, who had:
Henry I., King of France, who had:

Isabel, *m.* William, Earl of Surrey, and had:
Ada, *m.* Henry, Prince of Scotland, and had:
Margaret, *m.* Humphrey de Bohun, and had:
Henry, Earl of Hereford, who had:
Margery, *m.* Waleran de Newburg, and had:
Alice, *m.* William, Lord Mauduit, and had:
Isabel, *m.* William de Beauchamp, and had:
William, Earl of Warwick, who had:
Isabel, *m.* Patrick, Lord Cnaworth, and had:
Maud, *m.* Henry, Earl of Lancaster, and had:
Joan, *m.* John, Lord Mowbray, and had:
John, Lord Mowbray, who had:
Jane, *m.* Sir Thomas de Grey, and had:

WILLIAM THE CONQUEROR, had:
Henry I., King of England, who had:
Maud, *m.* Geoffrey, Count of Anjou, and had:
Henry II., King of England, who had:
John, King of England, who had:
Henry III., King of England, who had:
Edward I., King of England, who had:
Joan *m.* Gilbert de Clare, and had:
Margaret, *m.* Hugh d'Audley, and had:
Margaret, *m.* Ralph de Stafford, and had:
Hugh, Earl of Stafford, who had:
Margaret, *m.* Ralph de Neville, and had:

    Sir Thomas de Grey, of Heton = Alice de Neville.
    Elizabeth de Grey = Sir Philip, Lord d'Arcy.
    John, Lord d'Arcy = Margery de Grey, of Wilton.
    Philip, Lord d'Arcy = Eleanor Fitzhugh.
    Margaret d'Arcy = Sir John Coniers, of Hornby Castle.
    Eleanor Coniers = Sir Thomas de Markenfield, Yorks.
    Sir Nian de Markenfield = Dorothy Gascoigne, of Bentley, Yorks.
    Alice de Markenfield = Robert Mauleverer, of Wothersome, Yorks.
    Dorothy Mauleverer = John Kaye, of Woodersome, Yorks.
    Edward Kaye, of Woodersome = Anne Tirwhitte, of Ketelby, Yorks.
    Margaret Kaye, see Ped. 86 = William Lawrence, of Ramsey, Hunts.
William Lawrence, of St. Albans, Herts = Catherine Beamond.
    John Lawrence, of St. Albans = Margaret Robets.
    Thomas Lawrence, of St. Albans = Joan Anterbus, of St. Albans.
William Lawrence, of Long Is., N. Y. = (Name unknown.)
    William Lawrence, of Flushing, L. I. = Deborah Smith, of Smithtown, L. I.
    Samuel Lawrence, of Black Stump, L. I. = Mary Hicks, of Little Neck, L. I.
    Abigail Lawrence = James James, of Philadelphia, Pa.
    Sarah James = Gideon Scull, of Gt. Egg Harbor, N. J.
    Gideon Scull, of Salem, N. J. = Lydia Ann Rowan, of Salem.
    Alfred Penrose Scull, of Philadelphia = Mary James Reeves, of Phoenixville.
    Ellen Madeleine Scull = James Boyd Nixon, of Bridgeport, N. J.
    Sarah Boyd Nixon = Henry McCoy Norris, of Trenton, and Cincinnati.
    Nixon Grosvenor Norris, *b.* Cincinnati, 24 Oct., 1898.

THE ROYAL DESCENT
OF
MRS. THOMAS S. McCLELLAND,
OF CHICAGO, ILL.

CHARLEMAGNE, Emperor of the West = Lady Hildegarde, of Suabia.

Pepin, 777-810, King of Italy = (Bertha, dau. William, Duke of Thoulouse?)

Bernard, 799-818, King of Lombardy = Lady Cunegonde.

Pepin de Peronne, Palatine Count of Vermandois = (Name unknown.)

Pepin, Count de Senlis, Berengarius de Bayeaux, and de Valois = (Name unknown.)

Lady Papie de Senlis = Rollo, the Dane, first Duke of Normandy, 876.

William, Longue-epee, second Duke of Normandy = Lady Leutgarde de Vermandois.

Richard, Sans-peur, third Duke of Normandy = Lady Gunora (dau. Sweyn, King of Denmark?)

Godfroi, Count de Brione, and d'Eu = (Name unknown.)

Gislebert, Count de Brione, and d'Eu = (Name unknown.)

Baldwin Fitzgislebert, Sheriff of Devonshire, 1100 = Lady Albreda d'Auveranches.

Richard d'Auveranches, Earl of Devon, d. 1137 = Lady Adeliza Fitzosborne de Bréteuil.

Baldwin de Redvers, 2nd Earl of Devon, d. 1155 = Lady Lucia de Balm.

William de Redvers, 6th Earl of Devon, d. 1216 = Lady Mabel de Meulent.

Lady Mary (widow Robert Courtney, d. 1242) = Peter le Prouz, or de Preux, of Eastervale, Devon.

William le Prouz, of Eastervale, Devonshire, 1260 = (Name unknown.)

Walter le Prouz = Daughter of Lord Dinham.

William le Prouz = Daughter and heir of Giles de Gidley Castle, Devon.

Sir William le Prouz, Lord of Gidley Castle = Alice, dau. Sir Fulke Ferrers.

Sir William le Prouz, of Orton, Devon = Alice, dau. and heiress Sir Hugh de Widwor.

Lady Alice le Prouz, heiress = Sir Roger Moelis, of Newmarch, d. 1295.

Alice Moelis, heiress = John Wotton, Jr., of Widworthy, Devon.

Alice Wotton = Sir John Chichester, of Rawleigh, b. 1385, a knight at Agincourt.

Richard Chichester, 1424-1496, sheriff = Margaret, dau. Sir Nicholas Keynes.

Nicholas Chichester, of Rawleigh, b. 1447 = Christian, dau. Sir William Pawlet.

John Chichester, of Rawleigh, 1472-1538 = Joan, dau. Robert Brett, 2nd wife.

Amias Chichester, of Arlington, Devon, 1527-1577 = Jane, dau. Sir Roger Giffard.

Frances Chichester = John Wyatt, of the Inner Temple, London, 157?

Margaret Wyatt = Matthew Allyn, 1605-1671, of Windsor, Conn. (See Pedigree IV.)

Capt. Thomas Allyn, of Windsor, Conn. = Abigail Warham, m. 21 Oct., 1658.

Jane Allyn, b. 22 July, 1670 = Lieut. Henry Wolcott, of East Windsor, Conn., b. 20 May, 1670, m. 1 April, 1696.

Henry Wolcott, b. East Windsor, 28 Feb., 1697 = Abigail Cooley, m. 27 Dec., 1716.

Martha Wolcott, bapt. 9 Dec., 1739 = Joseph Stoughton, b. East Windsor, Conn., 31 July, 1738.

Betsey Stoughton = John Gale, of Weathersfield, Vt., b. Worcester, Mass., m. 1798.

John Gale, Jr., b. Weathersfield = Margaret, dau. Samuel Norcross, m. 6 Feb., 18-

Ella Gale, a member of the Order of the Crown in America, the National Society of the Colonial Dames of America, etc. = Thomas S. McClelland, of Chicago.

Marion McClelland.   Ella McClelland.   Inez McClelland.

PEDIGREE XCIII.

LOUIS IV., King of France, *m.* Lady Gerberga, daughter of Henry I., Duke of Saxony, Emperor of Germany, 919, and had:

CHARLES, Duke of Nether Lorraine and Brabant, the heir, but excluded from the throne. He had by his first wife, Bonné, Countess d'Arderne:

GERBERGA, Countess of Lorraine, who *m.* Lambert I., Count de Mous, and had:

LAMBERT II., Count of Louvaine, Lord of Gemblours, *m.* Ode, daughter of Gothelon I., Duke of Lorraine, Marquis d'Anvers, *d.* 1043, a grandson of King Louis IV. of France, and had:

HENRY II., Count of Louvaine, Lord of Gemblours and Nivelle, who *m.* Adele, daughter of Otto, Margrave of Thuringia, and had:

GODFREY I., *Le* Grand, first Duke of Brabant, Lorraine and Lother. He *m.* first, Ida, daughter of Albert III., Count de Namur, and had:

ADELICIA, the Fair Maid of Brabant, widow of Henry I. of England, who *m.* secondly, 1138-9, William d'Albini, "The Lion Slayer," lord of Buckingham, in Norfolk, created Earl of Arundel, 1139, *d.* 1176, and had:

WILLIAM, second Earl of Arundel, *d.* 1196, who had by his wife, Maud de St. Hilliario, widow of Roger de Clare, third Earl of Hertford:

WILLIAM, Earl of Arundel and Sussex, *d.* 1222, *m.* Mabel de Meschines, daughter of Hugh de Cyveliok, Palatine Earl of Chester, and had:

MABEL DE ALBINI, who *m.* Robert de Tateshall, Yorks, *d.* 1249 (see Banks's "Extinct Baronages," and Andrews's "Bygone Lincolnshire"), and had:

EMMA DE TATESHALL, (see Pedigree CCXXXVII., 4th Edition), *m.* Osbert de Cailly, son of Adam de Cailly, lord of the Court Manors, and had:

SIR HUGH DE CAILLY, feudal lord of Owby and Hecham, in Norfolk, 1286, who had by his wife, Agnes, daughter of Hamo de Hamsted:

SIR WILLIAM DE CAILLY, lord of Owby and Hecham, 1317, who had:

JOHN DE CAILLY, of Owby, sheriff of Norfolk and Suffolk, who had:

JOHN DE CAILLY, of Owby, sheriff of Norfolk and Suffolk, who had.

WILLIAM CAYLEY, lord of Normanton Manor, Yorks, by tenure, second son, who had:

JENNET CAYLEY, sole heir, who *m.* (see Dugdale's "Yorkshire Visitations"), John Lake, of Normanton Manor, and had:

JOHN LAKE, of Normanton Manor, who *m.* (see Plantagenet-Harrison's "Yorkshire"), Jane, daughter of Robert Drax, or Drakes, and had:

JOHN LAKE, of Normanton Manor, Yorkshire, whose son,

LAUNCELOT LAKE, of Normanton, *m.* ("Yorkshire Visitations," 1612), Margaret, daughter of Henry Twisleton, of Cirdling Park, and had:

JOHN LAKE, of Normanton Manor, who *m.* Catherine, daughter of John Peake, or Pake, of Wakefield, Yorks, and had:

LANCELOT LAKE of Normanton Manor, who *m.* Emma, daughter of Orbert Northend, of Halifax, Yorks, and had:

JOHN LAKE, of Erby, Lincolnshire, who *m,* ———Osgarby, and had:

RICHARD LAKE, of Erby, who had by his first wife:

CAPT. THOMAS LAKE, of Boston, Mass, 1655, a merchant and selectman, (see Boston Evening Transcript, 7 December, 1904). He was described as of Boston, by his brother, Sir Edward Lake, first Baronet, who named him in his will, 1665, as executor. He was a captain in King Philip's war, and was slain in August, 1676, aged 61. He *m.* Mary, daughter of Stephen Goodyear, sometime deputy governor of Connecticut colony, and had:

ANN LAKE, *b.* 12 October, 1663, *d.* 29 March, 1737, *m.* August, 1686, Rev. John Cotton, of Hampton, N. H., *b.* 8 May, 1658, *d.* 27 March, 1700, and had:

1.—MARY COTTON, *d.* at Concord, 29 May, 1731, aged 42, who *m.* 1712, Rev. John Whiting, of Concord, Mass., *b.* 20 January, 1681, *d.* 4 May, 1752. Of their descendants are: Mrs. William B. Jackson, Utica, N. Y.; Mrs. Wallace Clarke, Montreal; Mrs. Henry W. Wilkinson, Providence, R. I.; Mrs. Samuel F. Smith, Davenport, Iowa. (see pp. 224-225).

2.—DOROTHY COTTON, *b.* 16 July, 1693, *d.* 20 May, 1748, who *m.* 21 December, 1710, Rev. Nathaniel Gookin, *b.* 15 April, 1687, *d.* 25 August, 1734, and had:

HANNAH GOOKIN, 1724-1756, *m.* 1749, Patrick Tracy, 1711-1789, and had:

HANNAH TRACY, 1754-1797, *m.* 1772, Jonathan Jackson, 1743-1810, and had:

JUDGE CHARLES JACKSON, 1775-1855, *m.* 31 December, 1809, Fanny Cabot, and had:

FANNY CABOT JACKSON, 1812-1878, who *m.* 29 October, 1832, Charles Cushing Paine, 1808-1874, son of Charles, son of Judge Robert Treat Paine, a signer of the Declaration of Independence, also of Royal Descent, see Ped. C., and had:

1.—GEN. CHARLES JACKSON PAINE, *b.* 26 August, 1833.

2.—WILLIAM CUSHING PAINE, 1834-1889.

3.—ROBERT TREAT PAINE, of Boston, *b.* October, 1835.

THE ROYAL DESCENTS
OF
MR. AND MRS. ISAAC W. BIRDSEYE,
OF BRIDGEPORT, CONN.

THE EMPEROR CHARLEMAGNE, had:
Louis I., King of France, who had:
Gisela, *m.* Everard, Duke of Frioul, and had:
Hedwige, *m.* Ludolph, of Saxony, and had:
Otto the Great, Duke of Saxony, who had:
Henry I., Emperor of Germany, who had:
Hedwige, *m.* Hugh, Duke of France, and had:
Hugh Capet, King of France, who had:
Robert I., the Pious, King of France, who had:
Henry I., King of France, who had:
Hugh the Great, Count Vermandois, who had:
Isabel, *m.* William de Warren, and had:
Gundred, *m.* Roger de Newburg, and had:
Waleran, Earl of Norfolk, who had:
Alice, *m.* William de Mauduit, and had:
Isabel, *m.* William de Beauchamp, and had:
William, Earl of Warwick, who had:
Guy, Earl of Warwick, who had:
Maud, *m.* Sir Geoffrey, Lord Say, and had:
Idonae, *m.* Sir John, Lord Clinton, and had:
Margaret, *m.* Baldwin de Montfort, and had:
Sir William de Montfort, Knt., who had:
Sir Baldwin de Montfort, Knt., who had:
Robert Montfort, of Bescote, Stafford, who had:
Catherine, *m.* George Booth, and had:
William Booth, of Dunham Massie, who had:
Edward Booth, of Twemlowe, who had:
William Booth, Twemlowe, Cheshire, who had:
Edward Booth, of Great Budworth, who had:
Richard Booth, *d.* Stratford, Ct., 1687, who had:
Bethia, *m.* Joseph Curtiss, Stratford, who had:
Ephraim Curtiss, of Stratford, Ct., who had:
Stiles Curtiss, of Stratford, Ct., who had:
Ephraim Curtiss, of Stratford, Ct., who had:
Rebecca, *m.* David Birdseye, and had:
Joseph Birdseye, of Huntington, Ct., who had:
  Isaac W. Birdseye, of Bridgeport, Conn.

THE EMPEROR CHARLEMAGNE, had:
Louis I., King of France, who had:
Charles II., King of France, who had:
Judith, *m.* Baldwin, of Flanders, and had:
Baldwin II., King of Jerusalem, who had:
Arnulph the Great, Count of Flanders, who had:
Baldwin III., Count of Flanders, who had:
Arnulph II., Count of Flanders, who had:
Baldwin IV., Count of Flanders, who had
Baldwin V., Count of Flanders, who had:
Maud, *m.* William the Conqueror, and had:
Henry I., King of England, who had:
Maud, *m.* Geoffrey, Count of Anjou, and had:
Henry II., King of England, who had:
John, King of England, who had:
Henry III., King of England, who had:
Edward I., King of England, who had:
Edward II., King of England, who had:
Edward III., King of England, who had:
John, Duke of Lancaster, who had:
Joan, *m.* Ralph, Earl of Westmoreland, and had:
Richard, Earl of Salisbury, K. G., who had:
Alice, *m.* Henry, Lord Fitzhugh, and had:
Elizabeth, *m.* William Parr, K. G., and had:
Sir William, Lord Parr, of Horton, who had:
Elizabeth, *m.* Sir Nicholas Woodhull, and had:
Fulke Woodhull, of Thenford, who had:
Nicholas Woodhull, of Wodehull, who had:
Anthony Woodhull, of Wodehull, who had:
Agnes, *m.* Richard Chetwood, and had:
Sir Richard Chetwood, of Wodehull, who had:
Grace, *m.* Rev. Dr. Peter Bulkley, and had:
Dr. Peter Bulkley, Fairfield, Conn., who had:
Peter Bulkley, of Fairfield, Conn., who had:
Sarah, *m.* Joseph Perry, of Fairfield, and had:
Mary, *m.* Gershom Banks, of Fairfield, and had:
Gershom Banks, Jr., of Fairfield, who had:
Huldah, *m.* Joseph Sherwood, and had:
Aaron Banks Sherwood, of Greenfield, who had:
Elizabeth Josephine Sherwood. (See p. 390.)

  Elizabeth Josephine Birdseye, *b.* 28 June, 1892.

PEDIGREE XCIV.

EDWARD I., King of England, had by his first wife, Princess Eleanor, of Castile:

PRINCESS ELIZABETH PLANTAGENET, who *m.* 14 November, 1302, Humphrey de Bohun, fourth Earl of Hereford and Essex, Lord High Constable, killed at Boroughbridge, in 1321, and had:

LADY MARGARET DE BOHUN, *d.* 16 December, 1391, who *m.* in 1325, Sir Hugh de Courtnay, K.G., second Earl of Devon, *d.* 1377, and had:

LADY ELIZABETH DE COURTNAY, who is named in her mother's will, proved 28 January, 1391-2, as "my daughter Lutterell" (given in Nicolas's "Testamenta Vetusta," p. 127). She *m.* secondly, (being the widow of John de Vere), Sir Andrew Luttrell, of Chilton, and Dunster, Somersetshire, and had:

LADY ELIZABETH LUTTRELL, who *m.* John Stratton, of Weston, and had:

ELIZABETH STRATTON, who *m.* John Andrews, of Stoke, and had:

ELIZABETH ANDREWS, who *m.* Thomas Wyndsore, and had:

SIR ANDREWS, LORD WYNDSORE, of Stanwell and Bardsley Abbey, *d.* 1549, who *m.* Lady Elizabeth, daughter of William Blount (eldest son and heir of Sir Walter le Blount, K.G., first Lord Montjoy, *d.* 1474), *d. v. p.*, and his wife, Lady Margaret Echingham, also of Royal Descent (*see* Ped. XXXII.), and had:

LADY EDITH WYNDSORE, who *m.* George Ludlowe, of Hill Deverill, Wilts, high sheriff in 1567, *d.* 1580 (*see* Hoar's "His. of Wiltshire," vol. I., p. 11), and had:

THOMAS LUDLOW, of Dinton, *d.* 1607, who *m.* Jane, sister of Sir Gabriel, and daughter of Thomas Pyle, of Bopton and Fisherton de la Mare, Wilts, and had:

ROGER LUDLOW, (brother of Gabriel, p. 131, George, of York County, Va., and others), *bapt.* 7 March, 1590. He was a cousin of Lieut- Gen. Edmund Ludlow, the regicide. He was an Assistant in Massachusetts Colony, 1630-34, Deputy Governor, 1634, and Deputy Governor of Connecticut, 1635, etc., (*see* N. E. His. Gen. Reg., 1886, p. 300, Waters's "Gleanings," Stiles's "Windsor," etc.) He *m.* a sister of Governor Endicott, of Massachusetts, and had:

SARAH LUDLOW, who m. Rev. Nathaniel Brewster, grad. H. C., 1642, B. D. (Trinity College, Dublin), d. Brookhaven, L. I. 1690, aged 70, and had:

1.—MARY BREWSTER, who m. Jonathan Owen, of Southold, L. I., and had:

JOSEPH OWEN, of Setauket, L. I., m. 1729, Hannah Helmes, and had:

JOSEPH OWEN, JR., of Setauket, m. 5 April, 1761, Milicent Horton, and had:

HORTON OWEN, of Bedford, N. Y., m. 30 September, 1807, Anna St. John, and had:

ST. JOHN OWEN, of Bedford, m. 12 November, 1833, Mary Ann Smith and had:

I.—ANNA LUCRETIA OWEN, a member of the Society of the Colonial Dames of America, who m. at Bedford, N. Y., 25 December, 1867, Asahel Sutton, of Colorado Springs, Colo. No issue.

II.—MARY ELIZABETH OWEN, b. New York, 24 May, 1841, d. 18 July, 1891, m. October, 1866, George H. Sutton, of Springfield, Mass., and had:

1.—CARRIE H. SUTTON, b. Madison, Conn., 26 January, 1868, m. at Springfield, August, 1898, Charles L. Kirschner, of New Haven, Conn.

2.—EDWARD O. SUTTON, of Springfield, Mass., b. Bedford, N. Y., August, 1871, m. at Springfield, May, 1901, Ada Mayo.

3.—HERBERT L. SUTTON, of Bridgeport, Conn., b. New Haven, August, 1874, m. Chicago, December, 1902, Frances Howe.

4.—MARIAN SUTTON, b. 15 April, 1877.

2.—SARAH LUDLOW BREWSTER, m. Joseph Hawkins, and had:

JOSEPH HAWKINS, who m. Mercy Riggs, and had:

FREEGIFT HAWKINS, who m. Hannah Tomlinson, and had:

MERCY HAWKINS, who m. David Short, and had:

DAVID HAWKINS SHORT, who had by his second wife, Mary Eliza Purdy:

REV. WILLIAM SHORT, D. D., of St. Louis, Mo., a member of the Society of Colonial Wars, etc., who m. Mary W. Hondlow, and had *Arthur C., Harold Hall, Edith Marian, William Chadwell,* and *Edwin Purdy.*

THE ROYAL DESCENT
OF
MR. INGERSOLL DAY TOWNSEND,
OF NEW YORK CITY

ALFRED THE GREAT, King of England, had:
Edward the Elder, King of England, who had:
Edmund I., King of England, who had:
Edgar the Peaceful, King of England, who had:
Ethelred II., King of England, who had:
Edmund II., King of England, who had:
Prince Edward the Exile, of England, who had:
Margaret, *m.* Malcolm III., King of Scotland, and had:
Matilda, *m.* Henry I., King of England, and had:
Maud, *m.* Geoffrey, Count of Anjou, and had:
Henry II., King of England, who had:
John, King of England, who had:
Henry III., King of England, who had:
Edmund Plantagenet, Earl of Lancaster, who had:
Henry Plantagenet, Earl of Lancaster, who had:
Joan, *m.* John, 3d Baron de Mowbray, and had:
John, 4th Baron Mowbray, of Axholm, who had:
Margery, *m.* John, 2d Lord Welles, and had:
Eudo de Welles, heir, d. v. p., who had:
Lionel, 3d Lord Welles=Joan Watertown.

Sir James Lawrence, of Ashton Hall=Eleanor.	Cicely=Sir Robert Willoughby, Knt. (p. 287).
John Lawrence, of Ramsay, who had:	Sir Christopher Willoughby, K. B., who had:
William Lawrence, of St. Ives, who had:	Sir Thomas Willoughby, Chief Justice, who had:
William Lawrence, of St. Albans, who had:	Christopher Willoughby, Chiddingstone, who had
John Lawrence, of St. Albans, Herts, who had:	Christopher Willoughby, Chiddingstone, who had
Thomas Lawrence, of St. Albans, Herts, who had:	Col. William Willoughby, of London, who had:
Thomas Lawrence, Newton, L.I., N.Y., who had:	Sir Francis Willoughby, Dep.Gov.Mass., who had
Capt. John Lawrence, Yorkshire, L. I., who had:	Sarah, *m.* Samuel Canfield, and had:
Judge John Lawrence, of New York, who had:	Abigail, *m.* Jonathan Rockwell, and had:
Major Jonathan Lawrence, of New York, who had:	David Rockwell, of Norwalk, Conn., who had:
Judith, *m.* John Ireland, of New York, and had:	Abijah Rockwell, of Ridgebury, Conn., who had
Margaret, *m.* Thomas Lawrence, of N.Y., who had:	Obil Rockwell, of Ridgebury, Conn., who had:
Louisa Anna, *m.* Bradish Johnson, N. Y., and had:	Eli Rockwell, of Ridgebury, Conn., who had:
William Martin Johnson, of New York, who had:	Belinda, *m.* Edward M. Townsend, and had:

Louisa Anna Johnson=Robert Cooper Townsend, of New York.

Ingersoll Day Townsend, *b.* 28 May, 1895.

THE ROYAL DESCENT
OF
MR. JOHN B. CLEMENT.

EDWARD I, King of England, had by his first wife:
LADY ELIZABETH, who *m.* Humphrey, Earl of Hereford, and had:
SIR WILLIAM, first Earl of Northampton, K.G., who had:
ELIZABETH DE BOHUN, *m.* Richard, Earl of Arundel, K.G., and had:
ELIZABETH FITZALAN, *m.* Sir Robert Goushill (pp. 91, 155), and had:
JOAN GOUSHILL, *m.* Sir Thomas, Lord Stanley, K.G., and had:
MARGARET STANLEY, *m.* first, Sir William Troutbeck, of Prynes Castle, slain at Bloreheath. Inq. P. M., 1465. (See Ormerod's "Cheshire," II., Cheshire Visitations, 1580, Dugdale's "Baronage," II., 248, Collins's "Peerage," 1779, III., 40), and had:
JANE TROUTBECK, widow of Sir William Boteler, who *m.* Sir William Griffith, K.B., of Penrhyn Castle (see Dwnn's Visita. of Wales, II., 154-5; Ped. 16, Nov. 1588, and Hengwrt MSS. No. 96, 603), and had:
SIR WILLIAM GRIFFITH, of Penrhyn Castle, chamberlain of North Wales, 1520, who *m.*, contract dated 2 August, 1522, second wife, Jane, daughter of John Puleston, of Carnarvon Castle, and had:
SIBILL GRIFFITH, who *m.* Owen ap Hugh, of Bodeon, high sheriff of Anglesea, *d.* 1613, (see Dwnn. Ped., CXLIX), and had:
JANE OWEN, who *m.* Hugh Gwyn, of Penarth, high sheriff of Carnarvonshire, 1600, (Dwnn, II., 172), and had.
SIBILL GWYN, who *m.*, *ante* 20 September, 1528, John ap Howel Gôch, of Gadfa, buried at Llanwddyn, 24 July, 1636 (parish register), (Dwnn, II., 172), and had:
ELIZABETH POWELL, who *m.* 1624-25, Humphrey ap Hugh, *d.* 1664-5, of Llwyn-du (see p. 156, and MS. pedigree by her grandson, Rowland Ellis, 1697), and had:
OWEN HUMPHREY, of Llwyn-du, Llangelynin parish, Talybont, Merionethshire, 1625-1699, eldest son, J. P., who had by his wife, Jane:
REBECCA OWEN HUMPHREY, who *m.* 11 March, 1678-9, Robert Owen, of Fron Gôch, Merionethshire. They removed to Pennsylvania, in 1690, where he was J. P. for Merion township, and a member of the Governor's Council, and *d.* 8 December, 1697, aged 33. See "Owen of Merion," Pennsylvania Magazine, XIII., and Glenn's "Merion in the Welsh Tract," Pa., p. 112, etc. They had:
ROBERT OWEN, of Philadelphia, who *m.* Susannah, daughter of Judge William Hudson, Mayor of Philadelphia, 1726, and had:
MARY OWEN, *m.* Henry Burr, of Burlington Co., N. J., and had:
RACHEL BURR, *m.* Josiah Foster, of Burlington Co., N. J., and had:
MARY FOSTER, *m.* Samuel Clement, of Haddonfield, N. J., and had:
ROBERT WHARTON CLEMENT, of Haddonfield, *m.* Sarah A. Mathes, and had:
SAMUEL M. CLEMENT, of Philadelphia, *m.* Anne Browning, and had:
JOHN BROWNING CLEMENT, of Philadelphia, *m.* Dessa W. Crowell, and had: *Dessa Crowell, John B., Jr., Gregory,* and *DeWitt Crowell.*

PEDIGREE XCV

HUGH CAPET, King of France, had by his wife, Adela:
PRINCESS HAVIDE, *m.* Raingerius IV., Count of Hainault, and had:
BEATRIX DE HAINAULT, who *m.* Eblo I., Count of Rouci, and had:
ADELA, Countess de Rouci, *m.* Hildwin, Count of Montdider, and had:
MARGARET DE ROUCI, who *m.* Hugh, Count de Clermont, and had:
ADELIZA DE CLERMONT, who *m.* Gilbert, Earl of Clare, and had:
ADELIZA DE CLARE, who *m.* Alberic, second Baron de Vere, and had:
JULIANA DE VERE, who *m.* Hugh Bigod, first Earl of Norfolk, and had:
ROGER BIGOD, second Earl of Norfolk, who had:
HUGH BIGOD, third Earl of Norfolk, who had:
SIR RALPH BIGOD, who *m.* Berta de Furnival, and had:
ISABEL BIGOD, who *m.* John Fitzgeoffrey, C. J. of Ireland, and had:
JOHN FITZJOHN, Chief Justice of Ireland, 1258, who had:
MAUD FITZJOHN, who *m.* William, first Earl of Warwick, and had:
SIR GUY DE BEAUCHAMP, second Earl of Warwick, who had:
MAUD DE BEAUCHAMP, *m.* Geoffrey, Baron de Say, Admiral, and had:
IDONAE DE SAY, who *m.* John, third Baron de Clinton, and had:
WILLIAM DE CLINTON, fourth Baron, who had:
JOHN DE CLINTON, fifth Baron, who had:
JOHN DE CLINTON, sixth Baron, who had:
JOHN DE CLINTON, seventh Baron, who had:
THOMAS DE CLINTON, eighth Baron, who had:
EDWARD DE CLINTON, ninth Baron, first Earl of Lincoln, who had:
HENRY DE CLINTON, K.B., tenth Baron, Earl of Lincoln, who had:
THOMAS DE CLINTON, eleventh Baron, third Earl of Lincoln, who had:
SUSAN DE CLINTON, who *m.* Gen. John Humfrey, of Dorchester, 1595-1661, Deputy Governor of Massachusetts Colony, 1629, and had:
ANNE HUMPHREY, who *m.* first, William Palmes, of Salem, *d.* 1677, and had:
SUSAN PALMES, 1665-1747, who *m.* Samuel Avery, 1664-1723, and had:

MARY AVERY, 1695-1739, who *m.* William Walworth, 1691-174--, and had:

1.--LUCY WALWORTH, 1732-1795, who *m.* Veach Williams, 1727-1804, and had:

ELIZABETH WILLIAMS, 1759-1839, who *m.* Ozias McCall, 1758-1826, and had:

DOROTHY MCCALL, 1793-1869, who *m.* Jabez Metcalf, 1786-1852, and had:

WILLIAM WILLIAMS METCALF, of Washington, D. C.; *b.* Susquehanna County, Pa., 15 January, 1824, who *m.* Glorianna Helen Maynard, *b.* Worthington, Ohio, 13 April, 1836, and had:

WILLIAM PARK METCALF, of Washington, D. C., a member of the Order of Runnemede.

2.--MARY WALWORTH, who *m.* Solomon Morgan, and had:

ELISHA MORGAN, who *m.* Abigail Morgan, and had:

ELISHA MORGAN, who *m.* Caroline Morgan, and had:

MARY ABBY MORGAN, who *m.* Nathan Denison Smith, and had:

FREDERIC MORGAN SMITH, who *m.* Annie Holt, and had:

NATHAN HOLT SMITH, of New York City, who m. 28 October, 1902, Mary Wilson, daughter of William Seeley and Mary (Needles) Little, of Philadelphia, and had: KATHARINE FORSYTH, *b.* 23 July, 1903.

THE ROYAL DESCENT
OF
FREDERICK HASTINGS RINDGE,
OF LOS ANGELES, CALIFORNIA

ALFRED THE GREAT, King of England=Lady Elswitha.
Edward the Elder, King of England=Lady Edgiva.
Edmund the Elder, King of England=Lady Elgifa.
Edgar, King of England=Lady Elfrida.
Ethelred II., the Unready, King of England=Lady Elgifa.
Edmund II., Ironside, King of England=Lady Algitha.
Edward the Exile, Prince Royal of England=Lady Agatha, of Germany.
Malcolm III. Canmore, King of Scots=Princess Margaret, of England.
Henry I., King of England=Princess Matilda, of Scotland.
Geoffrey Plantagenet, Count of Anjou=Empress Maud, of Germany.
Henry II., King of England=Lady Eleanor of Aquitaine.
John, King of England=Lady Isabella, of Angouleme.
Henry III., King of England=Lady Eleanor of Provence.
Edward I., King of England=Lady Eleanor of Castile.
Humphrey, Earl of Hereford=Princess Elizabeth Plantagenet.
Robert, Baron Ferrers, of Chartley=Lady Agnes de Bohun.
John, Baron Ferrers, of Chartley=Lady Elizabeth de Stafford.
Robert, Baron Ferrers, of Chartley=Lady Margaret le Despencer.
Edmund, Baron Ferrers, of Chartley=Lady Eleanor de la Roche.
William, Baron Ferrers, of Chartley=Lady Elizabeth Belknap.
Sir Walter Devereux, Baron Ferrers, of Chartley=Lady AAnne de Ferrers, of Chartley.
Sir James Baskerville, K. B., Sheriff of Hereford=Katherine Devereux.
Sir Walter Baskerville, K. B., Sheriff of Hereford=Anne, vch. Morgan ap Jenkyn.
Sir James Baskerville, Kt., of Eardisley=Elizabeth Breynton.
Sir Robert Whitney, M. P.=Sybil Baskerville.
Robert Whitney, of Whitney=Elizabeth, vch. William ap Morgan.
Thomas Whitney, of Westminster=Mary Bray.
John Whitney, London to Watertown, Mass., 1635=Elinor ———
John Whitney, of Watertown, 1621-1692=Ruth Reynolds.
Daniel Harrington, of Lexington, Mass.=Sarah Whitney.
Robert Harrington, of Lexington=Anna Harrington.
Ensign Robert Harrington, of Lexington=Abigail Mason.
Captain Daniel Harrington, of Lexington=Anna Munroe.
Levi Harrington, of Lexington=Rebecca Mulliken.
Captain Nathaniel Harrington, of Lexington=Clarissa Mead.
Samuel Baker Rindge, of East Cambridge, Mass.=Clarissa Harrington.
Frederick Hastings Rindge, of Los Angeles, Cal.=Rhoda May Knight.
Samuel Knight Rindge, Frederick Hastings Rindge, Jr., Rhoda Agatha Rindge.

PEDIGREE XCVI

EDWARD III., King of England, had:
SIR LIONEL, Duke of Clarence, K. G., who had:
LADY PHILIPPA, m. Edmund, Earl of Marche, and had:
LADY ELIZABETH, m. Sir Henry Percy, "Hotspur," and had:
SIR HENRY, Earl of Northumberland, K. G., who had:
SIR HENRY, Earl of Northumberland, who had:
LADY MARGARET, m. William Gascoigne, of Gawthorpe, and had:
LADY ELIZABETH, m. Sir George de Talboys, of Kyme, and had:
LADY ANNE, m. Sir Edward Dymoke, of Scirvelsby, and had:
LADY FRANCES, m. Thomas Windebank, of Haines Hill, and had:
LADY MILDRED, m. Robert Reade, gent., of Linkenholt, and had:
COL. GEORGE READE, of Virginia, member of the Governor's Council, 1657, (see p. 248), who had:

1.—THOMAS READE, of Ware Parish, Va., third son, will executed 4 January, 1694. He m. Lucy, daughter of Dr. Edmund Gwynne, and his wife, Lucy Bernard, also of Royal Descent (see p. 38), and had:

MILDRED READE, m. Philip Rootes, of "Rosewell," and had:
ELIZABETH ROOTES, m. Rev. John Thompson, and had:

I.—JUDGE JOHN THOMPSON, m. Elizabeth Howison, and had:
ROBERT COLEMAN THOMPSON, m. Sarah Wigglesworth, and had:
MARY FRANCES THOMPSON, m. Gen. Samuel Woodson Price, and had:
ROBERT COLEMAN PRICE, of St. Louis, m. Sally Green Humphrey, and had: *Jassamine, Edward Humphrey,* and *Mary Frances.*

II.—MILDRED THOMPSON, m. Capt. George Gray, and had:
JOHN THOMPSON GRAY, of Louisville, Ky., who m. Mary, daughter of Peter Benson Ormsby, of Ireland, and had:
CATHERINE GREY, who m. George G. Fetter, of Louisville, Ky., and had:

PEDIGREE XCVI. *Continued.*

GEORGE GRIFFITH FETTER, of Louisville, Ky., who *m.* Amanda S. Burks, and had *George Griffith,* and *John Burks.*

2.—MILDRED READE, *m.* Col. Augustine Warner, Jr., of "Warner's Hall," Gloucester Co., Va., 1642-1681, a member of the Governor's Council, 1680, son of Capt. John Augustine Warner, 1610-1674, a member of the Governor's Council, and had:

ELIZABETH WARNER, 1672-1720, *m.* Col. John Lewis, of "Warner's Hall," and member of the Governor's Council, 1715, and had:

COL. CHARLES LEWIS, of "The Byrd," Gloucester Co., who *m.* 17 May, 1717, Mary Howell, and had *Ann, John,* and *Howell* (see pp. 255-257), and

1.—ROBERT LEWIS, *b.* 29 May, 1739, who *m.* 20 February, 1760, Jane, daughter of Tucker Woodston, and had:

ROBERT LEWIS, *d.* 29 January, 1802, who *m.* 11 May, 1786, Mary Gilchrist Bryce, *d.* 2 January, 1800, and had:

JANE LEWIS, 1791-1848, who *m.* 2 June, 1825, Dr. Thomas Curd, of "The Forest," Goochland Co., Va., and had:

DR. JOHN ROBERT CURD, of "The Forest," who *m.* Sarah Virginia, daughter of William Bacon Miller, of "The Retreat," Halifax Co., Va., and had:

KATHERINE CURD, (see p. 430), who *m.* Robert Oscar Holt, of Washington, D. C., and had *Robert Pope,* and *Crenshaw Bacon.*

2.—ELIZABETH LEWIS, who *m.* 3 April, 1744, William Kennon, of Chesterfield Co., Va., and had *Richard, m.* Celia Ragland; *Charles, m.* Mary Lewis: *Mary, m.* Thomas Harrison; *Elizabeth, m.* John Lewis; *William, m.* first, Elizabeth Bullock, *m.* secondly, Elizabeth Harrison, and

LT. JOHN KENNON, of Granville Co., N. C., and of Putnam Co., Ga., who *m.* 11 February, 1779, Elizabeth, *d.* 15 December, 1793, daughter of John and Elizabeth (Hughes) Woodson, of Cumberland Co., Va., and had *John William, Richard,* (*m.* Jane, daughter of his uncle, William Kennon, by his second wife, and had Emily, of Warrior, Ala., *b.* 1813); *Charles, Robert Lewis, Howell Lewis,* and

ELIZABETH LEWIS KENNON, *b.* 12 May, 1783, who *m.* in Putnam Co., Ga., 6 July, 1809, Dr. David Lindsay White, and had seven sons and two daughters, and of these,

JUDGE PLEASANTS WOODSON WHITE, *b.* 25 May, 1820, *d.* at Quincy, Fla., November, 1902; *m.* Quincy, Fla., 10 October, 1848, Emily, daughter of Dr. Edward Reynolds Gibson, of Talbot Co., Md., and had *Jean-*

ette Gibson, Rebecca Smallwood, Edward Lindsay; Hanson Gibson, d. 1890; and

WOODSON TILTON WHITE, of Waco, Texas, *b.* 23 July, 1849, who *m.* in McLennan Co., Texas, 30 October, 1878, Louisiana Woolfolk Johnston, and had:

1.—CLARA HERIOT WHITE, *b.* 27 December, 1880, a member of the Society of Colonial Dames, in Virginia and Texas.

2.—PLEASANTS WOODSON WHITE, *b.* 27 August, 1882.

3.—EMILY REBECCA WHITE, *b.* 11 August, 1884.

4.—HUGH JOHNSTON WHITE, *b.* 2 May, 1886.

5.—TILTON HANSON WHITE, *b.* 22 November, 1896.

THE ROYAL DESCENT
OF
MR. FRANKLIN R. CARPENTER, Ph.D., F.G.S.A.,
OF DENVER, COLO.

EDWARD I, King of England, had by his second wife:

THOMAS, Earl of Norfolk; Earl Marshal of England, who *m.* Lady Alice, daughter of Sir Roger Halys, of Harwich, and had:

LADY MARGARET PLANTAGENET, Duchess of Norfolk, *d.* 1399, who *m.* John, Lord Segrave, and had:

LADY ELIZABETH SEGRAVE, who *m.* John, Lord Mowbray, and had:

SIR THOMAS MOWBRAY, K.G., Lord Mowbray, who *m.* Lady Elizabeth, daughter of Thomas Fitz-Alan, Earl of Arundel and Surrey, and had:

LADY MARGARET MOWBRAY, who *m.* Sir Robert Howard, and had:

LADY CATHARINE HOWARD (sister of John, Duke of Norfolk), who *m.*, his second wife, Edward Nevill, Lord Bergavenny, and had:

LADY MARGARET NEVILL, who *m.* John Brooke, Lord Cobham, also of Royal Descent (see Ped. XX), *d.* 1511, and had:

THOMAS BROOKE, Lord Cobham, *d.* 1529, who *m.* first, Lady Dorothy, daughter of Sir Henry Heydon, and had:

LADY ELIZABETH BROOKE, who *m.* first, 1520, Sir Thomas Wyatt, of Allington Castle, Kent, Poet to King Henry VIII., 1503-1544, and had:

SIR THOMAS WYATT, executed on Tower Hill, 11 April, 1554. He *m.*, 1536, Lady Jane, daughter of Sir Thomas Hawte, of Bishop Bourne, Kent, and had: JANE, wife of Charles Scott, of Egerton, Kent, (brother to Sir Thomas Scott, of Scott's Hall, Kent, p. 54, sons of Sir Reginal Scott, of Scott's Hall), and grandmother of Dorothea Scott (see p. 89), and

GEORGE WYATT, of Allington Castle, and Boxley, Kent, *d.* 1625, who *m.* Jane, daughter of Thomas Finch, of Eastwell, and had:

1.—SIR FRANCIS WYATT, of Boxley, 1575-1644. He was twice Governor of the Virginia Colony, 1621-26, and 1639-41. He *m.* Lady Margaret, daughter of Sir Samuel Sandys, of Ombersley, son of the Bishop of York. Issue.

2.—Rev. HAWTE WYATT, minister at Jamestown, Va., 1626, *d.* at Boxley, 31 July, 1683. The Wyatt mural monument at Boxley, erected in 1701, states that the Rev. Hawte Wyatt had "issue now living in Virginia." He was twice married, first, before he was ordained, to Elizabeth, *d.* 31 October, 1626, secondly, to Anne, *d.* February, 1631. By his first wife he had: 1, *Edward,* of Middle Plantation, or York Co., Va., 1644-63, of Gloucester Co., Va., where he had a seat called "Boxley," 1663; *d.* about 1714, having, son and heir named Conquest, sheriff of Gloucester Co., 1705. 2, *Thomas, bapt.* 17 October, 1626, *d.* inf., and 3, *George* (see below). By his second wife he had *John,* and *Ann, b.* January, 1631. There were several other Wyatts in Colonial Virginia, who have not been identified with this family. (See William and Mary Quart., III.; N. E. Gen. Reg., XL., 43; Va. His. Soc. Coll.,VIII., 102; Va. His. Mag., III., 177.)

GEORGE WYATT, a son of Rev. Hawte Wyatt, patented land in York Co., 4 October, 1645, and was living in 1660; *m.* Susanna ———, who was living in 1660. His son and heir,

HENRY WYATT, *b.* 1647, sold his father's plantation in 1671, and removed into New Kent Co., where he *d.* about 1705. He was a vestryman of St. Peter's, 1686. His wife, Alice, was living in 1686. His son,

RICHARD WYATT, of New Kent Co., probably *d. v. p.*, having a son and heir, Henry, of New Kent and Spottsylvania Cos., a legatee of his grandfather, Henry Wyatt, deceased, in 1705 (who had *Richard,* of King and Queen Co., 1706, and *Henry,* of Prince George Co., 1723), and

SUSANNA WYATT, who *m.*, first, ——— Day, and *m.*, secondly, Thomas Davis, and had:

SUSANNA DAVIS, who *m.* William Bartlett, of Spottsylvania Co., and had: MAJOR HENRY WILLIAM, of Berkley Co., Va., and three daughters, Mrs. Montague, Mrs. Graves, and Mrs. Collins, and

CAPT. THOMAS BARTLETT, of the Virginia Line, Continental Army, who had:

REBECCA BARTLETT, who *m.* John Taylor, and had:

CAPT. REUBEN BARTLETT TAYLOR, who had:

SARAH RERECCA TAYLOR, who *m.* John Woodward Carpenter, and had: JOHN W., WILLIAM ANDREW, and

FRANKLIN REUBEN CARPENTER, Ph. D., F. G. S. A., of Denver Colo., who *m.* Annette Howe (see p. 277), and had issue (see p. 260).

THE ROYAL DESCENT

OF

MR. EDWIN FRASER GILLETTE,

OF CHICAGO, ILL.

THE EMPEROR CHARLEMAGNE=Lady Hildegarde of Suabia.

Louis I., King of France=Judith the Fair, of Bavaria.

Charles II., **ALFRED THE GREAT.** Gisela=Everard, Duke of Frioul.

Louis II., Edward the Elder. Hedwige=Ludolph, Duke of Saxony.

Charles III.,=Egiva of England. Otto, Duke of Saxony.=Hedwige, of Germany.
King of
France. Emperor Henry, of Germany=Matilda of
Ringleheim.

Louis IV., King of France=Princess Gerberga of Saxony.

Charles, Duke of Nether Lorraine=Bonne, Countess d' Arderne, dau. Ricuinus, Duke of the Moselle.

Gerberga, Countess of Lorraine=Lambert I., Count of Mous.

Lady Mahaut de Louvaine=Eustace I., Count of Boulogne.

Eustace II., Count of Boulogne, etc.=Ida de Bouillon, dau. Godfrey IV., Duke of Lorraine.

Geoffrey de Boulogne=dau. of Geoffrey de Mandeville.

William de Boulogne=unknown.

Pharamond de Boulogne de Tingry=Matilda, (family unknown).

Lady Sybilla de Boulogne de Tyngrie=Enguerrand de Fiennes, or Fynes.

William de Fienes, lord of Martock=unknown.

Daughter, name unknown=Bartholomew de Hampden, in Bucks.

Sir Reginald de Hampden, Bucks=Agnes, dau. Sir Ingram Burton.

Sir Alexander de Hampden, sheriff=Marian, dau. Sir Bryan Herdby.

Sir Reginald de Hampden=Nichola, dau. John de Grenville.

Sir John de Hampden, sheriff=Joan, dau. Sir Phillip d'Alesbury.

Sir Edmund de Hampden, sheriff=Joan, dau. Sir Robert Belknap.

Sir John de Hampden, sheriff=Elizabeth de Walesbury.

Lady Anne de Hampden=William de Puttenham, of Penn, etc.

Nicholas Putnam, of Penn, Bucks, 1492=unknown.

Henry Putnam, of Eddlesborough, 1526=unknown.

Richard Putnam, of Woughton, Bucks=Joan (family unknown).

John Putnam, of Rowsham, Bucks, 1573=unknown.

Nicholas Putnam, of Stewkeley, 1598=Margaret Goodspeed.

John Putnam, d. Salem, Mass., 1662. Ped. XCVII.=Priscilla (family unknown).

Lt. Thomas Putnam, 1615-1686=Mrs. Mary Varen, second wife.

Joseph Putnam, b. 1669, m. 1690=Elizabeth Porter.

Huldah Putnam, b. 1716, m. 1734=Capt. Francis Perley, of Boxford.

Capt. William Perley, 1736-1812=Sarah Clarke, 1737-1796.

Rev. Humphrey Clark Perley, 1761-1838=Elizabeth Mighill, 1776-1830.

Humphrey Clark Perley, 1802-1884=Hester Malvinia Wilcox, 1812-1881.

Josephine Mighill Perley, m. 1860=Edwin Lewis Gillette, 1811-1892.

Edwin Fraser Gillette, of Chi-=Mabel Hyde. Delphine May Gillette,=William S. Jenks,
cago, m. 27 Oct., 1902, Mem- m. 31 Oct., 1892. of Chicago,
ber of Society of Colonial
Wars.

PEDIGREE XCVII.

LOUIS IV., King of France, *d.* 954, had, by his wife, *m.* 939, **Lady Gerberga de Saxe,** *d.* 968, daughter of Henry I., the Fowler, Duke of Saxony, and Emperor of Germany, 919:

CHARLES, DUKE OF NETHER LORRAINE AND BRABANT, heir to the throne of France, but excluded; *d.* 992. He *m.* first, Bonné, Countess d'Arderne, daughter of Ricuinus, Duke of the Moselle, and had:

GERBERGA DE BRABANT, Countess of Lorraine, who *m.* Lambert I., Count de Mous, and Count de Louvaine, in right of his wife, *d.* 1015, son of Rainier, third Count of Hainault, and had:

MAHAUT DE LOUVAINE, who *m.* Eustace I., Sovereign Count of Boulogne, *d.* 1049, and had:

EUSTACE II., Sovereign Count of Boulogne, Arderne, etc. He accompanied William of Normandy in his conquest of England, and received grants of many English manors. (See Freeman's "Norman Conquest," IV., 129, 744, etc.). He is depicted in the Bayeux Tapestry. He *m.* first, about 1050-1, Princess Gode, or Godoia, a widow, sister to Edward the Confessor of England, ("Anglo-Saxon Chronicle"). She *d.* 1054. He *m.* secondly, in December, 1057 (see Chronicle of William of Malmesbury), Ida, daughter of Godfrey IV. de Bouillon, Duke of Lorraine, *d.* 1069. Count Eustace took a monk's vow, and his wife became a nun, and *d.* in a convent, 13 August, 1113. He *d.* in 109—, having by Lady Ida, six children of record (see Ellis's "Introduction to Domesday"). Of these were the celebrated Crusaders, Count Godfrey de Bouillon, *b.* 1060, and Count Baldwin de Boulogne, *b.* 106—, both Kings of Jerusalem, and Count Eustace III., *b.* 1059, who was in the first Crusade with his brothers (Chronicle of Matthew of Paris), who *m.* the daughter of the King of the Scots (see the Chronicle of Pierre de Langtoft), and was the father of the wife of Stephen de Blois, "King of the English." (See "L'Art de Verifier les Dates des Faits Historiques;" "Monumenta Germaniæ Historica;" "Manuel Histoire de Genealogie et Chronologie;" Anderson's "Royal Genealogies," etc., for above pedigree). Another son of Count Eustace II. and Lady Ida, was

GEOFFREY DE BOULOGNE, *b.* about 1062. It has not been found that he was a Crusader with his brothers, but about 1093-4, he was "in the odour of sanctity," being a monk, according to a letter by the then Archbishop of Canterbury, St. Anselm, to Count Eustace II. (Lady Ida also corresponded with the Archbishop), at the instance of his son, "Geoffrey a monk at Bec." The Archbishop rebuked the Count for bigamy. His wife, Geoffrey's mother, had become a nun, and the Count himself had taken a vow, but nevertheless had married again, for the third time. The Archbishop argued that it was unlawful for him to marry in his wife's lifetime, although his wife was a nun. (See Letters of Archbishop Anselm, in Freeman's "William Rufus"). This is good proof that Eustace II., of Bolougne, had a son, "Goisfridus," or Geoffrey, although he is not mentioned in "L'Art de Verifier," and like works.

Geoffrey *m.* before the Domesday Survey, 1080-86. (as appears in "Domesday Book," I., fo. 36, under Aultone, Surrey, "De his hidis tenet Wesam VI hidas de Goisfrido filio comitis Eustachii, hanc terram deditei Goisfridus de Mannevil cum filia sua," see Round's "Feudal England," p. 330, and Ellis's "Domesday"), a daughter, name unknown, of "le Sire de Magnevile," or Geoffrey de Mandeville, lord of Aultone, Surrey, one of the heroes of Hastings, who was rewarded with 118 lordships in England, with his chief seat at Walden, in Essex, and was the first Norman constable of the Tower of London. (See Planche's "The Conqueror and His Companions"). Geoffrey's son,

WILLIAM DE BOULOGNE. d. before 1130. (See "Monasticon Anglicanum," VI., fo. 1017). Wife's name unknown. His son and heir was:

"FARAMUS DE BOLONIA DE TINGRY," in Boulogne, "nobilis et venerandus" lord of Martock, Somersetshire, of Wendover, Bucks, of Cotes, Cambridgeshire, etc. There are numerous references to this man and his distinguished ancestry, in contemporary charters and records. In a charter to St. Mary's Church, Bec Abbey, in Vimeux, 1171, it is related, "Faramus filius Willelmi de Bolonia quam antecessores mei, scilict Gaufridus filius comitis Eustachi de Bolonia, avus mea, et Willemus de Bolonia filius ipsius, pater meus, decerunt ecclesia Sanctæ Marias Becci." In a charter of King Stephen to Geoffrey de Mandeville, first Earl of Essex, dated Christmas, 1141, he signed "Pharam," as a witness, with eight earls and a bishop, and according to J. H. Round's "Geoffrey de Mandeville," this was "Pharamus fitz William de Boulogne, *nepos* of the Queen," (but in this and following item, rather the second cousin than the nephew or grandson of Queen Matilda). In this year, 1141. Faramus, or Pharamond, was in joint charge of the king's "familia," during his captivity: "Rexit antem familiam regis Stephani Willelmus d'Ipre, homo Flandrensis, et Pharamus nepos reginæ Matildis, et iste Bononiensis." (Sym. Dun., II., 310). Pharamond retained favor under Henry II., and is frequently of record in the Pipe Roll, and received sixty pounds annually from the royal dues in Wendover and Eton. At this time he held six fees of the honor of Boulogne. He also inherited the marriage portion of his grandfather, in Surrey, and the manor of Carshalton, a confiscated estate of Earl Geoffrey, grandson of the first Geoffrey de Mandeville. (See Brayley's "Surrey," IV., 65, and Collinson's "Somersetshire," III., 4, as to his other lands). Pharamond had by his wife, Matilda, *m.* before 1157, a son, William, who *d. v. p.*, and a daughter and heiress,

SYBILLA DE BOULOGNE DE TYNGRIE. She *m.* before 1171, Enguerrand, or Ingelram de Fienles, or Fiennes, a lord in Boulogne, who lost his life at Açon, 1189. "Faramus de Bolonia alias de Tyngrie cum uxore Matilda et Sibilla filia mea, et heredibus meis Ingeranno de Fienles et uxore ejus Sibilla filia mea." Bec Charter, 1171. (Cart. St. Josse, fo. 5, 20). Their son and heir:

WILLIAM DE FIENES, feudal lord of Martock, Somerset, of which manor he had livery, in 1207-8, on quit claim of his mother, (Rot. Claus. 8 John). He *d.* in 1240-1, having issue by his wife, whose name has not been preserved, Ingelram, his heir (who had livery of his father's estates in 1241, and was a knight at Eversham, and *d.* 1267, ancestor of the Lords Dacre of the South, the Lords Saye and Sele, etc.), and

A DAUGHTER, name unknown, who *m.* (see Lipscombe's "Bucks," Edmondson's "Baronagium Genealogicum," 412), Bartholomew de Hampden, Bucks, who had by this match certain lands in Wendover manor, Bucks, on which Pharamond, his wife's ancestor, was assessed a fine in 4 Hen. II., and which had been her father's in 2 Hen. III. Their son,

SIR REGINALD DE HAMPDEN, *d.* 1220, had, by his wife, Agnes, daughter of Sir Ingram Burton:

SIR ALEXANDER DE HAMPDEN, high sheriff of Bucks and Bedford, 1249 and 1260, *d.* 1262. He *m.* Marian, daughter of Sir Bryan Herdby, and had:

SIR REGINALD DE HAMPDEN, *d.* 1332, who *m.* Nichola, daughter of John de Grenville, of Wotton, and had:

SIR JOHN DE HAMPDEN, a knight of the shire, 1360-62, high sheriff of Bucks and Bedford, 1360, *d.* 1375. He *m.* Joan, daughter of Sir Philip d'Alesbury, and had:

SIR EDMUND DE HAMPDEN, a knight of the shire, 1399, high sheriff of Bucks and Bedford, 1390, *d.* 1420. He *m.* Joan, daughter of Sir Robert Belknap, and had:

SIR JOHN DE HAMPDEN, a knight of the shire, 1420 and 1430, high sheriff of Bucks and Bedford, 1450, *d.* 1450. He *m.* Elizabeth, daughter of Sir John de Walesbury, in Cornwall, and had a daughter:

ANNE DE HAMPDEN, who *m.* William de Puttenham, of Sherfield, Penn, Walhleton, Long Marston, etc., in Co. Bucks, *d.* 1492. Their third son,

NICHOLAS PUTNAM, of Penn, Bucks, who was named in his father's will, and in the Bucks "Visitations," (see Eben Putnam's "Putnam Family," and references therein). He had, by his wife, whose name has not been preserved: *John,* named in the Herald's Visitation Pedigree, and

HENRY PUTNAM (of Eddlesborough, 1526), named in the will of his brother, in 1526. He probably died intestate, having issue, by his wife, name unknown:

RICHARD PUTNAM, who removed from Eddlesborough to Woughton, will dated in 1556. He *m.* Joan, surname unknown, and had:

JOHN PUTNAM, of Rowsham, in Wingrave, Bucks, where he was buried, 2 October, 1573. He had, by his wife, name unknown:

NICHOLAS PUTNAM, named in his father's will, who *d.* in Stewkeley, will proved 27 September, 1598. He *m.* at Wingrave, 30 January, 1577, Margaret, daughter of John and Elizabeth Goodspeed, and had:

JOHN PUTNAM, *bapt.* at Wingrave, Bucks, 17 January, 1579-80, who came from Ashton Abbotts, Bucks, (where his children were baptized, 1612-1627), to New England, and *d.* at Salem, Mass., 30 December, 1662. He *m.* in England, Priscilla, surname unknown, and had:

LIEUT. THOMAS PUTNAM, of Lynn and Salem, Mass., *bapt.* at Ashton Abbotts, 7 March, 1614-5, *d.* at Salem, 5 May, 1686. He *m.* first, at Lynn, 17 October, 1643, Ann, daughter of Edward Holyoke, and had:

DELIVERANCE PUTNAM, *b.* 5 September, 1656, who *m.* 23 April, 1685, Capt. Jonathan Wolcott, of Salem, who *d.* 16 December, 1699, and had:

WILLIAM WALCOTT, of Attleboro, 1723, *b.* Salem, 27 March, 1691; *m.* at Salem, 6 August, 1711, Mary Felt, *b.* at Casco Bay, 13 October, 1687, and had:

BENJAMIN WALCOTT, of Attleboro, Mass., *b.* 16 October, 1729. He *m.* at Attleboro, Mary Foster, *b.* 19 November, 1729, *d.* 9 March, 1820, and had:

BENJAMIN STUART WALCOTT, *b.* Cumberland, R. I., 27 July, 1755, *d.* 5 May, 1824; *m.* 18 January, 1778, Mary Dexter, and had:

BENJAMIN STUART WALCOTT, JR., b. Cumberland, 29 September, 1785, d. at New York Mills, N. Y., in January, 1862; m. 10 June, 1810, Irena, d. at Whitestown, N. Y., in April, 1831 daughter of Gen. George and Grace (Wetmore) Doolittle, and had:

WILLIAM DEXTER WALCOTT, of New York Mills, b. Whitestown, N. Y., 29 July, 1813; m. 12 September, 1837, Hannah Coe Hubbard, b. Middletown, Conn., 3 July, 1817, and had:

ELIZABETH HAMILTON WALCOTT, member of the National Society of Colonial Dames of America, the Order of the Crown in America, etc., b. Whitestown, 10 March, 1840, who m. 15 June, 1859, Asa G. Pettibone, of New York Mills, N. Y., member of the Order of Runnemede, Society of Colonial Wars, etc., also of Royal Descent. (See Pedigree LXXXVII, and p. 362). No issue.

LIEUT. THOMAS PUTNAM, of Lynn and Salem, 1615-1686, m. secondly 14 November, 1666 Mrs. Mary Varen, d. 16 March, 1695, and had by her:

JOSEPH PUTNAM, b. 14 September, 1669; m. 21 April, 1690, Elizabeth Porter, and had:

HULDAH PUTNAM, b. Danvers, Mass., 29 November, 1716; m. 8 November, 1734, Capt. Francis Perley, of Boxford, Mass., b. 28 January, 1706, d. 8 March, 1765, and had:

CAPT. WILLIAM PERLEY, of Boxford, b. 11 February, 1735-6 d. 29 March, 1812; m. at Topsfield, 26 March, 1761, Sarah Clarke, of Topsfield, Mass., b., 15 March, 1737, d. 23 November, 1796, and had:

REV. HUMPHREY CLARK PERLEY, b. 24 December, 1761, d. at Georgetown, Mass., 9 April, 1838; m. 30 November, 1797, Elizabeth Mighill, of Georgetown, b. 20 October, 1776, d. 1 July, 1830, and had:

HUMPHREY CLARK PERLEY, JR., b. Methuen, Mass., 2 November, 1802, d. Lawrence Station, N. J., 31 July, 1884; m. New York, 10 February, 1833, Hester Malvinia Wilcox, b. Batavia, N. Y., 6 April, 1812, d. Washington, D. C., 27 June, 1881, and had:

JOSEPHINE MIGHILL PERLEY, b. 27 June, 1834; m. Chicago, 23 October, 1860, Edwin Lewis Gillette, b. Penn Yan, N. Y., 7 February, 1811. d. Chicago, 8 October, 1892 (see p. 424), and had:

1.—EDWIN FRASER GILLETTE, of Chicago, member of Society of Colonial Wars, etc., b. 19 October, 1863; m. at San Francisco, 27 October, 1902. Mabel Hyde, b. Oakland, Cal., 13 December, 1871. No issue.

2.—DELPHINE MAY GILLETTE. m. 31 October, 1892, William S. Jenks.

THE ROYAL DESCENT
OF
MRS. ROBERT OSCAR HOLT,
OF WASHINGTON, D. C.

THE EMPEROR CHARLEMAGNE, had:
Louis I., King of France, who had:
Charles II., King of France, who had:
Judith, *m.* Baldwin I. of Flanders, and had:
Baldwin II., Count of Flanders, who had:
Arnoul the Great, Count of Flanders, who had:
Baldwin III., Count of Flanders, who had:
Arnoul II., Count of Flanders, who had:
Baldwin IV., Count of Flanders, who had:
Baldwin V., Count of Flanders, who had:
Maud, *m.* WILLIAM THE CONQUEROR, and had:
Henry I., King of England, who had:
Maud, *m.* Geoffrey, Count d'Anjou, and had:
Henry II., King of England, who had:
John, King of England, who had:
Henry III., King of England, who had:
Edward I., King of England, who had:
Thomas, Earl of Norfolk, who had:
Margaret, *m.* John de Segrave, and had:
Elizabeth, *m.* John de Mowbray, and had:
Margery, *m.* Sir John de Welles, and had:
Eudo de Welles, heir, d. v. p., who had:
Sir Lionel, Baron Welles of Gainsby, who had:
Margaret, *m.* Sir Thomas Dymoke, and had:
Sir Robert Dymoke, of Scrivelsby, who had:
Sir Edward Dymoke, of Scrivelsby, who had:
Frances, *m.* Sir Thomas Windebank, and had:
Mildred, *m.* Robert Reade, Gent., and had:
Col. George Reade, of Virginia, who had:
Mildred, *m.* Col. Augustine Warner, and had:
Elizabeth, *m.* Col. John Lewis, and had:
Col. Charles Lewis, of "The Byrd," who had:
Robert Lewis, (Ped. LIX.), who had:
Robert Lewis, Jr. (See p. 420), who had:
Jane, *m.* Dr. Thos. Curd, "The Forest," and had:
Dr. John Robert Curd, of "The Forest," Gouchland Co., Va.

THE EMPEROR CHARLEMAGNE, had:
Pepin, King of Italy, who had:
Bernard, King of Lombardy, who had:
Pepin, Count de Vermandois, who had:
Hubert I., Count de Varmandois, who had:
Hubert, II., Count de Vermandois, who had:
Robert, Count de Chalons, who had:
Adeliza, *m.* Geoffrey, Count d'Anjou, and had:
Ermengarde, *m.* Conan I., of Brittany, and had:
Juetta, *m.* Richard II., of Normandy, and had:
Richard III., 5th Duke of Normandy, who had:
Alice, *m.* Radulfe, Viscount de Bayeaux, and had:
Randle, 1st Palatine Earl of Chester, who had:
Randle, 4th Palatine Earl of Chester, who had:
Hugh, 5th Palatine, Earl of Chester, who had:
Daughter, *m.* Reginald Bacun, and had:
Richard Bacun, (see p. 780, 4th edition), who had:
Sir Robert Bacon, of Baconsthorp, who had:
Sir Thomas Bacon, Knt., who had:
Sir Henry Bacon, Knt., who had:
Sir Henry Bacon, Knt., who had:
Sir Roger Bacon, Knt., who had:
Beatrice, *m.* Sir William Thorpe, and had:
William Thorpe, who had:
John Thorpe, (Ped. LXXXIV.), who had:
Margery, *m.* John Bacon, Drinkstone, and had:
Edmund Bacon, of Drinkstone, Suffolk, who had:
John Bacon, of Drinkstone, who had:
Robert Bacon, of Drinkstone, who had:
James Bacon, Alderman of London, who had:
Sir James Bacon, of Friston Hall, who had:
Nathaniel Bacon, of Friston Hall, who had:
Thomas Bacon, of Friston Hall, who had:
Gen. Nath. Bacon, the Rebel, of Va., who had:
Nathaniel (John) Bacon, of Va., who had:
Nathaniel Bacon, of Virginia, who had:
Sara, *m.* Charles Edwin Crenshaw, and had:
Agnes, *m.* William Miller, and had:
William Bacon Miller, "The Retreat," who had:
Sarah Virginia Miller, of "The Retreat," Halifax Co., Va.

Katherine Curd, member of the National Society of Colonial Dames of America. —Robert Oscar Holt, of Washington, D. C.

Robert Pope Holt.   Crenshaw Bacon Holt.

PEDIGREE XCVIII

ROBERT BRUCE, King of Scotland, had by his first wife, Lady Isabel, daughter of Donald, Earl of Mar:

LADY MARGERY BRUCE, who *m.* 1315, his second wife, Walter, lord high steward of Scotland, and had:

ROBERT II., KING OF SCOTLAND, who had by his first wife, Lady Elizabeth, daughter of Sir Adam Mure, of Rowallen:

LADY CATHARINE STEWART, who *m.* Sir David Lindsay, of Glenesk, Earl of Crawford, and had:

ALEXANDER LINDSAY, Earl of Crawford, who *m.* Lady Marietta, daughter of Sir David Dunbar, of Cockburn, a son of George, Earl of Dunbar and Marche, and had:

LADY ELIZABETH LINDSAY, only daughter, who *m.* Sir Thomas Maule, of Panmure, *d.* 1498, and had:

ALEXANDER MAULE, Master of Panmure, *d. v. p.*, who *m.* Lady Elizabeth, daughter of Sir David Guthrie, of Guthrie, high treasurer of Scotland, 1468, and had:

SIR THOMAS MAULE, of Panmure, killed at Flodden, 9 September, 1513. He *m.* Lady Elizabeth, daughter and co-heiress of Sir David Rollock, of Ballachie, and had:

ROBERT MAULE, of Panmure, *d.* 2 May, 1560. He had by his second wife, Isabel, daughter of James Arbuthnott, of Kellie:

WILLIAM MAULE, of Glaster, whose daughter (see Wood's Douglas's "Peerage of Scotland"),

ELEANOR MAULE, will proved 11 March, 1665, *m.* Sir Alexander Morison, of Preston Grange, a mansion and estate in Preston Pans parish, Haddingtonshire, which his father had purchased, in 1609, from the first Earl of Lothian. Sir Alexander was a lord of Sessions, or senator of the College of Justice, 1626-1632, and called "the lord of Preston Grange." His will proved at Edinburgh, 16 March, 1632. He had by his first wife, "Helenor Maule":

CATHERINE MORISON,* living in 1695, who *m.* George Home, or Hume, Master of Wedderburn, killed with his father, Sir David Home,

---

*Her sister, Bertha Morison, *m.* Sir Robert Spottiswood, 1596-1646. (See p. 290.)

seventh laird (son of Sir George Home, sixth laird of Wedderburn, comptroller of Scotland, 1597, *d.* 1616), at Dunbar, in 1650, and had:

GEORGE HUME, only son, eighth laird of Wedderburn, *b.* 1641, *d.* 1715. He succeeded, in 1664, to Wedderburn. He *m.* Lady Isobel, daughter of Sir Francis Liddell, and had two sons, GEORGE (see below) and FRANCIS HUME, of Quixwood, advocate, who was engaged in the Rebellion of 1714-15, with his brother and nephews. He took part in the battle at Preston, was captured and transported to Virginia, 16 April, 1716, where he was a factor of his cousin, Gen. Alexander Spotswood. He *d.* about 1718. A letter from his nephew, George Hume, of Virginia, to his brother-in-law, "Mr. Ninian Home, of Billie, att his lodgings forgainst the Magdalen chaple in the Cougate Edinburgh," dated "Rappahanock river, June 20, 1723," says: "We had no sooner landed in this country but was taken immediately with all ye most common distempers yt atten it, but ye most violent of all was a severe flux of wch my unkle died, being the governours factor att a place called Germawna, in the upper part of ye colony, whom ye buried their, and put pails about his berrial place, wch is not very common in ye country. I went and saw it as soon as I was able to ride." Francis Hume had married Lady Elizabeth Hume, *d.* in 1715-16, sister of his brother George's wife, and had issue Alexander, *d. unm.*, and John Home, the titular, twelfth laird of Wedderburn, whose son, Alexander Home was the titular thirteenth laird. There are letters in the possession of the Hume Genealogical Association of America, written by Francis, at Liverpool, before sailing "to the West Indies," dated 7 February, 1716, referring to his "transportation," and mentioning the death of his wife, and the disposition of "my poor children," and 14 March, 1716, in reference to the care and disposal of his property in Scotland. See Dr. John R. Hume's "History of the Hume Family," 1903, for full text of scores of family letters between the Virginia immigrants and their kin of Wedderburn, and elsewhere in Scotland. The eldest son of the eight laird of Wedderburn,

GEORGE HUME, ninth laird of Wedderburn, *d.* 1720. He was actively engaged in the Stewart Rebellion, of 1714-5, and was captured with his son, George, at the battle of Preston, fighting for the Pretender, 13 November, 1715. He and his son George were tried for treason, of which he wrote to his sister, Jean, from his prison at "Marishallsea, 7 July, 1716:" "I hope you will not be surprysed. On Thursday last John Winram and my tryalls came on and wer brought in guilty. * * * Yow need not be concerned, for our lives I hope ar in no hazzard, we haveing assurance no more heir ar to die. Every body was surprysed when the jure brought me in guilty, for ther wer two evidences against me who declaired they only see me once upon the road with the rebells without either sword or pistoll and no more. Ther wer other two of the King's evidences for me who declaired they see me brought in prisoner to Kelso, and see me carried on all the way prisoner till we came to Prestone, wher we wer taken by the King's forces. * * * As for Geordie (his son George, aged 18, the Virginian), we expect a *noli prosequi* for him, so he will be set at liberty." The laird was not executed, but forfeited his estates. Subsequently his widow petitioned the King for her rights. His contract of marriage, dated at Edinburgh and Wedderburn, 3d and 4th October, 1695, "between George Hume, younger of Wedderburn, eldest lawful son to George Hume, elder of Wedderburn, with consent of his said father; Dame Isabell Liddell, alias Hume, his mother, and Dame Katharine Morrison, widow of the deceased George Hume of Wedderburn, his grandmother, on the one part; and Mistress Margaret Hume, eldest lawful daughter of Sir Patrick Hume of Lumsden, Advocate, with her father's consent, on the other part," etc. They had nine children, born between 9 January, 1697, and 26 September, 1714. Their second child and second son, whose issue was omitted fraudulently from the new entail of Wedderburn, executed after the forfeiture, was

GEORGE HUME, eleventh laird of Wedderburn, *b.* 30 May, 1698. He was brother to David, the heir and tenth laird, who *d. s. p.* 1762, and to Patrick, third son, *b.* 16 July, 1699, *d. unm.* 1766, the titular eleventh laird of Wedderburn, it not being known or recognized at Wedderburn, that his elder brother, George, had male issue then alive in Virginia. Upon the decease *s. p.* of said Patrick, *his* three younger brothers having also *d. s. p.*, their cousin, John Home, aforesaid, as heir of line and heir of entail, became the twelfth titular laird of Wedderburn, and his son Alexander succeeded as the titular thirteenth laird. The latter dying *s. p.*, his three distant cousins, Patrick Home, George Home and John Home, who each *d. s. p.*, were respectively the fourteenth, fifteenth and sixteenth titular lairds. When it became known in Scotland that there were male descendants in the line of George, who went to Virginia, 1721, claim to the title and honors of Wedderburn, in this branch, were discontinued, though a lineal descendant of a sister of the Virginia immigrant, George Hume, retains possession of the estate of Wedderburn.

George Hume (*b.* 1698), after his imprisonment at Marshalsea, being pardoned because of his youth, came to Virginia in 1721, according to his letter of 24 February, 175—. In 1723, he wrote that he then resided "in the upper part of Essex Co." Subsequently he resided near Fredericksburg, Va., and died about 1760, in Culpeper Co. He was a surveyor, and was constantly employed in Orange Co., and the counties formed from it. In 1735-6, he was one of the surveyors on the part of the Crown to determine the bounds of the Fairfax patent, and in 1751, he was appointed a Crown surveyor.

He *m.* 1727-28, in Spotsylvania Co., Elizabeth, daughter of George Procter, of St. George parish, Orange Co., and had six sons, *George, Francis, John, William, James,* and *Charles,* and no daughters. Of these,

1.—GEORGE HUME, of Fredericksburg, Va., eldest son, *b.* in Orange Co., Va., 1729, *d.* 1802. He was a surveyor, and assisted his father. He *m.* in 1754, Jane Stanton, and had eight children. Of these,

"GEORGE HUME, *alias* Home," eldest son, *b.* 21 May, 1759, *d.* 1816. He made an attempt to recover for himself the Wedderburn estates in 1810-16. He *m.* in Culpeper, Co., Susannah Crigler, and had eight children. Of these,

I.—THOMAS HUME, *alias* Home," of Fredericksburg and Madison Va., eldest son, *b.* Culpeper Co., 21 February, 1785. He succeeded as "the claimant." He *m.* 12 June, 1828, Mary Helen Thomas, of Madison, and had two sons, STANTON, *d. unm.* 12 November, 1860, and

ROBERT HUME, eldest surviving son, *b.* 9 November, 1834, *d.* in Washington, D. C., 19 October, 1878, *s. p. m..* He *m.* 17 January, 1872, Jennie, daughter of Gen. Hill, of Madison, Va., and had only one child, FAY, *b.* 15 August, 1876, who *m.* Charles McMullen, of Culpeper, Va.

II.—LARKIN HUME, second son, of Madison Co., Ky., 1788-1835. He *m.* Nancy Moberly, and their eldest son,

THOMAS HUME, of Madison Co., Ky., *m.* Susan Miller, and had:

I.—IRVINE MILLER HUME, of Madison Co., Ky., *b.* 1881, eldest surviving son, and the heir male to the honors of Wedderburn, and the eighteenth laird, and, *jure sanguinis,* male representative and chieftain of this ancient Eastern Border clan of Scotland, as well as the House of Marchmont.

II.—GEORGE HUME, of Madison Co., Ky., *b.* 1884.

2.—FRANCIS HUME, second son, *d.* in Culpeper Co., Va., 1813. He *m.* Elizabeth Duncan, who died in Boone Co., Mo., 1821, aged 94, and had:

ARMISTEAD HUME, *d.* Culpeper Co., 19 January, 1815. He *m.* 25 December, 1798, Priscilla, daughter of John Colvin, and had:

CHARLES HUME, *d.* Washington, D. C., 25 June, 1863, *m.* 21 June, 1836, Frances Virginia Rawlins, and had thirteen children, of whom, FRANK HUME, of "Warwick," Va., and Washington, D. C., *b.* Culpeper Co., 21 July 1843. He served in the 21st Mississippi Regulars,

PEDIGREE XCVIII.—Continued.

U. S. Army, and was wounded at Gettysburg, and in 1st Battalion of Maryland Cavalry, C. S. A.; member of the Virginia Legislature three terms. He m. 22 June, 1870, Emma Phillips, daughter of John E. Norris, of Washington city, and had eleven children, *Charles, Alice, Frank Norris, Emma Norris, Robert Scott, Virginia, Annie Graham, Mabel Harmon, Howard, John, Edmund,* and *Alan Phillips.*

3.—WILLIAM HUME, of Fredericksburg, Va., fourth son, b. 1734, d. before 1782. He m. twice, and had by his second wife, Miss Granville:

REV. GEORGE HUME, b. Fredericksburg, 1755-6, served seven years in the American army, and was discharged in 1781. He removed to Harrodsburg, Ky., in 178—, and d. at Rising Sun, Ind., in 1821. He m. three times, and had by his first wife and cousin, m. 1780-1, Elizabeth Procter, d. 1797:

LEWIS HUME, b. 8 August, 1793, at Independence, Ky., d. in Sullivan Co., Ind., 23 December, 1875, a soldier in the "1812 War." He m. secondly, 1818, Mary Roberts, of Verona, Ky., and had by her:

JOSEPH C. HUME. b. Dearborn Co., Ind., 25 August, 1833, m. 26 November, 1860, Rebecca, daughter of Lt. Israel Benefield, of Jasper Co., Ill., an officer in the Mexican War (and his wife, Sarah, daughter of Daniel, son of Gen. William Lee Davidson, of the American army, killed at Cowan's Ford, a signer of the Mecklenburg Declaration), son of Col. John Benefield, d. in 1840, in Sullivan Co., Ind., and had ten children. Of these,

PROF. JOHN ROBERT HUME, A. M., M. D., PH. D., of St. Louis, Mo., b. Sullivan Co., Ind., 10 August, 1862, author of the "History of the Hume Family," 1903. He m. 18 April, 1899, Eugenia Williamson, who d. in September, 1899.

THE ROYAL DESCENT
OF
MRS. WILLIAM McCREERY RAMSAY,
OF "WESTOVER," CHARLES CITY CO., VA.

EDWARD III., KING OF ENGLAND, K. G.=Lady Phillippa of Hainault.

Thomas, Duke of Gloucester, K. G.=Lady Alianore de Bohun, dau. Humphrey, Earl of Hereford, Essex and Northampton, K. G.

Lady Anne Plantagenet, (widow of two Earls of=Sir William de Bourchier, Count d' Eu. Stafford).

Sir John de Bourchier, K. G., Lord Berners=Lady Margery, dau. Sir Richard, Lord Berners.

Sir Humphrey de Bourchier, eldset son, k. v. p.=Lady Elizabeth, dau. Sir Frederick Tilney, and widow of Sir Thomas Howard.

Sir John Bourchier, 2d Lord Berners=Lady Katharine Howard, dau. Sir John, Duke of Norfolk, K. G.

Lady Joan Bourchier d. 1561=Edmund Knyvett, of Ashwelthorpe, d. 1539.

Anne Knyvett=Richard Sayre, b. at Colchester, Essex, 1508, d. in Holland, 1540.

John Sayre, b. 1528, d. in Holland=Elizabeth, 1532-1595, dau. John Hawkins.

John Bourchier Sayers, d. at Amsterdam, 1629=Marie Lamoral Van Egmonte.

Richard Sears, b. 1590, d. at Yarmouth, Mass.,=Dorothy Thacher, d. 1680. 26 Aug., 1676, came from Leyden to Plymouth m. in England before 1630. Colony in 1630. Deputy to the Gen'l Court, 1662

Capt. Paul Sears, of Marblehead, Mass.=Deborah Willard, m. at Yarmouth, 1658.

Paul Sears, b. Yarmouth, 15 June, 1669, d. 14=Mercy, dau. Thomas and Rebecca Bangs ((Sparrow) Freeman, of Harwich, Mass, son of John Freeman, and Mercy, dau. Gov. Thomas and Patience (Brewster) Prince.

Daniel Sears, b. Yarmouth, 16 July, 1710, d. 28=Mercy, dau. Micajah Snow, of Eastham, Mass. Nov., 1771; m. 13 Jan. 1736.

Capt. Paul Sears, b. Yarmouth, 2 June, 1750, d.=Eleanor Smith, b. 23 July, 1760, d. 3 Aug., 1824. Ashfield, Mass., 3 Sept., 1808; m. at Buckland, Mass., 25 Oct., 1782.

Nathan Sears, M. D., b. Ashfield, Mass., 14 Feb.,=Grace Newkirk, b. 28 Jan., 1788, d. 24 Nov., 1863, 1791, d. 1 Feb., 1848; m. at Portsmouth, Ohio, dau. Judge William Loper, of Pittsville, N. J. in 1818.

Clarissa Sears, b. Marietta, Ohio, 3 Apr., 1820;=Ephraim Brown Bishop, of Elk Creek, Preble m at Swartzburg, Wayne Co., Mich., 17 July, Co., Ohio, b. 10 Apr., 1809. 1836.

Mary Elizabeth Bishop, b. Mount Carmel, Ill., 21=Joseph Henry Risley, of Westover, Somerset Co., Oct., 1840; m. first, at Mount Carmel, Ill., in Md. (first husband). 1860, and m. secondly, at San Francisco, Jonathan Bentley Harris, of Steuben Co., N. Y.

Clarise Sears Risley, b. at Westover, Md., a mem-=William McCreery Ramsay, of Lawrence Co., Pa., ber of the National Society of Colonial Dames resides at "Westover," Va. of America, in the States of Mass. and Va., m. at "Westover," Va.

Jonathan Ramsay. Bishop Ramsay. Elizabeth Sears Ramsay.

PEDIGREE XCIX.

MALCOLM III., King of Scotland, had by his wife, Margaret, daughter of Edward the Exile, son of Edmund II., "Ironsides," King of England:

DAVID, King of Scotland, *m.* Mathilda of Northumberland, and had:

HENRY, Earl of Huntingdon, *d. v. p.* 1152. He *m.* 1139, Ada de Warren, daughter of William second Earl of Surrey, and had:

LADY MARGARET, widow of Conan, Count de Bretagne, who *m.* Humphrey, fourth Baron de Bohun, Lord of Hereford, constable of England, and had:

HENRY DE BOHUN, Earl of Hereford and Essex, constable of England, a Surety for the Magna Carta, *d.* 1220. He *m.* Maud, daughter of Geoffrey de Mandeville, Earl of Essex, justice of England, and had:

LADY MARGERY DE BOHUN, *m.* Waleran, Earl of Warwick, and had:

LADY ALICE DE NEWBURGH, who *m.* William, sixth Baron of Mauduit, fourth Baron of Hanslape, heritable chamberlain of England, and had:

LADY ISABEL DE MAUDUIT (sister to William, seventh Earl of Warwick), *m.* William, Baron de Beauchamp, of Elmley, *d.* 1268, and had:

WILLIAM DE BEAUCHAMP, created Earl of Warwick. He *m.* Maud, daughter of John Fitzjohn, chief justice of Ireland, 1258, and had:

GUY, Earl of Warwick, *d.* 1315, who had by his wife, Alice de Toni:

SIR THOMAS, Earl of Warwick, K. G., *d.* 1369, who had, by his wife, Lady Catherine de Mortimer, daughter of Roger, first Earl of March:

LADY MAUD BEAUCHAMP, *m.* Roger, Lord Clifford, of Appleby, and had:

LADY PHILIPPA CLIFFORD, *m.* William, Lord Ferrers, of Groby, and had:

LADY MARGARET FERRERS, *m.* Richard, Lord Grey, of Wilton, and had:

LADY ALICE GREY, *m.* Sir John Burley, of Bromcroft, Salop, and had:

JOAN BURLEY, who *m.* Sir Thomas Littleton, King's Justice, and had:

SIR WILLIAM LITTLETON, of Frankley, Staffordshire; *m.* first, Elena, daughter and co-heiress of Thomas Welshe, of Onlep, Leicester, and had:

JOAN LITTLETON, heiress, *m.* Sir John Aston, of Tixall, *d.* 1523, and had:

SIR EDWARD ASTON, of Tixall, *d.* 1568, who *m.* Jane Bowles, and had:

LEONARD ASTON, of Longton, Gent., *m.* the Widow Creswell, and had:

WALTER ASTON, of Longton, Gent., *m.* Joyce Nason, of Rougham, and had:

LT. COL. WALTER ASTON, Gent., (see Va. Mag., III., p. 401). He purchased land in Charles City Co., Va., in 1634, and had subsequent grants. He was a justice and lieutenant-colonel, and a member of the House of Burgesses in Virginia. He was buried in the Westover churchyard, with a stone bearing the inscription: "Here Lyeth interred the body of leftenant Colonell Walter Aston, who died the 6th April, 1656. He was Aged 49 years And Lived in this county 28 years. Also here lyeth the Body of Walter Aston, the son of Leftenant Collonel Walter Aston, who departed this life ye 29th of Ianuair, 1666, Aged 27 yeares and 7 monthes." (See the William and Mary Quarterly, January, 1896). He *m.* first, according to land-patents, a lady named Norbrow (or Warbrow), and had a second wife named Hannah, whose surname is unknown, and it seems she *m.* Col. Edward Hill, Sr., of "Shirley," Va. *d.* 1663 (see Va. His. Mag., III., 401). He owned land in Shirley Hundred, adjoining Mrs. Aston's. Of the children of Lieut-Col. Walter Aston, SUSANNAH *m.* Lieut.-Col. Edward Major, who *d.* ante 1655; WALTER, JR., ELIZABETH (see p. 440), and

MARY ASTON, *m.* first, about 1647, his second wife, Lieut-Col. Richard Cocke, county lieutenant and burgess of Henrico Co., Va., *d.* 1665-6, aged about 65; will dated 4 October, 1665, [she *m.* secondly, Col. Edward Hill, Jr., of "Shirley," 1637-1700, who had several wives (see Va. His. Mag. III., 401, IV., 421), and it is uncertain which was the mother of his children, namely Col. Edward 3d, *d. s. p.* 1748; Martha, *m.* Hugh Gifford, and Elizabeth, *b.* about 169—, *m.* first, in 1723, John Carter, of "Carotoman," 1690-1743 (p. 135), and *m.* secondly, Bowler Cocke, 1696-1771, (Va. His. Mag., IV., 323)] and had:

1.—JOHN COCKE, of Henrico Co., first child, will dated 19 February, 1691-2, proved 1 February, 1696. He *m.* Mary Davis, probably daughter of John Davis, of Henrico Co., and had:

WILLIAM COCKE, *alias* Cox, will dated 10 February, proved June, 1712. He *m.* about 1695, Sarah Perrin, will dated 26 March, 1726, proved in Goochland Co., 20 January, 1747, probably daughter of Richard Perrin, of Gloucester Co., opposite Yorktown, Va., and had:

MARTHA COX, who *m.* at Bremo, Henrico Co., 13 October, 1723, Col. Henry Wood, *b.* 1696, first clerk of Goochland Co., Va., 1728, (Va. His. Mag., IV., 94, V., 78-9), and had: SALLY, *m.* Col. William Pryor (*issue,* PATTY, *m.* Capt. William Merriwether), and

COL. VALENTINE WOOD, J. P. in Albemarle Co., 1744, second clerk of Goochland Co., 1757; *bapt.* 23 October, 1724. He *m.* 3 January, 1764, Lucy, *b.* 29 March, 1743, *d.* 14 July, 1826, daughter of Col. John Henry, of Hanover Co., Va. (see Ped. XXIX), and sister to Gov. Patrick Henry, (p. 116), and had:

I.—MARTHA WOOD, *m.* Major Stephen Southall, *a quibus* VALENTINE W. SOUTHALL, and DR. PHILIP SOUTHALL, of Amelia Co., Va.,

II.—MARY WOOD, *m.* Judge Peter Johnson, *a. quibus* GEN. JOSEPH E. JOHNSON, C. S. Army, and BEVERLY JOHNSON, of Abingdon, Va.

III.—LUCY WOOD, *m.* Edward Carter, of "Blenheim," Albemarle Co., Va. (p. 135).

IV.—JOHN HENRY WOOD, *m.* Elizabeth Spencer.

2.—WILLIAM COCKE, 1655-1693, who *m.* first, about 1678, Jane, daughter of Lieut.-Col. Daniel Clarke, of Charles City Co., and had WILLIAM, and *m.* secondly, about 1689, Sarah Flower, of James City Co., and had:

I.—MARY COCKE, 1690-1754, *m.* Obadiah Smith, *d.* 1746, their wills proved in Henrico Co., and had: OBADIAH, of "Westham," Chesterfield Co., Va., *d.* 1765. *Issue.*

II.—ELIZABETH COCKE, who *m.* Lawrence Woodward.

3.—"RICHARD COCKE, the younger," of "Old Man's Creek Farm," Charles City Co., Va., had by his wife, whose name has not been preserved:

ANNE COCKE, who *m.* about 27 January, 1704-6, Major Robert Bolling, of "Farmingdale," Charles City Co., (or Prince Edward Co.), *b.* 25 January, 1682, *d.* 1749 (See Va. His. Mag., vol. IV., pp. 96, 329), son of Robert Bolling, of "Kippax," 1646-1709, by his second wife, *m.* about 1680, Anne Stith, of Brunswick Co., Va., and had, besides other issue (see Slaughter's "Bristol Parish"):

1.—ROBERT BOLLING, of "Bollingbrook," near Petersburg, Va., 1730-1775, who had, by his second wife, *m.* 1758, Mary Marshall, daughter of Col. Thomas Tabb, of "Clay Hill," Amelia Co., Va.:

ROBERT BOLLING, of "Centre Hill," who had, by his second wife, *m.* 1790, Catherine, daughter of Buckner Stith, of "Rockspring," Brunswick Co.:

COL. GEORGE W. BOLLING, who *m.* Martha, daughter of W. N. Nicholls, of Georgetown, D. C., and had:

1.—ROBERT BOLLING, *m.* Nancy Webster.

II.—WILLIAM N. BOLLING, *m.* Susan Meade.

III.—MARY TABB BOLLING, who *m.* 28 March, 1867, William Henry Fitzhugh Lee, Major-Gen. C. S. Army, a son of Gen. Robert E. Lee, Commander-in-Chief of the Armies of the Confederate States, also of Royal Descent (see Ped. LXV., 4th edition). *Issue.*

2.—JANE BOLLING, *b.* 1 April, 1722, *bapt.* Bristol parish, Va., 22 September, 1724, who *m.* 1745, Hugh Miller, of "Greenscroft," Bristol parish, *d.* London, 13 February, 1762; will at the Somerset House (see Va. Mag., vol. X., p. 323), and had:

1.—ANNE, first wife of Sir Peyton Skipwith, Bart. (see p. 233).

2.—JEAN, second wife of Sir Peyton Skipwith, Bart.

3.—LILIAS MILLER, (widow of John Ravenscroft, of "Maycox," Va.), who *m.* Patrick Stewart, of Cairnsmore, Kirkcudbright, Scotland, 1734-1814, and had:

JAMES STEWART, of Cairnsmore, *b.* 2 April, 1791, *d.* 19 September, 1887, who *m.* in London, 18 December, 1829, Elizabeth, daughter of Dr. Gilbert Macleod, and had:

ELIZABETH MACLEOD STEWART, who *m.* Patrick George Scot, of Edinburgh, a General in the British Army, and had:

1.—DR. WILLIAM SCOT, of Edinburgh, Scotland, and of the Orange River Colony, South Africa, a member of the Order of Runnemede; Diploma from the Royal College of Physicians and Surgeons, of Edinburgh and Glasgow.

2.—ELIZABETH MACLEOD; 3.—MARGARET, *d. unm.;* 4.—MARY;

5.—JAMES STEWART SCOT, of Edinburgh.

ELIZABETH ASTON, a daughter of Lieut.-Col. Aston, aforesaid, and a widow of Thomas Binns, *m.* Francis Mason, 1647-1697, a justice, 1680, son of James Mason, of Matthew's Mount, Va., and had:

FRANCES MASON, who *m.* Thomas Holt, of Hog Island, Surry Co., 1673-1730, a grandson of Randall Holt, who came to Virginia, 1621, and had:

ELIZABETH HOLT, who *m.* Nicholas Cocke, of Surry Co., Va., *b.* in England, *d.* in 1748, son of William Cocke, of Va., 1690, (see Va. His. Mag., V., 184), and had: *Frances Simmons,* and other daughters, and

1.—WILLIAM COCKE, will proved in 1763, *m.* Sarah, daughter of William and Mary Short, and sister to William Short, U. S. Minister to Spain, and had: *William, Susanna Buchanan, Martha Holt,* and

ELIZABETH COCKE, *m.* ——— Stewart, and had:

SARAH STEWART, *m.* John Minge, of "Sandy Point," on the James River, and had:

PEDIGREE XCIX.—Continued.

SARAH MELVILLE MINGE, *d*. 1854, *m*. Col. Robert Bolling, of "Centre Hill," Petersburg, Va.

2.—JOHN COCKE, of Cabin Point, Surry Co., Va., *m*. Elizabeth Peter, and had: *Thomas, Elizabeth, m*. William Cole; *Margaret, m*. Edward Wyatt, *Thomas Everard*, and

JAMES COCKE, of "Bon Accord," captain in the Va. Navy, 1771, *m*. ———— Poythress, of Prince George Co., and had: *John, m*. Elizabeth Peter; *Thomas, m*. Sarah Colley; *Benjamin, m*. Mary Eppes; *Elizabeth, m*. Jacob Hoffman, of Baltimore, and

DR. JAMES COCKE, of Baltimore, Md., *m*. Elizabeth Smith, and had:

I.—JAMES COCKE, *m*. Martha Cocke, and had: *Thomas, Henry T., James*, and *Nathaniel*.

II.—BENJAMIN COCKE, *m*. Mary Eppes, and had: *Elizabeth, Dr. "Richard Eppes," m* Josephine Horner, and Elizabeth Horner.

3.—ANNE COCKE, *m*. ———— Waddrup, and had: *Elizabeth*, and MARGARET WADDRUP, *m*. William Harwood, of Charles City Co., and had:

I.—AGNES, *m*. 1788, Fielding Lewis, of Gloucester Co., Va.

II.—MARGARET, *m*. Thomas Marshall.

III.—ELEANOR, *m*. ———— Douthat.

4.—ELIZABETH COCKE, who *m*. John Peter, of Cabin Point, *d*. 1765, a son of Thomas Peter, of Crossbasket, Lanarkshire, Scotland, and had:

ROBERT PETER, 1760-1791, who *m*. Claramond Holt, and had:

CLARAMOND PETER, who *m*. Walter Colquhoun, of Petersburg, Va., *b*. in Luss parish, Dumbartonshire, Scotland, 1769, *d*. 1813, and had:

CLARAMOND COLQUHOUN, who *m*. Gustavus B. C. Cleemann, of Petersburg, *b*. in Livonia, Russia, 1789, *d*. in Philadelphia, Pa., 1855. *Issue*:—

1.—FREDERICK VASQUEZ CLEEMANN, of Philadelphia, 1825-1863.

2.—WALTER COLQUHOUN CLEEMANN, 1827-1864.

3.—BERNARD CHRISTIAN CLEEMANN, 1829-1892.

4.—AMELIA LOUISA CLEEMANN, 1831-1833.

5.—CLARAMOND COLQUHOUN CLEEMANN, *b*. 1834, *m*. Joseph R. Smith, M. D., General in the Medical Dept., U. S. Army (retired), and had: *Claramond, Joseph Rowe*, and *Juliet de Hart;* all died young.

6.—MARGARETHA ELEONORA HILDA CLEEMANN, *b*. 1837.

7.—RICHARD ALSOP CLEEMANN, M. D., of Philadelphia, *b*. 1840.

8.—LUDOVIC COLQUHOUN CLEEMANN, of Philadelphia, *b*. 1840.

9.—THOMAS MUTTER CLEEMANN, 1843-1893.

THE ROYAL DESCENT OF MRS. EDW

WITEKIND, last King of Saxons.
Wigbert, Duke of Saxony. CHARLEMAGNE, Emperor of the West = Hildegarde of Suabia.
Buno, Duke of Saxony. = Louis I., Emperor of France, Germany, etc. = Judith of Bavaria.
EGBERT, first King of England. Everard, Duke of Frioul. = Gisela. Louis I., King of Bavaria.
Ethelwolf, King of England. Ludolph, Duke of Saxony = Hedwige. Carloman, King of Bavaria.
Alfred the Great, of England. Charles II., King of France. Arnoul, King of Germany.
Edward, King of England. = Emperor of Germany.
  Louis II., King of France. Otto, Duke of Saxony = Hedwige, of Germany.
  Princess Egiva = Charles III., King of France. Henry, Emperor of Germany = Matilda.
  King Louis IV. = Gerberga. Hubert II., de Vermandois. Hedwige = Hugh, Duke of France.
Edmund, King of England. Gerberga = Albert de Vermandois. Geoffrey d'Anjou = Adela. Hugh Capet, King of France.
Edgar, King of England. Hubert de Vermandois. Conan de Bretagne = Ermengard. Robert, King of France.
Ethelred, King of England. Otto de Vermandois. Richard, Duke of Normandy = Judith.
Edmund, King of England. Hubert de Vermandois. Robert, Duke of Normandy. Baldwin of Flanders = Ade
Edward, Prince of England. Adelheid = Hugh Magnus. William the Conqueror = Maud. Duncan I. King of Scotland.
  William, Earl of Surrey = Gundred. St. Margaret = Malcolm III., King of Henry I., K
                                                          Scotland.
Robert, Earl of Leicester = Isabella. = William, Earl of Surrey. St. David, King of Scotland. Maud, Emp.
Robert, Earl of Leicester. Ada = Henry, Earl of Huntingdon. LLEWELLYN, Prince of Wales = Henry II.,
Robert, Earl of Leicester. Earl David. William, King = John, Lord Braose = Margaret. John, King
                                       of Scotland.
Margaret = Saher de Quincey. Alan McDonal = Margaret. William, Lord Braose. Henry III.,
Roger, Earl of Winchester = Helen McDonal. Robert, Lord Ros = Isabel. William. Edward I., King of England =
William, Earl of Derby = Margaret. William, Lord Ros. John, Lord Mowbray = Alice. Joan = Gilbert, Earl
William, Lord Ferrers, of Groby. Robert, Lord Ros. Margaret de Clare = Hugh, Earl of Gloucester.
Anne = John, Lord Grey, of Ruthyn. William, Lord Ros. Margaret d'Audley = Ralph, Earl of Stafford.
Henry, Lord Grey, of Wilton. Alice = Nicholas, Lord Meinill. Hugh, Earl of Stafford. Cat.
Reginald, Lord Grey, of Wilton. Elizabeth = John, Lord d'Arcy. Margaret = Ralph, Earl of Westmor
Henry, Lord Grey, of Wilton = Elizabeth Talbot. Alice de Neville = Sir Thomas de Grey, of H
                            Philip, Lord d'Arcy = Elizabeth de Grey.
            Margaret de Grey = John, Lord d'Arcy.

John, Lord d'Arcy = J
Richard d'Arcy = E
Sir William, Lord d'Arcy = F
Sir Thomas, Lord d'Arcy, K. G. = D
Sir Arthur d'Arcy, Knt. = M
Sir Edward d'Arcy, of Dartford = u
Isabella d'Arcy = J
Mary Launce, d. Watertown, Ct., 1710 = R
Mary Sherman, b. 1657, m. 1679 = E
John Barron, of Dracut, Mass., m. 1721 = H
Lydia Barron, 1734-1824, m. 1753 = L
Silas Harris, of Green, Me., 1766-1844, m. 1790 = M
Anna Harris, d. Brooklyn Center, Minn., 1876 = N
George W. Allen, b. Exeter, Me., 1828, d. Cairo, Ill., 1866, m. 1857. = Mary Jane Smith,
Esther Allen, m. 1877, William V. Jobes, of Spokane, Wash. Lena Allen, m. 1888, Edward G. Stolber, o

ARD G. STOIBER, OF DENVER, COLO.

Pepin, King of Italy.
Bernard, King of Italy.
Pepin de Vermandois.
Hubert de Vermandois.   KING ACHAIUS.   GARSIAS XIMENES, first King of Superarabia.
BAZIL, Emperor of Constantinople.   King Alpin.   Garsias Ennicus, King of Superarabia.
Leo, Emperor of Constantinople.   King Kenneth II.   Fortunius I., King of Superarabia.
   King Constantine II.   Sancho Garsias, King of Superarabia.
Constantine, Emperor of Constantinople.   King Donal IV.   Ximen Inigo, King of Superarabia.
Romanus, Emperor of Constantinople.   King Malcolm I.   Inigo Arista, King of Superarabia.
Anne=Vladimer, Czar of Russia.   King Kenneth I.   Ximinius Eneco, Count of Aragon.
     Garsias Inigo, King of Superarabia.
Jarosalaus, Grand Duke of Russia=King Malcolm II.   Sancho I., Garsias, King of Navarre.
la, Henry I., King of France=Anne, Beatrix.   Garsias I., Sancho, King of Navarre and Aragon.
     Sancho II., Garsias, King of Navarre and Aragon.
     Garsias II., Sancho, King of Navarre and Aragon.
Philip I., King of France.   Sancho III., King of Navarre, Aragon, and Castile.
     Ferdinand I., King of Castile.
     Alphonso VI., King of Leon.   DIAMAID, King of all Ireland.
ing of England.   Louis VI., King of France.   Urraco, Queen of Castile.   Doncha, King of Leinster.
ress of Germany.   Louis VII., King of France.   Alphonso VII., King of Castile.   Dermot, King of Leinster.
King of England.   Philip II., King of France.   Ferdinand II., King of Castile and Leon.   Eva=Richard, Earl of Pembroke.
of England.   Louis VIII., King of France.   Alphonso X., King of Leon.   Isabel=William, Earl of Pembroke.
King of England. Robert. St.Louis, King of France.   St. Ferdinand, King of Castile and Leon.   Isabel=Gilbert, Earl of Gloucester.
leanor. Edmund=Blanche d'Artois.   Philip III., King of France=Richard, Earl of Hertford.
of Hertford.   Henry, Earl of Lancaster=Thomas, Earl of Norfolk=   Philip IV., King of France=Joan
John, Lord Mowbray=Joan.   Margaret=John, Lord Segrave.   Edward II., King of England=Isabel.
John, Lord Mowbray=Elizabeth Segrave.   Edward III., King of England=Philippa of Hainault.
ierine=Sir Thomas Grey, of Berwyke.
land.
ton.

an de Greystock, of Royal Descent.
leanor, dau. John, Lord Scrope, of Upsal.
uphemia, dau. Sir Thomas Langton, of Farnley.
owsabel, dau. Sir Henry Tempest, of Ridlesdale.
ary, dau. Sir Nicholas Carew, K. G.
iknown.
ihn Launce, of Penair, Cornwall.
ev. John Sherman, of Watertown, Ct., d. 1885.
llis Barron, 3d, of Lancaster, Mass., b. 1655.
annah Richardson, 1698-1746.
awrence Jackson Harris, of Dracut, Mass.
ercy Haskell, of New Gloucester, Me.
athaniel Smith, of Lincoln, Me., 1792-1876.
b. Lincoln, 1835.=J. Harrison, of Minneapolis, Minn., m. 1870.
Denver, Col.   Alfred W. Harrison, of Silverton, Col. b. 1872.   Marcia Laura Harrison, of Minneapolis, b. 1876.

PEDIGREE C.

HENRY I., King of France (descended from CHARLEMAGNE and HUGH CAPET), had, by his third wife, Anne, (see "The Genealogist," vol. XVI., 140), daughter of Czar Yaroslaff, the Halt, Grand Duke of Russia:

HUGH THE GREAT, Count of Vermandois. He commanded the French pilgrims in the first crusade, and *d.* at Tarsus, 18 October, 1101. He had by his third wife, Adelheid, or Hadwid, Countess of Vermandois and Valois, 1080-1117, daughter and heir of Hubert IV., Count of Vermandois, 1045-1080, a descendant of the EMPEROR CHARLEMAGNE and KING ALFRED THE GREAT, (see p. 289):

ISABELLA DE VERMANDOIS, (also called Elizabeth), *d.* 1131, who *m.* first, 1096, Robert de Beaumont, 1036-1118, Count of Meulent, first lord of Bellomont, by tenure, created in 1103, Earl of Leicester, (see Planche's "The Conqueror and His Companions"), and had:

ROBERT, second Earl of Leicester, justice of England, *d.* 1168. He *m.* Lady Amicia de Waer, daughter of Ralph, Earl of Norfolk, Suffolk, and Cambridge, 1066, and had:

ROBERT, third Earl of Leicester, steward of England, *d.* 1196. He *m.* Lady Petronella, daughter of Hugh, Baron de Grentemaisnil, steward of England, and had:

LADY MARGARET DE BELLOMONT, who *m.* Saher, second Baron de Quincey, of Bushby, Northants, created in 1207, Earl of Winchester; a Surety for the Magna Carta, *d.* 1219, and had:

ROGER, Earl of Winchester, constable of Scotland, *d.* 1264, who had, by his wife, Lady Helen, daughter of Alan McDonal, lord of Galloway, constable of Scotland, by his wife, Lady Margaret, daughter of David, Earl of Huntingdon, a grandson of DAVID I., King of Scots, 1124:

LADY MARGARET DE QUINCEY, who *m.* first (his second wife), William, Baron de Ferrers, of Tadbury Castle, seventh Earl of Derby, *d.* 1254. and had:

WILLIAM DE FERRERS (of Groby), second son, *d.* 1287-8, who *m.* first, Joan, sister of Hugh le Despencer, Earl of Winchester, and had:

ANNE DE FERRERS, who *m.* John, second Baron de Grey, of Ruthyn, and had:

HENRY, Baron de Grey, of Wilton Castle, *d.* 1342, who *m.* Anna, daughter of Ralph Rockley, by his wife, Elizabeth, daughter of William de Clare, a son of Richard, Earl of Hertford and Gloucester, *d.* 1262, and had:

REGINALD, Baron de Grey, of Wilton Castle, *d.* 1370, who *m.* Maud, daughter of John, first Baron Boutetourt, of Wesley, and had:

SIR HENRY, Baron de Grey, of Wilton Castle, *d.* 1394-6, who had:

MARGARET DE GREY, who *m.* John, fifth Baron d'Arcy, 1377-1411, and had:

JOHN, seventh Baron d'Arcy, second son, *d.* 1454; *m.* Joan, daughter of John de Greystock, *d.* 1435, by Elizabeth Ferrers, of Wemme, and had:

RICHARD D'ARCY, heir, *d. v. p.* He *m.* Eleanor, daughter of John, Baron Scrope, of Upsal, and had:

SIR WILLIAM, eighth BARON D'ARCY, 1450-1488; *m.* Euphemia, daughter of Sir Thomas Langton, of Farnley, (see Harrison's "Yorkshire"), and had:

SIR THOMAS D'ARCY, K. G., summoned to Parl. as Lord d'Arcy, of the North, in 1509. He had many honors from Henry VIII., but was finally accused of high treason, and beheaded on Tower Hill, London, 20 June, 1538. Before his execution, he made the request to be entombed with his second wife, Elizabeth, sister of William, first Lord Sandys, in Greenwich Priory, but this was refused, and he was buried at the church of St. Botolph, Aldgate, London. (See Drake's "History of the Hundred of Blackheath"). He *m.* first, Dowsabel, daughter of Sir Henry Tempest, of Ridlesdale, Northumberland, and had by her:

SIR ARTHUR D'ARCY, Kt., second son (brother to George, Lord d'Arcy, of Aston, *d.* 1558). The Abbey of Grace, on Tower Hill (where his father was executed), was granted to him by Henry VIII., on the dissolution of the monasteries, in 1539-40, and was demolished by him, (see Stowe's "London"). He *d.* in 1561. He *m.* Mary, daughter and co-heir to Sir Nicholas Carew, K. G., of Beddington, Surrey, (Sir Nicholas was buried in the D'Arcy vault, in Greenwich Priory), and had:

SIR EDWARD D'ARCY, Kt., third son, who resided at Dartford Manor, in Kent. The vast edifice, Dartford Priory, which had "reverted to the Crown," on the dissolution of the monasteries by Henry VIII., was reserved by him "as a house fit for a residence for himself and his successors." But James I. granted the old priory to Robert Cecil, Earl of Salisbury, the manor having been previously granted to Sir Edward d'Arcy. The Earl Robert conveyed the priory to Sir Edward's son,

Sir Robert d'Arcy, who was succeeded in it by his son, Sir Edward, of St. Ann, Blackfriars, 163—, in whose time it was known as Dartford Place. Sir Edward d'Arcy, aforesaid (see Cornwall Visitations, 1530-1620, edited by Col. Vivian, 1887), was the father of

ISABELLA D'ARCY, (sister to Sir Robert d'Arcy, of Dartford), who m. first, James Launce, of Penair, St. Clement's Parish, Cornwall, b. 1597, d. ante 1655. Isabella m. secondly, "Sydrack Sympson," of London, "Clerk (i. e., minister), Master of Pembroke Hall, Univ. of Cambridge," as he describes himself in his will, dated 2 April, proved 15 April, 1655, in which he mentions his wife, Isabella, and his children, probably by a former wife. (See Waters's "Gleanings in English Wills," p. 1185). The said Isabella (d'Arcy) Simpson, made her will, dated London, 29 May, 1668, proved 4 August, 1669, in which she devised to her son, James Launce, one hundred pounds, and some money to his daughter, Isabella; and also to him her "trunk at Exeter, at Mr. Pamors;" to his wife, Rebecca, a silver drinking-cup, with two handles; to her "son, Darcie Launce, five pounds," who admd. on the will, in place of his brother James. To "daughter Mary Sherman," she devised thirteen pounds, and "my caudel silver cup, with a silver porringer that covers it," and "a ring with three diamonds in it," one silver spoon, and her clothing, her watch, and household furniture, and some money to "daughter Mary's children who are unmarried". And "To my son, Sherman" (her daughter Mary's husband), five pounds, and "half of my books, with the great Bible I read." To her son Powell, twenty shillings to buy a ring, etc. (See Waters's "Gleanings," p. 1186). John Launce, of Penair, and his wife, Isabella d'Arcy, aforesaid, had:

MARY LAUNCE, b. after 1620, d. at Watertown, 9 November, 1710. She is said to have been a ward of Gov. Eaton, of the Conn. colony, in 1645, and m. in Conn., about 1648, Rev. John Sherman,* 1613-1691, of New Haven, and Watertown, Conn., his second wife, and had:

---

*Mather's "Magnalia Christi Americana," I., 466, or III., 164-5, Savage's "Genealogical Dictionary," under "Sherman," Bond's "Watertown," p. 432, N. E. His. Gen. Reg. IV. 307, and Am. Heraldic Journal, I. 64. It may be noticed that the statements herein as to Mr. Sherman's wife, Mary Launce, differ from those made by Mather, and subsequent biographers, Mather said, in part, of Mr. Sherman's second wife, that she was the daughter of a Puritan gentleman, whose name was Launce, and whose lands in Cornwall yielded him 1400 pounds a year. He was a Parliamentary man, a man learned and pious, who was killed in a duel over a religious dispute, and "whose wife was a daughter to the Lord Darcy, that was Earl of Rivers." This latter statement is incorrect, and it was Mrs. Sherman's brother, James Launce, of Penair, commissioner of the peace, for Cornwall, and surveyor of the Duchy of Lancaster, time of the Commonwealth, who was M. P. in 1650-1 for St. Clement's parish, and in 1658, for Michell, Cornwall. See "Diary of Thomas Burton." See "Launce" pedigree in "Polewhele" ped. in the "Parochial His. of Cornwall," I. 210.

1.—MARY SHERMAN, b. Watertown, 5 March, 1657, named in her father's will, 6 August, proved 6 October, 1685, who m. 27 May, 1679, Ellis Barron, Jr., or 3d, of Lancaster, Mass., b. 22 April, 1655, and had:

JOHN BARRON, of Concord, 1717-8, and of Dracut, Mass., from about 1718-21. He m. (published at Chelmsford, 22 April, 1721), Hannah, b. 28 September, 1698, daughter of Lieut. Josiah and Mercy (Parish) Richardson, of Chelmsford, Mass., and had by her, who d. 17 May, 1746:

LYDIA BARRON, b. at Dracut, 1 January, 1734, d. at Greene, Me., 1 January, 1824, who m. (published at Dracut, 31 October, 1753), second wife, Lawrence Jackson Harris, of Dracut, b. Medford, 9 January, 1713, d. Lewiston, Me., 10 November, 1784, and had:

SILAS HARRIS, b. at Dracut, 15 February, 1766, d. at Greene, Me., 13 January, 1844, who m. at New Gloucester, 28 November, 1790, Mercy Haskell, b. 15 December, 1771, d. at Greene, and had:

ANNA HARRIS, b. at Greene, 15 March, 1799, d. at Brooklyn Center, Minn., 29 February, 1876, who m. at Greene, 1 September, 1818, Nathaniel Smith, of Lincoln, Me., b. 30 November, 1792, d. Brooklyn, Minn., 24 August, 1876, and had:

MARY JANE SMITH, b. at Lincoln, 11 August, 1835, who m. first, at St. Anthony, Minn., 6 May, 1857, George W. Allen b. at Exeter, Me., 7 June, 1828, d. at Cairo, Ill., 19 August, 1866, and had:

I.—ESTHER ALLEN, m. 10 December, 1877, William V. Jobes, of Spokane, Wash. No issue.

II.—LENA ALLEN, b. at St. Anthony, 2 April, 1862, who m. at Chicago, 29 March, 1888, Edward George Stoiber, of Denver, Colo., b. New York city, in 1855. *No issue.*

MARY JANE SMITH, m. secondly, 20 December, 1870, J. Harrison, of Minneapolis, and had:

III.—ALFRED W. HARRISON, of Silverton, Colo., a member of the Order of Runnemede.

IV.—MARCIA LAURA HARRISON, of Minneapolis; *unm.*

2.—ABIGAIL SHERMAN, b. 1 February, 1647-8, d. 167—, who m. 8 August, 1664, (his first wife), Rev. Samuel Willard, of Boston, b. Concord, 31, January, 1639-40, d. 12 September 1707, pastor of the Old South Church, 1678-1707, and president of Harvard College, 1701-07, and had eight children (see the "Willard Memorial," 1858), of whom:

1.—ABIGAIL WILLARD, b. Groton, 5 July, 1665, d. 27 December, 1746, m. first, 29 November, 1694, Rev. Benjamin Estabrook, of Lexington, d.

July, 1697, and *m.* secondly, in 1700, Rev. Samuel Treat, of Eastham, (a son of Robert Treat, 1622-1710, governor of the Conn. colony, 1680), and had by him, who *d,* 18 March, 1717, aged 69:

EUNICE TREAT, 1704-1747, who *m.* 1721, Rev. Thomas Paine, of Weymouth, 1694-1757, and had:

ROBERT TREAT PAINE, 1731-1814, Att.-Gen. and Judge of the Supreme Court of Mass., etc., a member of the Continental Congress, and a signer of the Declaration of Independence. He *m.* 1770, Sarah Cobb, 1744-1816, sister of Gen. David Cobb, M. D., of Taunton, a member of the Provincial Congress, 1775, M. C., 1793-95, etc., and daughter of Col. Thomas Cobb, and had: *Robert Treat, Jr.,* a poet, *Antoinette, m.* Samuel Greele, of Boston; *Mary, m.* Rev. Elisha Clap, of Boston, and

CHARLES PAINE, 1775-1810, who *m.* 1799, Sarah Sumner Cushing, 1777-1859, and had:

CHARLES CUSHING PAINE. 1808-1874, who *m.* 29 October, 1832, Fanny Cabot Jackson, 1812-1878, also of Royal Descent (see Pedigree XCIII.), and had:

ROBERT TREAT PAINE, of Boston, *b.* 28 October, 1835, a member of the Society of Colonial Wars, etc., who *m.* 1862, Lydia Williams Lyman, 1837-1897.

2.—MARY WILLARD, *b.* 10 October, 1669, *d.* 2 August, 1723, *m.* (his first wife), David Melville, of Boston, Mass., and Newport, R. I. *Issue.*

3.—SIMON WILLARD, of Boston, *b.* 6 December, 1676, will 1709, proved 1713; *m.* 30 April, 1702, Elizabeth Alden a granddaughter of John Alden, the Pilgrim. *Issue.*

4.—MAJOR JOHN WILLARD, of Kingston, Jamaica, W. I., *b.* at Groton, 8 September, 1673, *d.* 1723. He *m.,* in Jamaica, 1703, Frances Sherburn, *d.* 1733, and had: *Nancy, m.* 1727, Capt. John Parris, of Kingston. *Issue: Frances, d. s. p.,* and

REV. SAMUEL WILLARD, *b.* Kingston, September, 1705, *d.* at Kittery, Me., 25 October, 1741. He *m.* 29 October, 1730, his cousin, Abigail, *b.* 19 February, 1708-9, daughter of Capt. Samuel Wright, of Rutland, and had:

1.—REV. DR. JOHN WILLARD, of Stafford, Conn., *b.* Biddeford, Me. *Issue.*

2.—EUNICE, wife of Rev. Benjamin Chadwick. *Issue,* two daughters.

3.—WILLIAM WILLARD, of Petersham, *b.* at Biddeford, 1735, *m.* 1763, Katherine Wilder, and had:

Rev. Samuel Willard, of Deerfield, Mass., *b.* at Petersham, 1776, *d.* 1859, *m.* 1808, Susan Barker, and had:

Samuel Willard, of Hingham, Mass., *b.* at Deerfield, 1814, *d.* 1885; *m.* 1848, Sarah J. Thaxter, and had:

Susan Barker Willard, of Hingham, *b.* at Deerfield.

4.—Rev. Dr. Joseph Willard, *b.* at Biddeford, 1738, *d.* in 1804, President of Harvard College, 1781-1804. He *m.* 1774, Mary Sheafe, and had seven sons and six daughters, of whom

1.—Sophia Willard, *m.* Francis Dana, of Cambridge, and had:

Francis Dana, of Cambridge, *m.* Isabella White, and had:

I.—George Hazen Dana, *m.* Frances Burke, and had:

Francis Dana, of New York, *b.* at Singapore.

II.—Isabella Hazen Dana, of Boston, Mass.

2.—Theodora Willard, *m.* Samuel Luther Dana, of Lowell, Mass., and had:

I.—James Jackson Dana, (deceased), who *m.* Thesta Dana, and had:

Richard Dana, of New York, *m.* first, Rosamond Upham; *m.* secondly, Elizabeth Upham.

II.—Lucy Dana, *m.* Benjamin Kittredge, of New York, and had:

I.—Sarah Kittredge (deceased), *m.* (first wife), George Canfield, of New York, and had:

George Canfield, *m.* Frances Maynard Marshall.

II.—Lucy Kittredge, *m.* George Miller Cumming, of New York.

III.—Samuel Dana Kittredge, *m.* 7 October, 1890, Anna Mattison.

IV.—Benjamin Rufus Kittredge, *m.* 1 June, 1899, Elizabeth M. Marshall.

3.—Prof. Sidney Willard, of Cambridge, *b.* 1780, *m.* first, 1815, Elizabeth Ann Andrews, and *m.* secondly, Hannah Staniford Heard, and had, with other issue:

Joseph A. Willard, of Boston, *b.* at Cambridge, 1816, *d.* 1904; *m.* Penelope Cochran, and had: *Elizabeth, m.* Henry Coolidge; *Edward; Mary, m.* Alvan Clark; *Penelope, m.* Henry Coolidge; *Edith,* and

Sidney Faneuil Willard, of Cambridge, *m.* Emma F. Wright, and had: Penelope, Edith, and Joseph.

4.—JOSEPH WILLARD, of Cambridge, 1798-1865, m. Susanna Hickling Lewis, and had:

1.—SIDNEY WILLARD, (deceased), who m. Sarah Ripley Fiske.

2.—THEODORA WILLARD (deceased).

3.—JOSEPH WILLARD, of Boston, Mass.

4.—ROBERT WILLARD, (deceased), who m. Caroline Cross Williamson, and had:

THEODORA WILLARD, of Boston, Mass.

5.—SUSANNA WILLARD, of Cambridge, b. Boston, member of the Massachusetts Society of the National Society of Colonial Dames of America, etc.

6.—RICHARD KENELM WILLARD (deceased).

THE ROYAL DESCENT
OF
MRS. ARTHUR DUDLEY CROSS,
OF SAN FRANCISCO, CAL.

THE EMPEROR CHARLEMAGNE had:
Louis, I., Emperor of France, etc., who had:
Louis I., King of Bavaria, who had:
Carloman, King of Bavaria, who had:
Arnoul, King of Germany, who had:
Hedwige, *m.* Otto of Saxony, and had:
Henry, Emperor of Germany, who had:
Hedwige, *m.* Hugh, Duke of France, and had:
Hugh Capet, King of France, who had:
Robert the Pious, King of France, who had:
Henry I., King of France, who had:
Philip I., King of France, who had:

Louis VI., King of France, who had:	HOWEL-DHA, PRINCE OF ALL WALES, had:
Louis VII, King of France, who had:	Ankaret, *m.* Tewdwr, Earl of Hereford, and had:
Philip II., King of France, who had:	Eikcon ap Tewdwr Trevor, heir, k.v.p., who had:
Louis VIII., King of France, who had:	Teudor-mawr, King of South Wales, who had:
Robert, Count of Artois, who had:	Rhys Tudor, Prince of South Wales, who had:
Blanche, *m.* Edmund, Earl of Leicester, and had:	Elizabeth, *m.* Edmund, Baron of Cayrowe, and had:
Henry, Earl of Leicester, who had:	Sir Edgar, Baron of Carew, who had:
Eleanor, *m.* Richard, Earl of Arundel, and had:	John, Baron of Carew, (p. 298) who had:
John Fitzalan, Lord Maltravers, who had:	Anne, *m.* Thomas Awbrey, and had:
John Fitzalan de Arundel, who had:	Thomas Awbrey, of Aberkynfrig, who had:
Sir Thomas Fitzalan, Knt., who had:	Thomas Awbrey-gòch, of Aberkynfrig, who had:
Eleanor, *m.* Sir Thomas Browne, and had:	Richard Awbrey, of Aberkynfrig, who had:
Sir Anthony Browne, standard bearer, who had:	Walter Awbrey, of Aberkynfrig, who had:
Elizabeth, *m* Henry, Earl of Worcester, and had	Morgan Awbrey, of Aberkynfrig, who had:
Eleanor, *m.* Sir Roger Vaughan, Knt., and had:	Jenkin Awbrey, of Aberkynfrig, who had:
Watkin Vaughan, of Talgarth, (p. 80), who had:	Hopkin Awbrey, of Aberkynfrig, who had:
Sir William Vaughan, of Porthaml, who had:	William Awbrey, of Aberkynfrig, who had:
Catherine, *m.* David ap Evan, of Neath, and had:	Richard Awbrey, of Aberkynfrig, who had:
Mary, *m.* Thomas Basset, of Miscin, and had:	Richard Awbrey, of Llanelyw, Brecknock, who had:
Catherine, *m.* Richard Evan, of Collenna, and had:	Thomas Awbrey, third son, (p. 299), who had:
Jane, *m.* Evan John, of Treverigg, and had:	William Awbrey, of Llanelyw manor, who had:

John Bevan, to Pa. in 1683, (p 80), who *m.* Barbara Awbrey, *d.* 1710, and had:
ELIZABETH BEVAN, who *m* Joseph Richardson, of Philadelphia, and had:
AUBREY RICHARDSON, of Philadelphia, who *m.* Sarah Thomas, and had:
ELIZABETH RICHARDSON, who *m.* Peter Miller, of Philadelphia, and had:
ANNA MILLER, who *m.* in Philadelphia, 9 Oct., 1794, Josiah Fox, *b.* Falmouth, England, 9 Oct., 1763, *d.* 1847, descended from Francis Fox, of St. Germans. Cornwall, *d.* 1670, (see Foster's "Descendants of Francis Fox"), and had:
ELIZABETH MILLER FOX, *b.* Philadelphia, 22 Aug., 1797, who *m.* Philadelphia, 22 June, 1813, Gen. Moses W. Chapline, an aide to Gen. Cass in the "1812 War," *b.* Md., 27 Oct., 1789, *d.* Wheeling, W. Va., 20 Oct., 1840, and had:
JOSEPHINE ISABELLA CHAPLINE, *b.* Wheeling, 1 March, 1832, who *m.* 11 Sep., 1866, Thomas B. Pheby (Phoebus), *b.* in Cornwall, England, 1 Oct., 1838, and had:
ELSIE CHAPLINE PHEBY, *b.* in Idaho, 11 July, 1868, a member of the Societies of Colonial Dames of America, Daughters of the American Revolution, United Daughters of the Confederacy, etc., who *m.* 15 May, 1893, Arthur Dudley Cross, of San Francisco, Cal., and had:
Elsie Hilton, *b.* 21 April, 1894, and *Arthur Dudley*, *b.* 2, April, 1898.

PEDIGREE CI.

EDWARD I., King of England, had, by his second wife, Princess Margaret, daughter of Philip III., King of France:

THOMAS DE BROTHERTON, Earl of Norfolk, earl-marshal of England, *m*. Alice, daughter of Sir Robert Halys, of Harwich, and had:

COUNTESS MARGARET PLANTAGENET, created Duchess of Norfolk, 1397, who m. John, third Lord Segrave, of Blackmere, *d*. 1353, and had:

LADY ELIZABETH SEGRAVE, *m*. John, Lord Mowbray, of Axholme, and had:

LADY MARGERY MOWBRAY, sister to Thomas, Duke of Norfolk, who *m*. John, second Lord Welles, of Gainsby, 1422, and had:

LADY MARGERY DE WELLES, widow of John de Huntingfield, who *m*. Sir Stephen, second Lord Scrope, of Masham, *d*. 1406, and had:

SIR HENRY, third Lord Scrope, K. G., treasurer of England, beheaded in August, 1415; *m*. Lady Philippa, daughter of Sir Guy de Brian, K. G., and had:

LADY JANE LE SCROPE, who *m*. Henry, second Lord Fitzhugh, of Ravensworth, by writ, *d*. 1389, and had:

LADY ELEANOR FITZHUGH, (sister to Sir Henry, Lord Fitzhugh, K. G., *d*. 1425), who *m*. Sir Thomas de Tunstall, in Lancashire, knight, feudal lord of Thurland Castle. (See pedigree in Harrison's "Yorkshire," Dugdale's "Yorkshire Visitations," "The Genealogist," XX., Part II.); Arms, Sa., 3 Cock's Combs, Ar., 2 and 1. Crest, A Cock, Ar., combed, etc., Or; in beak a scroll with motto, "Droit." (See "Surry Roll of Arms," Jenyns's "Ordinary," and Foster's "Feudal Arms"). He served, "armed and attended," by indenture with Henry V., dated 29 April, 1415, as a knight in France, and was at Agincourt, and was rewarded with the honor of Ponthieu, (see Rymer's "Fœdere," IX., 233, Carte's "List of Persons in the Calendar to the Norman Roll," Nicolas's "Agincourt," appendix, 8). He *d*. 5 November, 1415, Inq. P. M., January following. There was an effegy of him in St. Michael's, (St. John the Baptist), Tunstall. Of their children:

1.—WILLIAM DE TUNSTALL, heir, lord of Thurland Castle, *b*. 1391. He was with his father at Agincourt, and was appointed commissioner for musters, in Lonsdale, 28 April, 1418. He *d. s. p. m.* before 12 June,

1432, according to indenture of this date, between his relict, Lady Anne, and Nicholas Worthy, who *m.* his daughter, Isabella, (her will proved 21 March, 1491-2), mother of Sir Thomas Worthy, who was Knight of the Body to four kings ("Reliquary," XVIII.).

2.—ANNE, wife of Sir Thomas Parr, of Kendall, *d.* 1464, and mother of Sir William Parr, K. G., high constable of England, a celebrated Yorkist, grandfather of Queen Katherine Parr, the last wife of Henry VIII. (See Pedigree XCI., and pp. 5, 6, 678, 4th edition).

3.—SIR RICHARD DE TUNSTALL, K. G., lord of Thurland Castle, etc., *d.* 1491-2. He was chamberlain to Henry VI., and one of the commanders in his wars. He was the hero of Harlech Castle, which he held for King Henry, and which was the last fortress to surrender. Wauren's "Recuiel des Chroniques d'Engleterre," tells of his carrying off into safety of Henry VI., to Bolton Hall, after the battle of Hexam. In 1465-6, he was attainted, and forfeited all of his possessions, being a Lancastrian, but in 1473-4, he obtained a restitution. He was counsel to the corporation of York, 1490, steward of Pontefract, 1486, governor of York, 1489, member of the privy council to Henry VII., 1485-6, etc., and although a Lancastrian, he was made a Knight of the Order of the Garter, by Richard III., in 1483, in room of his nephew, Sir William Parr, deceased. His first wife, Elizabeth, daughter of Sir William Frank, took the vow of chastity and became a "half-nun," when he was attainted. She was living in 1470, but it was his widow, named Eleanor, who claimed dower, 26 May, 1501, in the estate of his son William. (See Hardynge's "Chronicle," Hodgson's "Northumberland," Richardson's "Border History," "Plumpton Correspondence," in Camden Soc. Pub.). His only son (he had daughters), *William,* lord of Thurland Castle, 1494, and of Sherburn Castle, 1483, constable of Scarborough Castle, 1485-1500, *d. s. p.* 10 November, 1500, will proved 21 January following. This *William m.* "Agnes," whom he names in his will, giving to her his silver basin and ewer. She was named as co-executrix, with his wife, to the will of Thomas Sage, Gent., of Scarborough, 20 February, 1496-7, and her husband, William de Tunstall, was a witness to the will, so it is possible that William's wife, Agnes, was said Sage's daughter. Agnes is also said to have been the child of Sir James Lawrence, of Aston, 1428-1490, by his second wife, Eleanor, daughter of Lionell, Lord Welles, 1406-1461. (See "The Miscell. Geneal. et Heral.," I., 199; but not the Dorset. Visita.) It is, by this presumed match, stated that this William *d. s. p.,* else his issue would have been heirs to Agnes Lawrence's brother, Sir John, *k.* at Flodden, whereas, the four daughters of Sir John's uncle, Sir Robert Lawrence, *k.* at Bosworth, were Sir John's heirs. See the Herald and Genealogist, VIII., 212.

4.—SIR THOMAS DE TUNSTALL, and "de Hornby Castle," in 1470, when he was enrolled as a member of the Guild of Corpus Christi, York city, his brother, Sir Richard, then being a member, and of which their uncle, John de Tunstall, had been the keeper in 1410. Sir Thomas *m.* Margaret, daughter of Sir Ralph Pudsey, of Bolton Hall, and had:

SIR THOMAS DE TUNSTALL, lord of Thurland Castle, by tenure, being the male heir of his cousin, William de Tunstall, in 1500. He was of age in 1485, and *m.* Alice Neville, said to have been the daughter of Richard Neville, of Chenet, Yorks, and had:

1.—THOMAS DE TUNSTALL, eldest son, *d. v. p. s. p.*

2.—SIR BRIAN DE TUNSTALL, second son and heir, slain at Flodden, 9 September, 1515, known as "the stainless knight. (See Scott's "Marmion," canto VI., sec. 24, and "The Gentleman's Mag.," January, 1775). He *m.* Isabella Boynton. She had a commission from the Archbishop of Canterbury, 6 November, 1513, to take the vow of chastity, and became a half-nun. She was a daughter of Henry Boynton, by his wife, daughter of Sir Martin de la Sea, of Banneston, Yorks, and sister to Martin Boynton, whose will, proved 2 September, 1518, says, "To nevoyes Marmaduke Tunstall, and Brian Tunstall, to each a stagg," and appoints "my sister, Isabella Tunstall," a supervisor of his will, and sister to Thomas Boynton, whose will, proved 23 April, 1532, has "To my sister Tunstall, my ringe with the blu stone." Of Sir Brian's issue, see below.

3.—WILLIAM DE TUNSTALL, third son, *b.* 148—, *d. ante* 1553, *s. p.* He was executor to his brother, Sir Brian's will, 1513. He *m.* "Margaret, of the Old Park, Durham," will dated 1553, proved 1558, widow of Thomas Wandisford, and daughter of Henry Pudsey, grandson of Sir Ralph Pudsey, aforesaid.

[4.—RT. REV. DR. CUTHBERT DE TUNSTALL, 1474-1559, Bishop of London, 1521, the last R. C. Bishop of Durham, Lord Keeper of the Privy Seal, Master of the Rolls, etc. See Gasquet's "Henry VIII., F. S. Thomas's "Historical Notes," Trail's "Social England." By Leland, in "Itinery," he is said to have been the "base son of Thomas de Tunstall by one of the Coniers daughters." He was not given by Tonge, Yorkshire Visitations, 1530, as a son of Sir Thomas.]

SIR BRIAN DE TUNSTALL, aforesaid, and Lady Isabella had:

1.—SIR MARMADUKE TUNSTALL, of Thurland and Scargill Castles, heir, a ward of Bishop Tunstall. He was constable of Durham Castle, and took a vigorous part in the destruction of the monasteries; suffered in the Aske Rebellion, and *d.* 26 March, 1566-7. His descendants at Scargill, Aldcliffe, Wycliffe, etc., were recusants, *temp.*, James I.

2.—BRIAN TUNSTALL, of Bathersea Manor, Ingleby parish, Cleveland, Yorks, second son, will dated 2 August, 1539, proved at York registry, 2 December, 1539. He had, by his wife, name unknown:

RICHARD TUNSTALL, of Burrow Manor, Tunstall parish, Lancashire, will proved at Richmond, in 1585, who had, by his wife, name unknown:

EDMUND TUNSTALL, of Netherburrow Manor, Tunstall parish, Lancashire, 1612, will proved at Richmond, in 1635, who had, by his wife, Margaret, will proved at Richmond, 1638, *Edmund, Barnard,* see below, and *Thomas,* formerly of Croston, Lancashire, alderman of Durham, 1639, who held the exclusive right, under the Great Seal, for selling tobacco at wholesale in and about Durham city, and had the monopoly of importing tobacco from Virginia to Durham. Thomas bore Sa., three Cock's Combs, Ar., a Mullet charged with a Mullet, for difference. Crest, a Cock, Ar., beaked, etc., Gu., which were, possibly, his father's arms, and those of the Tunstalls of Virginia.

EDMUND TUNSTALL, (son of Edmund, aforesaid), of Sutton Manor, Prescott parish, Lancashire, will proved at Chester, in 1635-6, (brother to Barnard, of Bury, will proved at York, 1610, father of *Edmund,* of Bury, will proved, 1658, and of *Brian,* of Burrow, will proved, 1654, the father of *Brian,* of Netherburrow, who d. 1723). Edmund, of Sutton, had: *Brian, Richard,* of Sutton, and *Edmund.*

"MR. EDMUND TUNSTALL" came with two servants to Virginia, about 1636, possibly as the factor of, or at the suggestion of Thomas Tunstall, the tobacco monopolist, as he was a tobacconist. He probably m. in Virginia this year, as he had a patent for land, 450 acres on the south side of the Appomattox river, in (Charles City) Henrico Co., part due his wife, Martha, on account of her former husband, Nicholas Greenhill, dated 21 November, 1636. Subsequently he had other large grants of land in Virginia. In January, 1639-40, he was a member of the Virginia House of Burgesses, for the Henrico plantations. (Va. His. Mag., II., 99). He was living in 1643, father of

1.—EDMUND TUNSTALL, of King and Queen Co., Va., 1691, a large land owner. He had, by his wife, Catherine, (who ṁ. secondly, Richard Wyatt, of King and Queen, 1707, son of Henry Wyatt, of New Kent Co.), three daughters, *Catherine,* wife of Samuel Matthews. of King and Queen; *Mary* and *Barbara,* living, 1722.

2.—"MR. RICHARD TUNSTALL," a large land owner in King and Queen Co., having several valuable grants of lands on the north side of the Mattapony, in 1667-1686. He had, by his wife, name unknown:

PEDIGREE CI.—Continued.

1.—COL. WILLIAM TUNSTALL, who m. Betsey Barker.

2.—CAPT. THOMAS TUNSTALL, of King William Co., Va., 1707.

3.—COL. RICHARD TUNSTALL, JR., eldest son, clerk of King and Queen Co., 1753, Burgess, 1766-68, on Com. of Safety, 1774, d. about 1782, who also had large grants of lands in New Kent (King and Queen) Co., 1756. He had, by his wife, Anne, daughter of Lieut.-Col. Edward Hill, of "Shirley," member of H. M. Va. Council, 1655, etc.:

1.—RICHARD TUNSTALL, 3d., clerk of King and Queen Co., 1782, M. C., 1783-4. He m. Catherine, daughter of Col. George Brooke, J. P., of "Mantipike," King William Co., also of Royal Descent, see Pedigree XCII., and had: *George Brooke, Ann,* and *Alexander,* grandfather of *Dr. Alexander Tunstall* and *Richard B. Tunstall,* of Norfolk.

2.—ROBERT TUNSTALL, grantee in King and Queen Co., 1745; a soldier.

3.—JOHN TUNSTALL, of "North Bank," King and Queen Co., 1776. He m. Sally, daughter of Joseph Temple, Gent.,* of "Presque Isle," King William Co., and had:

---

*Robert de Temple, of Temple Hall, Leicestershire, heir to his father, and elder brother to Thomas Temple, of Whitney (pp. 43, 332), and had, by his wife, Grace, daughter of William Turvyle, (see Temple Prime's "Temple" histories):

Richard de Temple, of Temple Hall, heir, d. circa, 1507. He m. Elizabeth, daughter of Richard Vincent, and had:

Roger Temple, of Temple Hall, heir, will proved, 16 April, 1522. He had, by his wife, Anne (who was buried with him in Tatyhull church), daughter of John Beaufoy:

Richard Temple, of Temple Hall, heir, buried in Sibbesdon church, 1556. He had, by his wife, Joice Lovet:

Richard Temple, of Temple Hall, heir, buried at Sibbesdon; will proved 24 March, 1567-8. He m. Elizabeth, daughter of John George, of Baudington; Gloucestershire, and had:

Edmund Temple, of Temple Hall, heir, a Puritan, will proved 18 October, 1618. Arms, Ar., five Martlets on a Chevron, Sa., between three Crescents. He m. Elizabeth, daughter of Robert Burgoine, of Wroxhall, Warwickshire (her will proved, 15 December, 1657), and had:

Joseph Temple, seventh child, b. at Temple Hall, in 1606. He was a brother to Peter Temple (heir to Paul, the eldest son), sheriff of Leicester, 1645, a member of the "Long Parliament," and sat on the trial of Charles I., and was, with his cousin, Col. James Temple, a signer of the warrant for the King's execution. In 1660 he was arraigned as a regicide, and sentenced to imprisonment for life in the Tower of London, when Temple Hall, and his other estates, were forfeited to the Crown. Joseph Temple became a Puritan, and d. in Bristol, will proved in 1699. He was twice married. His second wife, whom he survived, Milicent Flint, (widow of Robert Hall), d. at The Would, in Matlock parish, Derbyshire, where he resided; her will proved 20 November, 1655, by her executor, Francis Allyn, one of the celebrated Regicides. Her brother, Henry Flint, a teacher at Braintree, Mass., d. 1668, was named in her will as then in New England. Joseph Temple had, by his first wife, name unknown, an only child:

CAPT. JOSEPH TUNSTALL, 1755-1817. He removed from King and Queen Co., in 1797, to Louisville, Ky. He *m.* Jane Pearce, and had: *John,* (father of Judge Warrick Tunstall, of Floresville, Texas), *Henry Thòmas, Richard, Leonard, Maria, Sarah,* and

JOSEPH TEMPLE TUNSTALL, of Louisville, 1784-1857. He *m.* 1809, Elizabeth Apperson, 1789-1823, daughter of James Harper, of Petersburg, Va., lieutenant in the Va. Line, Continental Army, by his wife, Mary, daughter of Henry Green, and had: *Albert, d. unm., Logan, Marston, Maria, Martha, m.* John M. Duffield, *Elizabeth Harper, m.* James H. Spotts, and

JANE PEARCE TUNSTALL, who *m.* Harry Innes Spotts, of Louisville, son of Major Samuel Spotts, U. S. Army, and had:

1.—MARTHA TUNSTALL SPOTTS, a member of the National Society of Colonial Dames, etc., who *m.* Theodore Z. Blakeman, of San Francisco, and had an only child:

LÉONTINE SPOTTS BLAKEMAN, who *m.* 21 June, 1905, Robert Franklin McMillan, Captain of Artillery, U. S. Army.

2.—LÉONTINE SPOTTS, *m.* Charles McIntosh Keeney, and had, *Ethel Spotts, m.* 17 Dec., 1902, Theodore Edwin Tomlinson, and *Innes Spotts.*

3.—ALBERT TUNSTALL SPOTTS, *m.* first, Virginia Brown, *m.* secondly, Susanna Russell Johnstone. No issue.

Benjamin Temple, *b.* about 163—, (under 18 in 1654), named in his grandmother's will, 1657, and in that of his step-mother, 1654. He was a merchant in Bristol. Of his children, by his wife, Mary, surname unknown, will proved in 1712, his son, "William in America."

William Temple, came to Virginia, and in 1690 resided in Bristol parish, Charles City Co., where he had large grants of land. His wife's name has not been preserved. His son:

"Major Joseph Temple, Gent.",† resided at his seat, called "Presque Isle," on the Mattapony river, in King William Co., Va. He was as early as 1728, a merchant-planter, and had some large grants of land. He *m.* Anne, daughter of Benjamin and Anne Arnold, of New Kent (King and Queen) Co., Va., who had large grants of land in 1688, and had issue: Joseph, Liston, William, Samuel, Thomas, Benjamin, Mrs. Hannah Gwathmey, Mrs. Mary Elliott, Mrs. Martha Elliott, Mrs. Nancy Fleete, p. 470, and

Sarah, or Sally Temple, who *m.* John Tunstall, of "North Bank."

†The mistake is made by Burke of placing "Joseph Temple, Gent.," of "Presque Isle," as the son of William Temple, of Bishopstrow House, in Wiltshire, *d.* 1662. His "Landed Gentry," 1846, 1858, and 1868, says of "Joseph, *b.* 1666',' (son of said William), "Whose descendants are now living in Virginia," and in 1879, edition: "Whose descendants settled in Virginia." The impression is conveyed that some Virginian, of Temple blood, corresponded with a Temple, of Bishopstrow House, and suggested that Joseph, of "Presque Isle," was the "Joseph," son of said William, it being known in Virginia that Joseph's father was named William. Burke probably heard of this, and inserted it in his "Landed Gentry."

THE ROYAL DESCENT OF MISS SUSA

WITEKIND, last King of Saxons.

Wigbert, Duke of Saxony.　CHARLEMAGNE, Emperor of the West=Hildegarde of Suabia.

Buno, Duke of Saxony.=　Louis I., Emperor of France, Germany, etc.=Judith of Bavaria.

EGBERT, first King of England.　　Everard, Duke of Frioul.=Gisela.　　Louis I., King of Bavaria.

Ethelwolf, King of England.　　Ludolph, Duke of Saxony=Hedwige.　　Carloman, King of Bavaria.

Alfred the Great, of England.　Charles II., King of France.　　　　　Arnoul, King of Germany.
　　　　　　　　　　　　　　　　Emperor of Germany.
Edward, King of England.=　　Louis II., King of France.　Otto, Duke of Saxony=Hedwige, of Germany.

　　　Princess Egiva=Charles III., King of France.　Henry, Emperor of Germany=Matilda.

　　　　　King Louis IV.=Gerberga　Hubert II., de Vermandois.　Hedwige=Hugh, Duke of France.

Edmund, King of England.　Gerberga=Albert de Vermandois. Geoffroy d'Anjou=Adela　Hugh Capet, King of France.

Edgar, King of England.　　Hubert de Vermandois.　Conan de Bretagne=Ermengard.　Robert, King of France.

Ethelred, King of England.　Otto de Vermandois.　Richard, Duke of Normandy=Judith.

Edmund, King of England.　Hubert de Vermandois.　Robert, Duke of Normandy.　　Baldwin of Flanders=Ade

Edward, Prince of England.　Adelheid=Hugh Magnus. William the Conqueror=Maud.　Duncan I. King of Scotland.

　　　　　　　　　　William, Earl of Surrey=Gundred.　St. Margaret=Malcolm III., King of　Henry I., K
　　　　　　　　　　　　　　　　　　　　　　　　　　　　　　　　　　　Scotland.
Robert, Earl of Leicester=Isabella.=William, Earl of Surrey.　St. David, King of Scotland.　　Maud, Empr

Robert, Earl of Leicester.　Ada=Henry, Earl of Huntingdon.　LLEWELLYN, Prince of Wales=Henry II.,

Robert, Earl of Leicester.　Earl David. William, King=John, Lord Braose=Margaret.　John, King
　　　　　　　　　　　　　　　　　　　of Scotland
Margaret=Saber de Quincey. Alan McDonal=Margaret.　　William, Lord Braose.　　Henry III.,

Roger, Earl of Winchester=Helen McDonal. Robert, Lord Ros=Isabel.　William.　Edward I., King of England=E

William, Earl of Derby=Margaret.　　William, Lord Ros.　John, Lord Mowbray=Alice.　Joan=Gilbert, Earl

William, Lord Ferrers, of Groby.　Robert, Lord Ros.　　Margaret de Clare=Hugh, Earl of Gloucester.

Anne=John, Lord Grey, of Ruthyn.　William, Lord Ros.　Margaret d' Audley=Ralph, Earl of Stafford.

Henry, Lord Grey, of Wilton.　Alice=Nicholas, Lord Meinill.　Hugh, Earl of Stafford.　　Cath

Reginald, Lord Grey, of Wilton.　Elizabeth=John, Lord d'Arcy.　Margaret=Ralph, Earl of Westmore

Henry, Lord Grey, of Wilton=Elizabeth Talbot　　　Alice de Neville=Sir Thomas de Grey, of He

　　　　　　　　　　　　　　　　　　Philip, Lord d'Arcy=Elizabeth de Grey.

　　　　　　　　　　　　　　Margaret de Grey=John, Lord d'Arcy.

　　　　　　　　　　　　　　　　　　　　　　　John, Lord d'Arcy=Jo

　　　　　　　　　　　　　　　　　　　　　　　Richard d'Arcy=El

　　　　　　　　　　　　　　　　　　　　　　Sir William, Lord d'Arcy=E

　　　　　　　　　　　　　　　　　　　　Sir Thomas, Lord d'Arcy, K. G=D

　　　　　　　　　　　　　　　　　　　　　Sir Arthur d'Arcy, Knt.=M

　　　　　　　　　　　　　　　　　　　Sir Edward d'Arcy, of Dartford=un

　　　　　　　　　　　　　　　　　　　　　　　　Isabella d'Arcy=Jo

　　　　　　　　　　　　　　　　Mary Launce, d. Watertown, Ct., 1710=Re

　　　　　　　　　　　　　　　　　　Abigail Sherman, 1648-167--=Re

　　　　　　　　　　　　　Major John Willard, of Kingston, Jamaica, 1673-1723=Fr

　　　　　　　　　　　　　　Rev. Samuel Willard, of Kittery, Me., 1705-1741=Ab

　　　　　　　　　　　Rev. Dr. Joseph Willard, 1738-1804, President of=M
　　　　　　　　　　　　Harvard College, 1781-1804.

　　　　　　　　　　　　　Joseph Willard, of Cambridge, Mass , 1798-1865=Su

　　　　　　　　　　　Susanna Willard, of Cambridge, Mass , member of

NNA WILLARD, OF CAMBRIDGE, MASS.

```
Pepin, King of Italy.
                                        GARSIAS XIMENES, first King of Superarabia.
Bernard, King of Italy.                 Garsias Ennicus, King of Superarabia.
Pepin de Vermandois.                    Fortunius I., King of Superarabia.
Hubert de Vermandois.    KING ACHAIUS.  Sancho Garsias, King of Superarabia.
    BAZIL, Emperor of    King Alpin.    Ximen Inigo, King of Superarabia.
    | Constantinople.
    Leo, Emperor of      King Kenneth II.  Inigo Arista, King of Superarabia.
    | Constantinople.
    Constantine, Emperor of   King Constantine II.  Ximinius Eneco, Count of Aragon.
    | Constantinople.
    Romanus, Emperor of  King Donal IV.   Garsias Inigo, King of Superarabia.
    | Constantinople.
    Anne = Vladimer,     King Malcolm I.  Sancho I., Garsias, King of Navarre.
        Czar of Russia.
    Jarosalaus, Grand Duke of = King Malcolm II.  Sancho II., Garsias, King of Navarre and Aragon.
                     Russia
  la, Henry I., King of France = Anne. Beatrix.  Garsias II., Sancho, King of Navarre and Aragon.
                                        Sancho III., King of Navarre, Aragon, and Castile.
              Philip I., King of France.  Ferdinand I., King of Castile.
                                        Alphonso VI., King of Leon.   DIAMAID, King of all Ireland.
ing of England.   Louis VI., King of France.  Urraco, Queen of Castile.  Doncha, King of Leinster.
ess of Germany.   Louis VII., King of France.  Alphonso VII., King of    Dermot, King of Leinster.
                                              Castile.
King of England.  Philip II., King of France.  Ferdinand II., King of    Eva = Richard, Earl of Pembroke.
                                              | Castile and Leon.
of England.       Louis VIII., King of France.  Alphonso X., King of Leon.  Isabel = William, Earl of Pembroke.
King of England.  Robert.  St. Louis, King of France.  St. Ferdinand, King of    Isabel = Gilbert, Earl of Gloucester.
                                              | Castile and Leon.

  leanor.  Edmund = Blanche d'Artois.     Philip III., King of France = Richard, Earl of Hertford.

of Hertford.  Henry, Earl of Lancaster = Thomas, Earl of Norfolk =    Philip IV., King of France = Joan

    John, Lord Mowbray = Joan.     Margaret = John, Lord Segrave.   Edward II., King of England = Isabel.
    John, Lord Mowbray = Elizabeth Segrave.    Edward III., King of England = Philippa of Hainault.
erine = Sir Thomas Grey,
        of Berwyke.
land.
ton.
```

an de Greystock, of Royal Descent.

eanor, dau. John, Lord Scrope, of Upsal.

uphemia, dau. Sir Thomas Langton, of Farnley.

owsabel, dau Sir Henry Tempest, of Ridlesdale.

ary, dau. Sir Nicholas Carew, K. G.

known.

hn Launce, of Penair, Cornwall.

v. John Sherman, of Watertown, Ct., d. 1685.

v. Samuel Willard, President of Harvard College, 1701-'07.

ances Sherburn, of Jamaica.

igail Wright, of Rutland, Vt.

ary Sheafe.

sanna Hickling Lewis.

the National Society of Colonial Dames of America. (See p. 450)

THE ROYAL DESCENTS
OF
MR. RODERICK D. BARNEY, AND MR. HOWARD BARNEY,
OF WYOMING, OHIO.   OF CINCINNATI, OHIO.

EDWARD I, King of England, had by his first wife, Eleanor:

JOAN, *m.* Gilbert, Earl of Hertford and Gloucester, and had:

MARGARET, *m.* Hugh d'Audley, Earl of Gloucester, and had:

MARGARET, *m.* Ralph, Earl of Stafford, K. G., and had:

HUGH, Earl of Stafford, K. G., (p. 266), who had:

MARGARET, *m.* Ralph, Earl of Westmoreland, K. G., and had:

PHILIPPA, *m.* Thomas, Lord Dacre, of Gillesland, and had:

HUMPHREY, first Lord Dacre of the North, *d.* 1509, who had:

KATHERINE DE DACRE, *m.* Richard Loudenoys, (p. 267), and had:

MARY LOUDENOYS, *m.* Thomas Harlakenden, of Worthon, and had:

ROGER HARLAKENDEN, of Earle's Colne, Essex, who had:

RICHARD HARLAKENDEN, of Earle's Colne, 1565-1631, who had:

MABEL, *m.* John Haynes, Gov. of Mass., (p. 268), and had:

RUTH, *m.* Samuel Wyllys, of Hartford, (p. 268), and had:

MARY, *m.* Rev. Joseph Eliot, of Guilford, Conn., and had:

REV. JARED ELIOT, of Killingworth, Conn., (p. 272), who had:

NATHAN ELIOT, of Kent, Conn., *m.* 1754, Clarissa, daughter of Judge John Griswold, and had:

MATTHEW ELIOT, of Kent, *m.* 1804, Mary Ann., daughter of Capt. Jonathan Farrand, and had:

MARY ANN ELIOT, who *m.* 1831, Hiram H. Barney, the first State School Commissioner of Ohio, and had:

1.—LOUISA M. BARNEY, who *m.* William D. Yocum. No issue.

2.—RODERICK D. BARNEY, of Wyoming, Ohio, who *m.* Clara A. Yates, and had: *Clara Louise,* and *Ethel Wyllys.*

3.—HOWARD BARNEY, of Cincinnati, who *m.* Sadie A. Yates, and had: *John Eliot, Mildred Griswold,* and *Sara Adele.*

THE ROYAL DESCENT
OF
BENNET BERNARD BROWNE, M. D.
OF BALTIMORE MD.

THE EMPEROR CHARLEMAGNE=Hildegarde de Suabia.

- Louis I., King of France.
- Charles II. ALFRED THE GREAT.
- Louis II. Edward the Elder.
- Charles III.=Egiva, of England.
  - Louis IV., King of France.
  - Gerberga, Princess of France.=Albert I. de Vermandois.
  - Herbert III. de Vermandois. HUGH CAPET, King of France.
  - Otho de Vermandois. Robert I. King of France.
  - Herbert IV. de Vermandois. Henry I. King of France.
- Pepin, King of Italy.
- Bernard, King of Italy.
- Pepin de Peronne.
- Herbert I. de Vermandois.
- Herbert II. de Vermandois.

Adelheid de Vermandois=Hugh de Vermandois.
Isabel de Vermandois=Robert, Count of Meulent, Earl of Leicester. pp. 11, 163.
Robert de Bellomont, Earl of Leicester=Aurelia, dau. Ralph de Guader, Earl of Norfolk, Suffolk and Cambridge.
Robert de Bellomont, Earl of Leicester=Petronella de Grentemaisnil. p. 147.
Margaret de Bellomont=Sairer de Quincey, Earl of Winchester.
Roger, Earl of Winchester=Helen, dau. Alan McDonal, Lord of Galloway. p. 397.
Lady Elizabeth de Quincey=Alexander Cumyn, Earl of Buchan. p. 147.
Lady Agnes Cumyn=Gilbert d'Umfraville, Earl of Angus. p. 147.
Robert d'Umfraville, Earl of Augus=Lady Alianore.
Sir Thomas d'Umfraville, Lord of Holmaid=Joan, daughter of Adam de Rodam.
Sir Thomas d'Umfraville, Lord of Kyme=Lady Agnes. p. 147.
Lady Elizabeth d'Umfraville=Sir William d'Elmedon, Northumberland.
Lady Joan d'Elmedon=Thomas Forster, of Bucton. p. 397.
Thomas Forster, of Bucton=Elizabeth d'Etherstone.
Thomas Forster, of Etherstone=Elizabeth Featherstonehaugh, of Stanhope Hall.
Roger Forster, second son=——Hussey.
Thomas Forster, of Hunsdon, Herts=Margaret Browning, of Clemsford, Essex.
Sir Thomas Forster, Justice C. P. Court=Susan Forster, of Iden, Sussex.
Susan Forster=Thomas Brooke, M. P., White Church, Southants.
Gov. Robert Brooke (see Ped. XCII.), removed to=Mary, dau. of Thomas Baker, of Battel, Sussex. St. Mary's Co., Md., 1650.
Roger Brooke, of Calvert Co., Md., 1637-1700=Dorothy Neale.
Roger Brooke the younger, b. 1673=Elizabeth Hutchins.
Priscilla Brooke, 1717-1785=Charles Browne, of Queen Anne Co., Md.
Robert Browne, of Queen Anne Co., 1746-1794=Sarah ————.
Charles Cochrane Browne, of Queen Anne Co.=Martha T. Willson.
Charles Cochrane Browne, of "Wheatlands"=Mary Elizabeth Willson, of "Trumpington."
Bennet Bernard Browne, M.D., of Baltimore, a=Jennie R. Nicholson. member of the Order of Runnemede. See p. 406.

| Jennie Nicholson Browne, M.D. | Bennet Bernard Browne, Jr., M. D. | Mary Nicholson Browne, M.D. | DeCourcy Browne. | Ethel Nicholson Browne. |

THE ROYAL DESCENT
OF
MRS. EDWARD H. NEARY,
OF GOUVERNEUR, N. Y.

TEUDOR-MAWR, King of South Wales, a celebrated warrior, slain in battle in 993. His daughter,

LADY ELEEN (sister to Rhys ap Tewdor, or Tudor, Prince of South Wales, killed in a battle at Brecknock, in 1093; see p. 298), who *m*. (see Clark's "Glamorganiæ," pp. 193, 205), Bleddin, lord of Brycheiniog, or Brecknock, second son of Meynyrch (Maenarch, or Mayernick), lord of Brecknock, or Brecon (by his wife, Eleen vch. Einion ap Selyf, lord of Kwmmwd, see Meyrick's Dwnn's "Visitations of Wales," printed, vol. I., p. 107), son of Caridoc, Earl of Hereford, by his wife, Lady Tegayayr, daughter and heir of Pelinor, King of the Britains.

Lord Blethyn, or Bleddin, and the Lady Eleen had:

GWGAN, lord of Llangorse, etc., second son, who *m*. Marged, (or Gwellian, sister to "Syr Ffylib Gwys, L. off Wyston, Kt.," and daughter of "Ffylib Gwys, of Gwiston," in Pembroke; (see Clark's "Glamorganshire Pedigrees," p. 205), and had:

CAVIDOR AP GWGAN, *alias* Howel ap Gwrgan, of Glyn Tawe, in Brecknock, (brother of "Syr Water Wgan, Kt., L. off Wiston"), who *m*. Maud vch. Llewellyn Vychan ap Llewellyn, or "Mait, daughter and heir to Llewelyn-ychan ap Llewelyn ap Gwgan, and a great Gower heiress," and had: *Griffith Gwyr* (see "Bowen of Woodstock," Conn.), and MEYRICK, who had: GWILLIM, who had: CRADOC, who had: OWEN, who had, by his wife, Wenllian v. Einore Sais:

OWEN GETHYN, of Glyn Tawe, Brecon, who had:

GRIFFITH OWEN, of Glyn Tawe, who had:

OWEN GRIFFITH, of Glyn Tawe, who had by his first wife, a daughter of Richard Jenkin ap Richard David:

OWEN OWEN, third son, who *m*. Alison, daughter of Morgan ap Howel-melyn, and had: *Thomas Bowen* (grandfather of Thomas ap Harry Bowen, of Court House, father of Harry and Richard Bowen, of Court House, *temp.* 1500), and

MORGAN AP OWEN, or Bowen, of Swansea. In July, 1441, Geoffrey de la Mare executed a deed to him for Court House, and Mawr House, and lands pertaining, in Ilston parish, Glamorganshire. His second son,

RICHARD BOWEN, of Court House, was the father of

HARRY BOWEN, of Court House, heir to his grandfather. He had a confirmation of the deed of the manors inherited from Morgan Bowen. His will, dated 4 July, 1467, was proved, as was the custom then, in the church of St. Theliana, at Bishopstow, 12 February, 1467. He desired to be buried at St. Mary's, Swansea. Executors, his son, Richard, the heir, and uncle, Evan Bowen. His third son, *Thomas,* was the grandfather of William, whose son, Harry Bowen, went to New England in 163—, or before. His second son,

THEODORE BOWEN, was the father of

HARRY THOMAS BOWEN, of Court House, *d.* 1582, who had: *John,* (whose son, John, was the father of George Bowen, the sheriff of Glamorganshire, in 1650, founder of the Kittle Hill branch of the family), and

THOMAS BOWEN, of Court House, *d.* 1587, of whose sons, *Harry* succeeded to Court House manor, and

"MR. RICHARD BOWEN, SR.," *b.* 158—, probably at Court House, removed, probably *via* Bristol, to Weymouth, in 163—, resided at Rehoboth, Mass., 1643-1675, selectman, 1644, deputy to Plymouth Court, 1651, Town Clerk, 1654; moderator, deacon, etc., known in his latter years as "Father Bowen." He *d.* and was buried at Rehoboth, 4 February, 1675, and on his tomb were engraved his paternal arms, those of Bowen, of Court House Manor, Glamorganshire a stag trippant, with an arrow stuck in his back. He *m.* about 162—, Ann, surname unknown, who died also in 1675, at Rehoboth, and had: *Obadiah* (see p. 465); *Richard, Alice, m.* Robert Wheaton, and possibly *Samuel,* and

THOMAS BOWEN, of Rehoboth, will proved 11 April, 1663, names his son, Richard, and brother, Obadiah, who was buried at Rehoboth, 11 July, 1699. He *m.* Elizabeth ———, (widow of Samuel Fuller, of Plymouth, in 1668-9), and had: *Thomas,* of Rehoboth, 1689, *b.* January, 1664, and

DR. RICHARD BOWEN, of Rehoboth, *b.* 17 January, 1662, buried 12 February, 1736-7. He *m.* at Rehoboth, 9 January, 1683, Mercy Titus, and had: *Elizabeth, b.* 11 November, 1684, and

COL. THOMAS BOWEN, M. D., *b.* Rehoboth, 20 August, 1689. He *m.* 8 August, 1710, Sarah Hunt, *b.* 16 October, 1690, daughter of Ephraim and Rebecca Hunt, of Rehoboth, and had:

DR. EPHRAIM BOWEN, *b.* Rehoboth, 3 October, 1716, *d.* Providence, R. I., 1812. He *m.* twice. By his first wife, Mary Fenner, he had two sons, *Jabez, b.* Providence, 13 June, 1739, *d.* 8 May, 1815, chief justice of the Supreme Court of R. I.; Dep. Gov. of R. I., member of the National Constitutional Convention, chancellor of Brown University, etc., and *Oliver, b.* 1742, and by his second wife, *m.* 10 June, 1746, Lydia Mawney, he had: *Dr. William,* (whose daughter *m.* Como. Charles Morris, U. S. Navy); *Mary, Sarah, Lydia* (*m.* Mr. Clark, of Philadelphia, and their daughter *m.* Dr. Robert Hare, of Philadelphia), *Capt. Ephraim,* in the expedition against the "Gaspee;" *Nancy, Betsey, Fanny, Dr. Pardon,* and

BENJAMIN BOWEN, seventh child, *b.* Providence, 9 November, 1759, *d.* 16 October, 1824. He had by his first wife, *m.* 178—, Hannah Fenner: *Charles, Lydia, Eliza Betsey* (*m.* James Keith, of Newport, N. Y.), *Benjamin, Mary* (*m.* Philip Palmer, of Tuscumbia, Ala.; their daughter *m.* Key), *Lydia* (*m.* Col. Standish Berry, of Newport, N. Y.), and

NANCY BOWEN, third child, *b.* Providence, 17 August, 1785, *d.* Gouverneur, N. Y., 26 April, 1856, who *m.* 180—, Timothy Sheldon, of Pawtucket, R. I., and had: *Cordelia, Calista, Charles Bowen, Harriet, Eliza, Lucia, Timothy, Mary Ann, Benjamin Gray, Julia Preston, Hannah Maria,* and

HENRY SHELDON, fourth child, *b.* Gouverneur, 2 July, 1814, *d.* 2 May 1873. By his first wife, Betsey Botsford, he had:

1.—CHARLES HENRY SHELDON, of Ventura, Cal., *b.* Comstock, Mich., 9 June, 1839. He *m.* first, February —, 1861, Elizabeth Young, *b.* Headcom, England, *d.* at Ventura, 1881, and *m.* secondly, Mrs. Nellie Bradley, of Ventura, and had, by his first wife:

I.—FREDERICK HENRY, *b.* 1862; II.—EMMA CALISTA; III.—SARAH S.

IV.—CHARLES LEROY SHELDON, *b.* 1871, *m.* Nellie Beswick.

V.—HARRIET CORDELIA, *m.* James Costa Tyson, of Los Angeles, Cal.

VI.—MARY MAUD, *b.* Ventura, January, 1881.

2.—CALISTA SHELDON, *b.* Otsego, Mich., 19 March, 1841, who *m.* Lewis Morris, of Fowler, N. Y., and Auburn, Neb., and had, *Dora, Walter, Dewane, Frankie,* and *Ida.*

3.—GEORGE BOWEN SHELDON, *b.* Gouverneur, N. Y., 4 September, 1846, *d.* Ripley, N. Y., February, 1898; *m.* April, 1883, Fianna Brewer, and had: *Gray B., Ray F., Julia P.,* and *Clinton G.,* all *b.* in Union City, Pa.

HENRY SHELDON, by his second wife, Mrs. Martha Aldous Thompson, b. 16 April, 1824, d. 19 December, 1878, had, all b. at Gouverneur, N. Y.:

4.—JULIA S. SHELDON, b. 29 August, 1851, who m. 20 November, 1890, Judge Edward H. Neary, of Gouverneur, N. Y., b. Elphin, Co. Roscommon, Ireland, 10 November, 1834. *No issue.*

5.—THEODORE B. SHELDON, of Columbus, Ohio, b. 28 June, 1854, m. 19 October, 1887, Anna Brown.

6.—EMMA JANE SHELDON, of New York, b. 20 June, 1858; *unm.*

7.—ARTHUR TIMOTHY SHELDON, of Ilion, N. Y., b. 1 October, 1860, m. 5 June, 1889, Genevieve Hews, d. 16 February, 1903, and had: *Garth Grey, Martha Winnetta,* and *Henry,* d. 23 February, 1902.

8.—JAMES OTIS SHELDON, b. 7 April, 1863, m. 8 March, 1888, Lillian Taitt, b. 10 September, 1865, and had: *Marion Lou, James Douglas,* d. 23 April, 1902, and *Gertrude Alison.*

OBADIAH BOWEN, of Swansea (son of Richard Bowen, Sr., p. 463), Freeman, 1658, Deputy, 1681, d. 1699. He m. Mary Clifton. *Issue*: Lt. *Henry,* 1633-1724 (ancestor of Mrs. Emma Westcott Bullock, of Bristol, R. I., pp. 19, 20), and

OBADIAH BOWEN, JR., d. Swansea, 10 September, 1710; m. Abigail, daughter of Richard and Elizabeth (Ingraham) Bullock, and had: *Abigail,* m. Benjamin Fiske, and

LYDIA BOWEN, b. 23 April, 1666, d. 25 March, 1758; m. 4 September, 1686, Joseph Mason, of Swansea, and had:

CAPT. JOSEPH MASON, of Swansea, b. 30 April, 1687, Representative and Captain, 1732; m. 3 June, 1714, Elizabeth Barney, and had:

FREELOVE MASON, b. Swansea, 14 November, 1720, m. 1 May, 1738, Joseph Cole, and had:

URANIA COLE, of Scituate, b. 1746, d. 5 June, 1828; m. 27 February, 1763, James Rounds, Jr., of Clarendon, Vt., and had:

MARY ROUNDS, b. 9 April, 1773, m. Ezekiel Salisbury, of Starksboro, Vt., and had:

SABRA SALISBURY, b. 1804, d. 29 January, 1835; m. July, 1820, Joel Dodge, of Starksboro, and had:

MARY DODGE, b Starksboro, 27 June, 1826, d. Kingston, Wis., 25 December, 1890; m. 22 August, 1847, John Perkins Woodward, of Kingston, and had:

THERON ROYAL WOODWARD, of Chicago, (see pp. 372, 378).

THE ROYAL DESCENT
OF
THE DUKE OF MANCHESTER.

ROBERT BRUCE, King of Scotland, had:	ROBERT BRUCE, King of Scotland, had:
Mary, *m.* Walter, Lord High Steward, and had:	Margaret, *m.* Wm., Earl of Sutherland, and had:
Robert II., King of Scotland, who had:	John, Earl of Sutherland, who had:
Robert III., King of Scotland, who had:	Nicholas, Earl of Sutherland, who had:
James I., King of Scotland, who had:	Robert, Earl of Sutherland, who had:
Jean, *m.* George, Earl of Huntley, and had:	Alexander Sutherland, of Dunheath, who had:
Alexander, Earl of Huntley, who had:	Margaret, *m.* William, Earl of Orkney, and had:
John, Lord Gordon, of Huntley, who had:	Marjory, *m.* Andrew, Lord Leslie, and had:
George, Earl of Huntley, who had:	William, Earl of Rothes, who had:
George, Earl of Huntley, who had:	George, Earl of Rothes, who had:
George, Marquis of Huntley, who had:	Helen, *m.* Mark Ker, of Newbottle, and had:
George, Marquis of Huntley, who had:	Mark, Earl of Lothian, who had:
Louis, Marquis of Huntley, who had:	Jean, *m.* Robert, Master of Boyd, and had:
George, Duke of Gordon, who had:	James, eighth Lord Boyd, who had:
Alexander, Duke of Gordon, who had:	William, first Earl of Kilmarnock, who had:
Cosino, Duke of Gordon, who had:	Hon. Robert Boyd, of Kilmarnock, who had:
Alexander, Duke of Gordon, who had:	James Boyd, of Newburyport, Mass., who had:
Susan, *m.* Wm., Duke of Manchester, and had:	Frances, *m.* William Little, of Boston, and had:
George, Duke of Manchester, who had:	Maria Augusta, *m.* J. Clements, of La., and had:
William, Duke of Manchester, who had:	Ellen, *m.* Antonio Yznaga del Valle, and had:

George William Drogo Montague, Duke of Manchester, *d.* 18 Aug., 1892. = Consuelo Yznaga, *m.* Grace Church, N. Y. City, 22 May, 1876. Dowager Duchess of Manchester.

William Angus Drogo Montague, Ninth Duke of Manchester, *b.* 1877, *m.* at Marylebone Church, London, 14 Nov., 1900. See Ped. VIII. = Helena, *b.* 1879, dau. of Eugene Zimmerman, of Cincinnati, Ohio, and his wife, Etta Evans, of Urbana, Ohio.

Alexander George Francis Drogo Montague, Viscount Mandeville.   The Hon. Lady Mary Alice Montague.

THE ROYAL DESCENT
OF
MRS. JOSHUA WILBOUR.

CHARLEMAGNE, Emperor of the West, A. D. 800, had:
PEPIN, King of Italy, *d.* 810, who had:
BERNARD, King of Lombardy, *d.* 818, who had:
PEPIN, Count-Palatine de Vermandois, Peronne, etc., who had:
HUBERT I., second Count de Vermandois, *k.* 902, who had:
HUBERT II., Count de Vermandois and Troyes, *d.* 943, who had:
ROBERT, Count de Champagne, Troyes, etc., *d.* 968, who had:
ADELIZA DE CHALONS, who *m.* Geoffrey, Count d'Anjou, *d.* 987, and had:
ERMENGARDE, who *m.* Conan I., Count de Bretagne, *d.* 992 and had:
JUETTA, who *m.* Richard II., Duke of Normandy, *d.* 1026, and had:
RICHARD III., fifth Duke of Normandy, *d.* 1027, who had:
ALICE, who *m.* Radulfe, Count de Bayeux, and had:
RANDLE, Viscount de Bayeux, Earl of Chester, *d.* 1128, who had:
RANDLE, Earl-Palatine of Chester, *d.* 1153-55, who had:
HUGH, fifth Earl-Palatine of Chester, *d.* 1181, who had:
AGNES, who *m.* William, sixth Earl of Derby, *d.* 1246, and had:
JOAN DE FERRERS, who *m.* Thomas, first Lord Berkley, *d.* 1321, and had:
MARGARET, who *m.* Sir Anseleme Bassett, of Uley Manor, and had:
ISABEL BASSETT, heiress, who *m.* ———— Pynchard, and had:
SYMOND PYNCHARD, (see Pedigree LXXXVIII.), who had:
SIR EDMOND PYNCHARD, *alias* Bassett, of Uley Manor, who had:
SIR SYMOND BASSETT, of Uley Manor, Gloucestershire, who had:
ROBERT BASSETT, of Uley Manor, who had:
GILES BASSETT, of Uley Manor, who had:
ROBERT BASSETT, of Uley Manor, who had:
WILLIAM BASSETT, of Uley Manor, who had:
EDWARD BASSETT, of Uley Manor, who had:
JANE, who *m.* Dr. John Deighton, of Gloucester city, and had:
FRANCES, who *m.* Richard Williams, *d.* in Taunton, Mass., and had:
ELIZABETH WILLIAMS, who *m.* John Bird, and had:
DIGHTON BIRD, who *m.* Isaac Mysick, and had:
REBECCA MYSICK, who *m.* Nicholas Hatheway, of Dighton, and had:
STEPHEN HATHEWAY, who *m.* Hope Pierce, and had:
FREDERICK HATHEWAY, who *m.* Sally White, and had:
WILLIAM HENRY HATHEWAY, of Dighton, *m.* Fanny Arnold, and had:
BELINDA OLNEY HATHEWAY, a member of the Society of Colonial Dames, in Rhode Island, the Order of the Crown in America, etc. (see Pedigrees II., XXXV., and LXXXVIII.), who *m.* Joshua Wilbour, of Bristol, R. I., who *d. s. p.* in March, 1902.

THE ROYAL DESCENT

OF

MRS. ASA G. PETTIBONE,

OF NEW YORK MILLS, N. Y.

THE EMPEROR CHARLEMAGNE=Lady Hildegarde of Suabia.

Louis I., King of France=Judith the Fair, of Bavaria

Charles II., **ALFRED THE GREAT.** Gisela=Everard, Duke of Frioul.

Louis II., Edward the Elder. Hedwige=Ludolph, Duke of Saxony.

Charles III.,=Egiva of England. Otto, Duke of Saxony.=Hedwige, of Germany.
King of
France. Emperor Henry, of Germany=Matilda of
Ringleheim.

Louis IV., King of France=Princess Gerberga of Saxony.

Charles, Duke of Nether Lorraine=Bonne, Countess d' Arderne, dau. Ricuinus,
Duke of the Moselle.

Gerberga, Countess of Lorraine=Lambert I., Count of Mous.

Lady Mahaut de Louvaine=Eustace I., Count of Boulogne.

Eustace II., Count of Boulogne, etc.=Ida de Bouillon, dau. Godfrey IV., Duke of Lorraine.

Geoffrey de Boulogne=dau. of Geoffrey de Mandeville.

William de Boulogne=unknown.

Pharamond de Boulogne de Tingry=Matilda, (family unknown).

Lady Sybilla de Boulogne de Tyngrie=Enguerrand de Fiennes, or Fynes.

William de Fienes, lord of Martock=unknown.

Daughter, name unknown=Bartholomew de Hampden, in Bucks.

Sir Reginald de Hampden, Bucks=Agnes, dau. Sir Ingram Burton.

Sir Alexander de Hampden, sheriff=Marian, dau. Sir Bryan Herdby.

Sir Reginald de Hampden=Nichola, dau. John de Grenville.

Sir John de Hampden, sheriff=Joan, dau. Sir Phillip d'Alesbury.

Sir Edmund de Hampden, sheriff=Joan, dau. Sir Robert Belknap.

Sir John de Hampden, sheriff=Elizabeth de Walesbury.

Lady Anne de Hampden=William de Puttenham, of Penn, etc.

Nicholas Putnam, of Penn, Bucks, 1492=unknown.

Henry Putnam, of Eddlesborough, 1526=unknown.

Richard Putnam, of Woughton, Bucks=Joan (family unknown).

John Putnam, of Rowsham, Bucks, 1573=unknown.

Nicholas Putnam, of Stewkeley, 1598=Margaret Goodspeed.

John Putnam, d. Salem, Mass., 1662. Ped. XCVII.=Priscilla (family unknown).

Lt. Thomas Putnam, of Salem, Mass.=Ann Holyoke.

Deliverance Putnam=Capt. Jonathan Walcott, of Salem, Mass.

William Walcott, of Attleboro, Mass.=Mary Felt.

Benjamin Walcott, of Attleboro, Mass.=Mary Foster.

Benjamin Stuart Walcott, of Cumberland, R. I.=Mary Dexter.

Benjamin Stuart Walcott, of N. Y. Mills, N. Y.=Irena Doolittle.

William Dexter Walcott, of N. Y. Mills, N. Y.=Hannah Coe Hubbard.

Elizabeth Hamilton Walcott, Member of So-=Asa G. Pettibone, of N. Y. Mills, N. Y., Memb
ciety of Colonial Dames of America. No issue. of the Society of Colonial Wars. See Pe
See Ped. XCVII. and p. 362. LXXXVII. and p. 362.

PEDIGREE CII.

EDWARD I., King of England, had by his first wife:
LADY JOAN, *m.* Gilbert, Earl of Hertford and Gloucester, and had:
LADY ELEANOR DE CLARE, *m.* Hugh, Earl of Winchester, and had:
LADY ISABEL LE DESPENCER, *m.* Richard, Earl of Arundel, and had:
LADY PHILIPPA FITZALAN, *m.* Sir Richard de Sergeaux, and had:
LADY PHILIPPA DE SERGEAUX, *m.* Sir Robert Pashley, and had:
SIR JOHN PASHLEY, who *m.* Lowys Gower, and had:
LADY ELIZABETH PASHLEY, who *m.* Reginald de Pympe, and had:
ANNE DE PYMPE, who *m.* Sir John Scott, of Scott's Hall, and had:
SIR REGINALD SCOTT, of Scott's Hall, heir, sheriff of Kent, who had:
CHARLES SCOTT, of Egerton, who *m.* Jane, aunt of Francis Wyatt, Governor of Virginia, and a daughter of Sir Thomas Wyatt, of Allington Castle, also of Royal Descent, (see Pedigree XX.), and had:
DEBORAH SCOTT, who *m.* William Fleete, Gent., of Chartham, Kent., an incorporator of the third Virginia Charter (see Brown's "Genesis of the United States," Hayden's "Virginia Genealogies," p. 234; Va. His. Mag., II., 70; V., 254), and had:
LIEUT.-COL. HENRY FLEETE, of St. George's Hundred, Md., and Fleete's Bay, Northumberland Co., Va., *d.* 1660-1. He was associated with the Calverts in establishing the Province of Maryland, (see Neill's "Founders of Maryland"), a member of the first Assembly, 1637. He removed to Lancaster Co., Va., and had numerous grants of land, and became a justice and burgess. He *m.* Sarah ———, (who *m.* secondly, Col. John Walker, of Va.), and had:
HENRY FLEETE, Gent., a justice, 1695, and sheriff, 1718, of Lancaster Co. Will dated 31 January, 1728, printed in the Va. His. Mag., II., 72. He *m.* Elizabeth Wildey (whose mother's, Jane Wildey, will was proved 19 December, 1701), and had HENRY, sheriff of Lancaster Co., 1729, *d. unm.*, will dated 26 November, 1735, given in the Va. His. Mag., II., 74; MRS. BRENT, (issue); MRS. ELIZABETH CURRELL, (had *Ann* and *Harry*); JUDITH, *m.* William Hobson, of Northumberland Co., *m.* bond dated 28 June, 1723, (had *Sarah* and *Judith*); MARY, (or Margaret), *m.* Presley Cox, of Cople parish, Westmoreland Co., (had *Fleete* and

Mary Ann); ANNE, *m.* Leonard Howson, *m.* bond dated 10 June, 1722, (had *Elizabeth*), and

CAPTAIN WILLIAM FLEETE, sheriff of Lancaster Co., 1720; *m.* Sarah (Ann), daughter of Robert Jones, of King and Queen Co., and had MRS. MARY ANN TEBBS, (issue); JOHN, *b.* 12 August, 1724 (issue), and

WILLIAM FLEETE, of King and Queen Co., *b.* 19 October, 1726. He *m.* first, Ann, *d.* 7 May, 1754, daughter of Joseph Temple, of King William Co., (see Pedigree CI.), and *m.* secondly, Susannah, daughter of John Walker, of King and Queen Co., and had: JOHN, EDWIN, BAYLOR, MARY ANN, ELIZABETH, and

CAPT. WILLIAM FLEETE, of "Goshen," King and Queen Co., *b.* 18 December, 1757, *d.* 11 April, 1833, sheriff of King and Queen Co. He *m.* Sarah Tomlin, widow, daughter of Bennet Brooke, of Essex Co., Va., also of Royal Descent (see Pedigree XCII.) and had: COL. ALEXANDER, *b.* 26 April, 1798, justice and legislator, issue, and

1. BENJAMIN FLEETE, M. D., of King and Queen Co., *b.* 25 January, 1818, *d.* 8 March, 1865. He *m.* 1842, Maria Louisa, daughter of Jacob D. Wacker, M. D., of King and Queen Co., and had:

COL. ALEXANDER FREDERICK FLEETE, A. M., LL. D., Superintendent of the Culver Military Academy, Indiana, *b.* 6 June, 1843, member of the Order of Runnemede, etc. He *m.* Belle, daughter of Major John Seddon, of Stafford Co., Va., and had: *Mary, Belle, John Seddon, Henry Wyatt, William Alexander, Charles Preston,* and *Reginald Scott.*

2,—DOROTHEA ANN FLEETE, *m.* Richard Bagby, and had: PRISCILLA ELIZABETH, *m.* Thomas Meekins Henley, and had: MARIA LOUISA, *m.* Richard Warren Barkley, of New York, graduate U. S. Naval Academy; LL. M., Columbia Law School.

THE ROYAL DESCENT
OF
MR. CHARLES MARSHALL,
OF GERMANTOWN, PA.

THE EMPEROR CHARLEMAGNE had:
Louis I., the Pious, King of France, who had:
Charles II., the Bald, King of France, who had: | **ALFRED THE GREAT**, of England, had:
Louis II., King of France; who had: | Edward, the Elder, King of England, who had:
   Charles III., King of France=Egiva, of England.
Louis IV., King of England, who had:
Gerberga, *m.* Albert de Vermandois, and had:
Hubert III., Count of Vermandois, who had: | **HUGH CAPET**, King of France, had:
Otto, Count of Vermandois, who had: | Robert, the Pious, King of France, who had:
Hubert IV., Count of Vermandois, who had: | Henry I., King of France, who had:
   Adelheid de Vermandois=Hugh Magnus, Count of Vermandois.
Isabel, *m.* William, Earl of Surrey, and had:
Ada, *m.* Henry, Prince of Scotland, and had: | **WILLIAM THE CONQUEROR**, had:
Margaret, *m.* Humphrey de Bohun, and had: | Henry I., King of England, who had:
Henry, Earl of Hereford, who had: | Maud, *m.* Geoffrey, Count of Anjou, and had:
Margery, *m.* Waleran de Newburg, and had: | Henry II., King of England, who had:
Alice, *m.* William, Lord Mauduit, and had: | John, King of England, who had:
Isabel, *m.* William de Beauchamp, and had: | Henry III., King of England, who had:
William, Earl of Warwick, who had: | Edward I., King of England, who had:
Isabel, *m.* Patrick, Lord Chaworth, and had: | Joan *m.* Gilbert de Clare, and had:
Maud, *m.* Henry, Earl of Lancaster, and had: | Margaret, *m.* Hugh d'Audley, and had:
Joan, *m.* John, Lord Mowbray, and had: | Margaret, *m.* Ralph de Stafford, and had:
John, Lord Mowbray, who had: | Hugh, Earl of Stafford, who had:
Jane, *m.* Sir Thomas de Grey, and had: | Margaret, *m.* Ralph de Neville, and had:
   Sir Thomas de Grey, of Heton=Alice de Neville.
     Elizabeth de Grey=Sir Philip, Lord d'Arcy.
     John, Lord d'Arcy=Margery de Grey, of Wilton.
     Philip, Lord d'Arcy=Eleanor Fitzhugh.
     Margaret d'Arcy=Sir John Coniers, of Hornby Castle.
     Eleanor Coniers=Sir Thomas de Markenfield, Yorks.
    Sir Nian de Markenfield=Dorothy Gascoigne, of Bentley, Yorks.
     Alice de Markenfield=Robert Mauleverer, of Wothersome, Yorks.
Sir Edmund Mauleverer, of Arncliffe Hall, Yorks=Lady Mary Danby.
  William Mauleverer, of Arncliffe Hall=Eleanor Aldburgh, of Humburton.
  James Mauleverer, of Arncliffe Hall=Beatrice Hutton, of Marske, Yorks.
  Edmund Mauleverer, of West Ayton, Yorks=Ann Peirson, of Mowthorpe, Yorks.
    Anne Mauleverer=John Abbott, of Burlington Co., New Jersey.
    Jane Abbott=Joseph Burr, of Burlington Co., New Jersey.
  Henry Burr, of Burlington Co., N. J.=Elizabeth Foster.
    Hannah Burr=Henry Ridgway, of Burlington Co., N. J.
  Joseph Ridgway, of Philadelphia=Esther Coates, of Coatesville, Pa.
    Rebecca Ridgway=Wallace Marshall, of Philadelphia, Pa.
  Charles Marshall, of Germantown,=Julia A. Herring, of Baltimore.
  (see Ped. LXXXVI).
   Charles Marshall, Jr., of Germantown, Pa., b. 30 Dec. 1873.

THE ROYAL DESCENTS
OF
MR. AND MRS. HENRY WHIPPLE SKINNER,
OF DETROIT, MICH.

THE EMPEROR CHARLEMAGNE had:	**THE EMPEROR CHARLEMAGNE**, had:
Louis I., King of France, who had:	Louis I., King of France, who had:
Charles II., King of France, who had:	Gisela, m. Everard, Duke of Frioul, and had:
Louis II., King of France, who had:	Hedwige, m. Ludolph, of Saxony, and had:
Charles III., King of France, who had:	Otto the Great, Duke of Saxony, who had:
Louis IV., King of France, who had:	Henry I., Emperor of Germany, who had:
Charles, Duke of Lorraine, who had:	Hedwige, m. Hugh, Duke of France, and had:
Gerberga, m. Lambert, Count de Mous, and had:	Hugh Capet, King of France, who had:
Mahaut, m. Eustace, Count Boulogne, and had:	Robert I., the Pious, King of France, who had:
Eustace II., Count de Boulogne, who had:	Henry I., King of France, who had:
Geoffrey de Boulogne, who had:	Hugh the Great, Count Vermandois, who had:
William de Boulogne, who had:	Isabel, m. William de Warren, and had:
Pharamond de Boulogne de Tingrie, who had:	Gundred, m. Roger de Newburg, and had:
Sybilla, m. Enguerrand de Fynes, and had:	Waleran, Earl of Norfolk, who had:
William de Fienes, Lord of Martock, who had:	Alice, m. William de Mauduit, and had:
Daughter, m. Bartholomew de Hampden, and had	Isabel, m. William de Beauchamp, and had:
Sir Reginald de Hampden, Co. Bucks, who had:	William, Earl of Warwick, who had:
Sir Alexander de Hampden, Sheriff, who had:	Guy, Earl of Warwick, who had:
Sir Reginald de Hampden, who had:	Maud, m. Sir Geoffrey, Lord Say, and had:
Sir John de Hampden, Sheriff, who had:	Idonae, m. Sir John, Lord Clinton, and had:
Sir Edmund de Hampden, Sheriff, who had:	Margaret, m. Baldwin de Montfort, and had:
Sir John de Hampden, Sheriff, who had:	Sir William de Montfort, Knt., who had:
Anne, m. William de Puttenham, and had:	Sir Baldwin de Montfort, Knt., who had:
Nicholas Putnam, of Penn, Bucks, who had:	Robert Montfort, of Bescote, Stafford, who had:
Henry Putnam, of Eddlesborough, who had:	Catherine, m. George Booth, and had:
Richard Putnam, of Woughton, Bucks, who had:	William Booth, of Dunham Massie, who had:
John Putnam, of Rowsham, Bucks, who had:	Edward Booth, of Twemlowe, who had:
Nicholas Putnam, of Stewkeley, Bucks, who had:	William Booth, Twemlowe, Cheshire, who had:
John Putnam, Salem, Mass., (p. 428), who had:	Edward Booth, of Great Budworth, who had:
Sarah, m. John Hutchinson, Salem, and had:	Richard Booth, Stratford, Ct., (p. 385), who had
Sarah, m. Joseph Whipple, Ipswich, and had:	Elizabeth, m. Capt. John Minor, and had:
Joseph Whipple, who had:	Grace, m. Samuel Grant, of Windsor, and had
Capt. Joseph Whipple, of Manchester, who had:	Capt. Ebenezer Grant, of Windsor, Ct., who had
Major John Whipple, U. S. Army, who had:	Anne, m. John Marsh, Wethersfield, and had:
Catherine S., m. Edwin A. Skinner, and had:	Mary, m. William Watson, Hartford, and had
	Sarah, m. Richard Henry Dana, and had:
Henry Whipple Skinner, of Detroit=	=Henrietta Channing Dana.
Member of the Societies of Colonial Wars, Founders and Patriots of America, Sons of the American Revolution, Descendants of Colonial Governors, War of 1812, Military Order of the Loyal Legion, etc.	Member of the Societies Colonial Dames of America, Daughters of the American Revolution, Hon. Gov.-Gen. of the Order of Descendants of Colonial Governors, etc.

PEDIGREE CIII.

ROBERT BRUCE, King of Scotland, had by his first wife:

LADY MARJORY BRUCE, who m. Walter, lord high steward, and had:

ROBERT II., King of Scotland, who had by his first wife:

ROBERT, Duke of Albany, Regent of Scotland, who had:

LADY MARJORY STEWART, who m. first (his first wife), Sir Duncan Campbell, laird of Lochow; created in 1445, Lord Campbell, d. 1453; son of Sir Colin, son of Sir Archibald, son of Sir Colin, son of Sir Neil Campbell, of Lochow, d. 1316, and his wife, Lady Mary Bruce, sister to King Robert I. of Scotland, and had:

ARCHIBALD CAMPBELL, Master of Lochow (see p. 239), d. v. p, who m Lady Elizabeth, daughter of Sir John Somerville, laird of Carnwarth, and had:

COLIN, Lord Campbell, of Lochow, created in 1457, Earl of Argyle. He m. Lady Isabel Stewart, daughter of John, Lord Lorn, and had:

ARCHIBALD CAMPBELL, 2d Earl of Argyle, killed at Flodden. He m. Lady Elizabeth Stewart, daughter of John, Earl of Lennox, and had:

COLIN CAMPBELL, 3d Earl of Argyle. He m. Lady Janet Gordon, daughter of Alexander, Earl of Huntley, and had:

ARCHIBALD CAMPBELL, 4th Earl of Argyle. He had by his first wife, Lady Margaret Graham, daughter of William, Earl of Menteith:

SIR COLIN CAMPBELL, 6th Earl of Argyle. He had, by his second wife, Lady Agnes Keith, daughter of William, 4th Earl Marischal:

ARCHIBALD CAMPBELL, 7th Earl of Argyle. He had, by his first wife, Lady Agnes Douglas, daughter of William, Earl of Morton:

ARCHIBALD CAMPBELL, 8th Earl and 1st Marquis of Argyle, b. 1598. He crowned Charles II. at Scone, and by his command was beheaded at Edinburgh, 27 May, 1661. He m. Lady Margaret Douglas, daughter of William, second Earl of Morton, and had, besides others:

1.—LADY MARY, who m. Sir John Campbell, Earl of Breadalbane.

2.—ARCHIBALD CAMPBELL, 9th Earl of Argyle.*

---

*This Earl was beheaded at Edinburgh, 30 June, 1685. He had by his first wife, Lady Mary Stewart, daughter of James Earl of Moray:

PEDIGREE CIII.—Continued.

3.—LORD NEIL CAMPBELL, laird of Ardmaddie, Governor of Dumbarton castle, etc. He came to America in 1685, bringing a colony of Scots to Perth Amboy, and in 1686 became the Deputy Governor of East Jersey. He returned to Scotland, and d. in 1693. He m. first, 28 January, 1668, Lady Vere Ker, daughter of William, Earl of Lothian (see p. 41), and had ANNE, who m. Capt. James Menzies, CHARLES, an adherent of his uncle, was condemned to death, August, 1685, which sentence was commuted to banishment in 1689, and he died in America, and Rt. Rev. Dr. ARCHIBALD, P. E. Bishop of Scotland, consecrated 25 August, 1711, d. in London, 1744.

LORD NEIL CAMPBELL m. secondly, 1673-4, Lady Susan, daughter of Sir Alexander Menzies, of Weem, Bart., and sister to Capt. Menzies, aforesaid, (she m. secondly, Col. Alexander Campbell, of Finnab), and had by her: JOHN, ARCHIBALD, and

LADY JEAN CAMPBELL, b. 1675, only surviving child by second wife, (see Wood's Douglas's "Peerage of Scotland"), who m. 1693, John Campbell,* laird of Inverawe, Argyleshire; resided in Jamaica, W. I.; d. in Glasgow, 172—. He accompanied Lord Neil Campbell, to Perth Amboy. He m. secondly, 1708, Catherine, 1681-1715, daughter of

---

1. ARCHIBALD, tenth Earl and first Duke of Argyle, Marquis of Kintyre and Lorn, Earl of Campbell and Cowal, Viscount of Lochow, etc., d. 1703. His sons, John and Archibald, were Dukes of Argyle, and d. s. p. l.

2. JOHN CAMPBELL, of Mamore, M. P., d. 1730; m. Elizabeth, 1673-1758, daughter of John, Lord Elphinstone, and had:

JOHN CAMPBELL, of Mamore, b. 1693, who succeeded as the fourth Duke of Argyle, 1761. Of his children: JOHN, 1723-1806, succeeded as the fifth Duke of Argyle, and LORD WILLIAM CAMPBELL, Captain R. N., was Governor of Nova Scotia, 1766, and of South Carolina, 1773; d. at Southampton, 5 Sept., 1778. He m. 7 April, 1763, Sarah, d. 4 Sept., 1784, daughter of Ralph Izard, of Charleston, S. C. Issue.

---

*SIR DUNCAN, first Lord Campbell, of Lochow, aforesaid, d. 1453, (see p. 97), had by his second wife, Lady Margaret, only child of Sir John Stewart, of Blackhall:

DUNCAN CAMPBELL, first laird of Auchenbreck, whose descendant (see Douglas' Peerage of Scotland):

SIR DUGALD CAMPBELL, laird of Auchenbreck, was created a Baronet of Nova Scotia, in 1628, d. 1643. He m. Lady Mary, daughter of Sir Alexander Erskine, of Gogar, brother to John, Earl of Mar, and had:

SIR DUNCAN CAMPBELL, of Auchenbreck, second Baronet, slain fighting against Montrose. He m. Lady Jean, daughter of Sir Alexander Colquhoun, of Luss. His second son,

SIR DUNCAN CAMPBELL, of Auchenbreck, fourth Baronet, m. Lady Muriel Lindsay, daughter of Alexander, second Lord Balcarres, and had:

Leonard Claiborne, a merchant, who had large grants of land on the Mattapony, in Virginia, and *d.* in Jamaica, 1694, son of Col. William Claiborne, of Virginia, 1587-1676 (see p. 64), but had no issue by her, who *d.* in Jamaica. Of Mr. Campbell's children, DUNCAN, a major in a Highland regiment, died of wounds received in battle at Fort Ticonderoga, New York (of whose descendants was the wife of Dr. William Norton, of Fort Edward, New York); FRANCIS, of Dublin, a merchant, *d.* 1745-6, (whose son, *Francis,* was a lieutenant in 13th Dragoons, and *d.* in Dublin, 1792); DR. EBENEZER, a physician, in Prince George Co., Va., who *d.* at Blandford, in 1751-2, where he had a well-stocked "shop" or drug store, according to the advertisement in the *Virginia Gazette* of the sale of his personal estate; JAMES, a merchant, at Port Tobacco, Md. (father of *Francis,* and ancestor of others in Charles Co., Md.); ARCHIBALD, second son, an advocate, who *d.* in Edinburgh, (he had by his wife, Margaret Stewart, of Ascog, Isle of Bute, widow of John MacArthur, of Milton; *Robert,* his heir, Rev. Dr. *Archibald,* of "Kirnan," Westmoreland Co., Va., and *Alexander,* of Falmouth, Va., 1750, and Glasgow, a merchant, *d.* in Edinburgh, in 1800-1, who *m.* 12 June, 1756, in Glasgow, Margaret Campbell, his cousin, and had issue, see below), and

JOHN CAMPBELL, *b.* at Inverawe, 1694, eldest son, *d.* Glasgow, 1736-7. He was a merchant at Glasgow and Jamaica, trading with Falmouth, Dumfries, and Blandford, in Virginia. He *m.* 1718-9, Mary, daughter of Robert Simpson, also a Glasgow merchant, engaged in the Virginia trade, and had MARGARET, *b.* 1736, *d.* near Snow Hill, 1812, who *m.* as above, Alexander Campbell (and had: *Archibald, d. s. p.* in Richmond, Va., in 1830, aged 70; *Alexander,* who removed from Richmond to Glasgow, where he *d.* in 1826, aged 65; *John,* 1763-1806, *d.* in Demarara, S. A.; *Robert,* of Virginia, 1768-1807; *James, Daniel, Thomas,* of Virginia, the poet, 1777-1844, and three daughters, who *d. unm,* in Edinburgh); EBENEZER, *b.* 173—, a merchant at the Scotch settlement of Snow Hill, Md.; (he made application in May, 1768, and paid for a large tract of land on Dunning's Creek, Cumberland Co., Pa., near land Francis Campbell took warrant for in 1762); DANIEL, a merchant at Falmouth, Va., *d.* in Glasgow, in partnership with his brother-in-law, Alexander Campbell; JOHN, a lawyer, *m.* Ellen Parker, and

FRANCIS CAMPBELL, of Shippensburg, Pa., born about 1724-5. He is first of record in the Cumberland Valley as an unlicensed Indian trader, and the storekeeper at Shippensburg in 1747, and he was then well and

---

SIR JAMES CAMPBELL, of Auchenbreck, fifth Baronet. He *m.* Janet Macleod, and Susanna Campbell, and had six sons, and five daughters. One of his younger sons was JOHN CAMPBELL, of Inverawe House, aforesaid.

favorably known there; he had probably resided there several years, or as early as 1737, and bartered for peltry for the Scotch merchants at Falmouth, Va. In 1750, he received license to trade with Indians, and in that year was a land owner and taxpayer in Hopewell township, adjoining Shippensburg, and here, on his farm, called "The Forest," he generally resided. Governor Sharpe, of Maryland, in a letter, dated 27th December, 1754, to the Governor of Pennsylvania, at a time when any sympathy or intimacy with the French in Western Pennsylvania was looked upon as suggestive of possible treachery to the pioneers, charged that "Francis Campbell was dangerous as a Roman Catholic," and "on that account likely to sympathize with the French." To this, the Pennsylvania Governor replied, 7 January following, saying that Mr. Peters informs him that "Francis Campbell, a storekeeper at Shippensburg, was bred for the Church, as he has heard, among the Roman Catholics;" but that he was not "dangerous," he "being an honest, inoffensive man, and did not concern himself as to the French." It is possible that in early life Mr. Campbell was a Catholic, as then there were as many Catholic Campbells as Protestant, and the time was not distant when Campbells had forfeited their lives for being of either denomination, and that he was tutored by a priest in Glasgow, in Maryland, or in Virginia, for he certainly was a man of culture, well educated, and remarkable in this respect among the pioneers of the Cumberland Valley, but certainly he was affiliated by the Presbyterians, for as early as 1765, he was one of the guarantors of the salary of the minister of the Presbyterian Church at Middle Spring (near his residence), of which he was a trustee, and in 1767 a town-lot in Shippensburg was conveyed to him, in trust for a Presbyterian church there. Mr. Campbell was a man of affairs in Shippensburg from the first mention of him in the records, in 1746-7-8, when, in town meetings, he fought against the removal of the county seat from there to Carlisle. He was a clear and convincing writer, judging from his letters to the Provincial Council on local affairs and Indian matters. In 1764 the Governor appointed him a member of the Board of Justices of Cumberland Co., and several times re-appointed him, till in 1777. He served for several years as the County Surveyor. In 1758 he was appointed by the Provincial Council the Indian Agent at Fort Augusta (Sunbury, Pa.), but he declined to accept the commission. In 1754-56, he took active part in the defense of the settlement against the Indians, and was wounded in battle with them at Sidling Hill, in April, 1756. About this engagement he wrote a long letter, dated 17 April, to the Provincial Council. His will, dated 8 August, 1790, proved at Carlisle, 9 March, following, names his seven surviving children. Mr. Campbell (or "Campble," as he sometimes wrote the surname), was twice married. The name of his first wife has not been preserved. He married her before, or about 1750, and had two children. He married secondly, about 1754-5, Elizabeth, who survived him, and was residing in 1819, in Carlisle, daughter of John Parker, of Carlisle, *d.* before 1785 (and his wife, Margaret McClure, *d.* 1792), son of Richard Parker, will proved 7 September, 1774, who came from Ulster, with his father, John Parker, and family, and settled in 1725, on the Conodoguinet creek, three miles from Carlisle. See Note in the Corrigenda.

FRANCIS CAMPBELL had by his first wife:

1.—REV. JOHN CAMPBELL, D. D., *b.* 1752, graduate of College of New Jersey (Princeton), 1770; B. D. at Oxford University, ordained in London; rector of All Saints's, Hertford, near London, where he *m.* Catherine, daughter of Dr. Richard and Elizabeth Cutler. He returned to Philadelphia in May, 1784, and became rector of St. John's, York, Pa., 6 July, 1784, and of St. John's, Carlisle, Pa., 1789, till his death, 16 May, 1819. He was buried in the churchyard at Carlisle, with a monument. He had by his wife, Catherine, who was living in 1793:

I.—RICHARD CUTLER CAMPBELL, *b.* at York, Pa., 2 December, 1784, *d.* 23 April, 1818. By his second wife, *m.* 1808, Barbara Zimmerman, *b.* 12 February, 1783, *d.* 22 January, 1867, he had:

1.—CATHERINE CUTLER CAMPBELL, *b.* 22 May, 1809 *d. inf.*

2.—REV. JOHN FRANCIS CAMPBELL, a Lutheran minister, *b.* 17 February, 1811, *d.* 1889, in Albermarle Co., Va. *Issue.*

3.—GEORGE, 1812-1819; 4.—BLACKFORD, 1814-1866;

5.—ELIZABETH CUTLER CAMPBELL, 1815-1855;

6.—JANE CAMPBELL, *b.* 10 March, 1818.

II.—FRANCIS CALDWELL CAMPBELL, *b.* at York, 18 April, 1787, *d.* at Williamsport, Pa., 21 April, 1867. He was admitted to the York County Bar, 1810, and settled at Williamsport in April, 1812, where he *m.* in May, 1818, Jane, *b.* 19 March, 1795, *d.* 19 May, 1867, daughter of James Hepburn, of Williamsport, and had:

1.—MARY JANE CAMPBELL, *b.* 16 July, 1817, *d.* 24 May, 1849; *m.* 1836 (his second wife), Robert Faries, of Williamsport, civil engineer, *d.* 12 November, 1864, and had: *Francis Lee*, 1837-1904; *Robert Hamill*, of Williamsport, *b.* 1841; *James Campbell*, *b.* 1843; *Earnest Brannon*, *b.* 1845; *William*, 1847-1873, and *Mary Jane*, *b.* 1849, *m.* John Hamill of Philadelphia.

2.—JOHN RICHARD CAMPBELL, *b.* 5 September, 1818, *d.* Washington, D. C., 23 September, 1892; *m.* Elizabeth R. W., daughter of Judge Joseph B. Anthony, of Williamsport, and had: *Francis Caldwell*, of Washington, D. C., *b.* 4 August, 1844; *James Hepburn*, *b.* 7 February, 1848, and *Annie*, *b.* 9 November, 1860.

3.—JAMES HEPBURN CAMPBELL, *b.* 8 February, 1820, *d.* Wayne, Pa., 12 April, 1895. He was admitted to the Cumberland and Schuylkill Bars, represented the district of Pottsville, where he then resided, in Congress, 1855-57, and 1858-61; in 1864, was appointed United States Minister to Sweden, and in 1867, to United States of Columbia; this he declined. He *m.* Juliet, daughter of Judge Ellis Lewis, C. J., Supreme Court of Pennsylvania, and had: *Francis Duncan, James Hepburn, Ellis Lewis,* all *d. s. p.,* and *Julia Lewis,* who *m.* first, Mario Philip Verplanck, of New York, and *m.* secondly, Archibald Keightley, surgeon, of London, England.

4.—CATHERINE CUTLER CAMPBELL, of Washington, D. C., *m.* first, John F. Carter, and *m.* secondly, Lewis Jamison.

5.—WASHINGTON LEE CAMPBELL, *d.* Odell, Neb., 1893, aged 69, *m.* Martha Duncan, and had: *Jane, m.* J. R. C. Field, and had: *Herbert, Henry, d. s. p.,* 1897, and *Martha, d. s. p.,* 1897.

6.—CAROLINE CAMPBELL, *b.* 1826, *m.* Rev. John Henry Black, and had: *Francis, d. inf., Henry Campbell,* of Washington, D. C., *Caroline Lee, d. s. p.,* 1893, *m.* Charles F. Horne, of New York.

7.—ELIZABETH, *d. inf.* 8.—FRANCIS HEPBURN, *b.* 1830, *d. s. p.*

9.—ELIZABETH LEE CAMPBELL, 1832-1865; *m.* Seth W. Geer, of Wilkesbarre, and had: *Francis, Helen, m.* Mr. Patterson, and *James*.

10.—SARAH CAMPBELL, *b.* 1833, *m.* first, Capt. Appleton C. Ruggles, and had: *Jennie Hepburn, m.* Rev. John N. MacGonigle, and *Catharine,* and *m.* secondly, Col. J. D. Stanbury, of St. Augustine, Fla.

11.—ALFRED CAMPBELL, 1838-1866, *m.* Mary Bosworth, and had: *Eleanor, m.* Edward Lewis.

III.—ELIZABETH CUTLER CAMPBELL, *b.* York, 10 August, 1790, *d.* at Nanticoke, Pa., 8 December, 1865; *m.* 26 June, 1817, Col. Washington Lee, of Wilkesbarre. *No issue.*

IV.—JANE CAMPBELL, *d. unm.,* at Nanticoke, 30 November, 1864, aged 70.

2.—CAPT. ROBERT CAMPBELL, *b.* 1753-4, commissioned Lieut. (being then a private), 19 March, 1776, in 2d Batt., Pa. Rifles, and 8 April, 1777, Lieut., in "Congress's Own" Regiment. He lost an arm in an engagement on Staten Island, 22 August, 1777, was taken prisoner, and exchanged, in August, 1778, rejoined his old command, 5 August, and transferred to the Invalid Reg., at Philadelphia, January, 1779. On 4 October, 1779, he was mortally wounded, while helping to defend Mr. James Wilson, at Third and Walnut streets, Philadelphia, from a mob of American soldiers, during the militia riots. He *m.* at First Baptist Church, Philadelphia, 16 September, 1779, Mary Hall, of Philadelphia.

FRANCIS CAMPBELL had by his second wife, Elizabeth Parker:

3.—JAMES CAMPBELL, *b.* about 1755, a lawyer, admitted to the Cumberland bar, in 1778, and the York Bar, 29 July, 1788; *d.* at Natchez, Miss., 1807-8. He *m.* Cassandana, daughter of Gen. Henry Miller, of the Pa. Line, Continental Army, and had:

I.—SARAH CAMPBELL, *d. unm.*

II.—HENRY MCCONNELL CAMPBELL, an artillery officer with Pa. troops in the 1812 War. He *d. unm.* in Maryland.

III.—JULIANA WATTS CAMPBELL, *d. unm.,* at Carlisle, Pa., 1878.

4.—NANCY CAMPBELL, *m.* before 1790, Robert Tait. *Issue.*

5.—FRANCIS CAMPBELL JR. He was a private in Capt. Wilson's Co., 6th Batt., Pa. Line, 1777. He and his brother Ebenezer carried on their father's store in Shippensburg, after his decease. He was an elder of the Middle Spring Church, and *d.* intestate, in 1808, at Shippensburg. He *m.* Sally, daughter of Stephen Duncan, of Carlisle, and had:

I.—FRANCIS CAMPBELL, 3d, *d. unm.,* at Chillicothe, Ohio.

II.—DANIEL DUNCAN CAMPBELL, living in June, 1816.

III.—ELIZABETH CAMPBELL.

IV.—MARY ANN CAMPBELL, *b.* 1796; *m.* 1816, Charles S. Carson.

V.—ELLEN DUNCAN CAMPBELL, *m.* William McClure.

VI.—SAMUEL DUNCAN CAMPBELL, *d.* Chillicothe, Ohio. *Issue.*

VII.—JAMES PARKER CAMPBELL, 1806-1849, *d.* Cincinnati; *m.* Harriet, daughter of Dr. Daniel Drake, of Cincinnati, and had: FRANK D., *m.* Mammie, daughter of Patterson Brown, of Dayton, Ohio; JAMES P., who *m.* his brother's widow, and NELLIE, *m.*

PEDIGREE CIII.—Continued.

6.—EBENEZER CAMPBELL, who was an executor to his father's will, and his successor in the Shippensburg store. Subsequently he resided at Strasburg, and Washington, Pa., and Portsmouth, Ohio, and he and his wife died in Quincy, Ill. He *m.* before 1806, Eleanora, or Ellen, daughter of Capt. Samuel McCune, who resided near the "Forest," and had:

I.—ELIZABETH MCCUNE CAMPBELL, *d. unm.*, in Cincinnati.

II.—ELLEN CAMPBELL, *b.* Shippensburg, 26 February, 1820, *d.* at Atchison, Kansas, 25 March, 1874. She *m.* in Cincinnati, 3 May, 1836, James Henry Lea, *b.* Philadelphia, 9 December, 1809, *d.* Atchison, 4 June, 1890, buried, Alton, Ill., and had:

1.—HENRY NEVILL LEA, *b.* 25 March, 1837, *d.* 3 August, 1838.

2.—ELLEN MARIA LEA, *b.* 25 January, 1839, *m.* Atchison, 15 May, 1873, Nicholas Hume, of Atchison. *No Issue.*

3.—CHARLES GAZZAM LEA, *b.* 4 April, 1840, *d.* St. Joseph, Mo., 9 May, 1891; *m.* Alton, Ill., 24 April, 1866, Margaret Eliza Edwards and had:

1.—EDITH C. LEA, *b.* Alton, 31 March, 1867; *m.* 3 Novem. 189—, Joseph Chambers Baldwin, of St. Joseph, Mo.

II.—JOHN JAMES LEA, of Des Moines, Iowa, *b.* Alton, 10 August, 1870; *m.* Ida Virginia Patrick.

4.—CATHERINE LEA, *b.* 25 March, 1842, *d.* 7 August, 1843.

5.—ALICE LEA, *b.* 26 February, 1845, *d. s. p.*, Atchison, Kans., 26 October, 1883; *m.* 15 May, 1873, William H. McNeil.

6.—CATHERINE LEA, *b.* 28 February, 1847, *d.* 5 July, 1848.

7.—CATHERINE LEA, *b.* 29 June, 1849, *m.* Atchison, 20 February, 1870, George Oliver Cromwell, of Atchison, Kansas, and had:

I.—NELLIE CARRIE CROMWELL, *b.* 20 June, 1874, *d.* 13 September, 1879.

II.—ANDREW ELY CROMWELL, *b.* Tomah, Wis., 22 February, 1876.

8.—GRACE LEA, of Atchison, *b.* 13 April, 1854.

III.—MARY BARR CAMPBELL, *b.* Shippensburg, 14 May, 1818. She *m.* 17 October, 1839, Samuel Ogden, *b.* Elizabeth, N. J., *d.* Cincinnati, Ohio, 9 February, 1881, and had:

1.—GEORGE CAMPBELL OGDEN, M. D., of Norwood, Ohio, *unm.*

2.—CHARLES AUGUSTUS OGDEN, of Cincinnati, *d. s. p.*

3.—LAURA LOUISE OGDEN, of Norwood, Ohio, who *m.* first, 6 February, 1867, William A. Whaling, of Milwaukee, Wis., *d.* 23 May, 1874, and *m.* secondly, 6 June, 1875, John A. Trimble, of Cincinnati, from whom she was divorced, 6 May, 1882, and resumed her first husband's surname. *No issue.*

IV.—FRANCIS, *d.* young, *unm.* V.—ELLEN, *d.* young, *unm.*

7.—PARKER CAMPBELL, a minor in 1790, and an executor to his father's will. He was a lawyer; admitted to the Cumberland Bar, April, 1794; to the York Bar, June, 1794; and the Washington Bar, September, 1794. He settled in Washington, Pa., in 1794, was a deputy attorney of Washington Co., 1796; an aide on the staff of Gen. Tannehill, in the 1812 War; was town-council, 1810-16; made a Mason, 25 July, 1795, *d.* at Washington, 30 July, 1824. He *m.* Elizabeth Calhoun, of Chambersburg, Pa., who *d.* in 1846, in Natchez, Miss, and had:

I.—NANCY CAMPBELL, *d.* 1871, *m.* Samuel Lyon. *Issue.*

II.—ELIZABETH CAMPBELL, *d.* 1828, *m.* first, William Chambers, of Chambersburg, and *m.* secondly, John S. Brady, of Washington.

III.—ELEANOR CAMPBELL, *d.* 1872, *m.* John Ritchie.

IV.—FRANCIS CAMPBELL, of Washington, Pa., a lawyer, *d. unm.*

V.—JOHN CAMPBELL, *d. unm.*

VI.—PARKER CAMPBELL, JR., 1815-1880, *d.* Richmond, Va. He *m.* Isabella, 1823-1876, daughter of Samuel Sprigg, and his wife, Amelia, widow of William McKillum, and daughter of Samuel Hay, and his wife, Elizabeth, daughter of William and Mary (Langley) Mallom, of London, and had:

1.—SAMUEL SPRIGG CAMPBELL, of Richmond, Va., *b.* 1846.

2.—ELIZABETH CALHOUN CAMPBELL, *b.* 1848; *m.* Channing M. Bolton, Major C. S. Army.

3.—IDA MALLOM CAMPBELL, *b.* 1854, *m.* 10 April, 1878, John Lawrence Schoolcraft, of Richmond, Va.

4.—PARKER CAMPBELL, 3d, 1860-1864.

8.—ELIZABETH CAMPBELL, a minor in 1790, *d. unm.*

9.—GEORGE CAMPBELL, a minor in 1790.

THE ROYAL DESCENT OF DR. WILLI

WITEKIND, last King of Saxons.

Wigbert, Duke of Saxony.   CHARLEMAGNE, Emperor of the West=Hildegarde of Suabia.

Buno, Duke of Saxony.=   Louis I., Emperor of France, Germany, etc.=Judith of Bavaria.

EGBERT, first King of England.   Everard, Duke of Frioul.=Gisela.   Louis I., King of Bavaria.

Ethelwolf, King of England.   Ludolph, Duke of Saxony=Hedwige.   Carloman, King of Bavaria.

Alfred the Great, of England.   Charles II., King of France.   Arnoul, King of Germany.
                            Emperor of Germany.

Edward, King of England.=   Louis II., King of France.   Otto, Duke of Saxony=Hedwige, of Germany.

      Princess Egiva=Charles III., King of France.   Henry, Emperor of Germany=Matilda.

            King Louis IV.=Gerberga.   Hubert II., de Vermandois.   Hedwige=Hugh, Duke of France.

Edmund, King of England.   Gerberga=Albert de Vermandois.   Geoffrey d'Anjou=Adela.   Hugh Capet, King of France.

Edgar, King of England.   Hubert de Vermandois.   Conan de Bretagne=Ermengard.   Robert, King of France.

Ethelred, King of England.   Otto de Vermandois.   Richard, Duke of Normandy=Judith.

Edmund, King of England.   Hubert de Vermandois.   Robert, Duke of Normandy.   Baldwin of Flanders=Ad

Edward, Prince of England.   Adelheid=Hugh Magnus.   William the Conqueror=Maud.   Duncan I. King of Scotland.

            William, Earl of Surrey=Gundred.   St. Margaret=Malcolm III., King of   Henry I.,
                                                      Scotland.

Robert, Earl of Leicester=Isabella.=William, Earl of Surrey.   St. David, King of Scotland.   Maud, Em

Robert, Earl of Leicester.   Ada=Henry, Earl of Huntingdon.   LLEWELLYN, Prince of Wales=Henry II.,

Robert, Earl of Leicester.   Earl David.   William, King=John, Lord Braose=Margaret.   John, King

Margaret=Saher de Quincey.   Alan McDonal=Margaret.   of Scotland   William, Lord Braose.   Henry III.,

Roger, Earl of Winchester=Helen McDonal.   Robert, Lord Ros=Isabel.   William.   Edward I., King of England=

William, Earl of Derby=Margaret.   William, Lord Ros.   John, Lord Mowbray=Alice.   Joan=Gilbert, Earl

William, Lord Ferrers, of Groby.   Robert, Lord Ros.   Margaret de Clare=Hugh, Earl of Gloucester.

Anne=John, Lord Grey, of Ruthyn.   William, Lord Ros.   Margaret d' Audley=Ralph, Earl of Stafford.

Henry, Lord Grey, of Wilton.   Alice=Nicholas, Lord Meinill.   Hugh, Earl of Stafford.   Cat

Reginald, Lord Grey, of Wilton.   Elizabeth=John, Lord d'Arcy.   Margaret=Ralph, Earl of Westmor

Henry, Lord Grey, of Wilton=Elizabeth Talbot.   Alice de Neville=Sir Thomas de Grey, of H

                                        Philip, Lord d'Arcy=Elizabeth de Grey.

                            Margaret de Grey=John, Lord d'Arcy.   Jo

                                Philip, Lord d'Arcy=Eleanor Fitzhugh.   S

                                    Margaret=Sir John Coniers, of Horton, Yorks.

                                    Eleanor=Sir Thomas de Markenfield, Yorks.

                                            Sir Nyan de Markenfield=Doro

Robert Mauleverer, of Wothersome, Yorks=Alice Markenfield, who was descended f
                                                  of the 25 Sureties for Magna Carta, p.

                           Dorothy Mauleverer=John Kaye, of Woodsome, Yorks, also of

                            Robert Kaye, of Woodsome=Anne, dau. John Flower, of Whitewell.

                               Grace Kaye=Sir Richard Saltonstall, of Huntwick. One

                             Major Richard Saltonstall, of Ipswich, Mass., 1610

                            Judge Nathaniel Saltonstall, of Salem, Mass.

               Elizabeth Saltonstall, 1668-1726, second wife, m. 22 Sept.,

                                                   Joanna Cotton, 169?-

                                                      Elizabeth Br

                                             Elizabeth Chipman, 1756-

                                               Henry Gray, 1784-

                                           Ellen Cordis Gray, 1830-

                                         William Gray Brooks, of

AM GRAY BROOKS, OF PHILADELPHIA.

Pepin, King of Italy.

Bernard, King of Italy.

Pepin de Vermandois.

Hubert de Vermandois.

BAZIL, Emperor of Constantinople.

Leo, Emperor of Constantinople.

Constantine, Emperor of Constantinople.

Romanus, Emperor of Constantinople.

Anne=Vladimir, Czar of Russia.

Jaroslaus, Grand Duke of Russia=King Malcolm II.

ela, Henry I., King of France=Anne. Beatrix.

GARSIAS XIMENES, first King of Superarabia.

Garsias Ennicus, King of Superarabia.

Fortunius I., King of Superarabia.

KING ACHAIUS. Sancho Garsias, King of Superarabia.

King Alpin. Ximen Inigo, King of Superarabia.

King Kenneth II. Inigo Arista, King of Superarabia.

King Constantine II. Ximinius Eneco, Count of Aragon.

King Donal IV. Garsias Inigo, King of Superarabia.

King Malcolm I. Sancho I., Garsias, King of Navarre.

King Kenneth I. Garsias I., Sancho, King of Navarre and Aragon.

Sancho II., Garsias, King of Navarre and Aragon.

Garsias II., Sancho, King of Navarre and Aragon.

Sancho III., King of Navarre, Aragon, and Castile.

Philip I., King of France. Ferdinand I., King of Castile.

Alphonso VI., King of Leon. DIAMAID, King of all Ireland.

King of England. Louis VI., King of France. Urraco, Queen of Castile. Doncha, King of Leinster.

press of Germany. Louis VII., King of France. Alphonso VII., King of Castile. Dermot, King of Leinster.

King of England. Philip II., King of France. Ferdinand II., King of Castile and Leon. Eva=Richard, Earl of Pembroke.

of England. Louis VIII., King of France. Alphonso X., King of Leon. Isabel=William, Earl of Pembroke.

King of England. Robert. St. Louis, King of France. St. Ferdinand, King of Castile and Leon. Isabel=Gilbert, Earl of Gloucester.

Eleanor. Edmund=Blanche d'Artois. Philip III., King of France=Richard, Earl of Hertford.

of Hertford. Henry, Earl of Lancaster=Thomas, Earl of Norfolk= Philip IV., King of France=Joan

John, Lord Mowbray=Joan. Margaret=John, Lord Segrave. Edward II., King of England=Isabel.

John, Lord Mowbray=Elizabeth Segrave. Edward III., King of England=Philippa of Hainault.

herine=Sir Thomas Grey, of Berwyke. John, Duke of Lancaster=Lionel, Duke of Clarence.=Thomas, Duke of Gloucester.

eland. Robert Ferrers=Joan. Edmund, Earl of March=Philippa.

eton. Ralph de Neville=Margaret. Henry Percy.=Elizabeth. William, Earl of Eu=Anne.

John Neville, of Oversley.=Henry, Earl of Northumberland=John Bourchier, Lord Berners=

an=Sir William Gascoigne, Henry, Earl of Northumberland=Humphrey, Earl of Buckingham=

lr William Gascoigne, of Whalten=Margaret Percy. Sir John Lord Berners=Catherine Howard, of Royal Descent.

Joan Bourchier=Sir Edmund Knyvett, of Ashwellthorpe, 1490-1546.

John Knyvett, of Plumstead, 1524-156—.=Agnes Harcourt.

thy Gascoigne. Sir Thomas Knyvett, 1544-1617=Muriel Parry, d. 1616, dau. Sir Thomas Parry.

rom 18
355.
Royal Descent.

Muriel=Sir Martin Sedley, of Morley, Suffolk, 1531-1609.

of the patentees of Mass. and Conn. Muriel=Bramton Gurdon, of Assington Hall, Sheriff of Suffolk, 1625-29, d. 1649.

-1694.=Muriel Gurdon.

, 1639-1707.=Elizabeth Ward, gr. dau. Rev. John Ward.

l692.=Rev. Roland Cotton, of Sandwich, Mass., 1667-1721, gr. son Rev. Dr. John Cotton, of Boston, England.

1772=Rev. John Brown, of Haverhill, Mass., 1696-1742.

own=John Chipman, 1722-1768.

1823=William Gray, 1750-1825.

1854=Frances Peirce, 1794-1830.

1901=Rev. W. Henry Brooks, S. T. D., 1831-1900,

Philadelphia (see pp. 354-360).

THE ROYAL DESCENT

OF

MRS. HARLEY CALVIN GAGE,

OF WASHINGTON, D. C.

This pedigree represents more than fourteen hundred years of Royal Descent from GUELPH, Prince of the Scyrri, ancestor of the present Royal Family of England, from CHARLEMAGNE, HUGH CAPET, PRIAM, King of the Franks, A. D. 382, ALFRED THE GREAT, WILLIAM THE CONQUEROR, and hundreds of Emperors, Kings, Princes, Dukes, Counts, Knights of the Golden Fleece, including the Founder of the Order, Knights of the Order of the Garter, etc., also the actual Founders of Christian civilization in Holland, Germany, France, Italy, and America, and the great Protectors of the Christian Church.

SANCHO III., Emperor of Spain, King of Navarre and Castile, *d.* 1035. He *m.* 1001, Munie-Elvire, or Nunnia, daughter of Sancho-garcia, Count of Castile, and had:

FERDINAND I., King of Castile and Leon, *d.* 1065. He *m.* Sanctia, daughter of Alphonso V., King of Leon, and had:

ALPHONSO IV., King of Castile and Leon, *d.* 1092. He *m.* thirdly, Constance, widow of Hugh II., Count de Chalons, and daughter of Robert I., le Vieux, Duc de Bourgogne, and had:

URRAQUE, Queen of Castile and Leon, heiress, *d.* 1126. She *m.* 1090, Raimond, Comte de Bourgogne, and de Galice, (Amous), *d.* 1108, and had:

ALPHONSO-RAIMOND VIII., Emperor of Spain, King of Castile and Leon, *d.* 1157. He *m.* first, Bérengere, *d.* 1148, daughter of Raimond-Bérenger III., Count de Barcelona, and had:

SANCHO III., King of Castile, *d.* 1158, He *m.* Blanche, *d.* 1156, daughter of Sancho VI., King of Navarre, by his wife, Sanche, sister to this Sancho III., and had:

ALPHONSO IX., King of Castile, d. 1214. He *m.* 1170, Eleanor, Duchess of Gascogne, *d.* 1214, daughter of Henry II., King of England, and had:

BLANCHE, of Castile, *d.* 1252, who *m.* 1200, LOUIS VIII., King of France, a lineal descendant of the Emperor CHARLEMAGNE, and King HUGH CAPET, and had:

LOUIS IX., King of France, who *m.* 1234, Margaret, daughter of Raimond de Bérenger, Count de Provence, and had:

PHILIP III., King of France, le Hardi, who *m.* first, 1262, Isabella, *d.* 1271, daughter of JAMES I., King of Arragon, the Conqueror, by his wife, Yolande, daughter of ANDREW, II., King of Hungary, and had:

CHARLES DE FRANCE, Comte de Valois, Anjou, and Maine, founder of the Royal House of Valois, *d.* 1325. He *m.* Margaret, daughter of CHARLES II., King of Sicily and Naples, Comte De Provence and Forcalquier, by his wife, Mary, daughter of STEPHEN V., King of Hungary, and had:

PHILIP VI., King of France, the first of the Valois monarchs. He *m.* first, in July, 1313, Jeanne, daughter of Robert II., Duc de Bourgogne, and had:

JEAN II., LE BON, King of France, Duc de Normandy. He *m.* first, 1332, Bonne, daughter of JEAN DE LUXEMBERG, King of Bohemia, and had:

PHILIPPE, LE HARDI, *b.* 15 January, 1342, created, 1384, Duc de Bourgogne, *d.* 27 April, 1404. He *m.* 19 June, 1369, Marguerite, *d.* 16 March, 1405, only child of Louis, le Male, Comte de Flandre, and first Comte de Bourgogne, and had:

JEAN, Sans Peur, Duc de Bourgogne, *b.* 28 May, 1371, murdered 10 September, 1419. He *m.* 9 April, 1385, Marguerite, *d.* 23 January, 1425, daughter of Albert de Baviere, Comte de Hainaut and Holland, and had:

PHILIPPE LE BON, Duc de Bourgogne and the Netherlands, *b.* 30 June, 1396, *d.* 15 June, 1467. He was the Founder and the first Grand Master of the Order of the Golden Fleece, 10 January, 1429. He *m.* three times; first, June, 1409, Michelle de France, daughter of King Charles VI., *d.* 8 July, 1422; secondly, 30 November, 1424, Bonne d'Artois, daughter of Philippe, Comte d'Eu; *d.* 17 September, 1425, and thirdly, 10 January, 1429, Isabella, daughter of John I., King of Portugal; *d.* 17 December, 1472. His son,

BAUDOUIN DE BOURGOGNE, 1445-1508, Seigneur de Falais, Bredam, etc., envoy to Spain, 1488; *m.* 1488, Marie de Manuel de la Cerda, daughter of Jean Manuel de Villena, and had:

MAGDELAINE DE BOURGOGNE, 1489-1511, who *m.* Philippe, Seigneur de Lannoye*, Chevalier de la Toison d'Or, *b.* 1501, *d.* 1543, and had:

JEAN DE LANNOYE, 1511-1560, Chevalier de la Toison d'Or, Seigneur de Conroy, etc., Chamberlain to Emperor Charles V., of the Holy Roman

---

*Guelph, Prince of the Scyrri, A. D. 476, had:
Guelph, Prince of Bavaria, 590, who had:
Guelph, Chamberlain of France, 613, who had:
Guelph, Comte de Bavaria, 670, who had:
Adelbertus, Comte de Bavaria, 756, who had:
Wolfhardus, Comte de Lucca, 823, who had:
Boniface, Comte de Lucca, 850, who had:
Adelbert, Duc de Tuscany, 871, who had:
Boniface, Comte de Lucca, 884, who had:
Segisfrede, Prince de Lucca, 900, who had:
Adelbert, Marquis de Tuscany, 950, who had:
Otbert, Comte-Palatine, 974, who had:
Otbert, Marquis de Liguria, 1014, who had:
Azo, Marquis d'Este, 1030, who had:
Azo, Marquis d'Este, 1097, (also descended from the Actii of ancient Rome, B. C. 600, through Kings of Rome), who had:
Guelph, Comte d'Altdorf, Duc de Bavaria, 1101, who had:
Henry III Duc de Bavaria, 1120, who had:
Henry IV, Duc de Bavaria and Saxe, 1141, who had:
Henry V, Duc de Bavaria and Saxe, 1195, who had:
Henry VI, Duc de Bavaria and Saxe, 1200, who had:
Agnes *m.* 1225 Othon, Duc de Bavaria, and had:
Agnes, *m.* Helin, Marquis de Franchimont, and had:
Helin II, Marquis de Franchimont, who had:
Jean, Marquis de Franchimont, *m.* 1312 Mahaut de la Noye, and de Lys, heiress, and had:
Hugues de Franchimont, Seigneur de Lannoye, de Lys, &c., *d.* 1349, who had:
Guibert de Lannoye, second son, Seigneur de Santes and de Beaumont, who had:
Baudouin le Begue, de Lannoye, lord of Molembais, governor of Lille, Grand Master of the Order of the Golden Fleece, *d.* 1474, who had:
Baudouin de Lannoye, Chevalier de la Toison d'Or, who had:
Philippe de Lannoye, (†) Chevalier de la Toison d'Or, aforesaid.

(†) The present hereditary Chief of the House de Lannoy, is His Princely Grace, Edgar Honore Marie de Lannoy, Comte de Lannoy de Clervaux, and Prince de Rheina-Wolbec (Fürst von Rheina-Wolbec).

Arms: 1 and 4; *Ar.*, 3 lions, (2 and 1), rampant; vert., armed and tongued, *gu.*, crowned, *or.* (Lannoy). 2 and 3; *Ar.*, 3 lions, (2 and 1), rampant; *gu.*, armed, tongued and crowned, *or.* (Barbançon). Crest: Head and neck of a unicorn, *ar.*, accornée, crinée and onglée, *or.* on a ducally crowned helmet. Mantling, *ar*, and *vert.* Motto: "Bonnes Nouvelles." Supporters: Two unicorns, *ar.*, accornées, crinées, and onglées, *or.* with banners; dexter, bearing Lannoy arms; sinster, Barbançon arms.

Empire. He m. Jeanne, daughter of Louis de Ligne, Seigneur de Barbançon, and had.

GYSBERT DE LANNOY, b. 1545, the first Protestant of his family, Seigneur de Tourcoing, in Flanders. He had:

JEAN DE LANNOY, 1570-1604. He removed from Tournai to Leiden, Holland, 1599. He m. 1601, Walloon Church, Leiden, Marie le Mahieu, and had:

PHILIPPE DE LANNOY, b. Leiden, 1602, *bapt.* in Walloon Church, Leiden, 7 December, 1603. His mother (Marie le Mahieu), established twelve Houses of Refuge (Hospices), for the persecuted Huguenots and Protestants, who came from all countries to Leiden. The famous Pastor, John Robinson, leader of the Pilgrims, there sought refuge, and remained several years. Marie and her husband, Jean, were for many years the Patrons and Protectors of the fugitive Huguenots and the Mayflower Pilgrims. Two portraits of this philanthropic lady are preserved in the Leiden Museum. Philippe de Lannoy came in the ship "Fortune," in 1621, to New England, being the first French Huguenot to set foot on American soil. He served as a volunteer in the Pequot War, 1637, besides fitting out, at his expense, fifty-six men for service in that war. He d. at Bridgewater, Mass., in 1681, leaving a valuable estate, and a large collection of books. (See "Delano Family History.") He m. in Duxbury, Mass., 19 December, 1634, Hester Dewsbury, and had:

DR. THOMAS DE LANNOY, (or Delano), second son, b. Duxbury, 21 March, 1642, d. 13 April, 1723. He m. 1667, Mary, daughter of John and Priscilla Alden, both Mayflower pilgrims, and had:

JONATHAN DE LANNOY, (Delano), Sr., b. 1676, d. Duxbury, 6 January, 1765. He m. 12 January, 1699, Hannah, b. Plymouth, 28 December, 1675, daughter of Thomas and Mary (Churchill) Doty, both Mayflower pilgrims, and had:

HANNAH DE LANNOY (Delano), b. Duxbury, 28 December, 1711, d. Woolwich, Me., 25 Sept., 1768; m. Duxbury, 14 January, 1733, Ezekiel Soule, b. Duxbury, 11 February, 1711, d. Woolwich, Me., 8 December, 1768, son of Joshua Soule, of Duxbury, 1681-1767, son of John Soule, of Duxbury, 1632-1707, (and his wife, Esther Delano, 1638-1678), son of George Soule, a Mayflower pilgrim, and had:

WILLIAM SOULE, b. Duxbury, 1738, d. Alburgh, Vt., 23 March, 1811. He was a Loyalist, and had a command under Burgoyne, at Saratoga, He m. at Duxbury, Anna Sewall, d. at Alburgh, 27 March, 1825, aged 86, and had:

JOHN SOULE, b. Spencertown, N. Y., 19 March, 1772, d. Alburgh, 30 March, 1812. He m. 25 March, 1794, Sylvia Marvin, b. Brookhaven, L. I., 20 January, 1776, d. Alburgh, 17 August, 1830, daughter of Capt. Benjamin Marvin, a distinguished soldier of the "Old French War," and of the Revolutionary War, and recorded in history as one of the "Thirty-seven Patriots," and had:

ANNA SOULE, b. Alburgh, 1 November, 1796, d. Moira, N. Y., 25 June, 1852; m. at Alburgh, 20 March, 1817, Jacob Mott, of West Alburgh, Vt., b. 12 March, 1788, d. 18 November, 1849, one of the original landed proprietors of Grand Isle Co., Vt., son of Major Jacob Mott, of Dutchess Co., N. Y., a Loyalist, and British officer, and had:

ASHLEY MOTT, b. West Alburgh, 4 July, 1822, d. Poultney, Vt., 12 March, 1878. He was a temperance, educational and political leader. He m. at Essex, N. Y., 18 October, 1847, Rosetta Abigail Graves, b. Elizabethtown, N. Y., 22 February, 1822, and had:

MARY ELDORA MOTT, of Washington, D. C., b. West Alburgh, 20 June 1859, grad. Vassar College, 1880; A. B., 1885; life member of Vassar College Alumnæ Association, and Vassar Students' Aid Society; charter member of the Woman's Uni. Club, of New York; founder and president of the National Society of Colonial Daughters of American Founders and Patriots; member of Society Daughters of American Revolution; Society of Mayflower Descendants; life member of New York Genealogical and Biographical Society, the Society for the Promotion of Hellenic Studies (London), and the Classical Association, of England and Wales, etc. She m. at Minneapolis, Minn., 21 February, 1883, Harley Calvin Gage, b. Penacook (Concord), N. H., 10 November, 1852, and had: *Margaret Vivian*, of Washington, and *John Baron*, d. infant, 12 April, 1889.

THE ROYAL DESCENT
OF
MRS. WILLIAM ALFRED GILL
OF COLUMBUS, OHIO.

THE EMPEROR CHARLEMAGNE had,
Louis I., Emperor of France, who had,
Louis I., King of Bavaria, who had,
Carloman, King of Bavaria, who had,
Arnould, King of Germany, who had,
Hedwige, m. Otto of Saxony, and had,
Henry, Emperor of Germany, who had,
Hedwige, m. Hugh, of France, and had,
HUGH CAPET, King of France, who had,
Robert I., King of France, who had,
Henry I., King of France, who had,
Philip I., King of France, who had,
Louis VI., King of France, who had,
Louis VII., King of France, who had,
Philip II., King of France, who had,
Louis VIII., King of France, who had,
St. Louis, King of France, who had,
Philip III., King of France, who had,
Philip IV., King of France, who had,

THE EMPEROR CHARLEMAGNE had,
Louis I., Emperor of France, who had,
Charles II., King of France, who had,
Judith m. Baldwin, of Flanders, and had,
Baldwin II., King of Jerusalem, who had,
Arnulph the Great, Count of Flanders, who had,
Baldwin III., Count of Flanders, who had,
Arnulph II., Count of Flanders, who had,
Baldwin IV., Count of Flanders, who had,
Baldwin V., Count of Flanders, who had,
Maud, m. WILLIAM THE CONQUEROR, and had,
Henry I., King of England, who had,
Maud, m. Geoffrey, Count of Anjou, and had,
Henry II., King of England, who had,
John, King of England, who had,
Henry III., King of England, who had,
Edward I., King of England, who had,

Princess Isabella de France, m. Edward II., King of England, and had,
Edward III., King of England, who had,
John, Duke of Lancaster, who had,
Joan de Beaufort, m. Ralph, Earl of Westmoreland, and had,
Richard, Earl of Salisbury, who had,
Catherine de Neville, m. William, Lord Bonville, and had,
Cecily de Bonville, m. Thomas, Marquis of Dorset, and had,
Elizabeth de Grey, m. Gerald, 9th Earl of Kildare, and had,
Hon. Edward Fitzgerald, second son, who had,
Hon. Thomas Fitzgerald, third son, who had,
George, 16th Earl of Kildare, who had,
Hon. Robert Fitzgerald, third son, who had,
Margaret Fitzgerald, m. Toby Hall, of Mount Hall, Down, and had,
Elizabeth Hall, m. Robert Neilson, of Ballinderry, Antrim, and had,
Mary Neilson, m. John-mor Campbell, of Ballinderry, Antrim, and had,
Elizabeth Campbell, m. Henry Mitchell, of Virginia, and had,
Belinda Strother Mitchell, m. William A. Gill, Columbus, O., and had,

1. Lillie Thomas, wife of Earle Clarke Derby, Columbus, O,
2. Frances Eugenia, wife of William Theo. Smith, Columbus, O.

PEDIGREE CIV

EDWARD III, King of England, had, by his wife, Lady Philippa, daughter of William, Count of Holland and Hainault, also of Royal Descent:

JOHN OF GAUNT, Duke of Lancaster, who had by his third wife, Lady Katherine, daughter of Sir Payn Roet, of Hainault, and widow of Sir Otes Swynford:

LADY JOAN DE BEAUFORT, widow of Robert, Lord Ferrers, of Wemme, who *m.* secondly, Sir Ralph de Neville, first Earl of Westmoreland, K. G. (second wife), and had:

RICHARD DE NEVILLE, first Earl of Salisbury, who *m.* Lady Alice, daughter of Thomas de Montacute, fourth Earl of Salisbury, and had:

LADY CATHERINE DE NEVILLE, who *m.* William de Bonville, Lord Harrington, and had:

LADY CECILY DE BONVILLE, of Chuton, who *m.*, first, Sir Thomas Grey, Earl of Huntingdon, 1471, Marquis of Dorset, 1475, and had:

LADY ELIZABETH GREY, who *m.*, 1519 (second wife), Geraldoge Fitzgerald, ninth Earl of Kildare, High Treasurer and Lord Deputy in Ireland, one of the prominent characters in the history of Ireland. He was attainted of high treason, his honors forfeited and died a prisoner in the Tower of London, 12 Dec., 1534. His eldest son was executed at Tyburn, with five of his great-uncles, for alleged treason. The Earl's second son, by Lady Grey:

HON. EDWARD FITZGERALD, *b.* 17 Jan., 1528, Lieut. of Gentlemen Pensioners of England, brother to Sir Gerald, who was restored to the honors of his House, and was the eleventh Earl of Kildare, *m.* Lady Mabel, daughter of Sir John Leigh and widow of Sir John Paston, and had:

HON. THOMAS FITZGERALD, third son, brother to Gerald, fourteenth Earl of Kildare, who *m.* Lady Frances, daughter of Thomas Randolph, Postmaster-General of England in Elizabeth's reign, and had:

GEORGE FITZGERALD, who succeeded as the sixteenth Earl of Kildare. He m., 15 Aug., 1630, Lady Joan Boyle, d. 11 March, 1655, daughter of Richard, Earl of Cork, and had:

HON. ROBERT FITZGERALD, third son, b. 17 Aug., 1637, d. in 1697, brother to Wentworth, seventeenth Earl of Kildare, the father of John, eighteenth Earl, who d. s. p. m. 1707. He m., in 1663, Mary, daughter of James Clotworthy, of Monnimore, County Londonderry, brother to John, Viscount Massereene, and had by her, who d. 31 March, 1734:

LADY MARGARET FITZGERALD, d. 8 Dec., 1758, sister to Robert Fitzgerald, 1675-1743, who succeeded as nineteenth Earl of Kildare, and was the father of James, 1722-1773, twentieth Earl of Kildare, and first Duke of Leinster. She m., 16 Dec., 1712, Toby Hall, Esq., of Mount Hall, Downshire, Ireland, son and heir of Roger Hall, Esq., of Mount Hall (and his wife m., 1686, daughter of Sir Toby Pointz, Kt., of Acton, County Armagh), son of Francis Hall, of Mount Hall, will proved 1706 (and his wife, Mary, daughter of Judge Lyndon), son of William Hall, who purchased forfeited estates in County Antrim and died at his seat, Red Bog, in County Antrim, in 1640. Lady Margaret had by Toby Hall, of Mount Hall, one son and five daughters.

Their youngest daughter,

ELIZABETH HALL, sister to Roger Hall, of Narrow Water House, near Warine Point, County Down, 1713-1797, who had issue, and to Catherine Watts ("my aunt Lady Kitty Watts," so referred to in correspondence of Mr. Hall Neilson). Her other sisters died unmarried. She m. Robert Neilson, Gent., of Ballinderry parish, County Antrim, who d. there in 1800. From "Marron Family Bible,"—"Elizabeth Hall, wife of Robert Neilson, Sr., died in Ireland, 22 Sept., 1803." They had ten children, who removed to the United States after the '98 rebellion. Of these,

1.—JOHN NEILSON, b. 26 Aug., 1771. He m., in 1810, Maria Dent, and resided in Alabama and Florida. It is thought he was buried at Blandford, near his brother Thomas. His son, *Robert*, b. 1827, m. Charlotte Warren.

2.—MARY HALL NEILSON, b. 17 March, 1773, d. at Brownsville, Ill., 28 July, 1834. She m., in 180-, in Ballinderry parish, County Antrim, John More Campbell, of this parish, and resided near the ruins of Portmore Castle, near Glenavy and near Lough Neagh Lake in County Antrim, where their children were born. They removed to America, and finally settled at Brownsville, Ill., where Mr. Campbell *d.* 20 July, 1834. Their children were:

I.—ELIZA NEILSON CAMPBELL, *b.* in 1810, *d.* in Sept., 1871. She *m.*, in Augusta County, Va., Feb., 1839, George Henry Mitchell, of Augusta County, Va., *d.* 1863 (son of Henry Mitchell, of Augusta County, Va., and his wife *m.*, 20 Nov., 1811, Mary, sister of Joseph Tuley, of "Tuleyries," Millwood, Clarke County, Va., 1764-1825), and had:

1.—BELINDA STROTHER MITCHELL (see page 489). She *m.*, 3 Oct., 1867, in Philadelphia, Pa., William Alfred Gill, of Columbus, Ohio, and had:

1.—LILLIE THOMAS GILL, *b.* 24 Aug., 1870, who *m.* 15 Nov., 1892, Earle Clarke Derby, of Columbus, Ohio, *b.* 13 Aug., 1865.

II.—FRANCES EUGENIA GILL, *b.* 17 Feb., 1873, who *m.*, 3 June, 1896, William Theodore Smith, of Columbus, Ohio, *b.* 17 June,, 1869.

2.—MARY FRANCES MITCHELL, *m.* Henry Huntington Fitch, and had:

I.—MARY LEE FITCH, *m.* William Egbert Fairchild Steele, and had: WILLIAM CULLEN BRYANT STEELE.

II.—EDWARD HUNTINGTON FITCH, *unm.*

3.—REV. ROBERT HALL MITCHELL, Chaplain C. S. Army, *d. unm.*, 1862.

4.—THOMAS NEILSON MITCHELL, *d. unm.*, in C. S. Army.

II.—SARAH NICHOLSON CAMPBELL, *m.*, 1838, Joseph Tuley Mitchell, of Augusta County, Va. (a brother of George Henry Mitchell, aforesaid), and had:

1.—MARY ELIZA MITCHELL, *unm.*

2.—JOSEPH TULEY MITCHELL, JR., of Roanoke, Va., *m.* Bettie W. Young, and had:

I.—ARCHER MITCHELL, *m.* Margaret Callum.

II.—ELEANOR, wife of Dr. Richard W. Frey, of Roanoke, Va.

III.—BELINDA TULEY MITCHELL, *unm.*

3.—ELNA MORE MITCHELL, *m.*, first, Augustus W. Greene, and *m.*, secondly, Rev. Alfred N. Anson, son of Canon Frederick Anson, Chaplain to Queen Victoria. Issue by first *m.*, *Frances W.*, *m.* A. N. Barr; *Joseph Campbell*, and *Mary Newport*, and by second *m.*, *Hilda Vernon* and *Edith Vernon*.

4.—WILLIAM CAMPBELL MITCHELL, of "Hillcrest," near Staunton, Va. He *m.* Laura Rennie and had: *Ellen Douglas*, *Ethel Warren*, *Florence Thomas* and *Norman Tuley*.

5.—EDMONIA LEE MITCHELL, *m.* R. L. B. Lorraine, of Richmond, Va., and had:

    I.—NED M. LORRAINE, *m.* Susie Elain.
    II.—MARIE L., wife of William Colvin.
    III.—EDMONIA LEE,
    IV.—CAMERON R.
    V.—GRACE N.

6.—HENRY ARCHER MITCHELL, *d. unm.*, in C. S. Army.

7.—FRANCES ANN MITCHELL, *m.* Dr. Henry C. Perrow, of Nelson County, Va., and had:

    BELLE PERROW, *m.* Charles Wright, of Nelson County, Va., and had: *Perrow Gilmer*, *Mary Mitchell*, *Eleanor* and *Tuley Allen*.

III.—ANN PORTER CAMPBELL, *m.* William Limerick, of Brownsville, Ill. *Issue.*

IV.—MARY MORE CAMPBELL, *m.* William Thompson, of St. Louis, Mo. *Issue.*

V.—EVELYN HALL CAMPBELL, *unm.*

3.—THOMAS NEILSON, *b.* 2 Feb., 1775, *d. s. p.*, 4 Oct., 1847, buried in the Blandford Churchyard, near Petersburg, Va., with a monument. He *m.* Anna ——, in Ireland. His wife died there, and was buried with her husband at Blandford, with two of his brothers.

4.—WILLIAM HALL NEILSON, *b.* 28 Feb., 1777, *d. unm.* at Brownsville, Ill., 20 April, 1834. He resided in Louisville, Ky., and in 1825 was of the local committee to entertain General Lafayette upon his visit to that city. His portrait was engraved by St. Memin in 1810.

PEDIGREE CIV.—Continued.

5.—ANNE NEILSON, *b.* in Jan., 1779; *m.*, 8 Nov., 1798, Constantine Marron, a son of Bernard Marron, of County Antrim, and his wife, Margaret O'Neill, presumed to have been a sister to John O'Neill, Viscount O'Neill, of Shane's Castle, who was slain at Antrim by some '98 rebels, 7 June, 1796. Constantine Marron and wife and infant son came to America in June, 1800, and settled near Augusta, Ga., where he *d.*, 21 March, 1821, aged 51 years. Of their children,

> I.—JOHN MARRON, *b.* in County Antrim, near Shane's Castle, 6 Oct., 1799, *d.* 3 March, 1859. For many years, until his death, he was Third Assistant Postmaster General at Washington, D. C. He *m.*, 23 Feb., 1832, Eliza Ann, daughter of Thomas Baker and Mary Pamela (Davis) Dyer, and had:
>
>> MARY PAMELA MARRON, eldest daughter, who *m.*, 21 Sept., 1865, William Oswald Dundas, son of William Hepburn Dundas, sometime Second Assistant Postmaster General, a son of John Dundas, of Alexandria, Va., *b.* 1759, a son of James Dundas, of Manor and Philadelphia, 1734-1788, whose Royal Descent is in p. 100.
>
> II.—ELIZABETH MARRON, *b.* 15 Aug., 1802.
>
> III.—ROBERT HALL MARRON, *b.* 27 March, 1804, *d.* at Shawneetown, Ill. He *m.* 21 Aug., 1842, Adeline Lynch.
>
> IV.—MARY ANN MARRON, *b.* 9 April, 1806.
>
> V.—SAMUEL NEILSON MARRON, *b.* 15 Dec., 1807.
>
> VI.—THOMAS WILLIAM HARRISON MARRON, *b.* 31 Jan., 1810.
>
> VII.—ELIZA MARRON, *b.* 9 April, 1812.
>
> VIII.—MARGARET ANN MARRON, *b.* 20 April, 1815.
>
> IX.—MARIA MARRON, *b.* 8 Feb., 1817.
>
> X.—ELIZA ELEANOR MARRON, *b.* 24 Dec., 1819.

6.—JAMES NEILSON, *b.* in Feb., 1781, *d. unm.*, Brownsville, Ill., 24 Aug., 1828.

7.—ROBERT NEILSON, *b.* 5 March, 1783, *d. unm.*, Louisville, Ky., 2 July, 1833.

8.—SAMUEL NEILSON, of New York City, *b.* 30 March, 1785, *d.* 21 Nov., 1834. He *m.*, in Sept., 1825, Joanna Bayard, *b.* 17 July, 1802, *d.* 18 Jan., 1846, a daughter of John Gardiner and Ann Hude (Kearney) Warren, of New York. Their only child:

ROBERT HALL NEILSON, *m.* Mary, daughter of Rev. Alexander McClelland, and had:

JOANNA BAYARD NEILSON, who *m.* Henry Augustus Neilson, of New Brunswick, N. J., son of John Butler Coles Neilson (and his wife, Helena, daughter of Dr. John Neilson, son of Brigadier General John Neilson, of New Brunswick, 1745-1833, Colonel of the Second Regiment, Middlesex County militia in the Revolutionary War), son of William, and grandson of William Neilson, of New York City, 1763, and his first wife, Susanna Hude (his second wife was Kitty Duer, of New York), and had:

    I.—ROBERT HUDE NEILSON, of New York.

    II.—MARY NEILSON.

    III.—HELENA BLEECKER NEILSON.

    IV.—KATHARINE MCCLELLAND NEILSON.

9.—HALL NEILSON, *b.* 30 March, 1787, *d.* in Washington, D. C. He resided in Norfolk and Richmond, Va. He *m.*, first, about 1833, Edmonia Lee, *b.* about 1815, daughter of William Byrd Page, of "Fairfield," Clarke County, Va. (son of Mann Page, of "Fairfield," who was of Royal Descent, see p. 334, A. R. D. IV.), and his wife, Ann, sister of General "Light Horse Harry" Lee and daughter of Hon. Richard Henry Lee, of Virginia. He *m.*, secondly, Feb., 1839, Mary Archer, daughter of Henry and Mary (Tuley) Mitchell, aforesaid. Hall Neilson had by his first wife:

I.—EDMONIA LEE NEILSON, *b.* 1834, living at Norfolk, *unm.*

II.—ANN NEILSON, *d. unm.*

III.—WILLIAM BYRD PAGE NEILSON, *d. unm.*

Hall Neilson had by his second wife:

I.—MARY TULEY NEILSON, who *m.* Rev. Augustus Jackson, of Washington, D. C., and had:

    1.—FANNY ARCHER JACKSON, of Washington, *unm.*

    2.—MARY ROWAN JACKSON, a vice-president general of the Society Daughters of the American Revolution. She *m.* William Dunham Kearfott, of Mount Clair, N. J., and had:

        I.—THORNTON CAMPBELL; II.—MARY TULEY.

3.—HALL NEILSON JACKSON, of Cincinnati. *Issue.*

4.—STUART WELLS JACKSON, of New York. *Issue.*

5.—REGINALD HEBER JACKSON, of New York.

II.—THOMAS HALL NEILSON, of New York, *m.* CATHERINE, daughter of George Barton, of Philadelphia. No issue.

III.—FRANCES ANN NEILSON, *m.* Stuart Wells, M.D., Surgeon in U. S. Navy.

10.—ELIZA NEILSON, *b.* 9 January, 1791. *d. unm.*, 14 May, 1815, at Bandon, near Cork, Ireland.

PEDIGREE OF MRS. PHILIP H. COOPER, MORRISTOWN, N. J.

- Roger Bigod.
- Hugh Bigod.
- Ralph Bigod. = Saire de Quincy.
- Isabel Fitzgeoffrey. Roger de Quincy.
- Isabel Vipount. Elene le Zouche.
- Idonia de Leybourne. Geoffrey de Saye. Eudo le Zouche.
- William de Leybourne. William de Saye. Eva de Berkeley.
- Idonia de Leybourne. = Geoffrey de Saye. Isabel de Saye. William d'Albini.
  - Juliana de Northwode. Thomas de Musgrave. William d'Albini.
  - John de Northwode. Thomas de Musgrave. Isabel d'Albini. = Robert de Roos.
  - Juliana Digges. Richard de Musgrave. Robert de Roos.
  - Elizabeth Aucher. Richard de Musgrave. Sacer de Roos.
  - Henry Aucher. Elinor Thornborough. Robert de Roos.
  - Henry Aucher. William Thornborough. Margery Gifford.
  - John Aucher. Rowland Thornborough. John Gifford.
  - James Aucher. Anne Roos. William Gifford.
  - Anthony Aucher. Anne Dixon. Margery Chauncy.
  - Edward Aucher. Margaret Sandys. John Chauncy.
  - Elizabeth Lovelace. Edwin Sandys. John Chauncy.
  - William Lovelace. = Anne Barne. John Chauncy.
    - Anne Barne. Henry Chauncy.
    - Anne Gorsuch. = George Chauncy.
    - Anne Todd. Charles Chauncy.
    - Thomas Todd. Sarah Chauncy.
    - William Todd.
    - Elizabeth Hubbard.
    - Anne Taylor.
    - James Taylor.
    - Keturah Leitch Taylor. = Horatio Turpin Harris.
      - George Washington Ward. = Josephine Bonaparte Harris. Jordena Cannon Harris. = John Taintor Foote.
        - Elizabeth Johnson Ward. = Charles Avery Doremus. Katharine Jordena Foote. = Philip Henry Cooper.
          - Katharine Ward Doremus. Dorothy Bradford Cooper. Leslie Bradford Cooper.

- Henry de Bohun.
- Humphrey de Bohun.
- Alice de Toni.
- Ralph de Toni. Robert Fitzwalter.
- Alice de Beauchamp. Walter Fitzwalter.
- Thomas de Beauchamp. Robert Fitzwalter.
- Joan Basset. Ida de la Warde.
- Alice Basset. Joan de Meynell.
  - Hugo de Meynell.
  - Richard de Meynell.
  - Ralph de Meynell.
  - Thomasine de Dethick.
  - Margaret Basset.
  - William Basset.
  - Elizabeth Beresford.
  - Thomas Beresford.
  - Ellen Chetwode.
  - Roger Chetwode.
  - Richard Chetwode. = Richard Chetwode.
    - Grace Bulkley.
    - Gershom Bulkley.
      - John Bulkley.
      - Gershom Bulkley.
      - Sarah Taintor.
      - John Taintor.
      - Sarah Foote.

- William Malet. = Helewyse de Wahull.
- Mabel Vyron. John de Wahull.
  - Thomas de Wahull.
  - John de Wahull.
  - Nicholas de Wahull.
  - Thomas de Wahull.
  - Thomas de Wahull.
  - John de Wahull.
  - Fulke de Wodehull.
  - Nicholas de Wodehull.
  - Anthony de Woodhull.
  - Agnes de Woodhull.

PEDIGREE CV.

HENRY I., King of France (see p. 444), had,

HUGH THE GREAT, Duke of France (pp. 444, 83, 11), who had,

ISABEL, *m.* secondly, William, second Earl of Surrey, and had,

WILLIAM DE WARREN, third Earl of Surrey (p. 11), who had,

COUNTESS ISABEL, *m.* secondly, Hameline Plantagenet, and had,

ISABEL, *m.* Roger, Earl of Norfolk, a Magna Charta Surety, and had,

HUGH BIGOD, a Magna Charta Surety, Earl of Norfolk, who had,

SIR RALPH BIGOD, knt., third son (see pp. 11, 83), who had,

ISABEL, *m.* secondly John Fitzgeoffrey, of Barkhampstead, and had,

ISABEL FITZGEOFFREY (sister to John fitz John, lord justice of Ireland, p. 11), who *m.* Robert, third Baron de Vipount, of Totney Castle, high sheriff of Westmoreland, *d.s.p.m.*, 1265, and had,

IDONEA DE VIPOUNT, who *m.* Roger de Leybourne, *d.* 1272, and had

WILLIAM DE LEYBOURNE, constable of Pevensay Castle, father of

IDONEA DE LEYBOURNE, *m.* Geoffrey, Baron de Saye, *d.* 131-, and had,

JULIANNA DE SAYE, who *m.* Sir Roger de Northwode, in Kent, who succeeded his grandfather as second baron, *b.* 1307, *d.* 1361. He was the son and heir of John de Northwode, *d.v.p.* (and his wife, Lady Agnes, daughter of William, first Baron de Granson, or Grandison, *d.* 1335, see Beltz's "Order of the Garter"), son and heir of Sir John, first Baron de Northwode, *d.* 26 May, 1319. In 1319-20, Sir Bartholomew de Badlesmere was given by Edward II., the custody and marriage of Roger de Northwode, aged 13 years, and he sold the "marriage" to "Lady Idonea de Leybourne, late wife of Sir Geoffrey de Saye, Sr.," who married him to her daughter Julianna, he being then between 14 and 15 years old. See a XIV century pedigree of the Northwode family in Vol. 2, "Archaelogia Cantiana." Sir Roger had by Lady Julianna,

SIR JOHN DE NORTHWODE, third Baron, *d.* 27 Feb., 1379. He *m.* Joan, daughter of Robert Harte, of Feversham, Kent, and had,

LADY JULIANNA DE NORTHWODE. In the settlement of the Granson, or Grandison, estate, in 1382, she was one of the heirs, and wife of John

Digges, of Barham manor, in Kent. See Arch. Canti., Vol. 2., pp. 11, 25, &c. Their daughter,

ELIZABETH DIGGES, *m.* Henry Aucher, 1370-1400 (see Burke's "Extinct Baronetages" pp. 27-8, Berry's "Kent," p. 222, and Hasted's "Kent"), and had,

HENRY AUCHER, of Losenham Manor, Kent, who had by his second wife, Joane, daughter of Thomas St. Leger, of Otterden Manor, Kent, *d.* 1409, second son of Sir Ralph St. Leger, of Ulcombe, Kent.

HENRY AUCHER, of Otterden Manor, 1448, *m.* Alice Boleyne, and had,

JOHN AUCHER, of Otterden Manor, *d.* 23 April, 1503; *m.* Alice Church, and had,

JAMES AUCHER, of Otterden Manor, *d.* 6 Jan., 1508, who *m.* Alice, daughter of Thomas Hilles, of Eggerton, Kent, and had,

SIR ANTHONY AUCHER, of Otterden, Bishopsbourne, and Hautesbourne manors, in Kent 1530. He *m.* Lady Affra, daughter of Sir William Cornwallis, K. B., of Suffolk Co., ancestor of the Earls of Cornwallis, and his wife, Elizabeth, daughter of John Stanford, and had,

EDWARD AUCHER, second son, who inherited the manors of Bishopsbourne and Hautesbourne, He *m.* Mabel, living 1563, daughter of Sir Thomas Wrothe, and had,

ELIZABETH AUCHER, who *d.* 3 Dec., 1627, and is buried in the Canterbury Cathedral. She *m.* Sir William Lovelace, of Bethersden, Kent, knighted in July, 1599; buried 12 October, 1629, age 68, and had,

SIR WILLIAM LOVELACE, of Woolwich, Kent, 1583-1628, knighted in 1609, killed at the seige of Grolle; will proved in 1628. He *m.* Anne, daughter of Sir William Barne, of Woolwich; will proved in 1633, and had,

ANNE LOVELACE, *d.* in Virginia, 1657, sister to Gov. Francis Lovelace and Sir Richard Lovelace, poet and dramatist. She *m.* in 1628, Rev. Dr. John Gorsuch, rector of Walkeholme, Herts, who was sequestered, and murdered, in 1642, son of Daniel Gorsuch, of London, merchant (see Chauncy's "Hertfordshire," II, 88; London "Visitations," 1633; Walker's "Sufferings of the Clergy;" Cussan's "Hertfordshire," II, 77, &c.), and had *Daniel, John, William* and *Catherine,* named in the "Visitation" pedigree of their grandfather, 1633, and *Anne, Charles, Richard, Lovelace,* and *Robert,* who came to Virginia and Maryland (see Va. His. Mag. III. 83). Their daughter,

ANNE GORSUCH, living in 1675, who m. in 1655, Captain Thomas Todd, of "Toddsbury," in Ware parish, Gloucester Co., Va., and of Baltimore Co., Maryland, 1664, of which he was a Burgess in 1674. He died at sea in 1676; will proved 30 May, 1677. Their son,

MAJOR THOMAS TODD, 1660-1725, of "Toddsbury," J. P. in Gloucester Co., 1698-1702; d. 16 Jan., 1725 (see "William and Mary Quaterly," III. 116). He m. Elizabeth (Bernard?), and had,

WILLIAM TODD, of King and Queen Co., Va., Justice of the Peace, will signed in 1736. He m. 1709, Martha Vicaries, b. 1680, and had,

ELIZABETH TODD, b. 1710; m. in 1728, Benjamin Hubbard, of Gloucester Co., Va., 1702-1784. Member of the Committee of Safety, Gloucester Co., and had,

ANNE HUBBARD, b. 26 March, 1738; m. 1 June, 1758, his first wife, Col. James Taylor, Jr., of "Midway," Caroline Co., Va., Burgess 1732-1814, and had,

GENERAL JAMES TAYLOR, b. 19 April, 1769, at "Midway," d. 7 November, 1848, at Newport, Kentucky. See Collins' History of Kentucky, Appleton's Enc. Am. Bio. Dict., etc. He m. 15 Nov., 1795, at Tuckahoe, Ky., Keturah Moss, 1774-1866, and had,

KETURAH LEITCH TAYLOR, 1802-1871, m. in 1821, Horatio Turpin Harris, 1790-1855, son of Major Jordan Harris, and grandson of Lieut. John Harris, of Powhattan Co., Va., both of whom were original members of the Society of the Cincinnati. Mr. Harris was a member of the Kentucky Legislature, in 1832, and Mayor of Newport, Ky., and had by his wife, Keturah,

1.—JOSEPHINE BONAPARTE HARRIS, b. 17 July, 1823, d. 13 Oct., 1902; m. 15 June, 1847, George Washington Ward, b. Georgetown, Ky., 1808, d. at Leota Landing, Miss., 2 March, 1870 (son of Col. William Ward, b. Somerset Co., Md., and his wife, Sarah, daughter of Col. Robert Johnson, of Scott Co., Ky., m. in 1795), and had,

I.—KATHARINE WARD, m. William W. Richards, of New York.

II.—EDWARD; III. WILLIAM HARRIS;

IV.—ELIZABETH JOHNSON WARD, b. 24 May, 1853; m. in Washington city, 4 August, 1880, Prof. Charles Avery Doremus, M.D., Ph.D., of New York, b. 6 Sept., 1851, son of Robert Ogden Doremus, M.D., Ph.D., of New York, 1824-1906, and had,

KATHARINE WARD DOREMUS, b. 25 March, 1889.

V.—ANNA HARRIS, *d. unm.*, VI. HELEN JOHNSON; VII. ROBERT J., *d. unm.*

VIII.—DAVID LEITCH WARD, *m.* 1888, Anna Lee Gaskell, and had,

    1.—GEORGE, *b.* 1889; 2. JOSEPHINE, *b.* 1896.

2.—JORDENA CANNON HARRIS, 1827-1853, *m.* 3 Sept., 1845, John Taintor Foote, *b.*, New York, 27 May, 1819; *d.* Morristown, N. J., 5 July, 1902, son of Israel Foote, of New York, and Sarah Taintor, his wife, and had,

  I.—LOUISE FOOTE, *m.* 12 Oct., 1876, John Stuart, of Detroit, Mich., and had,

    1.—ELLEN STUART, *m.* 17 Oct., 1899, Victor Blue, Comd'r. U. S. Navy, and had,

      STUART BLUE, *b.* in 1902.

    2.—MARION STUART, *m.* 1903, Charles Terry, M.D.

  II.—ELLEN FOOTE, *d.* in 1878.

  III.—GEORGE WARD FOOTE, of Newport, R. I., *m.* in 1879, Margaret Moore, and had,

    1.—JOHN TAINTOR; 2. HAROLD GODWIN; 3. KENNETH MOORE.

  IV.—KATHARINE JORDENA FOOTE, *b.* 18 Oct., 1853, *m.*, New York, 24 June, 1884, Philip Henry Cooper, Rear Admiral, U. S. Navy (retired), and had,

    1.—DOROTHY BRADFORD COOPER, *b.* 9 March, 1889.

    2.—LESLIE BRADFORD COOPER, *b.* 24 March, 1894.

3.—ANNA MARIA HARRIS, *m.* 13 June, 1855, James J. O'Fallon, of St. Louis, Mo., *b.* 31 July, 1852, *d.* 5 April, 1902, and had,

  HARRIS TAYLOR O'FALLON, of St. Louis, Mo.

4.—VIRGINIA MOSS HARRIS, *b* 16 April, 1843, *d.* 14 Nov., 1908, *m.* 5 July, 1870, his second wife, James Van Voast, Colonel, U. S. Army (retired), of Cincinnati, and had,

  I.—VIRGINIA REMSEN VAN VOAST, of Cincinnati.

  II.—RUFUS ADRIAN VAN VOAST, *m.* 1908, Phoebe Bogart.

PEDIGREE CVI.

HUGH CAPET, King of France, 987, *m.* Lady Adela, daughter of Guillaume I., *tete d' etoupe,* Count of Poitiers and Auvergne, 951, created Duke of Aquitaine, *d.* 963, and his first wife, *m.* 933, Lady Gerloc, daughter of Rollo the Dane, first Duke of Normandy, and had,

ROBERT THE PIOUS, King of France, who *m.* secondly in 998, Lady Constance, daughter of William III., Count of Toulouse, and had by her,

LADY ADELA DE FRANCE, *d.* 1079, sister to Queen Matilda of England, and widow of Richard III., Duke of Normandy, who *d. s. p.,* the uncle of William the Conqueror, who *m.* 1027-8, Baldwin V., de l'Isle, Count of Flanders, 1036, and of Artois, *d.* 1067, and had,

LADY JUDITH DE FLANDERS, *d.* 1091, widow of Tostin, brother of Harold II., King of England, who *m.* his second wife, Guelph IV. (or I.). Duke of Bavaria, 1071, *d.* 1101, and had,

HENRY VII. (or III.), *le noir. d.* 1120, who *m.* Lady Wulfhilde de Saxe, daughter of Magnus, the last sovereign Duke of Saxony, of his line, *d.* 1106, by his wife, Sophie, *m.* in 1070, and had,

HENRY VIII., Duke of Bavaria and Saxony, *d.* 10 Sept. 1139. He *m.* Lady Gertrude, daughter of the Emperor Lothaire, and had by her, who *d.* 1143,

HENRY X., Duke of Bavaria and Saxony, 1154, *d.* 1195. He *m.* 1168, Lady Matilda, second wife, *d.* 1189, daughter of Henry II., King of England, and had,

HENRY DE SAXE, *le Jeune,* Palatine Count of the Rhine, *d.* 1200, who had by his wife, Lady Agnes,

LADY AGNES DE SAXE, who *m.* 1225, Otto II., (or Othon), Palatine Count of the Rhine, 1227, in right of his wife, and Duke of Bavaria, 1231, *d.* 29 Nov. 1253, son and heir of Louis I., Duke of Bavaria, 1183, (and his wife, *m.* 1204, Lady Ludomille, widow of Albert, Count of Bogen, and daughter of Przemislas, Duke of Bohemia), son of Otto, *le Grand,* Count Palatine of Wittelsbach, who was appointed, in 1180, Duke of Bavaria, succeeding Henry X., by his wife, Lady Agnes, daughter of Thierre, Count of Wassersburg (see "L'Art," vols. 15 and 16), and had,

LADY AGNES DE BAVARIA, who m. Hellin, Margrave, or Marquis of Franchimont, 1225, and had,

HELLIN II., Marquis of Franchimont, 1275, who m. Lady Agnes, daughter of Guilbert, Count of Duras, and had,

JEAN, Marquis of Franchimont, d. 1310, who m. Lady Mayenne (or Mahaut, or Matilda), heiress de la Noye and de Lys, and had,

HUGUES DE FRANCHIMONT, Seigneur de la Noye, de Lys, &c., d. 1349, who m. 1329, Lady Marguerite, daughter of Gilles le Maingoral, lord of Chateau de Béthune, and had,

GUILLEBERT DE LANNOYE, Seigneur de Santes, and de Beaumont, second son. He m. Lady Catherine de Molembais, an heiress, and had,

BAUDOUIN DE LANNOYE, *le Begue,* or Baldwin the stutterer, lord of Molembais, in right of his wife, Governor of Lille, Grand Master of the Order of the Golden Fleece, d. 1474, who had by his second wife, Lady Adrienne de Berlaymont,

BAUDOUIN DE LANNOYE, Chevalier de la Toison d'Or, d. 1501; m. Michele d'Esne, 1493-1519, and had,

PHILIPPE DE LANNOYE, Chevalier de la Toison d'Or, 1501-1543, who m. Lady Magdelaine, 1489-1511, daughter of Baudouin de Bourgogne, *le Batard,* 1445-1508, Seigneur de Falais, and de Lille, whose father, Philippe, *le Bon,* 1396-1467, Duke of Burgundy and the Netherlands, was the founder, and first Grand Master of L'Ordre de la Toison d'Or, and had,

JEAN DE LANNOYE, Seigneur de Conroy, Falais, Bredam, etc., Chamberlain to Charles V., Emperor of the Holy Roman Empire, d. 1560. He m. Jeanne, daughter of Louis de Ligne, Seigneur de Barbancon, and had,

GYSBERT DE LANNOYE, Seigneur de Tourcoing, in Flanders, who was the first Protestant of his family, b. 1545, d. 16—. He m. ———, and had,

JEAN DE LANNOYE, 1570-1604, who removed from Tournai, in Belgium, to Leiden, in Netherlands, in 1599, where he m., in 1601, at the Walloon Church, Marie le Mahieu, and had,

PHILIPPE DE LANNOYE, *bapt.* at the Walloon Church, 7 Dec., 1603; came to New England in 1621 (see page 487); m. at Duxbury, Mass., 19 Dec., 1634, Hester Dewsbury, and had, besides other children, JONATHAN (see below), and

1.—HESTER DELANO, 1638-1678, *m.* John Soule, 1632-1707 (see page 487), and had,

> MOSES SOULE, 1676-1751, *m.* Mercy Southworth, 1670-1728, and had,
>
> > BARNABAS SOULE, of Freeport, Me., *b.* 25 Mar., 1758; *d.* 25 Jan., 1823; *m.* 17 May, 1781. Jane, *d.* 5 Mar., 1825, daughter of David Dennison, and had,
> >
> > > ESTHER SOULE, *d.* at Mobile, Ala., in 1862, aged 77; *m.* at Freeport, 4 Aug., 1805. Clement Jordan, *b.* Gorham, Me., *d.* at Tuscaloosa, Ala., in 1840, aged 61, and had,
> > >
> > > > JANE BRADBURY JORDAN, *b.* Sparta, Tenn., 27 Jan., 1822; *d.* Washington, D. C., 8 Nov., 1894; *m.* at Montevallo, Ala., 14 Sept., 1845, Hermon Osgood Parker, of Suncook, N. H., *b.* Allentown, N. H., 11 July, 1816, lost at sea, 25 Oct., 1865, and had,
> > > >
> > > > > EMMA JOSEPHINE PARKER, *b.* Mobile, Ala., 12 Nov., 1856; *m.* at Washington, D. C., 23 Nov., 1881. William Wesley Karr, of Memphis, Tenn.; *b.* New Orleans, 19 Feb. 1833, and had,
> > > > >
> > > > > > I.—CHARLES HENDERSON, b. 30 Mar., 1883; II. ARTHUR JAMIESON, *b.* 12 Mar., 1886; III. EMMA FABER, *b.* 26 May, 1888; IV. WILLIAM MIDDLETON, *b.* 7 May; *d.* 9 May, 1894.

2.—JONATHAN DELANO, of Duxbury, who *m.* Mercy Warren, a granddaughter of Richard Warren, *d.* 1628, who came in the Mayflower, 1620, and had,

> JONATHAN DELANO, JR., of Tolland, Conn., who *m.* Hannah Doten, a granddaughter of Edward Doten, *d.* 1655, who came in the "Mayflower," 1620, and had,
>
> > SUSANNA DELANO, *b.* 23 June, 1724; *m.* 5 Nov., 1746, Capt. Noah Grant, Jr., of Tolland and Coventry, Conn., 1718-175—, an officer in the French and Indian War, and had,
> >
> > > CAPT. NOAH GRANT, 3D., *b.* at Tolland, 20 June, 1748, an officer in the Revolutionary Army; *d.* at Maysville, Ky., 14 Feb., 1819. He *m.* at Greensburg, Pa., 4 March, 1792, Mrs. Rachel (Miller) Kelly, and had by her, who *d.* 10 April, 1805.
> > >
> > > > JESSE ROOT GRANT, *b.* Greensburg, Pa., 23 Jan., 1794, sometime postmaster at Covington, Ky., where he *d.* 29 June, 1873. He *m.* at

Point Pleasant, Ohio, 24 June, 1821, Hannah Simpson, *b.* Montgomery County, Pa., 23 Nov., 1798, *d.* Jersey City, N. J., 11 May, 1883, and had, with other children,

ULYSSES S. GRANT, 1822-1885, General of U. S. Army, and twice elected President of the United States. He *m.* at St. Louis, Mo., 22 Aug., 1848, Julia Boggs, daughter of Col. Fred. Dent, U. S. Army (see **A. H.** Grant's "Grant Family"), and had,

1.—FRED. DENT GRANT, *b.* 30 May, 1850, Maj. Gen. U. S. Army; *m.* at Chicago, 20 Oct., 1874, Ida M. Honore, and had,

    I.—JULIA, *b.* 7 June, 1876; II. ULYSSES S., *b.* 4 July, 1881.

2.—ULYSSES S. GRANT, *b.* 22 July, 1852; *m.* at New York, 1 Nov., 1880, Fanny J. Chaffee, and had,

    I.—MIRIAM; II. CHAFFEE; III. JULIA DENT; IV. FANNY; V. ULYSSES S.

3.—NELLIE WRENSHALL GRANT, *b.* 4 July, 1855; *m.* at Washington city, 21 May 1874, Algernon C. P. Sartoris, *d.* 3 Feb, 1893, and had,

    I.—GRANT, *d.* 21 May, 1876; II. ALGERNON EDWARD; III. VIVIEN MAY; IV. ROSEMARY.

4.—JESSE R. GRANT, b. 6 Feb. 1858; *m.* 21 Sept., 1880, Elizabeth Chapman, and had,

    I.—NELLIE; II. CHAPMAN.

PEDIGREE CVII.

DAVID I., King of Scotland, 1124, *d.* 1153, (see pp. 194, 437), had by his wife, Lady Matilda, *d.* 1134, daughter of Waltheof, Earl of Northumberland, etc., who was executed by order of William the Conqueror, in 1075,

PRINCE HENRY, Earl of Huntingdon, etc., only son, *d. v. p.* 1152. He *m.* 1139, Lady Ada, daughter of William de Warren, second Earl of Surrey, and had by her, who *d.* 1178,

PRINCESS MARGARET, widow of Conan le Petit, Count of Bretagne, and Earl of Richmond, *d.* 20 Feb., 1171. She *m.* secondly, Humphrey IV., Baron de Bohun, lord of Hereford, constable of England, and had,

HENRY DE BOHUN, fifth feudal baron, created in 1199, Earl of Hereford, and Earl of Essex, hereditary constable of England. He was active in securing the Magna Charta from King John, and became one of the twenty-five sureties for it in 1215. He *d.* 1220, having issue by his wife, Lady Maud, sister to Geoffrey de Mandeville, a surety for the Magna Charta, and daughter of Geoffrey fitz Piers, Baron de Mandeville, who was created in 1199, Earl of Essex, lord justice of England,

HUMPHREY V., DE BOHUN, sixth baron, Earl of Hereford and Essex, and lord high constable, but being taken prisoner while in rebellion was not permitted to enjoy his honors. He *m.* first, Lady Maud, daughter of Henry, 4th feudal Baron d'Eu, and had by her,

LADY ALICE DE BOHUN, who *m.* Ralph, seventh feudal Baron Toni, of Flamsted, in Herts, and had,

RALPH DE TONI, lord of Flamsted, who had by his wife, Clarissa,

LADY ALICE DE TONI, 1285-1325, sister and heir to Robert, Baron de Toni, of Flamsted, and widow of Sir Thomas de Leyborne. She *m.*, his first wife, Sir Guy de Beauchamp, second Earl of Warwick, *d.* 1315, also of royal descent, and had,

LADY LUCIA DE BEAUCHAMP (sister to Sir Thomas and Sir John de Beauchamp, both original members of the Noble Order of Knights of the Garter), who *m.* Sir Robert de Napton, feudal lord of Napton, in Warwickshire, and had,

ADAM DE NAPTON, heir, lord of Napton, *d.* 1371. He *m.* Margaret Holiar, or Helier, and had,

PEDIGREE CVII.—Continued.

CLEMINTINA DE NAPTON, who *m.* Robert de Keverell, in Warwickshire, and had,

AUGUSTUS DE KEVERELL, who *m.* Agnes, daughter of William de Frankton, in Warwickshire, and had,

WILLIAM DE KEVERELL (see Warwickshire Visitation) whose daughter,

JOHANNA DE KEVERELL, heiress, *m.* "Thomas Jeames de Tisho," and had,

JOHN JEAMES, of Tisho parish, Warwickshire, who had,

JOHANNA JEAMES, heiress, who *m.* Richard Willis, feudal baron by tenure of Napton manor aforesaid, and had,

THOMAS WILLIS, of Napton manor, whose son and heir,

RICHARD WILLIS, of Napton manor, had,

THOMAS WILLIS, of Priors Marston manor, in Warwickshire, who had,

RICHARD WILLIS, of Feny Compton manor, Warwickshire. Will signed 24 Jan., 1531-2, proved 11 May, 1532. He *m.* Joan Grant, of Norbrooke, Warwickshire, and had,

RICHARD WILLIS, of Newbold Comyn manor, Warwickshire, 1539, second son, will signed 30 Sept., 1559, proved 4 Nov., 1564. His second son,

RICHARD WILLIS, *m.* daugher of Humfrey Wright, of Hobsford manor, Warwickshire, and had,

HENRY WILLIS, *b.* about 1600. He became a Quaker, married, and removed Devizes, and to Westbury, in Wiltshire, where he *d.* in Oct., 1675. His only son,

HENRY WILLIS, *b.* Westbury, 14 Sept., 1628, a Quaker, removed from Devizes to Shoreditch, London, in 1667, subsequently to Spittalfield, and then to the Quaker settlement on Long Island, N. Y., about 1674, and founded the town of Westbury, where he *d.* 11 July, 1714. He *m.* Mary Peace, *d.* Westbury, 23 April, 1714, who came over with him and seven of their children, and had,

ELIZABETH WILLIS, b. at Devizes, who *m.* first, his third wife, Robert Zane, Sr., of Newton tp., Gloucester County, N. J., will signed 27 Jan., 1694-5, proved 1 March following, and had,

PEDIGREE CVII.—Continued.

ROBERT ZANE, JR., of Deptford tp., Gloucester County, N. J., 1681-1774, will proved 19 March, 1774. He *m.* Jane Satterthwaite, 1694-1778, and had,

ROBERT ZANE, 3D, of Deptford tp., 1716-1763. He *m.* Mary Chattin, and had,

SIMEON ZANE, of Upper Greenwich tp., Gloucester County, *b.* 29 March, 1758. Will dated "in 1811," filed in 1832. He *m.* Margaret Macomson, and had,

REBECCA ROBERTS ZANE, 1781-1857, who *m.* in Gloucester County, 16 July, 1816, Charles Shuster, 1792-1853, and had. *John Henry, b.* 28 Jan. 1819, *Joseph Cooper, b.* 12 Nov., 1821, and

KITURAH ANN SHUSTER, *b.* Camden, N. J., 22 June, 1817, *d.* in Stockton tp., Camden Co., N. J., 12 Nov., 1889. She *m.*, Philadelphia, 30 Jan., 1840, Thomas Sinex, of Philadelphia, 1820-1899, and had,

1.—MARY ANN SINEX, 1840-1888, who *m.* Richard S. Bartine, of Camden, N. J., 1836-1891, and had,

> I.—CATHERINE SHUSTER; II. ELLA AMELIA; III. RICHARD STOUT; IV. MARY CUSTER; V. THOMAS HENRY; VI. LOUISA READING.

2.—CHARLES FREDERICK SINEX, *b.* 16 Sept. 1842; *m.* Eugenia Boone, and had, LAWRENCE, only child.

3.—CATHARINE ELIZA SINEX, 1845-1893, *m.* 18 June, 1868, Joseph Henry Wilkinson, of Merchantville, N. J., and had,

> I.—MARIAN LILLIE, 1870-1874; II. FRANK EASTBURN.

4.—REBECCA SHUSTER SINEX, *d. unm.* 7 May, 1851.

5.—JOHN HENRY SINEX, of Philadelphia, and Edgewater Park, N. J., *b.* Philadelphia, 7 Dec., 1850, member Society Sons of the Revolution, in Pennsylvania; Colonial Society of Pennsylvania. He *m.* Mary McGonigal, second wife, and had by her,

> MARY MCCLELLAND SINEX, only child.

PEDIGREE CVIII.

EDWARD I., King of England, had by his second wife,

PRINCE THOMAS, Earl of Norfolk, Earl Marshal, who had,

MARGARET, Duchess of Norfolk, *m.* John, Lord Segrave, and had,

LADY ELIZABETH SEGRAVE, *m.* John, Baron Mowbray, and had,

LADY ELEANOR MOWBRAY, *m.* John, second Lord Welles, and had,

EUDO DE WELLES, *d. v. p.*, who *m.* Lady Maud Greystock, and had,

SIR LIONEL, K. G., sixth Lord Welles, *k.* in 1461, who had,

LADY MARGARET DE WELLES, *m.* Sir Thomas Dymoke, and had,

SIR LIONEL DYMOKE, Knt., of Scrivelsby, *d.* 7 Aug., 1519, who had,

LADY ALICE DYMOKE, who *m.* (his second wife) Sir William Skipwith, of South Ormsby, Lincolnshire, 1488-1547, [see Pedigree LIV, also Lincolnshire "Visitations," in "The Genealogist," Vol. IV., Maddison's "Lincolnshire Pedigrees," III., (Harlein Society Pub., 1904)], and had, *Sir Henry,* page 232, and

JOHN SKIPWITH, of Walmsgate, Lincolnshire, second son by second wife. His estate was adm. by his relict, 5 Nov., 1585. He *m.* Eleanor, daughter and heiress of John Kingston, of Great Grimsby, Linc. She *d.* 4 June, 1599. Her will signed 2 Jan., 1593-4. (See Massingbred's "South Ormsby," pp. 95-6, "Newcomen" ped., Maddison's Linc. Pedigree II. 716, and Allaben's "Ancestry of L. H. Crall," pp. 197-8, 153-4). John and Eleanor (Kingston) Skipwith had,

MARY SKIPWITH, legatee of her mother, will proved 20 Oct., 1627. She *m.* John Newcomen, of Saltfleetby, Linc., buried here 1 May, 1621, and had,

ELEANOR NEWCOMEN, *bapt.* Saltfleetby, 10 Nov., 1576, legatee of grandmother, Eleanor Skipwith, aforesaid, and of her mother, Mary Newcomen. She *m.* at Saltfleetby, 20 April, 1597, William Asfordby, of Saltfleetby-All-Saints, and Newark-on-Trent, (see Allaben's "Crall" ancestry, pp. 94, 98, 350, etc.), and had,

JOHN ASFORDBY, of Saltfleetby, heir, and signer of the Herald's pedigree, in the "Visitation" of 1634; *d.* after 11 Nov., 1657. He *m.* at

Cumberworth, 14 Oct., 1634, Alice, buried at Saltfleetby All Saints, 16 June, 1658, daughter of William Wolley, of Cumberworth, and had.

WILLIAM ASFORDBY, of Stayne-in-the-Marsh, Linc., heir, *bapt.*, Saltfleetby, 29 Mar. 1638, a legatee of his uncle, William Wolley, 15 Feb., 1676-7. After baptizing and burying a child, in Nov., 1669, at Marblethorpe, he and his wife, Martha (daughter of William Burton, of Burgh-in-the-Marsh, Linc.), and one child, removed to New York, and resided at Kingston and Marbletown, Ulster County, of which county he became high sheriff, (see authorities recited in Allaben's "Crall" ancestry). His will signed 6 Nov., 1697, proved 24 Feb., 1698. He had issue by his wife, Martha, who *d.* before 30 April, 1711, three daughters, co-heiresses, Eleanor, Catherine, and

SUSANNA ASFORDBY, oldest surviving child (Ulster Co. Deed. 20 April, 1711), *d.* Frederick Co. Md., will signed 20 June, 1742, proved 30 Oct., 1742. She *m.* 7 Nov., 1691, John Beatty, of (Esopus) Kingston, and Marbletown, will signed 26 April, 1720, proved 9 March, 1721, and had ten children, of these,

WILLIAM BEATTY, second son, *bapt.* 9 June, 1695, at Dutch Church, Kingston, will signed 18 May, 1757, recorded in Frederick County, Md., where he died. He *m.* Elizabeth, daughter of Cornelius Carmack, and had,

MARY BEATTY, third child. She *m.*, first, Isaac Eltinge, and *m.*, secondly, 21 May, 1757, John Cary, of Frederick County, Md., his will dated 23 Nov., 1773, proved in May, 1777, and had,

WILLIAM CARY, second son, *b.* 19 June, 1760, at Fredericktown. He enlisted and served in Seventh Regiment, Md. Line, 1778-80, over two years, and *d.* in Montgomery County, Md., 12 Oct., 1806. He *m.* 2 June, 1793, Maria Barbara, daughter of Dr. Casper Fritchie, and his wife, Susan Whithare, and had,

1.—ROBERT CASPER JEFFERSON CARY, *m.* Frances Crome Mathews, and had,

ROBERTA CARY, *m.* first, Richard Corbin, of Moss Neck, Fredericksburg, Md., and *m.* secondly, Rev. Ovid A. Kinsolving, D.D., rector of P. E. Church, Middleburg, Va., and had,

REV. WYTHE LEIGH KINSOLVING, rector of P. E. Church, Barton Heights, Richmond, Va.

2.—WILLIAM CARY, of Lewisburg, Va., second son, *b.* Georgetown, D. C., 23 July, 1798, member Va. Legislature, from Greenbrier County,

1833, etc., presiding justice of the county, *d.* 1 April, 1857. He *m.* 2 April, 1828, Ophelia, daughter of John and Catherine (Pope) Mathews, of Greenbrier County, and had,

1.—HENRIETTA HARRISON CARY, *m.* Judge Adam Clarke Snyder, of Lewisburg, West Va., and had.

    I.—JULES VERNE; II. KENTON MATHEWS; III. FREDERICK WILLIAM; IV. ZULIEME AUSTIN.

2.—LOUISE MADDEN CARY, *m.* Thomas Lewis Feamster, of Lewisburg, West Va., and had,

    I.—DAISY PATTON; II. WILLIAM CARY; III. ROYDEN KEITH; IV. CLAUDIUS NEWMAN; V. OTEY TURK; VI. OPHELIA MATHEWS; VII. ZOE LOUISE.

3.—SALLIE MATHEWS CARY, *m.* Flavius Josephus Snyder, of Lewisburg, West. Va., and had,

    I.—OTEY LOUISE; II. ADAM CARY; III. HENRIETTA ELIZABETH; IV. WILLIAM HOLT; V. ROBERT LEE.

4.—WILLIE ANNE CARY, youngest child member Society Colonial Dames of America, in Virginia, Society Daughters of the American Revolution, National Society of Americans of Royal Descent, etc. She *m.* in Lewisburg, W. Va., Rudolph Samuel Turk, of Staunton, Va. No issue.

THE ROYAL DESCENTS
OF
MR. AND MRS. GEORGE MASON CHICHESTER
OF "ST. MARY'S," ARDMORE, PA.

EDWARD I., KING OF ENGLAND, had,
Edward II., King of England, who had,
Edward III., King of England, who had,
John, Duke of Lancaster, who had,
Joan, m. Ralph, Earl of Westmoreland, and had,
Edward Nevill, Lord Bergavenny, p. 54, who had,
Sir George Nevill, Lord Bergavenny, who had,
Sir George Nevill, Lord Bergavenny, who had,
Ursula, m. Sir Warham St. Leger, and had,
Sir Anthony St. Leger, of Ulcombe, who had,
Sir Warham St. Leger, of Ulcombe, who had,
Ursula, m. Rev. Daniel Horsmanden, and had,
Col. Warham Horsmanden, of Purleigh, who had,
Maria, m. Col. William Byrd, of Va., and had,
Anne, m. Robert Beverley, p. 58, and had,
Col. William Beverley, "Blandfield," who had,
Robert Beverley, "Wakefield," p. 187, who had,
Robert Beverley, of Va., who had,
Bradshaw Beverley, of Va., who had,
Mary, m. Arthur Mason Chichester, Va., and had,

EDWARD I., KING OF ENGLAND, had,
Elizabeth, m. Humphrey de Bohun, and had,
William, Earl of Nottingham, K.G., who had,
Elizabeth, m. Richard Fitzalan, K.G., and had,
Elizabeth, m. Sir Robert Goushill, and had,
Joan, m. Thomas, Lord Stanley, K.G., and had,
Margaret, m. Sir William Troutbeck, and had,
Jane, m. Sir William Griffith, K.B., and had,
Sir William Griffith, of Penrhyn, who had,
Sibill, m. Owen ap Hugh, p. 155, and had,
Jane, m. Hugh Gwyn, of Penarth, Gent., and had,
Sibill, m. John Powel, of Gadfa, and had,
Elizabeth, m. Humphrey, of Llwyn-du, and had,
Owen Humphrey, of Llwyn-du, p. 156, who had,
Rebecca, m. Robert Owen, of Fron Goch, and had,
Gainor, m. Jonathan Jones, p. 160, and had,
Owen Jones, of Merion tp., Pa., who had,
Lowry, m. Daniel Wister, p. 160, and had,
John Wister, Germantown, Philadelphia, who had,
Louis Wister, of Ardmore, Pa., who had,

GEORGE MASON CHICHESTER, Ardmore, Pa., m. Sara Edythe Wister. (See p. 160). *No issue.*

DESCENT FROM 18 OF THE 25 SURETIES FOR THE MAGNA CHARTA OF MR. ARTHUR PETERSON, OF PHILADELPHIA.

ROGER BIGOD.
HUGH BIGOD.
Ralph Bigod.
Isabel Fitzpiers.
John Fitzjohn.
Maud Beauchamp.
Isabel Chaworth.
Maud Plantagenet.
Joan Plantagenet. =

WILLIAM MALET.
Hawise Muscegros.
John de Muscegros.
Robert de Muscegros.
Hawise de Ferrers.
Robert de Ferrers.
Robert de Ferrers. = Elizabeth Boteler.
Robert de Ferrers.
Mary de Ferrers. = Ralph de Neville.

GEOFFREY DE SAYE.
William de Saye.
William de Saye.
Lady de Sudley.
John de Sudley.
Joan le Boteler.

JOHN FITZROBERT.
Roger Fitzjohn.
Robert Fitzroger.
Euphemia de Neville.
Ralph de Neville.
John de Neville.
Ralph de Neville.
Ralph de Neville.
John de Neville.
Joan de Gascoigne.
William de Gascoigne. = Margaret de Percy.

WILLIAM DE LANVALLEI.
Hawise de Burgh.
John de Burgh.
Margaret de Burgh.
John de Burgh.
William de Burgh.
Elizabeth Plantagenet.
Philippa de Mortimer.
Elizabeth de Percy.
Henry de Percy.
Henry de Percy.

ROBERT FITZWALTER.
Walter Fitzwalter.
Ela d' Odingsells.
Margaret de Grey.
John de Grey.
Robert de Marmyon.
Elizabeth Marmyon. =

Robert Mauleverer, of Wot
Edmund Mauleverer, Arncliff Hall, Yorks, = Mary
William Mauleverer, Arncliff Hall, Yorks, = Elean
James Mauleverer, Ayton manor, Yorks, = Beatri
Edmund Mauleverer, West Ayton, Yorks, = Ann

Births.	Deaths.		Marriages.	
circa 1660.	6 mo., —, 1737.	John Abbott,	3 mo., 26, 1696,	Anne
11 mo., 5, 1693.	4 mo., 13, 1767.	Joseph Burr,	12 mo., 16, 1726.	Jane
6 mo., 2, 1741.	2 mo., 5, 1794.	David Ridgway,	5 mo., 19, 1762,	Jane
1 mo., 21, 1768.	6 mo., 21, 1841.	John Evans,	6 mo., 5, 1792.	Rachel
4 mo., 21, 1785.	5 mo., 10, 1872.	George Peterson,	1 mo., 9. 1812,	Jane
December 7, 1818.	October 10, 1891.	Henry Peterson,	October 28, 1842,	Sarah
September 20, 1851.		Arthur Peterson.	March 30, 1891,	Georgi

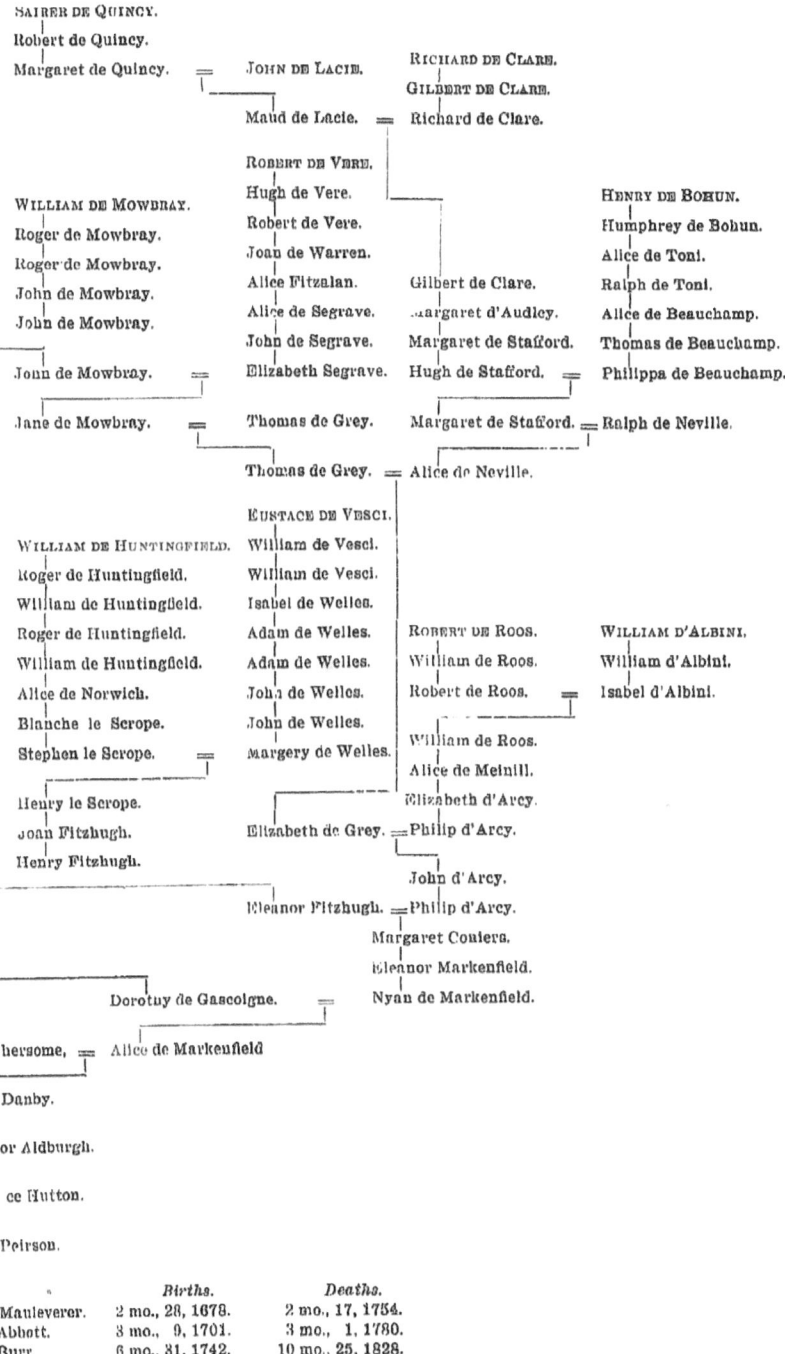

	Births.	Deaths.
Mauleverer.	2 mo., 28, 1679.	2 mo., 17, 1754.
Abbott.	3 mo., 9, 1701.	3 mo., 1, 1780.
Burr.	6 mo., 31, 1742.	10 mo., 25, 1828.
Ridgway.	6 mo., 12, 1766.	8 mo., 1, 1808.
Evans.	3 mo., 29, 1793.	6 mo., 20, 1859.
Webb.	November 9, 1820.	April 19, 1891.
ana Harrah.	October 16, 1852.	No issue.

PEDIGREE CIX.

EDWARD I., King of England, had by his first wife,

JOAN, *m.* Gilbert, Earl of Hertford and Gloucester, and had,

MARGARET DE CLARE, who *m.* Hugh, Earl of Gloucester, and had,

MARGARET D'AUDLEY, who *m.* Ralph, Earl of Stafford, and had,

HUGH, EARL OF STAFFORD, K. G., (see p. 37), whose daughter,

MARGARET DE STAFFORD, *m.* Ralph, Earl of Westmoreland, and had,

ALICE DE NEVILL, who *m.* Sir Thomas de Grey, of Heton, and had,

ELIZABETH DE GREY, who *m.* Sir Phillip, Baron d'Arcy, and had,

JOHN D'ARCY, fifth Baron, 1377-1411, (see p. 296), father of

SIR JOHN D'ARCY, seventh Baron, (see p. 445), whose daughter,

LADY JOAN D'ARCY, widow of John de Beaumont, *m.* secondly Giles, fourth feudal Baron d'Aubeney, 1403, high sheriff of Bedford and Bucks, 1432, *b.* at Kempstead, Bedford, 20 Oct. 1393, buried at South Petherton, Somerset, 11 Jan. 1445-6, and had,

WILLIAM D'AUBENEY, fifth Baron by tenure, and Lord of South Petherton manor, *b.* 11 June, 1424, *d.* 2 Jan. 1460. He *m.* Lady Alice, daughter of John de Stourton, of Preston, (King Henry VII, was descended from his sister, Lady Edith), and had,

JAMES DAUBENEY, second son, *d.* 1 Oct. 1528, (brother to Sir Giles Daubeney, K. G., Baron by writ, 1485-6, lord chamberlain to Henry VII., &c., father of Henry, first Earl of Bridgewater), eventual heir to Elias d'Albini, first Baron d'Aubeney, by writ, 1295. He *m.* Elizabeth, daughter and heir of Robert Pauncefote, and had,

GILES DAUBENEY, of Wayford manor, in Somerset, heir, *d.* 22 March, 1559. He *m.* ——————— Coles, and had, John, of Gorwell, * and

---

*JOHN DAUBENEY, of Gorwell, Litton Cheney parish, Dorset, fourth son, will dated 1 Aug., proved 25 Nov., 1570 (see "Magna Charta Barons and their American Descendants," p. 365); *m.* Alice, dau. of Giles Penny, of East Coker, Somerset, and had,

GEORGE DAUBENEY, of Gorwell, *d.* 6 Sep., 1612, aged 54; *m.* Elizabeth, *d.* 23 July, 1639, dau. of Thomas Cocker, of Maypowder, Dorset, and had.

HENRY DAUBENEY, of Gorwell, heir, will dated 28 Dec., 1655, proved 19 May, 1656; *m.* Edith Symonds, *d.* 22 Jan., 1650, and had,

GEORGE DAUBENEY, of Gorwell, heir, *bapt.* 16 Dec., 1616, will dated 3 Oct., 1689, proved 17 Oct., 1690; *m.* Judith Bryant, *d.* 27 June, 1655, and had,

DOROTHY DAUBENEY, buried at Widworth, 18 Oct. 1598. She *m.* at Shute parish church (see parish register), 24 Feb. 1570, John Chichester, of Widworthy, Devon, (see Vivian's "Devonshire Visitations"), buried at Widworthy, 19 Feb. 1609, will proved, in 1609, in Archdeacon's Court, Exeter. Son of John, of Widworthy, fourth son of John Chichester, of Rawleigh, 1472-1538, see p. 261, 408. Their son,

HUGH CHICHESTER, of Widworthy, heir, *bapt.* at Widworthy, 7 June, 1573. He certified the Herald's "Chichester" pedigree, 1619-20. His will, signed 28 Sep. 1640, was proved 10 May, 1642, and he was buried at Widworthy, 22 Feb. 1641-2. He *m.* Martha, daughter of Richard Duke, of Otterton, Devon, and had,

RICHARD CHICHESTER, of Widworthy, heir, *bapt.* at Widworthy, 13 June, 1600, and buried here, 17 March, 1638. Administration on his estate was granted to a creditor, his relict, Joan, renouncing, 1 June, 1639. He *m.* at Kington, Somerset, 22 May, 1625, Joan Smiths, of that parish, and had by her, who was buried at Widworth, 5 Aug. 1643,

JOHN CHICHESTER, of Widworthy, heir, *bapt.* at Widworthy, 11 Oct. 1626, and buried here, 11 June, 1661. He was named in will of his

---

ANDREW DAUBENEY, of Pulham, Dorset, *bapt.* 14 April, 1653, at Little Cheyney, buried at Pulham, 12 Sep., 1734; *m.* Sarah, dau. of Richard Blackall, of Britwell, Oxon, widow of Charles Revett, and had,

GEORGE DAUBENEY, heir, *b.* Buckshaw Hill, Holwell, Somerset, buried at St. James' Church, Bristol, 28 Feb., 1740, will proved 23 May, 1741; *m.* Jane Lloyd, buried at St. James', 15 Sep., 1761, and had,

LLOYD DAUBENEY, *bapt.* at St. Nicholas' Church, Bristol, 9 Nov., 1718, buried at St. James', 22 Dec., 1754; *m.* 4 Feb., 1742, at St. James', Ducibella Saxbury, and had,

LLOYD DAUBENEY, only surviving son, *b.* 22 Nov., 1746, came to New York city, and became owner of considerable land in various New York counties, 1768. He *m.* 24 Jan., 1770, Mary, *b.* New York, 15 July, 1743, *d.* 6 Oct., 1813, widow of James Calder, and dau. of William Coventry, of New York city, nephew of William, Earl of Coventry, and Viscount Deerhurst, and had,

ELIZA MARTIN DAUBENEY, heiress, *bapt.* at Holy Trinty, New York, 10 Nov., 1779; *m.* 8 Nov., 1800, Capt. Henry Waddell, of New York, 1767-1819, son of William Waddell, Lieut. Col. N. Y. "Loyalists" regiment, and had,

WILLIAM COVENTRY HENRY WADDALL, of New York, heir, 1802-1884; *m.* Jan., 1828, Julia Anna Cobb, and had,

SUSAN ALICE WADDELL, *m.* 8 April, 1868, George Washington Smith, of Morris Co., N. J., and had,

PHILIP HENRY WADDELL SMITH, of Pittsburgh, Pa., a founder of the Order of Runnemede, and member of Society of Colonial Wars, Society Sons of the Revolution,

He *m.* at Princeton, N. J., 28 May, 1903, Isabella Williamson, daughter of Rev. Donald MacLaren, D.D., chaplain U. S. Navy (retired) (son of Rev. Donald MacLaren, Geneva, N. Y.), and Elizabeth, daughter of Prof. Jacob Green (son of President Ashabel Green, of Princeton), and Elizabeth, daughter of Samuel McCulloch, of Baltimore, and had,

1. ALICE WADDELL SMITH, *b.* 24 Jan., 1906.
2. COVENTRY WADDELL SMITH, b. 23 July, 1909.

grandfather, 1640. His will, dated 3 June, 1661, administration granted to his relict, Margaret, 12 Sep. 1661. He *m.* Margaret, will dated 17 May, 1711, proved 3 Dec. 1714, daughter of John Ware, of Hallerton, and Silverton, Devon, and had, *John,* 1649-1702, the heir, and

RICHARD CHICHESTER, second son, *b.* 5 Mar. and *bapt.* 16 Mar., 1657, at Silverton. Named in his father's will. He removed to Virginia, and by deed, 12 Oct. 1702, bought farm land in Lancaster Co., where he died, will dated 14 April, proved 12 June, 1734. He was high sheriff, 1722-23, He *m.* first, in England, Anna, whose surname has not been preserved, and secondly, on 11 July, 1719, (Lanc. Co., marriage bonds), Ann Chinn, will 14 Apr., 1734, widow of William Fox. No issue by her. By his first wife, he had,

JOHN CHICHESTER, heir, *bapt.* at Widworthy, 10 May, 1681, who came to Virginia with his father, and *d. v. p.,* in Oct. 1728. He *m.* Elizabeth, daughter of Thomas Symes, of Beamister, Dorset, (see N. E. His. Gen. Reg. XLI. 63, and "Virginia Heraldica"). He is named in the will of his grandmother, 1711, and in the "Chichester" pedigree, Vivian's "Devonshire Visitations." He had by his wife, who was buried at Powerstock, Dorset, 28 Jan. 1728-9,

RICHARD CHICHESTER, of "Fairweathers", Lancaster Co., Va. Named in will, 1736, of his grandmother, Mary Symes, and was heir to paternal grandfather. He *d.* at Exeter, England, 30 Dec. 1743, and was buried at Powerstock, Dorsetshire, 3 Jan. following, will dated 16 May, 1743, proved 10 Aug. 1744, Lanc. Co. He *m.* 3 July, 1734, (Lanc. Co., Va., marriage bonds), Ellen, daughter of Col. William and Hannah (Beale) Ball, of Lancaster Co., (see Hayden's "Virginia Genealogies, p. 91), and had,

COL. RICHARD CHICHESTER, of "Newington", Fairfax Co., Va., County Lieutenant, a justice, &c., Fairfax Co., *d.* 22 Aug. 1796, will dated 10 Oct. 1793. He *m.* first, 9 June, 1759, Ann Gordon, *d.* 20 Apr. 1765, and *m.* secondly, Sarah, daughter of Col. Daniel and Sinah (Ball) McCarty, of Fairfax Co., ("Va., Geneal." pp. 89, 106-7), and had seven children by her, who *d.* 25 June, 1826, of these, *Mary Symes,* who *m.* Bernard Hooe, Jr., will proved in Prince William Co., 7 May, 1810, and had *Sarah McCarty,* who *m.,* his second wife, 6 Feb. 1812, Mordecai Throckmorton, of "Meadow Farm", Loudoun Co., *b.* 10 March, 1777, *d.* 7 April, 1838, [son of Thomas, *d.* in Nicholas Co., Ky., 27 April, 1826, son of Mordecai, sheriff of King and Queen Co., 1740, *d.* 1767, (and his wife, Mary, daughter of Thomas Reade, of Gloucester Co., also of Royal Descent. see p. 248), son of Gabriel Throckmorton. *d.* Jan. 1737, also of Royal

Descent, see p. 297], and had, *John Aris Throckmorton*, 1815-1891, Loudoun and Culpeper Cos., major Sixth Va. Cavalry, C. S. Army, who *m.* 13 March, 1839, Mary Barnes, daughter of Col. Charles Pendleton Tutt, of Loudoun Co., 1780-1832, and his wife, Anne Mason, 1789-1882, daughter of Richard McCarty Chichester, 1769-1817, hereafter, and had, *Charles B. Throckmorton*, of New York City, Major U. S. Army, retired, who *m.* at Bardstown, Ky., 8 Oct. 1863, Fanny Hall, daughter of Robert Logan Wickliffe, and had *Charles Wickliffe Throckmorton*, of New York, a founder of the Order of Runnemede, and member of Society of Colonial Wars, Society Sons of the Revolution, etc.

Col. Richard Chichester, also had by his wife, Sarah McCarty,

RICHARD MCCARTY CHICHESTER, *b.* at "Newington", 27 Feb. 1769, *d.* Fauquier Co., 29 Aug. 1817. He *m.* Ann Thomson, *d.* 29 Aug. 1817, aged 48, daughter of Thomson Mason, of "Raspberry Plain", Loudoun Co., (brother to the celebrated George Mason, of "Gunston Hall"), and had,

GEORGE MASON CHICHESTER, *b.* at "Newington", 2 March, 1793, *d.* 12 Dec. 1835. He *m.* first, 14 April, 1818, Sarah C. Elliott, *d.* 20 Mar. 1820, *issue;* and *m.* secondly, 23 Dec. 1824, Mary, *b.* 1 July, 1802, *d.* 31 July, 1872, daughter of Washington and Margaret (Johns) Bowie, of Georgetown, D. C., by whom he had,

1. WASHINGTON BOWIE CHICHESTER, *b.* 11 Feb 1828; *m.* 17 Jan. 1854, Lydia H. R. Brown.

2. ARTHUR MASON CHICHESTER, of "Ivon", Loudoun Co., Va., *b.* 6 April, 1831. He served through the Civil War as Captain of Engineers, C. S. Army. He *m.* 25 Oct. 1854, Mary Beverly, also of Royal Descent, and had issue

  1. GEORGE MASON CHICHESTER, of St. Mary's," Ardmore Pa., who *m.* Sara Edythe Wister, see pp. 160, 516. *No issue.*

  2. ARTHUR MASON CHICHESTER, *m.* 1st. Marie Mathilde de Benneville, of Royal Descent, see p. 281, *d.* Aug., 1906, and had, *Arthur Mason Chichester*, 3rd., and *m.* 2nd. Ethel Langhorne Wister, of Philadelphia.

  3. BRADSHAW BEVERLEY CHICHESTER, *m.* Clara G. Canby, and had, *James Beverley Chichester.*

  4. SARAH BYRD CHICHESTER, *m.* Fred. Mann Page, Captain, U. S. Army. He *d.s.p.*, at Havanna, Cuba.

  5. JANE BEVERLEY CHICHESTER, *m.* Dr. Joseph M. Fox, and had, *Mary Beverley, Jean Beverley, Sarah,* and *Joseph M.*

  6. MARY BEVERLEY CHICHESTER, *m.* J. Willcox Jenkins, and had, *Mary Beverley, Carroll,* and *J. Willcox.*

DESCENT FROM 18 OF THE 25 SURETIES FOR THE MAGNA CHARTA OF MRS. JOHN SCOTT, JR., OF PHILADELPHIA.

Roger Bigod.
Hugh Bigod.
Ralph Bigod.
Isabel Fitzpie
John Fitzjohr
Maud Beauch
Isabel Chawo
Maud Plantas
Joan Plantag

William Malet.	Geoffrey de Saye.	John Fitzrobert.	William de Lanvallei.	
Hawise Muscegros.	William de Saye.	Roger Fitzjohn.	Hawise de Burgh.	
John de Muscegros.	William de Saye.	Robert Fitzroger.	John de Burgh.	Robert Fitzw
Robert de Muscegros.	Lady de Sudley.	Euphemia de Neville.	Margaret de Burgh.	Walter Fitzw
Hawise de Ferrers.	John de Sudley.	Ralph de Neville.	John de Burgh.	Ela d' Odings
Robert de Ferrers.	Joan le Boteler.	John de Neville.	William de Burgh.	Margaret de G
Robert de Ferrers. =	Elizabeth Boteler.	Ralph de Neville.	Elizabeth Plantagenet.	John de Grey.
	Robert de Ferrers.	Ralph de Neville.	Philippa de Mortimer.	Robert de Mar
	Mary de Ferrers. =	Ralph de Neville.	Elizabeth de Percy.	Elizabeth Mar
		John de Neville.	Henry de Percy.	
		Joan de Gascoigne.	Henry de Percy.	
		William de Gascoigne. =	Margaret de Percy.	

Robert Mauleverer, of Wothersome, =
Edmund Mauleverer, Arncliffe Hall, Yorks, =
William Mauleverer, Arncliffe Hall, Yorks, =
James Mauleverer, Arncliffe Hall, Yorks, =
Edmund Mauleverer, West Ayton, Yorks, =
Anne Mauleverer, 1678-1754, =
Jane Abbott, 1701-1780, =
Henry Burr, Burlington Co., N. J., 1731-1804, =
Henry Ridgway, Burlington Co., N. J., = (*first husband*).
Henry Paxson Landis, 1790-1824. =
Henry D. Landis, of Philadelphia, 1824-1895. =
Mary Lane Landis, *m.* 17 July, 1884. –
John Fulton Reynolds Scott, of Philadelp

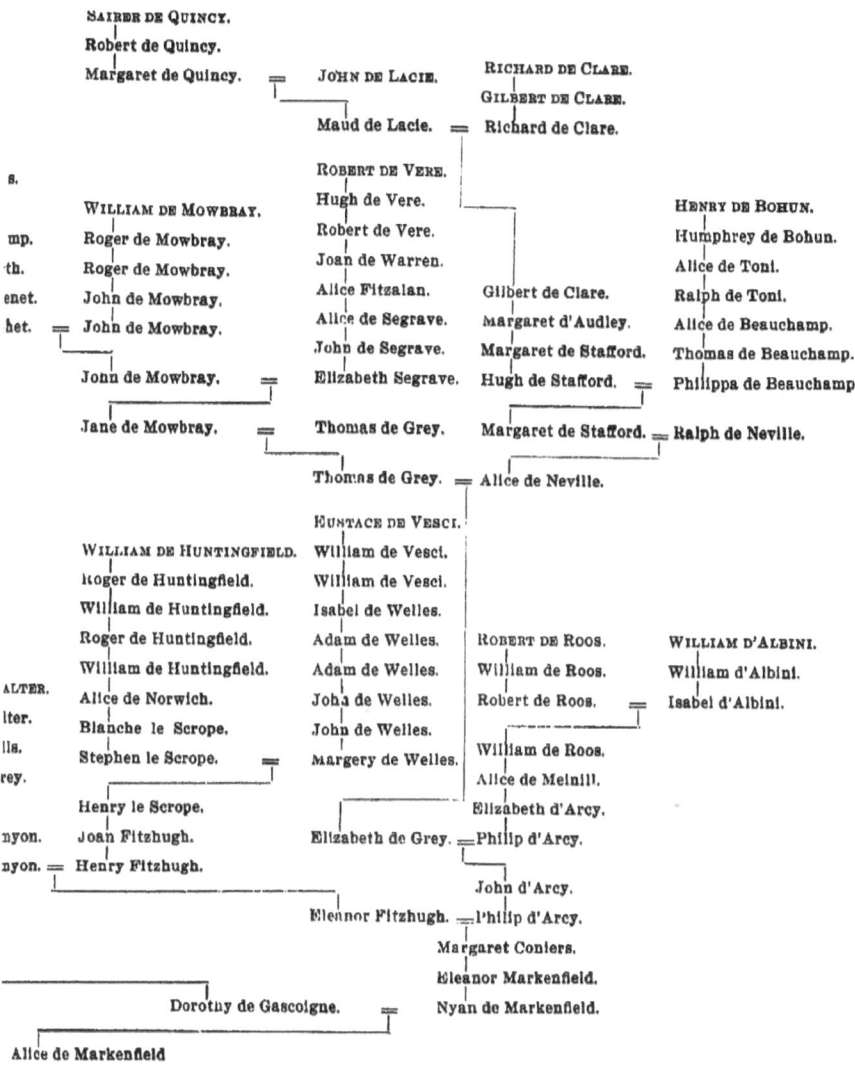

THE ROYAL DESCENT
OF
MR. LEWIS JONES LEVICK
OF BALA, PA.

HUGH CAPET, KING OF FRANCE, had,
Havide, *m.* Rainier de Hainault, and had,
Beatrix, *m.* Eblo, Count de Rouci, and had,
Alix, *m.* Hildwin de Montdidier, and had,
Marguerite, *m.* Hugh de Monchi, and had,
Adeliza, *m.* Gilbert, de Clare, p. 43, and had,
Richard de Clare, Earl of Hertford, who had,
Roger de Clare, Earl of Hertford, who had,
Richard de Clare, Earl of Hertford, who had,
Joan, *m.* Rhys Gryd, of Yestradtywy, and had,
Rhys Mechyllt, lord of Llandovery, who had,
Rhys-vaughn, lord of Yestradtywy, who had,
Rhys-gloff, lord of Cymcydmaen, who had,
Madoc ap Rhys-gloff, who had,
Trahairn-gôch, lord of Penllech, who had,
David-gôch, lord of Penllech, who had,
Ievan, lord of Penllech and Grainoc, who had,
Madoc, lord of Grainoc, who had,
Deikws-ddu, lord of Grainoc, who had,
Einion, lord of Grainoc, who had,
Howel ap Einion Deikws-ddu, who had,
Griffith ap Howel, who had,
  Lewis ap Griffith Howel, lord of Yshute,=

KING ALFRED THE GREAT, had,
Edward, King of England, who had,
Edmund I., King of England, who had,
Edgar, Peaceful, King of England, who had,
Ethelred, Unready, King of England, who had,
Edmund, Ironsides, King of England, who had,
Prince Edward, the Exile, who had,
Margaret, *m.* Malcolm, King of Scots, and had,
Matilda, *m.* Henry I., of England, and had,
Maud, *m.* Geoffroi, Count of Anjou, and had,
Henry II., King of England, who had,
John, King of England, who had,
Eleanor, *m.* Simon de Montfort, and had,
Eleanor, *m.* Leoline, of No. Wales, and had,
Catherine, *m.* Philip of Cardigan, and had,
Eleanor, *m.* Thomas of Trefgarned, and had,
Eleanor, *m.* Gryffyth of Glendwdwyn, and had,
Lowry, *m.* Robert Puleston, of Emral, and had,
John Puleston, lord of Emral, (p. 190), who had,
Margaret, *m.* David Ievan Einion, and had,
Einion David, lord of Cryniarth, who had,
Llewelyn ap Einion, who had,
Griffith ap Llewelyn, who had,
Catherine, *m.* Edward ap Ievan, p. 190, and had,
  Ethli, or Ellen v. Edward, p. 47.

Robert Lewis, lord of Rhiwlas,= Gwyrryl v. Hewelyn, lord of Llan Rwst.

Ievan Robert Lewis, lord of Rhiwlas, and of Fron Gôch, = Jane ——.

Evan Evan, of "Fron Gôch farm," Merion, Wales, (p. 191) =

Cadwalader Evans, 1664-1745, removed to Gwynedd, Pa. = Ellen, dau. John Morris, of Bryn Gwyn.

Sarah Evans, = John Hank, of White Marsh, Montgomery Co., Pa.

Jane Hank, = John Roberts, of "Woodlawn,"

Job Roberts, of "Woodlawn," Penllyn, = Mary Naylor.

Jane Roberts, = Charles Mather, of "Woodlawn," Penllyn, Pa.

Susanna Morris Mather, =Samuel Jones Levick, of Philadelphia.

Lewis Jones Levick, of Bala, Phila. Co., Pa. = Mary d'Invilliers, of Philadelphia.

Henry Lewis Levick.   Mary Sabina Levick. = Winthrop C. Neilson, Philadelphia.   Louise J. Levick.   Suzanne Levick.

Lewis Winthrop Neilson.

PEDIGREE CX.

EDWARD, I., King of England, had by his second wife,

THOMAS, EARL OF NORFOLK, earl-marshal of England, who had,

MARGARET, DUCHESS OF NORFOLK, *m.* John Lord Segrave, and had

LADY ELIZABETH DE SEGRAVE, who *m.* John, Lord Mowbray, and had,

LADY JANE DE MOWBRAY, *m.* Sir John de Grey, of Berwyke, and had,

THOMAS DE GREY, (p. 296), who *m.* Lady Alice de Nevill, and had,

LADY MAUD DE GREY, *m.* Robert Ogle, high sheriff of Northumberland, 1418, *d.* 1437, and had,

WILLIAM OGLE, (brother of Robert, first Lord Ogle, d. 1469). He *m.* Margaret ―――――. She was living 28 Dec. 1552, when her grandson, Gregory Ogle, granted her an annuity (see Hodgson's "Northumberland"). Their son,

GAWEN OGLE, of Choppington, Northumberland, (see Foster's "Visittations of Northumberland," 1615, and 1666), father of

JOHN OGLE, of Ogle Castle, will dated 4 April, 1565, (Surtees Society publication, "Northumberland Wills and Inventories," I. 247). He *m.* ――――――, daughter of William Barnaby, of Gunerby, Lancashire, and had,

PHILLIS OGLE, (see Foster's "Visit. No'd", 1615, and Surtees No'd, W. & I. II. 130). She *m.* secondly, John Ogle, of Newsham, *d.* 1585-6. Her will dated 22 June, 1606. She *m.* first, Edward de la Val, *d.* before 21 Dec. 1572, son of Sir John de la Val, of Seaton-De la Val, and his wife Mary Cary (Nort'd Visit. 1615, 1666), daughter of Thomas Cary, of Chilton-Foliot, Wilts, and his wife Margaret, daughter of Sir Robert Spencer, and his wife, Lady Alinore de Beaufort, (widow of James Boteler, Earl of Wiltshire), daughter of Edmund, Duke of Somerset, K. G., see p. 103. Their daughter

BARBARA DE LA VAL, was named in his will, dated 21 Dec. 1572, by her uncle, Sir John de la Val, heir to Seaton-De la Val. She *m.* John Watson, Jr., of Newcastle-on-Tyne, merchant, I. P. M., 1612, (See North'd Visita., 1666). His father was sheriff, 1567, and mayor of Newcastle-on-Tyne, 1574. Their daughter,

MARY WATSON, (sister of Thomas Watson, mayor of Stockton, Durham, 1623), *m.* Christopher Wetherell, of Stockton, where he was buried.

in the parish church, 25 May, 1622. His will dated 24 May, 1622, proved at Durham Registry, 4 Dec. 1624. His brother, Rowland, (father of Gyles, mayor of Stockton, 1630, etc.), was mayor of Stockton, 1619, and was buried in the church, 6 Dec. 1636. Their father, Gyles Wetherell, of Stockton, will dated 12 July, proved 18 Aug., 1604. Christopher and Mary (Watson) Wetherell had,

THOMAS WETHERELL, of the parish of All Saints, Newcastle-on-Tyne, merchant, a minor in Dec. 1624, buried 28 Dec. 1672, will dated 23 Dec. 1672, proved in Durham Registry, Jan. 1672-3. He was twice married, and had issue by each wife. He *m.* secondly, 12 Sept. 1658, Jane Heighington, widow, will proved in 1678. By his first wife, whose name is not preserved, he had five children, of these, his son,

CHRISTOPHER WETHERILL, removed from Sherburne, Yorks, with his wife, to Burlington Co., West Jersey, 1683. He was a member of the Proprietary Council, 1688, 1703-6-7. He *d.* at Burlington, 25 Jan. 1711, will proved 6 April, 1711. He *m.* 7 Feb. 1672, at York, Mary Hornby, of Hull, *d.* 1680. *Issue.*

The following are of Royal Descent through Christopher Wetherill:

FRANK D. WETHERILL.
H. EMERSON WETHERILL.
HERBERT J. WETHERILL.
ISABELLA M. WETHERILL.
REBECCA WETHERILL.
I. CORTRIGHT WETHERILL.
RICHARD WETHERILL.
ROBERT WETHERILL.
BRINTON WETHERILL.
JOHN PRICE WETHERILL.
THOMAS WETHERILL.
GEORGE D. WETHERILL.
A. LAWRENCE WETHERILL.
CHARLES WETHERILL.
EDWARD WETHERILL.
SAMUEL PRICE WETHERILL.
SAMUEL WETHERILL.
WILLIAM H. WETHERILL.
WILLIAM D. WETHERILL.
MRS. CHRISTINE NORTHROP WETHERILL.

LEWIS J. LEVICK, see p. 522.
WASHINGTON BLEDYN POWELL.
SAMUEL WHITE LEVIS.
SARA ROXY CORLIES.
MRS. WALTER E. COX.
BENJAMIN W. RICHARDS.
HENRY LEVIS.
ALICE CUSHMAN.
IDA CUSHMAN.
ANNIE GODLEY.
JAMES DUNDAS LIPPINCOTT.
MRS. MORRIS HACKER.
MRS. FRANK K. HIPPLE.
MRS. WILLIAM WURTZ DUNDAS.
MRS. E. IUNGERICH SMITH.
MRS. WINTHROP C. NEILSON.
MRS. JAMES ORNE MCHENRY.
MRS. ROBERT R. LOGAN.

THE ROYAL DESCENT

OF

MRS. L. MONTGOMERY BOND, JR.,

OF ELIZABETH, N. J.

LOUIS VIII., King of France =Blanche, daughter of Alphonso VIII. of Castile.

Robert, Count of Artois=Lady Matilda of Brabant.

Blanche, widow of Henry I., King of Navarre=Edmund, son of Henry III., King of England.

Henry, Earl of Lancaster=Lady Maud de Chaworth.

Lady Maud Plantagenet=Sir William de Burgh, Earl of Ulster.

Lady Elizabeth de Burgh =Lionel, Duke of Clarence.

Lady Philippa Plantagenet= Edmund de Mortimer. Earl of Marche.

Lady Elizabeth de Mortimer= Sir Henry de Percy, K. G., "Hotspur."

Henry, Earl of Northumberland=Lady Eleanor de Neville.

Henry, Earl of Northumberland= Lady Eleanor Poynings.

Lady Margaret de Percy=Sir William Gascoigne, of Gawthrope.

Lady Elizabeth Gascoigne= Gilbert de Talboys, of Kyme.

Sir George de Talboys, of Kyme (Name unknown.)

Lady Anne de Talboys= Sir Edward Dymoke, of Scrivelsby, Lincolnshire.

Lady Frances Dymoke= Thomas Windebank, of Haines Hill, Berkshire.

Lady Mildred Windebank=Robert Reade, Linkenholt Manor, Southampton.

Col. George Reade, of Gloucester Co., Va.= Elizabeth Martian, of York Co., Va.

Mildred Reade= Col. Augustine Warner, Jr., of "Warner's Hall."

Mildred Warner= Lawrence Washington, of "Bridge's Creek," Va.

Augustine Washington, of Stafford Co., Va. =Mary Ball, of "Epping Forest," Va.

Col. Samuel Washington, of Va., (a brother of=Anne Steptoe (fourth wife).
President Washington)

George Steptoe Washington, of "Harewood," Lucy Payne (sister of Dolly, wife of President
Jefferson Co., W. Va. Madison).

Samuel Walter Washington, M.D., of "Harewood." Louisa Clemson.

Lucy Washington John Bainbridge Packett, of "Harewood."

Frances H. Washington Packett, of Elizabeth, L. Montgomery Bond, Jr., of Philadelphia.
New Jersey, a member of the N. J. Society of
the Colonial Dames of America, the Order of
the Crown, etc.

William de Hertburne Washington Bond. Mary Carolena Washington Bond.

PEDIGREE CXI.

PHILIP III., King of France, 1270-1285 (see pp. 484-5), *m.* Isabel, daughter of James I., King of Arragon, and had,

CHARLES III., Count of Valois, Anjou, and Maine, founder of the Royal House of Valois, brother to Philip IV., King of France. He *m.* Margaret, daughter of Charles II., King of Naples and Sicily, by his wife, Mary, daughter of Stephen V., King of Hungary, and had,

JOANNA DE VALOIS (sister to Philip VI., King of France), who *m.* William III., Sovereign Count of Hainault, Holland, Zeeland, and Friezland, and had,

PHILIPPA DE HAINAULT, who *m.* Edward III., of England, and had,

EDMUND, DUKE OF YORK, who had by his wife, Isabel, daughter of Peter, King of Castile and Leon.

RICHARD, EARL OF CAMBRIDGE, beheaded in 1415. He *m.* Lady Anne de Mortimer, a descendant of Edward III., of England, and had,

RICHARD, DUKE OF YORK, the Protector, starter of the War of Roses, killed in battle, 1460. He *m.* Lady Cecily de Nevill, a descendant of Edward III., of England, and had,

GEORGE, DUKE OF CLARENCE, K.G., murdered in 1477, brother to Kings Richard III., Edward IV. and Elizabeth, Queen consort of Henry VII., and uncle of Henry VIII. and of Edward V., and Richard, Duke of York, brothers, murdered in the Tower of London. He *m.* Lady Isabel de Nevill (whose sister, Anne, *m.* first, Edward, Prince of Wales, only son of Henry VII., and after his murder, *m.* secondly, King Richard III.), a descendant of Edward III., of England, and daughter of Richard, Earl of Warwick, "the king maker," and had an only daughter,

LADY MARGARET PLANTAGENET, Countess of Salisbury, beheaded in 1541, aged 72 years, sister of Edward, "the last of the Royal Plantagenets," beheaded in 1499. She *m.* Sir Richard Pole, K.G., *d.* Nov., 1505, and had,

SIR HENRY POLE, created Lord Montagu, beheaded in 1539. He *m.* Lady Jean de Nevill, a descendant of Edward III., of England, and had,

LADY KATHERINE POLE, who *m.* Sir Francis Hastings, K.G., second Earl of Huntingdon, *d.* 20 June, 1561, and had,

LADY CATHERINE HASTINGS, who *m.* Sir Henry Fienes, tenth Baron Clinton, K.B., second Earl of Lincoln, a descendant of Edward III., of England, and had,

THOMAS, THIRD EARL OF LINCOLN, and eleventh Baron Clinton, *d.* 15 Jan., 1619. He *m.* Elizabeth, daughter of Henry Knyvett, of Charlton manor, in Wiltshire, and had,

LADY SUSAN FIENES, who *m.* "John Humfrey, Esq.," 1595-1661, a lawyer, of Dorchester, Dorsetshire (see p. 146). Mr. Humphrey was a shareholder in the Mass. Bay Company, of London, and removed with his wife and family to New England, in July, 1634, and resided at Lynn, of which he was one of the founders. They returned to England in 1641, and resided at Sandwich, in Kent. Their daughter,

ANNE HUMPHREY, *b.* 1621, *m.* first, at Salem, Mass., William Palmes (? Palmer), who came from Ardfinan, Ireland, and had,

SUSAN PALMER, 1665-1747 (N. E. His. Gen. Reg., XXXI, p. 307). She *m.* Samuel Avery, of New London, Ct., 1664-1723, and had,

JONATHAN AVERY, who had by his wife, Preserved,

ROBERT AVERY, who had by his wife, Anna,

ANNA AVERY, who *m.* George Haliburton, and had,

ANNA HALIBURTON, who *m.* Henry McClintock, and had,

CAROLINE MCCLINTOCK, who *m.* Richard Jenness, and had,

CLARA JENNESS, a member of the National Society of Colonial Dames of America. She *m.* Hon. William Thomas Hamilton, of "Oak Hill," Hagerstown, Md., Governor of Maryland, &c., and had,

1. RICHARD JENNESS HAMILTON.

2. JULIA H. HAMILTON, *m.* James Thompson Briscoe. *No issue.*

3. CLARE HAMILTON, *m.* Harold Hayden Eames, and had *Clare Jenness, Emma Hayden, Julia Hamilton,* and *Hamilton.*

4. JOSEPHINE HAMILTON, *m.* Hiram Percy Maxim, and had *Hamilton* and *Percy.*

5. WILLIAM T. HAMILTON, *m.* Mary Vincent Jamison, and had *Mavin.*

6. LEONORE HAMILTON, *m.* 28 April, 1909, Marshall M. Wilson.

THE ROYAL DESCENT
OF
MRS. ANNIE W. L. KERFOOT
OF CHICAGO, ILLINOIS.

THE EMPEROR CHARLEMAGNE=Hildegarde de Suabia.

- Louis I., King of France.
- Pepin, King of Italy.
- Charles II. ALFRED THE GREAT.
- Bernard, King of Italy.
- Louis II. Edward the Elder.
- Pepin de Peronne.
- Charles III.=Egiva, of England.
- Herbert I. de Vermandois.
- Louis IV., King of France.
- Herbert II. de Vermandois.
- Gerberga, Princess of France.=Albert I. de Vermandois.
- Herbert III. de Vermandois.
- HUGH CAPET, King of France.
- Otho de Vermandois.
- Robert I. King of France.
- Herbert IV. de Vermandois.
- Henry I. King of France.
- Adelheid de Vermandois=Hugh de Vermandois.
- Isabel de Vermandois=Robert, Count of Meulent, Earl of Leicester. pp. 11, 163.
- Robert de Bellomont, Earl of Leicester=Aurelia, dau. Ralph de Guader, Earl of Norfolk, Suffolk and Cambridge.
- Robert de Bellomont, Earl of Leicester=Petronella de Grentemaisnil. p. 147.
- Margaret de Bellomont=Sairer de Quincey, Earl of Winchester.
- Roger, Earl of Winchester=Helen, dau. Alan McDonal, Lord of Galloway. p. 397.
- Lady Elizabeth de Quincey=Alexander Cumyn, Earl of Buchan. p. 147.
- Lady Agnes Cumyn=Gilbert d'Umfraville, Earl of Angus. p. 147.
- Robert d'Umfraville, Earl of Angus=Lady Alianore.
- Sir Thomas d'Umfraville, Lord of Holmaid=Joan, daughter of Adam de Rodam.
- Sir Thomas d'Umfraville, Lord of Kyme=Lady Agnes. p. 147.
- Lady Elizabeth d'Umfraville=Sir William d'Elmedon, Northumberland.
- Lady Joan d'Elmedon=Thomas Forster, of Bucton. p. 397.
- Thomas Forster, of Bucton=Elizabeth d'Etherstone.
- Thomas Forster, of Etherstone=Elizabeth Featherstonehaugh, of Stanhope Hall.
- Roger Forster, second son=———Hussey.
- Thomas Forster, of Hunsdon, Herts=Margaret Browning, of Clemsford, Essex.
- Sir Thomas Forster, Justice C. P. Court=Susan Forster, of Iden, Sussex.
- Susan Forster=Thomas Brooke, M. P., White Church, Southants.
- Gov. Robert Brooke (see Ped. XCII.), removed to=Mary, first wife, daughter of Thomas Baker, of Battel, Sussex. St. Mary's Co., Md., 1650.
- Major Thomas Brooke, of Brookefield Manor,=Eleanor Hatton. Calvert Co., Md., 1632-1676.
- Col. Thomas Brooke, of "Brookefield," Prince=Anne, first wife, surname unknown. George Co., Md., 1660-1730.
- Thomas Brooke, of "Brookefield," Prince George=Lucy, dau. of Major Walter Smith, of "Hallscroft," Calvert Co., Md. Co., Md.
- Mary Brooke, of "Brookefield"=Dr. Patrick Sim, of Prince George Co.
- Col. Joseph Sim, of Prince George Co., Md.,=Catherine, dau. of William Murdock, member of first Continental Congress. eldest son.
- Mary Brooke Sim=Capt. Roger Nelson. 5th. Reg. Md. Line, Bvt. Brig. Gen., member of the Cincinnati.
- Catherine Murdock Nelson=Otho Williams Lawrence, of "Elk Ridge," Anne Arundel Co., and Hagerstown, Md.
- Annie Warfield Lawrence, member of Society of=Samuel Humes Kerfoot, youngest son of Richard Kerfoot, of Castle Blaney, Monaghan Co., Ireland. Colonial Dames in Md., organizer of the society in Ill., and its first President, in 1895.

| Nannie Lawrence, dec'd., mem. Ill. S. C. D. m. Franklin Beckwith, of Chicago, Ill. | Katherine Nelson Kerfoot. Dec'd. | Alice Gray Kerfoot. 2d. V. P. Ill. S. C. D. | Samuel Humes Kerfoot. Chicago. | John Barrett Kerfoot. New York |

PEDIGREE CXII.

EDWARD III., King of England, had,

LIONEL, DUKE OF CLARENCE, (see p. 351), who had,

LADY PHIIIPPA, who *m.* Edmund, Earl of Marche, and had,

LADY ELIZABETH, who *m.* Sir Henry Percy, and had,

LADY ELIZABETH, who *m.* John, Lord Clifford, and had,

LADY MARY, who *m.* Sir Philip Wentworth, and had,

SIR HENRY WENTWORTH, of Nettlested, Suffolk, who had,

LADY MARGARET, who *m.* Sir John Seymour, *d.* 1536, and had,

EDWARD, DUKE OF SOMERSET, beheaded 22 Jan. 1551-2, brother to Lady Jane Seymour, a wife of Henry VIII., and mother of Edward VI. He *m.* Lady Anne, 1497-1587, daughter of Sir Edward Stanhope, of Sudbury, Suffolk, and had,

LADY ANNE SEYMOUR, *d.* Feb. 1587-8. She *m.* 29 April, 1555, Sir Edward Unton, of Wadley, Berks, and had,

LADY CECELIA UNTON, *d.* 16 June, 1618, aged 57. She *m.* John Wentworth, of Gosfield, Essex, buried 11 Feb. 1613-4, and had,

ANNE WENTWORTH, *bapt.* at Gosfield, 3 March, 1589-90, *d.* 6 July 1633. She *m.* 11 April, 1608, Sir Edward Gostwick, Bart., of Wellington, Bedford, *d.* 20 Sept. 1630, and had,

LADY MARY GOSTWICK, who *m.* first, Nicholas Spencer, of Cople, Bedford, *d.* 1644, and had,

COL. NICHOLAS SPENCER, of Cople parish, Westmorland Co., Va. President of the Virginia Council, 1683-4, *d.* 13 Sep. 1689. See Va. His. Mag. XVII, 215. He *m.* Frances, daughter of Col. John Mottram, Burgess of Northumberland Co., 1645, (see Hayden's "Va. Geneal." p. 100), and had,

MARY SPENCER, who *m.* Capt. Joseph Ball, of "Coan", North'd Co., will proved 15 Sep. 1721, (see Hayden's "Va. Geneal." p. 65), and had,

SPENCER BALL, of "Coan", Lieut. Col. of North'd Co., 1753, burgess, 1755-58, will proved 9 March, 1767. He *m.* ———— Mottrom, and had,

PEGIGREE CXII. Continued.

SPENCER MOTTROM BALL, of "Coan", burgess, 1772, sheriff, 1773. He *m.* Elizabeth, daughter of Francis Waring, of "Goldsberry", justice of Essex Co., 1740-60, and had,

1. SPENCER BALL, of "Coan," 1762-1832, justice of Prince William Co., 1793, and of North'd Co., 1801. He *m.* Elizabeth Landon, daughter of Robert Carter, of "Nomini", descended from Col. Robert Carter, p. 132, also of Royal Descent, and had,

> LUCY ELIZABETH BALL, *m.* 5 March, 1807, William Fitzhugh Carter, of "Mountain View", son of John, of "Sudley", son of Col. Landon Carter, of "Sabine Hall", also of Royal Descent, p. 186. *Issue.*

2. MOTTROM BALL, M.D., of "Woodbury", Fairfax Co., 1767-1842, *m.* 25 Jan. 1800, Martha Corbin, daughter of Maj. John Turberville, and had,

COL. SPENCER MOTTROM BALL, Fairfax Co., 1801-1859. He *m.* 7 May, 1833, Mary Dulany, also of Royal Descent, see p. 45, and had, besides other children,

1. MOTTROM DULANY BALL, Lt. Col. C. S. Army, 1835-1887, U. S. Dist. Att'y, Alaska. He *m.* 17 Oct. 1860, Sallie Stuart, daughter of Stephen O. Wright, and his wife, Mary Louise, daughter of Dr. Samuel Stuart Griffin, son of Judge Cyrus Griffin, and his wife, Lady Christina Stuart, also of Royal Descent, see p. 114. *Issue.*

2. REBECCA FRENCH BALL, *m.* 11 Dec. 1872, John Addison, of Richmond, Va., Lieut. C. S. Army. See p. 45.

PEDIGREE CXIII.

HUGH CAPET, King of France, 987, had:

LADY HEDEWIGE, *m.* Raginerus IV., Count of Hainault, and had:

LADY BEATRIX, who *m.* Eblo, Count of Rouci and Reimes, and had:

LADY ADELA, *m.* Hildwin, Count of Montdidier and Rouci, and had:

LADY MARGARET, *m.* Hugh de Clermont, Count of Beauvois, and had:

LADY ADELIZA, *m.* Gilbert, second Earl of Clare, and had:

LADY ADELIZA DE CLARE, who *m.* Alberic, second Baron de Vere, and had:

SIR ROBERT DE VERE, second son (brother to Alberic, Earl of Oxford, see p. 43), feudal lord of Drayton and Adington Manors, Northants. He *m.* Matilda, daughter of Robert de Furnell, and had:

SIR HENRY DE VERE, lord of Drayton and Adington; who had, by Hildeburga, his wife: SIR ROBERT DE VERE, second son, who inherited Adington Magna Manor, and was ancestor of Sir Richard de Vere, see below, and

SIR WALTER DE VERE, lord of Drayton Manor, *d.* 12 John. He *m.* Lucia, daughter of Gilbert Basset, of Weldon, and had:

SIR HENRY DE DRAYTON, who had his surname from his lordship, *d.* 34 Henry III. He *m.* Ivetta, daughter of Sir William Bourdon, and had:

SIR BALDWIN DE DRAYTON, *d.* 6 Edward I., lord of Drayton Manor, who *m.* Idonea, daughter of Robert de Gimeeges, and had:

SIR JOHN DE DRAYTON, lord of Drayton Manor, *d.* 20 Edward I., who *m.* Philippa, daughter of Sir Ralph d'Arderne, and had:

LADY CATHERINE DRAYTON, who *m.* Sir Henry de Greene, Lord Chief Justice of England, in 1353; *d.* 1369, also of Royal Descent (see Pedigree LXV, 4th edition), and had:

SIR HENRY DE GREENE, of Drayton, second son, who *m.* Maud, daughter of Sir Thomas Mauduit, of Warminster, Wilts, and had:

JOHN DE GREENE, of Drayton, second son and heir, *d.* 1433, who *m.* Margaret, daughter of Walter Greene, of Bridgnoth, and had:

PEDIGREE CXIII.—Continued.

ISABELLA DE GREENE, who m. Sir Richard de Vere, of Adington Magna (see above, and also see Bridge's "History of Northamptonshire," and Baker's), and had:

ELENE DE VERE (sister of Henry de Vere, Sheriff of Northamptonshire, 1 Henry VII.), who m. Thomas Isham, lord of Pytchley Manor, in Northamptonshire, b. 1456, and had:

EUSEBY ISHAM, lord of Pytchley, eldest son, who m. Anne, daughter of Giles Poulton, of Desborough, by Catherine, his wife, daughter of Thomas Lovet, of Artwell, and had 21 children, of whom:

GREGORY ISHAM, of Braunston, merchant, third son, d. 4 Sep., 1558. He m. Elizabeth, daughter of Matthew Dale, of Bristol, and had:

SIR EUSEBY ISHAM, of Braunston Manor, Northants. heir, b. 26 Feb., 1552-3, succeeded his uncle, Giles Isham, in Pytchley, and erected the manor house, in 1559, was sheriff of Northants in 1584; knighted by King James I., 11 May, 1603. He d. at Pytchley, and was buried in the church, 12 June, 1626. His will, signed 7 June, 1626, was administered by his relict, Anne (daughter of John Borlace, of Little Marlow, Bucks), whose will, signed 1 Dec., was proved 1 Jan., 1627-8, by whom he had (see "Victoria Histories," Barron's Northamptonshire Families, pp. 146-7), six sons and six daughters, of whom,

WILLIAM ISHAM, third son, bapt. at Braunston, 20 March, 1588. He had a legacy of £200 under his mother's will, and his wife, "a border of goldsmith's work." He m. at Foddington, in Bedfordshire (see Blogde's "Geneal. Bedford."), 15 Aug., 1625, Mary, daughter of William Brett, of Toddington (see London Visitations, 1568), and sister to Sir Edward Brett, of Bexley, Kent, sergeant-porter to the King, whose will (see N. E. His. Gen. Reg. July, 1890, and William and Mary Quart, vol. I, 108-9), signed 22 Dec., 1682, mentions his Virginia nephew, Henry Isham, deceased, and the latter's two daughters.

William and Mary Isham had a daughter, *Anne,* and two sons, *Euseby,* and

HENRY ISHAM, second son, a legatee in the will of his uncle, Sir Edward Brett. He was named as "Capt. Harry Isham, of Bermuda Hundred," on the James river, Henrico Co., Va. (where he patented land in 1661), in will of John Smith, of Bristol, 1676, and d. before 1680. He m. Katherine Banks, presumed to be of a Canterbury family, relict of —— Ryall, or Royall (by whom she had a son, "Joseph Ryall"), and had by her, whose will, dated 10 Oct., was proved in Va., 1 Dec., 1686, one son and two daughters, namely,

1.—HENRY ISHAM, of Henrico Co., Va., to whom Thomas Isham, of the Middle Temple, London, his cousin-german, gave a legacy in his will, dated 13 June, 1676, on condition that Henry should come back and spend a year in England. Henry died *s. p.* at sea, returning from England to Va., and his will, signed 13 Nov., 1676, was proved in London, 5 June, 1680, and in Va., by the executor, William Randolph, 1 Feb., 1678-9. He gave legacies to his mother, Katherine, and her son Joseph, and bequeathed his plantation, "Doggams," in Charles City Co., Va., to his sisters, Mrs. Randolph and Mrs. Eppes, and the residue of his estate, in Va. and Eng., to his executor.

2.—ANNE ISHAM, who *m.* before 1676, Francis, son and heir of Col. Francis Eppes, of Va. *Issue.*

3.—MARY ISHAM, *b.* 1659. She *m.* before 1676, Col. William Randolph, of Turkey Island, James river, Va., a member of the Virginia House of Burgesses, and the Governor's Council, *d.* 21 April, 1711, aged 60, and had, besides other issue (see Pedigree CCXV, Fourth Edition, of which this royal descent is a correction and pp. *ante* 136, 168, 180).

1.—ISHAM RANDOLPH, of "Dungeness," *d.* 1742, *m.* 1717, Jane Rodgers, and had:

JANE RANDOLPH, b. 1720, *m.* 1739, Peter Jefferson, of "Shadwell," Va., 1708-1757, and had:

THOMAS JEFFERSON, President of the United States, 1801-1809, who *m.* 1772, Martha, daughter of John Wayles, of "The Forest," Va., and widow of Bathurst Skelton. For descendants, see p. 719, 4th Edition.

2.—ELIZABETH RANDOLPH, *d.* 1719, *m.* 1701, second wife, Richard Bland, of "Jordans Point," Va., *d.* 1720, and had:

RICHARD BLAND, of "Jordans Point," 1710-1776, a member of the Continental Congress. He *m.* first, in 1729, Anne, 1712-1758, only daughter of Peter Poythress, of "Fleur de Hundred," Va., and had by her:

LUCY ATKINSON BLAND, who *m.* Rev. Theodorick Bland Pryor, of Dinwiddie Co., Va., and had:

JUDGE ROGER A. PRYOR, LL.D., of New York. He *m.* Sara Agnes Rice. For her Royal Descent, and descendants, see p. 349.

3.—MARY RANDOLPH, *b.* 1692, *d.* before May, 1738. She *m.* 1712, William Stith, of Williamsburg, Va., and had:

MARY RANDOLPH STITH, 1715-1785, sister to Rev. William Stith, third President of William and Mary College, 1752-55. She *m.* 1733, Rev. William Dawson, D.D., 1704-1752, second President of William and Mary College, 1743-52, and had:

MARY DAWSON, *b.* Williamsburg, 28 June, 1734, *d.* 29 June, 1788. She *m.* 1752, Ludwell Grymes, of "Brandon," Middlesex Co., Va., *b.* 26 April, 1733, and had:

MARY GRYMES, *b.* Williamsburg, 25 Aug., 1753, *d.* 23 Sep., 1839. She *m.* 7 March, 1777, Rev. Walker Maury, D.D., of Norfolk, Va., 1752-1788, son of Rev. James Maury, of Albemarle Co., Va., and had:

PENELOPE FONTAINE MAURY, *b.* 3 June, 1785, *d.* 5 May, 1833. She *m.* Robert Polk, of Washington, D. C., 1788-1818, and had:

ROBERT I. W. POLK, of Washington, D. C., *b.* 28 March, 1818, *d.* 11 Oct., 1861; *m.* 19 Jan., 1842, Sarah, *b.* 8 June, 1817, *d.* 12 June, 1889, daughter of James Somerville, of Frederick Co., Va., and had:

PENELOPE FONTAINE MAURY POLK, *b.* Winchester, Va., 17 Aug., 1843, residing in Philadelphia, a member of the Pa. Society of the Colonial Dames of America. She *m.* 15 Feb., 1865, Philip Leidy, M.D., of Philadelphia, 1838-1891, and had:

1.—JOSEPH LEIDY, M.D., of Philadelphia, *b.* 11 April, 1866, *m.* Helen Redington, daughter of William T. Carter, of Philadelphia.

2.—JAMES FONTAINE LEIDY, *b.* 11 Jan, 1869, *d.* June, 1869.

3.—C. FONTAINE MAURY LEIDY, M.D., *b.* 28 June, 1873, *m.* Margaret, daughter of John Ridgely, of Hampton, Md.

4.—GERTRUDE LEIDY, *b.* 31 Oct. 1879.

5.—KATHRYN MELLICK LEIDY, *b.* 2 May, 1882, *m.* Waln Morgan Churchman, of Philadelphia, also of Royal Descent, see p. 126.

PEDIGREE CXIV.

EDWARD, I., King of England, had by his second wife:

THOMAS, Earl of Norfolk, Earl Marshal of England, who had:

MARGARET, Duchess of Norfolk, m. John, Lord Segrave, and had:

LADY ELIZABETH SEGRAVE, who m. John, Lord Mowbray, and had:

SIR THOMAS MOWBRAY, K.G., Lord Mowbray, who had:

LADY MARGARET MOWBRAY, who m. Sir Robert Howard, and had:

LADY CATHERINE HOWARD, m. Sir Edward Nevill, K.G., and had:

LADY MARGARET NEVILL, m. John Brooke, Lord Cobham, and had:

THOMAS BROOKE, Lord Cobham (see p. 422), who had:

ELIZABETH BROOKE, m. Sir Thomas Wyatt, of Allington, and had:

SIR THOMAS WYATT, of Allington Castle, Kent Co., who had:

GEORGE WYATT, of Allington Castle, and Boxley, Kent, who had:

REV. HAWTE WYATT, d. at Boxley, 31 July, 1638 (p. 423), who had:

EDWARD WYATT, of "Boxley," Gloucester Co., Va., d. 1714. He m. Jane Conquest, living in 1667, and had:

CONQUEST WYATT, of "Boxley," heir, high sheriff of Gloucester Co., 1705-09; a vestryman of Petsworth parish, 1690, whose son,

CONQUEST WYATT, Jr., a vestryman of Petsworth parish, 1727-9, removed to Prince William Co., Va. He m. ——Sayres, and had:

ELIZABETH WYATT, m. Samuel Owens, of Prince William Co., and had:

CONQUEST WYATT OWENS, 1803-1860, of Mason Co., Ky., a magistrate for forty years. He m. Susanna Beverley, b. 8 Sep., 1800, daughter of Francis Preston, 1778-1874, of Fayette Co., and his wife, Elizabeth Beverley, 1781-1852, daughter of George, son of George Stubblefield, will proved Spotsylvania Co., Va., 2 June, 1752, and his wife, Catherine, b. 7 Dec., 1708, will proved 20 Dec., 1778, daughter of Capt. Harry Beverley, will proved, Spotsylvania Co., 2 Feb., 1730 (see Va. His. Mag. III. 173), and his wife, Elizabeth Smith (granddaughter of Maj. Gen. Robert Smith, of Va.), son of Major Robert Beverley, burgess and justice in Middlesex Co., will proved 4 April, 1687, and had:

COL. FRANK SAMUEL OWENS, of Maysville, Ky., *b.* near Washington, Mason Co., Ky., 28 June, 1829, *d.* 10 Jan., 1895. He *m.* 26 Oct., 1859, Mary Parry, *d.* 19 Dec., 1898, daughter of Theodrick Lee Browning, 1810-1865 (and his wife, Frances Dobyns Parry), of Mason Co., son of Thomas Browning, 1767-1834 (and his wife, Elizabeth Le Wright), removed, in 1795, to Mason Co. from Culpeper Co., Va., son of Joshua Browning, removed from Culpeper Co., Va., to Ky., 1795, *d.* in Bourbon Co., Ky., 20 Dec., 1814 (and his wife Nancy Scott), and had:

1.—FRANCES BROWNING OWENS, *m.* Ephraim Robert Blaine, of Clifton, Cincinnati, Ohio, no issue.

2.—ROBERT BUCHANAN OWENS, *m.* Julia Nelson Wood, and had *George Wood, Frank,* and *Robert Buchanan.*

3.—HARRY BARKLEY OWENS, *m.* Lottie Perrine, and had *Perrine.*

4.—ELIZABETH HALL OWENS, *m.* George Cox Keith, and had, *Owens, Elizabeth Barkley,* and *John.*

5.—LIDA BROWNING OWENS, *m.* Samuel S. English, and had *Mary Owens,* and *Samuel Owens.*

EDWARD I., King of England, *m.* Princess Eleanor of Castile, and had,

JOAN D'ACRE, *m.* Gilbert, Earl of Hertford and Gloucester, and had,

ELEANOR DE CLARE, *m.* Hugh, Earl of Winchester, and had,

ELIZABETH LE DESPENCER, *m.* Maurice de Berkeley, of Beverston, and had,

ISABEL DE BERKELEY, *m.* Robert de Clifford, heir to Appleby, and had,

ROGER, SECOND BARON CLIFFORD, of Appleby, *m.* Lady Maud Beauchamp, and had,

PHILIPPA DE CLIFFORD, *m.* William, Baron Ferrers, of Groby.

From this couple descended (see pages 437-8)—

LT. COL. WALTER ASTON, Gent., 1607-1656, of Virginia, whose daughter,

ELIZABETH ASTON (see p. 440), *m.* Francis Mason, Jr., 1647-1697, and had,

JAMES MASON, a justice and burgess of Surry Co., Va., will dated Sep. 1702, had by his wife Elizabeth, will was dated in Sep. 1713,

ELIZABETH MASON, will dated 4 March, 1708-9, proved 3 May; *m.* Capt. Thomas Holt, a justice and a burgess in Surry Co., *d.* before 1708, and had,

JANE HOLT, who, with her husband, was named in her mother's will. She *m.* John Hancock, will proved in Henrico Co., in 1726, and had,

SUSAN HANCOCK, who *m.* Samuel Watkins, of Henrico Co., Va., and had,

SAMUEL WATKINS, of Petersburg, Va., who *m.* Elizabeth, daughter of Bennet Goode, of "Fine Creek" plantation, Cumberland Co., Va., and his wife, Martha, an aunt of President Thomas Jefferson, and daughter of Capt. Thomas Jefferson, Jr., of "Osborne's" plantation, a justice, and sheriff of Henrico Co., and his wife, Mary, daughter of Major Peter Field, 1647-170-, who resided in several counties in Va., and served as sheriff, burgess, and coroner, and his wife, Judith, daughter of Henry Soane, or Soame, of James City Co., a member and speaker of the House of Burgesses, 1660-61, and had,

ALICE GOODE WATKINS, *d.* 7 June, 1866, aged 91 years. She *m.* 1792, Reuben Vaughan, Jr., *b.* in Lunenburg Co., Va., in 1750; *d.* at "Battersea" plantation, in Marengo Co., Ala., in 1837, and had,

MARTHA JEFFERSON GOODE VAUGHAN, *b.* 1805, buried in the Blanford cemetery, Petersburg, Va., 28 June, 1874. She *m.* William A. Gasquet (Guillaume Amédée de Gasquet), who removed from Petersburg to New Orleans, La., and had,

1. FRANCIS JONES DE GASQUET, of New Orleans, *d.* 1908, who *m.* Louise Lapayere.
2. VICTOIRE DE GASQUET, *d. s. p.* 1864, *m.* Philippe de la Chaise, of New Orleans
3. EVELYN E. DE GASQUET, who *m.* John R. Marshall, of New Orleans, and New York, and had,
    I. MARTHA, wife of John J. Wysong, of New York. *No issue.*
    II. MARIE MARSHALL. *Unmarried.*
    III. LOUISE GASQUET MARSHALL, who *m.* first, John A. Kernochan, of New York, and had,
        MARSHALL RUTGERS KERNOCHAN, of New York.
        She *m.* secondly, William Pollock, of New York, and "Holmesdale," Pittsfield, Mass., *No issue.*
4. LOUISE DE GASQUET, who *m.* Andrew Broadus James, of Petersburg, Va., and New Orleans, La., and had,

AMEDEE JAMES, or Guillaume Amédée, Comte de Gasquet-James, of "La Belle Issue," Dinard, France, who *m.* Elizabeth T., daughter of George Watson, (and Anna Tibbits) Pratt. *Issue.*

DESCENT FROM 18 OF THE 25 SURETIES FOR THE MAGNA CHARTA OF MR. AND MRS. ROBERT PITFIELD BROWN, OF "ARNCLIFFE," GERMANTOWN, PHILADELPHIA.

Roger Bigod.
Hugh Bigod.
Ralph Bigod.
Isabel Fitzpiers.
John Fitzjohn.
Maud Beauchamp.
Isabel Chaworth.
Maud Plantagenet.
Joan Plantagenet.

William Malet.
Hawise Muscegros.
John de Muscegros.
Robert de Muscegros.
Hawise de Ferrers.
Robert de Ferrers.
Robert de Ferrers.

Geoffrey de Saye.
William de Saye.
William de Saye.
Lady de Sudley.
John de Sudley.
Joan le Boteler.
Elizabeth Boteler.
Robert de Ferrers.
Mary de Ferrers. = Ralph de Neville.

John Fitzrobert.
Roger Fitzjohn.
Robert Fitzroger.
Euphemia de Neville.
Ralph de Neville.
John de Neville.
Ralph de Neville.
Ralph de Neville.
John de Neville.
Joan de Gascoigne.
William de Gascoigne. = Margaret de Percy.

William de Lanvallei.
Hawise de Burgh.
John de Burgh.
Margaret de Burgh.
John de Burgh.
William de Burgh.
Elizabeth Plantagenet.
Philippa de Mortimer.
Elizabeth de Percy.
Henry de Percy.
Henry de Percy.

Robert Fitzwalter.
Walter Fitzwalter.
Ela d' Odingsells.
Margaret de Grey.
John de Grey.
Robert de Marmyon.
Elizabeth Marmyon.

Robert Mauleverer, of Wothersome, = All

Dorothy Mauleverer, m. 21 Jan. 1543, John Kaye.
Edward Kaye, m. Ann Tirwhitt.
Margaret Kaye, m. William Lawrence, buried 20 Dec. 1572.
William Lawrence, m. 25 Nov. 1559, Catherine Beaumond.
John Lawrence, m. 25 Jan. 1587, Margaret Robets.
Thomas Lawrence, m. 23 Oct. 1609, Joan Antrobus.
William Lawrence, 1622-1680, to New York, m. ....
Thomas Stevenson, m. 2. 1672, Elizabeth Lawrence.
Thomas Stevenson, 3d, m. 2. 10, 1704, Sarah Pennington Jennings.
Sarah Stevenson, m. 8. 29, 1724, Benjamin Field.
Ann Field, m. 7. 20. 1750, John Brown.
John Brown, Jr., m. 11. 13. 1777, Martha Harvye
David Brown, m. 11. 13, 1806, Sarah Williams.
George Williams Brown, m. 5. 10, 1836, Ann Eliza Pitfield.
Robert Pitfield Brown, of "Arncliffe," Philadelphia, m. 11, 24, 1886.
He m. first, Mary R. Tatnall, and had Henry Tatnall Brown

SAIRER DE QUINCY.					
Robert de Quincy.			RICHARD DE CLARE.		
Margaret de Quincy.	=	JOHN DE LACIE.	GILBERT DE CLARE.		
		Maud de Lacie.	= Richard de Clare.		
		ROBERT DE VERE.			
		Hugh de Vere.			HENRY DE BOHUN.
WILLIAM DE MOWBRAY.		Robert de Vere.			Humphrey de Bohun.
Roger de Mowbray.		Joan de Warren.			Alice de Toni.
Roger de Mowbray.		Alice Fitzalan.	Gilbert de Clare.		Ralph de Toni.
John de Mowbray.		Alice de Segrave.	Margaret d'Audley.		Alice de Beauchamp.
= John de Mowbray.		John de Segrave.	Margaret de Stafford.		Thomas de Beauchamp.
		Elizabeth Segrave.	Hugh de Stafford.	=	Philippa de Beauchamp.
John de Mowbray.	=				
Jane de Mowbray.	=	Thomas de Grey.	Margaret de Stafford.	=	Ralph de Neville.
		Thomas de Grey.	= Alice de Neville.		
		EUSTACE DE VESCI.			
WILLIAM DE HUNTINGFIELD.		William de Vesci.			
Roger de Huntingfield.		William de Vesci.			
William de Huntingfield.		Isabel de Welles.			
Roger de Huntingfield.		Adam de Welles.	ROBERT DE ROOS.		WILLIAM D'ALBINI.
William de Huntingfield.		Adam de Welles.	William de Roos.		William d'Albini.
Alice de Norwich.		John de Welles.	Robert de Roos.	=	Isabel d'Albini.
Blanche le Scrope.		John de Welles.			
Stephen le Scrope.	=	Margery de Welles.	William de Roos.		
			Alice de Meinill.		
Henry le Scrope.			Elizabeth d'Arcy.		
Joan Fitzhugh.		Elizabeth de Grey.	= Philip d'Arcy.		
= Henry Fitzhugh.					
			John d'Arcy.		
		Eleanor Fitzhugh.	= Philip d'Arcy.		
			Margaret Coniers.		
			Eleanor Markenfield.		
	Dorothy de Gascoigne.	=	Nyan de Markenfield.		

de Markenfield

SIR EDMUND MAULEVERER, d. 1571, m. Oct. 1541, Mary Danby.

WILLIAM MAULEVERER, 1557-1618, m. Apr. 1571, Eleanor Aldborough.

JAMES MAULEVERER, 1591-1664, m. Nov. 1613, Beatrice Hutton.

EDWARD MAULEVERER, 1640-1670, m. May 1676, Anne Pearson.
ANNE MAULEVERER, m. 26, 3, 1696, John Abbott.
JANE ABBOTT, m 16, 12, 1726, Joseph Burr.
JOSEPH BURR, m. .. 11, 1756, Rachel Coate.
JOSEPH BURR, 3d, m 20, 12, 1798, Mary Sloan.
MARY SLOAN BURR, m. 1, 5, 1822, Chalkley Atkinson.
RACHEL C. ATKINSON, m. 4, 10, 1853, James Willits.
Mary Burr Willits, second wife. No issue.

ADDENDA.

Page 498.—Mrs. Cooper has further discovered she is also descended from seven other Sureties, as below, thus showing her a lineal descendant of 17 of the 18 Sureties who had descendants:—

(Genealogical chart, printed sideways on the page)

Eustace de Vesci line:
- William de Vesci
  - William de Vesci = Isabel de Welles
    - Adam de Welles
      - Adam de Welles
        - John de Welles
          - John de Welles = Margery de Mowbray
            - Anne de Welles

William de Mowbray line:
- Roger de Mowbray
  - Roger de Mowbray
    - John de Mowbray
      - John de Mowbray
        - John de Mowbray
          - Margery de Mowbray (m. John de Welles above)

William de Lanvallei line:
- Hawyse de Burgh
  - John de Burgh
    - Margaret de Burgh
      - Joan d'Arcy
        - Elizabeth Butler
          - James Butler
            - James Butler = Elizabeth Butler (dau. of John de Talbot)

Richard de Clare line:
- Gilbert de Clare
  - Richard de Clare
    - Thomas de Clare
      - Thomas de Clare
        - Margaret Badlesmere
          - Elizabeth de Bohun
            - Elizabeth Fitzalan
              - Joan de Beauchamp = John de Talbot
                - Elizabeth Butler (m. James Butler above)

John de Lacie line:
- Maud de Lacie = John Fitzrobert
  - Roger Fitzjohn
  - Robert Fitzroger
    - Eupheme Neville
      - Ralph de Neville
        - John de Neville
          - Thomas de Neville
            - Maud de Neville = John de Talbot
              - John de Talbot = Elizabeth Butler
                - Gilbert Talbot
                  - John de Talbot
                    - John de Talbot
                      - John de Talbot
                        - Anne Needham
                          - *Robert Needham
                            - *Robert Needham
                              - *Dorothy Chetwode
                                - Grace Bulkley, see pp. 498, 84, 390, 392.

Robert de Vere line:
- Hugh de Vere
  - Robert de Vere
    - Joan de Warren
      - Alice Fitzalan
        - Richard Fitzalan
          - Mary le Strange
            - Ankaret de Talbot
              - John de Talbot

---

* Robert Needham, of Shavington, Sheriff of Shropshire, *temp.* Eliz.
* Sir Robert Needham, first Viscount of Kilmorrey, 1625.
* Dorothy Needham m. Sir Richard Chetwode, and had Grace, see Wotton's "Baronetage," IV. 86.

NOTES.

Pages 27, 409.—MARY ALLYN, of royal descent, d. Windsor, Conn., Dec. 14, 1703 (sister to Lt. Col. John Allyn, p. 27, and to Capt. Thomas Allyn, p. 409), m. at Windsor, June 11, 1646, Maj. Benjamin Newbury, d. Windsor, Sep. 11, 1689, and had:

SARAH NEWBURY, b. Windsor, June 14, 1650, d. Northampton, Mass., Oct. 3, 1716, m. Northampton, June 4, 1668, Capt. Preserved Clapp, b. Dorchester, Mass., Nov. 23, 1643, d. Northampton, Sept. 20, 1720, and had:

WAIT CLAPP, b. Northampton, 1670, d. Norwalk, Conn., Jan. 29, 1722, m. Northampton, 1689, Lieut. John Taylor, b. Northampton, Oct. 10, 1667, d. Norwalk, Nov. 18, 1744, and had:

REUBEN TAYLOR, b. Norwalk, Nov. 21, 1703, d. Norwalk, 1754, whose daughter,

MARY TAYLOR, b. Norwalk, Dec. 3, 1731, d. Richmond, Mass., Sept. 11, 1807, m. Norwalk, Conn., June 5, 1754, Samuel Comstock Betts, b. Norwalk, Mar. 2, 1732, d. Richmond, May 16, 1823, and had:

URIAH BETTS, b. Wilton, Conn., Feb. 25, 1761, d. Newburg, N. Y., Aug. 10, 1841, m. Guilford, Conn., Oct. 14, 1783, Sarah, dau. of Nathan and Rossiter, Jr., b. Guilford, Aug. 28, 1763, d. Richmond, June 10, 1796, and had:

SAMUEL ROSSITER BETTS, b. Richmond, June 8, 1786, d. New Haven, Conn., Nov. 3, 1868, m. Williamstown, Mass., Nov. 4, 1816, Caroline A., dau. of Daniel Dewey, Jr., b. Williamstown, Apr. 8, 1798, d. New Haven, June 9, 1882, and had:

MARIA CAROLINE BETTS, b. Newburg, N. Y., Aug. 15, 1818, m. New York City, July 12, 1842, James Whiting Metcalf, b. New York City, Oct. 28, 1815, d. Westfield, Mass., Apr. 14, 1856, and had:

JAMES BETTS METCALF, b. New York, May 13, 1843, d. New York, Feb. 1, 1896, m. New York, Mar. 31, 1869, Annie Tiffany, b. Westfield, Mass., July 4, 1845, dau. of Franklin H. Cutting, and had:

BRYCE METCALF, of New York, b. New York, Dec. 10, 1874, member of the Society of Colonial Wars.

Pages 28, 385.—Should read:

SIR WILLIAM DE MONTFORT, d. 1453, m. Lady Margaret, dau. Sir John Peche, of Hampton-in-Ardly, and had:

ROBERT DE MONTFORT, of Bescote, Stafford, second son, who had,

KATHERINE MONTFORT, who m. Sir George Booth, etc.

"Margery de Newburg" was not the mother of "Alice de Mauduit," nor was "Maud Fitzjohn" the mother of "Guy de Beauchamp." This correction eliminates the "Magna Carta Barons," Bohun and Bigod, from this claim.

Collins's Peerage, 1779, vol. II, 247, and 1812, vol. II, 185-8, states that Lady Margaret de Clinton, wife of Sir Baldwin de Montfort, of Coleshill, Warwick, was the dau. of Sir John, 2d Lord Clinton, of Maxtock, b. 1303, and his wife, m. 1327-8, Margery Corbet. If this statement was true, Sir William de Montfort, and his descendant "Mary Bruen" (p. 29), would not be of Royal Descent. But it was an error, for Margaret de Clinton's age would not allow her to have been a sister of Sir John, 3d Lord Clinton, son of the 2d Baron, as she m. in 11 Ric. II., 1387, Sir Baldwin,

(541)

according to Dugdale in his "Warwickshire" history. She would have then been about 53 years old, if she was the dau. of the 2d Lord Clinton, as he was dead in March, 1335. Therefore, Lady Margaret was, as on p. 28, the only dau. of Sir John, 3d Baron, by his first wife, Lady Idonia de Say, who d. about 1388, as 3d Lord Clinton m. 2d., in 1389-90, Elizabeth de la Planche, by whom he had no issue. For further particulars as to this matter, see the Boston *Evening Transcript,* Feb. 23, 1909.

Page 32.—Rev. James Bacon m. between 1623-29, Martha Woodward, who d. 25 Aug., 1670, dau. George Woodward and his second wife, Elizabeth, will 8 Aug., 1631, dau. Robert Honeywood, d. 22 Apr., 1576, by his wife, —— Atwater, d. 16 May, 1620.

Martha Bacon, d. before 1667, was second wife of Anthony Smith, a tanner, of Colchester, Eng., will proved 1667. Their dau. Abigail, was *bapt.,* at St. James, Colchester. See Keith's "Harrison," p. 25.

Page 38.—Col. William Bernard was entered at Gray's Inn, London, 1 Nov., 1631. His wife, m. in 1657, Lucy, d. Nov., 1675. She was the widow of Major Lewis Burwell, 1621-1656. See Va. His. Mag., IV, 204. "Virginia Carolorum," p. 260.

Pages 54, 89, 469.—This is also a correction of Pedigree CLXII, 4th edition.

ANNE PYMPE, only daughter and heir of Reginald Pympe, of Nettlestead, by his wife, Lady Elizabeth Pashley (of Royal Descent), according to Inq. P.M., taken in 1576, married Sir John Scott, of Scott's Hall, knighted by Prince Henry, of Castile, sheriff of Kent, 1528 (son and heir of Sir William Scott, K.B., of Scott's Hall, sheriff of Kent, 1490; lord Warden of the Cinque Ports, and constable of Dover Castle, by his wife, Lady Sybilla, daughter of Sir Thomas Lewknor), and had:

SIR REGINALD SCOTT, of Scott's Hall, and Nettlestead, heir, captain of Calais, sheriff of Kent, 1542, will dated 4 Sept., 1554 (see 4th Edition, "Bulletin," p. XXV). He was twice married, first to Lady Emeline, d. *ante* 1554, daughter of Sir William Kempe, of Ollantigh, Kent, and secondly to Lady Mary, who survived her husband, daughter of Sir Brian Tuke, secretary to Cardinal Wolsey. He had, by which wife it is uncertain:

CHARLES SCOTT, of Egerton, Kent. d. 1617, named in his father's will, and in the Inq. P.M., 1576. His oldest brother, *Sir Thomas,* was the heir (see below), and he also had brothers, *George, William* and *Henry,* living in 1576. He m. Lady Jane, daughter of Sir Thomas Wyatt, also of Royal Descent (see Ped. XX), and had:

    1. THOMAS SCOTT, of Egerton, 1567-1635, p. 89.

    II. DEBORAH SCOTT, who m. William Fleete, of Chartham, and had *Capt. Henry Fleete,* of Md. and Va., d. 1660. See pp. 469-70, and "The Magna Carta Barons and their American Descendants," pp. 328-335.

SIR THOMAS SCOTT, of Scott's Hall, sheriff of Kent, 1577, will dated 17 Dec., 1594 (see above), was thrice married, and had nine children. Of these:

    1. MARY SCOTT, m. Sir Anthony St. Leger, of Ulcombe, Kent, and had *Anthony,* and *Sir Warham St. Leger,* see p. 54.

    2. ELIZABETH SCOTT, m. 1589, Sir Richard Smyth, d. 1628 (see p. 803, A.R.D., 4th editon), and had *John* and *Richard.*

    3. DAUGHTER, m. Sir Henry Bromley.

    4. SIR JOHN SCOTT, of Nettlestead. His second wife was Lady Catharine, daughter of Sir Thomas Smyths, and widow of Sir Rowland Hayward, Lord Mayor of London, d. 1593, father of Mary Hayward, wife of Sir Warham St. Leger, p. 54.

    5. RICHARD SCOTT, m. Catharine Hayward, also a daughter of the Lord Mayor.

Pages 57, 64, 245.—Lucy Lyons, wife of John Hopkins, was not the daughter of Sarah Spotswood Waugh, but was the sister of Dr. James Lyons, husband of this Miss Waugh, and dau. of Judge Peter Lyons, of the first Court of Appeals of Va., and his wife, Mary Catherine, dau. of James Power, of Ireland. Therefore, John Hopkins, Jr., was not of royal descent. See p. 353.

Page 64.—"Sarah Fenn" was the name of wife of Lt. Col. Thomas Claiborne.

Page 132.—See Boston *Evening Transcript*, 29 July, and 19 Oct., 1908, as to parentage of "King" Robert Carter.

Page 142.—See "Fauntleroy" ped. in "Fragmenta Genealogica," VII, 44.

Pages 162, 244, 293.—"Elizabeth Moore" did not marry Col. James Macon. She m. William Penn Taylor, M.C., of Caroline Co., Va. See Richmond, Va., *Standard*, 3 Sep., 1881. Col. Macon's wife was Elizabeth, dau. Augustine Moore, and aunt of Bernard Moore, Jr., of "Chelsea," King William Co., Va. Therefore, Mary Macon, wife of Col. William Aylett, of "Fairfield," King William Co., d. 1781, was not of royal descent.

Page 170.—Another version of the descent of Capt. John-mor MacIntosh is given as follows, in Dr. Bullock's "Baillie of Dunain," p. 72:
LACHLAN MACINTOSH, the second of Borlum, by his wife Anne, had:
WILLIAM MACINTOSH, third of Borlum, m. 1656, Mary Baillie, and had:
LACHLAN MACINTOSH, of Knocknagail, who m. Mary Lockhart, and had:
Capt. John-mor MacIntosh, b. 1700, etc.

Page 227.—As it is questionable that Sir William Devereux was the son of Sir John Devereux, K.G., d. 22 Feb., 1392-3, by Lady Margaret de Vere, the royal line, in p. 418, is substituted.

Page 244.—Add to issue of Col. William Aylett, of "Fairfield," and his wife, Mary Macon, of "Chelsea":
3. ANNE DANDRIDGE AYLETT, 1778-1818, m. Alexander Alexander, of "Liberty Hall," Rockbridge Co., Va., 1768-1844, and had:
MARY ANNE ALEXANDER, 1806-1881, who m. Francis Thomas Anderson, Judge of the Supreme Court of Appeals of Va., son of Col. William Anderson, of "Walnut Hill," Botetourt Co., Va., and had:
ANNE AYLETT ANDERSON, m. Rev. William Finney Junkin, D.D., LL.D., of Montclair, N. J., b. 1831, son of Rev. George Junkin, D.D., LL.D., 1790-1868, and had:
1. FRANCIS THOMAS ANDERSON JUNKIN, A.M., LL.B., of Chicago.
2. WILLIAM DANDRIDGE ALEXANDER JUNKIN, of New York.

Pages 246, 249, 284, 286.—MISS ISA GLENN m., in New York City, 11 Nov. 1903, Samuel John Bayard Schindel, Captain, U. S. Army, and had John Bayard Schindel.

Page 301.—It is queried that "Margaret Erskine" was the dau. of "Margaret Stewart."

Page 354.—The descent from "Henry de Bohun" is incorrect in this page. It is derived in another way, for which see p. 514.

Page 369.—Ford Archer Hinchman was born 28 Aug., 1898.

Page 377.—"Mehitable Deane" was born 6 June, 1697.

Page 377.—Phœbe Richmond Townsend, b. at Barnard, Vt., and was m. there 14 March, 1822.

Page 377.—Norman Cornelius Thompson, was born 25 May, 1828.

Page 377.—Ralph Emerson Thompson was born 1 Feb., 1888.

Page 385.—SIR GEORGE BOTHE, of Dunham Massie was son of
SIR WILLIAM BOTHE, and Maud, daughter of
JOHN DE DUTTON (and Margaret Savage), son of
SIR PETER DE DUTTON (and Elizabeth Butler), son of
EDMUND DE DUTTON (and John Minshull), son of
SIR THOMAS DE DUTTON (and Ellen Thornton), son of
HUGH DE DUTTON, and Joan, daughter of
ROBERT DE HOLAND, and Maud, daughter of
ALAN, LORD DE LA ZOUCHE (and Eleanor de Segrave), son of
ALAN, LORD DE LA ZOUCHE, and Helen, daughter of
ROGER DE QUINCY, Earl of Winchester, d. 1264. See p. 444.

Pages 384-5, 437.—The name of the mother of Sir Guy de Beauchamp is unknown, and since Maud Fitzjohn was not his mother, cancel the descent from Roger and Hugh Bigod, the Sureties. Also cancel the descent in the same ped. from the Surety Henry de Bohun, since his dau. Margery was not the mother of Alice de Mauduit.

Page 387.—*Mrs. Augusta M. Lippincott* has also Deborah Scull. *John W. Muir, m.* Mary T. Brinley, and has John B., *Maria W. Muir, m.* Rev. Frank S. Ballentine.

Pages 391-2.—Make following correction:
Sir Nicholas Woodhull, of Wodehull, Bedfordshire, will signed 25 March, 1531, d. 1532, had two wives, both of royal descent. He *m.* first, Mary, dau. Richard (Edward) Rowleigh, of Farmburg, Warwick, and had Anthony, d. 1543, (p. 392), and *m.* secondly, Lady Elizabeth Parr, and had *Fulke* (p. 392).

Page 405.—Correct as follows (see Mackenzie chart-pedigree):
SARAH TAYLOR MACKALL, 1771-1816, *m.* Cosmo Mackenzie, of Calvert Co., 1770-1807, and had:
THOMAS MACKENZIE, of Baltimore, 1794-1866, *m.* Tacy Burges Norbury, 1799-1837, and had:
GEORGE NORBURY MACKENZIE, of Baltimore, 1824-1887.

Page 407.—GIDEON SCULL, of Great Egg Harbor, N. J., had by his wife, Sarah James,
PAUL SCULL, *b.* 1792, who *m.* Hope Kay, 1815-1844, and had,
DEBORAH SCULL, *b.* 7. 11mo. 1822, *d.* 15. 11mo. 1893. She *m.* John H. Lippincott, and had,
JOHN H. LIPPINCOTT, who *m.* 18 Nov. 1902, Augusta Elizabeth Muir, of Royal Descent, see p. 387, and had *Augusta Elizabeth, Deborah Scull,* and *Dorothy Muir.*

Page 422.—Lady Jane Wyatt's father was Sir William Hawte, of Hawtesbourne and Bishopsbourne manors, in Kent Co.

Page 436.—This is the ped. of the immigrant, "Richard Sares," which Mr. May, in his Sears' family history, gives evidence that it is questionable. It was put together by Mr. Somerby, deceased, who compiled the two Arnold (pp. 11, 321), the Wilkinson (p. 275), Browne (p. 137), Gov. Thomas Dudley, of Mass., etc., royal descents, all of which I have found to be fake pedigrees.

Page 437.—Lady Alice de Harcourt was the mother of Lady Alice de Newburgh. See p. 217, and note to pp. 28, 385.

Page 445.—Sir Thomas, first Lord Darcy of the North, was not a K.G.

Page 449.—Correct as follows:

Sarah Kittredge, m. as his first wife (his second wife was Frances Maynard Marshall), George Canfield, of New York, and had *George*.

Pages 463 and 464 are not "Pedigree CI," continued.

Page I., Corrigenda. The discovery of the correct lineage of Mary Isham, wife of Col. Randolph, of Va., may be found in Pedigree CIX.

Page 465.—Lieut. Henry Bowen, 1633-1724, was not an ancestor of Mrs. Bullock.

Page 467.—Correct to "Myrick." After "Nicholas Hatheway" his descendants wrote their surname "Hathaway."

Page 471.—Of course, Louis IV. was King of France, and not "of England."

Page 471.—CHARLES MARSHALL, JR, of Germantown, Philadelphia, m. 6 June, 1906, Katharine Marshall Rapplier, and had *Helen Repplier*.

Pages 491-2.—Ped. CIV was investigated in July, 1908, for the Society, by Rev. Dr. Hayden, genealogist employed by the Order of the Crown, and he pronounced it correct in all particulars and statements, when Mrs. William F. Gill, p. 498, was admitted to the Order. See Burke's "Royal Descents." Ped. XCVII, for the royal descent of Roger Hall, of Narrow Water House, p. 492.

Page 493.—Read "Dr. Richard W. Fry, of Roanoke, Va."

Page 494.—Read, "Elena More Mitchell." "Augustus N. Greene." "Rev. Alfred W. Anson." "Thomas Archer Mitchell, *d. unm.*"

The sixth child of Mrs. Edmonia Lorraine was:

"VI. WILLIAM LORRAINE. m. Johana, dau. of William Strother."

Page 495.—The children of Mrs. Mary M. Dundas are:

1. DE SALLES; 2. DOUGLAS; 3. MARRON.

Page 498.—In addition to the nine Magna Charta Sureties from whom Mrs. Philip H. Cooper lineally descends, she has descent as follows from another line discovered too late to insert in the chart:

ROBERT DE VERE, *m*. Lady Isabel de Bolebec.
Hugh de Vere *m*. Lady Hawise de Quincy.
Robert de Vere *m*. Lady Alice de Saundford.
Lady Joan de Vere *m*. William de Warren.
Lady Alice de Warren *m*. Edmund Fitzalan.
Richard Fitzalan *m*. Lady Eleanor Plantagenet.
Lady Mary Fitzalan *m*. John le Strange.
Lady Ankaret le Strange *m*. Richard de Talbot.
Lady Mary de Talbot *m*. Thomas de Greene.*
Lady Anabel de Greene *m*. John de Chetwode.*
Lady Elizabeth de Chetwode *m*. Thomas de Wahull, Sr.,* etc.

Page 500.—The full will of "Daniel Gorsuch, of Walkerne, Herts., Gent.," "late citizen and mercer of London," signed 6 Oct., and proved 24 Nov., 1638, may be seen in the Va. His. Mag., July, 1909. See in same the "Lovelace" pedigree.

Page 505.—Capt. Noah Grant, Jr., was son of Noah Grant (and Martha Huntington), son of Samuel Grant, by his second wife, Grace Minor, dau. of Capt. John Minor, and his wife, Elizabeth Booth, dau. of Richard Booth, of Stratford, Conn., 1608-1687, whose pedigree is in pages 385, 411 and 472.

---

*See Baker's "Northamptonshire," vol. I, p. 32 and p. 739.

Royal Descent of the VENTRESS family.

ROBERT BRUCE, King of Scotland, had,

MARGERY, *m.* Walter, lord high steward of Scotland, and had,

ROBERT II., King of Scotland, who had,

ROBERT STEWART, Duke of Albany, who had,

MARGARET, *m.* Sir Duncan, Lord Campbell, of Argyle, and had,

SIR COLLIN CAMPBELL, laird of Glenurchy, who had,

HELEN, *m.* William Stewart, laird of Balquhidder, and had,

JOHN STEWART, laird of Glenbucky, second son, (p. 337), who had,

DUNCAN STEWART, laird of Glenbucky, heir, who had,

ALEXANDER STEWART, laird of Glenbucky, heir, who had,

PATRICK STEWART, laird of Glenbucky, heir, (p. 337), who had,

WILLIAM STUART, laid of Ledereich, heir, who had,

PATRICK STUART, laird of Ledereich, heir, who had,

ALEXANDER STUART, laird of Ledereich, heir, who had.

1. PATRICK STUART, laird of Ledereich, Balgheider, Perthshire, heir. *Issue.* He removed to No. Car., in 1739, (see p. 337-8). His son Charles wrote out the above pedigree, which his father signed 18 Jan. 1763, and which is extant; printed in full in "American Historical Register," (Jan. 1895), vol. I., the following is correction of Note thereto.

2. WILLIAM STUART, youngest son, who came over with Patrick. He *m.* in Bladen Co., N. C., second wife, Jone McDougal, from Ayr, widow of Daniel Williamson, and had by her, 1. *Catherine;* 2. *Duncan Stewart,* of Wilkinson Co., Miss., *m* Penelope, daughter of Tignal Jones, Raleigh, N. C., (and had Jones; Eliza *m.* Col. Hamilton, U. S. A., (and had Col. William S. Hamilton, San Anton Co., Texas), William; Catherine, *m.* Harry Cage; James, and Charles Duncan, father of John Black Stewart, of N. Y.); 3. *James Stewart, m.* Catherine Knowlton, Wilmington, N. C.; 4. *Jane, m.* Capt. "Jack" Stewart, Woodville, Miss.; 5. *Ann. m.* Dr. James Carroway; 6. *Elizabeth,* see below; 7. *Charles;* 8. *Eleonor.*

ELIZABETH STEWART, *d.* 182-, *m.* in N. C., Lovick Ventress, and removed from Tenn. to Wilkinson Co., Miss., 1809. Their son,

JAMES ALEXANDER VENTRESS, 1805-1867, of Woodville, Miss., *m.* at Woodville, 29 May, 1848, Charlotte Davis Pynchon, 1815-1877, *b.* Brimfield, Mass., and had,

1. LAWRENCE TRASK VENTRESS, of "La Grange," Woodville, *b.* 5 Aug. 1850, *m.* Mary Ellen Holmes.

2. JAMES ALEXANDER VENTRESS, of "Greenwood," West Feliciana parish, La., *b.* 14 Feb. 1853, *m.* Sallie Mathews.

3. JUDGE WILLIAM PYNCHON STEWART VENTRESS, of Woodville, *b.* 28 May, 1854, *m.* Willie Galloway.

THE PEDIGREE OF WILLIAM SCOT, M. D.

Roger Bigod.

Saher de Quincey. — Hugh Bigod. — Henry de Bohun.

Robert de Quincey. — Richard de Clare. — Ralph Bigod. — Margery de Bohun.

Margaret de Quincey = John de Lacie. — Gilbert de Clare. — Isabel Bigod. — Alice de Newburgh.

Maud de Lacie. = Richard de Clare. — John Fitzjohn. — Isabel de Mauduit.

Thomas de Clare. = Amy Fitzmaurice. — Maud Fitzjohn. = William de Beauchamp.

Thomas de Clare = (unknown). — Guy de Beauchamp. = Alice de Toni.

Maud de Clare. = Robert de Clifford. — Thomas de Beauchamp. = Catharine de Mortimer.

Roger de Clifford. = Maud de Beauchamp.

Philippa de Clifford. = William, 5th Lord de Ferrers, of Groby.

Margaret de Ferrers. = Richard, 6th Lord de Grey, of Wilton.

Alice de Grey. = Sir John Burley, of Bromcroft Castle, Salop.

Joan Burley, co-heiress. = Sir Thomas Westcott, *alias* Littleton, King's Justice.

Sir William Littleton, of Frankley. = Elena, dau. Thomas Welshe, of Onlep, Leicester.

Joan Littleton, heiress. = Sir John Aston, of Tixall, Staffordshire, d. 1523.

Sir Edward Aston, Knt., of Tixall, d. 1568. = Jane Bowles (second wife).

Leonard Aston, of Longdon, Gent. = ———, widow of ——— Creswell.

Walter Aston, of Longdon, Gent. = Joyce Nason, of Rougham.

Lt. Col. Walter Aston, of Westover parish, Va., Gent, d. 1656, aged 49. = ——— Norbrow (or Warbrow). (1st wife).

Mary Aston, (second wife). m. circa 1647. = Lt. Col. Richard Cocke, of Henrico Co., Va., d. 1665-6.

"Richard Cocke, the Younger," of Charles City Co., Va. = ——— (unknown).

Anne Cocke. = Major Robert Bolling, Jr., of "Farmingdale," Prince George Co., Va., 1683-1749.
m. circa 27 Jan., 1704-6.

Jane Bolling, b. 1 April, 1722. = Hugh Miller, Gent., of "Greenscrofts," Bristol parish, Va. M. 1745. d. London, 13 Feb., 1762. (Will at Somerset House).
Bapt. Bristol parish, Va., 22 Sep., 1724.

Lillias Miller = Patrick Stewart, Esq., of Cairnsmore, Kirkcudbright, Scotland, 1734-1814.
(widow of John Ravenscroft, of "Maycox," Va.).

James Stewart, of Cairnsmore. = Elizabeth, dau. of Dr. Gilbert MacLeod.
2 Apr., 1791. m. London, 18 Dec., 1829,
d. 19 Sep. 1887.

Elizabeth MacLeod Stewart. = General P. G. Scot, of the British Army.

William Scot, M. D., of Edinburgh, Scotland, and Lindley, Orange River Colony, South Africa. A member of the Order of Runnemede, etc.

CORRIGENDA.

ARNOLD, Pedigree II.—This pedigree is a copy of the one compiled by the late Mr. H. G. Somerby. Since printing it, I have learned that Thomas Arnold, of Cheselbourne parish, Dorsetshire, father of William Arnold, the immigrant of Providence, R. I., was not, as Mr. Somerby stated, "Thomas, son of Richard Arnold, of Bagbere manor," as on pp. 12, 13, hence the royal descent of the said William Arnold remains to be discovered. I have given a fuller explanation of the faults of this claim in the "Boston Transcript," 1 February, 1904, and retain it in this collection in the hope that it will be a guide to its improvement.

ARNOLD, Pedigree LXXVI. Since it is claimed that the immigrant, Thomas Arnold, of Providence, was the half brother of William Arnold, the immigrant, of Providence, the same remarks on the royal descent claim for the said William are applicable to this Thomas. But there is no evidence that the said William's half-brother, Thomas, came to America, and there is evidence that the immigrant, Thomas Arnold, of Watertown, Mass., and Providence, R. I., were the same man, and that he was born in 1605-6, while the real half brother of William was born in 1599. I am retaining this claim to royal descent, hoping that it may be improved on the lines assumed. See further as to the faults in this claim, my criticism of it in the "Boston Transcript," 1 February, 1904.

BROWNE. Pedigree XXXIII. This claim to royal descent is reproduced from the American Heraldic Journal, II., 23 (vouched for by Col. Chester and Mr. Whitmore). The doubt about it arises from there being no evidence found, or produced, that "Simon Browne, Barrister, of Browne Hall, 1540," (the alleged ancestor of the immigrant, William Browne), was the son of Sir George Browne, of Beechworth Castle, executed in 1483, and because he was not named in the Herald's Surry Visitation, pedigree, 1530, with the children of the said Sir George. I have discussed this matter in the "Boston Transcript," 14 March, 1904, but retain the "pedigree" in this collection, as a guide to its revisal. See p. D.

CHAUNCEY.—Pedigrees XV. and XIX.—This pedigree is reproduced from "The Chauncey Memorial." Since printing it, I find that the prominent Chauncey genealogists, Messrs. Fowler, Cluterbuck, Chauncy, etc., failed to agree on who was the father of "Joan Bygot," who is, through her several alleged fathers, the link connecting the Chauncys with Royalty. For this reason, this claim to royal descent could be classed as uncertain, for it cannot be positively stated which one of the Bigods, of royal descent, was the father of said Joan. I have written of this question more fully in the "Boston Transcript," 23 February, 1904. See "The Bulletin," p. II., 4th edition, as to the false claim of royal descent for the Chaunceys through "Catherine Eyre."

DELAFIELD. Pedigree XXIV.—This "pedigree" was reproduced from Burke's History of the Commoners, I., 544, and I regret to say that I find the claim to royal descent false. John Delafield, 1748-1824, of New York, was not a Count of the Holy Roman Empire by inheritance. Nor was his grandfather, John Delafield, who was bapt. at Waddeston, 14 August, 1692, and buried at Aylesbury, 7 January, 1737, of the paternal descent Burke claimed, therefore he was not of the royal descent set forth in p. 102. See further as to this false claim, "The Ancestor," October, 1904, and the "Boston Transcript," 21 December, 1904.

HAYNES, SYMONDS. Pedigrees LXII. and LXIV.—The royal descent, in this line, was compiled by two American gentlemen, Messrs. Chauncey and Jones, about 1860, on the authority of a chart pedigree in the British Museum, in Additional MSS. No. 6065, fo. 76b, which was compiled by Raven in the Richmond Herald, in 1612, a fac simile of which is in the Conn. Mag. of March, 1904. This Herald's pedigree states that Richard Loudenoys (p. 267), married "Katherine, daughter to the Lord Dacres." It is presumed by Chauncey and Jones that this lady's father was Sir Thomas Fienes, second Lord Dacre of the South, as in p. 266, because Raven described the arms of Fienes with this statement, thus giving the impression that Catherine's surname was Fienes, and that her father was of the Fienes line of Lords Dacre. But it seems, from all peerage books, that this second Lord Dacre of the South had only one daughter, namely, Lady Mary Norreys, and that no Lord

A

B.

Dacre, of the Fienes blood, had a daguhter named Catherine. See further as to this in the "Boston Transcript," 13 January, 4 April, and 30 November, 1904. The only "Lord Dacres," of proper age, who had a daughter named Catherine, was Humphrey de Dacre, the seventh feudal baron of Gillesland, and the first Baron Dacre of the North, by writ. See Additional MSS. No. 5530, fo. 17, British Museum, or Nichols's "Coll. Geneal. Topog., Vol. I., 302 and 407, and "Boston Transcript," 8 May, 1905, and p. 460.

FARWELL. Pedigree LXXXV.—After printing this "Pedigree" in good faith, I discovered that the immigrant, Henry Farwell, was not of the parentage given to me. I find that his alleged mother was born in the year he came to New England! And "Henry," a younger son of John Farwell, of Hill Bishop, was born about thirty years after the immigrant came over! I have referred to this "fake pedigree" in the "Boston Transcript," 24 February, 1904.

LYMAN. Pedigree XXXVI.—This claim is reproduced from Dr. Coleman's "Lyman Genealogy." It seems that Sir "William" Lambert, of Owlton, and his wife, Lady Joan de Umfraville, had no son named "Robert," and that the "Robert Lambert, of Owlton," his alleged son, was the son and heir of Sir John Lambert, of Owlton, the son and heir of the said Sir "William," by the Lady Joan. Since printing this claim to royal descent, I find that there is some uncertainty about it, because there is no evidence, and only assumption, by Dr. Coleman, that Henry Lambert, of Ongar, in Essex, 1447, was the son of Robert Lambert, of Owlton, in Durham. I am retaining the claim, hoping that it may be substantiated. See further as to it in the "Boston Transcript," 16 May, 1904.

READ. Pedigree LXXX.—Since printing this claim, I find that William Read, of Woburn, was not the son of Sir Thomas, nor was the immigrant's wife, Mabel Kendall, the granddaughter of Henry and Helen Kendall, as believed by the compilers of the "pedigree;" therefore the claim to royal descent in these lines falls. See further as to this claim in the "Boston Transcript," 29 February, and 16 May, 1904.

WHITING. Pedigree LII.—This claim of royal descent is reproduced from "The Whiting Memorial," and the N. E. His. Gen. Reg., XV., 61. Since printing it I have discovered that Lady Elizabeth St. John, 1605-1677, through whom the Whitings claimed royal descent, was not of all the descent claimed for her. She certainly was the daughter of Sir Oliver St. John, of Keysoe, M. P., d. 1625, but he was the son of Henry St. John, of Keysoe, Gent., and not of Sir John St. John, as on p. 218 (who was of royal descent), as is evident from the will of the said Sir Oliver's mother, proved 7 September, 1616. As the connection of the said Henry St. John with the Lords of St. John, of royal blood, has not been found, this claim may be said to rest in abeyance, and I retain it in the hope that it can be satisfactorily remodeled. See further as to the errors in this "pedigree," the "Boston Transcript," 30 December, 1903.

WILKINSON. Pedigree LXIII.—This was a "pedigree" compiled by Mr. H. G. Somerby, in the American Heraldic Journal, I., 85. Since I reproduced it, I have learned the claim that Lawrence Wilkinson was the son of William and Mary (Conyers) Wilkinson, cannot be substantiated by any evidence, and that there is no proof that the said Mary Conyers, p. 276, through whom the blood royal, was the wife of the said William Wilkinson. I am retaining the claim, hoping that it may be improved. I have given more details as to the unreliability of this claim in the "Boston Transcript," 27 July, 1904.

Pages 10, 76.—Nora Digges, who m. Dr. James E. Morgan, had

1. Ethelbert Carroll, d. unm. 2. George Atwood, d. inf.

3. Eleanora Digges, m. Judge Emory Speer, Macon, Ga. No issue.

4. Anna, m. James Mosher. No issue.

5. James Dudley Morgan, m. Mary Abell, of Baltimore, and had: Edward F. Abell, Eleanora Carroll, Dudley Digges and Charles Carroll.

6. Ada, m. Richard Smith Hill, pp. 10, 76. Issue.

7. Cecil Morgan, m. Henrietta Dodson, and had: James Ethelbert.

Page 24.—Mrs. Martha Denning Van Rensselaer's issue: John Alexander, b. 5 July, 1872, and Frederick Harold, b. 6 January, 1874; m. Josephine Lucy Grinnell.

Page 26.—As to "the clarous family of Prouz," see Westcote's "Devonshire Pedigrees," p. 431.

Page 26, 1. 6.—"Sir Foulke Ferrers." See p. 408.

C.

Page 26.—Margaret (Wyatt) Allyn was also the mother of Mary Allyn, who m. Benjamin Newbury, (Stiles's "Windsor," II.), and had: Mary, m. John Moseley, and had: Joseph Moseley, m. Abigail Root, and had: Abner Moseley, of Glastonbury, m. 1722, Elizabeth Lyman, from whom descends William Ward Wight, of Milwaukee, a member of the Order of Runnemede. See pp. 424 and 427, 4th edition.

Page 26.—Pedigree on p. 408 is the corrected version of the descent of Lady Alice Wotton, wife of Sir John Cirencester, or Chichester, of Ranleigh. Her grandfather, Sir Roger Moels, or Moelis, Kt., was the feudal lord of Newmarch and North Cadbury, Somerset. He served in the war in Wales, 1277, and was appointed governor of Llanbadarn-mawr castle, and d. 1295.. His wife, Lady Alice, was the daughter and heiress of Sir William de Preux, or Prowse, Kt. His father, Nicholas de Molis, was a great personage in the Court of Henry III., and was ambassador, high sheriff, governor of Guernsey, Jersey, etc., and of the castles of Rochester, Canterbury, Shirborne, Corf, etc.

Page 31.—As to Bacon, of Shrubland Hall, see the East Anglican Mag., (N. S.), IV.

Page 32.—For will of Rev. James Bacon, see "Bury Wills," in Camden Soc. Pub.

Page 37.—See Mrs. Higgins's "The Bernards of Abington," Glover's "Kingthorpiana," and William and Mary Quart., III., 41.

Page 38.—Col. Bernard was brother to Sir Robert Bernard, Bart., of Brampton Hall, Hunts, 1600-1666.

Pages 39, 78, 250, 297.—Mr. Ashton A. Chapman, of Franklin, W. Va., is a member of the Order of Runnemede.

Page 42.—The death notice of James Boyd, the immigrant, in the "Columbian Centinel," Boston, Wednesday, 3 October, 1798, says: "Died, on Friday evening (September 28th), in this town, Mr. Boyd." And in same, October 6th, "Died in this town, James Boyd, Esq., Aet. 62." If Mr. Boyd was aged 62 when he died, in 1798, he was born about 1736, and for this reason the question was raised, could he have been the "James, b. and bapt. 3 and 4 May, 1732," the tenth child of Robert Boyd, of Kilmarnock, 1689-1762, who was m. 25 October, 1714, and had eleven children? See the "Boston Transcript," 27 April, 1904.

Page 47.—Dr. Charles E. Cadwalader and Howard Reifsnyder, both of Philadelphia, members of the Order of Runnemede, are of Royal Descent in Ped. X.

Page 51.—Armistead Peter, of New York, a member of the Order of Runnemede, is of Royal Descent in Ped. XI.

Page 53.—Joseph W. Woolfolk, of Anniston, Ala., a member of the Order of Runnemede, is of Royal Descent in Ped. XII.

Page 63.—See Jackson's "Cumberland and Westmoreland Papers."

Page 64.—Capt. William Claiborne's (second son) mother, Grace, 1558-1594, m. secondly, Gerard Lowther. Her tomb in the chancel of Chatterick Church, Yorks.

Page 67.—Roger Bigod, the last Earl of Norfolk, d. s. p. 1306, (it has been suggested that he was the father of King Edward I.), surrendered his titles and honors to the Crown, 29 Edw. I., and excluded his brother, Sir John (d. 1312), and Ralph, and the latter's son, Sir John Bigod, of Singes, Norfolk (d. 1305). Sir John (d. 1312), is supposed to have been the one who had two sons, John, his heir, and Roger, of Settrington, who had John and Roger, and, it is also claimed, was the father of Joan Chauncey (see p. A). See Canci or Chauncy Genealogy, in Banks's "Stemmati Anglican," pedigrees of families omitted by Dugdale.

Page 67.—As to John Chauncy, who d. 8 June, 1510; From Plea Rolls, de Banco, Easter, 20 Edw. IV., 1461, "Hereford:"—"Walter Patsyll and Rose, his wife, sued John Chauncy, late of Sabryggeworth, gentleman, for illegal entry by force into a tenement at Sabryggeworth. Ralph Gyfford, formerly seized of said tenement, had granted it to John Gyfford and Matilda, his wife, and to the heirs of their bodies. According to an Inq. P. M., taken 1448-9, on the death of John Chauncy, the manor of Great Swampford, called Giffords, had descended to John Gyfford, to William, his son, to Margaret, heir, wife of John Chauncy. Margaret had granted said Manor to John Chauncy, her eldest son, and John Chauncy, the elder, by his deed, had granted it to John Chauncy, the younger, his brother, to be held by him and his heirs forever." See The Genealogist, XX., Part II., p. 91.

D.

Page 68.—Some descendants of Rev. Dr. Chauncy:—

Charles S. Hall, of Binghamton, N. Y., and Daniel B. Childs, of New York, both members of the Order of Runnemede.

Page 72.—Inglis Stuart is a member of the Order of Runnemede.

Page 89.—David Scull Bispham, of New York, a founder of the Order of Runnemede, is of Royal Descent in Ped. XX.

Page 91.—See East Anglican Mag. V., for "Wingfield" data.

Page 92.—R. H. Ives Goddard, of Providence, R. I., member of the Order of Runnemede, is a descendant of James Claypoole, 1634-1687.

Page 92.—Sir John Claypool was knighted and created a baronet 16 July, 1657, by Cromwell. He was of Gray's Inn, London, 1651, and was buried in London, it is supposed. His wife, Mary Angell, was buried at Narboro, 19 April, 1661. Sir John was the father of fourteen children. His father, Adam Claypool, of Latham, etc., d. 1634, having m. secondly, 25 September, 1620, Jane Bird. He was the father of ten children.. James Claypool had been a merchant in London before he removed to Philadelphia. His brother, Benjamin, youngest child, bapt. 15 February, 1642, in a letter from London, dated 23 March, 1706, to a son of said James, sent a good account of his father's family, substantiating this pedigree. He said that his father was a J. P. in 1655, and M. P., 1654, and left him £900 per annum; that his brother, John, m. the Protector's daughter; that his mother, Mary Angell, was the daughter of a fishmonger in London. See Mrs. Graff's "Claypool."

Page 105.—For Drake of Ashe, etc., see Westcote's "Devonshire Pedigrees." The will of the immigrant's father was proved 6 May, 1625.

Pages 102, 140, 178, 200, 236, 247.—Lady Elizabeth Gascoighe, m. Sir George de Tailbois, or Talboys, of Kyme, and had: Lady Anne, who m. Sir Edward Dymoke, and had Lady Frances Windebank.

Page 105.—Melville M. Bigelow, of Cambridge, Mass., a founder of the Order of Runnemede, is of Royal Descent in Ped. XXV.

Pages 109, 121.—"Lady Antigone Plantagenet" was a bastard child of Humphrey, Duke of Gloucester (son of Henry IV. by his wife, Mary, daughter of Henry de Bohun), by Lady Jacqueline, wife of the Duke of Brabant (Dugdale). Lady Elizabeth de Grey, d. 1453, and her husband, Sir Roger Kynaston, d. 1496.

Page 115.—Spencer R. Thorpe, of Los Angeles, Cal., a member of the Order of Runnemede, is of Royal Descent in Ped. XXIX.

Page 131.—Thomas Ludlow was buried at Dinton, 25 November, 1607. Will proved in June, 1608. His wife, Jane's will, proved 6 July, 1650. She was sister to Sir Gabriel Pyle, of Bapton. Their son, Gabriel Ludlow, was bapt. at Dinton. He was a Bencher, in 1637, and was appointed (by patent, 5 Ch. I.), "Particular Receiver of the Duchy of Lancaster Possessions in Norfolk," etc., and resigned 23 June, 1639. His wife's, Phillis, will proved 30 September, 1659. See Waters's "Gleanings in English Wills," 276-7. Sarah Ludlow was their youngest and seventh child. She was named in her grandmother's, Jane Ludlow, will, 1650. The parentage of her husband, Col. John Carter, has not been discovered, nor is it known where he resided before coming to Virginia.

Page 137.—"Simon Browne, Barrister," is said to have removed "from Browne Hall, in Lancashire," to Brundish, near Framlingham, in Suffolk, about 1540, but proof of this is wanting. His wife, Elizabeth, d. 30 August, 1584. See p. A.

Page 138.—The immigrant, William Browne, b. 1 March, 1608, was apprenticed to a merchant at Southold, Suffolk, and came from Brundish to New England, when aged 26. See N. E. His. Gen. Reg., Oct., 1871, p. 352. His son, Major William Browne, m. first, 29 December, 1664, Hannah, 1646-1692, daughter of Capt. William Curwen, of Salem, Mass., (Essex Insti. His Coll., VIII., 225). Captain Curwen (or Corwin), is presumed to have been of the Curwen family of Workington Hall, (see p. 63). He was b. at Workington, Cumb., 10 December, 1610, (Savage). See Essex Insti. Coll., XXXII., 211.

Page 146.—Lady Susan's family name was "Fienes."

Page 155.—As to Stanley-Troutbeck intermarriage, see Cheshire Visitations, 1580; Dugdale's "Baronage," II., 248; Collins's "Peerages," (1779), III., 40; Ormerod's "Cheshire," II. As to Troutbeck-Griffith intermarriage, see Dwnn's Visitations of Wales, II., 154, and Hengwrt MSS., No. 96, fo. 603. As to Griffith-Owen Hugh intermarriage, see Dwnn's Visit

E.

of Wales, pedigree dated 8 November, 1588, and vol I., 1728, and MS. ped., by Rowland Ellis, 1697; (see Glenn's "Merion in the Welsh Tract," Pa.). The *m.* contract between Sir William Griffith and Jane Puleston, was dated 2 August, 1522. The Inq. P. M. on Sir William Troutbeck was in 1465.

Page 164, 209, 361.—Hon. Charles Francis Adams, *b.* 18 Aug., 1807.

Page 165.—See Waters's "Gleanings in English Wills," 418-20, for wills of Dr. Daniel Oxenbridge and wife, proved, respectively, 12 September, 1642, and 5 November, 1651, and will of his father, Rev John, 2 June, 1618.

Page 166.—Will of Rev. John Oxenbridge, proved 9 January, 1675 (Waters), and of his wife, Susannah (widow Abbott), 23 March, 1696 (Waters). It is queried: Was "Theodora," *d.* 25 July, 1659, the daughter of Susanuah, third wife, or of his second, Frances, daughter of Rev. Hezekiah Woodward See 4th edition, p. 679.

Page 169.—Frederick H. Winston, of Chicago, a founder of the Order of Runnemede, is of Royal Descent in Ped. XLI.

Page 184.—Sarah C. B. Shaw *m.* first, Summerville Bolling, of Virginia. Issue *d.* young. She *m.* secondly, in California, Albert H. Rose, *d.* May, 1872, and had: Selden and Anna Brooke, *b.* 22 February, 1872, a member of the Order of the Crown in America.

Page 195.—Rev. Dr. Edward P. Ingersoll, of Brooklyn, N. Y., a member of the Order of Runnemede, is of Royal Descent in Ped. XLVII.

Page 199.—William J. Walker, of Richmond, Va., a member of the Order of Runnemede, is also of Royal Descent in Pedigree LXXVII.

Page 205.—John Q. Adams Johnson, of New York, a member of the Order of Runnemede, is of Royal Descent in Pedigrees XXXVIII. and L.

Page 211.—John J. Riker, of New York, a founder of the Order of Runnemede, is of Royal Descent in Ped. LI.

Page 213.—Francis William Woodward, of Eau Clare, Wis., is a member of the Order of Runnemede.

Page 220.—Mrs. Tallant's children, Elsie, and Drury, *d.* 1888.

Page 228.—As to John Whitney, the immigrant, and his ancestry, see Henry Melville's "Whitney," and the "Boston Transcript," 18 May, 27 June, 24 August, and 30 November, 1904 and 25 January 1905.

Pages 246, 249, 284, 285.—Miss Isa Garterey Urquhart Glenn, of Atlanta, President-General of the Order of the Crown in America, *m.* in New York City, 11 November, 1903, Samuel John Bayard Schindel, Capt. U. S. Army.

Page 247.—Lady Elizabeth Gascoigne, *m.* Sir George de Talboys, of Kyme, and had: Lady Anne, who *m.* Sir Edward Dymoke (see Lodge's "Scrivelsby"), and had. Lady Frances, who *m.* Sir Thomas Windebank, who was buried at St. Martin's-in-the-Field, London, 25 November, 1607. Inq. P. M. 1609, (6 Jas. I., Part II., No. 200, of Harl. MSS., 1551. fo, 57b.). Sir Thomas was knighted by James I., 23 July, 1603. See William and Mary Quart., July, 1903, as to the baptism of his children at St. Martin's-in-the-Field. See also, "The Athenæum," London, 24 March, 1894, and Va. His. Mag., IV., 204.

Page 248.—Some descendants of Col.. George Reade:—

Charles F. Whitner, of Atlanta, Ga., a member of the Order of Runnemede, son of Mrs. Sarah Cobb Whitner, p. 249, also of Royal Descent, in Ped. VII.

Garrard Glenn, of New York, (p. 249), a member of the Order of Runnemede. Also of Royal Descent in Pedigrees VII. and LXV.

William Jacqueline Holliday, of Indianapolis, pp. 200, 251, and his son, Jacqueline S. Holliday, (see p. 162), are members of the Order of Runnemede. The latter is also of Royal Descent in Pedigrees XXIX., LVIII. and LXVIII.

Page 248.—Lady Mildred Windebank was bapt. as "Margareta," at St-Martin's-in-the-uly, 1600, when aged only 16 years, to RobertField 12 August, 1584. She was *m.* there, 31 J Reade, of Lincolnholt parish, Southants, and was his second (or third) wife. Her will, dated 15 August, 1630. His first (or second) wife, Alice Pooley, *d.* 12 October, 1598. He had issue by both Alice and Mildred. The date of the birth or baptism of his son, Col. George Reade, has not been found.

Page 250.—"Throckmorton," see William and Mary Quart., July, 1894.

F.

Page 250.—"John Reade," (who m. Mary, daughter of John Lilly), is called "Robert." in William and Mary Quart., III., 40.

Page 251, "Warner." See Va. His. Mag. II. 423; III., 11, and W. and M. Quart., IV., 48.

Page 252-3.—Major Courtland H. Smith, of "Hampton Farm," in Fairfax Co., Va., d. 27 January, 1902. His son, Courtland H. Smith, is a member of the Order of Runnemede, as are also Francis Lee Daingerfield, of Alexandria (p. 253), and Col. Francis Lee Smith, Jr., (p. 252).

Page 260.—Arthur Howe Carpenter, of Denver, is a member of the Order of Runnemede. (See p. 423).

Page 267.—Some descendants of Mrs. Mabel Haynes:—

A. Howard Clark, of Washington city, a member of the Order of Runnemede.

Charles C. Pomeroy, of New York, (deceased), a founder of the Order of Runnemede.

Gen. Charles W. Darling, of Utica, N. Y., a founder of the Order of Runnemede.

Charles S. Ward, M. D., of Bridgeport, Conn., (deceased), a founder of the Order of Runnemede.

Page 275.—Burke was followed in placing Lady Elizabeth Talbot as granddaughter of Gen. Sir John Talbot, Earl of Shrewsbury, but it seems that this is wrong, as Lord Thomas Talbot, the General's eldest son, who d. v. p., 145—, was older, of course, than his brother, John, second son, who succeeded as Earl of Shrewsbury, and was aged 47 years when he was killed in 1460, and the General's alleged grandson, Richard (son of said Lady Elizabeth), sixth Baron de Grey, of Wilton, was b. in 1391, which was twenty years before his alleged grandfather, Lord Thomas Talbot, was born.

Page 279.—"Dorothy Harlakenden" was of Royal Descent as in p. 460.

Page 282.—Mrs. Hanson's royal descent is corrected in p. 460.

Page 284.—Garrard Harris, of Jackson, Miss., son of Mrs. Gertrude Garrard Harris, is a member of the Order of Runnemede.

Page 285.—William Green was a "yeoman of the body-guard" to William of Orange, according to the "Census of the Officers of the Court," of William III., taken 1693-4. See the printed membership book of the S. A. R., p. 722. His wife, Eleanor Duff, was sister to William Duff, a Quaker, of King George Co., Va., who came to Va. about 1710-17. The will of Henry Green, of Fauquier Co., 6 September, 1782, proved 19 September, 1785, names his mother, Anne, brothers, William and Willis Green, and "sister Eleanor Duff Green." Robert Green, 1695-1748, came over with his uncle, William Duff. Will proved at Orange C. H., in 1748.

Page 290.—Dandridge Spottswood, of New York, a founder of the Order of Runnemede, is of Royal Descent in Pedigrees XXXII., LVIII. and LXVIII.

Page 291.—A letter from John Pratt, in Manor street, Chelsea, near London, 2 April, 1725, "Now tell you that Colo. Spotswood was married about a month ago to a daughter of Mr. Braine, who was formerly a steward of Chelsea College. Ye young lady is said to be wonderfully pretty, but no money. Ye Colo. hath taken a house in Duke street, near ye park, where he now lives, and doth not intend to return to Va. any more." See "Roger Jones's Family," of Va., p. 125. The evidence of the descent of Gen. Alexander Spotswood, as set forth, may be found in a book, "Published by John Spotiswoode, of that Ilk, Advocate, the Author's Grandson," entitled, "Practicks of the Laws of Scotland, Observed and collected by Sir Robert Spotiswoode, of Penland, President of the College of Justice, and Secretary of State to K. Charles the I," etc., Printed and sold in Edinburgh, in 1706. In this work, the Advocate included a memoir by himself of Sir Robert Spotiswoode's "Life and Trial for an alleged Crime of High Treason against the States, in the Pretended Parliament at St. Andrew's, in Dec., 1645, and Jan., 1646." The Advocate says, at p. XL., "It remains that we give account of Sir Robert's Marriage, Children, and Fortune. In the year 1629, he married Mrs. Bethia Morison, eldest daughter of Sir Alexander Morison, of Prestongrange, one of the Senators of the College of Justice, who did bear him four Sons and three Daughters, of which Children at the time of his death there were only three Sons alive:

1.—Mr. John Spotiswoode, who died unmarried, before the restoration of King Charles II., in the year 1660.

G.

2.—Mr. Alexander Spotiswoode, of Crumstain, Advocate, who died in the year 1675, and left behind him three Sons and two Daughters.

3.—Robert Spotiswoode, a Physician, who died in the year 1680, and left behind him one Son, who at present is Lieutenant-General, Quartermaster of the English Army in Holland, under the Command of the Duke of Marlborough."

This army officer referred to is no other than Gen. Alexander Spotswood, *b*. at Tangier British garrison, in 1676, where his father was the surgeon. Gen. Spotswood arrived in Virginia in the man-o'-war, Depford, 20 June, 1710, and became a high Colonial official. In a letter, dated 14 April, 1718, he says he "had the honor to serve nine years under my Lord Cadigan, as Lieut.. Quart. Master Gen, of his late Majesty's Army in Flanders." See "Spottswood's Letters," vol. II., p. 298. See also "The Spottswood Miscellany," vol. I., p. 188; Douglas's "Peerage of Scotland," 1798, under "Spottiswoode;" Playfair's "British Family Antiquity," vol. VIII.; Note, p. 305. Gen. Spotswood's mother was Catherine Mercer, widow of William Elliot, of Wells, by whom she was the mother of Maj. Gen. Roger Elliot, Gov. of Gibraltar, 1707, whose will, 7 March, 1713, mentions his half-brother, Alexander Spotswood, see Va. His. Mag., July, 1905.

Page 297, Charles W. Throckmorton, of New York, a member of the Order of Runnemede, is of Royal Descent in Ped. LXX, 209.

Page 309.—Some descendants of Mrs. Elizabeth Digby Lynde:—
Calvin W. Fitch, of St. Louis; Esek S. Ballord, of Davenport, Ia., and Lynde Sullivan, of Boston, who is also of Royal Descent, through Master John Sullivan, pp. 203. They are members of the Order of Runnemede.

Page 313.—Henry M. Duffield, Jr., of Detroit, is a member of the Order of Runnemede.

Page 318.—Philip Barton Warren, of Springfield, Ill., is a member of the Order of Runnemede.

Page 319, 1, 13.—Elna Warren Leib, *m*. 8 October, 1901, William Hammond Wright, also of Royal Descent, see pp. 184, 216, 220.

Page 324.—Capt. Horace Edward Dyer, of "Dyer Place," Rutland, Vt., is a member of the Order of Runnemede.

Page 330.—Dr. Joseph C. Bulloch, of Savannah, is a member of the Order of Runnemede.

Page 331.—The genealogical chasm of 200 years between "Edwin de Temple," 1075, and "Henry de Temple," 1275, has not yet been bridged with connecting generations.

Page 343.—Judge James Logan's "Autobiography" says: "My father was born in East Lothian, in Scotland, was educated for the clergy, and was a chaplain for some time; but turning Quaker, he was obliged to go to Ireland, and to teach Latin school there." "My mother was Isabel Hume, daughter of James Hume, a younger brother of the House of St. Leonards, of the shire of Mers (as I think), in the south of Scotland. He was a manager of the estate of the Earl of Murray, and lived in the shire of Fife." "My grandmother, before she married, was Bethia Dundas, sister of the Laird of Dundas, of Didiston, about eight miles west of Edinburgh, a fine seat. She was nearly related to the Earl of Panmar" (Panmure). See "Immigration of Irish Quakers to Pennsylvania," p. 238

Page 361.—"Abigail Brooks Brown," *d*. 6 June, 1889.

Page 393.—James Goodrich, *d*. New Haven, 17 Oct., 1864. His son, William Goodrich, *d*. Philadelphia, 4 July, 1883. The latter's wife was a granddaughter of Maj. Gen. John Cocke. Casper F. Goodrich. is now a Rear Admiral, U. S. N.

Page 406.—Mrs. Francis T. Redwood has two brothers, Robert Dorsey Coale and George William Coale. Her children are George B. and Francis T.

Page 417.—Mrs. William S. Little was "Mary Wilson."

II.

Of the Presidents of the United States, these apparently were of Royal Descent: Washington, John Quincy Adams, William Henry Harrison, Buchanan, Lincoln, Benjamin Harrison, and Roosevelt.

PRESIDENT WASHINGTON'S royal descent was through Col. George Reade, of Virginia, (see Ped. LIX.), whose descendant, Mildred Warner (p. 253), m. first, Lawrence Washington, d. 1697, and had: Augustine Washington, 1693-1743 (see p. 253), who had by his wife, Mary Ball (see Hayden's "Virginia Genealogies"), Gen. George Washington, twice President of the United States.

PRESIDENT JOHN Q. ADAMS' royal descent was through the Rev. William Norton, of Ipswich, Mass, 1610-1694 (see Ped. XXXVIII.).

PRESIDENT WILLIAM HENRY HARRISON'S royal descent was through Col. Robert Carter, of Virginia, 1661-1732. See Pedigrees XXXII., XLV., and p. 185.

PRESIDENT BUCHANAN'S royal descent was, it is claimed, through the Buchanans of Romelton, in County Tyrone, Ireland, cadets of the Buchanans of Blairlusk, and lairds of Buchanan, in Scotland, from ancient Kings of Ireland. See Ped. XIII., 3d edition. It was also claimed that President Buchanan and the Cassatt family, of Haverford, Pa., were descendants of King Robert Bruce, and the Stewart kings (see Ped. CL., 4th edition), through Lady Isabella Stewart (the alleged mother of Thomas Buchanan, first laird of Carbeth, third son of Sir Walter Buchanan, twelfth laird of that ilk), daughter of Murdach Stewart, second Duke of Albany, sometime Governor of Scotland, who was executed for treason in 1425, (grandson of Robert II., King of Scots), by his wife, Lady Isabella, daughter of Duncan, Earl of Lennox. Recent investigation into this claim has cast a doubt upon it. It seems that because Thomas Buchanan, of Carbeth, aforesaid, and his brothers, Patrick and Maurice, did not have part in the partition and settlement of the Lennox estate, (the aforesaid Lady Isabella Stewart, the alleged mother of the first laird of Carbeth, being the granddaughter of said Duncan, Earl of Lennox), it is doubtful that the said Thomas Buchanan, of Carbeth, was a son of the said Lady Isabella Stewart, but of another wife, name unknown. This naturally queries the lineal descent from the Royal House of Stewart of the lairds of Carbeth through Lady Isabella, whose anti-nuptial contract with Sir Walter Buchanan was dated 17 February, 1391-2. See "The Genealogical Magazine," London, September, 1899, p. 217. The Genealogist, vol. II., p. 497, also the introduction of Burnett's Exchequer Rolls of Scotland, IV., and the "Red Book of Menteith Reviewed." However, some reason may be discovered why these Buchanans did not participate in the division of the Lennox estate, for the younger brother, Maurice, was apparently of an age suitable to have been Lady Isabella's son, as he was in the suite of Sir John Stewart, of Darnley, in 1427, about twenty-five years after his father's marriage to Lady Isabella Stewart.

PRESIDENT LINCOLN'S royal descent was claimed by the late Howard M. Jenkins, of Philadelphia, in the following line (see "Boston Transcript," 21 February, 1905):

EVAN AP EVAN ROBERT LEWIS, of Fron Goch farm, near Bala, in Merionethshire, Wales, d. 166—, (p. 191), of royal descent, had:

CADWALADER EVANS, who removed to Gwynedd, Pa. He was b. at Fron Goch, in 1664, d. 30 May, 1745. He m. in Wales, Ellen, daughter of John Morris, of Bryn Gwyn, Denbighshire, by his wife, Eleanor v. Ellis Williams, of Cai Fadog, son of William ap Hugh, lord of Ciltalgarth, and had:

SARAH EVANS, who m. at Gwynedd M. H. Pa., 11 Dec., 1711, John Hank, of Whitemarsh, Pa., yeoman. His will dated 12 Dec., 1730, proved in May, 1731, his wife executrix, names seven children, of whom William, b. 1720, Samuel, b. 1723, Joseph, b. 1725, and

JOHN HANK, JR., b. 1712. He resided on a farm in Exeter township, near Reading, Pa., about a half mile from where "Mordecai Lincoln" resided, who was probably an ancestor or relative of President Lincoln. John Hank, Jr., sold his Pennsylvania farm, and with John and Benjamin Lincoln, his neighbors, removed to Rockingham Co., Va., in 1787, where other Lincolns had removed from Pennsylvania. From thence John Hank, Jr., removed to Fayette Co., Ky.

NANCY HANK, b. in Virginia, a daughter (or granddaughter) of the aforesaid John Hank, Jr., m. in Kentucky, in 1808, Thomas Lincoln, brother to Mordecai Lincoln, who died at Hancock, Ill., in 1831, and Isaac and Josiah Lincoln, sons of Abraham Lincoln, who was slain by Indians in Kentucky. Thomas and Nancy (Hank) Lincoln, aforesaid, of Larue Co., Ky., had an only child, born on their farm, near Hodgensville C. H., 12 Feb., 1809:

ABRAHAM LINCOLN, twice President of the United States.

I.

PRESIDENT BENJAMIN HARRISON'S royal descent may be seen in Pedigrees XXXII. and XLV.

PRESIDENT ROOSEVELT is a lineal descendant of the renowned Robert Bruce, King of Scots, through his ancestor,

DR. JOHN IRVINE, of royal descent, [see p. 329, and Am. His. Reg. (Phila.), III., 311], whose daughter,

ANNE IRVINE, m. first, 13 April, 1786, Capt. James Bulloch, of Georgia, and had:

JAMES STEPHENS BULLOCH, a major in Chatham's battalion, of the Georgia Line, in the Continental Army. He m. first, a daughter of U. S. Senator John Elliott, and m. secondly, Martha, daughter of General Daniel Stewart, of the Georgia Line, in the Revolutionary War, and by the latter had:

MARTHA BULLOCH (sister of Irvine Bulloch, the sailing-master of the "Alabama," at the time of her engagement with the "Kearsarge"), who m. Theodore Roosevelt, of New York, and had:

THEODORE ROOSEVELT, twice President of the United States.

Presidents John Adams (Ped. XVIII., 3d edition), and Andrew Jackson (Ped. VI., 1st edition), were claimed to have been of royal descent, but I have turned down their alledged pedigrees in the "Bulletin" of the 4th edition, pp. IV. and XXIV.

President Jefferson, being a lineal descendant of Col. William Randolph, of Virginia, and his wife, Mary Isham, (Ped. CCXV), was supposed to have been of royal descent through the said Mary Isham, till it was found that she was not of the lineage claimed for her. See William and Mary Quart., 1. 158; Water's "Gleanings in English Wills," p. 445, and N. E. His. Gen. Reg., July, 1890.

President Madison's wife, Dolly (Payne) Todd, was long supposed to have been of royal descent in the "Fleming," of Virginia line, (see Ped. XCIX., 3d edition), till it was discovered that the royal descent had no foundation in fact. See p. XVIII., "Bulletin," in 4th edition, and N. E. His. Gen. Reg., April, 1894.

J.

Note to Ped. CIII.—Mrs. Laura L. Whaling (p. 480), sends for insertion, the following versions of this Campbell family's pedigree, from Drs. Creigh's and Murray's "Parker" family, in "The Standard," Richmond, Va., 16 Oct., 1880, and Drs. Egle's and Brock's "Campbell" family in "The Standard," 17 July, 1880, and in Egle's Notes and Queries, July 24, August 14, and September 8, 1880.

DUNCAN CAMPBELL, (1), (of the lineage of the noble branch of Breadalbane), *b.* in Scotland; *m.* there, 1612, Mary McCoy, and removed that year to Ireland. Their son

JOHN (2), *b.* 1621; *m.* 1655, Grace, dau. of Peter Hay, and had:

I. DUGALD (3). His descendants settled in Rockbridge Co., Va.

II. ROBERT (3), *b.* 1656; *m.* 1695. His descendants settled in Augusta Co., Va., in 1740.

III. JOHN (3), *b.* 1656; *d.* 1734; *m.*, emigrated from Ireland to Lancaster Co., Pa., in 1726. He had:

I. PATRICK (4), *b.* 1690, removed from Pa. to Va., in 1738.

II. ROBERT (4), *d.* in Va., *m.* and had four daughters, and one son, *d.* young.

III. JAMES (4), *d.* in England.

IV. DAVID (4), went to Augusta Co., Va., in 1741; *m.* Margaret Hamilton.

V. Rev. JOHN (4), *b.* 1692, P. E. minister at York, Pa., *d.* 1764; *m.*, and had:

I. JAMES (5), *b.* 1731; removed to Va. in 1760.

II. ELLEN (5), *b.* 1733, *d.* 1735.

III. FRANCIS (5), *b.* 1737. (See p. 475).

IV. JOHN (5), lawyer, *b.* 1740, *d.* 1797; *m.* Ellen Parker, and had:

I. Rev. JOHN (6), educated in England, had charge first of the P. E. parish of York, and afterwards of that of Carlisle, Pa., *m.* and had issue.

II. FRANCIS (6).

III. JAMES (6), removed to Chillicothe, Ohio, *m.* the sister of the mother of Hon. Fred'k Watts, of Carlisle. He read law with the father of Mr. Watts. He *d.* about 1807, at York, Pa. Issue.

IV. PARKER (6), *b.* 1768, at Carlisle; *m.* Elizabeth Calhoun (*d.* 1846, in N. O.), of Chambersburg, Pa. His son Parker, bred a civil engineer, is a banker, in Richmond, Va.

And again ("Egle's version"), that the aforesaid

JOHN (3), 1656-1734, had:

Rev. JOHN (4), 1692-1764, P. E. minister at York, Pa., who had:

FRANCIS (5), of Shippensburg, 1737-1791, who had:

Rev. JOHN (6), 1752-1819, P. E. minister at Carlisle, Pa. (half-brother to Ebenezer, p. 480).

Page 477.—Rev. John Campbell was ordained a deacon, 1 June, 1773, and five days later, Sunday, a priest, by the Lord Bishop of London, Richard Terrick, in the chapel of the Episcopal Palace, at Fulham. He became curate of St. John's, Bury, in 1777, and curate of All Saints, Hertford, 1782, where he *m.*, in 1784, Catharine Cutler, who *d.* Sunday, 24 July, 1836, aged 84. Mr. Campbell's monument in the Watts lot, Carlisle, gives him the degree of D. D., but it was not discovered what college conferred it.

ADDENDA.

Page 16.—*Mrs. Julia Sweet Weir*, d. 19 March, 1900. She had only one child, *Laura*, d. 5 August, 1865, aged 12 years.

Page 22.—Mrs. John Kilgour is a member of the Georgia and Ohio Societies of the Colonial Dames of America.

Page 24.—Mrs. Maria Denning King Van Rensselaer was a member and founder of "the original" Society of the Colonial Dames.

Page 24.—Mr. Frederic Bronson d. in March, 1900.

Page 26.—*Matthew Allyn*, 1605-1670, and his wife Margaret Wyatt, of Royal Descent, had:
Mary Allyn, m. 11 June, 1646, Captain Benjamin Newberry, and had:
Sarah Newberry, m., 4 June, 1668, Captain Preserved Clapp, and had:
Roger Clapp, m., 20 November, 1706, Elizabeth Bartlett, and had:
Aaron Clapp, m., 1747, Jemima Bartlett, and had:
Achsah Clapp, m., 16 September, 1780, John Dewey, and had:
Sarah Dewey, m., 19 December, 1804, Gurdon Lord, and had:
Sarah Naomi Lord, m., 12 June, 1849, Renel Kimball, Jr., of Leyden, New York, and had:
Lucy Lord Kimball, a member of the New York Society of the Colonial Dames of America, the Order of the Crown, etc., who m., 29 August, 1877, Henry Gilbert Hart, of Utica, New York, and had: *Henry Gilbert*, b. 25 January, 1879; *Merwin Kimball*, b. 25 June, 1881, and *Richard Seymour*, b. 13 March, 1887.

Page 32.—Abigail Smith, the first wife of Major Lewis Burwell, Jr., was heir to Colonel Bacon, her uncle. She was *bapt.* at St. James's Church, Colchester, Virginia.

Page 32.—Rev. James Bacon had apparently two wives, and it is uncertain which was the mother of Colonel Nathaniel Bacon, who d. 16 March, 1692, and Mrs. Martha Smythe, or Smith (see Keith's "Ancestry of Benjamin Harrison," p. 22). His second wife was Martha, daughter of George Woodward and his second wife, Elizabeth Honeywood.

Page 33.—Mrs. Thomas Marshall Colston was Miss Eliza Jacqueline Fisher.

Page 33.—Mary Eloise Howard, m. Francis Eliot Shoup.

Page 38.—*Judge R. Augustine Thompson's* daughter (by his first wife), *Sarah Elizabeth*, m. G. W. Huie, and had: *Sallie Helena Huie*, who m., in 1899, William Thompson. Judge Thompson's daughter (by his second wife), *Ruth Hairston Thompson*, m. William Craig.

Page 39.—Belle Chapman, m. William Moncure on 12 December, 1878.

Page 40.—The mother of Princess Joan Plantagenet was Princess Eleanor of Castile.

Page 42.—*Miss Augusta Dearborn Boyd*, of Portland, Maine, is a member of the Order of the Crown.

Page 47.—The m., in September, 1293, of Henry III., Comte de Bar, and Princess Eleanor Plantagenet, and the pedigree which follows, are from Burke's "Royal Families," Ped. XXXI. in Vol. i., and his "Royal Descents," Ped. CX. But "L'Art de Verifier les Dates," vol. xiii., p. 457, mentions only one daughter of this marriage: "Jeanne, femme de Jean de Varennes, Comte de Sussex." However, Burke's "Royal Families," vol. i., Ped. LII., gives the following royal descent for Eleanor, wife of Gryffyth Vychan, fourth Lord of Glyndfrdwy: JOHN, KING OF ENGLAND, had by his wife Isabel: ELEANOR, who had by her second husband, Simon de Montfort, Earl of Leicester, d. 1238: ELEANOR, d. 1280, who m. Llewelyn ap Gryffyth, Prince of North Wales, and had: CATHERINE, heiress, who m. Philip ap Ivor, lord of Cardigan, and had: ELEANOR, heiress, who m. Thomas ap Llewelyn, and had: ELEANOR, wife of the aforesaid Gryffyth Vaughn.

Page 48.—Mr. John Hone resides at Red Bank, New Jersey.

Page 48.—The wife of Archibald McCall, Jr., of Philadelphia, was Elizabeth Cadwalader, 1773-1824.

Page 63.—Christopher Curwen and his son Thomas were both knighted, and were high sheriffs. Sir Christopher was one of the truce commissioners between England and Scotland, in 1438. He d. 17 July, 1450, aged 46. His wife was a daughter of Sir John Huddleston, of Millom.

Page 64.—Lieutenant-Colonel Thomas Claiborne, 1647-1683; *m*. Sarah Fenn.

Page 71.—*Mrs. Roswell Smith*, who *d*. 21 January, 1900, aged 73 years. Sent the first telegram for Mr. Morse, the inventor, which was, "What hath God wrought?" Her daughter, Julia Smith, *m*., 23 April, 1879, George Innes, Jr., of New York, and had: *Elizabeth*, *b*. New York City, 22 March, 1880; *Juliet*, *b*. Montclair, New Jersey, 17 June, 1881, and *George Ellsworth*, *b*. at Montclair, 10 October, 1882.

Page 72.—*Mrs. Katharine Stuart Dunscomb's* son, Cecil, was *b*. 20 September, 1887.

Page 72.—*Homer Hine Stuart, Jr.*, *m*. Margaret Beckwith Kenny.

Page 77.—*Mrs. Peterfield Trent*, *d*. before May, 1900.

Page 84.—Mary Sage was *b*. 9 April, 1699, at Cromwell, Connecticut.

Page 85.—Cephas Smith, Sr., resided at Sandisfield, Massachusetts.

Page 85.—Names of children of *Judge Jesse and Roxa (Francis) Booth*: *Walter Bulkeley*, *m*. Eliza Banner; *Pembroke Somerset*; *George Washington*, *m*. Hester Look; *Mary Elizabeth*, *m*. Hugh Beatie Cochran; *Roxa Lyman*, *m*. L. R. Slade; *Thyrza Angeline*, *m*. Julius Austin; *Flora Sylvia*, *m*. Selah Look; *Julia Portia*, *m*. Earl Hollingsworth, and *Ella Cordelia*, a member of the Connecticut and California Societies of the Colonial Dames of America, who *m*. Byron Coleman Dick.

Page 87.—William Henry Bulkeley, *m*., September, 1863, Emma Gurney.

Page 87.—The issue of *Mrs. Sarah T. (Bulkeley) Macauley*: *Richard Bulkeley*, *Frances Gurney*, *b*. 1 December, 1897, and *Sally*.

Page 88.—It is only a tradition that Horatio T. Harris was ever connected with United States Navy, and the statement has not been verified.

Page 90.—Richard Wood, *b*. 1755, resided at Greenwich, New Jersey. His wife Elizabeth, *b*. 1776, was the daughter of John Bacon, *b*. 1725 (see "Family Sketches," by Mrs. Richard D. Wood).

Page 92.—*Miss Susan Kidder Meares* is a member of the North Carolina Society of the Colonial Dames of America.

Page 92.—*James Claypoole*, 1634-1687, of Royal Descent; had:

Nathaniel Claypoole, of Philadelphia, 1672-172–; *m*. Elizabeth ——, and had:

James Claypoole, *m*. Mary Hood, and had:

James Claypoole, *m*. Mary Kemp, and had:

James Claypoole, *m*. Elizabeth Morrison, and had:

John Claypoole, *m*. Martha Ann Browne, and had:

Julia Ann Claypoole, *d*. 1899, a member of the Order of the Crown, who *m*. Isaac Freeman Rasin, of Baltimore, Maryland, and had:

1.—*Helen Ringgold Rasin*, a member of the Order of the Crown, *m*. Hugo Albert Rennert.

2.—*Julia Angela Rasin*, of Baltimore, a member of the Order of the Crown.

3.—*Gertrude Browne Rasin*, of Baltimore, a member of the Order of the Crown.

Page 94.—*Rebecca Wallace*, 1778-1867, of Royal Descent, *m*. Judge Jacob Burnet, and had: *William Burnet*, of Cincinnati, who had by his second wife, Susan M. Clark:

Josephine Clark Burnet, a member of the Order of the Crown, who *m*. (his second wife) Peter Rudolph Neff, of Cincinnati, and had: *Rudolph*, *Robert Burnet*, *Rebecca*, and *Susan Clark Neff*, of Cincinnati, a member of the Order of the Crown.

Page 95.—*Lucy Wortham James* was *b*. at St. James, Missouri, 13 September, 1880.

Page 98.—*Mrs. Nannie Jenifer Triplett*, of Richmond, had also: 1. *John Richards Triplett*, *m*. Sallie Ross, of Mobile, and had: *Mary Amanda*, *Sallie Ross*, *Nannie T.*, and *Helen Lyons*. 2. *Mary Jenifer*, wife of Philip Haxall, of Richmond. *No issue*. Mrs. Lizzie Campbell Price was the second child and Mrs. Montague the fourth child of Mrs. Nannie O. J. Triplett.

Page 104.—Count John Delafield, 1786-1853; *m*., first, at the Hillingdon Church, in Middlesex county, England, 22 January, 1812. His eldest son, John, *b*. in East Street, St. George's, Bloomsbury, London, 21 October, 1812, *d*. 12 December, 1866; *m*., 14 June, 1833, Edith Wallace, and had: Count Wallace Delafield, of St. Louis, Missouri, a member of the Order of Runnemede, *etc*.

Page 106.—*Ursula Wolcott*, 1724-1788, of Royal Descent, *m*. Governor Matthew Griswold, of Connecticut, and had:

Governor Roger Griswold, of Connecticut, who *m.* Fanny Rogers, and had:

Eliza Woodbridge Griswold, who *m.* Charles Leicester Boalt, and had:

Fanny Griswold Lane Boalt, a member of the Connecticut Society of the Colonial Dames of America, the Order of the Crown, *etc.,* who *m.* Jay Osborne Moss, of Sandusky, Ohio, and had:

1.—*Cornelia Emily Moss,* a member of the New York Society of the Colonial Dames of America, who *m.* George Hunter Brown, Jr., and had: *Ursula Wolcott.*

2.—*Augustus Leicester Moss, m.* Carrie Babcock Curtiss, of Hartford, Connecticut, and had: *Wolcott Griswold.*

Page 107.—Dr. Elijah F. Reed, *m.* 6 January, 1792.

Page 108.—Mary Reed, *m.,* 17 August, 1863, Samuel Francis Smith.

Page 136.—Emily Slaughter was the second wife of Samuel K. Bradford, Jr.

Page 136.—*Mrs. Mary Wright Wootton's* son is *Herbert Wright Wootton.*

Page 139.—Harriot Tynge Walter, *m.* John Odin.

Page 140.—Gilbert de Clare was Earl of Hertford.

Page 149.—*Arthur Collins Ketcham, m.,* New York City, Margaret Bruce Allen, and had: *Margaret Bruce* and *Arthur Collins.*

Page 149.—*Charles* and *Mary Hall (Terry) Collins,* of New York City, also had issue: *Charles Terry Collins, d.* 1883, second child, who *m.* Mary A. Wood, and had: 1. *Charles.* 2. *Clarence Lyman,* 2d. 3. *Mary Terry.* 4. *Arthur Morris,* and *Arthur Morris Collins,* fourth child, who *d.* young, *unm.*

Page 150.—*Clarence L. Collins,* also had *Maude, d. inf.*

Page 150.—*Mrs. William Allen Butler, Jr.,* was the fifth child.

Page 152.—General William Lyman, *d.,* at Cheltenham, 22 September, 1811. He did not *m.,* on 11 *June,* 1803, Jerusha Welles.

Page 152.—James S. Cox was *b.* 13 February, 1822.

Page 171.—*Charlotte Kilgour, m.* Captain Ashton B. Heyl, surgeon, United States army.

Page 177.—Mercy Floretta Fairfax, *m.* Rev. Samuel Haggings.

Page 177.—Mr. and Mrs. M. F. H. Gouverneur had issue: *Fairfax Heiskell.* Mr. and Mrs. Donald MacRae have no issue.

Pages 177, 231.—*Mrs. Virginia Dunbar* is a member of the Order of the Crown.

Page 188.—*Mrs. Henry F. Le H. Lyster,* of Detroit, is also of Royal Descent through *Colonel William Digges,* deputy-governor of Maryland, and his wife, Elizabeth Sewell (p. 76), who had: *Anne,* who *m.* Governor Henry Darnall, and had:

Eleanor, who *m.* Daniel Carroll, *d.* 1751, and had:

Eleanor, who *m.* William Brent, of "Richland," Stafford county, Virginia, and had: *Daniel Carroll Brent,* who *m.* Anne Fenton Lee, and had: *William Brent,* who *m.* his cousin, Winifred Beale Lee (also of Royal Descent, *see* p. 187), and had: *Thomas Lee Brent,* father of *Mrs. Lyster,* whose daughter, *Mrs. Edward H. Parker,* of Detroit, is a member of the Michigan Society of the Colonial Dames of America.

Page 189.—Anna Lee is the name of Mrs. Alfriend's daughter, and not Maria Lee.

Page 193.—Brigadier-Major Edward Bulkeley was the son of Charles, son of Edward, of Wethersfield, 1673-1748, as on pp. 84, 85.

Page 198.—*Rev. Robert Rose,* of Virginia, 1704-1751, of Royal Descent, had by his wife, Anne Fitzhugh:

Charles Rose, of "Bellivat," Nelson county, Virginia, third son, who *m.* —— Jordan, and had:

Dr. Joseph Rose, 1776-1849, who had by his second wife, Nancy Armstrong:

U ——— M. Rose, b. 5 March, 1834, *m.* Margaret Gibbs, and had:

Fanny Rose, b. 5 November, 1863, a member of the Virginia and Arkansas Societies of the Colonial Dames of America, who *m.,* 1 January, 1884, Wallace W. Dickinson, of Little Rock, and had: *Wallace W., b.* 15 January, 1885; *Rose, b.* 18 April, 1886, and *Benjamin F., b.* 23 July, 1888.

Page 198.—*Colonel Hugh Rose,* of "Geddes," had by his wife, Caroline Jordan:

Anne Fitzhugh Rose, m. Samuel Irvine, and had:

Mary Fleming Irvine, m. Samuel Anthony, and had:

Samuel Irvine Anthony, m. Nancy B. Emery, and had:
Mary Jeanette Anthony, a member of the Virginia Society of the Colonial Dames of America, the Order of the Crown, etc., who m. Charles Gifford Dyer, and had:
Stella Dyer, a member of the Order of the Crown.

Page 199.—Benjamin Powell Walker's son is Bradford Hastings.

Page 199.—*Mrs. Maria Rose Fisher* had issue: *Rose, Helen*, and *Edith*.

Page 199.—*Mrs. Caroline Walker Fisher* is a member of the Virginia and Illinois Societies of the Colonial Dames of America.

Page 199.—*Mrs. Rose Fisher Kennedy* has issue: *Jane*.

Page 199.—*Mrs. William James Walker* (Columbia Stanard Hayes), of Richmond, a member of the Virginia Society of the Colonial Dames of America, is of Royal Descent through Colonel Robert Carter, page 132, she being a sister of Mrs. Eaches, page 136.

Page 208.—Samuel Sergeant Newbury was k. in battle in 1865.

Page 208.—*Mrs. Katherine Sedgewick (Newbury) Robb* has issue: *Marion* and *Russell*.

Page 208.—Egbert Starr Newbury m. F. Kellogg, and had: *Egbert, George, Katherine*, and *Sergeant*.

Page 208.—*Mrs. Mary Newbury Adams* is a member of the Connecticut and Iowa Societies of the Colonial Dames of America, Order of Colonial Governors, Order of the Crown, etc.

Pages 209, 341.—Mrs. John Judson Bagley died at Colorado Springs, Colorado, 7 February, 1897.

Page 215.—"The Long Island Lawrences" are descendants of "Thomas Lawrence, of St. Albans," Herts, 1588-1624. It has long been presumed by these descendants that they were of Royal Descent through the Lawrences of Lancashire, but recently the particular pedigree connecting these two branches has been found so defective the claim of Royal Descent is suspended.

Page 216.—Lady Edith Wyndsor m. George Ludlowe, of Hill Deverill.

Page 220.—*Roberta E. Lee Wright* m. George H. Hellman, and had: *Mary S., Katherine*, and *Roberta Lee Wright*, b. July, 1899.

Page 224.—*Mrs. Anna Reed Wilkinson* is also of Royal Descent through John Drake, p. 105, being a sister of Mrs. Samuel Francis Smith, p. 108.

Page 229.—*Lady Anna von Rydingsvärd* is a member of the Vermont Society of the Colonial Dames of America.

Page 239.—*Mrs. Paul Wayland Bartlett*, a member of the Order of the Crown, is of Royal Descent through William Montgomery.

Page 248.—*Mrs. Burton Smith* (Frances Gordon), *Mrs. John B. Gordon* (Frances R. Haralson), and *Miss Caroline Lewis Gordon*, of "Kirkwood," Atlanta, members of the Georgia Society of the Colonial Dames of America, are of Royal Descent through Colonel George Reade.

Page 251.—Mary Warner m., 17 February, 1680, John Smith, of "Purton," Gloucester county, Virginia.

Page 267.—*Mrs. James Henry Parker*, of New York City, a member of the New York Society of the Colonial Dames of America, the Order of the Crown, etc., is of Royal Descent through Mabel Harlakenden.

Page 304.—*Colonel Charles Carroll*, of "Homewood," d. 1861, had:
Charles Carroll, of Donghoregan Manor, only son, 1801-1862, who m., 1825, Mary Digges, daughter of John Lee, of Needwood, Frederick county, Maryland, son of Thomas S. Lee, Governor of Maryland, and had:
Albert Henry Carroll, Confederate States army, k. in battle in 1862; m. Mary Cornelia, daughter of William George Read, and his wife, Sophia Catherine, daughter of Colonel John Eager Howard, thrice Governor of Maryland, United States Senator, etc., and had:
Mary Sophia, Mary Elinor, and
Agnes Carroll, Countess Henssenstamm, of Matzleinsdorf, Austria, a member of the Order of the Crown.

Page 315-319.—This royal descent is a revise and correction of Mrs. Samuel F. Leib's pedigree printed in "Americans of Royal Descent," vol. ii., pp. 859-863.

INDEX TO AMERICANS OF ROYAL DESCENT.

Abbot, 151, 218
Acton, 129
Adams, 65, 164, 208, 209, 257, 320, 325, 348, 356
Addison, 45
Alexander, 22, 23, 24
Alfriend, 189, 245, 291, 355
Allen, 60, 86, 148, 310
Allin, 127
Allison, 50
Allyn, 26, 27, 353
Alsop, 70
Alston, 332, 334
Alvord, 170, 226
Ambler, 33, 132
Ames, 19
Anderson, 23, 171, 178, 182, 215, 256, 257, 292, 341
Andrews, 18, 225
Angell, 260
Ansley, 284
Anson, 148
Anthony, 356
Armistead, 34, 55, 183
Arnold, 13, 14, 17, 20, 146, 223, 322, 326
Ashley, 272, 273, 312
Atkinson, 93
Atterbury, 267
Atwood, 10
Austin, 260, 277, 354
Avery, 146
Awbrey, 299
Aylett, 116, 162, 200, 244, 293

Bacon, 32, 346-349, 353
Baggett, 199
Bagley, 209, 341, 356
Baird, 127, 160, 192, 318
Bailey, 90, 205, 236, 254
Baker, 280
Balch, 322
Baldwin, 29
Ball, 45
Ballord, 310
Barr, 70, 348
Barrett, 348
Barron, 224
Barrow, 214
Bartlett, 356
Bassett, 32, 254, 255
Baughman, 76
Baxter, 58
Bayard, 22, 306
Bayne, 134
Beall, 60
Beckwith, 144
Beekman, 84
Bell, 81
Bennett, 116, 162, 200, 244, 251, 293
Benning, 258
Berkeley, 34, 133, 134, 188, 250
Bernard, 38, 246
Berry, 87
Bethell, 140, 256
Bettle, 129, 158
Bevan, 80, 81

Beverley, 58, 168, 187
Bibby, 323
Biddle, 129, 154, 157, 158, 159, 240
Billings, 312
Bingham, 260, 277
Blackford, 157
Bladen, 44
Blanton, 293
Blood, 224
Boalt, 355
Boardman, 86
Bolling, 180, 344
Boone, 304
Booth, 85, 152, 193, 318, 354
Borie, 93, 94, 101
Bowdoin, 313
Bowers, 244, 292
Boyd, 42, 353
Boyden, 262
Bradford, 136, 270, 355
Brady, 87
Brainerd, 222
Braxton, 183, 216
Brent, 187, 355
Brevard, 180
Brinley, 71
Briscoe, 317
Brockerbrough, 143, 144
Bronson, 24, 353
Brooke, 183, 216, 299
Brookfield, 74
Brooks, 209
Brown, 48, 128, 170, 209, 223, 304, 323, 341, 349, 355
Browne, 138, 182
Browning, 161
Bruen, 29
Brundage, 87
Bryan, 55
Bryant, 158
Bucklin, 18
Buckner, 32, 58, 66, 138, 183, 187, 243, 254
Buell, 248
Buffum, 326
Bugg, 348
Bulkeley, 84-88, 152, 193, 306, 347, 354
Bullitt, 116
Bullock, 19, 20, 330
Burbank, 148
Burgess, 268
Burlingame, 14, 29
Burnet, 94, 354
Burr, 235
Burrill, 326
Burwell, 32, 33, 34, 77, 132, 133, 189, 245, 291, 353
Butcher, 235
Butler, 150, 172, 215, 271, 355
Butterick, 341
Butts, 66, 242
Buzby, 80
Byrd, 54, 57, 58

Cabell, 334
Cadwalader, 48, 49, 240
Caldwell, 318

Call, 180
Calvert, 52, 61
Cameron, 151
Campbell, 244, 292
Canby, 281
Caner, 300
Carey, 61
Cargill, 17
Carlyle, 176
Carpenter, 13, 14, 18, 127, 130, 139, 260, 277, 314, 344
Carroll, 10, 60, 61, 76, 304, 355, 356
Carter, 33, 55, 56, 131-136, 143, 181-188, 216, 255, 326, 344
Cass, 222
Castleman, 186, 284, 286
Caulkins, 61
Chalkley, 35, 186, 238
Chamberlayne, 54
Chambers, 94
Chapin, 69, 322
Chapman, 39, 78, 159, 166, 221, 250, 280, 297
Charbonnier, 247
Chase, 69
Chauncey, 68-72, 83-88, 193, 263, 278, 306
Cheny, 271
Chew, 24, 48, 325
Christian, 116
Christophers, 206, 207
Chrystie, 325
Churchill, 55, 182
Churchman, 126
Claiborne, 32, 64-66, 138, 182, 242, 243, 254, 334, 354
Clapp, 353
Clark, 245, 277, 292
Clarke, 224
Claypoole, 92-96, 120, 354
Clinch, 23, 171, 215
Coates, 326
Cobb, 246, 248, 249, 257
Cobbs, 246, 248, 257
Cochran, 125, 354
Cocke, 66
Cockercraft, 166
Cockrill, 273
Coffin, 209, 221
Cole, 78
Coles, 116
Colket, 300
Collins, 122, 149, 150, 151, 152, 172, 355
Colston, 33, 132, 143, 353
Colton, 86
Colvin, 259
Comfort, 119, 161, 192, 295
Comstock, 322, 324
Conarroe, 154, 158
Converse, 268
Cook, 71, 95
Cooper, 88, 306
Cordner, 209, 221
Corson, 55, 119, 143, 161, 187, 191, 192, 295
Cotton, 208, 209, 320, 341

Coward, 270
Cox, 152, 153, 355
Coxe, 93, 120, 166, 344
Craig, 38, 65, 250, 353
Craik, 97, 98
Cranage, 313, 314
Cranston, 260, 277
Crawford, 85, 112, 185
Crenshaw, 349
Crittenden, 230
Crockett, 148
Crouch, 293
Crux, 84
Culbertson, 65
Cullen, 245, 292
Cummings, 229, 351
Curtis, 86
Curtiss, 355
Cushing, 68
Custis, 52
Cutter, 311
Czaykowski, 150, 172

Dabney, 251
Daingerfield, 253
Dale, 140, 178, 256
Dalton, 166, 221
Damon, 276
Dandridge, 189, 200, 242, 243, 244, 245, 291, 292
Danielson, 223
Darling, 146
Darnall, 355
Darneal, 65, 242
Dashiell, 186, 168
Davidson, 144
Davis, 18, 90, 127, 176, 177, 196, 201, 203, 214, 229, 336, 351
Day, 178, 257
de Benneville, 281
Deering, 267, 279
Delafield, 103-104, 354
Denman, 76
Dent, 317
Devereux, 22
Dewey, 353
Dexter, 18, 206
Dick, 85, 152, 193, 354
Dickinson, 124, 356
Digges, 10, 76-78, 355
Dillard, 299
Dilworth, 281
Dodge, 349
Dooley, 78
Dorr, 139, 314
Dorrance, 214
Douglas, 58
Dowd, 86
Downing, 284
Drake, 105-108, 289, 356
Drinker, 345
Duer, 24
Duffield, 313
Dugan, 304
Dulany, 45, 187
Dun, 95
Dunbar, 72, 177, 231, 263, 355
Dundas, 100
Dunlap, 154, 158, 228
Dunlop, 66, 242, 243

(357)

Dunscomb, 72, 263, 354
Durkee, 129
Dutcher, 69
Dwight, 149. 172
Dyer, 149, 225, 324, 356

Eaches, 136, 356
Earle, 323, 326
Eaton, 73
Edrington, 140, 256
Eliot, 68, 272, 273, 312
Ellet, 130
Ellsworth, 71, 278
Ely, 24, 302
Emerson, 273
Emlen, 125, 126
Emmet, 215
Empie, 236, 254
Epes, 281
Erwin, 248
Este, 35, 112, 185
Evans, 191, 295
Everard, 180
Evertson, 210, 213
Ewing, 126

Fairfax, 176, 231, 355
Farnsworth, 311
Farnum, 14
Farrington, 338
Farwell, 351
Fauntleroy, 55, 142–144
Fearing, 326
Fergusson, 123
Ferrill, 248
Fessenden, 276
Filer, 199, 328
Fink, 134
Firth, 128
Fisher, 23, 83, 132, 166, 199, 328, 344, 356
Fiske, 14, 29, 332
Fitch, 107, 108, 222
Fitts, 332
Fitzhugh, 78, 116, 162, 200, 244, 293
Flournoy, 257
Foote, 88, 306
Force, 218
Ford, 70
Forde, 234, 235
Foster, 140, 256
Foulke, 118, 119, 160, 161, 191, 197, 295
Fowler, 70, 94, 148, 208
Fowlkes, 333
Fox, 242
Francis, 85, 152, 190
Frazer, 270
Freeman, 273
Frishmuth, 158
Frothingham, 71
Fry, 270
Fürst, 319

Gano, 319
Gaines, 332
Gardiner, 127, 207
Garland, 274, 328
Garner, 284
Garrard, 186, 249, 284, 286
Garterey, 284
Gaskell, 238
Gaylord, 108
Gerry, 146
Gibbons, 88
Gignoux, 208
Gill, 90
Gladding, 14
Glascock, 348
Glendinning, 344
Glenn, 246, 249, 284, 286
Goan, 320
Goddard, 223

Goodrich, 69, 71, 263, 278
Gordon, 107, 132, 142, 289, 356
Gotherson, 90
Gould, 348, 349
Gouverneur, 177, 355
Grafton, 312
Graham, 69
Granger, 85
Grant, 257, 258
Gray, 110, 208, 218, 256, 273, 312
Green, 135, 286
Greene, 19
Greenough, 281
Gregory, 255
Griffin, 114, 135
Griscom, 129, 158
Grissim, 319
Griswold, 106, 312, 355
Groesbeck, 94
Groves, 333
Gwynne, 38, 95, 246, 248
Gwathmey, 236, 254

Hagan, 248
Haggins, 177, 231, 355
Haines, 267–273
Hale, 165, 195
Hall, 149, 172, 209, 238, 284
Halsey, 208
Hamilton, 146
Hancock, 238
Hansell, 235
Hanson, 280, 282
Haralson, 356
Hardaway, 56
Hardy, 126, 203
Hare, 94, 265
Harlakenden, 267, 279
Harrington, 311
Harris, 19, 199, 279, 284, 286
Harrison, 34, 35, 36, 66, 78, 112, 116, 124, 185, 186, 233, 243, 292
Hart, 353
Hastings, 49
Hathaway, 18
Hatheway, 146
Haxall, 354
Hayes, 135, 136, 356
Hazlehurst, 93, 101
Heiskill, 280, 282
Hellman, 220, 356
Henry, 80, 81, 115-116, 162, 243, 274, 292, 328
Henssenstamm, 356
Hepburn, 45
Herbert, 176
Hering, 166
Heyl, 28, 171, 355
Hickok, 130
Hill, 10, 76, 92, 120, 122, 248, 304
Hillhouse, 222, 325
Hinsdale, 22
Hitchcock, 149, 225, 324
Hobart, 94, 221
Hobson, 348
Hodge, 305
Hoffman, 49, 132
Hoge, 85, 180, 186, 233
Holden, 16
Holladay, 180
Holliday, 116, 162, 200, 244, 251, 293
Hollingsworth, 156, 345, 354
Hone, 48, 353
Hooe, 176, 353
Hooper, 184, 219
Hopkins, 57, 64, 90, 174, 184, 245, 277

Horn, 215
Horsey, 304
Horsmanden, 54
Horton, 269
Hosmer, 341
Houghton, 15
Howard, 33, 132, 249, 351, 353
Howe, 260, 267, 277
Howell, 129
Hubbard, 269, 270
Huber, 126
Huidekoper, 190
Huie, 38, 250, 353
Hulburt, 280, 282
Hulett, 225, 324
Hulse, 122, 129
Hume, 116, 162, 200, 244, 251, 293
Humphreys, 82, 146, 156
Hunter, 17
Huntington, 153, 240
Hurd, 69
Hurlburt, 206

Innes, 71, 278, 354
Irvine, 329, 330, 356
Ives, 223

Jackson, 224, 257
James, 95, 354
Janney, 50
Jarboe, 222
Jefferies, 349
Jenifer, 98
Jenkins, 312
Jenness, 146
Jewell, 69
Johnson, 15, 22, 248, 318, 326
Jones, 73, 76, 108, 128, 160, 182, 191, 230, 267, 293, 295
Jordan, 81
Jouett, 184, 219

Kebler, 151
Keeler, 208, 320, 341
Keeney, 170, 226
Keith, 160, 192
Keim, 66
Kennedy, 199, 328, 356
Kenney, 318, 319
Kennon, 52
Kent, 153, 333
Ketcham, 149, 172, 355
Key, 254
Kilgour, 22, 171, 353, 355
Kimball, 353
Kimber, 318
King, 23, 24, 153
Kinzie, 106, 289
Kirkpatrick, 112
Kling, 177, 231
Knight, 271

Lafferty, 189, 245, 291
Lamar, 153
Lammot, 93, 101
Landreth, 122
Lane, 235
Latimer, 236, 254
Law, 14, 15
Lawrence, 215, 356
Lawton, 144, 171, 182
Leaming, 110, 265
Ledyard, 223
Lee, 58, 187, 355, 356
Leeds, 139, 314
Leffingwell, 70
Leib, 319, 356
Leigh, 107
Lemmon, 45, 187
Lennig, 207, 265

Lewis, 46, 93, 96, 101, 110, 140, 157, 178, 236, 246, 254, 255, 257, 258, 259, 299, 323
Lightfoot, 259
Lilly, 61
Lincoln, 196
Lippincott, 281
Lippitt, 14, 16, 17
Lisle, 148
Little, 271, 338
Livingston, 22
Lloyd, 121-130
Logan, 124, 343, 345
Long, 256
Look, 353
Loomis, 107
Lord, 288, 306, 312, 323, 353
Lough, 45
Low, 107
Lowell, 122
Lowndes, 45, 46
Lukens, 119, 161, 191, 295
Lusson, 84
Lynde, 87, 139, 288, 309, 314
Lyman, 148-153, 172, 193, 355
Lyons, 64, 116, 242, 243, 245, 292
Lyster, 188, 355

McAfee, 186, 347, 284, 286
McAllister, 88
McCall, 48, 49, 353
McCandlish, 54, 248
McClelland, 87
McCluney, 126
McClure, 57, 64, 184, 219, 245
McCown, 65
McCurdy, 106, 288, 313
McDonald, 348
McGowan, 347
Mac Gehee, 284
Mac Gregor, 284
McIntosh, 22, 170, 171, 226
McKean, 80, 93, 100, 101
McKee, 185
McKittrick, 311
McLean, 132
McMechen, 55, 183
McMurphy, 348
McWhorter, 347
Maben, 244, 292
Macalester, 174
Macauley, 87, 354
Maccubin, 60, 61
Mackubin, 61
Macon, 162, 293
Mac Rae, 177, 355
Madden, 140, 256
Madison, 39, 250, 297
Magill, 106, 289
Maltier, 348
Malsan, 128
Manning, 269
Manson, 189, 245, 291
Marshall, 126, 243
Martin, 332
Mason, 94, 101, 221
Mather, 108
Matthewson, 323
Mauran, 17
May, 78
Mayfield, 332
Maynard, 267
Mayo, 33, 133
Meade, 180
Meares, 92, 93, 854
Meredith, 265, 274, 328

Meigs, 161, 240
Meriwether, 258
Merritt, 123
Metcalf, 269
Middleton, 166
Miller, 23, 50, 142, 171, 347
Milner, 249
Minor, 34, 56, 133, 134, 136, 168, 183, 188, 250, 255
Mitchell, 49
Moncure, 39, 78, 250, 297, 353
Montague, 98, 354
Montgomery, 239, 240
Moore, 66, 122, 126, 127, 140, 162, 178, 243, 244, 255, 256, 292, 293, 318
Morgan, 10, 73, 74, 76, 268
Morris, 15, 49, 50, 122, 123, 128
Morson, 126
Morton, 128
Moseley, 151
Moss, 355
Müller, 134
Mumford, 204, 207, 208, 224
Munds, 93
Murphey, 280
Myles, 146

Neely, 104
Neff, 354
Neilson, 96
Nelson, 33, 56, 57, 77, 132, 133, 135, 250, 318
Nevins, 267, 270
Newberry, 353
Newbury, 208, 209, 320, 341, 356
Newhall, 27
Newman, 198, 199
Newton, 34
Nicholas, 57, 132, 133, 134
Nicoll, 210-214
Nicolls, 210, 212
Nicolson, 77
Nightingale, 18
Noblit, 123
Norris, 124, 125
Norton, 164
Nye, 84

Ober, 58, 135
Odin, 139, 314, 355
O'Fallon, 132
Ogden, 157
Ogle, 46
Oglesby, 207
Okie, 280, 282
Olney, 15, 16
Ormsbee, 14
Osborne, 215
Otey, 65, 242
Otis, 312
Owen, 154, 157, 160, 191
Oxenbridge, 165

Packard, 90
Page, 34, 56, 57, 132, 133, 134, 135, 143, 152, 183, 216, 235
Palmer, 23, 146
Parker, 71, 107, 188, 256, 313, 355, 356
Parkman, 71, 209, 221
Parran, 317
Parrish, 191
Parsons, 271
Patten, 206, 262
Payson, 304

Peacock, 280
Pearsall, 48
Pearson, 348
Peirce, 245, 291
Pelham, 195
Pendexter, 345
Pendleton, 110, 153
Penhallow, 229
Penn, 237, 238
Penn-Gaskell, 238
Pennington, 127
Pepper, 150
Perkins, 39, 78, 250, 268, 272, 297
Perot, 299
Perry, 347
Peter, 52
Peterkin, 55
Peyton, 168
Philler, 159
Phillips, 159, 255
Phinizy, 347
Pillow, 140, 256
Pinckney, 55
Pitkin, 271, 272
Pitts, 313
Platt, 280
Pleasants, 87, 345
Poisson, 236, 254
Pomeroy, 152, 193, 269
Poole, 336
Pope, 127
Pordage, 313
Porter, 255
Potter, 93, 120
Poultney, 54, 132, 157
Powell, 305
Power, 223
Pratt, 93, 100
Preston, 60, 127
Price, 98, 354
Proudfit, 345
Prouty, 325
Pryor, 349
Putnam, 210, 214
Pynchon, 208, 320, 341

Quincy, 164, 209, 268

Randall, 54, 76, 132
Randolph, 136, 168, 180
Rasin, 354
Rathbone, 348
Rathburn, 225
Rantoul, 205
Raymond, 312
Read, 336
Reade, 38, 40, 62, 140, 178, 200, 236, 246-259, 336, 356
Reed, 107, 108, 224, 225, 336, 355
Redd, 116, 162, 200, 244, 251, 293
Rennert, 354
Reynolds, 35, 112, 185, 259
Rhodes, 15, 16, 42, 94, 101, 223
Rice, 349
Richards, 58, 187
Richardson, 36, 186, 299
Ricketts, 23
Ridgway, 270
Ridley, 256
Rives, 56
Robb, 49, 356
Roberdeau, 262
Roberts, 86, 127, 161, 191, 233, 235, 299
Robertson, 178, 256, 257
Robins, 33, 77, 133
Robinson, 159, 182, 218, 258, 293

Rockwell, 267
Rodney, 340
Rogers, 160, 166, 192, 220, 221
Roman, 45
Rootes, 38, 246, 248, 249
Rose, 184, 198, 199, 219, 274, 328, 355, 356
Royall, 115, 242
Rucker, 35, 95, 186, 283
Ruggles, 220
Russell, 269, 271, 348
Rutherfurd, 23, 301, 302

Sabin, 87
Sage, 230
Salisbury, 106, 288, 313
Saltonstall, 204, 209, 320, 341
Sanborn, 313
Sanders, 132
Savage, 86
Sawyer, 69
Sayles, 16, 276
Schäffer, 139, 314
Scollay, 235
Scoville, 224
Scott, 89, 142, 157, 265
Screven, 107, 142
Sears, 151
Sergeant, 208, 320, 341
Settle, 93, 120
Sever, 196
Seymour, 272
Shaw, 161, 183, 184, 216, 218, 219, 221
Shearer, 344, 345
Sheldon, 277
Shepherd, 96
Sherman, 224, 341
Shober, 262
Shoemaker, 127
Short, 134
Shoup, 353
Skeel, 70
Skinner, 86
Skipwith, 232, 233
Skyren, 292, 293
Slade, 354
Slaton, 258
Slaughter, 135, 136
Smith, 17, 18, 32, 40, 62, 71, 85, 108, 123, 128, 130, 164, 200, 215, 222, 225, 235, 246, 249, 251, 252, 253, 278, 311, 343, 345, 354, 356
Solomon, 332
Speer, 76
Spence, 61
Spencer, 222, 258
Spotswood, 162, 189, 245, 290-293
St. George, 84
Stanard, 135
Starkweather, 268
Starr, 191
Stearns, 68
Steedman, 17
Steele, 203
Steere, 323
Steinmetz, 50
Steuart, 76, 77
Stevens, 23
Stevenson, 184
Stewart, 55, 146, 248
Stewartson, 156
Stiles, 71
Stimson, 267, 279
Stockton, 94
Stone, 318
Stovall, 347
Stow, 86
Stribling, 311
Strong, 102, 151, 214, 252

Stuart, 72, 263, 337, 354
Sullivan, 203
Sweet, 16
Symonds, 279-282

Taintor, 88, 306
Talbot, 324
Talcott, 272
Tallant, 184, 220
Talmadge, 149, 172
Tarleton, 259
Tasker, 45, 46
Tayloe, 46
Taylor, 50, 140, 178, 255, 258, 268
Temple, 293, 332
Terry, 149, 172
Thacher, 168
Thayer, 84, 159
Thiot, 257
Thomas, 222, 299, 300, 317
Thompson, 38, 65, 207, 249, 250, 353
Thornton, 254
Thorpe, 93
Throckmorton, 38, 250, 297
Thurmond, 251
Tiffany, 76
Tillinghast, 277
Topp, 338
Trent, 77, 354
Trevilian, 326
Trezevant, 66
Triplett, 98, 354
Trippe, 199, 328
Trott, 93, 101
Troubetskoy, 56
Trumbull, 269
Tudor, 270
Turnbull, 60
Turner, 182, 293
Turney, 318
Tutt, 110

Urquhart, 249, 284

Valentine, 310, 311
Vance, 338
Vanderbilt, 96
Van Hoose, 332
Van Rensselaer, 24, 267, 353
Van Vranken, 325
Van Wyck, 55, 56, 183, 230
Vaux, 124
Verplanck, 72
Von Rydingsvärd, 229, 336, 351, 352, 356
Vowell, 40, 62, 252

Walker, 56, 180, 199, 221, 274, 328, 349, 356
Wallace, 94, 293, 354
Waller, 114, 135
Waln, 110, 123, 124
Walter, 139, 314, 355
Waring, 332
Warner, 40, 62, 140, 178, 200, 236, 246, 251, 253
Warren, 196, 316-319
Washburn, 16, 61, 204, 208, 276
Washington, 33, 138, 236, 253, 254, 255
Watkins, 332
Watson, 258, 323
Waugh, 64, 245
Webb, 139, 314
Webster, 14, 29
Weeden, 17, 284
Weir, 16, 353
Wells, 123, 203, 267

West, 189, 195, 200, 242–245
Westcott, 19, 20
Wetherill, 215
Wharton, 101, 125, 126, 157
Wheat, 262
Wheeler, 122, 129
Wheelock, 198
Wheelwright, 205
Whelen, 270
Whipple, 280, 282
White, 184, 215, 258, 279, 326
Whiting, 27, 218–225
Whitner, 249
Whitney, 228–230
Whittlesey, 69, 70
Whitwell, 270
Wight, 66, 243
Wilbour, 18, 146
Wilcox, 84
Wilhelmi, 128
Wilkinson, 224, 235, 260, 276, 277, 356
Williams, 14, 15, 76, 143, 158, 222, 224, 256, 257
Williamson, 55
Willis, 255
Willoughby, 288
Wilson, 58
Winchester, 259
Winship, 24, 218, 325
Winslow, 184, 195, 350
Winn, 60
Winsor, 159
Wise, 58
Wistar, 119, 128, 157, 161, 191, 295
Wister, 160, 192
Wolcott, 71, 72, 106, 289, 355
Wood, 80, 90, 110, 158, 224, 265
Woodbridge, 228, 269, 271
Woodbury, 104
Woodhull, 210–215
Woodnutt, 129
Woodruff, 35, 85, 112, 185
Woodward, 210, 213, 214
Woolf, 332
Woolfolk, 57, 58, 135
Wootton, 136, 355
Wright, 57, 64, 92, 93, 120, 136, 184, 216, 219, 220, 245, 344, 356
Wyatt, 161
Wyllys, 268, 269, 271, 272

Young, 114, 135

Zabriskie, 74

SECOND INDEX TO AMERICANS OF ROYAL DESCENT.

NOTE: Figures 353, 4, 5, 6, in the First Index refer to pages of "Addenda," and letters A. B. C. &c., in this Index, refer to pages in "Corrigenda."

Abbott, 357, 358, 471.
Abel, 400.
Abell, B.
Abernethy, 301.
Adams, 208, 361, 376, E. H. I.
Albini, 354.
Aldbaugh, 356.
Alden, 448, 487.
Alesbury, 424, 427.
Alexander, 301, 308.
Allen, 86, 370, 393, 442-3, 447.
Allin, 375.
Allyn, 408, 456, C.
Amory, 167.
Andrews, 360, 412, 419.
Angell, D.
Anterbus, 407.
Anthony, 478.
Apperson, 457.
Apthorp, 377.
Arbuthnott, 431.
Aris, 359.
Armstrong, 479.
Arnold, 457, 467, A.
Arundel, 137, 380, 381.
Ashe, 574.
Ashton, 38?.
Aston, 437-441.
Aubrey, 298, 451
Auchenleck, 329.
Audley, 37, 51, 109, 266, 296, 335, 354.
Austin, 379.
Avery, 416, 417.
Awbrey, 451.

Bacon, 430, C.
Bagby, 470.
Bagley, 209, 376.
Baker, 396, 398, 418.
Baldwin, 384, 387, 388, 480.
Ball, 253, H.
Ballord, G.
Bamforth, 275.
Bangs, 436.
Banks, 390, 395, 411.
Barclay, 237, 290.
Bardolf, 167.
Barker, 449, 456.
Barkley, 470.
Barney, 460, 465.
Barr, 480.
Barrington, 179.
Barron, 442, 443, 447.
Bartlett, 370, 423.
Barton, 317.
Baskerville, 227, 228, 380, 381, 418.

Basset, 80, 141, 364, 372, 374, 467.
Baughman, 400.
Baxter, 239.
Beall, 44, 60, 398, 401.
Bearden, 393.
Beare, 360.
Beauchamp, 12, 28, 75, 165, 217, 321, 339, 354, 384, 385, 437.
Beaufort, 79, 103.
Beaufoy, 456.
Becket, 48—.
Beckwith, 398.
Bedles, 358.
Beirne, 402.
Beler, 308.
Belkap, 418, 424, 427.
Bell, 376.
Bellomont, 111, 141, 147, 163, 227, 396.
Belt, 402.
Benefield, 435.
Bermingham, 60.
Berkley, 372, 373.
Bernard, 38, 419, C.
Barners, 436.
Berry, 87, 393, 464.
Beswick, 464.
Betts, 370.
Bevan, 299, 451.
Bidwell, 379.
Bigod, 11, 67, 83, 117, 201, 321, 354, 385, 416, A, C.
Bigelow, D.
Binns, 440.
Bird, 375, 467, D.
Birdseye, 386, 390, 395, 410.
Bishop, 436.
Bispham, D.
Bissell, 379.
Black, 478.
Blackmer, 377.
Blagdon, 353.
Blair, 264.
Blakeman, 457.
Blakiston, 356, 402.
Blois, 307.
Blount, 131, 181, 412.
Boarman, 399.
Bohun, 59, 89, 91, 105, 194, 275, 315, 354, 385, 415, 437, D.
Bolling, 439, 440, 441, E.
Bolton, 481.
Bonneson, 262.

Bonville, 379.
Booth, 29, 384, 385, 404, 411, 472.
Bostwick, 366, 368, 371.
Boteler, 355, 415.
Bothe, 385.
Botsford, 464.
Bouchier, 266, 279, 372, 436.
Boutetourt, 445.
Bowen, 462, 465.
Bowers, 377.
Bowet, 266.
Bowles, 438.
Boyd, 252, 398, 407, 466, C.
Boynton, 454.
Bradley, 464.
Brady, 87, 393, 481.
Braine, F.
Braose, 362, 363, 364.
Braxton, 404.
Bray, 418.
Braybrooke, 89.
Brent, 396, 399, 404, 405, 469.
Bretagne, 307.
Brett, 408.
Breus, 364.
Brewer, 464.
Brewes, 364.
Brewster, 413, 436.
Breynton, 418.
Brintnall, 379.
Bromflete, 357.
Bromsall, 358.
Brooke, 89, 347, 382, 396-406, 422, 456, 461, 470.
Brooks, 360, 361, 482.
Brown, 355, 356, 360, 457, 465, 479, 482, D.
Browne, 9, 406, 451, 461, A, D.
Browning, 355, 358, 396, 397, 415.
Bruce, 97, 99, 197, 327, 342.
Bruen, 384, 386, 387.
Brun, 79.
Brundage, 87, 393.
Bryce, 420.
Buchanan, 337, 398, 403, 406, H.
Buell, 371.
Buckley, 390, 392-395, 411.
Bulloch, G, I.
Bullock, 20, 420, 465.
Burges, 405.

Burgh, 355.
Burghersh, 202.
Burgoine, 456.
Burgoyne, 362, 365.
Burguillon, 332.
Burke, 449.
Burks, 420.
Burley, 437.
Burnet, 239.
Burr, 357, 415, 471.
Burton, 424, 427.
Butler, 59, 275.
Bygot, 364.
Bytton, 373.

Cabell, 366.
Cabot, 410, 448.
Cadwalader, 389, C.
Caesar, 340.
Cailly, 409.
Cairncross, 301.
Caldwell, 478.
Calhoun, 480, J.
Calkins, 384, 387.
Calthorpe, 167, 374.
Calvert, 381, 399.
Cameron, 379.
Campbell, 97, 173, 239, 252, 262, 337, 393, 473-481, J.
Canfield, 414, 449.
Cantilupe, 194.
Carew, 298, 445.
Carnegy, 113.
Carpenter, 422, 423, F.
Carroll, 402.
Carson, 479.
Carter, 438, 439, 478, D, H.
Cassatt, H.
Cecil, 335.
Chadwick, 357, 448.
Chamberlain, 347.
Chambers, 481.
Champernon, 351.
Chandler, 395.
Chapline, 451.
Chapman, 359, C.
Chardon, 360, 361.
Chauncey, 393, A, C, D.
Chaworth, 354.
Cheney, 279.
Cherleton, 109, 118, 121.
Chester, 364, A.
Chetwood, 390, 392, 411.
Chew, 403.

Second Index to Americans of Royal Descent.

Chichester, 26, 387, 408, C.
Childs, D.
Chipman, 360, 482.
Cholmoneley, 176.
Claiborne, 353, 475, C.
Clap, 448.
Clapp, 372, 378.
Clare, 37, 43, 51, 109, 117, 167, 197, 201, 339, 354, 363, 445.
Clark, 356, 372, 378, 464, F.
Clarke, 308, 394, 410, 424, 429, 439.
Claxton, 275.
Claypool, D.
Cleburn, 63, 353.
Cleemann, 441.
Clement, 415.
Clements, 466.
Clifford, 175, 351, 437
Clifton, 465.
Clinton, 28, 384, 385, 416.
Coale, 403, 406, G.
Coates, 357, 471.
Cobb, 448.
Cobham, 89.
Cochran, 449.
Cocke, 393, 438-441, G.
Coe, 429.
Coffin, 209, 376.
Colden, 366.
Cole, 371, 441, 465.
Coleman, 367, 419, B.
Coles, 392.
Colesworthy, 377.
Coleville, 362, 364.
Colley, 441.
Collins, 371, 377, 423.
Colquhoun, 441, 474.
Colston, 402.
Colvin, 434.
Comyn, 285.
Coniers, 296, 355, 407.
Coutee, 402.
Conyers, 275, B.
Cocke, 297, 359, 381, 393.
Cooley, 408.
Cooper, 88, 306, 389, 392, 393.
Copley, 241.
Cordner, 209, 376.
Corbet, 332.
Cordis, 360, 482.
Cordoba, 400.
Cornwall, 335.
Corwin, D.
Cotton, 360, 410, 482.
Courtnay, 79, 89, 105, 379, 412.
Cox, 438, 469.
Crane, 398.
Crawford, 253.
Crenshaw, 430.
Creswell, 433.
Crichton, 115, 327.
Crigler, 434.
Crittenden, 367, 370.
Cromwell, 480.
Cross, 451.
Crowell, 415.
Crowshaw 242.
Cumyn, 111, 147, 396.
Cumming, 449.
Cunningham, 239.
Cunyngham, 262.

Curd, 420, 430.
Currell, 465.
Curtis, 371.
Curtiss, 385, 386, 395, 411.
Curwen, 63, 353, D.
Cusack, 103.
Cushing, 448.
Cutler, 477.

Dacre, 266, 351, 427, A.
Daingerfield, F.
Dana, 449, 472.
Danby, 335.
Dandridge, 353.
d'Arcy, 275, 296, 354, 379, 407, 445.
Darling, F.
Darnall, 382.
Darrell, 403.
Davenport, 316.
Davidson, 435.
Davis, 373, 423, 438.
Day, 414, 422.
Deane, 377, 378.
Deighton, 372, 374.
Delafield, A.
Delano, 487.
Denman, 398.
Dennys, 379.
Dent, 401.
Despencer, 75, 165.
Deuprey, 384, 388.
Devereux, 418, 227.
Dewsbury, 487.
Dexter, 428, 429, 468.
Dick, 85, 152, 193, 393.
Digby, 308.
Digges, 359, B.
Dighton, 467.
Dodson, B.
Dodge, 465.
Doolittle, 429.
Dorney, 374.
Dorsey, 406.
Doty, 487.
Douglas, 21, 234, 237, 285, 301, 329, 342.
Douthat, 441.
Dowling, 405.
Drake, 379, 479, D.
Drayton, 367.
Drax, 410.
Drummond, 374, 378.
Dudley, 141, 375, 376.
Duff, 285, F.
Duffield, 457, G.
Duke, 405.
Dunbar, 261, 342.
Duncan, 434, 479.
Dundas, 343, G.
Dushane, 398.
Duval, 402, 406.
Dwight, 379.
Dyer, G.
Dymoke, 232, 247, 419, 430, D, E.

Earle, 122, 386.
Earp, 394.
Eaton, 287, 446.
Echyngham, 131, 181, 412.
Edwards, 480.
Eglington, 239, 261.
Eliot, 370, 460.
Elliott, 457, I.
Ellis, E.
Elmedon, 396, 397.

Elys, 309.
Emerson, 377.
Emery, 378.
Emlen, 343, 367.
Emmes, 377.
Emory, 405.
Endicott, 412.
Engham, 398.
Eppes, 441.
Ergadia, 115, 301.
Erskine, 290, 301, 329.
Estabrook, 447.
Etterstone, 396, 397.
Evans, 47, 80, 367, 466, H.
Evelette, 380, 383.
Everard, 180.
Eyre, A.

Faires, 477.
Fairfax, 44.
Farnum, 376.
Farrand, 460.
Farwell, B.
Featherstonehaugh, 397.
Felt, 428, 468.
Fenner, 464.
Fenwick, 404.
Ferrers, 163, 339, 355, 408, 418, 437, 444.
Fetter, 419, 420.
Fitzalan, 9, 79, 91, 131, 137, 181, 211, 315, 391, 451.
Fitzgerald, 59, 169, 202.
Fitzhugh, 211, 266, 296, 354, 391, 452.
Fitzjohn, 12, 321, 385.
Fitzmaurice, 59.
Fitzpiers, 385.
Fitzrobert, 354, 355, 385.
Fitzwalter, 354, 385.
Field, 358.
Fienes, 146, 266, 279, 362, 424, 427, A.
Fillol, 351.
Finch, 422.
Fish, 368.
Fiske, 450, 465.
Fitch, G.
Fleete, 405, 406, 457, 469, 470.
Fleming, 262, I.
Flint, 456.
Flower, 359, 439.
Forbes, 237, 285, 329.
Forster, 396, 397, 461.
Fortibus, 354.
Forwood, 405.
Foster, 357, 377, 415, 428.
Fotheringham, 290.
Foulke, 389.
Fowlee, 369.
Fox, 386, 451.
Foxcroft, 395.
Francis, 365, 393.
Frank, 453.
Fraser, 197, 424, 429.
Frazier, 368.
Freeman, 436.
Freville, 362, 365.
Fuller, 463.

Gage, 484-488.
Gale, 408.
Gamage, 12, 20, 321.

Gardiner, 394.
Garmendia, 400.
Garneys, 365.
Gascoigne, 205, 247, 296, 355, 419, D, E.
Gaylord, 379.
Geer, 478.
Genevill, 117, 389.
George, 456.
Gernon, 362, 364.
Gibbs, 371.
Gibson, 377, 420.
Gidley, 408.
Giffard, 408.
Gifford, 438, C.
Gilbert, 377, 378, 379.
Gillette, 424, 429.
Glenn, 415, D, E.
Gobaud, 364.
Goddard, D.
Goodrich, 369, 393, 394, G.
Goodspeed, 424, 428.
Goodyear, 410.
Gookin, 410.
Gordon, 173, 197, 198, 353, 402, 466.
Gorges, 379.
Gorham, 360.
Gorter, 398.
Goushill, 91, 155, 315, 415.
Graeff, 403.
Graham, 261, 285.
Granger, 85, 393.
Grant, 285, 472.
Graves, 423, 487.
Granville, 435.
Gray, 208, 264, 360, 376, 419, 482.
Green, 353, 457, F.
Greenhill, 455.
Gregg, 402.
Gregory, 369.
Greele, 448.
Grey, 109, 121, 164, 275, 296, 354, 407, 437, 445.
Grenville, 105, 379, 424, 427.
Grevstock, 445.
Griffin, 309.
Griffith, 109, 155, 415, E.
Griggs, 370.
Grinnell, B.
Griswold, 379, 460.
Grosvenor, 407.
Groves, 393.
Guiteau, 362, 366.
Gully, 322.
Gun, 283.
Gunter, 298.
Gurdon, 359, 482.
Guthrie, 431.
Gwathmey, 457.
Gwyn, 155, 415.
Gwynne, 419.

Hagburne, 375, 376.
Haighburn, 374, 375.
Hall, 375, 401, 456, 478, D.
Halsey, 208, 376.
Halys, 422.
Hamill, 477.
Hamilton, 99, 234, 285, 342, 429.
Hampden, 362, 424, 427, 428, 468.

Second Index to Americans of Royal Descent.

Hank, H.
Hanson, 402, 421, F.
Harby, 165.
Harcourt, 308.
Hardell, 354, 355.
Hardres, 279.
Hare, 464.
Harlakenden, 267, 279, 460, F.
Harper, 457.
Harrington, 418.
Harris, 436, 442, 443, 447, F.
Harrison, 403, 420, 442, 443, 447, H, I.
Harwell, 373.
Harwood, 441.
Haskell, 447.
Haskins, 378.
Hassylden, 167.
Hastings, 145, 179, 394, 418.
Hatheway, 467.
Hatton, 400.
Hawkins, 413, 436.
Hawte, 422.
Hawthornden, 329.
Hay, 481, J.
Hayden, 365, G.
Haynes, 460. A, F.
Headley, 387.
Heard, 449.
Hedsworth, 275.
Helmes, 413.
Henley, 470.
Henry, 439.
Hepburn, 262, 477.
Herdby, 424, 427.
Heriot, 262.
Heritage, 332.
Herring, 357, 471.
Hews, 465.
Heydon, 422.
Hickling, 449.
Hicks, 407.
Hill, 384, 387, 400, 405, 434, 438, 456, B.
Hillyer, 388.
Hinchman, 369.
Hinsdale, 369.
Hoadley, 370.
Hobart, 267.
Hobson, 469.
Hoffman, 441.
Hogg, 456.
Holbrook, 369, 370.
Holford, 29, 384, 386.
Holland, 79, 103, 121, 211, 391.
Holliday, E.
Holt, 417, 420, 433, 440, 441.
Holyoke, 428.
Home, 431, 432, 433.
Hondlow, 413.
Hooe, 359.
Hooker, 369, 370.
Horn, 329.
Horner, 441.
Horsmanden, 54.
Horton, 413.
Houghton, 394.
Howard, 380, 422, 436.
Howe, 277, 413, 423.
Howell, 109, 255, 420.
Howison, 419.
Howson, 470.
Hubbard, 429.
Hubbart, 267.

Hubbell, 395.
Hudson, 360, 415.
Hughes, 389, 420.
Hume, 343, 431-435, 479, G.
Humfrey, 109, 416.
Humphrey, 362, 366, 415, 419.
Hungerford, 241, 317.
Hunt, 405, 463.
Hunter, 360.
Huntingfield, 354.
Huntingdon, 342.
Hurd, 400.
Hutchins, 405, 461.
Hutchinson, 472.
Hutton, 353, 356.
Hyde, 371, 424, 429.

Ingraham, 465.
Ingersoll, E.
Innes, 457.
Irvine, I.
Isaac, 115, 301.
Isham, I.
Izard, 347, 474.

Jackson, 275, 410, 448, I.
James, 407.
Jameson, 399.
Jamison, 478.
Jefferson, I.
Jekyle, 332.
Jenkins, 405.
Jenks 424, 429.
Jenney, 287.
Jobes, 442, 443, 447.
Johns, 401.
Johnson, 414, 439, E.
Johnston, 421.
Johnstone, 457.
Johnstoun, 237.
Jones, 76, 398, 371, 470, F.
Jordan, 369
Jykett, 332.

Kaye, 205, 296, 355, 358, 407, 482.
Kean, 368.
Keeney, 457.
Keightley, 478.
Keith, 111, 197, 237, 285, 464.
Kendall, B.
Kennon, 420.
Ker, 41, 466.
Kerfort, 398.
Key, 464.
Keyser, 405.
Keynes, 408.
Kidder, 180.
Kimball, 398.
King, 353, 378, 380.
Kirby, 394.
Kirschner, 413.
Kittredge, 449.
Knight, 418.
Knyvett, 372, 436, 483.
Kynaston, 109, 121, D.

Le Grosse, 347.
L'Hommedieu, 366.
Le Roy, 367.
Lacie, 354.
Lacy, 117, 201, 389.
Lake, 409, 410.

Lambert, 147, B.
Lamoral, 436.
Lancaster, 404.
Lane, 391.
Langton, 445.
Lannoy, 485, 487.
Lanvallei, 354.
Larkin, 434.
Launce, 442, 443, 446.
Laurie, 358.
Lawrence, 358, 361, 386, 398, 404, 407, 414, 453.
Lawson, 403.
Lea, 480.
Leakin, 398.
Lee, 52, 332, 361, 369, 440, 478.
Leete, 362, 365, 366.
Leib, G.
Lenthall, 353.
Leslie, 41, 99, 283.
Leverett, 376.
Lewis, 47, 109, 190, 359, 420, 430, 441, 447, 458, 478.
Liddell, 432, 433.
Lilly, F.
Lindsay, 21, 113, 290, 420, 431.
Lincoln, 196, H.
Lippincott, 387.
Liston, 457.
Little, 417, 466, G.
Littleton, 437.
Livingston, 262, 342, 368.
Lloyd, 73, 109, 118, 294, 371.
Logan, G.
Loudenoys, 267, 279, 460.
Loper, 436.
Lord, 394.
Lovet, 456.
Lowther, 381, 382, C.
Luce, 384, 387.
Ludlow, 131, 181, 412, 413, D.
Ludwell, 38.
Lugg, 376.
Luman, 371.
Lumley, 275.
Lumsden, 237.
Luthrell, 412.
Lygon, 374.
Lyle, 239.
Lyman, 448, C.
Lynch, 358.
Lynde, 87, 393, G.
Lynn, 406.
Lyon, 481.
Lyons, 353.

McAllister, 88, 393.
McCall, 417.
McClelland, 408.
McClure, 477, 479.
McCoy, 407, J.
McCreery, 436.
McCune, 479.
McDonal, 396.
McDonald, 402.
McDonnell, 327.
McEachern, 383.
McGaw, 384, 388.
McIntyre, 377.
McKean, 403.
McKillum, 481.
McLarin, 337.

McMillan, 457.
McMullen, 434.
McNeil, 480.
McVean, 401.
Macauley, 87, 393.
MacCarthy, 202.
Macdonald, 169, 283.
MacDuff, 285.
Mackall, 401, 405.
Mackenzie, 169, 283, 405.
Mackenneth, 169.
MacLeod, 283, 440.
MacMurcha, 339.
Macomber, 376.
Macon, 253.
Madison, 359, I.
Mainwaring, 398.
Magna Charta Barons 354, 355.
Malet, 339, 354, 355.
Mallom, 481.
Mandeville, 354, 436, 437.
Manly, 398.
Mansfield, 389.
Markenfield, 205, 296, 355, 407, 471, 482.
Marmyon, 354.
Marsh, 472.
Marshall, 197, 201, 339, 354, 357, 376, 441, 449, 471.
Marston, 457.
Marvin, 487.
Mason, 396, 400, 402, 418, 465.
Mather, 366, 446.
Mathes, 415.
Matson, 369.
Matthews, 401, 455.
Mauduit, 28, 217, 354, 384, 385, 437.
Mattison, 449.
Maule, 290, 431.
Mauleverer, 296, 355, 356, 357, 358, 407, 471, 482.
Maulsby, 398.
Mawney, 464.
Maxwell, 261.
Major, 438.
Maynadier, 405.
Maynard, 417.
Mayo, 413.
Mead, 418.
Meade, 440.
Meddaugh, 369.
Meekins, 470.
Meigs, 367.
Meinill, 354.
Melville, 448, E.
Menzies, 337, 474.
Mercer, 237.
Merriwether, 438.
Merrills, 379.
Metcalf, 417.
Mickle, 360.
Middlecott, 361.
Mighill, 424, 429.
Milbourne, 227.
Miller, 430, 434, 420, 440, 451, 479.
Milnor, 393.
Minge, 441.
Minor, 472.
Moberly, 434.
Moels, 26, 408, C.
Mohun, 194.
Molineux, 315.

Second Index to Americans of Royal Descent.

Molis, C.
Monaghan, 389.
Montacute, 211, 391.
Montagne, 386.
Montague, 423, 466.
Montcrief, 264.
Montfichet, 354.
Montford, 28.
Montfort, 294, 384, 385, 411.
Montgomery, 173, 239, 261, 343, 384.
Moore, 367, 383.
Moreton, 241.
Morgan, 382, 394, 417, B.
Morison, 290, 431, 432, F.
Morris, 464, H.
Morrison, 432.
Mortimer, 117, 175, 247, 389, 437.
Moseley, C.
Mosher, B.
Mott, 487.
Mowbray, 232, 241, 287, 353, 354, 380, 422.
Muir, 387.
Muirhead, 343.
Muirland, 262.
Mulliken, 418.
Munroe, 418.
Mure, 239.
Murray, 368.
Muscegros, 355.
Myrick, 467.

Napier, 97.
Nason, 438.
Neale, 399, 404, 461.
Neary, 462-465.
Needham, 392.
Needles, 417.
Negus, 376.
Neville, 37, 51, 53. 75, 165, 211, 247, 266, 335, 354, 355, 391, 422, 454.
Newkirk, 436.
Newburg, 217, 385.
Newburgh, 28, 354, 384, 437.
Newbury, C.
Nicoll, 392.
Nicholl, 392.
Nicholls, 439.
Nicholson, 406, 461.
Nixon, 407.
Norbrow, 438.
Norbury, 405.
Norcross, 408.
Norreys, A.
Norris, 407, 435.
Northend, 410.
Northrop, 368.
Norton, 475, H.
Norville, 164.
Nowers, 356.
Norwich, 354.

O'Brien, 59.
O'Carroll, 60, 303.
O'Conor, 60.
O'Shaughnassie, 59.
O'Sullivan, 202.
Odingsells, 354, 385.
Ogden, 361, 480.
Ogilive, 264.

Ognal, 316.
Olney, 467.
Ormsby, 419.
Owen, 155, 413, 415.
Oxenbridge, E.

Paddock, 372.
Padelford, 376, 377.
Paganel, 141.
Page, 183, 404.
Paine, 410, 447.
Pake, 410.
Pakeman, 308.
Palmer, 446, 464.
Palmes, 146, 416.
Pancoast, 358.
Parkhurst, 322.
Parish, 447.
Parker, 475, 477, J.
Parmenter, 377.
Parmalee, 384.
Parmlee, 387.
Parr, 211, 340, 391, 411, 453.
Parran, 317, 380, 382, 383, 398.
Parris, 448.
Paston, 335.
Patrick, 480.
Patsyll, C.
Patterson, 370.
Pawlet, 408.
Payne, 353, 366, I.
Peake, 410.
Pearce, 457.
Pearre, 402.
Peche, 384.
Pierce, 360, 482.
Peirson, 357.
Pendleton, 255.
Penniman, 398.
Penrose, 407.
Perley, 424, 429.
Perrin, 438.
Percy, 53, 175, 205, 247, 351, 354, 355.
Perkins, 372.
Perry, 390, 394, 395, 411.
Perwich, 309.
Peter, 441, C.
Petre, 10.
Pettibone, 362, 366, 429, 468.
Peyton, 362, 365.
Pheby, 451.
Phenix, 398.
Philpot, 398.
Phoebus, 451.
Pickering, 297, 358.
Pierce, 467.
Pinkney, 353.
Pinney, 386.
Pinto, 386.
Pitt, 386.
Pitts, 376.
Plantagenet, 145, 155, 165, 179, 181, 232, 241, 247, 287, D.
Pleasants, 420.
Pointz, 374.
Pole, 89, 145, 179.
Pomeroy, F.
Pooley, E.
Pope, 420, 430.
Porter, 424, 429.
Powell, 156, 415.
Poynings, 247.
Poythress, 441.
Pratt, F.

Prentice, 394.
Presburg, 383.
Prescott, 393.
Presson, 380, 383.
Preux, C.
Prideaux, 379.
Price, 294, 402, 419.
Prime, 456.
Prince, 436.
Procter, 434, 435.
Prouz, 26, 408, C.
Pryor, 438.
Pudsey, 454.
Puleston, 190, 415, E.
Purdy, 413.
Putnam, 353, 362, 424, 428, 429, 468, 472.
Puttenham, 362, 424, 428.
Pyle, 412, D.
Pynchard, 372, 373.

Quincy, 111, 147, 163, 209, 227, 354, 376, 396, 444.

Raborg, 396, 400.
Ragland, 420.
Ramsey, 329, 436.
Randolph, 342, I.
Ratcliffe, 315.
Ravenscroft, 440.
Rawlins, 435.
Read, 343, B.
Reade, 287, 297, 335, 359, 419, 430, E, H.
Redvers, 25, 408.
Redwood, 406, G.
Reeder, 382.
Reeves, 407.
Reid, 327.
Reynolds, 418, 420.
Rice, 379.
Richardson, 447, 451.
Richmond, 377.
Riddle, 301.
Ridgway, 357, 358, 471.
Riggs, 413.
Riker, E.
Rindge, 418.
Ringgold, 402.
Risley, 436.
Ritchie, 358, 481.
Roberts, 435.
Robertson, 115, 327.
de la Roche, 418.
Rockley, 445.
Rockwill, 414.
Rodam, 396.
Rodburg, 321.
Rodgers, 379.
Rogers, 367, 376.
Rohan, 308.
Rohe, 384, 388.
Rollock, 431.
Rooker, 403.
Roos, 354.
Roosevelt, H, I.
Rootes, 419.
Root, C.
Rose, E.
Rosewell, 360.
Rosseter, 252, 370.
Rounds, 465.
Rousby, 382.
Rowan, 407.
Rowleigh, 392.

Ruggles, 362, 366, 367, 368, 371, 478.
"Runnemede," 319, 358, 359, 360, 361, 369, 370, 377, 384, 386, 388, 392, 394, 402, 405, 406, B. C. D. E.
Sage, 393, 394, 453.
Salisbury, 391. 465.
Saltonstall, 359, 360, 361, 482.
Sanders, 361.
Sanderson, 368.
Sandys, 332, 422, 445.
Satterthwaite, 358.
Sawier, 381.
Sawtell, 387.
Say, 28, 354, 355, 384, 385.
Sayer, 372.
Sayers, 372, 436.
Sayre, 436.
Schindel, E.
Schoolcraft, 481.
Scot, 440, 48—.
Scott, 239, 422, 469.
Scoville, 370.
le Scrope, 452.
Scrope, 37, 51, 335, 354, 445.
Scull, 407.
de la Sea, 454.
Sears, 372, 436.
Seaton, 237.
Seddon, 470.
Sedley, 48—.
Seeley, 417.
Segrave, 354, 380, 422.
Seton, 198, 234, 283.
le Seur, 383.
Sewall, 400, 403, 487.
Seymour, 321, 339, 351.
Shaw, E.
Sheafe, 370, 449, 458.
Sheffield, 44.
Sheldon, 464, 465.
Shepard, 374.
Shephard, 383.
Shepherd, 361.
Shepey, 332.
Sherburn, 448, 458.
Sherill, 394.
Sherman, 442, 443, 446, 447, 453.
Sherwood, 386, 390, 395, 411.
Shillowe, 374.
Shipman, 369.
Short, 413, 440.
Shute, 362, 365.
Sim, 401.
Simson, 265.
Simpson, 446, 475.
Sinclair, 41, 327.
Sioussat, 398.
Skeene, 237.
Skelton, 389.
Skinner, 86, 393, 472.
Skipwith, 440.
Smallwood, 420.
Smith, 380, 381, 382, 399, 401, 392, 398, 401, 402, 407, 410, 417, 436, 439, 441, 442, 447, E, F.
Smyth, 392.
Snow, 436.

Second Index to Americans of Royal Descent.

Snowden, 406.
Sollers, 380.
Somerby, A. B.
Somerie, 141.
Somerset, 10, 80, 380, 381, 382.
Somerville, 111, 239, 380.
Sothern, 382.
Southall, 439.
Soule, 487.
Sparrow, 403, 436.
Speer, B.
Spencer, 332, 402, 439.
Spotiswoode, F, G.
Spotswood, 432.
Spotts, 457.
Spottswood, F, G.
Sprigg, 481.
Spycer, 374.
St. John, 51, 218, 413, B.
St. Lawrence, 103.
St. Leger, 54, 75.
St. Maur, 339.
Stafford, 37, 51, 109, 266, 296, 335, 354.
Stanbury, 478.
Stanley, 155, 315, 384, 387, 415.
Stansbury, 389.
Stanton, 434.
Stapylton, 167.
Steele, 398.
Stevens, 371.
Stewart, 111, 113, 115, 169, 173, 239, 261, 262, 264, 285, 301, 327, 329, 337, 342, 360, 410, 441, G, I.
Stirling, 337.
Stith, 439.
Stolber, 442, 443, 447.
Stone, 353, 369, 399.
Stonestreet, 400.
Stoughton, 408.
Stourton, 142.
Strange, 118, 241.
Stratton, 412.
Strong, 379.
Stuart, 97, 428, D.
Studley, 48—.
Sudley, 355.
Sullivan, 398, G.
Sutherland, 41, 327.
Sutherlin, 252.
Sutton, 365, 403, 413.
Symonds, A.

Tabb, 439.
Taillefer, 79.
Taintor, 394.
Taitt, 465, 479.
Talbot, 12, 20, 275, 321, F.
Talboys, 247, 419, D. E.
Talcott, 377.
Tallant, D.
Talvas, 321.
Taney, 382, 399, 404.
Tasker, 400.
Tate, 479.
Tateshall, 409.
Taylor, 405, 423.
Teall, 394.
Tebbs, 470.
Tempest, 445.
Temple, 456, 457, 470, G.
Thacher, 436.
Thaxter, 449.
Thomas, 396, 400, 402, 434, 451.
Thompson, 377, 398, 419, 465.
Thomson, 396, 400.
Thorley, 241.
Thornton, 253.
Thorpe, 430, D.
Throckmorton, 165, 358, 359, E, G.
Tilney, 436.
Tilton, 421.
Tirwitte, 296, 358.
Titus, 463.
Todd, I.
Tolle, 366.
Tomlin, 405, 470.
Tomlinson, 413, 457.
Tompkins, 387.
Toni, 384.
Tottishurst, 287.
Townsend, 377, 414.
Tracy, 369, 370, 410.
Treat, 410, 447.
Trimble, 480.
Triplett, 403.
Troutbeck, 155, 415, E.
Turberville, 12, 20, 80, 321.
Tunstall, 404, 452-457.
Turvyle, 456.
Tutt, 359.
Twisleton, 410.
Tyng, 375.
Tyson, 398, 464.

Ufford, 266, 364.
Umfraville, 147, 396, 397.
Upham, 449.
Url, 371.

Van Egmonte, 436.
Van Rensselaer, B.
Von Glode, 388.
Varen, 424, 429.
Vaughan, 80, 190, 299, 451.
Vere, 43, 117, 227, 354.
Vernon, 202, 384.
Verplanck, 478.
Vesci, 354.
Vincent, 265, 456.
Vyvon, 339.

Wacker, 470.
Waddrup, 441.
Wade, 375, 387.
Wadhams, 371.
Wadsworth, 367.
Wainwright, 361.
Walcott, 362, 366, 428, 429, 468.
Walesbury, 424, 428.
Walker, 469, 470, E.
Wallace, 343.
Wallace, 209, 376, 227, 354, Wallingford, 387.
Walworth, 84, 394, 417.
Wandisford, 454.
Warbrow, 438.
Ward, 360, 370, 379, 482, F.
Warham, 408.
Warner 366, 420, 430, F, H.
Warr, 241, 353.
Warren, 28, 67, 79, 83, 321, 354, 384, G.
Washburn 208, 376.
Washington, 253, H.
Waters, 359, 364, 365, 374, 376, 392, 398, 412, 446, E, H.
Watkins, 353.
Watson, 357, 472.
Waugh, 353.
Wayne, 392.
Webster, 371, 439.
Weems, 403.
Wehn, 384, 388.
Welch, 362, 366.
Weld, 401.
Welles, 232, 287, 354, 414, 430, 452, 453.
Welsh, 437.
Wentworth, 339, 351, 358.
West, 353.
Wetmore, 429.
Whaling, 480.
Wheaton, 463.
Whelpley, 395.
Whipple, 472.
White, 361, 420, 421, 449, 467.
Whiting, 410, B.
Whitleigh, 379.
Whitner, E.
Whitney, 418, E.
Whitridge, 402.
Wicliffe, 359.
Widworthy, 408.
Wight, C.
Wightman, 387.
Wilbour, 467.
Wilcox, 394, 424, 429.
Wilder, 448.
Wildey, 469.
Wilkinson, 382, 410, B.
Willard, 436, 447, 448, 450, 458.
Willetts, 389.
Williams, 368, 369, 372-378, 403, 417, 467, H.
Williamson, 435, 450.
Willing, 402.
Willoughby, 414.
Willson, 406, 461.
Wilson, F.
Wingfield, 91, 351, D.
Windebank, 247, 419, 430, D, E.
Winn, 398.
Winston, 353, E.
Winthrop, 360.
Witmer, 353.
Wolcott, 408, 428.
Wood, 378, 438, 439.
Woodbridge, 366, 362.
Woodhull, 390, 391, 392, 411.
Woodruff, 356.
Woods, 398.
Woodson, 420.
Woodston, 420.
Woodward, 372, 378, 428, 439, 465, E.
Woolfolk, C.
Workington, 63.
Worthington, 402.
Worthy, 453.
Wotton, 26, 408, C.
Woulf, 369.
Wrigglesworth, 419.
Wright, 356, 393, 448, 449, 458, G.
Wurts, 387.
Wyatt, 26, 89, 408, 422, 423, 441, 455, 469.
Wyllys, 460.
Wyndham, 335.
Wyndsore, 131, 181, 412.

Yarnall, 389.
Yates, 460.
Yergason, 370.
Yocum, 460.
Yorke, 375.
Young, 322, 329, 383, 398, 464..
Yznaga, 466.

Zimmerman, 466, 477.
Zouche, 308.

THIRD INDEX

Abbott, 514, 520, 538.
Addison, 530.
Aldborough, 538.
Aldburgh, 514.
Aldbury, 520.
Alexander, 543.
Allaben, 510, 511.
Allen, 525.
Allyn, 541.
Anderson, 543.
Anson, 494, 525, 545.
Antrobus, 538.
Archer, 496, 543.
Arnold, 544.
Asfordby, 510, 511.
Aston, 515, 587.
Atkinson, 538.
Atwater, 542.
Aucher, 500.
Avery, 501.
Avery, 528.
Aylett, 543.
Bacon, 542.
Badlesmere, 227.
Baillie, 543.
Baker, 495.
Ball, 518.
Ball, 518, 529, 530.
Ballentine, 544.
Banks, 532.
Barkley, 536.
Barnaby, 523.
Barne, 500.
Barnes, 519.
Barr, 494.
Bartine, 509.
Barton, 497.
Basset, 531.
Bayard, 495, 543.
Beale, 518.
Beatty, 511.
Beauchamp, 507, 540, 541, 544.
Beaufort, 523.
Berkeley, 587.
Berlaymont, 504.
Bernard, 501, 542.
Bethune, 504.
Betts, 541.
Beverley, 513, 519, 535.
Bigod, 499, 514, 520, 523, 541, 544.
Blackall, 517.
Blaine, 536.
Bland, 533.
Blue, 502.
Bogart, 502.
Boggs, 506.
Bohun, 507, 513, 514, 520, 525, 541, 543.
Bolebec, 545.
Boleyne, 500.
Bolling, 525.
Bonville, 491, 525.
Boone, 509.
Booth, 541, 545.
Borlace, 532.
Boteler, 523.
Bothe, 544.

Bourdon, 531.
Bourgogne, 504.
Bowen, 545.
Bowie, 519.
Bowles, 525.
Boyle, 492, 525.
Bradbury, 505.
Bradford, 502.
Bradshaw, 519.
Brett, 532.
Brinley, 544.
Briscoe, 528.
Broadus, 537.
Bromley, 542.
Brooke, 535.
Brown, 519, 538.
Browne, 544.
Browning, 536.
Bruen, 541.
Bryant, 516.
Bryce, 541.
Buchanan, 536.
Bullock, 545.
Burges, 544.
Burley, 525.
Burr, 514, 520, 538.
Burton, 511.
Burwell, 542.
Butler, 540, 544.
Byrd, 513.
Cage, 546.
Calder, 517.
Callum, 493.
Campbell, 492-7, 489, 546.
Canby, 519.
Canfield, 545.
Cannon, 502.
Carmack, 511.
Carroway, 546.
Carter, 530, 534, 543.
Cary, 511, 512, 523.
Chaffee, 506.
Chapman, 506.
Chattin, 509
Chetwode, 540, 545.
Chichester, 513, 517, 518, 519.
Chinn, 518.
Church, 500.
Churchman, 534.
Claiborne, 543.
Clapp, 541.
Clarke, 512, 525.
Clifford, 520, 537.
Clinton, 541.
Clotworthy, 492, 525.
Coats, 538.
Cobb, 517.
Cocker, 516.
Coles, 496.
Colvin, 494.
Comstock, 541.
Coniers, 538.
Conquest, 535.
Cooke, 525.
Cooper, 498, 502, 540, 545.
Corbet, 541.
Corbin, 511, 530.
Corlies, 524.

Cornwallis, 500.
Cortright, 524.
Coventry, 517.
Cox, 524, 536.
Crall, 510, 511.
Creswell, 525.
Crome, 511.
Cushman, 524.
Custer, 509.
Cutting, 541.
d'Albini, 514, 516, 520.
d'Arcy, 516.
d'Arderne, 531.
d'Aubeney, 516.
d'Audley, 516.
de Benneville, 519.
de Clare, 514, 516, 520, 522, 531.
d'Esne, 504.
d'Eu, 507.
de Gasquet, 537.
d'Invilliers, 522.
de Lannove, 504.
de Sales, 525.
de la Chaise, 537.
de la Noye, 504.
de la Planche, 542.
de la Val, 523.
de la Zouche, 544.
Dale, 500.
Danby, 514, 520, 538.
Dandridge, 543.
Darcy, 545.
Daubeney, 516, 517.
Davis, 495.
Dawson, 534.
Deane, 543.
Delano, 504, 505.
Dennison, 505.
Dent, 492, 506.
Derby, 489, 493, 525.
Devereux, 543.
Dewey, 541.
Dewsbury, 504.
Digges, 500.
Dobyns, 536.
Doremus, 498, 501.
Doten, 505.
Drayton, 531.
Dudley, 544.
Duer, 496.
Duke, 517.
Dulaney, 530.
Dundas, 495, 524, 525, 545.
Duras, 504.
Dutton, 544.
Dyer, 495.
Dymoke, 510.
Eames, 528.
Eastburn, 509.
Elain, 494.
Elliott, 519.
Eltinge, 511.
Emerson, 524
English, 586.
Eppes, 533.
Erskine, 543.
Evans, 514, 522.
Faber, 505.

Fairchild, 493.
Fauntleroy, 543.
Feamster, 512.
Fenn, 543.
Ferree, 520.
Ferrers, 537, 538.
Field, 587, 538.
Fienes, 528.
Finney, 543.
Fitch, 493, 525.
Fitzalan, 513, 545.
Fitzgerald, 491-2, 525.
Fitzgeoffrey, 499.
Fitzhugh, 530, 538.
Fitzjohn, 499, 541, 544.
Fitzpiers, 507.
Fitzrobert, 514, 520.
Fitzwalter, 514, 520.
Fleete, 542.
Fontaine, 534.
Foote, 502.
Foster, 520.
Fox, 518, 519.
Franchimont, 504.
Frankton, 508.
French, 530.
Fritchie, 511.
Fry, 493, 545.
Fulton, 520.
Furnell, 531.
Galloway, 546.
Gardiner, 495.
Gascoigne, 514, 520, 539.
Gaskell, 502.
Gasquet, 537.
Gasquet-James, 537.
Gill, 489, 493, 525, 545.
Gimeeges, 531.
Glenn, 543.
Godley, 524.
Goode, 537.
Gordon, 518.
Gorsuch, 500, 545.
Gostwick, 529.
Goushill, 513.
Grandison, 499.
Granson, 499.
Grant, 505, 506, 508, 545.
Grey, 491, 516, 525.
Green, 517.
Greene, 494, 525, 531, 532, 545.
Griffin, 530.
Griffith, 513.
Grymes, 534.
Hacker, 524.
Haliburton, 528.
Hall, 492-7, 519, 525, 536.
Hamilton, 528, 546.
Hancock, 537.
Hank, 520.
Harcourt, 544.
Harlan, 520.
Harrah, 514.
Harris, 501.

(547)

Harrison, 542.
Harte, 499.
Harvey, 538.
Harvye, 538.
Hastings, 10, 527.
Hatheway, 545.
Hawte, 544.
Hayden, 528, 545.
Hayward, 542.
Heber, 497.
Heighington, 524.
Henderson, 505.
Herbert, 10, 80.
Hilles, 500.
Hinchman, 543.
Hipple, 524.
Holand, 544.
Hollar, 507.
Holmes, 546.
Holt, 512, 537.
Honeywood, 542.
Honore, 506.
Hooe, 518.
Hopkins, 543.
Hornby, 524.
Horsmanden, 513.
Howard, 535.
Hubbard, 501.
Hude, 495-6.
Humfrey, 528.
Humphrey, 513, 528.
Huntingfield, 514, 520.
Huntington, 493, 545.
Hutton, 514, 520, 538.
Isham, 532, 533, 545.
Iungerich, 524.
Jackson, 496-7, 525.
James, 537, 544.
Jamieson, 505.
Jamison, 528.
Jeames, 508.
Jefferson, 533, 537.
Jenkins, 519.
Jenness, 528.
Jennings, 538.
Johns, 519.
Johnson, 501.
Jones, 513, 522, 546.
Jordan, 505.
Junkin, 543.
Karr, 505.
Kay, 544.
Kaye, 538.
Kearfoot, 496, 525.
Kearney, 495.
Keith, 512, 536.
Kelly, 505.
Kempe, 542.
Kernochan, 537.
Keverell, 508.
Kingston, 510.
Kinsolving, 511.
Kittredge, 545.
Knowlton, 546.
Knyvett, 528.
Lacie, 514, 520.
Landis, 520.
Landon, 530.
Lane, 520.
Langhorne, 519.
Lanvallei, 514, 520, 525.
Lapeyre, 537.
Lawrence, 539.
Le Despencer, 469, 537.
Le Fèvre, 520.
Le Mahieu, 504.
Le Strange, 545.
Le Wright, 536.

Lee, 496, 536.
Leidy, 534.
Leigh, 491, 525.
Leitch, 501.
Levick, 522, 524.
Levis, 524, 512.
Lewknor, 542.
Leybourne, 499, 507.
Ligne, 504.
Lillie, 509.
Limerick, 494.
Lippincott, 524, 544.
Littleton, 525.
Lloyd, 517.
Lockhart, 543.
Logan, 519, 524.
Lorraine, 494, 525, 545.
Lovelace, 500, 545.
Lovet, 532.
Lovick, 546.
Lyndon, 492.
Lynch, 495.
Lyons, 543.
McCarty, 518, 519.
McClelland, 496, 509.
McClintock, 528.
McCulloch, 517.
McDougal, 546.
McGonigal, 509.
McHenry, 524.
MacIntosh, 543.
Mackall, 544.
Mackenzie, 544.
MacLaren, 517.
Mac Leod, 525.
Macomson, 509.
Macon, 543.
Madden, 512.
Maingoral, 504.
Malet, 514, 520.
Mandville, 507.
Mann, 519.
Markenfield, 514, 520, 538.
Marmyon, 538.
Marron, 492-5, 525, 545.
Marshall, 537, 545.
Martin, 517.
Mason, 513, 537, 519.
Mather, 522.
Mathews, 511, 512, 546.
Mauduit, 531, 541, 544.
Mauleverer, 514, 520, 538.
Maury, 534.
Maxim, 528.
May, 544.
Maynard, 545.
Mellick, 534.
Metcalf, 541.
Middleton, 505.
Miller, 505, 525.
Minor, 545.
Minshull, 544.
Mitchell, 493-4, 525, 545.
Molembais, 504.
Monchi, 522.
Montacute, 525.
Montfort, 522, 541.
Montdidier, 531, 522.
Moore, 502, 543.
Morris, 522.
Mortimer, 527.
Moss, 501, 503.
Mottrom, 529, 530.
Mowbrey, 510, 514, 520, 535, 540.

Muir, 544.
Myrick, 545.
Napton, 507, 508.
Nason, 525.
Naylor, 522.
Needham, 540.
Neilson, 492-7, 520, 525.
Nelson, 536.
Nevill, 513, 516, 527, 540.
Newburg, 541, 544.
Newbury, 541.
Newcomen, 510.
Newman, 512.
Norbury, 544.
Northrop, 524.
Northwode, 499.
O'Fallon, 502.
O'Neill, 495.
Ogden, 501.
Ogle, 523.
Orne, 524.
Osgood, 505.
Otey, 512.
Owen, 513.
Owens, 535, 536.
Page, 496, 519.
Palmer, 528.
Palmes, 528.
Parker, 505.
Parr, 544.
Parry, 536.
Pashley, 542.
Paston, 491.
Patton, 512.
Pauncefote, 516.
Paxson, 520.
Peace, 508.
Pearson, 588.
Peche, 541.
Peirson, 514.
Peirson, 520.
Pendleton, 519.
Pennington, 538.
Penny, 516.
Percy, 528, 529, 538.
Perrine, 536.
Perrow, 494.
Peterson, 514.
Pitfield, 525.
Plantagenet, 527.
Pointz, 492.
Pole, 527.
Polk, 534.
Pollock, 537.
Pope, 512.
Porter, 494.
Poulton, 532.
Powell, 524.
Power, 543.
Poythress, 533.
Pratt, 537.
Preston, 535.
Price, 524.
Pryor, 525, 533.
Puleston, 522.
Pympe, 542.
Pynchon, 546.
Quincy, 514, 520, 525, 544, 545.
Randolph, 491, 525, 533, 534, 545.
Rappiler, 545.
Reade, 518.
Reading, 509.
Redington, 534.
Rennie, 494.
Revett, 517.
Reynolds, 520.
Rice, 533.
Richards, 501, 524.

Ridgely, 534.
Ridgway, 514, 520.
Roberts, 538, 522.
Robinson, 183.
Rodgers, 533.
Roos, 520, 514.
Root, 505.
Rossiter, 541.
Rouci, 531.
Rowan, 496, 525.
Rowleigh, 544.
Royall, 532.
Rutgers, 537.
Ryall, 532.
St. Leger, 500, 513, 542.
Sares, 544.
Sartoris, 506.
Satterthwaite, 509.
Saundford, 545.
Savage, 544.
Saxbury, 517.
Saye, 499, 514, 520, 542.
Sayres, 535.
Schindel, 543.
Scot, 525.
Scott, 520, 536, 542.
Scull, 544.
Sears, 544.
Segrave, 510, 523, 544.
Selden, 64.
Seymour, 529.
Shuster, 509.
Sinex, 509.
Simpson, 506.
Skelton, 533.
Skipwith, 510.
Sloan, 538.
Smith, 489, 493, 517, 524, 525, 535, 532, 542.
Smiths, 517.
Smyth, 542.
Smyths, 542.
Snyder, 512.
Soame, 537.
Somerby, 544.
Somerville, 534.
Soule, 505.
Southworth, 505.
Spencer, 523, 529.
Spotswood, 543.
Stafford, 516.
Stanhope, 529.
Stanley, 513.
Steele, 493, 525.
Stevenson, 538.
Stewart, 525, 543, 546.
Stith, 533, 534.
Stourton, 516.
Stout, 509.
Strother, 493, 525, 545.
Stuart, 502, 530, 546.
Stubblefield, 535.
Symes, 518.
Symonds, 516.
Taintor, 502.
Talbot, 540, 545.
Taylor, 501, 541, 543.
Terry, 502.
Thacher, 166.
Thomas, 498.
Thompson, 494, 528, 544.
Thomson, 519.
Thornton, 544.
Throckmorton, 518, 519.

(548)

Tibbits, 537.
Tiffany, 541.
Tignal, 546.
Tirwhitt, 538.
Todd, 501.
Toni, 507.
Townsend, 543.
Trask, 546.
Troutbeck, 513.
Tuke, 542.
Tuley, 493, 525.
Turberville, 530.
Turk, 512.
Turpin, 501.
Tutt, 519.
Unton, 529.
Valois, 527.
Van Voast, 502.
Vaughan, 537.

Ventress, 546.
Vere, 514, 520, 525, 531, 532, 543, 545.
Vesci, 514, 520.
Vicaries, 501.
Vipount, 499.
Waddell, 517.
Wahull, 545.
Waln, 534.
Ward, 498, 501.
Ware, 518.
Waring, 530.
Warren, 492, 495, 499, 505, 507, 545.
Watkins, 537.
Watson, 523, 537.
Watts, 492.
Waugh, 543.
Wayles, 533.

Webb, 514.
Welles, 510, 540.
Wells, 497, 525.
Welshe, 525.
Wentworth, 529.
Wesley, 505.
Westcott, 525.
Wetherell, 523, 524.
White, 524.
Whithare, 511.
Whiting, 541.
Wickliffe, 519.
Wilkinson, 509, 544.
Willcox, 519.
Williams, 538.
Williamson, 517, 546.
Willis, 508.
Willits, 538.
Wilson, 528.

Winthrop, 522.
Wister, 513, 519.
Wolley, 511.
Wood, 530.
Woodhull, 544.
Woodward, 542.
Wormley, 183.
Wrenshall, 506.
Wright, 494, 508. 530.
Wrothe, 500.
Wurtz, 524.
Wyatt, 161, 535, 542, 544.
Wysong, 537.
Young, 493.
Zane, 508, 509.

AMERICANS

OF

ROYAL DESCENT.

PEDIGREE OF MRS. WILLIAM ALFRED GILL

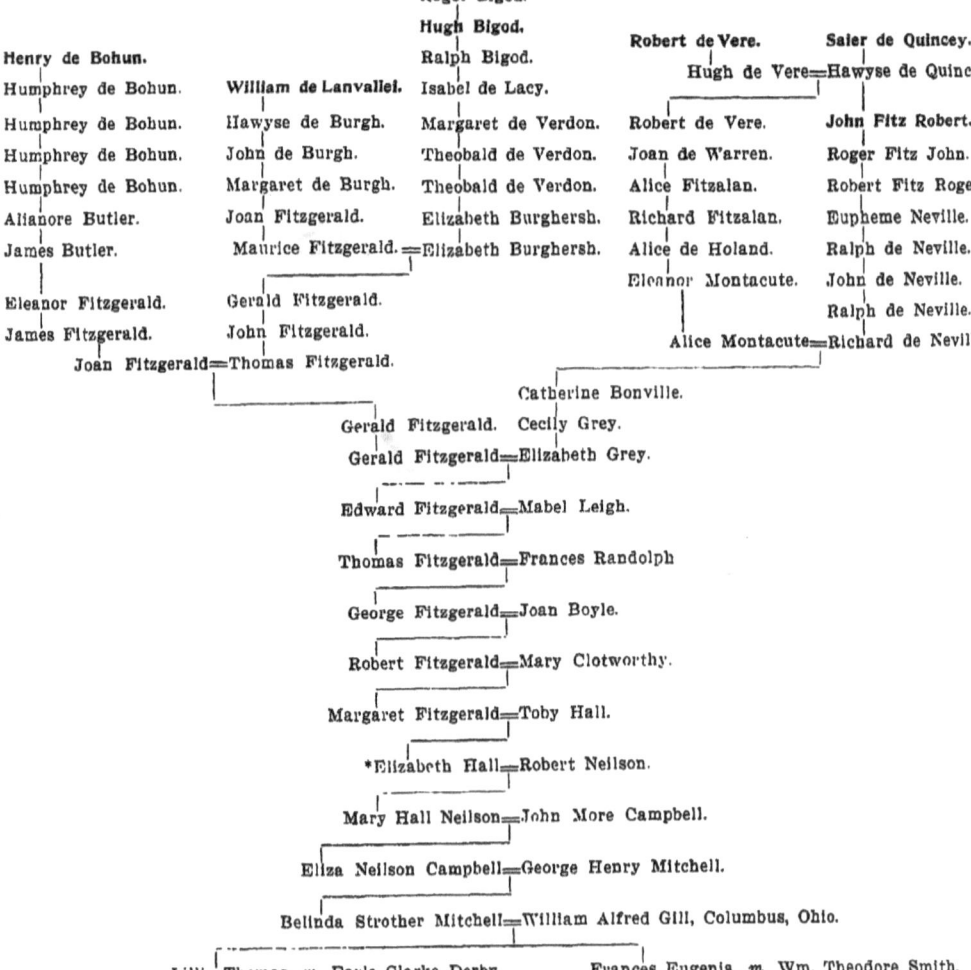

*The following are also lineally descended from these Sureties for the Magna Charta, through Mrs. Robert Neilson, and from Charlemagne. Rev. Robert Hall Mitchell, Thomas Neilson Mitchell, Mrs. Mary Frances Mitchell Fitch, Mrs. Mary Lee Fitch Steele, William Cullen Bryant Steele, Miss Mary E. Mitchell, Mrs. Mary Tuley Neilson Jackson, William Byrd Page Neilson, Mrs. Mary Rowan Jackson Kearfoot, Thornton Campbell Kearfoot, Miss Mary Tuley Kearfoot, Joseph Campbell Greene, Miss Hilda Vernon Anson, Norman Tuley Mitchell, Tuley Pryor Mitchell, Tuley Allen Wright, Stuart Wells Jackson, de Sales Douglas and Marron Dundas, Cameron Richard Lorraine.

www.ingramcontent.com/pod-product-compliance
Lightning Source LLC
Chambersburg PA
CBHW030537080526
44585CB00012B/183